PHONETICS and PHONOLOGY

VOLUME 4

PHONETICS and PHONOLOGY

Editors

STEPHEN R. ANDERSON

Department of Cognitive Science
The Johns Hopkins University
Baltimore, Maryland 21218

PATRICIA A. KEATING

Department of Linguistics
University of California, Los Angeles
Los Angeles, California 90024

A list of titles in this series appears at the end of this book.

PHONETICS and PHONOLOGY

VOLUME 4

Studies in Lexical Phonology

Edited by

Sharon Hargus
Ellen M. Kaisse

Department of Linguistics
University of Washington
Seattle, Washington

ACADEMIC PRESS, INC.
A Division of Harcourt Brace & Company

San Diego New York Boston
London Sydney Tokyo Toronto

This book is printed on acid-free paper. 

Academic Press, Inc.
1250 Sixth Avenue, San Diego, California 92101-4311

United Kingdom Edition published by
Academic Press Limited
24–28 Oval Road, London NW1 7DX

Library of Congress Cataloging-in-Publication Data

Studies in Lexical phonology / edited by Sharon Hargus and Ellen M. Kaisse.
p. cm. – (Phonetics and phonology ; v. 4)
Includes index.
ISBN 0-12-325070-6 (Hardcover)
ISBN 0-12-325071-4 (Paperback)
1. Lexical phonology. I. Hargus, Sharon. II. Kaisse, Ellen M.
III. Series.
P217.62.L49 1993
414–dc20 92-23535
CIP

PRINTED IN THE UNITED STATES OF AMERICA
93 94 95 96 97 98 QW 9 8 7 6 5 4 3 2 1

CONTENTS

Modeling the Phonology–Morphology Interface

Deriving Cyclicity

Interaction between Modules in Lexical Phonology

The Structure of the Slave (Northern Athabaskan) Verb

Looking into Words

PART II. ON SOME BASIC TENETS OF THE THEORY

On the Word Level

Structure Preservation and Postlexical Tonology in Dagbani

(Post)Lexical Rule Application

Blocking in Nonderived Environments

Are Strict Cycle Effects Derivable?

PART III. APPLYING THE THEORY TO HISTORICAL CHANGE

The Chronology and Status of Anglian Smoothing

CONTRIBUTORS

Numbers in parentheses indicate the pages on which the authors' contributions begin.

Geert Booij (23), Vakgroep Taalkunde, Vrije Universiteit, 1007 MC Amsterdam, The Netherlands

Toni Borowsky (199), Department of Linguistics, University of Sydney, Sydney, New South Wales 2006, Australia

B. Elan Dresher (325), Department of Linguistics, University of Toronto, Toronto, Ontario, Canada M5S 1A1

Sharon Hargus (1, 45), Department of Linguistics, University of Washington, Seattle, Washington 98195

Larry M. Hyman (235), Department of Linguistics, University of California, Berkeley, California 94720

Sharon Inkelas (75), Department of Linguistics, University of California, Berkeley, California 94720

Gregory K. Iverson (255), Department of Linguistics, University of Wisconsin—Milwaukee, Milwaukee, Wisconsin 53201

Ellen M. Kaisse (1, 343), Department of Linguistics, University of Washington, Seattle, Washington 98195

Paul Kiparsky (277), Department of Linguistics, Stanford University, Stanford, California 94305

Rochelle Lieber (23), Department of English, University of New Hampshire, Durham, New Hampshire 03824

David Odden (111), Department of Linguistics, Ohio State University, Columbus, Ohio 43210

William J. Poser (315), Department of Linguistics, Stanford University, Stanford, California 94305

Keren D. Rice (145), Department of Linguistics, University of Toronto, Toronto, Ontario, Canada M5S 1A1
Richard Sproat (173), Linguistics Research Department, AT&T Bell Laboratories, Murray Hill, New Jersey 07974
Draga Zec (365), Department of Modern Languages and Linguistics, Cornell University, Ithaca, New York 14853

PREFACE

What do lexical phonologists believe about phonology? To what uses are they putting the theory? What core of theorems remains from the "classical" version of lexical phonology, and what has been widely rejected or seriously challenged? Although we consider ourselves to be well within the lexical phonology fold, we have nonetheless found ourselves uncertain about these points and about others as well. At the time we first voiced these uncertainties to each other, in late 1989, there had been no major conferences on lexical phonology for many years, and the last sizable collection of papers with an emphasis on lexical phonology had appeared in 1985 in *Phonology Yearbook 2*. With a recent workshop on the phonology–syntax interface as an inspiration (see Inkelas and Zec, 1990), we decided to apply to the National Science Foundation for funding to host a workshop on lexical phonology. When funding was approved, we organized this workshop, which took place at the University of Washington in June, 1990. The present volume contains many of the papers presented at that workshop, since revised in the light of comments from participants and referees, plus additional papers from lexical phonologists who did not attend. We trust that other phonologists who have been wondering the same things that we wondered in 1989 will find this collection of articles useful.

For general introductions to lexical phonology, the reader is referred to Booij and Rubach (1991), Kaisse and Shaw (1985), and works cited therein. Our introduction concentrates on subjects that call for special explication and on topics treated in several articles in the volume. Our original call for papers suggested that authors concentrate on two of our favorite subfields: phonology–morphology interaction and the application of lexical phonology to diachronic investigations. The reader will therefore notice some bias toward these areas, but almost every dimension of lexical phonology receives some attention in the dozen or so papers in this volume.

We thank the NSF for providing funding (NSF grant #BNS-8919475). We also thank Siri Tuttle for doing most of the nuts-and-bolts organization which resulted in a successful workshop.

We each contributed equally to the task of editing; our names are printed below in alphabetical order.

Sharon Hargus
Ellen M. Kaisse

REFERENCES

Booij, G., and Rubach, J. (1991). Lexical phonology. In *International Encyclopedia of Linguistics* (W. Bright, ed.), **2**, pp. 327–330. Oxford University Press, New York.

Inkelas, S., and Zec, D. (1990). *The Phonology–Syntax Connection.* CSLI Publications and University of Chicago Press, Chicago.

Kaisse, E. M, and Shaw, P. (1985). On the theory of lexical phonology. *Phonology Yearbook* **2**, 1–30.

INTRODUCTION

ELLEN M. KAISSE
SHARON HARGUS

Department of Linguistics
University of Washington
Seattle, Washington 98195

1. THEORETICAL COMMON DENOMINATOR[1]

It may at times seem to the observer that there is no common core of beliefs that all lexical phonologists adhere to. And indeed, the papers in this volume reflect differences on practically every tenet of "classical" lexical phonology, including the source of word-internal phonological domains, phonology–morphology interaction, structure preservation, and the strict cycle condition. Yet there is a pervasive similarity in the sorts of questions that lexical phonologists ask when they describe a language, questions which might not have even been thought of ten years ago. Not many phonologists in the early eighties would have tried as a matter of course to find out whether a rule they were studying applied between words; whether it was sensitive to syntactic, prosodic, or morphological domains; whether it had exceptions; whether it applied only in morphologically derived contexts; whether the rule was neutralizing or rather supplied allophonic features; whether it was cyclic; whether it was crucially ordered with a rule already known to be lexical or postlexical; and so forth. Even if some of these questions might have been addressed individually, there would have been no overarching theoretical viewpoint that would make such pieces of information interrelated and critical to the overall picture of how the rule fit into the grammar as a whole.

In addition to agreeing on the essential information that belongs in phonological description, many lexical phonologists continue to agree on the following gen-

Phonetics and Phonology, Volume 4
Studies in Lexical Phonology

eral points. First, languages have rules with different clusters of characteristics (as posited by Kiparsky, 1983, for example), usually associated with the labels LEXICAL and POSTLEXICAL. We will see, however (Section 7), that this rule typology is not as simple and straightforward as was first suggested.

Second, languages may have word-internal phonological domains which are derived from morphological structures in various ways but do not necessarily correspond to either morphological or metrical phonological structures. This hypothesis, discussed in greater detail in Section 3, is now generally regarded as superseding the level ordering hypothesis of Siegel (1979) and Allen (1978), with improved empirical and theoretical consequences.

Finally, languages do not allow postlexical rules, be they syntactic or phonological, to refer to word-internal structure. In the past, this has been explained by positing a bracketing erasure convention, which erases word-internal brackets at some point in the lexical derivation. Again, the issue is not as simple as it first appeared. The invisibility of lexical junctures has been challenged by the existence of postlexical rules which appear to refer to word-internal phonological domains (Sproat, this volume, and Section 2.1 of this Introduction), and an alternative theory ("precompilation") has been developed by Hayes (1990) to handle such cases as well.

We see then that there is agreement concerning the gross characteristics of the model and about the kinds of questions that are of interest in arriving at a phonological analysis. In much of the rest of this introduction, we discuss more controversial aspects of the theory.

2. MORPHOLOGICAL QUESTIONS

A large number of articles in this volume (Booij and Lieber, Borowsky, Hargus, Inkelas, Odden, Sproat) deal with questions concerning the interaction of phonology and morphology.

2.1 Bracket Erasure

Like Inkelas (1990), Sproat (this volume) suggests that reference to morphological bracketing may be blocked by locality conditions on phonological rules. English /l/ has "light" and "dark" allophones, the major determinants of lightness and darkness being the length of a preboundary rime and the degree of tongue dorsum retraction. Because of the noncategorical nature of its structural change, /l/-Darkening is considered to be a postlexical rule of phonetic implementation, yet, as Sproat shows, the degree of darkening depends on the kind of (lexical) boundary (%) which follows /l/ in the context /Vl%V/. Laterals following + and

boundaries pattern together, but compound boundaries are treated differently: i.e., in nonsense words *beel-ic* and *beel-ing* /l/ is lighter than it is in *beel equator*. Sproat suggests that the increased darkness of /l/ before the compound boundary might be attributed to indirect visibility of word-internal structure via metrical or phonological domain constructs, raising the question of whether or not there is any erasure of morphological brackets.

2.2 Interactionism

The classical theory of lexical phonology was based in part on a seemingly well established number of analyses in which phonological rules apply cyclically (e.g., Brame, 1974; Chierchia, 1983; Cohn, 1989; Mascaró, 1976; Rubach, 1984; etc.; see Cole, 1991, for a recent overview of the phonological cycle). Following Mascaró (1976), cyclic rules were considered to be typically neutralizing, rather than allophonic. The hypothesis adopted by Pesetsky (1979) and Kiparsky (1982) was that the distinction between cyclic and postcyclic rules coincided with the lexical–postlexical distinction. The explanation for this correlation was that cyclicity followed from the interleaving of phonological and morphological rules, with the bold theoretical consequence that phonological rules were then predicted to be able to precede morphological ones.

However, as discussed in the next section, it is now firmly established that morphological and phonological (cyclic) structure need not be isomorphic, but that there may be a more indirect correspondence between them. Furthermore, the hypothesis that all lexical rules are cyclic has been challenged recently by Booij and Rubach (1987) who propose, largely on the basis of theory-internal considerations, that the last set of rules in the lexical component applies noncyclically. Borowsky (this volume) proposes an even more restrictive version of this hypothesis, in which the lexical component contains two phonological domains, the stem level and the word level, with word-level phonological rules applying noncyclically to the outputs of the stem level and also to the word-level morphemes prior to their concatenation with the output of the stem level.

The remaining hypothesis of the cluster of related hypotheses within the "classical" lexical phonology position—that phonological rules may precede morphological ones in some cases—is what has come to be known as INTERACTIONISM, the focus of a number of papers in this volume. Interactionism is defended by Hargus (this volume), who presents a typology of analyses which support the interactionist position, including morphological rules which refer to derived phonological properties (e.g., stress-sensitive affix allomorphy in Finnish, Dutch, German, etc.), and phonological rules whose domains crucially exclude some phonological process (e.g., infixation rules in Sanskrit and Sundanese whose outputs normally block or fail to undergo the phonological rules in question). Booij and Lieber (this volume) similarly conclude that an interactionist model is to be preferred over the more restrictive noninteractionist model (below) or alternative models proposed by Anderson (1988) and Aronoff (1988). However, there are certain facts about the kinds of analyses which supposedly support interactionism which classical lexical phonology fails to explain, as pointed out to us by Donca Steriade (personal communication). First, if an affix subcategorizes for a base with certain derived phonological properties, those properties are almost always suprasegmental (e.g., stress). Second, if a phonological rule fails to apply to the output of a word formation rule, that morphology is almost always nonconcatenative (e.g., reduplication or infixation). Interactionism would be better supported if a broader range of types of morphology and phonology interacted in the manner predicted.

A return to the Chomsky and Halle (1968) noninteractionist model, in which all morphology precedes all phonology (albeit a version of the phonological component which is enriched to include word-internal phonological domains), has recently been proposed by Halle and Vergnaud (1987a, 1987b), and also adopted by Halle, Harris, and Vergnaud (1991, HHV) and Odden (this volume). Odden provides an interesting empirical argument against interactionism using data from Maltese. An ordering paradox arises in an interactionist analysis, which can be avoided if all morphemes are concatenated before any phonological rules apply. But the noninteractive analysis is itself somewhat odd, requiring that one of the phonological rules in question be analyzed as precyclic, applying before the demonstrably cyclic stress rules (Brame, 1974); precyclic phonological rules are not otherwise known to exist. Less controversially, the Maltese data seem to support Hayes's (1990) theory of precompilation. A precompilation analysis of the data involves neither precyclicity nor the ordering paradox of the interactive analysis.

A point which is made by several authors (HHV; Hargus, this volume; Odden, this volume) is that support for interactionist and noninteractionist positions in some cases relies on one's particular conception of morphology with respect to phonology. Consider the Spanish rule of *la–el* Replacement, discussed by HHV.[2] This dissimilatory rule accounts for alternations between *la,* the feminine singular definite article, and *el,* a form of this article which is used if a noun begins with stressed *a: la aguáda* 'the water supply', *la alméja* 'the clam', but *el água* 'the water', *el álma* 'the soul'. Complications arise when *el* occurs instead of *la* even before certain unstressed *a*'s: *el aguíta* 'the water' (diminutive), *el aguaniéve* 'the sleet'. To account for these facts, HHV note that forms with unstressed *a* which take *el* instead of *la* always alternate with forms with stressed *á.* They suggest that these are forms which either contain "a noncyclic derivational affix" (diminutive *-it-* vs. cyclic *-ad-* in *la aguáda*) or occur as the first component of a compound. Thus HHV posit a crucial distinction between cyclic and noncyclic affixes and also assume that *la–el* Replacement precedes Conflation (a rule which removes crucial stresses). Thus the input to *la–el* Replacement will be *la aguáda* (which surfaces with *la*) versus *la águita* (which surfaces with *el*). The theoretical point which arises from this discussion is, as mentioned above, that *la–el* Replacement, a rule which obviously refers to a derived phonological property (stress), could be analyzed in one of two ways; as a phonological rule (1), as they choose (p. 153), or as "a contextually determined lexical choice," as suggested by Harris (1989).

(1)

$$\begin{array}{r} * \\ * \\ la \rightarrow l / [_{N} \underline{\qquad} [_{N} a \end{array}$$

Their rationale for formalizing *la–el* Replacement as in (1) is as follows (HHV, p. 157).

> [If formalized as in (1),] then this phenomenon involves no interaction between morphological rules and those of the phonology. . . . On the other hand, if the phenomenon is treated by multiple listings in the lexicon, then the separateness of morphology from phonology is compromised (insofar as this type of lexical choice is a matter of morphology).

This sort of analytical uncertainty can be found in other languages, as pointed out by Hargus (this volume) and Odden (this volume).

Like Booij and Lieber, Inkelas (this volume) argues for a model in which phonological structure[3] is constructed in tandem with morphological structure, as discussed in more detail in the next section. While Inkelas's theory incorporates various hypotheses, her proposal that the distribution of cyclic and noncyclic rules is predictable provides general support for interactionism. A further assumption made by a number of noninteractionists (e.g., Halle and Vergnaud, 1987a, 1987b; cf. also Halle and Mohanan, 1985) is that word-internal phonological domains are unpredictably cyclic or noncyclic. Inkelas proposes that cyclicity be formalized as the automatic application of phonological rules upon construction of a new P-CONSTITUENT (nonmetrical phonological domain), a proposal which is directly supported by Cohn's (1989) cyclic analysis of stress assignment in Indonesian. Inkelas's model accounts for the existence of noncyclic phenomena (or the nonapplication of cyclic rules) in two places within the lexicon. First, cyclic rules may fail to apply prior to the first phonological cycle, either because of a universal prohibition against cyclic rules applying to bound roots or because there is cross-linguistic variation in the ordering of affixation with respect to p-structure construction. Secondly, a language may have a set of noncyclic rules which apply at the end of the lexical component (à la Booij and Rubach, 1987). Inkelas suggests that the existence of the latter may follow from whether or not the language has morphemes which belong to the last lexical phonological domain. These relatively new predictions should be further examined but for the moment appear to offer general support for interactionism.

It should be noted that even the hypothesis that phonological rules apply cyclically has been controversial throughout the history of generative phonology, partly because cyclic analyses of individual languages tend to be based on abstract morphological and/or phonological analysis, and partly because theoretical refinements have rendered individual analyses obsolete. The cycle in Spanish provides a good example of the latter. Brame (1974) argued that stress was assigned cyclically in Spanish on the basis of the stress-conditioned raising of *e* to *i* in adverbs derived from the past participles of second conjugation verbs: *cono***ci***damente* < *conoc-e-r* 'knowingly', *de***bi***damente* < *deb-e-r* 'justly'. In order for stresses to appear in the proper locations, stress assignment must precede suffixation of *-mente;* that is, stress must be assigned cyclically. The need for the cycle disappears, however, if *-mente* is analyzed as constituting a separate phonological domain, as does Suñer (1975) (cf. also Lantolf, 1977), who provides morphological and phonological evidence for this analysis.

3. WORD-INTERNAL PHONOLOGICAL DOMAINS

As mentioned above, lexical phonologists generally recognize that, in some languages, it is necessary to posit one or more phonological domains which are smaller than the phonological word (the latter being a domain which may or may not exclude clitics; see Zec, this volume; Zec and Inkelas, 1991). There have been two recent and related developments in the theory of word-internal phonological domains which are reflected in many of the papers in this volume. The first concerns the recognition and explanation of the fact that word-internal phonological domains may exhibit varying degrees of independence from morphological representations. The second concerns the viability of the level ordering hypothesis.

Due to work by Booij (1985), Booij and Rubach (1984), Inkelas (1990, this volume), and Sproat (1985), there is now something of a consensus that word-internal phonological domains (dubbed P-STRUCTURE by Inkelas) may be derived from, but need not be isomorphic with, morphological or morphosyntactic structure. Polish, as analyzed by Booij and Rubach (1984), provides an example of this nonisomorphism. These authors argue that [rozɨjimitsa] 'truce maker' has the following phonological and morphological structures.

(2) [[[rozɨ [jim]] its] a] morphological representation
[rozɨ [[[jim] its] a]] phonological representation

The morphologically motivated structure incorporates their observation that "prefixed stems may, while inflected forms may not, function as bases for further word-formation" (p. 19). Yet the cyclic derivation required for the correct application of the phonological rules of Yer Lower and Yer Deletion is one in which the prefix /rozɨ-/ must belong to the last cycle. Booij and Rubach propose that both morphological prefixes and inflected stems in Polish are phonological words (members of the category *mot*), and that the morphological word corresponds to a higher-order phonological constituent, the phonological compound, or *mot'*:

(3)

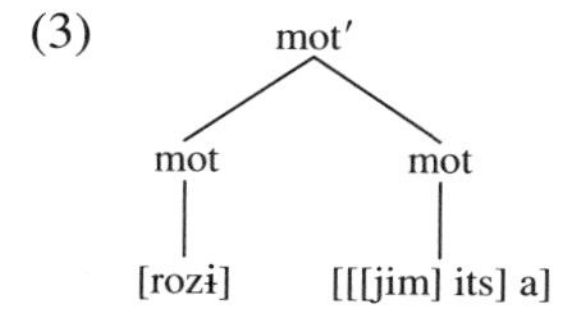

Such data, once considered unusual and puzzling, have turned up in a variety of languages, and analyses similar to that proposed by Booij and Rubach for Polish can be found in Nespor and Vogel (1986), Cohn (1989), Kang (1992), and Inkelas (1990, this volume). For example, Kang (1992) shows that Ahn's (1985) four-level analysis of the lexical phonology of Korean, which required the loop, yields to a prosodic analysis with no extraordinary theoretical devices and only one word-internal phonological domain once the independence of morphological representations and p-structure is recognized. Following Inkelas (1990), the version of lexical phonology which recognizes this independence may be called prosodic lexical phonology (PLP).

The level ordering hypothesis (LOH), once considered a tenet of classical lexical phonology, attempted to explain an observed correlation between affix order and phonological rule domains by positing a strict ordering between affixes which belong to different phonological rule domains (termed LEVELS or STRATA in the theory of level ordering). Yet in recent years a number of authors have challenged the descriptive adequacy of the correlation in a number of languages (see, e.g., Aronoff and Sridhar, 1987; Hargus, 1988; Mohanan, 1986; Strauss, 1982). For example, Aronoff and Sridhar note for English that the (stress-affecting) level 1 affix *-ity* attaches quite productively to words containing the (stress-neutral) level 2 affix *-able,* counterexemplifying the LOH. Moreover, Spencer (1989) has demonstrated that much of the work attributed to the LOH in the regulation of affix order in English must be accomplished by more restrictive morphological subcategorization frames. In PLP, with its looser connections between morphological and phonological representations, there is no role for the LOH. Instead, like word-external phonological domains, word-internal p-structure in PLP is assumed to be nested, regulated by the strict layer hypothesis (SLH) (Selkirk, 1984; Nespor and Vogel, 1986), in which smaller phonological domains are strictly contained within larger ones.

It is legitimate to ask whether or not the SLH is simply a reincarnation of the LOH. While the ordering restrictions imposed by the LOH and the SLH are both hierarchical, PLP allows that affixes not be underlyingly specified for domain but may instead CLITICIZE to the phonological domain of an adjacent morpheme, thereby accommodating what were previously considered to be level ordering violations. An Aronoff and Sridhar–style analysis of English words like *ungrammat-*

icality and *turnability* would have the following components. First, affixes within the domain of the English Stress Rule, like *-ity,* would be underlyingly specified as stem-level or level 1, whereas affixes like *-able-* and *un-* would be unspecified for domain assignment. Second, some sort of algorithm would be required for converting morphological representations (which include underlying affixal domain assignment, if any) into phonological representations. The following is a paraphrase of one such algorithm proposed by Aronoff and Sridhar.

(4) The edge of a phonological word (W) is the edge of any element which is a member of a major lexical category, unless that edge is adjacent to a stem-level affix.

This algorithm predicts the following mapping between morphological and phonological representations for words like *ungrammaticality* and *turnability.*[4]

(5)

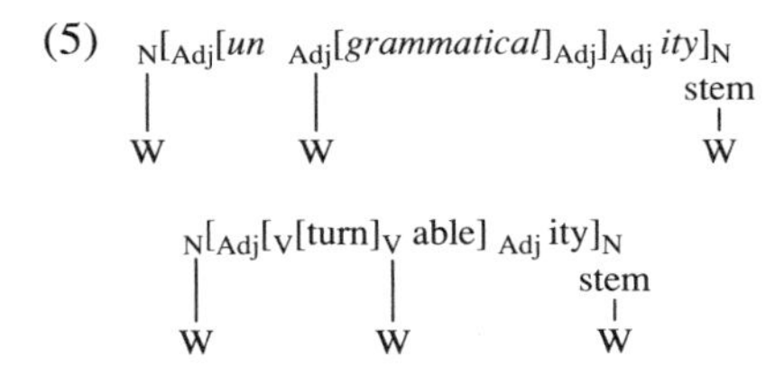

The Aronoff and Sridhar–style algorithm predicts that no W-boundary can be inserted between *grammatical* and *-ity,* even though *grammatical* is a member of a major lexical category, because *-ity* is a stem-level affix. Similarly, *-able* and *-ity* are correctly predicted to form a phonological unit. Note further that the preceding derived phonological representations are in accord with the SLH, whereas representations in which *-able* and *un-* are considered level 2 morphemes violate the LOH.

(6) $[[\text{un}[\text{grammatical}]]_2\ \text{ity}]_1$
$[[[\text{turn}]\ \text{abil}]_2\ \text{ity}]_1$

To summarize, then, the relationship between morphological and phonological representations is less restrictive in several ways: structures such as the phonological word and the morphological word are not required to be identical, and affixes may have empty domain specifications. One current, unresolved issue in PLP concerns the extent to which p-structure is predictable. Inkelas (1990, this volume) and Borowsky (this volume) adopt the traditional view that rule domains are lexically specified information included in the subcategorization frames of affixes. The alternative position, based on Selkirk (1986), is that word-internal p-structure is basically predictable, a position adopted by Kang (1992) and by Rice (this volume). Kang (1992) shows that the phonological word in Korean can be determined from the left edge of a morphological constituent, thereby correctly predicting that the left branches of compounds and prefixed words are independent phonological constituents. Rice (this volume) proposes three word-internal phonological rule domains for Slave, an Athabaskan language, the SMALL WORD, WORD, and PHONOLOGICAL PHRASE, the latter being the phonological domain usually thought of as the entire "verb word" in previous analyses of Athabaskan languages. Rice suggests that the word-internal morphological structure of verbs in Slave is basically syntactic, rather than morphological, and that Slave has in fact very little true morphology. Basing her analysis on earlier work by Speas (1990), Rice argues that this morphosyntactic constituent structure is not determined by phrase structure rule but is derived from universal notions of syntactic SCOPE. Thus, in Rice's analysis, the edges of phonological domains follow from the particular morphosyntactic structure adopted.

4. THE STRICT CYCLE CONDITION: IS IT DERIVABLE FROM UNDERSPECIFICATION?

The strict cycle condition (SCC), a development of previous concepts introduced by Kiparsky over two decades, such as the (revised) alternation condition (RAC), is a constraint on the application of certain rules which prevents them from applying within a morpheme or from applying in environments which were already available on a previous cycle. Lexical phonologists generally agree that there is a robust set of phenomena which motivate something roughly like the SCC or the RAC. In his contribution to this volume, Kiparsky argues that the SCC suffers from empirical difficulties while the RAC suffers from theoretical weaknesses and argues instead that the phenomena they cover can be derived from segmental underspecification. The applicability of the SCC to a rule was a clear indication of its lexical status in classical lexical phonology, but this hypothesis is under attack from all directions, including that of its originator, for Kiparsky now argues that true lexical rules, word-level rules, and postlexical rules may all exhibit or fail to exhibit such effects. Iverson, in his contribution, argues for a return to the position that strict cycle effects are a characteristic simply of neutralization rules, while nonneutralizing rules may fail to exhibit them even if lexical. Both Kiparsky (1985) and Borowsky (1986, this volume) have argued that whatever the precise form of the condition blocking rule application in nonderived environments, it should turn off at the last level of the lexicon, the word level, rather than postlexically. Finally, Poser suggests in this volume that the derived environment condition should be divided into constraints on a requirement for concatenation versus a requirement of previous application of phonological rule.

Kiparsky (1985, this volume) has introduced a sort of contextual underspecification which he uses in his attempt to account for nonderived environment effects.

Since this version of underspecification figures in Iverson's article as well, and because it may be less familiar to our readers, we summarize it briefly here. We have made up a simple example below, but the explanation is transferable to more complicated cases such as Trisyllabic Shortening in English, and Iverson's Korean Palatalization as well.

Consider a language which has nasalized vowels underlyingly but also has a natural sort of phonological process which nasalizes vowels before nasals. Vowel Nasalization is thus neutralizing or "structure preserving." Now assume that Vowel Nasalization shows the derived environment effect, so that within a single morpheme, it fails to apply—there are monomorphemes with a nonnasalized vowel preceding a nasal.

Recall now Kiparsky's (1971) discussion of opaque rules. Paraphrasing, a rule is opaque to the extent that there are surface forms which contradict it. Contradiction can take the form of strings where the rule should have applied but has not, and cases where the rule should not have applied, but has. More technically, as Kiparsky puts it, a rule P, $A \rightarrow B/C\_\_\_ D$, is opaque to the extent that there are strings *CAD* in its output (in other words, underapplication); or strings *CBD* not derived from P.

We can now see that a neutralizing rule subject to the derived environment condition results in both kinds of opacity. We have strings that look like they should have undergone the rule but do not (apparent underapplication), in the form of morpheme-internal oral vowel plus nasal sequences. And we have strings that look like they have undergone the rule but shouldn't have, in the form of underlying nasalized vowels followed by nonnasal consonants (apparent overapplication). Opaque forms are marked. Kiparsky's method of underspecifying therefore reserves the unmarked value for vowels which underlyingly accord with what the rules of the language will produce. That is, the more natural, morpheme-internal sequences of nasal vowel plus nasal consonant and of nonnasal vowel plus nonnasal consonant will be unmarked. Those opaque cases of nasal vowel followed by nonnasal consonant and nonnasal vowel followed by nasal consonant will be marked.

(7) Nonnasalized vowels: [−nasal] before nasals in the same morpheme;
[0nasal] elsewhere
Nasalized vowels: [+nasal] before nonnasals;
[0nasal] elsewhere

Thus the case of [VN] within a morpheme, the case where the nonderived environment effect appears, is achieved by having the vowel prespecified for nonnasality. The 'overapplication' case, [ṼT], is derived by prelinking the vowel to a [+nasal] specification. The morpheme-internal and -external cases where a vowel nasalizes before a nasal are both handled by Vowel Nasalization filling in the feature on the underlying [0nasal] vowel. Implicit in this system is the claim that there is no possible representational contrast between morpheme-internal [ṼN] deriving from an underlying nasal vowel and an underlying nonnasal vowel. The environment is one in which the vowel is simply [0nasal]. Thus we rediscover the RAC, which prevented a neutralization rule from applying to every instance of a morpheme. By the RAC, Sanskrit *ṣ* before morpheme-internal *r, u, k,* or *i* had to be a real underlying *ṣ* and our Ṽ before nasal had to be a real underlying nasalized vowel. Now the *ṣ* and the Ṽ must be unmarked for retroflexion and nasality respectively and thus cannot contrast with an underlying /s/ or /V/ which undergoes the *ruki* rule or Nasalization.

The final step in Kiparsky's disposal of the SCC is to say that rules delinking features, that is, structure-changing rules, are marked. Rules building structure, that is, filling in features such as [+nasal] or [−nasal] on previously underspecified segments, are unmarked. Thus, unless the language in our nasalization example has an unusual, specific rule removing prespecified linkages, we should not expect underlying prenasal, morpheme-internal oral vowels to nasalize, since they are already linked to [−nasal]. However, a morpheme-final oral vowel will have no specification for nasality. Thus when it is prefixed to a nasal-initial morpheme, spreading can occur without any marked delinking rule being present in the language, and we achieve the derived environment effect.

5. STRUCTURE PRESERVATION

The basic concept of structure preservation is a simple one, though we shall see that its proper technical instantiation may be anything but that. The general idea is that the prototypical lexical rule preserves the basic underlying segment and tonal inventory of the language and the basic arrangement of strings of segments as well. There will be a lexical vocabulary of segments and tones, which does not alter during the derivation of words, and an enriched array of allophones, which is derived postlexically.

We have already seen that Borowsky and Kiparsky (1985) both propose that structure preservation turns off a bit earlier than this simple dichotomy of lexical versus postlexical rules would predict. In work in this volume and in her 1986 dissertation, Borowsky suggests that new allophones can be created within the lexicon, at the word level. Extending the possible relevance of structure preservation in the other direction, Hyman (this volume) considers the effects of structure preservation in postlexical applications of a rightward High Tone Spread in the Gur language Dagbani. He concludes that there are two very similar High Tone Spread rules. HTS-1 obeys structure preservation, for it does not create contour tones, which are otherwise prohibited in the language. HTS-2, on the other hand, does not obey structure preservation—it creates contour tones. The straightforward expectation in standard lexical phonology would have been that HTS-1 applies in an earlier stratum than HTS-2. One might be lexical, the other postlexical; one might be an early lexical rule, the other a word-level rule; or, if there are two postlexical levels, as argued by Kaisse (1985) and by Mohanan (1986), we might expect that HTS-1 applied at the earlier of the postlexical strata, called P1 by Kaisse, where lexical characteristics persist.

The rub is that, as Hyman demonstrates, BOTH HTS-1 and HTS-2 must be utterance-level rules. In a theory like Kaisse's (1985, 1990), the first postlexical level, P1, should correspond loosely to the small prosodic domain known as the phonological phrase. Rules restricted to the phonological phrase will apply, roughly, between the head of a syntactic phrase and its various arguments. Such rules, applying immediately after lexical rules, should be expected to exhibit more lexical characteristics than later, so-called P2 rules. But utterance-level rules, corresponding to P2 rules, apply between all words in the same sentence, or even between closely bound sentences. Thus we are forced to the conclusion, if Hyman is correct, that even within a single component (in this case, the last postlexical stratum, P2), structure preservation may arbitrarily be or not be a characteristic of a rule. Typically, Hyman concludes, structure preservation will characterize the application of lexical rules, while failure to preserve structure will be a hallmark of postlexical ones, as in the standard theory. But this is only a tendency. Since an utterance-level rule is clearly P2, we do not have two separate components here to segregate the rules into. The example is weakly consistent with Kaisse's and Kiparsky's theories in the sense that in these theories, no postlexical rule is REQUIRED to create novel segments or sequences, so that HTS-1's inability to create a contour tone does not mean it cannot be a P2 rule. Things could also be worse in that at least HTS-1 precedes HTS-2, but the phenomenon is puzzling nonetheless, for it shows that structure preservation may turn off arbitrarily, rather than at a well-defined level provided by the lexical phonology.

Recent work by McFarland and Pierrehumbert (1991) has the potential to make irrelevant many invocations of structure preservation as a block to the application of lexical rules. We discuss their proposal here, for Hyman's results may turn on whether we accept McFarland and Pierrehumbert's interpretation. These authors contend that the proper interpretation of structure preservation, as spelled out in Kiparsky (1985), does not rule out the lexical derivation of segments which are novel but derived by feature spreading. In such cases, the number and configuration of association lines may be critically different from what a lexical marking condition rules out. A strict application of Hayes's (1986) linking constraint and of the theory of feature geometry shows that rules spreading a feature from one segment to another create structures with double linkages of the assimilated feature. These double linkings do not match the single linkages of lexical conditions intended to rule out the association of a segment type with a certain feature. Consider Kiparsky's (1985) own use of structure preservation to prevent the lexical participation of Russian sonorants in voicing assimilation. MacFarland and Pierrehumbert point out that the lexical prohibition against (8)

(8) [+son]
|
[αvoice]

does not rule out the lexical spread of voicing onto a sonorant, because in a form derived by spreading, [voice] is linked to TWO association lines, and lines of association must be interpreted exhaustively.

(9) [+son] [−son]
[−voice]

The relevance of McFarland and Pierrehumbert's meticulous interpretation of structure preservation to Hyman's Dagbani case may now be apparent to the reader. The High Tone Spread rules, as their names imply, of course create linked structures. If the lexical constraint in Dagbani rules out contour tones as in (10); tbu = 'tone-bearing unit',

(10) * Tone Tone
tbu

it will not rule out the structure derived by spreading (11),

(11)
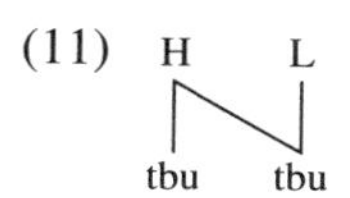

because in this latter structure, the first tone is doubly linked. It is only singly linked in the lexical constraint. By the strict interpretation of structure preservation, therefore, no tone spreading rules can be prohibited from applying in Dagbani merely as a consequence of the fact that Dagbani has no underlying contour tones. We will have to have a specific lexical condition ruling out tone-bearing units with more than one tone attached to them, regardless of whether those tones have additional lines of association.

(12)
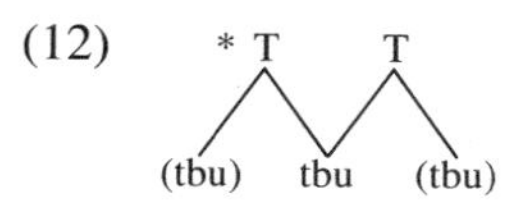

In the absence of the relevance of structure preservation to spreading rules, such an unpalatable condition is indeed needed, since there are lexical rules which would otherwise produce contour tones.

The strict interpretation of the applicability of structure preservation gets us out of the difficulty Hyman's case raises, though at significant cost, both to the simplicity of the grammar of Dagbani and perhaps to phonological theory in general. Rather than worrying why structure preservation turns off at an arbitrary point in Dagbani grammar, we will say it was never relevant—spreading rules of this form are not blocked by structure preservation. Instead we impose a condition on derived contour tones that does not stem organically from Dagbani's lack of underlying contour tones. And we must still stipulate that that condition is applicable to HTS-1 but not to HTS-2.

McFarland and Pierrehumbert conclude their article by pointing out that the strict and consistent interpretation of structure preservation will rule out many otherwise appealing analyses which used that principle to prevent assimilations within the lexical phonology. These cases include some of Kiparsky's own, such as Russian Voicing Assimilation and Finnish Vowel Harmony, as well as numerous others in the literature of lexical phonology. We agree with McFarland and Pierrehumbert's assessment: phonologists must either revise structure preservation to allow it to rule out those assimilations that it appeared to prevent so appealingly, or they must consistently interpret structure preservation in the light of the results of feature geometry and the linking constraint and rework the analyses that incorrectly invoked it. We cannot help but feel that the most rigorous interpretation of structure preservation leaves it too weak to deal with the very cases it was designed to explain.

6. APPLYING LEXICAL PHONOLOGY TO DIACHRONIC CHANGE

Three contributions to this volume, those of Dresher, Kaisse, and Zec, deal not so much with controversies within the theory as with the uses of its basic premises to elucidate diachronic change. The addition, generalization, and movement of rules has long been the basis for describing the bulk of historical changes within generative phonology. Because lexical phonology has developed a sophisticated view of the position or domain of rules in a grammar, it allows one to understand the progress of a rule over time in a much more detailed and revealing fashion.

Both Kaisse and Zec flesh out the idea that rules are added postlexically and gradually move up through the levels. Zec traces the development of a rule spreading high tones leftward in Serbo-Croatian. The grammaticization of Spreading is seen by Zec as the withdrawal of Spreading from successive lower (i.e., later) levels of the grammar. Different dialects have frozen the progression of the rule at various stages. In addition, changes in the level at which phonological words (the *mots* discussed in Section 3) are created accounts for another dialect divergence.

Kaisse looks at rules which may have gone even farther along the path of change. She suggests that once rules have become lexical, a further possible path of development is for them to again begin spreading or moving their domains to later levels and into the postlexical component, where they have access to redundant features and thus appear to have generalized. Indeed, she claims that it may be possible to do away altogether with the notion of rule generalization as an independent mechanism of historical change and simply to derive generalization from underspecification. Recall that Kiparsky proposed to derive the SCC from underspecification as well. It is apparent that while no one is yet able to agree on exactly how underspecification works, it is a powerful tool.

Dresher argues that apparent synchronic and diachronic ordering problems involved in the analysis of the rule of Anglian Smoothing can be resolved if the rule was at some point reanalyzed as a constraint holding over the lexicon but turning off at the word level. As Dresher remarks, the chronological status of Smoothing was always obvious from the Old English texts, but earlier researchers doubted the chronology nonetheless, for their theories could not account for the facts. Again, the power of lexical phonology to resolve longstanding difficulties in diachronic change is made evident.

The arguments of Kaisse and Zec rest in part on the notion that historical change is profitably viewed not only as the progression of rules from one component to another, but that it is possible for a rule to remain in the domain in which it began while extending its application to another domain or component. This view of rule progression is implicitly challenged by Iverson's contribution to this volume. Iverson wishes to return to the early versions of lexical phonology, in which rules had well-defined domains—they belonged to particular strata. In lexical phonology dating from 1984 and beyond, Kiparsky (1984) argues in fact that the natural state of a rule is not to be restricted to a particular component or stratum (the strong domain hypothesis). Rules will apply at Level 1 and throughout the lexicon and will extend into the postlexical component as well, unless they are turned off by a specific statement in the grammar. But the characteristics of the extended rule will differ from component to component, in accordance with the precepts of the theory. Kiparsky's best examples, Catalan Nasal Assimilation and Russian Devoicing, are challenged in Iverson's article. Booij and Rubach (1987) also challenge the change in the theory which allowed, indeed expected, rules to apply in several strata and components; this remains then a controversial modification. Historical studies should provide a good avenue for resolving the question of the unmarked extension of a rule's domain of application.

7. RULE TYPOLOGY

Among the more compelling hypotheses of the early lexical phonology model was the proposal that phonological and morphological rules which belonged to different components of grammar had different characteristics. Consider the summary of such characteristics provided by Kiparsky (1983).

(13)

	LEXICAL	POSTLEXICAL
a.	word-bounded	not word-bounded
b.	access to word-internal structure assigned at same level only	access to phrase structure only
c.	precede all postlexical rules	follow all lexical rules
d.	cyclic	apply once
e.	disjunctively ordered with respect to other lexical rules	conjunctively ordered with respect to lexical rules
f.	apply in derived environments	apply across the board
g.	structure-preserving	not structure-preserving
h.	apply to lexical categories only	apply to all categories
i.	may have exceptions	automatic

With nearly a decade of subsequent work, we now know that many of these characteristics cannot be considered diagnostic of the lexical or postlexical status of a rule.

It has been suggested, somewhat controversially (Hayes, 1990; but cf. Kaisse, 1990), that not all lexical rules are word-bounded (13a) or even restricted to information provided within their own phonological domain (13b) (as seen in Maltese; Odden, this volume). As discussed in Section 2.2, it has been suggested that not all lexical rules are cyclic (13d), and the existence of lexical postcyclic rules similarly makes characteristic (13f) problematic. In some languages, structure preservation (13g) appears to hold of postlexical rules (Hyman, this volume), whereas in other languages, some rules which are clearly lexical (albeit word-level) may not be structure-preserving (Borowsky, this volume). In contradiction to (13h), there are postlexical rules which may be indirectly or directly sensitive to syntactic category (Kaisse, 1985; Nespor and Vogel, 1986; among others), and some postlexical rules have exceptions (Kaisse, 1986) (13i). The role of characteristic (13e) seems to have been primarily to regulate word formation, enforcing (via the elsewhere condition) the blocking of regular derivatives like **borer* 'one who bores' by the existence of special/exceptional forms like *bore*. However, since it was also claimed that there was no postlexical word formation, the utility of this characteristic in diagnosing postlexical versus lexical morphology does not seem to us to have been very great.

Yet it is striking that many lexical and postlexical rules do have at least some of the characteristics given in (13) above. A conceivable alternative to (13) would be to weaken the ordering prediction (13c) and to remove the labels on the columns so that these characteristics are not rigidly associated with particular components but that for each erstwhile lexical characteristic, a rule in a particular language with that property precedes a rule with the complementary postlexical characteristic. Alternatively, the list in (13) could be viewed as constituting the unmarked set of characteristics of lexical and postlexical rules.

To a suitably weakened version of the list it may also be possible to add a few more characteristics.

(13′)

	"LEXICAL"	"POSTLEXICAL"
j.	not transferred to a second language	transferable to L2
k.	outputs subject to lexical diffusion	subject to Neogrammarian sound change
l.	apply categorically	may have gradient outputs

We take these more recently proposed characteristics from Rubach (1984), Kiparsky (1988), and Kiparsky (1985), respectively.

8. AN INVITATION

To the reader who feels the need of more certainty or at least more concrete detail than we have been able to provide in this introduction, we suggest turning directly to the papers offered by our contributors. They present their cases more cogently than we could hope to do here.

NOTES

[1] The order of names is arbitrary; authorship was shared equally. Our remarks owe much to discussion by workshop participants; in particular, Geert Booij, Elan Dresher, Jim Harris, Paul Kiparsky, and Bill Poser. We also thank Jurek Rubach and Donca Steriade for helpful comments.

[2] An earlier version of this article was presented by Harris at the 1990 Workshop on Lexical Phonology.

[3] Inkelas (1990, this volume) distinguishes metrical and nonmetrical phonological domains.

[4] We assume, following Cohn (1989) and Inkelas (1990), that the morphological structure is more basic.

REFERENCES

Ahn, S.-C. (1985). *The Interplay of Phonology and Morphology in Korean.* Doctoral dissertation, University of Illinois, Urbana-Champaign.

Allen, M. (1978). *Morphological Investigations.* Doctoral dissertation, University of Connecticut, Storrs.

Anderson, S. R. (1988). Inflection. In *Theoretical Morphology* (M. Hammond and M. Noonan, eds.), pp. 23–43. Academic Press, San Diego.

Aronoff, M. (1988). Head operations and strata in reduplication: a linear treatment. *Yearbook of Morphology* **1,** 1–15.

Aronoff, M., and Sridhar, S. (1987). Morphological levels in English and Kannada. In *Rules and the Lexicon* (E. Gussmann, ed.), pp. 9–22. Katolickiergo Uniwersytetu Lubelskiego, Lublin, Poland.

Booij, G. (1985). Coordination reduction in complex words: A case for prosodic phonology. In *Advances in Non-linear Phonology* (H. van der Hulst and N. Smith, eds.), pp. 143–160. Foris, Dordrecht.

Booij, G., and Rubach, J. (1984). Morphological and prosodic domains in lexical phonology. *Phonology Yearbook* **1,** 1–28.

Booij, G., and Rubach, J. (1987). Postcyclic versus postlexical rules in lexical phonology. *Linguistic Inquiry* **18,** 1–44.

Borowsky, T. (1986). *Topics in the Lexical Phonology of English.* Doctoral dissertation, University of Massachusetts, Amherst.

Brame, M. (1974). The cycle in phonology: Stress in Palestinian, Maltese, and Spanish. *Linguistic Inquiry* **5,** 39–60.

Chierchia, G. (1983/1986). Length, syllabification, and the phonological cycle in Italian. *Journal of Italian Linguistics* **8,** 5–34.

Chomsky, N., and Halle, M. (1968). *The Sound Pattern of English.* Harper and Row, New York.

Cohn, A. (1989). Stress in Indonesian and bracketing paradoxes. *Natural Language and Linguistic Theory* **7,** 167–216.

Cole, J. (1991). Arguing for the phonological cycle: A critical review. In *Proceedings of the First Meeting of the Formal Linguistics Society of Midamerica.* Department of Linguistics, University of Wisconsin, Madison.

Halle, M., Harris, J., and Vergnaud, J.-R. (1991). A reexamination of the stress erasure convention and Spanish stress. *Linguistic Inquiry* **22,** 141–159.

Halle, M., and Mohanan, K. P. (1985). Segmental phonology of Modern English. *Linguistic Inquiry* **16,** 57–116.

Halle, M., and Vergnaud, J.-R. (1987a). *An Essay on Stress.* MIT Press, Cambridge, Mass.

Halle, M., and Vergnaud, J.-R. (1987b). Stress and the cycle. *Linguistic Inquiry* **18,** 45–84.

Hargus, S. (1988). *The Lexical Phonology of Sekani.* Garland, New York.

Harris, J. (1989). The stress erasure convention and cliticization in Spanish. *Linguistic Inquiry* **20,** 339–364.

Hayes, B. (1986). Inalterability in CV phonology. *Language* **62,** 321–352.

Hayes, B. (1990). Precompiled phrasal phonology. In *The Phonology–Syntax Connection* (S. Inkelas and D. Zec, eds.), pp. 85–108. CSLI Publications and University of Chicago Press, Chicago.

Inkelas, S. (1990). *Prosodic Constituency in the Lexicon.* Garland, New York.

Kaisse, E. M. (1985). *Connected Speech: The Interaction of Syntax and Phonology.* Academic Press, Orlando.

Kaisse, E. M. (1986). Locating Turkish devoicing. *Proceedings of the West Coast Conference on Formal Linguistics* **5,** 119–128.

Kaisse, E. M. (1990). Toward a typology of postlexical rules. In *The Phonology–Syntax*

Connection (S. Inkelas and D. Zec, eds.), pp. 127–143. CSLI Publications and University of Chicago Press, Chicago.

Kang, O. (1992). Word-internal prosodic words in Korean. *Proceedings of the North Eastern Linguistics Society* **22,** 243–257.

Kiparsky, P. (1971). Historical linguistics. In *A Survey of Linguistic Science* (W. O. Dingwall, ed.), pp. 576–649. University of Maryland, College Park.

Kiparsky, P. (1982). Lexical morphology and phonology. In *Linguistics in the Morning Calm* (I.-S. Yang, ed.), pp. 3–91. Hanshin Publishing Co., Seoul.

Kiparsky, P. (1983). Word formation and the lexicon. *Proceedings of the 1982 Mid-America Linguistics Conference,* pp. 3–29.

Kiparsky, P. (1984). On the lexical phonology of Icelandic. In *Nordic Prosody III: Papers from a Symposium* (C. C. Elert et al., eds.), pp. 135–164. University of Umeå.

Kiparsky, P. (1985). Some consequences of lexical phonology. *Phonology Yearbook* **2,** 85–138.

Kiparsky, P. (1988). Phonological change. In *Linguistics: The Cambridge Survey* (F. J. Newmeyer, ed.), **1,** 363–415.

Lantolf, J. (1977). Stress subordination: Evidence from Spanish. *General Linguistics* **17,** 8–19.

McFarland, T., and Pierrehumbert, J. (1991). On ich-laut, ach-laut and structure preservation. *Phonology* **8,** 171–180.

Mascaró, J. (1976). *Catalan Phonology and the Phonological Cycle.* Doctoral dissertation, Massachusetts Institute of Technology, Cambridge.

Mohanan, K. P. (1986). *The Theory of Lexical Phonology.* Reidel, Dordrecht.

Nespor, M., and Vogel, I. (1986). *Prosodic Phonology.* Foris, Dordrecht.

Pesetsky, D. (1979). *Russian Morphology and Lexical Theory.* Unpublished manuscript, Massachusetts Institute of Technology, Cambridge.

Rubach, J. (1984a). *Cyclic and Lexical Phonology: The Structure of Polish.* Foris, Dordrecht.

Rubach, J. (1984b). Rule typology and phonological interference. In *Theoretical Issues in Contrastive Phonology* (S. Eliason, ed.), pp. 37–50. Julius Groos, Stuttgart.

Selkirk, E. O. (1984). *Phonology and Syntax: The Relation Between Sound and Structure.* MIT Press, Cambridge, Mass.

Selkirk, E. O. (1986). On derived domains in sentence phonology. *Phonology Yearbook* **3,** 371–405.

Siegel, D. (1979). *Topics in English Morphology.* Garland, New York.

Spencer, A. (1989). *Morphological Theory: An Introduction to Word Structure in Generative Grammar.* Blackwell, Oxford.

Speas, P. (1990). *Functional Heads and the Mirror Principle.* Unpublished manuscript, University of Massachusetts, Amherst.

Sproat, R. (1985). *On Deriving the Lexicon.* Doctoral dissertation, Massachusetts Institute of Technology, Cambridge.

Strauss, S. (1982). *Lexicalist Phonology of English and German.* Foris, Dordrecht.

Suñer, M. (1975). Spanish adverbs: Support for the phonological cycle? *Linguistic Inquiry* **6,** 602–605.

Zec, D., and Inkelas, S. (1991). Clitic groups and the prosodic hierarchy. *Proceedings of the West Coast Conference on Formal Linguistics* **5,** 505–519.

I

The Interaction of Morphology and Phonology

ON THE SIMULTANEITY OF MORPHOLOGICAL AND PROSODIC STRUCTURE

GEERT BOOIJ*
ROCHELLE LIEBER†

* *Vakgroep Taalkunde*
Vrije Universiteit
1007 MC Amsterdam
The Netherlands

†*Department of English*
University of New Hampshire
Durham, New Hampshire 03824

1. INTRODUCTION

In recent years, much attention has been devoted to the internal organization of complex words and to their prosodic structure. Less attention has been devoted to the relationship between prosodic and morphological structure. In this article we explore this relationship in some detail, arguing that there is good reason to believe that morphological and prosodic structure are built in tandem and are available simultaneously.[1] We show further that it must be possible to make reference to the two coexisting structures of a single string both in phonological rules and in the lexical entries of affixes. The theoretical benefits that we derive from this proposal are large and concern several outstanding problems in morphological theory, including head operations (Aronoff, 1988), bracketing paradoxes (Pesetsky, 1985; Sproat, 1985; among many others), and the status of clitics.

The theory of morphology we assume here is that of Lieber (1989, 1992), which shares with previous work in morphology the notion that complex words are hierarchically structured and with Lieber (1980) the idea that morphological struc-

Phonetics and Phonology, Volume 4
Studies in Lexical Phonology

tures are built from the bottom up, as follows. According to this theory, all morphemes have lexical entries which indicate their category and subcategorization (what category, if any, they attach to, and in what direction), as well as their phonological representations, lexical conceptual structures (LCSs), and predicate argument structures (PASs).[2] Morphemes are put together according to their morphological subcategorization requirements, and hierarchical structure is projected from lexical information and labeled using general principles of X-bar theory and feature percolation.

With respect to prosodic categories, we assume the following. Phonological segments are grouped into a number of hierarchically organized prosodic categories. It is relatively uncontroversial to include among these prosodic categories the syllable σ, the foot F, the phonological word Wd, and the phonological phrase ϕ. McCarthy and Prince (1986) argue that reference is sometimes necessary as well to particular sorts of syllables—the light syllable σ_{μ}, the heavy syllable $\sigma_{\mu\mu}$, and the core syllable σ_c (that is, a constituent consisting of a simple CV)—and to a constituent which they refer to as the minimal word (Wd^{MIN}, which is equal to a foot (see McCarthy and Prince, 1986 : 8, for technical details). Nespor and Vogel (1986) also argue for a number of prosodic constituents above the level of the word. For our purposes it is not necessary to determine what the exact inventory of prosodic constituents is. We will be most concerned with constituents at or below the level of the prosodic word: σ (with variants σ_{μ} $\sigma_{\mu\mu}$, σ_c), F ($=Wd^{MIN}$), and Wd.

Another point in prosodic theory that we take to be uncontroversial is that morphological structure and prosodic structure need not always be isomorphic. Syllable and foot boundaries do not always coincide with morpheme boundaries, nor does the phonological word always match exactly with the morphological word (see Booij, 1985; Booij and Rubach, 1984).

It is at this point, however, that we part company with the abovementioned theories of prosodic phonology. Both Selkirk (1984) and Nespor and Vogel (1986) assume that prosodic structure is built only after construction of words and sentences has been completed. Selkirk (1984 : 82) dubs this a SYNTAX-FIRST approach. Prosodic structure is created in two stages. Below the word level, prosodic structure is built after all morphological operations have been completed. Above the word level, prosodic structure is built as part of the postlexical phonology. Nespor and Vogel (1986) are somewhat less explicit than Selkirk about the overall organization of the grammar, but the picture that emerges from their work is one in which all prosodic structure is created as part of the postlexical phonology.

We argue in what follows that neither of these models is correct. Rather, there is good reason to believe that morphological and prosodic structure are built at the same time, from the bottom up, so that representations of words consist of two simultaneous structurings coexisting on distinct planes. This assumption has always been made in the standard version of the theory of lexical phonology, as proposed in Kiparsky (1982, 1985), but not always very explicitly. It is our aim to show that this assumption is correct and that there is substantial evidence that below the word level, morphology and prosodic phonology interact and apply in tandem.

2. EVIDENCE FOR SIMULTANEITY

In this section we argue that lexical entries of morphemes may refer simultaneously to both syntactic and prosodic requirements on their environment, and that therefore the syntactic and prosodic structuring of segmental strings must be derived in tandem.

A first example comes from Dutch. In this language, there are a number of productive nonnative suffixes that derive adjectives from nonnative nouns ending in *-ie* [i], among them *-isch* /is/ and *-ief* /iv/. The choice between these two suffixes with respect to base nouns in *-ie* crucially depends on the stress patterns of the base words: *-isch* is selected if the final syllable of the base noun bears main stress, whereas *-ief* is the correct suffix for nouns in unstressed *-ie*. This is illustrated in (1).

(1)	a.	*sociologíe*	'sociology'	*sociologisch*	'sociological'
		blasfemíe	'blasphemy'	*blasfemisch*	'blasphemous'
		allergíe	'allergy'	*allergisch*	'allergic'
	b.	*prevéntie*	'prevention'	*preventief*	'preventive'
		constrúctie	'construction'	*constructief*	'constructive'
		integrátie	'integration'	*integratief*	'integrating'

The final segment [i] of the base noun is subsequently deleted before the initial [i] of the suffix.

The two suffixes are also different in that *-ief* only productively attaches to nouns in unstressed *-ie*, whereas *-isch* also occurs with nouns that do not end in *-ie*. In the latter case, there is no stress condition involved.

(2)	*proféet*	'prophet'	*profetisch*	'prophetical'
	álgebra	'algebra'	*algebraïsch*	'algebraic'
	organisátor	'organizer'	*organisatorisch*	'organizational'

That is, the stress properties of the base noun are only relevant in the domain in which the two suffixes compete.

Given these facts, the lexical entries for the morphemes *-ief* and *-isch* must contain the following subcategorization.

(3) *-ief* (i) $\sigma_w\,]_N$ ——$]_A$
-isch $]_N$ ——$]_A$

We assume that attachment of an affix with a more specific subcategorization takes precedence over that of a competing affix with a more general subcategorization (the elsewhere principle, cf. also van Marle, 1985). Therefore, it suffices to mention the prosodic condition in the lexical entry of *-ief.* This lexical entry then requires both the morphological and the prosodic properties of the base word to be available. Note that stress properties of words are to be expressed in terms of strong/weak labeling of prosodic categories such as the syllable and the foot. Therefore, a word must be prosodified before the stress rules can assign a prominence pattern.[3,4]

The relevance of prosodic information for morphology is not restricted to information concerning stress. In Polish, the choice between one of the two allomorphs of both the comparative and the imperative suffix appears to depend on another prosodic property of the base word, namely, whether its final consonant can be syllabified by the syllabification algorithm of Polish, or remains extrasyllabic. The facts are as follows (we base ourselves here on the analysis in Rubach and Booij, 1990). The comparative morpheme is either *sz* [s] or *ejsz* [ejs]. The general form is *sz,* and the allomorph *ejsz* has to be selected when the stem ends in an extrasyllabic consonant. For instance, in the following examples the stem ends in a cluster of an obstruent followed by a sonorant consonant, which is an impossible coda because it violates the universal sonority sequencing generalization (Selkirk, 1984) (4a), or by a cluster of two sonorant consonants (4b), an ill-formed coda in Polish, and therefore, the final consonant of these stems remains unsyllabified (*-y* is the nominative singular ending; the *i* before *ejsz* indicates palatalization of the preceding consonant).

(4)		ADJECTIVE:	COMPARATIVE:
	a.	*podł-y* 'mean'	*podl-ejsz-y*
		szczodr-y 'generous'	*szczodrz-ejsz-y*
	b.	*czarn-y* 'black'	*czarn-iejsz-y*
		ogóln-y 'general'	*ogóln-iejsz-y*
		skromn-y 'modest'	*skromn-iejsz-y*
		fajn-y 'nice'	*fajn-iejsz-y*

Therefore, the lexical entry for the more specific comparative allomorph *ejsz* will be as follows, where C^* indicates an extrasyllabic consonant.

(5) *ejsz* $C^*]_A$ ——$]_A$

As above, we assume that in the case of competing affixes, the more specific one takes precedence over the more general, unrestricted one.[5]

Normally, the imperative morpheme of Polish does not surface directly, but only indirectly, in the form of palatalization of the stem-final consonant. Therefore, it is assumed that it consists of a so-called *yer,* a floating segment that only surfaces phonetically in specific contexts. For our purposes it suffices to point out here that we also find an allomorph in which the *yer* is preceded by the sequence *ij* [ij]. This allomorph only occurs when the final consonant of the stem is extrasyllabic, as is illustrated in (6). As in the previous case, there are two types of coda clusters that give rise to extrasyllabic consonants: clusters that violate the universal sonority sequencing generalization (6a), and clusters that violate the Polish prohibition on clusters of sonorants (6b).

(6)		VERBAL STEM:		IMPERATIVE:
	a.	*nagl-*	'to hurry'	*nagl-ij*
		spulchn-	'to make soft'	*spulchn-ij*
	b.	*zwoln-*	'to cover'	*zwoln-ij*
		utajn-	'to cover up'	*utajn-ij*

Hence, the allomorph /ijE/ (E stands for the *yer*) is subcategorized as follows.

(7) /ijE/ $C^*]_V$ —— $]_V$

In sum, for the selection of the proper allomorph of both the comparative and the imperative morpheme it is crucial that both the morphological and the prosodic structuring of the stem be available. These facts thus support both the theory of lexical phonology that claims that phonology and morphology are interspersed, and the claim that is the subject of this article, the simultaneity thesis.

The requirement of simultaneity not only manifests itself in the subcategorizations of bound morphemes in the lexicon, but also in the fact that there are phonological rules that refer simultaneously to both types of structuring. Let us call such rules BIPLANAR RULES.[6]

Hayes (1982) proposed such a biplanar rule for English, namely the rule of Adjective Extrametricality. This rule states that in English adjectives the final syllable is extrametrical. Thus, we get correct stress assignments such as *magnánimous* and *relúctant* instead of the incorrect **magnanímous* and **reluctánt.* This rule is a typically biplanar rule, because it refers to both morphosyntactic information (the notion "adjective") and to prosodic structure (the notion "extraprosodic syllable").

A second example of such a rule is the stress rule for Dutch nominal compounds. This rule assigns main stress to the left constituent of such compounds (Visch, 1989: 84).

(8) DUTCH COMPOUND STRESS RULE:
In a configuration $[AB]_N$, A is strong.

Visch correctly restricts this rule to nominal compounds because adjectival compounds such as *reuze-sterk* 'very strong' and *donker-groen* 'dark green' clearly have a different stress pattern in which both constituents are felt to be equally stressed. Therefore, rule (8) must refer to morphosyntactic information, the category label N. On the other hand, this rule clearly refers to prosodic structure, since the constituents that receive the labels "strong" and "weak" are prosodic categories (usually called PROSODIC WORDS) which dominate prosodic categories like syllable and foot.

The stress rule for nominal compounds of Dutch is a typical lexical rule, because it can also have exceptions (cf. Booij, 1977). That is, it cannot simply be part of the mapping procedure that maps morphosyntactic structure into prosodic structure. It is, therefore, an instance of a lexical phonological rule that refers simultaneously to the two kinds of hierarchical structuring of words discussed here.

A final example of a biplanar rule is the German rule of Schwa Insertion in nouns (Hall, 1989; Wiese, 1988). This rule inserts the German default vowel schwa before an extrasyllabic consonant. For instance, the underlying form of *Uebel* 'evil' is /ybl/. When we syllabify this underlying form, the /l/ remains extrasyllabic, because a coda cluster /bl/ would violate the sonority sequencing generalization. A schwa is then inserted to "save" the /l/. As Hall (1989:835) points out, this rule only applies to nouns: Schwa Insertion before consonants also occurs in adjectives, but at a later level, and not only before extrasyllabic consonants. Therefore, the structural description of this rule has to refer simultaneously to the morphosyntactic category "noun" and the prosodic notion "extrasyllabic consonant."

The conclusion of this section is that both subcategorizations of morphemes and phonological rules sometimes have to refer simultaneously to morphological and prosodic information, and both thus have a biplanar character. In the next section we show how the concept of biplanarity can be used to solve a number of theoretical problems with respect to the interaction of phonology and morphology.

3. THEORETICAL CONSEQUENCES

3.1. Head Operations

The first problem we consider concerns the existence of what Aronoff (1988), following Hoeksema (1985), calls head operations.[7] Hoeksema (1985) defines the notion HEAD OPERATION as in (9).

(9) F is a head operation if $F(Y) = Z$ and $W = XY$ (where Y is the head of W) together imply that $F(W) = X + F(Y) = X + Z$.

(9) says simply that a morphological rule is a head operation if it reaches into a word W to perform an operation on its head Y, changing Y to Z. Aronoff applies the notion of head operation to several recalcitrant cases of reduplication, among them a classically problematic case in Tagalog. Tagalog has a prefix *pang-* which

attaches to nouns. As the data in (10a) show, [ŋ] plus a following stop appears in the derived form as a single nasal homorganic with the underlying stop.

(10) a. *atip* 'roofing' *pang-atip* 'that used for roofing'
pu:tul 'cut' *pa-mu:tul* 'that used for cutting'
b. *pa-mu-mu:tul* 'a cutting in quantity'

The example in (10b) shows further that when the second form in (10a) is reduplicated, the reduplicating stem shows the effects of having already undergone affixation; the stem-initial [p] has become [m] prior to reduplication. This analysis is of course problematic in traditional frameworks in which morphology strictly precedes phonology; in such cases the sandhi rule operating between prefix and stem seems to have "overapplied." The ordering of the phonological rule with respect to reduplication is not necessarily problematic in frameworks where morphological rules can apply to the output of phonological rules and vice versa, as in the theory of lexical phonology we assume here. Nevertheless, even in frameworks in which phonological and morphological rules can be interspersed, it must still be explained why the reduplication rule seems to reach into an already prefixed word.

Aronoff suggests that the derivation of the form in (10b) involves a head operation. After affixation of *pang-*, which triggers sandhi, reduplication reaches into the word to copy the first two segments of the stem. The notion that certain morphological operations must be "head operations" is a problematic one. It is not at all clear that the item operated on by the "head operation" is actually the head of the word. Lieber (1992) shows that Tagalog word formation is largely left-headed; the majority of Tagalog prefixes are category-changing. In the case outlined above as well, it is very likely that it is the outermost prefix rather than the stem which is the head. Specifically, according to Schachter and Otanes (1972), *pang-* attaches to noun or verb stems to form adjectives. Although Aronoff's glosses, taken from Bloomfield (1933), suggest that the *pang-* forms are nouns, a native speaker of Tagalog confirms that they are adjectives instead with the glosses 'for roofing' and 'for cutting', in conformity to Schachter and Otanes (1972).[8] Reduplication then changes the *pang-* adjective to a noun. And if the reduplicative affix changes category, it must be the head. The stem therefore cannot be the head, and the operation cannot be a head operation.

We therefore suggest that Tagalog reduplication and other similar cases are not head operations. Rather, they appear to involve what Broselow and McCarthy (1984) and McCarthy and Prince (1986) call AFFIXATION TO A PROSODIC CONSTITUENT. In fact, we propose that the Tagalog reduplication process sketched above is one in which the reduplicative morpheme is subcategorized for both morphological and prosodic constituents, and that this simultaneous biplanar subcategorization gives rise to nonisomorphic prosodic and morphological structures in this case.

Let us first illustrate the notion of biplanar subcategorization with a somewhat simpler case. McCarthy and Prince (1986: 12) show that it is sometimes necessary to subcategorize affixes to attach to prosodic constituents (e.g., Wd, Wd^{MIN}, etc.), rather than to purely morphological constituents (that is, an X^0 of some sort).[9] They argue, for example, that the reduplicative affix in the Australian language Yidiny (Dixon, 1977) must attach to Wd^{MIN}, rather than simply to N^0. Consider the examples in (11).

(11) YIDINY NOMINAL REDUPLICATION:[10]

mulari	'initiated man'	*mulamulari*	'initiated men'
kintalpa	'lizard sp.'	*kintalkintalpa*	'lizards'

The Yidiny reduplicative prefix is, according to McCarthy and Prince (1986), the prosodic constituent Wd^{MIN} (which is to say a foot—two syllables in Yidiny). If the Wd^{MIN} prefix were to attach to the morphological constituent N^0, with concomitant copying of the phonemic melody of this constituent, we would expect the derivations illustrated in (12). Note that in (12) prosodic structure is illustrated above the phonemic melody, morphological structure below.

(12)

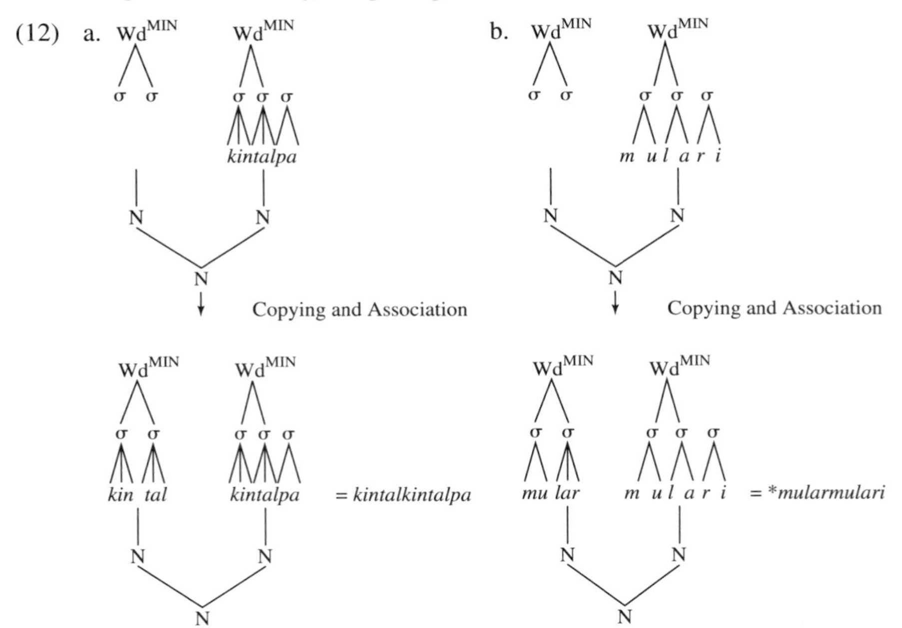

The derivations in (12) are presumed to go as follows. In both (12a) and (12b) the reduplicative prefix Wd^{MIN} is attached to the noun, and morphological structure is built. The phonemic melody of the verb stem is copied and the prosodic affix incorporates as much of the phonemic melody as can be fitted into its two syllables. The result is correct for the case in (12a); *kintalpa* reduplicates as *kintalkintalpa.* But (12b) is not; reduplication based on the whole noun stem yields **mu-*

larmulari, rather than the correct *mulamulari.* The question raised is thus how to get the *l* of *kintalpa* to reduplicate without also getting the *r* of *mulari* showing up in the reduplicative prefix.

McCarthy and Prince argue that this pattern of facts follows if the reduplicative prefix $\mathrm{Wd}^{\mathrm{MIN}}$ attaches to the prosodic constituent $\mathrm{Wd}^{\mathrm{MIN}}$ rather than simply to N^0, and if we make the following crucial assumption: ONLY THE PHONEMIC MELODY OF THE PROSODIC CONSTITUENT TO WHICH THE REDUPLICATIVE AFFIX ATTACHES IS AVAILABLE FOR COPYING. For the example in (12a), the prosodic constituent $\mathrm{Wd}^{\mathrm{MIN}}$ which is copied is *kintal,* since the *l* forms the coda of the second syllable of the $\mathrm{Wd}^{\mathrm{MIN}}$. But for (12b) the constituent which is copied is *mula,* the *r* being the onset of the third stem syllable, and therefore not part of the $\mathrm{Wd}^{\mathrm{MIN}}$. This is illustrated in the derivations in (13), where the plane of morphological structure is again beneath the melody and that of prosodic structure above the melody.

(13)

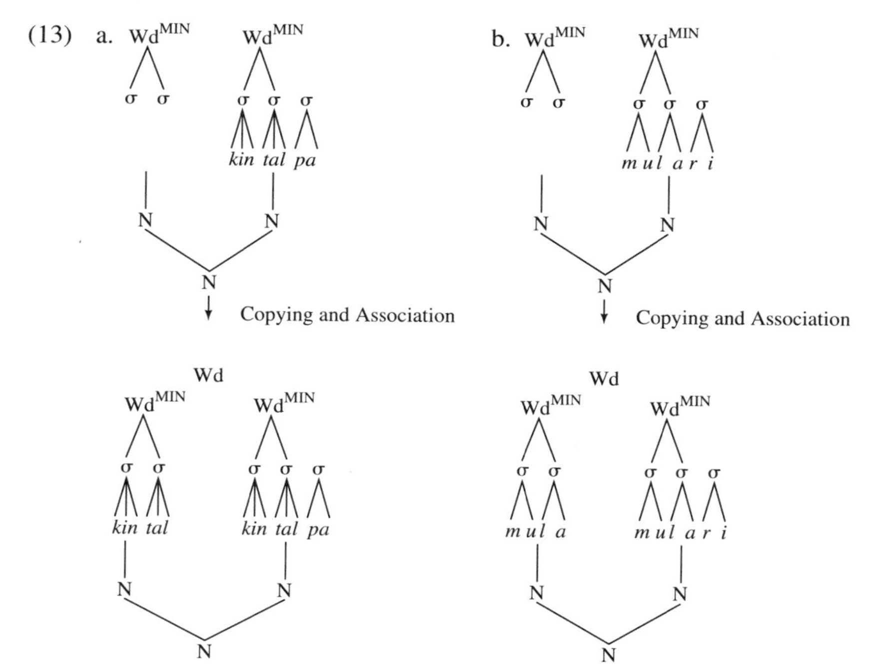

The pattern of reduplication illustrated in Yidiny can thus be accounted for if we assume that a reduplicative affix can sometimes be subcategorized for a prosodic constituent alongside a morphosyntactic constituent. In the theory of Lieber (1992), the Yidiny reduplicative prefix will therefore have the biplanar subcategorization in (14).

(14) YIDINY REDUPLICATION:
$\mathrm{Wd}^{\mathrm{MIN}} / [_{\mathrm{N}} \text{———} [_{\mathrm{N/Wd^{MIN}}}$

The notation in (14) should be interpreted as follows. The reduplicative prefix is a Wd^{MIN} which attaches to a Wd^{MIN} in prosodic structure and to a N^0 in morphological structure. Both morphological structure and prosodic structure must obviously be present simultaneously for such a subcategorization to be met.

The notion of biplanar subcategorization may now be used to account for the Tagalog case in (10). We assume that the particular reduplicative prefix in question is a core syllable (that is, CV), σ_c in the notation of McCarthy and Prince (1986), and that it has the subcategorization in (15).

(15) TAGALOG REDUPLICATION:

σ_c / [N ____ $[_{A/Wd^{MIN}}$

(15) says that the reduplicative prefix σ_c attaches morphologically to an A^0 and prosodically to the Wd^{MIN} (= a foot in Tagalog). Let us see what happens when this prefix is attached. We assume, first of all, that the prefix *pang-* is attached to a noun or verb stem, triggering the phonological rule of sandhi and giving rise to the simultaneous morphological and prosodic structure illustrated in (16).

(16) a.

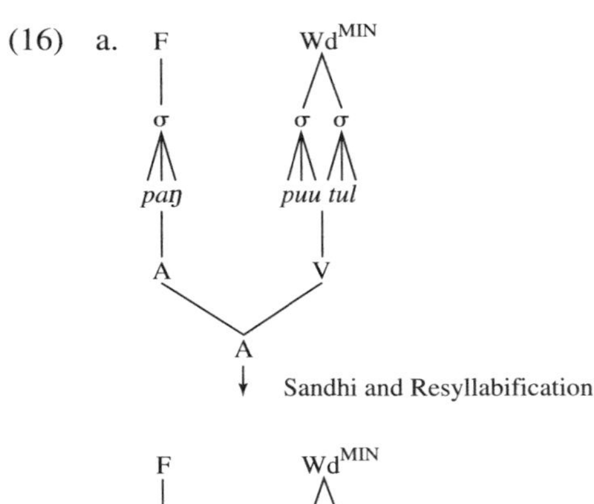

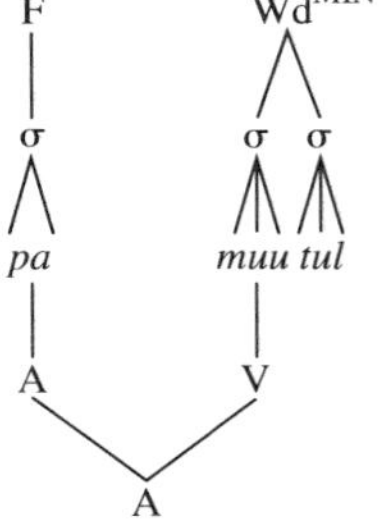

When we try to insert the reduplicative prefix, however, we find that we cannot fulfill the morphological and prosodic subcategorizations simultaneously. If we insert the σ_c to the left of *pa-*, in (16b), the σ_c will not be adjacent to the Wd^{MIN}, as illustrated in (17a). But if we try to insert the reduplicative prefix so that it is adjacent to the Wd^{MIN}, it will not be adjacent to the A, as shown in (17b); indeed, it is unclear how morphological structure could be projected at all in this structure, since to do so would involve creation of morphological structure on top of already existing morphological structure.

(17) a.* b.*

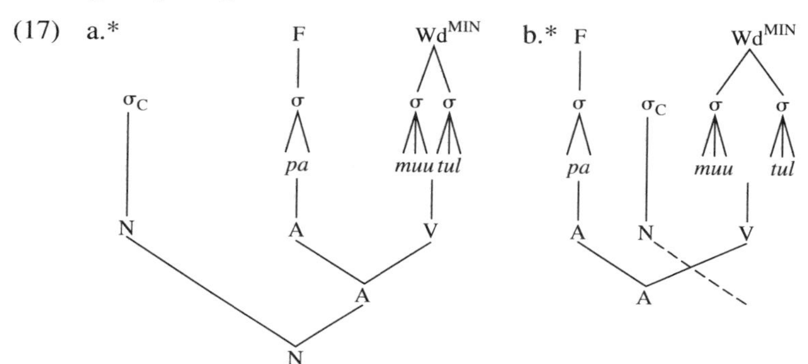

In order to get the reduplicative prefix in Tagalog to fulfill its morphological and prosodic subcategorizations simultaneously, we need to make one further assumption. It is clear that the lexical entry in (15) contains (at least) two sorts of requirements, both of which must be met. The reduplicative prefix consists of phonological information (it is a core syllable without any inherent segmental content) and morphosyntactic information (it is a bound noun, which presumably carries all of the morphosyntactic features of nouns in Tagalog). Given the dual content of the reduplicative prefix in Tagalog, we assume that the following occurs. Since it is not possible to satisfy its subcategorization if the prefix remains intact, we assume that a split occurs in the lexical representation of the prefix in order to meet both phonological and morphosyntactic requirements: the phonological material is inserted into the tree in (16b) adjacent to the $\mathrm{Wd}^{\mathrm{MIN}}$, thus satisfying the phonological part of the subcategorization, and the morphosyntactic part (the category features for N plus concomitant morphosyntactic features) is adjoined to the A, thus satisfying the morphosyntactic part of the subcategorization. This is illustrated in (18).

(18) a. b.

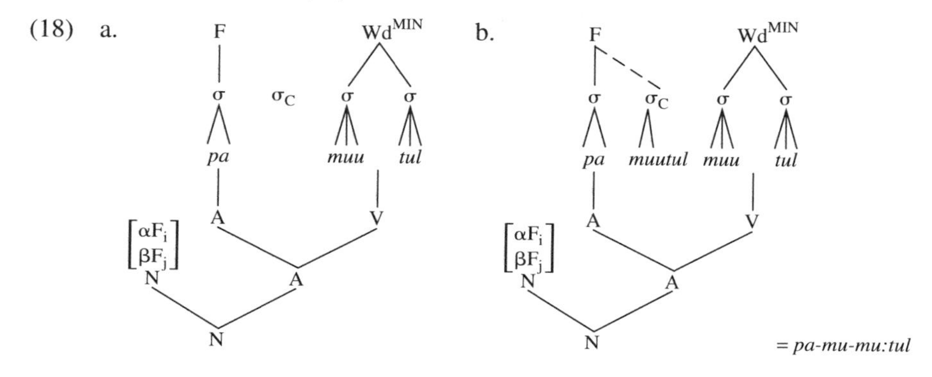

(18a) shows the splitting of the phonological and morphosyntactic parts of the entry. This is then followed by the copying of the phonemic melody of the Wd^{MIN} and association to the σ_c. We assume that the σ_c prefix is then incorporated into the existing prosodic structure by being absorbed into the preceding F. This is illustrated in (18b).

Note that we are not proposing that the reduplicative affix in Tagalog MOVES from one part of the word structure to another, but rather that the dual subcategorization requirement forces the lexical entry of the prefix to split upon insertion, so that the syllable template is severed from its categorial signature. The outermost layer of structure in (18b) does not contain a trace or an empty element of any sort, since there is no movement involved here; it merely carries the categorial signature of the prefix. Assuming that morphological and prosodic structure are built in tandem, and also that subcategorization of morphemes must sometimes satisfy both morphological and prosodic requirements thus allows us to explain the apparently odd behavior of the reduplicative prefix in Tagalog without invoking the special device of head operations. We will see in the next section that other theoretical benefits follow from these assumptions as well.

3.2. Bracketing Paradoxes

In this section we argue that a number of well-known bracketing paradoxes can be made to disappear if the simultaneity of morphological and prosodic structure is taken into account, and specifically if affixes are permitted to have both morphological and prosodic subcategorizations, as previously argued. We begin with a discussion of the well-known bracketing paradox of the English comparative form *unhappier* (see also Booij and Rubach, 1984, and Cohn, 1989, for discussion of similar paradoxes in Indonesian).

The problem presented by *unhappier* is as follows: the English comparative suffix *-er* can normally only be attached to adjectival bases consisting of one syllable, or consisting of two syllables of which the second one is light, a characteristic example of a prosodic condition on word formation. Pesetsky (1985) observes not only that *happy* allows for *-er* affixation, but also that it is possible to affix *-er* to the derived adjective *unhappy,* although it consists of three syllables. The so-called bracketing paradox is therefore that from the morphological point of view *unhappier* is derived from *unhappy,* whereas, given the prosodic condition on the comparative morpheme, *unhappier* seems to be derived from *happier.*

(19) morphology: [[*un*[*happy*]]*er*]
phonology: [*un*[[*happy*]*er*]]

Booij and Rubach (1984) propose to solve this problem by assuming that the prosodic condition on *-er*-affixation does not pertain to the whole word, but rather to the prosodic word to which *-er* is attached. The prosodic structure of *happy* consists of two syllables that together form one prosodic word. *Unhappy,* on the other hand, consists of two prosodic words, *un* and *happy.*

We propose to treat the comparative affix *-er* as an affix which has simultaneous morphological and prosodic subcategorization. The lexical entry for the English comparative morpheme *-er* thus looks like (20).

(20) *er* $]_{A}$ ___ $]_{A}$

[σ (σ_{C}) $]_{Wd}$ ___

Note that we do not need to stipulate here that the prosodic restriction to one or two syllables that *-er* is subject to pertains to the last prosodic word only. We assume that subcategorization requires strict locality. An affix subcategorized to attach to a prosodic constituent X must attach to the closest X. In the case of *-er,* this is the last prosodic word of the base word, since *-er,* like all cohering suffixes (i.e., suffixes that do not form a prosodic word of their own) fuses prosodically with the last prosodic word of the word to which it is attached, with concomitant resyllabification. In other words, prosodic subcategorizations of morphemes can only see the prosodically adjacent material.

(21)

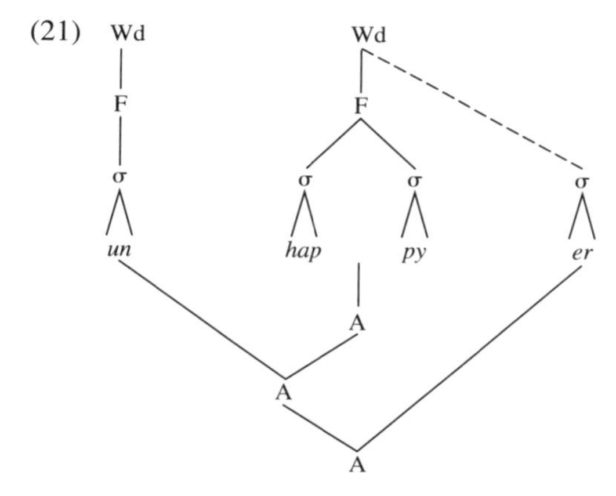

A related bracketing paradox is the case of *ungrammaticality* and similar words in *-ity* and *-ation.* Morphologically, *ungrammaticality* is to be considered as a derivation from *ungrammatical.* However, phonologically it should be seen as a case of prefixation of *un-* to *grammaticality,* because in the current analyses of lexical phonology the stress-neutral prefix *un-* should be added after (i.e., at a later level than) the stress-shifting suffix *-ity.* This is a problem for morphology, because *un-* is subcategorized for adjectives, not for nouns.

As Booij and Rubach (1984) point out, this problem can be solved by realizing two things. First, the domain of the Word Stress rule of English is not the morphological word but rather the prosodic word. Thus in compounds, which consist of at least two prosodic words, the Word Stress rule applies in at least two domains. Note also that the Word Stress rule is a rule that specifies prominence relations between syllables within a prosodic word. Secondly, as pointed out above, the prefix *un-* can be assumed to form a prosodic word of its own. This implies that there is no phonological problem created anymore by the correct morphological structure [[*un*[*grammatical*]]*ity*]. The relevant domains for the assignment of word stress are (*un*) and (*grammaticality*). In other words, although morphologically *-ity* attaches to the whole base word *ungrammatical,* prosodically it is only attached to the last prosodic word, with which it fuses: (*grammatical*). The lexical entry for *-ity* will therefore be as follows.

(22) *-ity* $]_A$ ——$]_N$

Note that it is not necessary to subcategorize *-ity* for a preceding prosodic word, because normally suffixes become part of the preceding prosodic word.

The representation of *ungrammaticality* will thus be as follows (the asterisk indicates the designated terminal element of the prosodic word *grammaticality*).

(23)

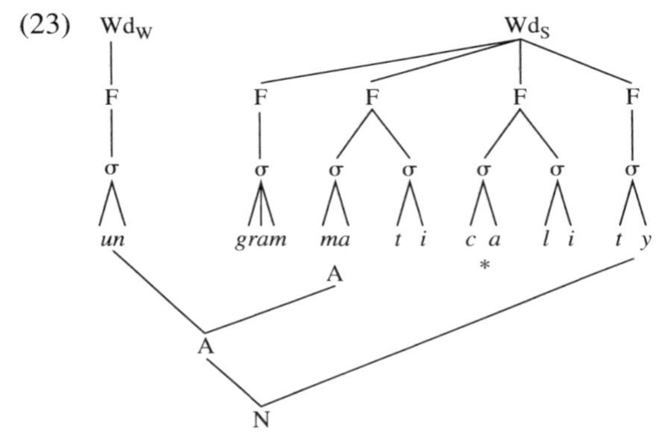

The same analysis can be applied to similar cases such as *underestimation* and *extrametricality,* since *under-* and *extra-* can also be considered to be prosodic words of their own. Note, by the way, that we also have to specify prominence relations within so-called stress-neutral prefixes; both in *under-* and *extra-* the first syllable is strong, in conformity with the word stress rule. That is, it is impossible to account for the so-called stress-neutral character of English prefixes even by ordering prefixation after the word stress rules, since polysyllabic prefixes conform to the patterns of metrical structure assignment that we find for words, and therefore they have to undergo the rule for (prosodic!) word stress.

It should be observed that the solution to this particular bracketing paradox, although it shows the necessity for an analysis in which the two sorts of structuring are available, does not necessarily require these two structures to be present simultaneously. Nevertheless, we deal with these phenomena here for two reasons.

First, the hypothesis of biplanarity provides us with a natural solution for this kind of bracketing paradox. Secondly, this analysis does imply that rules may have to refer to both planes: whereas in English compounds consisting of two prosodic words the Compound Stress rule correctly predicts the first to be strong, the situation is just the opposite in prefixed structures where the second prosodic word is the strongest one. That is, the metrical rules that assign prominence relations above the level of the prosodic word are sensitive to morphological information, namely the difference between nominal compounds and prefixed complex nouns. Thus, this case is parallel to the Dutch one discussed above concerning the stress differences between nominal and adjectival compounds in Dutch.

We therefore conclude that by making use of the biplanar nature of the structuring of words, there are no bracketing paradoxes that have to do with a conflict between phonology and morphology, and we do not need to introduce multiple levels of representation and rules relating these levels in morphology, as proposed by Pesetsky (1985) and Sproat (1985, 1988).[11]

3.3. Clitics

Clitics form classical examples of the nonisomorphy between morphosyntactic and prosodic structure. This can be seen most clearly in the case of so-called simple clitics (Zwicky, 1977) that have the same syntactic distribution as their nonclitic counterparts but are prosodically dependent on either the following prosodic word (proclisis) or the preceding prosodic word (enclisis). In this section we argue that simple clitics are elements that have only prosodic subcategorization but no morphological subcategorization and that they are distinct from affixes, which do have morphological subcategorization. The present framework therefore makes available a convenient typology in which clitics can be distinguished from other bound morphemes.

We illustrate this with the Dutch third person singular clitic pronoun *ie* [i] that is syntactically equivalent to its strong counterpart *hij* 'he'.[12] *Ie* is an enclitic because it always fuses prosodically with the preceding prosodic word, which functions as its host. This host provides the necessary prosodic support. The following sentences illustrate the syntactic equivalence of *hij* and *ie*.

(24) a. *Komt hij? / Komt ie?*
lit. 'Comes he? Does he come?'
b. *dat hij komt / dat ie komt*
'that he comes'
c. *wat hij doet / wat ie doet*
'what he does'

That *ie* forms one prosodic word with the preceding word is clear from the syllabification patterns $(kom)_\sigma$ $(tie)_\sigma$, $(da)_\sigma$ $(tie)_\sigma$, and $(wa)_\sigma$ $(tie)_\sigma$, which show that the syntactic boundary before *ie* does not create a prosodic word boundary [compare *komt aan* 'comes at (i.e., arrives)' with the syllabification pattern $(komt)_\sigma$ $(aan)_\sigma$]. Note also that *ie* is a typical clitic in that it combines with words of completely different syntactic categories, namely verbs, complementizers, and relative (or interrogative) pronouns. We can express this prosodic property of the clitic *ie* by assigning the following prosodic subcategorization to its lexical entry.

(25) *ie* N, 3rd pers. sing. $]_{Wd}$ ——

This lexical entry for *-ie* states that *ie* can only be inserted after a prosodic word. This clearly requires that at the level of lexical insertion the prosodic structuring of words up to the word level is already available, and this is exactly what is predicted by our view of the role of prosodic structure in the lexical phonology: since morphological and prosodic structure are derived simultaneously, both kinds of information are available at the level of lexical insertion. We also assume that, like affixes, such clitics become part of the prosodic category for which they are subcategorized. But, unlike affixes, they do not have a syntactic subcategorization, and hence they cooccur with words of different syntactic categories.

This prosodic subcategorization of *ie* also correctly predicts that *ie* cannot occur at the beginning of a sentence, because in that case there is no host available.

(26) *Hij komt. / *Ie komt*
'He comes.'

That is, the exclusion of *ie* from the sentence-initial position does not need to be accounted for by a special stipulation in the syntax, but simply follows from its prosodic subcategorization.[13] Similarly, *ie* cannot be used as a one-word sentence (for instance as an answer to a question) because in that case it would also lack a prosodic host. From this we may conclude that the concept of "prosodic subcategorization" is not only necessary for expressing prosodic conditions in morphology, but also to account for the behavior and distributional restrictions of simple clitics. Moreover, this analysis supports our view that prosodic and morphosyntactic properties of morphemes and words must be simultaneously available.

The concept of prosodic subcategorization can also be used in accounting for the observations concerning clitics made by Klavans (1985). The main theme of this interesting article is the independence of syntax and phonology in cliticization. For instance, the following situation obtains in Nganhcara, an Australian language: the clitics *ngku* 'you' and *nhcara* 'us' occur either before or after the verb, which is always sentence-final (otherwise, word order is free in this language). Therefore, Klavans considers the verb as the syntactic host of these clitics. However, phonologically, these clitics are always attached to the preceding word. This is a phonotactic necessity, because Nganhcara does not allow for the consonant clusters *ngk* and *nhc* in word-initial position. Therefore, the first consonant of the cluster has to form a syllable with the final vowel of the preceding word. This is illustrated by the following sentence taken from Klavans (1985:104).

(27) *nhila pama-ng nhingku ku?a=ngku wa:*
he.NOM man.ERG 2sg.DAT child.DAT=2sg.DAT give=DAT
'The man gave a dog to you.'

The enclitic nature of *ngku* is indicated by '='. Klavans (1985:98) remarks that the direction of phonological attachment is a property of the clitic itself. In our analysis, this can be expressed by providing the lexical entry for such clitic pronouns with the prosodic subcategorization $]_{Wd}$ ——. We also assume that, just as in the case of the English comparative suffix dealt with above, clitics that are subcategorized for a prosodic word become part of that prosodic word by convention.

Although Klavans's observations about the behavior of clitics appear to be correct, her own formalization of the enclitic property of such pronouns is inadequate. She proposes to consider clitics as "phrasal affixes," that is, as words that are subcategorized (in the sense of Lieber, 1980) for a phrasal host. For instance, the general form of the subcategorization frame of clitics that she proposes (p. 117) is as follows.

(28) $_{X'}[$——$]_{X'}$ = enclitic
proclitic = $_{X'}[$——$]_{X'}$

Note, however, that such a subcategorization frame is impossible in those cases where an enclitic is subcategorized for a syntactic host on its right side, unless we also allow for subcategorization frames of the following type, with the boundary symbol "=" nonadjacent to the category for which the clitic is subcategorized.

(29) = enclitic $_{X'}[$——$]_{X'}$
$_{X'}[$——$]_{X'}$ proclitic =

This amounts to using the symbol "=" as a diacritic for the prosodic requirement "follows/precedes a prosodic host." That is, subcategorization frames of the form proposed by Klavans do not make it possible to account for the difference between the prosodic host and the syntactic host of a clitic, which are not necessarily identical, as Klavans has argued convincingly [cf. (27)]. This is only possible by making use of a separate prosodic subcategorization.

In fact, it is unlikely that we need syntactic subcategorization at all for clitics. In cases such as the Dutch clitic discussed above, the pronominal clitic shows up only in places where the independently needed phrase structure principles of Dutch would allow pronouns. Similarly, in the cases of the Greek definite article *ho* and the Kwakwala determiner particles that Klavans discusses, the clitics show up only where the phrase structure principles of these languages would independently allow articles and determiner particles. Since the syntactic positions of these clitics follow from the phrase structure rules of the languages in question, it would be superfluous (and incorrect) to subcategorize them for syntactic phrasal hosts, as Klavans proposes to do. Clitics are prosodically, not syntactically, dependent, and we propose to express this prosodic dependence through prosodic subcategorization.

Note that there are, however, items which we would consider to be bona fide phrasal affixes, that is, bound morphemes which subcategorize for a phrasal host. Lieber (1992) gives a number of examples of phrasal affixes, including the English possessive marker *-s* which Klavans assumes to be a clitic. Whereas clitics can have words of different syntactic categories as prosodic hosts, a real phrasal affix such as the possessive suffix *-s* occurs only with phrases of a specified type, in this case NP; prosodically it is absorbed into the closest phonological word to its left, as most suffixes without special prosodic subcategorization are.

We consider then that it is correct to characterize simple clitics as items which are syntactically independent, but prosodically dependent, and therefore that a theory that allows simultaneous reference to prosodic and morphological structure is superior to one that does not.

4. CONCLUSION

We have argued in this article that there are a number of reasons to believe that prosodic structure and morphological structure must be built in tandem. There are phonological rules that must refer to both sorts of structure simultaneously and affixes whose subcategorizations must be biplanar as well. Assuming simultaneity of prosodic and morphological structure allows us to eliminate the notion of "head operation" from morphology, to account simply for several sorts of bracketing paradoxes, and to characterize simple clitics in an appropriate way. Finally, by using the notions of morphological and prosodic subcategorization we can arrive at a typology of morphemes that allows us to distinguish clitics from both free morphemes and affixes.

ACKNOWLEDGMENT

The second author would like to acknowledge the generous support of the NWO, the Netherlands Organization for Scientific Research, during the time that this article was written.

NOTES

[1] Cf. Anderson (1975), Booij (1988), Booij and Rubach (1984), and Cohn (1989). Similar ideas have been developed in an unpublished dissertation by Inkelas (1989).

[2] See Jackendoff (1987), Levin and Rappaport (1986), and Rappaport and Levin (1988) for discussion of LCS, PAS, and the relationship between them.

[3] Note that even the grid-only theory of word stress requires that information about the syllabification of words be available.

[4] It is probably useful at this point to discuss some conceivable alternatives to the analysis proposed here. First, note that the difference in stress pattern between, e.g., *sociologíe* and *prevéntie* cannot be predicted on the basis of the segmental composition of these words. All present analyses of Dutch stress (e.g., Van der Hulst, 1984; Kager, 1989) assume that in the normal case main stress falls on the penultimate syllable of words ending in *-ie,* and therefore words in *-ie* with final stress have to be marked diacritically with a feature, say [+F], that takes care of this. Note, however, that we cannot make use of this feature [+F] instead of stress to select the proper suffix, since it is the distributionally more restricted suffix *-ief* that requires that its class of base words be characterized, whereas the words in *-ie* that are marked by the feature [+F] are those that cooccur with the more general suffix *-isch* (note that there is no evidence in Dutch that the distribution of *-ief* is determined by a diacritic feature [latinate]).

Observe, furthermore, that we cannot derive the adjectives from nominal stems without *-ie* such as *sociolog-* and *prevent-*, because in that case the property that distinguishes the bases of *-ief* and *-isch* would not be available, since it is located on the final syllable with [i]. That is, this is a typical case of word-based morphology.

Another conceivable analysis is based on the idea expressed in Chomsky and Halle (1968) that morphology precedes phonology, as suggested more recently by Halle and Vergnaud (1987). The facts discussed here might be analyzed within such as theory as follows. The morphology attaches both *-ief* and *-isch* to nouns in *-ie.* Prosodic structure is created cyclically on the basis of the morphological structure of the complex words, and there is a filter that states that words in which the suffix *-ief* is preceded by a syllable with main stress are ill-formed. Note, however, that the final [i] of the base noun that bears main stress before the suffix is added is deleted by rule before suffixes beginning with [i]. Therefore the filter could only do its work if it applied before the application of the [i]-deletion rule. Similarly, the filter would also have to apply before the application of the stress rules that derive the stress pattern of the adjectives, because otherwise the crucial information would get lost. That is, the filter cannot function as a prosodic well-formedness condition on the surface form of these adjectives, as one would expect from filters. One could of course envision a theory in which filters could be cyclic checking mechanisms, but such a theory would be far less restrictive than the theory of lexical phonology we assume here; it would, for example, leave the way open for the ordering of filters after particular rules in a cycle. Thus, the filter approach that one is forced to accept here, if one rejects the basic tenet of lexical phonology, seems to be completely ad hoc.

A final alternative analysis of the *-ief*/*-isch* facts might seem to be the following. We might assume a surface filter at the end of the lexicon for checking the stress patterns of words with these suffixes, with a postlexical rule deleting [i] before [i]. This alternative is not correct either, however; such a postlexical filter would incorrectly apply to words ending in [i] followed by the clitic *ie* [i], for example, *wie-ie is* 'who he is' (note that *-ie* forms one prosodic word with the preceding word).

[5] Alternatively, one might assume a phonological rule that inserts *ej* in this context. Note, however, that this cannot be a general rule of epenthesis, because *ej* is only inserted in comparatives. It is therefore more natural to analyze these facts in terms of two competing suffixes. If one preferred to assume a phonological insertion rule here, this would still make the point that lexical phonological rules have to refer to both morphological and prosodic structure.

Parallel to the discussion above with respect to Dutch, one might consider an alternative analysis in which a filter forbids the long allomorph to occur after a syllabified consonant. Again, such a filter could not be a condition on the surface form of these words, because at the surface all consonants will be syllabified due to the recursive application of syllabification procedures.

[6] Note that the examples which we discuss below provide direct evidence against the claim in Cohn (1989 : 197) that, in languages which have prosodic structure not isomorphic with morphological structure, the phonology will not refer to morphological structure.

[7] This section is adapted from Lieber, *Deconstructing Morphology. Word Formation in Syntactic Theory,* with permission from the publisher, the University of Chicago Press. Copyright © 1992 by the University of Chicago.

[8] Thanks to Patrocinio Schweikart for the Tagalog data. Further evidence that *pang-* forms are adjectives is that they can occur in the position of modifiers of nouns, as in *papel pang-sulat* 'paper for writing'.

[9] McCarthy and Prince (1986) do not state the facts below in terms of morphological subcategorization, so here we are taking the liberty of translating their basic idea into the morphological framework we have adopted.

[10] McCarthy and Prince (1986) label this reduplication "Verbal Reduplication," but in Dixon (1977) these examples are given as examples of Nominal Reduplication.

[11] See also Hoeksema (1987) for a critical appraisal of Pesetsky's (1985) proposal.

[12] See also Booij and Rubach (1987) and the references cited there for data concerning Dutch clitics.

[13] The general distribution of *ie,* as with other pronouns, is accounted for by syntactic principles such as X-bar theory, θ-theory, case theory, and so on.

REFERENCES

Anderson, S. (1975). On the interaction of phonological rules of various types, *Journal of Linguistics* **11,** 39–62.

Aronoff, M. (1988). Head operations and strata in reduplication. *Yearbook of Morphology* **1,** 1–15.

Bloomfield, L. (1933). *Language.* Holt, New York.

Booij, G. E. (1977). *Dutch Morphology: A Study of Word Formation in Generative Grammar.* Foris, Dordrecht.

Booij, G. E. (1985). Coordination reduction in complex words: a case for prosodic phonology. In *Advances in Non-linear Phonology* (H. van der Hulst and N. Smith, eds.), pp. 143–160. Foris, Dordrecht.

Booij, G. E. (1988). On the relation between lexical and prosodic phonology. In *Certamen Phonologicum. Papers from the 1987 Cortona Phonology Meeting* (P. M. Bertinetto and M. Loporcaro, eds.), pp. 63–75. Rosenberg & Selier, Turin.

Booij, G. E., and Rubach, J. (1984). Morphological and prosodic domains in Lexical Phonology. *Phonology Yearbook* **1,** 1–28.

Booij, G. E., and Rubach, J. (1987). Postcyclic versus postlexical rules in Lexical Phonology. *Linguistic Inquiry* **18,** 1–44.

Broselow, E., and McCarthy, J. (1984). A theory of internal reduplication. *The Linguistic Review* **3,** 25–88.

Chomsky, N., and Halle, M. 1968. *The Sound Pattern of English.* Harper & Row, New York.

Cohn, A. (1989). Stress in Indonesian and bracketing paradoxes. *Natural Language and Linguistic Theory* **7,** 167–216.

Dixon, R. M. W. (1977). *A Grammar of Yidiny.* Cambridge University Press, Cambridge.

Hall, T. (1989). German syllabification, the velar nasal, and the representation of schwa. *Linguistics* **27,** 807–842.

Halle, M., and Vergnaud, J.-R. (1987). *An Essay on Stress.* MIT Press, Cambridge, Mass.

Hayes, B. (1982). Extrametricality and English stress. *Linguistic Inquiry* **13,** 227–276.

Hoeksema, J. (1985). *Categorial Morphology.* Garland, New York.

Hoeksema, J. (1987). Relating word structure and logical form. *Linguistic Inquiry* **18,** 119–126.

Hulst, H. van der. (1984). *Syllable Structure and Stress in Dutch.* Foris, Dordrecht.

Inkelas, S. (1989). *Prosodic Constituency in the Lexicon.* Doctoral dissertation, Stanford University, Stanford, Calif.

Jackendoff, R. (1987). The status of thematic relations in linguistic theory. *Linguistic Inquiry* **18,** 369–412.

Kager, R. W. J. (1989). *A Metrical Theory of Stress and Destressing in English and Dutch.* Doctoral dissertation, University of Utrecht, Utrecht, Netherlands.

Kiparsky, P. (1982). Lexical morphology and phonology. In *Linguistics in the Morning Calm* (Linguistic Society of Korea, ed.), pp. 3–91. Hanshin, Seoul.

Kiparsky, P. (1985). Some consequences of lexical phonology. *Phonology Yearbook* **2,** 85–138.

Klavans, J. (1985). The independence of syntax and cliticization. *Language* **61,** 95–120.

Levin, B., and Rappaport, M. (1986). The formation of adjectival passives. *Linguistic Inquiry* **17,** 623–662.

Lieber, R. (1980). *On the Organization of the Lexicon.* Doctoral dissertation, Massachusetts Institute of Technology, Cambridge.

Lieber, R. (1989). On percolation. *Yearbook of Morphology* **2,** 95–138.

Lieber, R. (1992). *Deconstructing Morphology: Word Formation in Syntactic Theory.* University of Chicago Press, Chicago.

Marle, J. van. (1985). *On the Paradigmatic Dimension of Morphological Creativity.* Foris, Dordrecht.

McCarthy, J., and Prince, A. (1986). *Prosodic Morphology.* Unpublished manuscript, University of Massachusetts, Amherst, and Brandeis University, Waltham, Mass.

Nespor, M., and Vogel, I. (1986). *Prosodic Phonology.* Foris, Dordrecht.

Pesetsky, D. (1985). Morphology and logical form. *Linguistic Inquiry* **16,** 193–248.

Rappaport, M., and Levin, B. (1988). What to do with θ-roles. In *Syntax and Semantics* **21** (W. Wilkins, ed.), pp. 7–36. Academic Press, New York.

Rubach, J., and Booij, G. (1990). Syllable structure assignment in Polish. *Phonology* **7,** 121–158.

Schachter, P., and Otanes, F. (1972). *Tagalog Reference Grammar.* University of California Press, Berkeley.

Selkirk, E. (1984). *Phonology and Syntax: The Relation between Sound and Structure.* MIT Press, Cambridge, Mass.

Sproat, R. (1985). *On Deriving the Lexicon.* Doctoral dissertation, Massachusetts Institute of Technology, Cambridge.

Sproat, R. (1988). Bracketing paradoxes, cliticization, and other topics. In *Morphology and Modularity* (M. Everaert, A. Evers, R. Huybregts, and M. Trommelen, eds.), pp. 339–360. Foris, Dordrecht.

Visch, E. (1989). *The Rhythm Rule in English and Dutch.* Doctoral dissertation, University of Utrecht, Utrecht, Netherlands.

Wiese, R. (1988). *Silbische und lexikalische Phonologie. Studien zum Chinesischen und Deutschen.* Niemeyer, Tübingen.

Zwicky, A. (1977). *On Clitics.* Distributed by the Indiana University Linguistics Club, Bloomington.

MODELING THE PHONOLOGY–MORPHOLOGY INTERFACE

SHARON HARGUS

Department of Linguistics
University of Washington
Seattle, Washington 98195

1. INTRODUCTION

This article offers a defense of interactionism, the hypothesis that phonological rules may precede morphological rules. As discussed below and also by Kaisse and Hargus (this volume), interactionism has been challenged by a number of recent authors, including Halle and Vergnaud (1987a, 1987b) and Odden (this volume). In this article I have tried to assemble the best available evidence for interactionism, summarized in Section 3. In Section 4, I consider the theoretical implications of the analyses discussed in Section 2 and possible reanalyses of these data. I begin with a brief discussion of interactionism and noninteractionism.

2. RECENT THEORIES OF PHONOLOGY–MORPHOLOGY INTERACTION

2.1. Lexical Phonology May Precede Any Morphology

As is well known, the hypothesis that phonology and morphology apply in the same component is traceable to an unpublished paper by Pesetsky (1979:48) (cf. Pesetsky, 1985): We propose that the process of word formation consists of the following steps: . . . Apply an affix . . . to a base . . . Apply all cyclic phonological

Phonetics and Phonology, Volume 4
Studies in Lexical Phonology

rules, subject to the Strict Cycle Condition . . . Erase inner brackets, according to the BEC. Following the recognition that phonological rules can be broadly divided into two types, lexical and postlexical, Pesetsky's hypothesis could be restated as in (1).

(1) Lexical phonological rules may precede morphological rules.

Pesetsky's model might be called the "standard" theory of phonology–morphology interaction in lexical phonology, incorporating several hypotheses—lexical phonological rules apply cyclically in the unmarked case, the lexical phonology may precede (some) word formation, and word-internal structure is invisible to certain later processes.

Hypothesis (1) predicts that any lexical phonological rule which belongs to the same or an earlier phonological domain as a morphological rule should be able to precede that morphological rule. Somewhat more restrictive versions of this hypothesis have been proposed by Kiparsky (1985), Aronoff (1988), and Borowsky (this volume).

According to Kiparsky (1985), there are universally only two word-internal phonological domains, LEVEL 1 or the STEM LEVEL, and the WORD LEVEL, with the stem level being cyclic and the word level being noncyclic. Kiparsky's version of the model thus predicts that stem-level phonological rules may precede stem- and word-level morphological rules, but that word-level phonological rules should follow word-level morphological rules, since the latter domain is noncyclic. Borowsky (this volume) proposes not only that the word-level phonology is noncyclic, but that word-level phonology precedes word-level morphology, basing this conclusion on a number of studies of different dialects of English in which monomorphemic forms and those with word-level suffixes pattern together as opposed to forms with stem-level affixes.

The model proposed by Aronoff (1988), a slightly evolved version of Aronoff (1976), is very similar to these models. Aronoff (1976), assuming the distinction between two kinds of phonological rules, cyclic and word-level (= postcyclic, last-cyclic), proposed in Chomsky and Halle (1968) (henceforth *SPE*), had suggested that phonological and morphological rules may interact with each other in limited ways, with morphological rules restricted to applying in one of three places in the phonology: "first, before the [cyclic] phonology . . . ; second, before the word-level rules; third, after the phonology" (p. 73), with the first type of morphological rule applying in a block prior to the cyclic phonology.

Aronoff (1988) is primarily concerned with showing how cases of apparent "misapplication" of phonological rules (under- and over-application) in reduplication can be accounted for without the nonlinear, simultaneous models of reduplication that have been proposed by Clements (1985), Mester (1988), and Uhrbach (1987). He maintains that misapplication can be accounted for by allowing "a restricted type of morphological rule to follow certain phonological rules" (p. 4). As in the model of Kiparsky (1985), two word-internal phonological domains are posited as universal (stem- and word-level), and morphological processes are classes as stem-level or word-level depending on their phonological domain assignment. Putting aside the question of the existence of morphology which follows word-level phonology, Aronoff's model (both 1976 and 1988 versions) makes two predictions.

1. Languages may contain maximally two word-internal phonological domains, to which morphological processes are assigned.
2. Stem-level (cyclic, lexical) phonological rules may precede word-level, but not stem-level, morphology.

The main difference between Kiparsky's and Borowsky's lexical phonology models on the one hand, versus that of Aronoff (1988), is that Aronoff's model predicts the absence of analyses in which stem-level phonology precedes stem-level morphology, whereas the models of Kiparsky and Borowsky at least implicitly predict that they do exist.[1]

2.2. Phonology May Not Precede Any Morphology

A number of phonologists (Halle, Harris, and Vergnaud, 1991; Halle and Vergnaud, 1987a, 1987b; Odden, this volume; Szpyra, 1987) have recently espoused a resurrection of the previous "standard" theory of phonology–morphology interaction, that proposed in *SPE* and further elaborated by Halle (1973). Though differing in details, all these "noninteractionist" models posit a morphological component which precedes the (possibly level-ordered) phonological component. The noninteractionist position is well summarized by Halle and Vergnaud (1987a:78).

> We make the traditional assumption that [morphological] rules are the province of a special module, the *morphology*. In our theory, then, as in *SPE*, morphology is distinct and separate from the phonology. Morphology interacts with phonology in that it creates the objects on which the rules of phonology operate.

Odden (this volume) provides the best defense of noninteractionism, examining much of the often-cited evidence for lexical phonology and concluding that this evidence can be reanalyzed in a way which does not support it. Odden also offers an empirical argument against interactionism from Maltese.

However, while some of the evidence usually cited for interactionism can and should be reanalyzed, I suggest in the following section that not all the evidence can easily be dismissed.

3. PHONOLOGY PRECEDING MORPHOLOGY

McCarthy and Prince (1990) discuss a number of analyses of morphological rules which apply to a "prosodically circumscribed" portion of a morphological base, with the additional restriction that the prosodically defined base be identical to the Minimal Word in a particular language. The usual conception of the Minimal Word is that of metrical foot, a phonologically defined unit. McCarthy and Prince adduce a number of morphological rules from various languages which operate on a prosodically circumscribed base in this manner. This well-supported conclusion presupposes and thus provides support for interactionism; that is, phonologically defined circumscription of a base precedes some morphological process in a number of languages.

Below I summarize other types of analyses in which a phonological rule must precede a morphological one, segregating analyses into three tables. In Table 1 I include the better known type of analysis, in which a morphological process refers to a derived phonological property [English, Finnish, Koasati, Hebrew, German (Case 1), Dutch (Case 1)], followed by a brief discussion of one of these types of cases. Table 2 contains a short list of languages (Kihehe, Tagalog, Mende) in which phonological rules are known to overapply in reduplicative structures. While interactionism can easily accommodate these rules, alternative representational analyses are also available. Table 3 contains analyses in which the domain of a phonological process crucially excludes a (presumably later) morphological process, which, unlike the Table 1 analyses, does not refer to the output of the phonological rule [Sundanese, Sanskrit, Javanese, Luiseño, Icelandic, Danish, German (Case 2), Dutch (Case 2)]. Since this type of evidence for interactionism is not as well known as those summarized in Tables 1 and 2, I illustrate this type with several languages—Sundanese, German, Luiseño, and Javanese.

3.1. Morphology Which Refers to a Derived Phonological Property

The phonological processes in Table 1 are diverse, ranging from metrical structure construction or alteration (stress, syllabification, syncope, epenthesis) to changes in feature content (mutation) to metathesis. The morphological operations are equally varied, including affixation (English), allomorph selection (Finnish, Lappish, German, Dutch), and rhyme deletion (Koasati).

3.1.1. German

Let us now consider one of the cases from Table 1 in more detail, stress and *-ei*/*-erei* allomorphy in German. These data involve the distribution of allomorphs of the deverbal, nominalizing (with slightly pejorative connotations), stem-level suffix *-ei*/*-erei*.

Hall (1990) analyzes the distribution of the allomorphs of this suffix as follows (cf. also Giegerich, 1987): *-erei* is added to verb stems with final stressed syllables, including verb stems derived by the addition of *-ier; -ei* is added to other verb stems.[2]

TABLE 1

MORPHOLOGY REFERRING TO A DERIVED PHONOLOGICAL PROPERTY

Language	Phonology	Morphology	Reference
English			
Case 1	Stress	Expletive infix	McCarthy (1982)
Case 2	Stress	*-ize*	Marchand (1969), Hayes (personal communication)
Finnish	Stress	Illative allomorphy	Kiparsky (this volume), Kanerva (1987), Keyser and Kiparsky (1984)
Lappish	Stress	Various allomorphy	Bergsland (1976)
Koasati	Syllabification	Plural formation	Kimball (1982), Martin (1988)
Hebrew	Metathesis	Extraction	Bat-El (1986)
German			
Case 1	Stress, epenthesis	*-er/-erei* allomorphy	Hall (1990), Giegerich (1987)
Dutch			
Case 1	Stress	*-ie/isch* allomorphy	Booij and Lieber (this volume)

(2)

INFINITIVE	NOMINAL	
síng-en	*Sing-eréi*	'singing'
láuf-en	*Lauf-eréi*	'running'
éss-en	*Ess-eréi*	'eating'
báck-en	*Back-eréi*	'baking'
wídm-en	*Widm-eréi*	'dedicating'
órdn-en	*Ordn-eréi*	'arranging'
lack-íeren	*Lackier-eréi*	'lacquering'
spion-íer-en	*Spion-ier-eréi*	'spying'
árbèit-en	*Arbeit-eréi*	'working'
trompét-en	*Trompet-eréi*	'trumpeting'

The verb stem is provided in the infinitive column: the forms in (2) consist of the verb stem, the infinitival suffix /-n/, and an epenthetic vowel (Hall, 1987).

Insofar as the distribution of *-erei* refers to stress, which is a derived phonological property in German (although, as Hall notes, stress is sensitive to a native/nonnative lexical distinction, as are other rules of German phonology), these data are problematic for Odden's noninteractionist model. The preceding data require an analysis in which stress assignment precedes the selection of *-ei* or *-erei.*

Selection of the allomorph *-ei* is illustrated by the liquid-final verb stems in (3), which also undergo a stem-level rule of preliquid schwa epenthesis (Giegerich, 1987; Hall, 1987):

(3) /se:gl/ *ségel-n* *Segel-éi* 'sailing'
/trö:dl/ *trödel-n* *Trödel-éi* 'loitering'
/bü:gl/ *bügel-n* *Bügel-éi* 'ironing'
/plaʊdr/ *pláuder-n* *Plauder-éi* 'chatting'

Both the epenthesis rule and the rule assigning stress to the forms in (3) must apply prior to the allomorphy rule, since epenthesis inserts a schwa before the stem-final unsyllabified liquid, thereby creating a final unstressed syllable which determines that the *-ei* allomorph be selected.

An alternative, phonological account of this allomorphy has been suggested to me by Donca Steriade (personal communication). Suppose the suffix has the underlying representation -/ərái/. Following its attachment to /l/-final stems, /l+ə/ → syllabic [l] ([əl]), which then triggers a dissimilatory deletion of /r/ following the syllabic [l]: /se:gl+əraɪ/ → [se:gəlrai] → [se:gəlai]. While this analysis seems reasonable, Hall (personal communication) notes that there is no other evidence for liquid dissimilation in German, and that the directionality of the rule /lə/ → [əl] is the opposite of that required to account for other [ə] ~ ø alternations in German (Hall, 1987). Finally, I note that a phonological analysis of these data somewhat undermines the notion of morphology, since the alternation discussed is confined to a single morpheme.

3.1.2. Lapp

In Lapp there are suffixal allomorphy processes which refer to whether or not the final syllable of the stem is stressed.[3] I mention two such cases here, allomorphs of the illative plural suffix and allomorphs of a nominal diminutive suffix. All information about Lapp presented here comes from Bergsland's (1976) grammar.

3.1.2.1. Stress. According to Bergsland, main stress usually falls on the leftmost syllable, with every other syllable to the right receiving stress as well, with the exception of word-final syllables, which are never stressed, even in words with odd-numbered syllables.[4]

(4) [oap.pa.hæd.dji rek.ke.nas.ti.goat.ta] 'the teacher starts to count'

(5) [boar.rá.seb.mu.sat gud.ne.jat.tu.juv.vu.jit] 'the oldest are honored'

Clearly, Lapp contains an alternating stress rule. I suggest that the lack of word-final stresses is due to a general prohibition against monosyllabic feet, and that these stray, footless syllables as in (5) are adjoined to the foot to their left following word formation. While Bergsland also notes some words with exceptional, lexically specified mono- or trisyllabic feet, which are said to be mainly loanwords, compounds, and words with frozen derivational suffixes, the regular alternating stress rule appears to be the norm. Thus stress is basically predictable in Lapp.

3.1.2.2. Illative Plural Allomorphy. Bergsland notes that it is very important to distinguish between words which contain odd- or even-numbered syllables in the description of Lapp word formation. Many suffixes have one allomorph that is used after stems ending in an odd number of syllables, and another after even numbers of syllables. Following Hayes's (1982b) analysis of Yidiny, I suggest that these allomorphy rules are sensitive to foot structure—in particular, whether or not the final syllable of the base ends in a foot. Since Lapp has an alternating stress rule, it seems that the suffixal allomorphs that Bergsland refers to are selected in accordance with whether or not the final syllable of the stem belongs to a foot.

One such allomorphy rule is that which determines the shape of the illative plural suffix. According to Bergsland, the allomorph *-ide* is used after stems with even numbers of syllables (i.e., unstressed stem-final syllables), whereas *-ida* is used after stems with odd numbers of syllables (i.e., stressed stem-final syllables).

(6) *-ide* ALLOMORPH:

[čie.ga-ide]	'corner (ill.pl.)'
[boa.lo-ide]	'button (ill.pl.)'
[reŋ.ku-ide]	'stool (ill.pl.)'

(7) *-ida* ALLOMORPH:

[mál.lá.si-ida]	'feed (ill.pl.)'
[bæd.na.gi-ida]	'dog (ill.pl.)'

3.1.2.3. Diminutives. One type of nominal diminutive in Lapp is formed by adding a suffix whose shape also varies according to base syllable count. The form of the suffix is -(*a*)*š* in the singular. In the plural, the suffix has the shape *-žat* following even-numbered stems (also requiring the weak stem grade and a stem-internal vowel height alternation) (8), but -(*a*)*žžat* (with the strong grade of the noun stem) following odd-numbered stems (9).

(8) *-žžat* ALLOMORPH:

[bæ.na.ga-žžat]	'dogs (dim.)'
[us.ti.ba-žžat]	'friends (dim.)'

(9) *-žat* ALLOMORPH:

ful.ke.žat]	'relatives (dim.)'
[jå.ga-žat]	'rivers (dim.)'
[viel.lja-žat]	'sisters (dim.)'

3.1.2.4. Summary. In the analysis proposed here, the apparent reference to syllable count in the above-mentioned allomorphy rules is interpreted as a reference to foot structure. Thus stress assignment to stems must precede selection of the allomorphs of the suffixes discussed here. Many more allomorphy rules of this sort (e.g., attributive adjective suffix allomorphy) are found in Lapp.

3.1.3. HEBREW

Modern Hebrew as described by Bat-El (1986; cf. also Bat-El, 1989) also provides support for interactionism. The relevant morphological process involves a somewhat typologically unusual process Bat-El terms Extraction, a productive way of deriving members of one lexical category from another, as in the following denominal or deadjectival verbs.

(10) [koxav] 'star'
[kixev] 'to star'

(11) [telefon] 'telephone'
[tilfen] 'to telephone'

(12) [varod] 'pink'
[hivrid] 'to become pink'

Extraction is described as an essentially delinking process, one which separates the consonantal root tier from the syllable structure. Following Extraction of the consonantal tier from a lexical item, such as a noun, the consonantism is reassociated with a verb template.

Bat-El shows that the consonantism of derivational, but not inflectional, affixes is Extracted and subsequently reassociated to appear in derived forms. In the following example, both the initial and final /t/'s in 'pattern' are affixes; both appear in the derived verb.

(13) [tavnit] 'pattern'
[tivnet] 'to structure'

(14) [toxnit] 'plan'
[tixnen] 'to plan'
[tixnet] 'to program (a computer)'

In the second example, the older denominal verb 'to plan' is Extracted from the nominal root without the feminine /-t/ suffix, whereas the inclusion of the /-t/ suffix in the more newly derived verb contributes to the semantic difference between 'to plan' and 'to program'.

Of greater interest for present purposes, Bat-El also shows that the output of a productive phonological rule of Metathesis is also reflected in Extracted forms. Metathesis, the interchange /t/ and /s/, applies in morphologically complex forms only. The failure of Metathesis to apply in nonderived forms can be seen in (15) and (16).

(15) [tsisa] 'fermentology'

(16) [hitsis] 'to ferment'

The viability of Metathesis as a synchronic rule can be illustrated with forms which contain the verbal template /hitCaC(C)eC/. Bat-El notes that newly derived verbs which match this template undergo Metathesis, as shown in (17), for example.

(17) [zanav] 'tail'
/hit-zanev/ → [hizdanev] 'to plod along'

The following example illustrates that Extraction applies to the output of Metathesis, since in the derived agentive noun the order of the consonants is [st]:

(18) /skl/ (root)
/hit-sakel/ → [histakel] 'to observe'
[staklan] 'observer'

Metathesis must apply to the verb 'observe', rather than to the derived noun, on account of the monomorphemic status of the latter.[5] Somewhat more controversially, Bat-El also suggests that Extraction applies to the output of a phonological rule of Spirantization.

3.2. Overapplication of Phonological Rules

The second class of cases which are potentially supportive of interactionism are relatively well known. These are cases in which phonological rules OVERAPPLY in reduplicative structures; for instance, Tagalog /paŋ+putul/ → (phonology: Nasal Substitution) [pamutul] → (morphology: reduplication) [pamumutul]. Only a small sample of these sorts of cases are listed in Table 2.

TABLE 2
OVERAPPLICATION OF PHONOLOGICAL RULES

Language	Phonology	Morphology	Reference
Tagalog	Nasal Substitution, syncope	Various reduplication	Carrier (1979), Carrier-Duncan (1984), French (1988)
Mende	Mutation	Reduplication	Innes (1971), Hayes (1990)
Kihehe	Glide Formation	Reduplication	Odden (this volume), Odden and Odden (1986)

The rules in Table 2 constitute weaker evidence for interactionism, since there are competing, representation-based explanations for overapplication in this context, proposed by Mester (1988) and Clements (1985).

Clements's proposal is that reduplication is a multistage operation, some of whose structural changes are morphological and some phonological [in particular, sequencing of the reduplicative affix with respect to the base (left, right, or internally) would be considered phonological]. Mester's model is similar. Adopting this type of approach, Odden (this volume) argues that the apparent overapplication of a phonological rule of glide formation in Kihehe reduplicative forms can be accounted for in a noninteractionist model if transfer of the base melody to the reduplicative template is considered to be a phonological operation. Thus the glide formation process does not crucially precede the morphological operation. However, it seems premature to disallow all the cases in Table 2, as there seems to be some disagreement on the best nonlinear representation of reduplication (cf. Steriade, 1988; Hayes and Abad, 1989; Aronoff, 1988).

3.3. The Domain of a Phonological Rule Excludes a Morphological Process

Consider next a third class of cases which provide evidence for interactionism (Table 3). As pointed out by Steriade (personal communication), many, but not all, of these cases involve prosodic, nonconcatenative types of morphology, such as reduplication or infixation, a point I return to in Section 4. I next review several of these cases in more detail.

TABLE 3

DOMAIN OF PHONOLOGICAL RULE EXCLUDES MORPHOLOGICAL PROCESS

Language	Phonology	Morphology	Reference
Sundanese	Nasal Harmony	Plural infix	Robins (1957), Cohn (1989)
Sanskrit	*Ruki* rule	'Augment' infix	Murti (1984), Kiparsky (1982)
Luiseño	Spirantization	Various reduplication	Munro and Benson (1973), Davis (1976)
Javanese	*a*-Raising, Laxing	Elative, reduplication	Dudas (1974, 1975)
Icelandic	Syllabification	Subtraction	Kiparsky (1984), Stong-Jensen (1987)
Danish	Lengthening	Subtraction	Anderson (1975), Sobel (1981)
German			
Case 2	Nasal Assim., *g*-Deletion	Various suffix	Hall (1990)
Dutch			
Case 2	Shwa Deletion	*-eur/-ris* allomorphy	Booij (1981)

3.3.1. Sundanese

I begin with a fairly simple case. In Sundanese, there is a rule of rightward-spreading Nasal Harmony, which spreads nasality from nasal consonants to vowels, blocked only by supralaryngeal consonants. The following data are from Cohn (1989).

(19)	/ɲiar/	[ɲĩãr]	'seek (active)'
	/ɲaian/	[ɲãĩãn]	'wet (active)'
	/mihak/	[mĩhãk]	'take sides (active)'
	/ŋatur/	[ŋãtur]	'arrange (active)'
	/ŋuliat/	[ŋũliat]	'stretch (active)'
	/marios/	[mãrios]	'examine (active)'
	/ŋarahɨtan/	[ŋãrahɨtan]	'wound (active)'

As noted by Cohn, Nasal Harmony both precedes and follows a rule of *-al-/* *-ar-* plural infixation.

(20)	Stem	Singular	Plural	
	/ɲiar/	[ŋĩar]	[ɲãlĩãr]	'seek (active)'
	/niis/	[nĩĩs]	[nãrĩʔĩs]	'relax in a cool place'
	/ɲaian/	[ɲãĩãn]	[ɲãrãĩãn]	'wet (active)'

Comparing the two sets of data, note that the occurrence of nasal vowels following the liquid of the plural suffix is unusual. However, as Cohn suggests, the distribution of nasal vowels is easily accounted for if Nasal Harmony precedes (and follows) infixation.

(21)		/ɲaian/
	Nasal Harmony	ɲãĩãn
	Plural infixation	ɲ-ar-ãĩãn
	Nasal Harmony	ɲ-ãr-ãĩãn

The placement of Sanskrit in Table 3 is for completely parallel reasons, involving the well-known phonological *ruki* rule and various infixation rules.

3.3.2. German

The following data (from Hall, 1990; cf. also Borowsky, this volume) involve forms containing the velar nasal, which is traditionally analyzed as derived from an /Ng/ cluster via rules of Nasal Assimilation and *g*-Deletion. I suggest that the latter rule must follow the suffixation of certain vowel-initial morphemes but precede the suffixation of other vowel-initial morphemes.

The monomorphemic forms in (22) contain surface [ŋg].

(22)	*Tango*	[táŋgo]	'tango'
	Evangelium	[evaŋgéliʊm]	'gospel'

Ganges	[gaŋgɛs]	'Ganges (River)'
Singular	[zíŋgulaɐ]	'singular'
Kongo	[kɔŋgo]	'Congo'
Ungarn	[ʊŋgarn]	'Hungary'
Singapur	[zíŋgapuɐ]	'Singapore'
Angina	[aŋgína]	'angina'

[g] surfaces in these forms because the rule of *g*-Deletion is analyzed as applying only to syllable-final /g/ (preceded by [ŋ]), and in the forms in (22), [g] occurs in an onset. In the forms in (23), [g] is also preserved because a stem-level vowel-initial suffix has been added to the root, thereby causing the /g/ to be syllabified as the onset of the suffix syllable.

(23)	*tang-ier-en*	[taŋgí:rən]	'to touch'
	fing-ier-en	[fɪŋgí:rən]	'to fake'
	prolong-ier-en	[prolɔŋgí:rən]	'to prolong'
	laryng-al	[larüŋgá:l]	'laryngeal'
	Laryng-itis	[larüŋgí:tɪs]	'laryngitis'
	Angl-ist	[áŋglɪst]	'anglicist'
	angl-isier-en	[aŋglizí:rən]	'anglicize'

However, when a word-level vowel-initial suffix is added, [g] is deleted even where it would form a permissible onset, as in the forms in (24).

(24)	*Spreng-ung*	[ʃprɛŋʊŋ]	'explosion'
	läng-lich	[lɛŋlɪç]	'longish'
	Jüng-ling	jüŋlɪŋ]	'youth'
	hungr-ig	[hʊŋrɪç]	'hungry'

Clearly, if all surface instances of the velar nasal are to be derived from /Ng/, then Nasal Assimilation and *g*-Deletion must apply to the stem-final /Ng/ sequences in (25) prior to the addition of the word-level suffixes.

(25)		/ʃprɛ N g/
	Nasal Assimilation	ŋ
	g-Deletion	ø
	word-level morphology	-*ʊng*

Hall (1990) argues that *g*-Deletion is a cyclic, stem-level rule, and that morphological roots are not cyclic domains [thereby prohibiting *g*-Deletion from applying to the forms in (23)]. However, the rule fails to apply to stem-final /Ng/ sequences in *diphthongier-en* [dɪftɔŋgí:rən] 'diphthongize' and *monophthongier-en* [monɔftɔŋgí:rən] 'monophthongize', which are derived with stem-level morphemes. Borowsky (this volume) analyzes German and English *g*-Deletion as a word-level rule, where in her model, all word-level phonology precedes word-level morphology. The crucial aspect of this analysis is that *g*-Deletion precedes some suffixation rules.

3.3.3. Luiseño

In Luiseño, there is a phonological rule of Spirantization, the problematic underapplication of which has attracted considerable attention from theoretical phonologists (Munro and Benson, 1973; Anderson, 1975; Aronoff, 1976; Marantz, 1982; Aronoff, 1988).[6]

By most accounts, Luiseño contains the consonant inventory given in (26). Note that /v ð/ have [−cont] allophones; their status as underlying fricatives is debatable.

(26)
```
p t   č  k kw q qw ʔ
  s  ṣ (š) x xw
v ð
m n      ŋ
  l r y    w       h
```

One important point on which analysts disagree is the phonemic status of [š], a marginal phoneme at best. Munro and Benson (1973) and Davis (1976) analyze [č] and [š] as allophones which are in complementary distribution. To account for the distribution of [č]/[š], Munro and Benson formulate the rule of Spirantization given in (27).

(27) $\check{c} \rightarrow \check{s} \;/\; \_\_\_ \begin{Bmatrix} \# \\ [-\text{cont}] \end{Bmatrix}$

I will refer to the first subrule of Spirantization as WORD-FINAL SPIRANTIZATION and the second subrule as DISSIMILATORY SPIRANTIZATION. The rule accounts not only for the distribution of [č] and [š] but also for widespread alternations, shown in (28)–(29).

(28) [š] / ___ #

/qe:nič/	[qé:niš]	'squirrel'
/qe:nič-um/	[qé:ničum]	'squirrels'
/ki:-ča]	[kí:ča]	'house (nom.)'
/ki:-č/	[kíš]	'house (acc.)'

(29) [š] / ___ [−cont]

/čapomkat/	[čapómkat]	'liar'
/čačapomkat-um/	[čášpumkatum]	'liars'
/čoka:yla-č/	[čoká:ylaš]	'walking stick (abs.)'
/no-čoka:yla/	[nošká:yla]	(construct form)
/pu:či-l/	[pu:čil]	'eye (acc.)'
/pu:či-la/	[pu:šla]	'eye (nom.)'
/yo:vi-č-um-i/	[yo:višmi]	'meadow mice (acc.)'
/po-čuróʔa/	[pušróʔax]	'his leveling'
/čuróʔa/	[čuroʔa]-	'to level'

/čikwi:-la/	[čikwí:la]	'to be sad'
/čikwi:-čikwi:/	[čikwíškwi]	'to suffer'

In some cases, Spirantization is fed by a stress-sensitive Syncope rule. Stress does not appear to be completely predictable.

As noted by Marantz (1982), morpheme-internally, [č] and [š] are not in perfect complementary distribution. [č] occurs almost exclusively before [+cont] segments.

(30) [puʔéčva] 'his left hand'
[wačxat] 'shoe'
[čáčwumal] '*Gilia capitata ssp. staminea*' (a type of flower)

But there are a few examples of [č] before [+son] segments.

(31) [poxečla] 'its point (of an arrow)'
[čačmis] 'a stone tool'

Non-alternating [š] is rare, but a few instances are shown in (32).

(32) a. [mašxai] 'isn't it?'
b. [tóšnu]- 'to order'
c. [šóx] (exclamation, indicative of surprise)

(32c) is apparently the only recorded form in which [š] occurs word-initially before a vowel. Note that in (32a) and (32c) [š] occurs before a [+cont] segment, not as predicted by Spirantization. Marantz concludes that an underlying contrast between /č/ and /š/ must be recognized, and that Spirantization is thus a neutralization rule, restricted to derived contexts, not simply a rule of allophony. I will follow Marantz on this point.

Next consider the domain of Spirantization, which Munro and Benson (1973) suggest is a late rule, apparently not ordered before any other phonological rules. Comparative evidence also supports their view. Kroeber and Grace (1960) note that a contiguous language to the north, Juaneño (spoken in what is now Orange County), "is little more than a dialect [of Luiseño] and must have been largely intelligible" to its speakers (p. 1; cf. also Miller, 1961). In Juaneño (Bean and Shipek, 1978), there is no rule of Spirantization.

(33)

Juaneño	Luiseño	
[qé:ʔeč]	[qé:ʔeš]	'Mission San Luis Rey'
[ʔaxáčme]	[ʔaxášmay]	'town of Mission San Luis Rey'

However, there is other evidence that Spirantization is not a late rule, in that Spirantization appears to precede several morphological processes. Kroeber and Grace, Munro and Benson, and Davis (1976) all note certain constructions in which Spirantization appears not to apply. The best summary of these is provided by Davis, from which the examples in subsequent sections are taken.

Adjectival (deverbal) reduplication is the most celebrated example of this (it is the case discussed by Anderson, 1975, for example) but is by no means the only example. Davis remarks (p. 201):

> The surprising thing about the Munro/Benson article is that the authors approach the subject as if the failure of the č to š rule is found only in connection with one particular form of reduplication and furthermore only when this produces adjectives.

Adjectival reduplication has been (successfully, I think) reanalyzed by Marantz (1982) as reduplicative suffixation, and the nonapplication of Spirantization in these morphemes can be accounted for by positing the appropriate suffixal template. However, while Marantz's solution will account for adjectival reduplication, it will apparently not work for the following cases. These are noted by Marantz, who, significantly, suggests that their analysis necessarily involves some sort of "boundary phenomenon."

Reduplicative Plurals

Plurals may be formed from nominal or verbal roots via reduplication of the initial CV- of the base. Kroeber and Grace note that this sort of reduplication appears to be frozen and only found on personal nouns. One of the regular plural suffixes, *-m, -um,* or *-am,* also occurs on these forms.

(34)	/ṣuŋa:-l/	[ṣuŋá:l]	'woman'
	/ṣu-ṣŋa-l-um/	[ṣúṣŋalum]	'women'
(35)	/ča-čapomka-t-um/	[čačpómkatum]	'liars'
	/čapomka-t/	[čapómkat]	'liar'

Reduplicative Protracted Action Verbs

Protracted action verbs are formed via reduplication of the first CVC- of the verbal base (Davis, 1976:201).

(36)	/neč-neči-q/	[néčničiq]	'pays in dribs and drabs'
	/neči/-	[néči]	'to pay'
(37)	/nuč-nuči-q/	[núčnučiq]	'keeps going and squashing things'
	/nuči/	[núči]-	'to squash'

Causatives *-ki, -xami, -kixa, -kixani*

These data from Kroeber and Grace could not be reelicited by Davis.

(38)	/hakwáči-kixa/	[hakwáčkixa]	'to hurry someone (caus.)'
	/hakwáči/	[hakwáči]	'to hurry someone'
(39)	/tuč-kixa/	[túčkixa]	'to tie up (caus.)'
	/tu:či/	[tú:či]	'to tie up'

(40)	[non poi nečkixaniq]	'I got him to make (someone else) pay up'
	[neči]	'to pay up'

Agentive-forming and Adjectival [-kawut]/[-ku:t]

(41)	/miči-ku:t/	[míčku:t]	'strangler'
	/miči/-	[míči]-	'to strangle'
(42)	/neči-kawut/	[néčkawut]	'one who pays'
	/neči/-	[néči]-	'to pay'
(43)	/tu:či-ku:t/	[túčku:t]	'(something) which often gets entangled'
	/tu:č-kawut/	[tučkawut]	'often entangled'
	/tu:či/	[tú:či]	'to tie up'

Tense/Aspect Markers *-q(a), -qat, -quṣ*

(44)	/wač-qa/	[wačqa]	'are a few (of things)'
	/wač-qat/	[wačqat]	'were a few (yesterday)'
	/wač-quṣ/	[wačquṣ]	'used to be a few'

An Analysis

I suggest that a solution to the underapplication of Spirantization in the preceding morphological contexts is available in a theory which incorporates interactionism. An ordering solution, similar to those suggested by Munro and Benson (1973) and by Anderson (1975), is sketched in (45).

(45)	STEM-LEVEL:	Intensive Reduplication	*č* → *š* / ___ [−cont]
	WORD-LEVEL:	Plural Reduplication	*č* → *š* / ___]$_{word}$
		Protracted Reduplication	
		agentive and adjectival *-kawut*/*-ku:t*	
		causative suffixes *-ki, -kixa, -xami, -kixani*	
		tense/aspect suffixes *-q(a), -qat, -quṣ*	

The various morphological processes discussed above are assigned to one of two domains,[7] and the two subrules of Spirantization apply in different domains, as predicted by general principles. The crucial aspect of this analysis is that dissimilatory Spirantization, a stem-level rule, precedes the word-level morphology.

3.3.4. JAVANESE

Like Luiseño, Javanese appears to distinguish two word-internal phonological domains, referred to here as stem- and word-level. I propose an analysis in which a number of phonological rules must be assigned to the stem level since there are some (word-level) morphemes that do not undergo these rules.

Javanese has been insightfully described and analyzed by Dudas (1974, 1975), with later reanalyses of some of the data provided by Kenstowicz (1986), Mester (1988), and Schlindwein (1989). Unless otherwise noted, all forms are from Dudas. A small number of forms are from Suharno (1982).[8] My transcriptions differ slightly from those of both Dudas and Suharno.

Since most of the rules discussed here involve the vocalic phonology of Javanese, the vowel inventory is given in (46).

(46)

i		u
e	ə	o
	a	

The rules to be discussed apply in a variety of morphological contexts, primarily suffixal.

(47)

-[ku]	first person possessive
-[mu]	second person possessive
-[(n)e]	third person possessive or demonstrative
-[an]	substantive or verb-forming
-[ʔake]	causative
-[ɔ]	imperative, subjunctive
-[(ʔ)nɔ]	causative imperative
-[(n)ɔnɔ]	locative imperative

The prefixes are generally uninteresting for present purposes. The only vowels which occur in prefixes are [ə] and [a], and [ə] does not alternate in quality.

3.3.4.1. Mid Vowel Laxing. Lax variants [ɛ ɔ] of the mid vowels occur in three well-defined contexts.

1. A mid vowel is lax in a stem-final closed syllable and remains lax regardless of whether later suffixation results in a surface open or closed stem-final syllable.

This is illustrated in the following morphologically related forms [cf. (47)].

(48) [kəṭɛʔ] 'monkey'
[kəṭɛʔe]
[kəṭɛʔku]

(49) [doŋɛŋ] 'story'
[doŋɛŋku]
[doŋɛŋe]

2. Stem-internally, before a high vowel in an open syllable (which will surface as tense), mid vowels are lax.

(50) [klɛru] [klɛrune] 'mistaken'
[eḍʊm] [eḍume] 'shady, sheltered'

(51) [kɔpi] [kɔpine] 'coffee'
[tomɪs] [tomise] 'rice-accompanying dish'

3. Before a stem-final syllable containing [ə] (which does not occur in open syllables stem-finally), mid vowels are lax.

(52) [bɔsən] 'tired of'

(53) [ɛmpər] 'resemblance'

I refer to these three rules collectively as Mid Vowel Laxing (MVL).

Another source of mid lax vowels is the phenomenon Dudas calls Mid Vowel Harmony (MVH). A mid vowel in a final closed syllable is lax by MVL, and a vowel in a penultimate syllable agrees in laxness with the final vowel by MVL. However, as suggested by Kenstowicz (1986) and Mester (1988), this appears to be a case of sharing of vowel melodies by separate vowels, rather than harmony.

(54) [boḍo] 'stupid'
[bɔḍɔl] 'come out (hair)'
[ḍeḍe] 'sun oneself'
[ḍɛḍɛl] 'rip'

3.3.4.2. High Vowel Laxing. In a process related to MVL, lax variants [ɪʊ] of the high vowels occur in closed syllables, as discussed by Dudas (1975:59).

(55) V → [−advanced tongue root] / ___ $C]_{syll}$
[+high]

The high stem vowels in (56) alternate between tense and lax, whereas those in (57) and (58) invariably fall in open or closed syllables respectively and are thus always tense or lax respectively.

(56) [apɪʔ] [apiʔe] 'good, nice'
[ɟupʊʔ] [ɲupuʔɔ] 'go get'
[kluwʊŋ] [kluwuŋe] 'rainbow'
[wiwɪt] [wiwitan] 'beginning'

(57) [ibu] [ibune] 'mother'
[tuku] [nukuɔ] 'buy'

(58) [ɟamʊr] [ɟamʊrku] 'mushroom'
[murɪt] [murɪtku] 'student'
[tandʊʔ] [tandʊʔmu] 'actions'

Dudas notes that exceptions to High Vowel Laxing are found in loan words.

(59) [bɛnsin] 'gas'
[pərsis] 'precise'
[kɔrnɛt bif] 'corned beef'

3.3.4.3. a*-Raising.* Both Dudas and Suharno note that there are basically no Javanese morphemes ending in word-final *a*. Dudas defends the rule given in (60), hereafter called *a*-Raising (cf. also Kenstowicz, 1986; Mester, 1988).

(60) *a* → ɔ / ____ #

a-Raising accounts for widespread alternations, with stem-final /a/ appearing as [a] when non–word-final (in suffixed forms).

(61)			
	[ɟiwɔ]	[ɟiwaku]	'soul, spirit'
	[kənɔ]	[ŋənaʔake]	'can, may'
	[meɟɔ]	[meɟamu]	'table'
	[atmɔ]	[atmane]	'soul, spirit'
	[brastɔ]	[mbrastani]	'wipe out'
	[swargɔ]	[swargane]	'heaven'

a-Raising also applies to suffixal /a/ as well as to stem-final /a/.

(62) -[ɔ] imperative, subjunctive
-[(ʔ)nɔ] causative imperative
-[(n)ɔnɔ] locative imperative

The imperative suffixes appear to be the only suffixes which contain suffix-final /a/ in an open syllable. Examples of the first of these suffixes are given in (63).

(63)		Imperative		
	[turu]	[turuɔ]	'sleep'	(S22)
	[ginanɟar]	[ginanɟarɔ]	'rewarded'	(S22)

Dudas does not provide examples of the causative imperative and locative imperative, and these suffixes are not in Suharno.

Dudas notes that "the Imperative is the only formation in the language where a suffixed stem-final /a/ appears on the surface with [ɔ] as its final segment" (p. 110).

(64)		Imperative	
	[luŋɔ]	[ŋluŋɔɔ]	'go away'
	[təkɔ]	[nəkɔɔ]	'come'

In all other formations throughout the language, stem-final /a/ does not appear as [ɔ] on the surface unless it is in absolute word-final position.[9]

Suharno and Dudas note various exceptions to *a*-Raising, mainly in loanwords and place names.

(65)	[kɔlɛra] ~ [kɔlɛrah]	'cholera'	
	[ora]	'no'	
	[ɟakarta]	'Jakarta'	(S6)
	[ɟayapura]	'Jayapura'	(S6)
	[ɟakaria]	'Zakaria'	(S6)

Dudas suggests that the phonological rules discussed above must precede a number of morphological rules.

3.3.4.4. Elative Formation. Elative formation (EF) derives intensive forms of adjectives. For present purposes, the most important mark of EF is an obligatory segmental change, the raising of the rightmost vowel of the stem to [i] or [u], depending on the backness of the final stem vowel.[10]

(66)	PRIMARY	ELATIVE	
	[aŋɛl]	[aŋil]	'hard, difficult'
	[luwe]	[luwi]	'hungry'
	[abɔt]	[abut]	'heavy, heard'
	[adɔh]	[aduh]	'far'
	[iɟo]	[iɟu]	'green'
	[rinḍɪʔ]	[rinḍiʔ]	'slow'
	[wani]	[wani]	'bold, daring'
	[alʊs]	[alus]	'refined, smooth'
	[lugu]	[lugu]	'ordinary'

There is a complication to EF which arises with stem-final /a/. The elative forms of adjectives with stem-final /a/ vary according to whether /a/ occurs in a closed syllable or an open syllable.

(67)				
		[laraŋ]	[lariŋ]	'high in cost'
		[gampaŋ]	[gampiŋ]	'easy'
		[kəras]	[kəris]	'hard, harsh'
	/rosa/	[rosɔ]	[rosu]	'strong'
	/kəmba/	[kəmbɔ]	[kəmbu]	insipid, without spirit'

If /a/ occurs in an open syllable, then the elative form contains [u]. Otherwise, /a/ raises to [i] in the elative.

Dudas suggests that EF should be analyzed as applying to the output of *a*-Raising, which creates a back vowel from a vowel which is not clearly marked for backness (/a/). High Vowel Laxing must also precede EF. This counter-feeding order is required because the output of EF is a tense vowel, even if it occurs in a closed syllable.

3.3.4.5. Doubling. A second morphological process which lies outside the domain of the above phonological rules is a kind of reduplication which Dudas calls Doubling. This reduplication of entire stems generally indicates plurality of objects or actions, but as Dudas notes, Doubling is also used in conjunction with affixes which change the meaning of the base.

(68)	/meɟa/	[meɟɔ]	[meɟɔ-meɟɔ]	'table'
	/kodoʔ/	[kɔḍɔʔ]	[kɔḍɔʔ-kɔḍɔʔ]	'frog'
	/abur/	[abʊr]	[abʊr-abʊr]	'flight'

Dudas notes (p. 210) that "the operation of Doubling must be deferred until after nearly all phonological rules in the grammar have applied." *a*-Raising apparently precedes Doubling, since, as can be seen in 'table' in (68), the derived vowel [ɔ] appears in both portions of the doubled form. These forms could be easily handled by analyzing compounds as consisting of two phonological words (cf. Nespor and Vogel, 1986). However, there are forms which have undergone both Doubling and suffixation, which indicate that *a*-Raising is a stem-level process, whereas Doubling must be word-level.

(69)	[doŋɔ]	[doŋɔ-doŋɔ]	[doŋa-doŋane]	'prayer'
	[dɔwɔ]	[dɔwɔ-dɔwɔ]	[dawa-dawane]	'long'
	[meɟɔ]	[meɟɔ-meɟɔ]	[meɟa-meɟane]	'table'[11]

As noted by Schlindwein (1989), Doubling must distinguish between stem and suffix, since only the stem reduplicates in *a*-Raising. This is easily accomplished via prosodic circumscription of the base (McCarthy and Prince, 1990). However, the fact that the final vowel of the Doubled form contains [a], rather than [ɔ], indicates that *a*-Raising must counterfeed Doubling.

(70)			/doŋa/	/doŋa/
	STEM-LEVEL:	suffixation	—	*doŋane*
		a-Raising	ɔ	—
	WORD-LEVEL:	Doubling	*doŋɔ-doŋɔ*	*doŋa-doŋane*

If Doubling preceded *a*-Raising, the Doubled form *[doŋɔ-doŋane] would result.

(71)			/doŋa/		/doŋa/	
	MORPHOLOGY:	suffixation	—		*doŋane*	
		Doubling	*doŋa-doŋa*		*doŋa-doŋ*	*ane*
	PHONOLOGY:	*a*-Raising	ɔ	ɔ	ɔ	—
			doŋɔ-doŋɔ		**doŋɔ-doŋane*	

Similarly, High Vowel Laxing also precedes Doubling.

(72)	[abʊr]	[abʊr-abʊr]	[abur-abure]	'flight'
	[apɪʔ]	[apɪʔ-apɪʔ]	[apiʔ-apiʔe]	'good, nice'

[ḍuḍʊʔ]	[ḍuḍʊʔ-ḍuḍʊʔ]	[ḍuḍuʔ-ḍuḍuʔe]	'place'
[gilɪk]	[gilɪk-gilɪk]	[gilig-gilige]	'cylindrical'
[murɪt]	[murɪt-murɪt]	[murid-muride]	'student'

Again, following Dudas (1975), I suggest that suffixation precedes *a*-Raising, which precedes Doubling.[12]

3.3.4.6. An Analysis. An analysis of the facts presented is given in (73).

(73)

	Rules		Suffixation
Stem-level:	High Vowel Laxing	-[(n)e]	3rd p. possessive, demonstrative
	a-Raising		
	Consonant Neutralization	-[ku]	1st p. possessive
		-[mu]	2nd p. possessive
	Mid Vowel Laxing	-[ʔake]	simple causative
	h-Deletion	-[(n)i]	simple locative
		-[ɔ]	imperative, subjunctive
		-[ʔnɔ]	causative imperative
		-[(n)ɔnɔ]	locative imperative
Word-level:	Mid Vowel Laxing	Elative Formation	
		Doubling	

In support of the early application of *a*-Raising, Dudas notes (p. 106) that "there are a number of things about the behavior of [*a*-Raising] which indicate that it may be a very early rule of the grammar." In support of the relatively late location of EF in the grammar of Javanese, I note that it is preceded by Tier Conflation, since shared melodies are split up in this process: /laraŋ/, elative [lariŋ] 'high in cost'.

3.4. Summary

A number of seemingly interactive analyses do not appear in Tables 1–3. Among proponents of noninteractionism, Odden (this volume) in particular has challenged the validity of a number of the cases which have been adduced to support the interactionist lexical phonology model on a number of grounds, as discussed in Section 4. One objection with which I am in agreement concerns analyses which involve unproductive morphology, hence lexically listed or non–rule-governed morphology.

For this reason, I have not included English deverbal *-al* suffixation in Table 1, although, as is well known, *-al* only appears on verbs with final stress on their bases. The attachment of *-al* must be considered a lexical property of the bases to which *-al* is attached, as indicated by minimal pairs like *arrival* versus **derival* (*derivation*); *refusal* versus **confusal* (*confusion*); *recital* versus **incital* (*incitement*); and so on. For this reason, it makes no sense to analyze the suffixation of *-al* as crucially following the assignment of stress to verbs.[13]

It should also be noted that the strength of individual cases which have been included in Tables 1–3, such as Dutch *-eur*/*-ris* allomorphy, relies on information not provided by my sources. It is possible that the same objection raised above for English *-al* could be raised with respect to the Dutch *-eur*/*ris* alternation. Similarly, the validity of the analysis can be questioned if the phonological process turns out to be unpredictable. If stress in Dutch is "not transparently predictable," as suggested by Odden (this volume), then there is no stress rule and hence no phonological process which precedes the selection of the *-ief* or *-isch* allomorphs.

Finally, some apparent ordering cases can be reduced to nonordering given appropriate representations. This can be illustrated with another example from Javanese.

The habitual-repetitive (hereafter Hab-Rep, following Dudas), is a type of reduplication that is accompanied by obligatory changes to the vocalism of the base. The semantics of the Hab-Rep is 'be continually doing V' or 'be continually saying N' (see Dudas, 1975:229).

The shape of the Hab-Rep is determined by three templates, summarized and exemplified in (74).[14]

(74) a. $CV_1CV_2(C)$, where V_2 is not [a] → CV_1C*a*(C)-$CV_1CV_2(C)$

[boḍo]	[boḍa-boḍo]	'stupid'
[ḍeḍe]	[ḍeḍa-ḍeḍe]	'sun oneself'
[elɪŋ]	[elaŋ-elɪŋ]	'remember'

b. C*a*$CV_2(C)$ → C*o*$CV_2(C)$-C*a*$CV_2(C)$

[adɔh]	[odah-adɔh]	'far'
[bali]	[bola-bali]	'return'
[adʊs]	[odas-adʊs]	'take a bath'

c. CV_1C*a*C → CV_1C*a*C-CV_1C*ɛ*C

[gombal]	[gombal-gombɛl]	'rag'
[dolan]	[dolan-dolɛn]	'engage in recreation'
[edan]	[edan-ɛdɛn]	'crazy'
[rewaŋ]	[rewaŋ-rɛwɛŋ]	'servant'

Dudas argues that *a*-Raising precedes Hab-Rep formation, because forms with stem-final, open-syllable /a/ [ɔ] do not select template c, as do forms with stem-final closed-syllable /a/ [a], but instead they select template a.

(75)

/ɟiwa/	[ɟiwɔ]	[ɟiwa-ɟiwɔ]	*[ɟiwa-ɟiwɛ]	'soul, spirit'
/doŋa/	[doŋɔ]	[doŋa-doŋɔ]	etc.	'prayer'
/meɟa/	[meɟɔ]	[meɟa-meɟɔ]		'table'
/sida/	[sidɔ]	[sida-sidɔ]		'succeed in doing'

Moreover, if both stem vowels are /a/, and the rightmost occurs in an open rather than closed syllable, these forms select template a, rather than template b or c, as was the case for /a/ in a closed stem-final syllable.

(76)	/lara/	[lɔrɔ]	[lora-lɔrɔ]	'ill, painful'
	/dawa/	[dɔwɔ]	[dowa-dɔwɔ]	'long'
	/rasa/	[rɔsɔ]	[rosa-rɔsɔ]	'(the) taste (of)'

Dudas suggests that the distinction in Hab-Rep forms between closed and open syllable stem-final /a/ bases is best accounted for by assuming that their bases are in fact phonetically distinct at the time that Hab-Rep formation has applied, as shown in the derivations in (77).

(77)	/lawas/ 'old'	/dawa/ 'long'
a-Raising		ɔ ɔ
Hab-Rep		*dɔwa-dɔwɔ*
a.		
b.	*lowas-lawas*	
c.	*lawas-lɛwɛs*	
Mid Vowel Laxing		*dowa-dɔwɔ*
also,	[lowas-lɛwɛs]	

Dudas notes and argues against a syllable-based alternative to this analysis. If template c were altered so that it referred only to stems with final-syllable /a/ which ONLY occurred in closed syllables, then in the case of stems like /dawa/, only template b would be applicable, with Hab-Rep formation resulting in [dowa-dawa], followed by the application of *a*-Raising, resulting in [dowa-dɔwɔ]. Dudas's argument against this alternative analysis is that the syllable structure of the base is not relevant for determining the shape of the output template for any of the other Hab-Rep forms, and that this condition duplicates exactly the effect of *a*-Raising. While the syllable structure condition does encode the effect of *a*-Raising, we now know that reduplicative or other templates may indeed refer to the syllable structure of the base (McCarthy and Prince, 1990), and it seems best to disregard Javanese Hab-Rep formation as providing an argument for interactionism.

4. THEORETICAL IMPLICATIONS

A noninteractionist might raise either of two remaining objections to the cases included in Tables 1–3.

The first issue concerns the separation between morphology and phonology; that is, whether a given phenomenon is in fact morphological or phonological.

Thus, Halle, Harris, and Vergnaud (1991) assume that the rule of Spanish which accounts for alternant forms *la* and *el* of the feminine singular definite article is phonological (although they note that it could in fact be analyzed as morphological). Similarly, Odden (this volume) proposes that the subtractive morphology found in Danish, Icelandic, and Koasati (from Tables 1 and 3) and in Kimatuumbi (Locative Truncation, discussed by Odden) be reanalyzed as phonology (with morphological conditioning) rather than morphology. For the Danish alternation, Odden posits the rule in (78).

(78) $ə \rightarrow \emptyset \quad / \_\_\_\_]_{\omega}$
[IMPER]

Odden hypothesizes that morphological operations are restricted to concatenation through a PRINCIPLE OF MORPHOLOGY–PHONOLOGY SEGREGATION (PMPS), and thus that a rule like (78) must be considered phonological. For this reason, Odden argues that a rule of Chimwiini which changes stem-final dental /l/ to an alveolar in passive forms is a phonological rule which is conditioned by the morphological category passive. Similarly, a noninteractionist would need to analyze the German *-ei/-erei* allomorphy rule as phonological dissimilation and resyllabification, as sketched above in Section 3. Schlindwein (1989) argues that reduplication in Javanese is phonological, rather than morphological. However, her conclusion is based on the controversial assumption that the bracketing erasure convention is cyclic (see Mohanan, 1986, for discussion). The fact remains that the PMPS is simply a hypothesis, and in fact there exists a competing proposal that the possible operations in morphology are exactly those found in phonology (Martin, 1988). Indeed, if a morphological category has a consistent phonological realization, albeit of a negative (subtractive) nature, it seems plausible to consider this a morphological regularity, a consistent pairing of phonology and semantics.

Secondly, as pointed out by Steriade (personal communication), nearly all the cases presented in Tables 1–3 have certain unexplained similarities. Most of the Table 1 cases involve phonological rules which assign suprasegmental properties (e.g., stress, syllable structure), whereas most of the Tables 2 and 3 cases involve morphological rules which are prosodic (e.g., reduplicative, infixational), extensively manipulating phonological structure. We might expect a wider range of morphological and phonological rules to occur in all of Tables 1–3 if phonology can genuinely precede morphology.

Alternative explanations for the Tables 2 and 3 rules might invoke one of the ideas in the theory of reduplication proposed by Clements (1985) discussed above in Section 3.2. However, not all the Table 3 morphological rules involve prosodic morphology. The German word-level morphology that follows *g*-Deletion is suffixational. In a noninteractionist analysis of these data, it would be necessary to posit either underlying velar nasals or a separate rule of *g*-Deletion, which would apply to /g/ before vowels in word-level suffixes. Moreover, even some of the morphology that does appear to be prosodic does not uniformly fail to undergo a given phonological rule, as seen in Luiseño. In a noninteractionist analysis, the morphology which fails to undergo Spirantization would have to be represented on a plane separate from the morphological base, and Spirantization would have to apply before plane conflation. However, this analysis would not explain why some nonconcatenative morphology, such as Intensive Reduplication, does undergo Spirantization. Presumably the output of Intensive Reduplication would be represented in the same way that (e.g.) Protracted Reduplication is. The noninteractionist model would still need to recognize that morphological processes may belong to separate phonological domains, a solution which is similar to that predicted by lexical phonology. Planar segregation of morphemes appears to be irrelevant to the analysis of Luiseño.

Finally, although all of the Table 1 cases involve the manipulation of suprasegmental information (stress, syllable structure—Hebrew Metathesis), there is no obvious explanation for this. It was an oft-noted fact in the history of the phonological cycle that much of the best evidence for cyclicity involved stress rules, but this fact has to my knowledge resisted explanation.

ACKNOWLEDGMENTS

I thank the following for comments on earlier versions of this paper: Ewa Czaykowska-Higgins, Tracy Hall, Ellen Kaisse, Paul Kiparsky, Ove Lorentz, David Odden, Bill Poser, Keren Rice, Yasushi Sato, Pat Shaw, Donca Steriade, Margaret Strong-Jensen, and an anonymous reviewer.

NOTES

[1] Aronoff notes that his prediction is empirically supported, at least by the reduplicative cases he discusses in the 1988 paper: "To my knowledge, . . . there are no cases in the literature where a cyclic phonological rule can be shown to misapply in a demonstrably stem-level reduplication" (p. 6).

[2] The following forms are cited in German orthography, with stress marked with an acute accent.

[3] I thank Paul Kiparsky and Ove Lorentz for drawing Lapp to my attention.

[4] The following words are cited in Bergsland's transcription system, which uses, among other diacritics, acute accents to mark vowel quality distinctions. Stress is therefore indicated by underlining the stressed nuclei. I have also added [.] to mark syllable division (not provided in Bergsland's transcriptions).

[5] The /h/ fails to be extracted in the above example because it is a tense affix, one of a set of inflectional affixes which fail to appear in Extracted forms.

[6]Additional primary sources consulted on Luiseño are Bright (1965), Kroeber and Grace (1960), and Davis (1976).

[7]Adjectival reduplication could be assigned to either domain, given the analysis proposed by Marantz.

[8]These are marked S with a page number.

[9]Other word-internal instances of the output of *a*-Raising are due to sharing of vowel features by more than one vowel, as seen above with MVL.

(i)	[gɔwɔ]	[ŋgawani]	'bring'
	[lɔrɔ]	[larane]	'ill, painful'

In support of this, Dudas notes that *a*-Raising results in violations of her rule of MVH.

(ii)	[goḍɔ]	[goḍane]	'temptation'
	[polɔ]	[polane]	'design, pattern'
	[rosɔ]	[rosane]	'strong'
	[sogɔ]	[sogane]	'bark of the indigo tree'

[10]The elative is also optionally prosodically marked by lengthening the final vowel and/or raising its pitch.

[11]Doubling must retain stem brackets since only the stem reduplicates in affixed forms. Word-internal structure persists from an earlier level in these forms.

[12]Dudas also shows that Doubling must follow two additional phonological rules, Consonant Neutralization and *h*-Deletion.

[13]Moreover, given (e.g.) Hayes's (1982a) analysis of English stress, the stress contours of *-al* nominals could be correctly assigned even if stress followed *-al* suffixation.

[14]There is a complication to template c which will not be discussed here. See Dudas for details.

REFERENCES

Anderson, S. R. (1975). On the interaction of phonological rules of various types. *Journal of Linguistics* **11,** 39–62.

Aronoff, M. (1976). *Word Formation in Generative Grammar.* MIT Press, Cambridge, Mass.

Aronoff, M. (1988). Head operations and strata in reduplication: A linear treatment. *Yearbook of Morphology* **1,** 1–15.

Bat-El, O. (1986). *Extraction in Modern Hebrew Morphology.* Master's thesis, University of California, Los Angeles.

Bat-El, O. (1989). *Phonology and Word Structure in Modern Hebrew.* Doctoral dissertation, University of California, Los Angeles.

Bergsland, K. (1976). *Lappische Grammatik mit Lesestücken* (Veröffentlichungen der Societas Uralo-Altaica, 11.) Harrasowitz, Wiesbaden.

Bean, L. J., and Shipek, F. C. (1978). Luiseño. In *California* (R. F. Heizer, ed.) (Handbook of North American Indians, 8), pp. 550–563. Smithsonian Institution, Washington, D.C.

Booij, G. (1981). Rule ordering, rule application, and the organization of grammars. In *Phonologica 1980* (W. U. Dressler et al., eds.), pp. 45–56. Innsbrucker Beiträge zur Sprachwissenschaft.

Bright, W. (1965). Luiseño phonemics. *International Journal of American Linguistics* **31,** 342–345.

Carrier, J. (1979). *The Interaction of Morphological and Phonological Rules in Tagalog: A Study in the Relationship between Rule Components in Grammar.* Doctoral dissertation, Massachusetts Institute of Technology, Cambridge.

Carrier-Duncan, J. (1984). Some problems with prosodic accounts of reduplication. In *Language Sound Structure* (M. Aronoff and R. Oehrle, eds.), pp. 260–286. MIT Press, Cambridge, Mass.

Chomsky, N., and Halle, M. (1968). *The Sound Pattern of English.* Harper and Row, New York.

Clements, G. N. (1985). The problem of transfer in nonlinear morphology. In *Cornell Working Papers in Linguistics* **5,** 38–73.

Cohn, A. (1989). Phonetic evidence for configuration constraints. In *Proceedings of the North Eastern Linguistics Society* **19,** 63–77.

Davis, J. F. (1976). Some notes on Luiseño phonology. *International Journal of American Linguistics* **42,** 192–216.

Dudas, K. (1974). A case of functional opacity: Javanese elative formation. *Studies in the Linguistic Sciences* **4,** 91–111.

Dudas, K. (1975). *The Phonology and Morphology of Modern Javanese.* Doctoral dissertation, University of Illinois, Champaign-Urbana.

French, K. M. (1988). *Insights into Tagalog Reduplication, Infixation and Stress from Nonlinear Phonology.* Summer Institute of Linguistics, Arlington, Tex.

Giegerich, H. (1987). Zur Schwaepenthese im Standarddeutschen. *Linguistische Berichte* **112,** 449–469.

Hall, T. (1987). *Schwa–Zero Alternations in German.* Master's thesis, University of Washington, Seattle.

Hall, T. (1990). *Syllable Structure and Syllable-related Processes in German.* Doctoral dissertation, University of Washington, Seattle.

Halle, M. (1973). Prolegomena to a theory of word-formation. *Linguistic Inquiry* **4,** 3–16.

Halle, M., Harris, J., and Vergnaud, J.-R. (1991). A reexamination of the stress erasure convention and Spanish stress. *Linguistic Inquiry* **22,** 141–159.

Halle, M., and Vergnaud, J.-R. (1987a). *An Essay on Stress.* MIT Press, Cambridge, Mass.

Halle, M., and Vergnaud, J.-R. (1987b). Stress and the cycle. *Linguistic Inquiry* **18,** 45–84.

Harris, J. (1989). The stress erasure convention and cliticization in Spanish. *Linguistic Inquiry* **20,** 339–364.

Hayes, B. (1982a). Extrametricality and English stress. *Linguistic Inquiry* **13,** 227–276.

Hayes, B. (1982b). Metrical structure as the organizing principle of Yidiny phonology. In *The Structure of Phonological Representations,* part 1 (H. v.d. Hulst and N. Smith, eds.), pp. 97–110. Dordrecht, Foris.

Hayes, B. (1990). Precompiled phrasal phonology. In *The Phonology–Syntax Connection* (S. Inkelas and D. Zec, eds.), pp. 85–108. CSLI Publications and University of Chicago Press, Chicago.

Hayes, B., and Abad, M. (1989). Reduplication and syllabification in Ilokano. *Lingua* **77,** 331–374.

Innes, G. (1971). *A Practical Introduction to Mende.* School of Oriental and African Studies, London.

Kanerva, J. (1987). Morphological integrity and syntax: The evidence from Finnish possessive suffixes. *Language* **63,** 498–521.

Kenstowicz, M. (1986). Multiple linking in Javanese. In *Proceedings of the North Eastern Linguistics Society* **16,** 230–248.

Keyser, S. J., and Kiparsky, P. (1984). Syllable structure in Finnish phonology. In *Language Sound Structure* (M. Aronoff et al., eds.), pp. 7–31. MIT Press, Cambridge, Mass.

Kimball, G. (1982). Verb pluralization in Koasati. In *1982 Mid-America Linguistics Conference Papers* (F. Ingemann, ed.), pp. 401–411. Department of Linguistics, University of Kansas, Lawrence.

Kiparsky, P. (1982). Lexical morphology and phonology. In *Linguistics in the Morning Calm* (I.-S. Yange, ed.), pp. 3–91. Hanshin Publishing Co., Seoul.

Kiparsky, P. (1984). On the lexical phonology of Icelandic. In *Nordic Prosody III: Papers from a Symposium* (C. C. Elert et al., eds.), pp. 135–164. University of Umeå, Umeå, Sweden.

Kiparsky, P. (1985). Some consequences of lexical phonology. *Phonology Yearbook* **2,** 85–138.

Kroeber, A. L., and Grace, G. (1960). *The Sparkman Grammar of Luiseño* (University of California Publications in Linguistics, 16). University of California Press, Berkeley and Los Angeles.

Marantz, A. (1982). Re reduplication. *Linguistic Inquiry* **13,** 435–482.

Marchand, H. (1969). *The Categories and Types of Present-Day English Word-Formation,* 2nd ed. Beck, Munich.

Martin, J. (1988). Subtractive morphology as dissociation. *Proceedings of West Coast Conference on Formal Linguistics* **8,** 229–240.

McCarthy, J. (1982). Prosodic structure and expletive infixation. *Language* **58,** 574–590.

McCarthy, J., and Prince, A. (1990). Foot and word in prosodic morphology: The Arabic broken plural. *Natural Language and Linguistic Theory* **8,** 209–284.

Mester, R.-A. (1988). *Studies in Tier Structure.* Garland, New York.

Miller, W. (1961). Review of Kroeber and Grace, *The Sparkman Grammar of Luiseño. Language* **37,** 186–189.

Mohanan, K. P. (1986). *The Theory of Lexical Phonology.* Reidel, Dordrecht.

Munro, P., and Benson, J. (1973). Reduplication and rule ordering in Luiseño. *International Journal of Americal Linguistics* **39,** 15–21.

Murti, M. S. (1984). *An Introduction to Sanskrit Linguistics.* D. K. Publications, Delhi.

Nespor, M., and Vogel, N. (1986). *Prosodic Phonology.* Foris, Dordrecht.

Odden, D., and Odden, M. (1986). Ordered reduplication in Kihehe. *Linguistic Inquiry* **16,** 497–503.

Pesetsky, D. (1979). *Russian Morphology and Lexical Theory.* Unpublished manuscript, Massachusetts Institute of Technology, Cambridge.

Pesetsky, D. (1985). Morphology and logical form. *Linguistic Inquiry* **16,** 193–246.

Robins, R. H. (1957). Vowel nasality in Sundanese: A phonological and grammatical study. In *Studies in Linguistic Analysis,* pp. 87–103. Blackwell, Oxford.

Schlindwein, D. (1989). Reduplication in lexical phonology: Javanese plural reduplication. In *Arizona Phonology Conference,* vol. 2 (S. L. Fulmer et al., eds.) (Coyote Papers, 9), pp. 116–124. Department of Linguistics, University of Arizona, Tucson.

Sobel, C. P. (1981). *A Generative Phonology of Danish.* Doctoral dissertation, City University of New York.

Steriade, D. (1988). Reduplication and syllable transfer in Sanskrit and elsewhere. *Phonology* **5,** 73–155.

Strong-Jensen, M. (1987). Lexical overgeneration in Icelandic. *Journal of Nordic Linguistics* **10,** 181–205.

Suharno, I. (1982). *A Descriptive Study of Javanese.* Department of Linguistics, Australian National University, Canberra.

Szpyra, J. (1987). Inputs to WFRs—Phonological, intermediate or phonetic? The case of verbs and deverbal nouns in Polish. In *Rules and the Lexicon* (E. Gussman, ed.), pp. 169–203. Katolickiergo Uniwersytetu Lubelskiego, Lublin, Poland.

Uhrbach, A. (1987). *A Formal Analysis of Reduplication and Its Interaction with Phonological and Morphological Processes.* Doctoral dissertation, University of Texas, Austin.

DERIVING CYCLICITY

SHARON INKELAS

Department of Linguistics
University of California
Berkeley, California 94720

1. INTRODUCTION

The aim of this article is to present a particular model of the morphology–phonology interface from whose principles it follows that every process of word formation will trigger cyclic phonological rules. I call this model prosodic lexical phonology (PLP); one of its properties is that it derives cyclicity as the consequence of a regulated correspondence between two distinct levels of lexical representation: morphologically based constituent structure, and phonologically based constituent structure.

2. TERMINOLOGY

A notoriously ambiguous element in the literature on phonology and morphology is the term PROSODIC, which crops up also in the name of the theory discussed here. One application of this term has been to metrical constituents, such as the mora, the syllable, the foot, and the word tree. Notable examples of this usage are found in Itô's (1986) principle of prosodic licensing, which requires every segmental string to be incorporated into units of higher metrical structure; in work on prosodic morphology by McCarthy and Prince (1986, 1990); and in

Phonetics and Phonology, Volume 4
Studies in Lexical Phonology

the article by Booij and Lieber (this volume) on morphological sensitivity to prosodic structure.

The term "prosodic" is also commonly invoked to subsume stress and tone, and, most generally, all autosegmental effects, ranging over tone, vowel harmony, and the representation of length.

A third type of entity to which "prosodic" has been extended is the representation of rule domains. The theory of prosodic phonology, developed by Selkirk (1978, 1980, 1986) and Nespor and Vogel (1982, 1986), posits a prosodic hierarchy containing constituents such as the phonological phrase and phonological word, whose main function is to delimit the strings within which phonological rules apply. These relatively abstract constituents differ from the metrical constituents in lacking a universal phonological or phonetic reflex.

In this work, I take the position, developed in more detail in Section 3, that there is a crucial distinction between phonological rule domains, the main topic of the paper, and the phonological structure created by phonological rules applying within those domains. To refer to phonologically derived constituents such as the foot, the syllable, and the mora, I use the term METRICAL CONSTITUENT. To refer to rule domains such as the phonological phrase, I use the terms P-STRUCTURE and P-CONSTITUENT (Selkirk, 1986). M-STRUCTURE and M-CONSTITUENT refer to morphological constituent structure.

3. PROSODIC LEXICAL PHONOLOGY

PLP (Inkelas, 1989) is a model of the phonology–morphology interface which captures the empirical generalization that word-internal lexical rule domains correspond (roughly) to morphological constituents, while adhering to the restrictive position that phonological rules do not access m-structure or syntactic phrase structure directly.

3.1. Prosodic Hierarchy Theory

The latter claim underlies an influential theory of the interface between syntax and the postlexical component of the phonology, alternately called prosodic phonology or the prosodic hierarchy theory (Selkirk, 1978, 1986; Nespor and Vogel, 1982, 1986; Hayes, 1989). The postlexical units of this hierarchy, that is, of p-structure, are widely assumed to include the following, from which I have omitted the controversial clitic group (Hayes, 1989; Nespor and Vogel, 1986; Vogel, 1989).[1]

(1) POSTLEXICAL PROSODIC HIERARCHY:

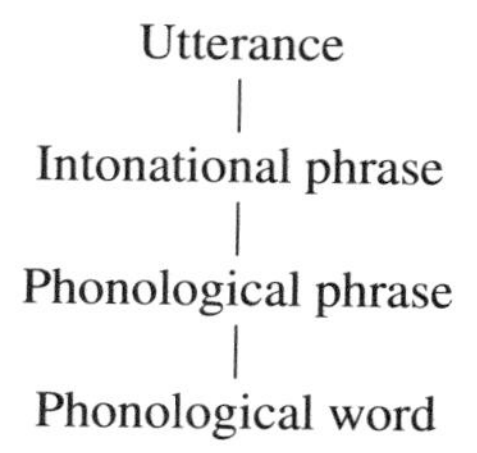

The appeal of this theory comes from its ability to constrain in a natural manner the amount of information made available to each component about the other. An important step in this direction is the indirect reference hypothesis (2), which prevents phonological rules from seeing any structure other than the string delimited by a particular p-constituent.

(2) INDIRECT REFERENCE HYPOTHESIS: phonological rules have access only to p-structure (i.e., not to m-structure or c-structure).

Along with some version of the indirect reference hypothesis, most implementations of the prosodic hierarchy theory have incorporated further conditions on the kind of syntactic information made available to the algorithms which generate p-structure (see, e.g., Bickmore, 1990; Cho, 1990; Nespor and Vogel, 1986; Selkirk, 1986; Zec and Inkelas, 1990). The most restrictive proposals limit algorithms to information about the configurationality of syntactic structure (with the possible inclusion of X′ level), specifically including information such as sisterhood and syntactic branchingness, while excluding reference to syntactic category or other morphosyntactic features.

Despite the prevalence of this general perspective on the phonology–syntax interface, the opposite view is assumed—and has generally proved unproblematic—in most theories of the interaction between morphology and phonology, about which the prosodic hierarchy theory says relatively little. Lexical phonology (Kiparsky, 1982; Mohanan, 1986; Pesetsky, 1979), for example, makes a certain amount of internal morphological bracketing accessible to phonological rules, but the domains of rule application themselves are provided by the interleaving of morphological operations and phonological rule application. Anderson (1986, 1988) also assumes a model in which the output of each morphological rule is fed directly to phonological rules.

A few significant exceptions to this general outlook occur in the work of Booij and Rubach (1984); Booij (1985); Sproat (1985, 1986); Booij and Rubach (1987); and Cohn (1989). These authors propose that WITHIN THE LEXICON there exist two distinct, copresent structures, one motivated by the morphology and the other by the phonology. The latter (crucially distinct from metrical structure) organizes morphemes into the constituents utilized as the domains of phonological rule application.

What is the nature of these lexical p-constituents? It was initially assumed by Selkirk (1978), and, following her, by Nespor and Vogel (1982, 1986), that the phonological phrase, the phonological word, the foot, and the syllable were directly related. Since the latter two constituents are smaller than most phonological words, a natural conclusion was that these metrical units formed the lexical end of the prosodic hierarchy. However, as foreseen by Nespor and Vogel (p. 18) and Selkirk (p. 385) in their respective 1986 expositions of the theory, this position has faltered under the more recent focus on lexical rules. Metrical constituents are sufficient in neither number nor size to describe adequately all the domains of lexical rules. Worse, they do not even form a consistent hierarchy with the lexical rule domains that are attested (Inkelas, 1989; Selkirk, 1986; Zec, 1988).

Significantly, in each of the works cited above in which p-structure is invoked to describe lexical phonological rule domains that do not coincide exactly with the corresponding morphological constituent structure, it is the p-units at the word level and higher—not the supposedly lexical metrical units—which are utilized.

In a paper on Dutch and German compounds, Booij (1985) shows that the ellipsis under coordination of certain elements of these compounds can be explained only under the assumption that their m-structure and p-structure are distinct. The omissible elements of compounds correspond not to morphological constituents, but rather to phonological words (p. 151).

Sproat (1986) argues along similar lines that the distinct treatment by phonological rules of subcompounds and cocompounds in Malayalam is best handled by treating the former as a single phonological word and the latter as two phonological words. Again, the appeal is to this relatively abstract member of the p-hierarchy, rather than to one of its hypothesized lower-end constituents.

Finally, Cohn (1989) argues persuasively that the cyclic application of stress rules in Indonesian yields the correct results only when p-structure is permitted to depart from m-structure. The complexity of Cohn's data requires reference to two different types of lexical p-constituents. Even so, her analysis conforms to those of Booij and Sproat in invoking only elements of the p-hierarchy at and above the level of the phonological word.

The generalization emerging from the work of Booij, Rubach, Sproat, and Cohn is that as it becomes clearer that units of the p-hierarchy must be invoked to handle lexical mismatches between m-structure and phonological rule domains, it becomes correspondingly obvious that the lexical units offered by standard prosodic hierarchy theory are not equal to the task. The only units that prove relevant in the lexicon are the NONMETRICAL units of that hierarchy.

If the only needed lexical p-constituent is the phonological word, then the problem is not severe: Booij and Rubach (1987) have argued that both the lexicon and the postlexical component possess word-level rules. Zec (1988, this volume) argues that the phonological word straddles the boundary between the lexical and the postlexical components and is thus accessible to both.

However, evidence such as Cohn's that more than one p-constituent is needed lexically poses a more serious problem. One possible solution, adopted in Cohn's article, is to draw the postlexical elements of the hierarchy (in her case, the clitic group) into the lexicon. However, doing so makes these p-constituents unavailable for postlexical use and also weakens the cross-linguistic claims that have been made as to the syntactic correlates of the various levels in the p-hierarchy.

The other type of solution is simply to jettison the useless (in this context) metrical units from the p-hierarchy and replace them with new, genuinely lexical p-constituents which will function as the lexical p-domains called for in the work of Booij, Sproat, Cohn, and others. Taking this idea to its logical extreme, I proposed (Inkelas, 1989) to supplement the lexical end of the p-hierarchy sufficiently that it can extend to all lexical phonological rules. Within the lexicon, just as outside it, phonological rules never apply to morphological strings directly. Rather, they always apply within domains described by p-constituents. Mismatch phenomena like those analyzed by Booij, Sproat, and Cohn are special not because the relevant rules refer to p-constituents, but rather because the relevant p-constituents do not match the corresponding morphological structure exactly.[2]

This approach thus unifies the theoretical treatment of lexical and postlexical rule application, while obviating the theoretically and empirically awkward position of forcing lexical rules to apply within metrical constituents or within postlexical p-domains.

In the two-structure model, the unmarked representation of a morphologically complex word will thus look something like that in (3).

(3)

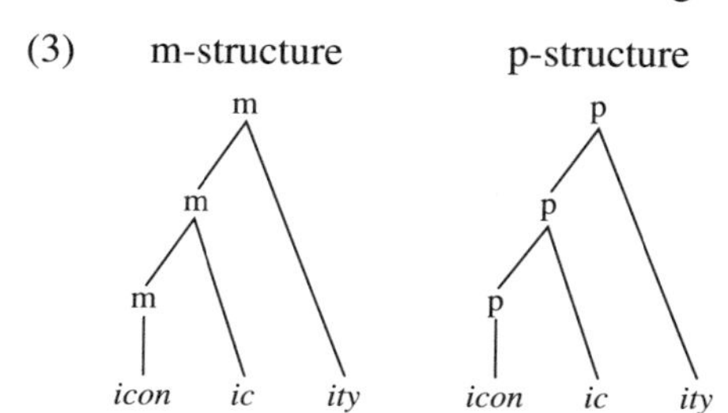

Despite its complexity, the model as illustrated in (3) still does not address Cohn's argument that more than one type of lexical p-constituent is needed. This conclusion, formed on the basis of Indonesian, patterns with a larger body of evidence accumulated from other languages that the lexicon may be stratified into more than one level, with corresponding differences in phonological rule application (see, e.g., Borowsky, 1986; Hargus, 1988; Kiparsky, 1982; Mohanan, 1982; Pesetsky, 1979; Zec, 1988).

To accommodate this complexity, I proposed (Inkelas, 1989) that lexical p-constituents may come in more than one type. Lexical stratification of phonological rules is thus comparable theoretically to postlexical stratification—the latter being more commonly recognized as the various layers in the (postlexical) prosodic hierarchy. Sublexical strata may simply be interpreted as different lexical p-categories, arranged in a fixed hierarchy dominated by the phonological word.

Assuming, for example, the stratification of the English lexicon into two levels (Kiparsky, 1985), we must posit two corresponding sublexical layers in p-structure. In the figure in (4), the category α corresponds to stratum 1 and the category β, to stratum 2.

(4) P-HIERARCHY (English):

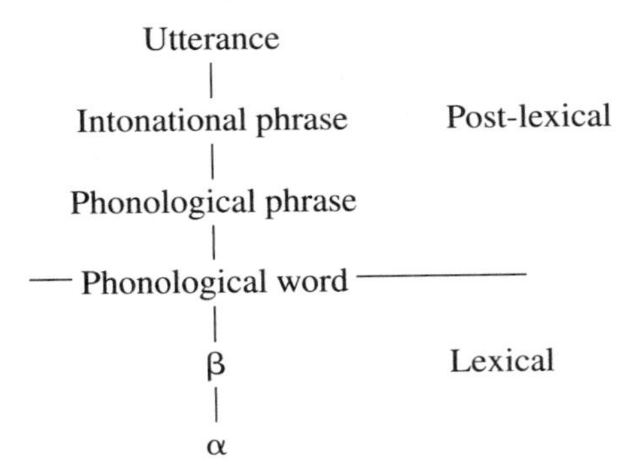

The parallel between these sublexical constituent types and traditional levels is close. Just as affixes select for attachment at a given level in standard lexical phonology, affixes subcategorize for attachment to a given constituent type in the model proposed here. (See Section 3.2.3 and Inkelas, 1989, for more details.)

To sum up, the proposal is that lexical phonological rule domains are to be represented neither as metrical constituents nor as morphological ones, but rather as elements of p-structure, a unique hierarchy whose coverage generally corresponds to that of morphological constituents. Metrical structure exists in a hierarchy distinct from p-structure. It is a different level of representation, and its units obey different constraints from those that govern p-structure. Just as phrasal stress is assigned by rules applying within the phonological phrase, so metrical constituents are built by phonological rules applying within p-constituents. Metrical constituents are built by phonological rules, whereas p-constituents are built by morphologically sensitive algorithms—a process to which I now turn.

3.2. Lexical P-Constituents

The correspondence between morphological structure and phonological rule domains that lexical phonology takes to be obligatory is treated in PLP as the unmarked case. The simple algorithm in (5) maps from m-structure into p-structure, providing for a perfect match between the two.[3]

(5) P-CONSTITUENT FORMATION ALGORITHM (PCF):

$\langle x \rangle_m \rightarrow \langle x \rangle_m \quad [x]_p$

The application of PCF, parallel to an unmarked phonological phrasing algorithm operating on syntactic constituents, presupposes the generation of the input m-structure. Though I cannot present the full details of a morphological theory here, I assume the existence of a parallel m-constituent formation which serves a function comparable to Selkirk's (1982) rewrite rules for morphology.

(6) M-CONSTITUENT FORMATION ALGORITHM (MCF):

$x \rightarrow \langle x \rangle_m$

In (6), the input x is a stem morpheme whose insertion is governed by the morphological component of the grammar. A derivation illustrating the simple interaction between m-structure and p-structure formation is given in (7).

(7)

INPUT:	stem	
MCF	$\langle \text{stem} \rangle_m$	
PCF	—	$[\text{stem}]_p$
PHONOLOGICAL RULES:		$[\text{stem}]_p$

Like theories in which phonological rules refer directly to syntactic structure (e.g., Kaisse, 1985), past theories in which phonological rules apply to morphological domains directly have restricted the access of those rules to the internal structure of the domains that they apply within. In lexical phonology, such restrictions have taken the form of bracket erasure conventions applying to morphological structure (Kiparsky, 1982; Mohanan, 1982; Pesetsky, 1979). Although less structure is available to phonological rules in PLP, it is still desirable to prevent phonological rules from accessing all of the internal p-structure generated in an extended derivation by invoking some notion of bracket erasure. Sproat (this volume) and Inkelas (1989) have proposed to view bracket erasure not as a transformational process destroying structure, but rather as a locality constraint on what phonological rules may access. The claim would thus be that phonological rules may only refer to the highest node in p-structure, thus limiting their access to internal complexity.[4]

Given this or any version of bracket erasure, it will be necessary for phonological rules to apply immediately upon the creation of each new p-constituent. Otherwise internal p-structure would be lost, and no word-internal rule application—or, extending the convention to the postlexical phonology, no rule application below the level of the utterance—could occur.

(8) Phonological rules apply automatically upon the construction of a new p-constituent.

So far I have discussed the generation of p-structure only in abstract terms. But insofar as we find it necessary to provide distinct types of lexical p-constituents in a level-ordered lexicon, the theory will need a mechanism for generating them in the appropriate order. The most straightforward method is to adjust the existing PCF algorithm such that instead of simply building generic p-structure, it creates p-constituents of the immediately higher category. The index *i* in the revised algorithm (9) ranges over the ordered set of category labels, with α being the lowest.

(9) P-CONSTITUENT FORMATION ALGORITHM (revised):

$$\langle x\rangle_{m_i} \quad [x]_{p_{i-1}} \rightarrow \langle x\rangle_{m_i} \quad [x]_{p_i}$$

Corresponding revisions are made to the M-CFA.

(10) M-CONSTITUENT FORMATION ALGORITHM (revised):

$$\langle x\rangle_{m_i} \rightarrow \langle x\rangle_{m_{i+1}}$$

A sample derivation showing the assignment of level 1 (α), level 2 (β), and word level (ω) structure to a simple stem follows.

(11) Underlying representation: stem

Level 1	MCF	$\langle\text{stem}\rangle_{m\alpha}$	
	PCF		$[\text{stem}]_{p\alpha}$
	phonological rules		$[\text{stem}]_{p\alpha}$
Level 2	MCF	$\langle\text{stem}\rangle_{m\beta}$	$[\text{stem}]_{p\alpha}$
	PCF		$[\text{stem}]_{p\beta}$
	phonological rules		$[\text{stem}]_{p\beta}$
Word level	MCF	$\langle\text{stem}\rangle_{m\omega}$	$[\text{stem}]_{p\beta}$
	PCF		$[\text{stem}]_{p\omega}$
	phonological rules		$[\text{stem}]_{p\omega}$

Instances in which PCF supplies p-structure to a representation that formerly lacked it, as seen in the sample derivation in (7) and in the first step of the derivation in (11), are simply the special case in which the index in the algorithm is instantiated as α.

3.3. Mismatches—or, PCF as the "Elsewhere Case"

Elsewhere (Inkelas, 1989) I have argued in favor of PLP on the grounds that it is eminently suited to describe in an insightful way the attested set of mismatches that occur between morphological constituency and phonological rule domains.[5] Though they may correspond exactly, as the preceding algorithm would suggest, the very assumption that p-structure and m-structure are represented separately predicts that mismatches should be possible. Mismatches between p-structure and syntactic structure are, of course, celebrated, forming one of the fundamental arguments in favor of the prosodic hierarchy theory (Nespor and Vogel, 1986; Selkirk, 1978, 1980). A basic tenet of PLP, in which sublexical p-structure now has many of the same properties as postlexical p-structure, is that mismatches should occur in the lexicon as well.

3.3.1. COMPOUNDS

One kind of lexical mismatch is already quite well known in the literature on the prosodic hierarchy, namely that occurring in a certain type of compound. In some languages, the two members of a compound word act as separate phonological rule domains. This is the case, for example, in Sanskrit (Selkirk, 1980); in Dutch and German (Booij, 1985); in Malayalam (Sproat, 1986); in Indonesian (Cohn, 1989); and in Italian, as described by Nespor and Vogel (1986; see also Nespor, 1984). For example, although all other words in Italian may contain at most one primary stress, compounds contain two. In addition, a word-bounded rule of nasal assimilation applies within each member of a compound but is blocked across the compound-internal boundary. A third rule, intervocalic voicing, also voices *s* word-medially—but not if its environment contains a compound boundary (Nespor and Vogel, 1986).[6]

Some compounds do behave as a unit for phonological purposes. For example, compounds in Greek (Nespor and Vogel, 1986) form a unitary domain for stress rules such that the surface stress of a compound need not reflect the surface stress of either component word. The internal morphological boundary of Greek compounds does not interfere with the domain of the stress rule.

This split in the behavior of compounds for phonological purposes has led to the hypothesis that while compounds of the type found in Greek correspond to a single p-constituent (12a), compounds like those in Italian correspond to two constituents (12b).

(12)	a.	⟨tɔsta⟩$_{m}$	[tɔ́sta]$_{p}$	'toaster'
		⟨pane⟩$_{m}$	[páne]$_{p}$	'bread'
		⟨tɔstapane⟩$_{m}$	[tɔ́sta]$_{p}$ [páne]$_{p}$	'bread toaster'
	b.	⟨kukla⟩$_{m}$	[kúkla]$_{p}$	'doll'
		⟨spiti⟩$_{m}$	[spíti]$_{p}$	'house'
		⟨kuklaspiti⟩$_{m}$	[kukláspiti]$_{p}$	'doll's house'

Thus, the array of phonological compound types provides evidence in favor of allowing mismatched morphological and p-structure.

3.3.2. Invisibility

A different type of mismatch involves the phenomenon characterized by Poser (1984) as INVISIBILITY. Often referred to in individual cases as extrametricality (Harris, 1983; Hayes, 1981), extratonality (Pulleyblank, 1986), or extraprosodicity (Kiparsky, 1985), invisibility involves the exclusion of some part of the phonological string from the domain of phonological rules.

In Amele, a language of Papua New Guinea (Roberts, 1987), there is an allophonic voicing alternation among labial and velar stops. These stops are voiced word-initially and intervocalically (13a), but voiceless word-finally (13b) (Roberts, 1987 : 333).

(13)	a.			b.		
		bæ	'today'		*gælæp*	'body ornament'
		æbə	*'brother'*		*bɔlɔp*	'trap'
		gæ : d	'crazy'		*bæmik*	'his scrotum'
		ɔgɔl	'tree species'		*ælɔk*	'raven'

However, just in case the word is monosyllabic, a final labial or velar stop will instead be voiced.

(14)	a.			b.		
		sib	'rubbish'		*ʔɔg*	'frog'
		næ : b	'termite'		*gug*	'basis'
		sub	'comb'		*lig*	'shrub species'

If we assume that these stops, for which voicing is not phonemic, undergo a word-level context-free rule inserting [+voice], then we may account for the voiceless status of word-final labial and velar stops with a rule of final consonant invisibility. Invisible consonants are enclosed in angled brackets.

(15)			
	INPUT:	*pɔlɔp*	*kuk*
	INVISIBILITY:	pɔlɔ⟨p⟩	—
	VOICING:	bɔlɔ⟨p⟩	gug
	OUTPUT:	[bɔlɔp]	[gug]
		'trap'	'basis'

Invisibility has often been treated diacritically in the past (though see Poser, 1984), a theoretical blemish handled with exception features (e.g., [+extrametrical]) whose restricted distribution is largely unexplained. In Inkelas (1989) I argued, to the contrary, that invisibility is an integrated facet of p-constituent formation: in particular, 'invisibility effects' result when certain elements of a morphological constituent are excluded from the corresponding p-constituent.

(16) <pɔlɔp>$_{m}$ [pɔlɔ]$_{p}$ p

The rule responsible for generating a p-representation like that in (16) is formulated in (17) and shown applying in (18).[7]

(17) FINAL CONSONANT INVISIBILITY: $[.... C]_p \rightarrow [...]_p\, C$

(18) $[\text{pɔlɔp}]_p \rightarrow [\text{pɔlɔ}]_p\, \text{p} \rightarrow [\text{bɔlɔ}]_p\, \text{p} \rightarrow [\text{bɔ́lɔp}]_p$
invisibility *voicing* *other rules*

The first advantage to treating invisibility as the adjustment of the p-constituent edge is that we can explain the blockage of invisibility in monosyllabic forms: removing the final consonant from the p-constituent would render these forms monomoraic, presumably in violation of a minimal size constraint in the language.[8]

A similar account can be given for any of the well-known examples of invisibility in the literature; final syllable extrametricality in English nouns (Hayes, 1981), for example, will derive forms of the sort depicted in (19).

(19) $\langle \text{Pamela} \rangle_m$ $[\text{Páme}]_p$ la

As in Amele, English invisibility assignment is blocked when the resulting form would dip below minimal size constraints: it is well known that monosyllabic nouns do not undergo the extrametricality rule, the best evidence being that they always surface with stress (Hayes, 1981).

(20) $\langle \text{dog} \rangle_m$ $[\text{dóg}]_p$ $(^*[\ ]_p\, \text{dog})$

Accounts in which extrametricality is a diacritic feature have had to stipulate its failure to be assigned to forms which it would exhaust (Hayes, 1981). But this prohibition follows naturally from the p-constituent approach, in which invisibility assignment directly affects the size of the p-domain.

In addition to obviating the need for an invisibility diacritic and explaining minimality conditions, the p-constituent treatment of invisibility also explains the best known condition on invisibility, namely its distribution: invisibility is found only at the edge (Buckley, 1992; Harris, 1983; Hayes, 1981; Poser, 1984; Pulleyblank, 1986).

This well known PERIPHERALITY CONDITION follows directly from the representation of invisible material as external to the p-constituent—thus necessarily in the environment of a p-constituent edge. It is no more possible on this approach to represent medial invisibility than it is to represent a discontinuous p-constituent. There is thus no source for medial invisibility in the theory.

In sum, the hypothesized existence of independent m- and p-structure yields a more restrictive theory of what information phonological rules can see directly. But possibly more importantly, it also provides a uniform treatment of compounding and invisibility mismatches, treating these otherwise troublesome phenomena as complementary facets of the regular process of p-constituent formation.

Representing invisibility and p-compounds as instances of p-structure mismatches has an important consequence for our interpretation of the PCF algorithm presented earlier. Intended to capture the generalization that m- and p-constituency correspond, this algorithm would clearly overgenerate if it applied in all the cases we have seen: it would incorrectly neutralize the distinction between compound types, and it would obscure representations of invisibility. We must therefore ensure that PCF applies only in the regular case and not in the exceptional case. This can be accomplished by construing the PCF as an elsewhere case, treating it as a purely structure-filling algorithm which applies only in the absence of the structure it would insert.[9]

3.3.3. P-SUBCATEGORIZATION

Positing separate structures in the lexicon makes possible the description of mismatches. It also enhances the representation of dependent morphemes, resulting in a principled classification of that complex set. Presented in (21), dependent (bound) morphemes are defined as those which are unable to stand alone. In this they contrast with underlyingly free stems.

(21)	FREE	BOUND
	Stem	Affix
		Bound root
		Clitic

Great differences separate bound roots, affixes, and clitics. Most salient is that clitics form their own syntactic terminals, their dependence seemingly phonological in nature. By contrast, affixes and bound roots display dependence of a more morphological ilk, requiring a morphological sister in order to constitute well-formed words capable of entering the syntax. Yet affixes and roots differ phonologically in that affixes typically trigger a cycle of phonological rules upon insertion and can be sensitive to phonological properties of sister morphemes—properties lacking in bound roots.[10]

These differences can be schematized as in (22), where the starting assumption is the distinctness of m- and p-structures, and the relevant parameter is best characterized as dependence.

(22)	M-DEPENDENT	NOT m-DEPENDENT
P-DEPENDENT:	Affix	Clitic
NOT p-DEPENDENT:	Root	Stem

The cells in (22) match the four categories of morphemes depicted in (21). We have thus factored apart the dependence properties of stems, roots, affixes, and clitics.

The question now arises as to how to encode the property of dependence in an enlightening and useful fashion. At least in the case of morphological dependence, we can make use of existing proposals by Lieber (1980), Selkirk (1982), Kiparsky (1983), Sproat (1985), and others to encode the requirement of a morphological sister in a subcategorization frame.

(23) AFFIX (e.g., the English suffix *-ity*): $_{N}\langle_{A}\langle\;\rangle_{m\alpha}\ \text{ity}\rangle_{m\alpha}$
ROOT (e.g., the English root *-mit*): $_{V}\langle_{[+Lat]}\langle\;\rangle_{m\alpha}\ \text{mit}\rangle_{m\alpha}$

A logical approach would be to propose a parallel notion for p-structure.[11]

(24) AFFIX (e.g., the English suffix *-ity*): $[[\;]_{p\alpha}\ \text{ity}]_{p\alpha}$
CLITIC (e.g., the English auxiliary *-'s*): $[[\;]_{p\omega}\ \text{z}]_{p\omega}$

Several advantages follow from the proposal to assign distinct p- and m-frames in the lexicon. One is the potential for a principled division of labor between the two types of entities. Working in a framework where m-frames and p-frames constrain the same constituents, Sproat (1985) proposed that m-frames could encode dominance relations in m-structure, while p-frames would encode linear precedence relations. While in our current proposal m-frames and p-frames refer to different constituent hierarchies, the idea that the responsibility for linear precedence might be consigned to p-frames is still applicable, thus eliminating some potential redundancy from the theory.

A further role that p-frames alone would perform under this approach would be encoding sensitivity of the bound form to phonological properties of its sisters. For example, affixes which are sensitive to the stress or syllabification or segment structure of the base would state these requirements in p-frames. This makes the prediction that bound roots, which lack such frames, will not impose this type of requirement, a prediction which as far as I know is correct.[12]

A third advantage to proposing distinct p- and m-subcategorization frames is the resulting ability to characterize exceptionality in one domain which does not carry over into the other. For example, the unpredictable invisibility inherent to particular suffixes in English, Japanese, and other languages can be stated purely in terms of their lexical p-frames, without complicating their perfectly normal morphological representation. If, like m-frames, p-frames encode basic information about the sister and the mother of the relevant affix, then the contrast between lexically invisible and (normal) lexically visible affixes becomes one of the relative location of the edge of the mother, relative to the subcategorizing affix.

(25) a. UNDERLYING REPRESENTATION OF A VISIBLE SUFFIX: $=[[\;]_{p}\ \text{suffix}]_{p}$
b. UNDERLYING REPRESENTATION OF AN INVISIBLE SUFFIX: $=[[\;]_{p}]_{p}\ \text{suffix}$

Our earlier decision to interpret the PCF algorithm as a purely structure-filling elsewhere algorithm saves the invisible suffix in (25b) from being immediately regularized in the derivation. More specifically, the information in the lexical frame of the affix about the p-status of its mother overrides the default algorithm and survives.

To exemplify, (26) provides a partial derivational history, in p-structure, of the suffixed form *historic-al.* Shown by Hayes (1981) to be inherently invisible, the suffix *-al* will be associated with the type of entry schematized in (25b). (The partial derivation takes place at stratum 1—that is, the p-constituents in question are of type α. I have omitted category labels to improve legibility.)

(26) INPUT: $[\text{historic}]_p$
AFFIXATION OF $[[\ ]_p]_p$ al: $[[\text{historic}]_p]_p$ al
PCF: —
PHONOLOGICAL RULES APPLY TO: $[\text{historic}]_p$ al

As can be seen in the above derivations, the bracket erasure, or locality convention, is assumed to be automatic, defining the amount of p-structure phonological rules can access at any given point in the derivation.

4. AFFIXATION AND CYCLICITY IN PROSODIC LEXICAL PHONOLOGY

Thus far we have identified the units of representation in a theory which construes lexical rule domains as units of p-structure and utilizes the distinction between m- and p-structure to capture certain asymmetries that have been observed to obtain between the two. We have also seen two sources for p-structure in the lexicon: PCF, and p-subcategorization.[13] Each of these is motivated independently of any discussion of cyclicity. PCF is required to supply p-constituency to nonderived stems, and p-frames are needed to represent direction of attachment, phonological constraints on possible sisters, and p-structure irregularities of affixes (and, in principle, clitics). We have also assumed that phonological rules apply automatically to the domain described by the uppermost node in p-structure immediately upon the creation of that node.

The relevance of this discussion to the issue of cyclic rule application is that the very elements of the theory presented thus far conspire to predict cyclicity at all word-internal stages of the derivation.

(27) All morphological processes will correlate with the construction of a p-constituent; thus, all will undergo cyclic phonological rules.

In this strong claim, PLP distinguishes itself from other theories of the morphology–phonology interface. For example, as we shall see later, other models have claimed that cyclicity or noncyclicity is a stipulated property of each lexical stratum (e.g., Halle and Mohanan, 1985)—or even that it is a diacritic property specified directly for each individual affix (e.g. Halle and Kenstowicz, 1991). But this kind of arbitrary variety is not possible within PLP. Due to the generic statement of PCF, all levels of m-structure will experience mapping to p-structure in the same fashion. And due to the existence of p-frames in the underlying representation of every affix, p-structure will be created anew with every instance of affixation.

In the following sections, we will explore three specific places in the derivation where PLP permits—or forces—rules to apply noncyclically. The noncyclicity of these three morphologically defined environments follows from independently needed properties of the theory. I argue, moreover, that they cover the data used in the literature to motivate less constrained models of morphology–phonology interaction (discussed in Section 5). These three noncyclic phenomena are: the apparently universal nonapplication of cyclic rules to bound roots; the language-specific nonapplication of cyclic rules to unaffixed stems prior to initial affixation; and the language-specific noncyclic application of phonological rules to words at the end of the lexical derivation. I turn first to the treatment of bound roots within PLP.

4.1. Bound Roots

Bound roots represent the one area in which past theories of the phonology–morphology interface have overgenerated cyclicity. In particular, the version of lexical phonology expounded in Kiparsky (1982) predicts a phonological cycle of rules after each morphological process, including the insertion of bound roots. But as Kiparsky observes (see also Brame, 1974; Harris, 1983), these morphemes do not constitute phonological rule domains on their own, failing to undergo such cyclic rules as stress assignment—and even, in some cases, to conform to morpheme structure constraints. The minimal morphological stature required for cyclic phonological rule application is that of free-standing stem, such as would be created when a bound root is supplied with a morphological sister.

The free stem is precisely the input required in order to trigger PCF (9). Past accounts have simply had to stipulate that bound roots do not qualify as phonological rule domains. However, this generalization follows naturally from the tenets of PLP, which is unable to assign such roots the requisite p-structure.

This point is illustrated in (28), which contrasts the 'derivation' of an unaffixed bound root (*-ceive*) with that of a free stem (*stem*).

(28)

	BOUND ROOT	STEM	
UNDERLYING REPRESENTATION:	$\langle\langle\ \rangle_{m_\alpha}$ ceive$\rangle_{m_\alpha}$	stem	
MCF:	—	$\langle$stem$\rangle_{m_\alpha}$	
PCF:	—		$[$stem$]_{p_\alpha}$
PHONOLOGICAL RULES:	—		$[$stem$]_{p_\alpha}$

Thus PLP derives the one instance of universally prohibited cyclic rule application without any extra stipulation.

The scenario predicted by PLP is thus far one of absolute extremes: rules never apply to bound roots, but always apply in a cyclic fashion to every (derived or nonderived) free stem. However, this rigidity is somewhat illusory. PLP in fact possesses flexibility at both ends of the lexical derivation. The flexibility derives from the interaction between the two sources of p-structure provided by the theory: affixation and PCF. As we will see, the order in which languages choose to tap these two devices allows for some variation in the construction of p-domains at both the very beginning and the very end of the lexicon. We turn first to the possibilities arising at the beginning.

4.2. Preaffixal Stem Cycle in Stratum 1

It is recognized that bound roots never constitute rule domains. But is it the case that nonderived stems always do? While PLP makes this situation possible, it does not force it.

The two sources of p-structure in the lexicon may in principle interact either in a feeding manner or in a bleeding manner. The former is what has been implicitly assumed thus far. That is, we have assumed that before acquiring an affix, a free stem will undergo PCF and, as an automatic consequence, a cycle of phonological rules.

(29) PCF FEEDS AFFIXATION:

INPUT:	stem
PCF:	$[\text{stem}]_p$
FIRST CYCLE OF PHONOLOGICAL RULES:	$[\text{stem}]_p$
AFFIXATION OF $[[\ ]_p\ \text{suffix}]_p$:	$[\text{stem-suffix}]_p$
SECOND CYCLE OF PHONOLOGICAL RULES:	$[\text{stem-suffix}]_p$

However, the opposite order of application is also logically possible. Under a unification-based view of subcategorization in which the combination of a subcategorization frame with another morpheme is permitted as long as the output is well-formed,[14] nothing will prevent an affix from attaching directly to a stem which itself lacks p-structure—thereby supplying the stem with that structure.

(30) AFFIXATION BLEEDS PCF:

INPUT:	stem
AFFIXATION OF $[[\ ]_p\ \text{suffix}]_p$:	$[\text{stem-suffix}]_p$
FIRST CYCLE OF PHONOLOGICAL RULES:	$[\text{stem-suffix}]_p$
PCF:	—

Due to the bracket erasure/locality conventions assumed here, there will be no representational difference between forms derived in the order shown in (29) and forms derived in the order shown in (30). Both produce $[\text{stem-suffix}]_p$ as output;

only (29), however, derives an intermediate stage where the input stem is an available constituent in p-structure. Only in (29) is there a pre-affixal stem cycle.

What I would like to argue here is that because PCF and Affixation lack intrinsic ordering, their order is parameterizable across languages. In other words, there ought to be languages in which Affixation bleeds PCF, predicting no stem cycles in case an affix is attached; and languages in which PCF always applies first, inducing obligatory stem cycles under all circumstances. The two typological possibilities are schematized below.

(31)

	Type A		Type B
Underlying representation:	stem	Underlying representation:	stem
PCF:	$[\text{stem}]_p$	Affixation:	$[\text{stem-suffix}]_p$
Affixation:	$[\text{stem-suffix}]_p$	PCF:	—
	(2 cycles)		(1 cycle)

(Of course, a stem which takes no affixes will be treated identically in both scenarios, as will stems which have already undergone affixation.)

This typological prediction is unavailable to direct-access versions of lexical phonology (Kiparsky, 1982; Mohanan, 1982; Pesetsky, 1979), which have no means of differentiating the two types of languages shown in (31). Thus, any evidence for the dichotomy in (31) has dual importance: it not only supports one particular proposal within PLP, but it also supports that model in general over direct-access models of lexical phonology.

With this in mind, let us now turn to the evidence. It has already been shown in the literature that languages of type A exist. Diyari (Poser, 1989), for example, presents a clear case in which the construction of metrical structure on monomorphemic stems crucially precedes any affixation. Pulleyblank (1986) makes similar arguments for Margi and Tiv, where rules of tone assignment (and in the case of Margi, tone spreading) must crucially apply to stems before the first suffix is attached (see, e.g., pp. 68, 74). Here I present one example of a candidate for Type B, namely Carib, a Cariban language spoken in Guyana. The analysis is amended from Inkelas (1989); the data come from Hoff (1968).

4.2.1. Carib

Stress in nonderived stems in Carib is perfectly alternating, subject to the restriction that word-final syllables are never stressed. Some nonderived stems display stress on odd-numbered syllables, while others display stress on even-numbered syllables. Phonetically, stress is correlated with vowel lengthening in the first two (nonfinal) stressed syllables of the word, and with associated high pitch with the second stressed syllable from the left. Only vowel length and stress will be marked, as in (32).

(32) ODD-NUMBERED STRESS:

No. of syllables	Stem	Gloss
1	*wo*	'to beat'
2	*é:ro*	'this'
	kú:pi	'bathe'
3	*é:maka*	'to comb a parting'
	tá:kuwa	'polishing-stone'
4	*á:rawá:ta*	'howling monkey'
	pá:yawá:ru	'cassava beer'
5	*aúwanó:pono*	'causing laughter'
	kó:kapó:take	'you will have me bitten'

(33) EVEN-NUMBERED STRESS:

No. of syllables	Stem	Gloss
3	*aká:mi*	'trumpeter bird'
	tonó:ro	'large bird'
4	*ará:mari*	'mythical snake'
	kurí:yara	'canoe'
5	*asá:pará:pi*	'species of fish'
	wotú:ropó:ro	'cause to ask'

As shown in (34), morphologically complex forms do not adhere to the perfectly alternating pattern. In particular, because stress is assigned cyclically and is structure-preserving, forms including prefixes or suffixes can exhibit nonalternating surface stress.[15]

(34)

akí:ma	'tease'	*kïn-á:kí:ma:-no*	'he teases her'
awó:mï	'to get up'	*ay-á:wó:mï-i*	'you must not get up'
epá:nopï	'help'	*ay-é:pá:nopï*	'your being helped'
emé:pa	'to teach'	*kïn-é:mé:pa:-no*	'he teaches them'
etámboka	'untie'	*kïn-é:támboka:-no*	'she unties it'
eyá:to	'call'	*kïn-é:yá:to-ya:-toŋ*	'they call him'
kurá:ma	'cure'	*si-kú:rá:ma-e*	'I cure him'
kurá:ma	'look after'	*kï-kú:rá:ma-ko*	'you must look after me'
		kï-kú:rá:ma-i	'you must not look after me'
		i-kú:rá:ma-ko	'you must look after him'

poró:pï	'stop'	*ni-pó:ró:pï-i*	'actually he has stopped'
		ni-pó:ró:pï:-se	'so that he may stop'
		a-pó:ró:pï-i	'you must not stop'

Both the derived and the nonderived words listed in the first and third columns of (34) exhibit stress on the second syllable. However, note that in each case the stems also exhibit stress on their own second syllable—that is, the third syllable of the derived word, where no postcyclic rule would place it. Of course, this stem-medial syllable is exactly where stress would be assigned were the prefix not present. We may thus conclude that these stems undergo stress assignment both before and after the prefix is added.[16]

Forms containing stems and suffixes only are consistent with the generalization that stress assignment is cyclic and structure-preserving.

(35)	a.	*kó:roka*	'scrub'	*kó:roká:no*	'he scrubbed'
		koró:mo	'recent'	*koró:mo-no*	'a recent thing'
	b.	*bá:siya*	'deputy-chief'	*bá:siyá:-koŋ̂*	'deputy-chiefs'
		pakó:to	'to cut wood'	*pakó:to-no*	'fact of wood-cutting'
	c.	*kurú:wese*	'palm shell'	*kurú:wesé-mbo*	'old palm sheath'
	d.	*eyá:to*	'call'	*kin-é:yá:to-yá:-toŋ̂*	'they call him'

Unlike prefixation, however, suffixation never results in adjacent stresses.

The contrast between odd- and even-numbered stress is phonemic only within stems, though preserved under subsequent derivation, as we have seen, by the structure-filling stress rule. Hoff indicates that of the two patterns, the odd-numbered stress pattern is less frequent (p. 73). This suggests that stems with the even-numbered stress pattern represent the unmarked case.

Given this, we still are faced with two options for the basic stress rule. Assuming that the rule operates from left to right, the basic stress foot could be iambic, or it could also be trochaic, in which case it would need to follow a rule assigning initial syllable extrametricality.

(36)	IAMBIC ANALYSIS	TROCHAIC ANALYSIS
CYCLE 1:	[kurá.ma]	ku [ráma]
CYCLE 2:	[ikú.rá.ma]	i [kú.ráma]

The iambic analysis would require newly inserted stress feet to overwrite weak stress foot terminals assigned on an earlier cycle (in order, for example, to produce the adjacent stresses in *i-kúráma*). By contrast, the trochaic analysis would require only that initial invisibility must be lost upon further prefixation, an assumption consistent with virtually all theories of extrametricality (including the one assumed here).

I will thus tentatively assume that the correct analysis is trochaic feet and that we require the two rules in (37) and (38).[17]

(37) INITIAL SYLLABLE INVISIBILITY: $[\sigma \ldots]_p \;\rightarrow\; \sigma[\ldots]_p$

(38) STRESS ASSIGNMENT: From the left edge, assign syllabic trochees.

I turn now to the question of how to capture the lexical distinction between stems falling into the odd-numbered pattern and those falling into the even-numbered pattern. One possibility is to annotate odd-numbered stems with an exception feature blocking the rule of extrametricality assignment from affecting them. But a feature of this type has no theoretical status, and we may thus reject it as nonexplanatory. A second possibility is to assign these words an initial stress foot in underlying representation. Since the stress foot assignment process is structure-preserving, this initial foot will remain intact, causing subsequent foot assignment to begin on the third syllable.[18]

(39)

	REGULAR	IRREGULAR
UNDERLYING REPRESENTATION:	*asaparapi*	*páyawaru*
PCF:	[asaparapi]	[páyawaru]
EXTRAMETRICALITY:	a [saparapi]	[páyawaru]
TROCHEE ASSIGNMENT:	a [sáparápi]	[páyawáru]
(other rules)	[asá:pará:pi]	[pá:yawá:ru]
OUTPUT:	'species of fish'	'cassava beer'

We are now prepared to examine the evidence against a preaffixal stem cycle in Carib. The first set of data is disyllabic stems.

Despite their adherence in citation form to the surface prohibition against final stress, disyllabic stems nonetheless separate into the same two groups into which larger stems are divided [see (32)–(33)]. Some surface with initial, or odd-numbered, stress in every environment (40); we may place these firmly in the odd-numbered category. However, the other set exhibits alternating stress (41). When uttered alone, without suffixes, these stems exhibit initial stress. But in the company of any suffix, they exhibit second-syllable, or even-numbered stress. We thus place them in the even-numbered category and require an explanation for their behavior in isolation.

(40) "ODD-NUMBERED STRESS":

é:ro	'this'	*é:ro-me*	'now'
ká:mi	'flame'	*ká:mi-ro*	'cause to become pale red'
ká:wo	'high'	*ká:wo-ná:ka*	'from above'
		ká:wo-nó:-koŋ̂	'high ones'

(41) "EVEN-NUMBERED STRESS":

á:pi	'red, ripe'	*apí:-ro*	'cause to ripen'
é:ta	'hear'	*etá:-topo*	'means of hearing'
ká:rai	'blackness'	*karái-ma*	'blacken'
ú:wa	'dance'	*uwá:-no*	'being dancing'

The analysis developed thus far would predict that the odd-numbered pattern is the marked case, requiring a lexically specified foot (42a). This is consistent with the nonalternating nature of the stress of these disyllabic stems. By contrast, disyllabic stems exhibiting the even-numbered pattern are lexically unspecified (42b)—correlating with the context-sensitivity of their stress patterns.

(42) UNDERLYING REPRESENTATION:

a. *karai* 'blackness' Unmarked "even-numbered"
b. *káwo* 'high' Marked "odd-numbered"

Given these underlying forms, we can now prove that disyllabic stems must not undergo a stem cycle prior to affixation (if any). To see why this must be so, let us start by assuming the opposite, namely that there IS a preaffixal stem cycle.

From the fact that all disyllabic stems (including those in the "even-numbered" category) possess initial stress in isolation, we know that the extrametricality rule must fail to apply on the cycle at which stress is assigned to them. This could plausibly be attributed to a minimality condition of the kind observed earlier in Amele. However, even assuming that we manage to block invisibility from applying to disyllabic stems, the subsequent assignment of initial stress poses a problem. Once stress is assigned to the first syllable of disyllabic stems, then it should thereafter exhibit the same nonalternating behavior exhibited by stems with underlying stress. But this is not the case: contrary to the predictions of a stem cycle account, the contrast between odd- and even-numbered disyllabic stems is not neutralized.

(43) "STEM CYCLE" ACCOUNT:

	REGULAR	IRREGULAR
UNDERLYING REPRESENTATION:	*karai*	*kámi*
PCF:	[karai]	[kámi]
INVISIBILITY:	[blocked by minimality]	
STRESS:	[kárai]	—
AFFIXATION:	[káraima]	[kámiro]
INVISIBILITY:	ká [raima]	ká [miro]
STRESS:	—	—
(late rules)	*[ká:raima] 'blacken'	[ká:miro] 'cause to become pale red'

We may thus conclude that there cannot be a preaffixal stem cycle for disyllabic stems. Instead, Affixation must bleed PCF, resulting in a stem cycle only on unaffixed stems.

(44) "NO STEM CYCLE" ACCOUNT:

	REGULAR	IRREGULAR
UNDERLYING REPRESENTATION:	*karai*	*kámi*
AFFIXATION:	[karaima]	[kámiro]
INVISIBILITY:	ka [raima]	ká [miro]
STRESS:	ka [raíma]	—
PCF:	—	—
(late rules)	[karaíma]	[ká:miro]
	'blacken'	'cause to become pale red'

The second set of data supporting the absence of a stem cycle in Carib comes from the behavior of a small set of "strong" suffixes which appear to alter the stress patterns of the bases to which they attach. As shown in (45), they cause stems otherwise exhibiting even-numbered stress (a) to switch to an odd-numbered stress pattern. The contrast between stems in the even-numbered category (a) and those in the odd-numbered category (b) is neutralized in the environment of these suffixes.

(45)

	ISOLATION	BEFORE "STRONG" SUFFIX	
a.	*kurí:yara*	*kú:riyá:ra-rï*	'canoe'
	yamá:tu	*yá:matú:-ru*	'basket'
b.	*sú:rabaŋ*	*sú:rabá:-nï*	'beam of roof'
	ká:rawá:si	*ká:rawá:si-rï*	'rattle'

Strikingly, this neutralization occurs only when the base is consonant-initial. The stress patterns of comparable vowel-initial words in the even-numbered category remain unaltered in the environment of "strong" suffixes, as seen in (46).

(46)

ISOLATION	BEFORE "STRONG" SUFFIX		
akí:nu	*akí:nu-ru*	'laziness'	(**á:kinú:-ru*)
iné:ku	*iné:ku-ru*	'liana'	(**í:nekú:-ru*)
ïrá:pa	*ïrá:pa-rï*	'bow'	(**ḯ:rapá:rï*)
okó:mo	*okó:mo-rï*	'wasp'	(**ó:komó:-rï*)

There are two puzzles here. First, why does the stress pattern shift at all in the forms in (45)? We know Carib possess no general cyclic stress erasure phenomenon. Second, why is the stress shift restricted to consonant-initial words? One possibility is to assume that the "strong" suffixes trigger a special rule of stress foot deletion, wiping the slate clean for the subsequent assignment of odd-numbered stress. However, this analysis is suspect for two reasons. First, odd-numbered stress is supposed to result only from lexical prespecification, not from tabula rasa environments. Second, there is no explanation for the correlation with initial consonants.

The solution I adopt instead is as follows. First, I conclude from the contrasting behavior of consonant- and vowel-initial stems that the rule of initial syllable invisibility proposed earlier must actually be broken down into two components, initial consonant invisibility and initial vowel invisibility.[19] When both apply, the consonant invisibility rule feeds the vowel invisibility rule, giving the appearance of initial syllable invisibility. However, should the consonant invisibility rule be blocked from applying, the vowel invisibility rule will also fail, and the initial syllable of the word will be visible for stress purposes.

To account for the contrast between consonant- and vowel-initial stems under "strong" suffixation, I further propose that consonant invisibility is actually part and parcel of Carib's version of the PCF algorithm.

(47) Initial Vowel Invisibility: [v . . .] → v [. . .]

(48) PCF (Carib): ⟨c . . .⟩$_m$ → ⟨c . . .⟩$_m$ c [. . .]$_p$

"Strong" suffixes block the imposition of initial consonant invisibility by blocking the application of P-Constituent Formation. That is, in Carib, Affixation precedes—and thereby preempts—PCF.

(49) Carib: Affixation < (MCF <) PCF

Derivations of unaffixed (50) and suffixed (51) consonant-initial stems are shown below:

(50)

	Regular	Irregular
Underlying representation:	*kuriyara*	*kárawasi*
MCF:	⟨kuriyara⟩$_m$	⟨kárawasi⟩$_m$
PCF:	k [uriyara]$_p$	k [árawasi]$_p$
Initial V Invisibility:	ku [riyara]$_p$	ká [rawasi]$_p$
Stress Assignment:	ku [ríyara]$_p$	ká [rawási]$_p$
(late rules)	[kurí:yara]$_p$	[ká:rawá:si]$_p$
	'canoe'	'rattle'

(51)

	Regular	Irregular
Underlying representation:	*kuriyara*	*kárawasi*
MCF	⟨kuriyara⟩$_m$	⟨kárawasi⟩$_m$
Affixation:	⟨kuriyararï⟩$_m$	⟨kárawasirï⟩$_m$
	[kuriyararï]$_p$	[kárawasirï]$_p$
Initial V Invisibility:	—	—
Stress Assignment:	[kúriyárarï]$_p$	[kárawásirï]$_p$
PCF:	—	—
(late rules)	[kúriyárarï]$_p$	[kárawásirï]$_p$
	'canoe'	'rattle'

Since the effect of blocking PCF by Affixation is manifested only in consonant-initial words, we correctly predict no alternations in the suffixed and unsuffixed forms of vowel-initial stems. The contrast between the behavior of regular consonant-initial and vowel-initial stems under "strong" affixation is generated as follows.

(52)

	VOWEL-INITIAL	CONSONANT-INITIAL
UNDERLYING REPRESENTATION:	*okomo*	*yamatu*
MCF:	⟨okomo⟩$_m$	⟨yamatu⟩$_m$
AFFIXATION:	⟨okomorï⟩$_m$	⟨yamaturï⟩$_m$
	[okomorï]$_p$	[yamaturï]$_p$
VOWEL INVISIBILITY:	o [komorï]$_p$	—
STRESS:	o [kómorï]$_p$	[yámatúrï]$_p$
PCF:	—	—
(late rules)	[okó : morï]$_p$	[yá : matú : rï]$_p$
	'wasp'	'basket'

Vowel-initial stems will undergo Initial Vowel Invisibility regardless of whether Affixation or PCF applies first and will exhibit the same stress patterns with or without a strong suffix:

(53)

	SUFFIXED	UNSUFFIXED
UNDERLYING REPRESENTATION:	*okomo*	*okomo*
MCF:	⟨okomo⟩$_m$	⟨okomo⟩$_m$
AFFIXATION:	⟨okomorï⟩$_m$	—
	[okomorï]$_p$	—
VOWEL INVISIBILITY:	o [komorï]$_p$	—
STRESS RULE:	o [kómorï]$_p$	—
PCF:	—	[okomo]$_p$
VOWEL INVISIBILITY:	—	o [komo]$_p$
STRESS RULE:	—	o [kómo]$_p$
(late rules)	[okó : morï]$_p$	[okó : mo]$_p$
	'wasp(poss.)'	'wasp'

Finally, irregular, that is, odd-numbered, stress pattern stems will be immune to the effects of the strong suffixes, because their underlying initial stress foot prevails regardless of the visibility or invisibility of their initial syllable.[20]

In summary, while stress assigned cyclically in Carib is normally preserved, the alternations exhibited between suffixed and unsuffixed stems shows that stress must not be assigned to stems prior to the insertion of the first suffix. This motivates the ordering of PCF following Affixation in Carib.

4.3. Noncyclic = Postcyclic

We noted earlier that the source from which PLP derives cyclic rule application is the presence of p-subcategorization frames in the lexical entries of affixes. Any stratum associated with affixation will necessarily be associated with cyclic phonological rule application.

However, this leaves open the possibility that a particular stratum might have no affixes associated with it. In fact, this is the case with the (postcyclic) lexical word stratum, as described by Kiparsky (1985) and Booij and Rubach (1987). The domain of word-level lexical rules, this stratum does not allow any morphology to take place.

In terms of PLP, we may capture the nonaffixational nature of a stratum with a constraint in underlying representation against affixes subcategorizing for constituents of the appropriate category. In other words, Affixation is turned off at a particular level of the hierarchy. In the corresponding constraint in (54), only the m-frame is mentioned; the assumption is that since affixes will always have m-frames, repeating the constraint on p-frames would at best be redundant.[21]

(54) $*\langle \mathrm{x}, \langle\, \rangle_{\mathrm{m}_i} \rangle_{\mathrm{m}_i}$, where $i \geq j$, j a category in the p-hierarchy

This constraint interacts with another constraint, that governing the level of the hierarchy up to which PCF operates in the lexicon. We know that constituents below the level of the phonological word are strictly lexical; those at the phrase level and above are strictly postlexical. This can be captured formally with a lexical constraint prohibiting the occurrence of constituents above some cutoff level k in the lexicon.

(55) $*[\ ]_{\mathrm{P}k}$ where $k \leq n$; n a category in the p-hierarchy

In fact, the constraint in (55) may be viewed as just a special case of structure preservation (Kiparsky, 1985).

Whether or not a system incorporating the constraint in (54) will possess a noncyclic level in the lexicon depends entirely on the instantiation of (55)—that is, on whether or not PCF is still operating at level j. If PCF persists for a level beyond the Affixation cutoff, then a noncyclic level will result. If, however, PCF and Affixation have the same cutoff point, then no noncyclic lexical level is expected.

(56) a. $j < n$: there will be a noncyclic word level
b. $j \geq n$: no effect, no noncyclic word level expected

It follows as a corollary of this prediction that only one stratum, in particular the last one, can be made noncyclic (57).

(57) At most one noncyclic lexical level will occur; if so, it will be the final level.

(57) corresponds to the claims about noncyclic lexical levels made by Kiparsky (1985) and Booij and Rubach (1987). Insofar as it follows from what we have proposed, the theory is supported.

Let us first examine the case in which a noncyclic level is generated. This will occur, I have said, when j in (54) is identified with a *non*-final stratum in the lexicon—that is, when j in (54) is lower in the hierarchy than the cutoff point n in (55). In such a case, PCF will continue to generate constituents above the cutoff level for affixation. Because of the lack of morphology, this level (or levels) will be noncyclic.

It is clearly necessary, given this source, for noncyclic levels to be at the end of the lexicon. But how do we ensure that there is only one? This, I argue, follows not from inherent constraints in the theory but rather from learnability. The evidence that some language has two or more contiguous levels at which affixation is impossible, as in (58), would be slim at best.

(58) . . .
affixational stratum k (cyclic)
non-affixational stratum $k+1$ (noncyclic)
non-affixational stratum $k+2$ (noncyclic)

Empirical evidence for such a situation would be identical to empirical evidence for stratum ordering in a language lacking affixes altogether. The learner would have no reason to divide up into levels a set of ordered rules ($k+1$ rules, $k+2$ rules) that would have the same effect if organized into a single level.

If, on the other hand, the category n in (55), at and above which no morpheme may attach, is above the lexical–postlexical cutoff j in (54), then the statement about subcategorization will be vacuous. Since constituents of level j cannot exist in the lexicon anyway, the ban on affixation at that level will have no noticeable effect. In particular, no noncyclic level j will occur.

Thus, PCF permits a single postcyclic lexical level, but it does not force one. This makes the prediction that there will be languages with such a stratum and languages without, a prediction I will attempt to support in this section (see also Zec, this volume).

Cases for a lexical noncyclic stratum have already been made in several places in the literature; see, for example, Kiparsky (1985), Booij and Rubach (1987) for an analysis of Polish, and Inkelas and Zec (1988), where a similar account for Serbo-Croatian is provided. Both works discuss rules which must follow all affixation but display distinctively lexical properties. I will not present these cases here, as they are available elsewhere, but concentrate instead on the less familiar category of languages which positively lack a postcyclic "word-level" stratum.

One source of positive evidence that a language lacked a postcyclic stratum would be a case in which lexically assigned invisibility persisted into the postlexical component. This would show that no word-level cycle of rules could have applied lexically, as the assignment by PCF of the word-level p-constituent would obliterate the trace of invisibility in embedded p-structure.

Such cases do occur. Zec (this volume) demonstrates that Štokavian dialects of Serbo-Croatian vary with respect to the parameter of whether or not the phonological word is available lexically. In my terms this amounts to a difference in whether or not the lexicon permits PCF to construct a ω constituent. Halle and Kenstowicz (1991) analyze data from Manam and Latin which motivate the absence of a noncyclic lexical ω level in both languages. I present the Manam case here as an illustration and then show how PLP generates facts of this kind.

4.3.1. Manam

Manam displays a basic stress pattern in which stress resides on the word-final syllable if it is heavy, and otherwise, on the penultimate syllable of the word (Lichtenberk, 1983). A way of stating the generalization without disjunctions is that stress surfaces on the syllable containing the penultimate mora of the word. This generalization is true of nonderived or prefixed words, and also of words ending in any of a particular set of suffixes.

(59)	Unsuffixed		Suffixed	
	i-panána	'he ran'	*ʔu-lele-ʔíʔo*	'I followed you'
	wabúbu	'night'	*tamá-da*	'our (inc.) father'
	u-zém	'I chewed (them)'	*tamá-ŋ*	'your (sg.) father'
	malabóŋ	'flying fox'	*tama-míŋ*	'your (pl.) father'

However, there is another set of suffixes which Lichtenberk terms AP (antepenult) suffixes. These cause stress to occur on the syllable containing the antepenultimate mora of words that they end; consequently, Halle and Kenstowicz analyze these as triggering a rule of final syllable extrametricality (p. 467).

(60)	*táma-(ma)*	'our (excl.) father'	*ʔa-malipi-lípi-(la)*	'you only work'
	táma-(da)	'their father'	*u-rapún-(di)*	'I waited for them'
	dí-te-(a)	'they saw me'	*mogáru(ŋa-Ø)*	'his nose'
	siŋába-(lo)	'in the bush'	*ú-do(ʔ-i)*	'I took it'

So far, these facts are compatible with two types of account. One possibility is that stress is assigned cyclically and there is no postcyclic word-level stratum; another possibility is that there is such a stratum, but no stress is assigned there. However, evidence from cliticization shows that only the former alternative is possible.

Manam has a number of enclitics. Convincingly argued by Lichtenberk and by Halle and Kenstowicz to be separate syntactic terminals, they are incorporated into the preceding word for phonological purposes, as shown by the fact that stress rules apply to the host–clitic combination. Stress shifts to a host-final unstressed mora in case a monosyllabic clitic follows.

(61)	HOST:	*ʔú-doʔ-i*	'you take it'
	HOST + CLITIC:	*ʔu-doʔ-í=ʔi*	'you take it or'

We may assume that Manam clitics form phonological words with their hosts and that stress is assigned postlexically on the domain of the phonological word.

What is crucial for our purposes is that this postlexical stress assignment is sensitive to a difference obtaining among host-final unstressed moras. The relevant difference is between those final moras which were extrametrical at the time the lexical stress rule applied, and those which were visible. Only the former (61), (62a)—never the latter (62b)—are eligible for stress assignment when a monosyllabic clitic is added.

(62)	a.	*ʔu-dóʔ-i*	'you take them'	*ʔu-dóʔ-i=ʔi*	'you take them or'
	b.	*ʔú-doʔ-(i)*	'you take it'	*ʔu-doʔ-í=ʔi*	'you take it or'

Halle and Kenstowicz conclude that it is only because the extrametrical suffixes were never metrified by the earlier, cyclic rules that they are subject to stress assignment at the noncyclic clitic level. Halle and Kenstowicz define two blocks of rule assignment; cyclic and noncyclic, and mark clitics diacritically as noncyclic. But the noncyclicity of clitics should not have to be stipulated; it ought to follow naturally from their postlexical nature.

The relevance of data of this kind to this paper is that there CANNOT be a postcyclic stratum in the lexical phonology of Manam. We know from the fact that it is only the outermost suffix which affects word stress that stress must be assigned cyclically in Manam, as Halle and Kenstowicz have argued. And we know that the same stress rule which applies lexically also applies postlexically (though postlexically it appears to respect existing metrical structure). If there were a postcyclic lexical level, we would incorrectly predict, given that invisibility disappears on the cycle (Inkelas, 1989), that all suffixed words would behave alike. A postcyclic level would neutralize the contrast provided by the difference between visible and invisible suffixes, a contrast which must persist until the postlexical level. In (63) a partial derivation shows how the contrast between forms with and without final invisible moras persists until the point of cliticization.

(63)	INVISIBLE SUFFIX	VISIBLE SUFFIX	
AFFIXATION:	$[\text{ʔudo}]_{P_i}$ ʔi	$[\text{ʔudoʔi}]_{P_i}$	Lexical phonology
STRESS RULE:	$[\text{ʔúdo}]_{P_i}$ ʔi	$[\text{ʔudóʔi}]_{P_i}$	
CLITICIZATION:	$[\text{ʔúdoʔiʔi}]_{P_i}$	$[\text{ʔudóʔiʔi}]_{P_i}$	Postlexical phonology
STRESS RULE:	$[\text{ʔudoʔíʔi}]_{P_i}$	—	
OUTPUT:	*ʔudoʔíʔi* 'you took it or'	*ʔudóʔiʔi* 'you took them or'	

The partial derivation in (64) shows the bad results of a neutralizing postcyclic level of lexical rules.

(64)

	INVISIBLE SUFFIX	VISIBLE SUFFIX	
AFFIXATION:	[ʔudo]$_{P_i}$ ʔi	[ʔudoʔi]$_{P_i}$	Lexical phonology
STRESS RULE:	[ʔúdo]$_{P_i}$ ʔi	[ʔudóʔi]$_{P_i}$	
PCF:	[ʔúdoʔi]$_{P_{i+1}}$	[ʔudóʔi]$_{P_{i+1}}$	
STRESS RULE:	[ʔudóʔi]$_{P_{i+1}}$	—	
CLITICIZATION:	[ʔudóʔiʔi]$_{P_{i+1}}$	[ʔudóʔiʔi]$_{P_{i+1}}$	Postlexical phonology
STRESS RULE:	—	—	
OUTPUT:	* *ʔudóʔiʔi*	*ʔudóʔiʔi*	
	'you took it or'	'you took them or'	

4.4. Summary of Predictions

Below is a summary of the predictions made by PLP, which forces cyclicity to be the unmarked case but does predict noncyclic rule application in a restricted number of environments.

(65) a. Cyclic rules do not apply to bound roots.
b. In some languages, nonderived stems always constitute cyclic rule domains, regardless of future affixation. In other languages, the application of rules to nonderived stems in preempted by the attachment of the first affix, if any.
c. The only noncyclic lexical rules will apply at the word-level stratum (i.e., postcyclically), though not all languages will have such a stratum in the lexicon.

In severely limiting the role of noncyclic rule application, PLP differs from models that have been proposed in the past. The version of standard lexical phonology developed by Kiparsky holds that all phonological rule application is cyclic, with stipulated exceptions for bound roots (Kiparsky, 1982) and word-level rules (Kiparsky, 1985). Taking the opposite view are Halle and Mohanan (1985) and Mohanan (1986), whose version of lexical phonology takes all levels to be noncyclic. A third perspective is that of Halle and Kenstowicz (1991), who propose that it is an arbitrary property of individual affixes whether they trigger a pass by cyclic phonological rules. All of these views are possible within a framework of the phonology–morphology interface in which the timing and amount of access by phonology to morphology is negotiable. Linguists have differed, given this flexibility, as to whether they take cyclicity to be the marked or the unmarked case.

Unfortunately, there is not space here to evaluate all the data spawning these diverse views. What I have attempted to do is rather different. Assuming, as argued compellingly by Hargus (this volume), the need for cyclic rule application in at least some cases, I have proposed a restrictive model of the phonology–morphology interface which derives cyclicity as the unmarked option.

5. CONCLUSION

Not every reader may agree that this paper has simplified the theory of when phonological rules may apply cyclically in the lexicon and when they may not. Although I have attempted to streamline the predictions about cyclicity triggered by affixation, I have introduced new complications regarding stem cycles and word cycles. The data are still quite complex and not perfectly understood, and the proposals made here may well turn out to be inadequate. But what I hope will prevail is the basic approach of relating cyclicity not to arbitrary diacritic properties of affixes or levels, but rather to independently needed representations, whose properties we understand.

ACKNOWLEDGMENTS

During the preparation of this paper I have benefitted from discussions with Sharon Hargus, Larry Hyman, Richard Sproat, Draga Zec, an anonymous reviewer, and participants in the Lexical Phonology Workshop at the University of Washington.

NOTES

[1] For arguments against treating the clitic group as a distinct p-constituent, see Buckley (1991), Inkelas (1989), Kanerva (1990), Zec (1988), and Zec and Inkelas (1991). Additions to this hierarchy have been proposed as well: Condoravdi (1990) has demonstrated that Modern Greek requires a constituent (the "minimal phrase") between the phonological phrase and the phonological word; Kanerva (1990) argues from Chicheŵa for a focal phrase between the intonational phrase and the phonological phrase.

[2] This move may also be seen as a meeting of prosodic hierarchy theory with Sproat's (1985) proposal that phonological structure and morphological structure are distinct, differing in the geometry of their bracketing.

[3] In (5) and subsequent examples, angle brackets indicate m-constituency, and square brackets indicate p-constituency.

[4] It may be necessary to relax this convention to permit access one constituent in, to

accommodate the apparent need for juncture rules. Another use to which access to internal structure has been put involves "strict cycle" rules, which putatively apply only across (internal) morpheme boundaries (Kiparsky, 1982; Mascaró, 1976); but see Kiparsky (this volume) for a reanalysis not requiring morphological boundary information.

[5] Notably excluded from this set are the bracketing paradoxes discussed by, among others, Sproat (1985). Certain apparent paradoxes can be handled elegantly in terms of p-structure; for example, Nespor and Vogel (1986) and Booij and Rubach (1987) have analyzed certain affixes that do not behave as though they are phonologically part of the word as exceptionally constituting phonological words on their own. However, I do not at present see a way to extend this approach to all of the cases discussed by Sproat (see also Harris, 1989), in particular to cases in which a level 2 affix appears to be inside a level 1 affix.

[6] It also fails to apply to prefix-final consonants, which Nespor and Vogel account for by assigning phonological word status to the prefixes in question (see previous footnote).

[7] Of course, not all invisibility effects result from the application of a general phonological rule such as that in (17). English, among other languages (e.g., Japanese), possesses suffixes which are inherently invisible. Especially in a theory which restricts access by phonological rules to morphological structure, these phenomena pose a challenge; I return to it in the next section.

[8] A problem for postulating a bimoraic minimum in Amele is the large number of monomoraic words [e.g., *be* 'neck (front)', *co* 'lips', *du* 'neck (back)', *su* 'breast (woman's)', *ca* 'add', *jo* 'house']. However, Itô and Hankamer (1989) have argued for Turkish that all the forms which appear to violate minimal size conditions in that language are underived; Itô (1990) has made a similar observation for Japanese. If minimality conditions are enforced only on (morphologically) complex words, then the Amele examples just cited would not constitute counterexamples to a bimoraic minimal word condition. Unfortunately, the derived environment hypothesis is difficult to falsify. For example, Amele has a process of possessive formation which has a zero allomorph in the third person. Whether we consider the monomoraic possessive *co-ø* 'his/her lips' to be derived or underived determines the success or failure of a derived environment minimal size condition in the language. I leave the issue open here, since there is another option: if necessary, we could always claim that minimal size constraints block phonological rules (such as invisibility assignment), but not morphological rules. Similar claims about other phonological well-formedness constraints are found elsewhere in constraint-based phonological theory (Hyman, 1991; Paradis, 1988).

[9] In this the lexical PCF algorithm conforms to a precedent already set by a number of postlexical phrasing algorithms in the literature. For example, phrasing algorithms developed for Greek (Condoravdi, 1990), Hausa (Inkelas, 1988), Korean (Cho, 1990), and Shanghai (Selkirk and Shen, 1990) possess explicit elsewhere clauses invoked whenever no more specific source is available to phrase the relevant material.

[10] I am assuming a general morpheme-based theory of morphology à la Lieber (1980) or Kiparsky (1983), in which all affixes, as well as stems and roots, are lexically listed items as opposed to rules (Anderson, 1986).

[11] Proposals for a notion of phonological subcategorization exist in the literature, but none involves the particular kind of phonological constituency at issue here. For example, Klavans's (1985) phonological subcategorization frames refer to syntactic constituents on which clitics phonologically lean; Booij and Lieber's prosodic subcategorization frames

(this volume) express the sensitivity of particular affixes to certain metrical properties of the base. Sproat's (1985) proposal is the closest relative. Separating out issues of linear precedence from issues of dominance, Sproat proposes to encode the former in the phonological entry and the latter in the morphological entry of an affix. Although Sproat did not invoke our notion of p-structure per se, his insight of separate phonological and morphological entries is also central to the proposal made here.

[12] If roots are inserted as the first step in a derivation, and if morphological sensitivity is always inward, then root sensitivity to phonological properties of adjacent morphemes would be ruled out on independent grounds, except perhaps in root–root compounding, as occurs, for example, in Japanese. Although the compounding process itself imposes phonological properties in that language, I am not aware of any root-specific allomorphy based on the phonological characteristics of the sister root there, or elsewhere.

[13] The morphological process not discussed here is compounding; Inkelas (1989) accounts for the two types of compounds mentioned earlier by positing two compounding rules. One (Mcompounding) refers only to m-structure, and its output feeds right into PCF. Such compounds correspond to a single p-constituent. The other compounding rule (Pcompounding) refers both to m- and to p-structure, imposing p-structure on its output such that the two elements of the compound correspond to distinct p-constituents. A more specific source of p-structure for the compound, Pcompounding overrides PCF exactly as affixation does. Both kinds of compounds, however, are associated with a cycle of phonological rules, either by virtue of triggering PCF by default, or by virtue of construction-specific p-structure assignment.

[14] For arguments in favor of such a view, see Inkelas (1989). Evidence that it is necessary comes from the ability of bound roots, which lack p-structure, to combine with affixes, which possess p-frames. The p-frame of the affix interprets the root as its p-sister.

[15] Note that the suffixes *-no, -toŋ̂, -se,* and *-ma* always impose length on the preceding vowel; the penultimate long vowels of words ending in these suffixes is thus a local effect and can be overlooked for present purposes.

[16] In possessing a cyclic, structure-preserving stress rule, Carib thus patterns with Diyari and Warlpiri, as analyzed in Poser (1989), and with Greek, as analyzed in Steriade (1988).

[17] A reviewer aptly points out that correlation between vowel quantity and stress is a property of iambic, rather than trochaic, systems (Hayes, 1987, 1991). To the extent that Carib violates this generalization, the analysis is suspect. However, in defense of the trochaic account proposed here, I note that vowel length is noncontrastive in Carib, assigned by a late rule that applies after stress foot construction. Moreover, note that vowel lengthening affects only the first two stress feet. On the assumption that words are exhaustively parsed by the footing algorithm, then vowel lengthening does not target all stressed syllables. Finally, although vowel lengthening occurs only in open syllables, suggesting that coda consonants contribute to weight, closed syllables do not interfere with the assignment of binary feet (*moxká:ro* 'they' vs. *túxkusi* 'arrow'; *maʔmá:taká:ra* 'species of fish' vs. *óxkotó:potï* 'the cutting of you into pieces'). The conclusion is that we are not dealing with prototypical quantity-sensitive feet.

[18] In Inkelas (1989) I instead assumed that odd-numbered stems possess an underlyingly long vowel and that the extrametricality rule only targeted an initial mora—thus failing to render the entire first syllable of such forms invisible. But this analysis is problematic in that vowel length is not otherwise phonemic in the language, and admitting it lexically

would violate structure preservation (Kiparsky, 1982). By contrast, stress feet are clearly needed in the lexical phonology. Admitting them in underlying representation is only a small extension of existing apparatus. For the use of underlying feet in the literature to capture exceptional stress patterns, see, e.g., Hayes (1981), Hammond (1989), and many others.

[19]The syllable canon in Carib is CV(C), such that removing the first CV from a word will eliminate the stress-bearing capacity of the initial syllable.

[20]What still remains to be explained is why "weak" suffixes, such as those illustrated in the examples involving disyllabic stems, do not display the sensitivity of "strong" suffixes to the initial consonant–vowel status of the stem. One possibility, explored in Inkelas (1989), is to assign to all "weak" suffixes the property of imposing invisibility on initial consonants. Though it may seem complex at first glance, this account has the advantage of making the more common, unmarked suffixes duplicate the effects of PCF, which is the case in, for example, English.

[21]At worst, it would incorrectly prohibit the representation of clitics, which subcategorize for word-level or higher constituents in the p-hierarchy (Inkelas, 1989; Zec and Inkelas, 1991).

REFERENCES

Anderson, S. R. (1986). Disjunctive ordering in inflectional morphology. *Natural Language and Linguistic Theory* **4,** 1–32.

Anderson, S. R. (1988). Inflection. In *Theoretical Morphology: Approaches in Modern Linguistics* (M. Hammond and M. Noonan, eds.), pp. 23–43. Academic, New York.

Bickmore, L. (1990). Branching nodes and prosodic categories. In *The Phonology–Syntax Connection* (S. Inkelas and D. Zec, eds.), pp. 1–17. CSLI Publications and University of Chicago Press, Chicago.

Booij, G. (1985). Coordination reduction in complex words: A case for prosodic phonology. In *Advances in Non-Linear Phonology* (H. van der Hulst and N. Smith, eds.), pp. 143–160. Dordrecht: Foris.

Booij, G., and Rubach, J. (1984). Morphological and prosodic domains in lexical phonology. *Phonology Yearbook* **1,** 1–27.

Booij, G., and Rubach, J. (1987). Postcyclic versus postlexical rules in lexical phonology. *Linguistic Inquiry* **18,** 1–44.

Borowsky, T. (1986). *Topics in the Lexical Phonology of English.* Doctoral dissertation, University of Massachusetts, Amherst.

Brame, M. (1974). The cycle in phonology: Stress in Palestinian, Maltese, and Spanish. *Linguistic Inquiry* **5,** 39–40.

Buckley, E. (1991). *Second-position Clitics in Alsea.* Unpublished manuscript, University of California, Berkeley.

Buckley, E. (1992). *Theoretical Aspects of Kashaya Phonology and Morphology.* Doctoral dissertation, University of California, Berkeley.

Cho, Y. Y. (1990). Syntax and phrasing in Korean. In *The Phonology–Syntax Connection*

(S. Inkelas and D. Zec, eds.), pp. 47–61. CSLI Publications and University of Chicago Press, Chicago.

Cohn, A. (1989). Stress in Indonesian and bracketing paradoxes. *Natural Language and Linguistic Theory* **7,** 167–216.

Condoravdi, C. (1990). Sandhi rules of Greek and prosodic theory. In *The Phonology–Syntax Connection* (S. Inkelas and D. Zec, eds.), pp. 63–83. CSLI Publications and University of Chicago Press, Chicago.

Halle, M., and Kenstowicz, M. (1991). The free element condition and cyclic versus noncyclic stress. *Linguistic Inquiry* **22,** 457–501.

Halle, M., and Mohanan, K. P. (1985). Segmental phonology of Modern English. *Linguistic Inquiry* **16,** 57–116.

Hammond, M. (1989). Lexical stresses in Macedonian and Polish. *Phonology* **6,** 19–38.

Hargus, S. (1988). *The Lexical Phonology of Sekani.* Garland, New York.

Harris, J. (1983). *Syllable Structure and Stress in Spanish.* MIT Press, Cambridge, Mass.

Harris, J. (1989). The stress erasure convention and cliticization in Spanish. *Linguistic Inquiry* **20,** 339–363.

Hayes, B. (1981). *A Metrical Theory of Stress Rules.* Doctoral dissertation, Massachusetts Institute of Technology, Cambridge.

Hayes, B. (1987). A revised parametric metrical theory. *Proceedings of the North Eastern Linguistics Society* **17,** 274–289.

Hayes, B. (1989). The prosodic hierarchy and meter. In *Rhythm and Meter* (P. Kiparsky and G. Youmans, eds.), pp. 201–260. Academic Press, Orlando.

Hayes, B. (1991). *Metrical Stress Theory: Principles and Case Studies.* Unpublished manuscript, University of California, Los Angeles.

Hoff, B. (1968). *The Carib Language.* Nijhoff, The Hague.

Hyman, L. (1991). *Imbrication in Cibemba.* Unpublished manuscript, University of California, Berkeley.

Inkelas, S. (1988). Prosodic effects on syntax: Hausa 'fa'. *Proceedings of the West Coast Conference on Formal Linguistics* **7,** 375–389.

Inkelas, S. (1989). *Prosodic Constituency in the Lexicon.* Doctoral dissertation, Stanford University, Stanford, Calif.

Inkelas, S., and Zec, D. (1988). Serbo-Croatian pitch accent: The interaction of tone, stress and intonation. *Language* **64,** 227–248.

Itô, J. (1986). *Syllable Theory in Prosodic Phonology.* Doctoral dissertation, University of Massachusetts, Amherst.

Itô, J. (1990). Prosodic minimality in Japanese. In *CLS 26-II: Papers from the parasession on the syllable in phonetics and phonology* (K. Deaton, M. Noske, and M. Ziolkowski, eds.), pp. 213–239.

Itô, J., and Hankamer, J. (1989). Notes on monosyllabism in Turkish. In *Phonology at Santa Cruz 1* (J. Itô and J. Runner, eds.), pp. 61–70. Syntax Research Center, University of California, Santa Cruz.

Kaisse, E. (1985). *Connected Speech.* Academic Press, New York.

Kanerva, J. (1990). Focusing on phonological phrases in Chicheŵa. In *The Syntax–Phonology Connection* (S. Inkelas and D. Zec, eds.), pp. 145–161. CSLI Publications and University of Chicago Press, Chicago.

Kiparsky, P. (1982). Lexical morphology and phonology. In *Linguistics in the Morning Calm* (I.-S. Yang, ed.), pp. 3–91. Hanshin Publishing Co., Seoul.

Kiparsky, P. (1983). Word formation in the lexicon. In *Proceedings of the 1982 Mid-America Linguistics Conference* (F. Ingemann, ed.), pp. 3–29. University of Kansas, Lawrence.

Kiparsky, P. (1985). Some consequences of lexical phonology. *Phonology Yearbook* **2,** 85–138.

Klavans, J. (1985). The independence of syntax and phonology in cliticization. *Language* **61,** 85–120.

Lichtenberk, F. (1983). *A Grammar of Manam.* University of Hawaii Press, Honolulu.

Lieber, R. (1980). *On the Organization of the Lexicon.* Doctoral dissertation, Massachusetts Institute of Technology, Cambridge.

Mascaró, J. (1976). *Catalan Phonology and the Phonological Cycle.* Doctoral dissertation, Massachusetts Institute of Technology. Distributed by the Indiana University Linguistics Club.

McCarthy, J., and Prince, A. (1986). *Prosodic Morphology.* Unpublished manuscript, University of Massachusetts, Amherst, and Brandeis University, Waltham, Mass.

McCarthy, J., and Prince, A. (1990). Foot and word in prosodic morphology: The Arabic broken plural. *Natural Language and Linguistic Theory* **8,** 209–284.

Mohanan, K. P. (1982). *Lexical Phonology.* Doctoral dissertation, Massachusetts Institute of Technology, Cambridge.

Mohanan, K. P. (1986). *The Theory of Lexical Phonology.* Reidel, Dordrecht.

Nespor, M. (1984). "The phonological word in Italian." In *Advances in Non-linear Phonology* (H. van der Hulst and N. Smith, eds.), pp. 193–204. Foris, Dordrecht.

Nespor, M., and Vogel, I. (1982). Prosodic domains of external sandhi rules. In *The Structure of Phonological Representations,* part 1 (H. van der Hulst and N. Smith, eds.), pp. 225–255. Foris, Dordrecht.

Nespor, M., and Vogel, I. (1986). *Prosodic Phonology.* Foris, Dordrecht.

Paradis, C. (1988). On constraints and repair strategies. *The Linguistic Review* **6,** 71–97.

Pesetsky, D. (1979). *Russian Morphology and Lexical Theory.* Unpublished manuscript, Massachusetts Institute of Technology, Cambridge.

Poser, W. (1984). *The Phonetics and Phonology of Tone and Intonation in Japanese.* Doctoral dissertation, Massachusetts Institute of Technology, Cambridge.

Poser, W. (1989). The metrical foot in Diyari. *Phonology* **6,** 117–148.

Pulleyblank, D. (1986). *Tone in Lexical Phonology.* Reidel, Dordrecht.

Roberts, J. (1987). *Amele.* Croom Helm, London.

Selkirk, E. (1978). On prosodic structure and its relation to syntactic structure. In *Nordic Prosody II* (T. Fretheim, ed.), pp. 11–40. TAPIR, Trondheim.

Selkirk, E. (1980). Prosodic domains in phonology: Sanskrit revisited. In *Juncture* (M. Aronoff, ed.), pp. 107–129. Anma Libri, Saratoga, Calif.

Selkirk, E. (1982). *The Syntax of Words.* MIT Press, Cambridge, Mass.

Selkirk, E. (1986). On derived domains in sentence phonology. *Phonology Yearbook* **3,** 371–405.

Selkirk, E., and Shen, T. (1990). Prosodic Domains in Shanghai Chinese. In *The Phonology–Syntax Connection* (S. Inkelas and D. Zec, eds.), pp. 313–337. CSLI Publications and University of Chicago Press, Chicago.

Sproat, R. (1985). *On Deriving The Lexicon.* Doctoral dissertation, MIT, Cambridge, Mass.

Sproat, R. (1986). Malayalam Compounding: a Non–Stratum Ordered Account. *Proceedings of the West Coast Conference on Formal Linguistics* **5,** 268–288.

Steriade, D. (1988). Greek accent: A case for preserving structure. *Linguistic Inquiry* **19,** 271–314.

Vogel, I. (1989). The clitic group in prosodic phonology. To appear in *Grammar in Progress: GLOW Studies for Henk van Riemsdijk.* (J. Mascaró and M. Nespor, eds.). Foris, Dordrecht.

Zec, D. (1988). *Sonority Constraints on Prosodic Structure.* Doctoral dissertation, Stanford University, Stanford, Calif.

Zec, D., and Inkelas, S. (1990). Prosodically constrained syntax. In *The Phonology–Syntax Connection* (S. Inkelas and D. Zec, eds.), CSLI Publications and University of Chicago Press, Chicago.

Zec, D., and Inkelas, S. (1991). The place of Clitics in the Prosodic Hierarchy. *Proceedings of the West Coast Conference on Formal Linguistics* **10,** 505–520.

INTERACTION BETWEEN MODULES IN LEXICAL PHONOLOGY

DAVID ODDEN

Department of Linguistics
Ohio State University
Columbus, Ohio 43210

1. INTRODUCTION

This article addresses questions in the theory of component interaction in lexical phonology (LP), questions which arise in giving a formal interpretation to the standard graphic metaphor in (1), adapted minimally from Kiparsky (1982).

(1)

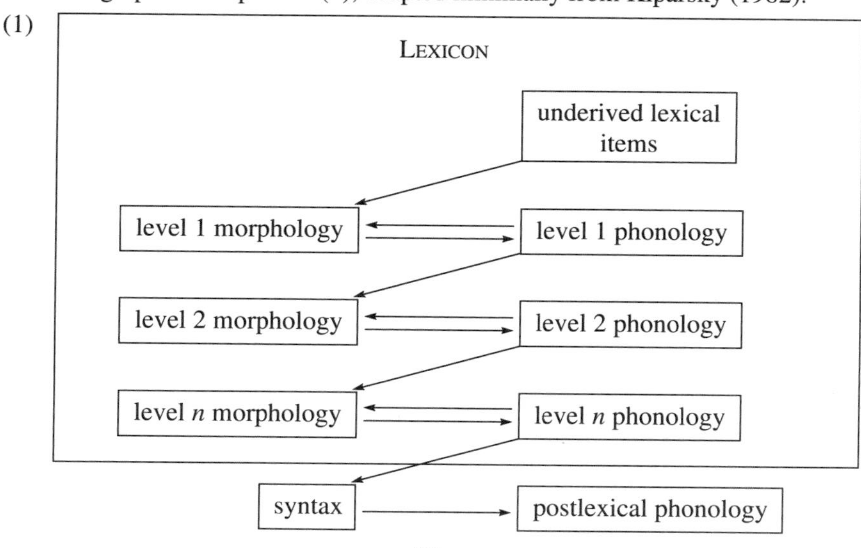

Phonetics and Phonology, Volume 4
Studies in Lexical Phonology

This display embodies a number of hypotheses, the most important being spelled out in (2).

(2) a. There is a construct "level" common to phonology and morphology.
 b. There are significant formal differences between lexical and postlexical phonology.
 c. Levels in phonology are the same as levels in morphology.
 d. Cyclic application of phonological rules derives from the interaction between lexical phonology and morphology as characterized above.
 e. Lexical phonology has no access to the output of the syntax.
 f. Lexical phonology and morphology interact so that morphology has access to phonological properties derived by applying phonological rules on some earlier level.

Claims (2a) and (2b) are the level-ordering claims, and are simply assumed here to be true. The related claim (2c) that phonological levels are the same as morphological levels has less support, in light of certain bracketing paradoxes. I also maintain without comment (or commitment) the standard assumption of lexical phonology that phonological levels are isomorphic with morphological levels, since the identity of morphological and phonological levels is entirely orthogonal to the question of interaction between phonology and morphology. Claim (2d), that cyclic behavior CAN be derived from a phonology–morphology interaction, is a purely theory-internal claim. As we will see, other models can derive cyclic behavior without this interaction.

1.1. Noninteractive Lexical Phonology

The purpose of this article is the presentation of a theory of phonology and morphology which captures the relevant generalizations regarding level ordering and cyclicity, without the LP theory of component interaction. Therefore, claims (2e) and (2f) are the focus; they are the main hypotheses about the organization of components into grammars and about the information available to each component. I consider the alternative organization of components in (3), a theory to be referred to as noninteractive lexical phonology (NLP).

(3)

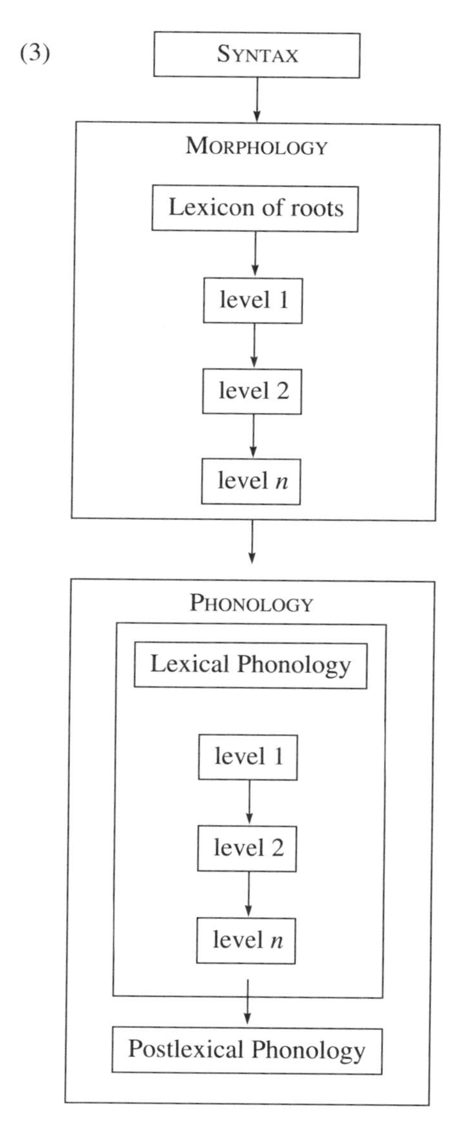

In effect, the proposal is to retain the more traditional ordering of components but also adopt the notion of level and the lexical–postlexical split. Halle and Vergnaud (1987) similarly adopt this ordering of morphology before phonology.

In calling into question certain assumptions of LP, it is important to distinguish the claims under investigation from interesting but tangential issues. The claim which is most important to this theory, the one which most obviously differentiates the models, is the relative ordering and noninteraction of components. To facilitate comparison with LP, the level-ordering claims (2a,b,c) are retained from LP, though the formal mechanisms which generate these types of behavior are not the same in the two theories: it may well turn out that the distinction between lexical and postlexical phonology is spurious, or that "level" is a purely phonological notion, but these questions are not investigated here.

NLP assumes, as does LP, that there is a primitive notion of level, L_1 to L_n. The putative identity of morphological and phonological levels would be in NLP a consequence of assumptions about how levels in phonology are defined. As in LP, each morphological rule is encoded for a specification of the level where it applies. Word construction starts by selecting a root, and morphological rules apply to this structure, concatenating appropriate material with it. In NLP each morphological rule provides a labeled bracketing as well as the segmental content of its affix, so rules take the form of those in (4).

(4) $[_X \text{Y}] \rightarrow [_Z [_X \text{Y}]\ \text{W}]$ $\qquad$ $[_X \text{Y}] \rightarrow [_Z \text{W}\ [_X \text{Y}]]$

The labels attached to these structures indicate the level on which the operation applies; it is this labeled bracketing which phonology reacts to, in applying rules to morphologically defined domains.

In (5) we see the morphological derivation of the Maltese Arabic form *ḥàtfit-kúmš* 'she didn't snatch you' which has two Level 1 morphemes, the root *ḥataf* and the subject marker *it,* and two Level 2 morphemes, the object suffix *kum* and the negative *š*.

(5)

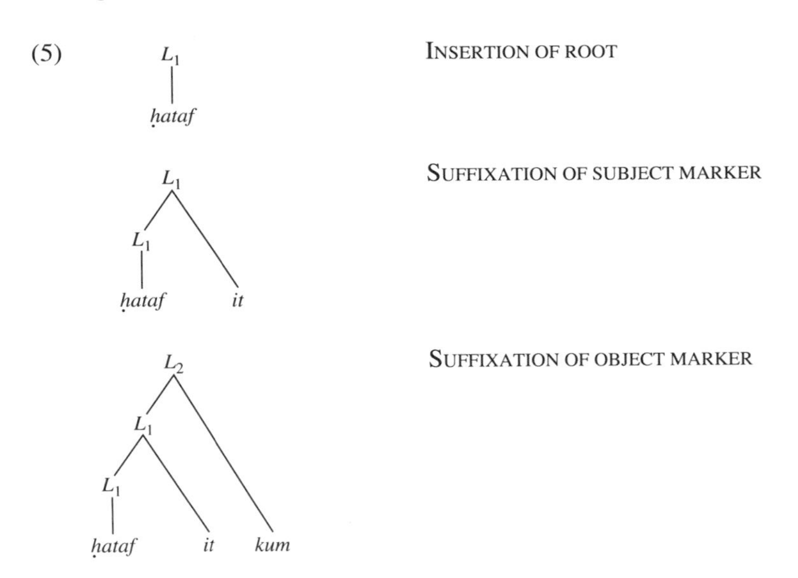

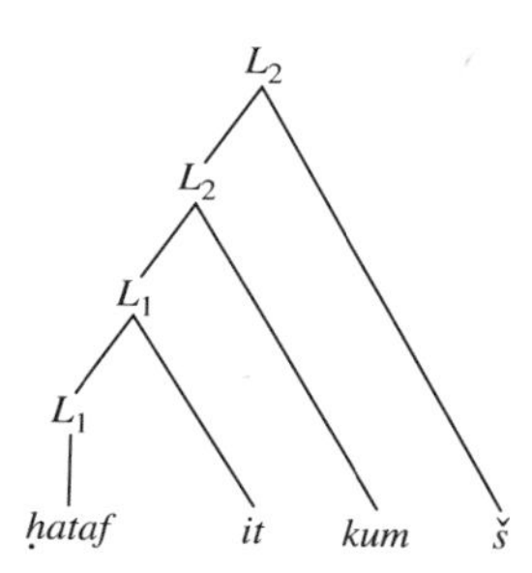

SUFFIXATION OF NEGATIVE

'she didn't snatch you'

The only difference between this and standard lexical phonology is the inclusion of labels on the brackets which indicate distinctions of level: Inkelas (1989), who assumes the orthodox theory of LP, adopts a model quite similar to this, employing the labels α, β, γ.

In the phonological component, rules are encoded for domain of application, specifically the lowest- and highest-numbered levels where the rule may apply. This is the same as specifying, for instance, that a rule is "in" Level 1 phonology. In NLP, cyclicity is achieved in a manner analogous to that of LP. As is well known, cyclicity in LP can be expressed in two ways. First, if a rule resides in two consecutive levels, cyclicity arises when the rule applies at level L_{n-1} and at level L_n (interstratal cyclicity). Second, if L_n is deemed cyclic, cyclicity result when some rule applies to each substring resulting from morphological operations within L_n (stratum-internal cyclicity).

Now consider how NLP expresses cyclicity. I consider first interstratal cyclicity, using the Maltese Arabic form *ḥàtfitkúmš* as an illustration. The highest constituent dominated by L_1 becomes the initial input to the phonology, and phonological rules encoded for application at L_1 apply to this string. Thus the boxed constituent in the first step of (6) is the domain where Level 1 phonological rules apply, beginning in this case with stress assignment. After the last rule defined at L_1 applies (Apocope), the highest constituent dominated by L_2 becomes the string subject to phonological rules, and rules encoded for L_2 apply to this string. This continues to the last lexical level and into postlexical phonology.

(6)

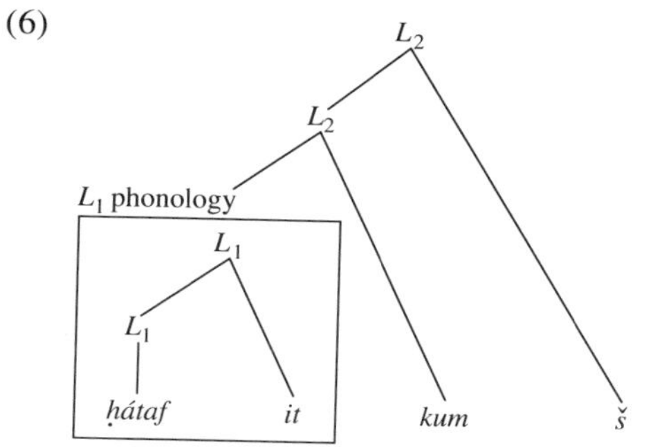

STRESS

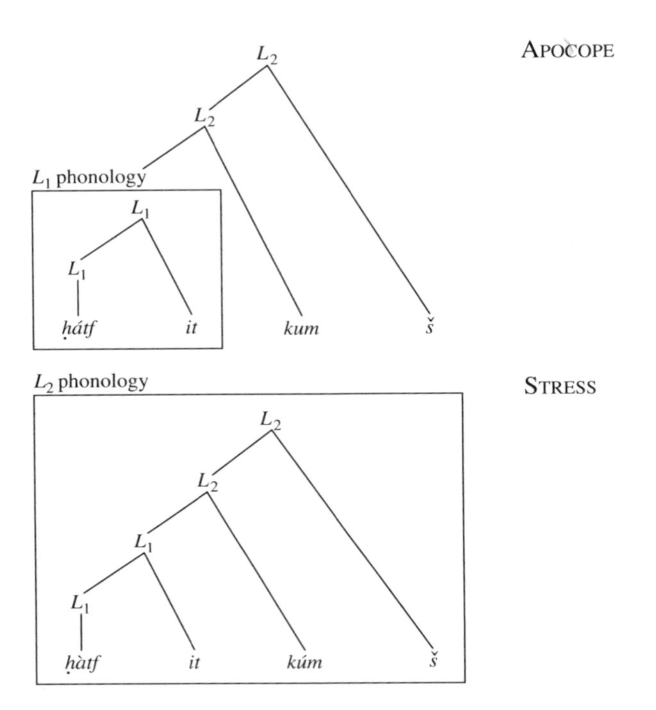

NLP handles stratum-internal cyclicity by applying phonological rules of level L_n to the lowest unprocessed constituent dominated by L_n. Suppose that L_2 in Maltese Arabic had been cyclic. Then in the derivation (6), the lowest constituent dominated by L_2 would have defined the first domain of rule application; then the next lowest constituent dominated by L_2 would define the next domain of rule application, and so on. In this way, we keep cyclicity and level ordering, without interaction between phonology and morphology: the issue of cyclicity in no way distinguishes NLP from LP.

1.2. The Interpretation of Boxes

The literature of LP has been virtually silent regarding the formal interpretation of displays like (1). Consider the fact that in (1), the boxes called "level 1 phonology" through "level *n* phonology," and the boxes called "level 1 morphology" through "level *n* morphology" are contained in a larger box called "lexicon." A conceivable interpretation of such structures is that things sharing a box have similar properties which things outside the box do not have. But it is quite unclear what the shared formal properties of morphology and lexical phonology are, except that in LP, these components define the lexicon. In fact, taking displays like (1) to be a claim about similarity in formal properties, we would conclude that lexical phonology and morphology are more similar than lexical and postlexical phonology. We might even conclude that lexical and postlexical phonology have no shared properties, since they share no box. This is clearly absurd, and other arrangements of the boxes have been proposed, for instance Kaisse and Shaw (1985), where boxes overlap, or Mohanan (1986), where phonology and morphology do not even share a box. If display (1) has a meaning, it cannot be a claim about similarity of components.

More plausibly, these structures could be taken as graphic metaphors for claims about the ordering of processes; thus, lexical phonology precedes syntax, and postlexical phonology follows syntax. Since we have no substantive evidence for the real-time interpretation of component ordering, a claim about ordering reduces to a claim about the information available to a given module. If module *M* "follows" module *L* and "precedes" module *N*, then *M* has access to the results of operations defined in *L*, but not to the results of operations defined in *N*. In this sense, when we say that lexical phonology precedes syntax, we mean that information provided by syntax is not available to lexical phonology. This has been taken to entail that no rule of lexical phonology has access to properties of other words in the sentence, or to any fact about the syntactic structure of the sentence which the word appears in. Supposing that we had criteria for deciding whether a rule is lexical, then this seems to make the prediction that certain types of languages will not be found.

The issues separating NLP and LP are the following two. First, NLP claims that rules of lexical phonology have access to information from syntax. Second, NLP disallows morphology access to information coming from phonological rules. These two issues are separable—one could have an interactive model of phonology and morphology, and reorder syntax relative to lexical phonology. Or one could retain the ordering of phonology and morphology relative to syntax but reject the interactive aspect of LP. I thus consider these claims separately.

Two conclusions regarding what languages do will emerge in the course of this paper. First, we will see that systems exist with exactly the properties which LP predicts should not exist, namely lexical rules accessing the output of syntax. Second, it will be argued that there are no compelling cases of rules of morphology applying after rules of phonology. Taken together, this should argue for noninteractive model (3) over model (1).

However, an extension to LP, specifically Hayes's theory of precompiled phonology, can be called on to handle any counterexamples where a phonological rule acts as though it sees outside its domain, such as a lexical rule seeing between words, or for that matter, a Level 1 rule seeing material only available on Level 2. This extended version of LP (ELP) has access to all the information available to the noninteractive model, plus it allows for rules of morphology which are sensitive to derived phonological information, a situation which is disallowed in the noninteractive model.

2. SYNTAX AND PHONOLOGY

The first problem I look into briefly is the ordering between lexical phonology and syntax. More extensive discussion of the data and issues involved here can be found in Odden (1990a) and Odden (1987), as well as Hayes (1990). A general description of Kimatuumbi phonology and morphology can be found in Odden (1992).

2.1. Ordering Sandhi Rules in the Lexicon

The problem I consider here is that some rules of Kimatuumbi phonology must be lexical, but they also have access to syntactic structure and phonological properties of surrounding words. The first rule is the phrase-level rule Shortening, which shortens a long vowel if it is the head of a phrase and is followed by material within its phrase. This vowel length alternation is seen in (7).

(7)	*kįkóloombe*	'cleaning shell'
	kįlólombe chaángu	'my cleaning shell'
	kįtúumbili	'monkey'
	kįtúmbili ywáawįįlé	'monkey who died'
	naakį-twéetį	'I took it'
	naakį-twétį kįkóloombe	'I took a cleaning shell'

Since this rule involves multiple words and syntactic structures, LP requires the rule to be a postlexical rule.

(8) SHORTENING

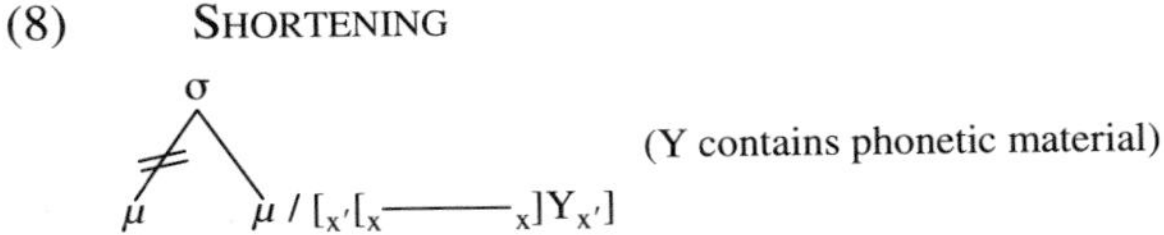

The second rule is Glide Formation (GF), a strictly word-internal lexical rule. That rule desyllabifies a prevocalic high vowel and compensatorily lengthens the following vowel. Examples of the vowel–glide alternation and compensatory lengthening are seen in (9).

(9)	/kį-kálaango/ Cl. 7-frying pan	*kį-kálaango*	'frying pan'
	/kį-ų́lá/ Cl. 7-frog	*ky-ųų́lá*	'frog' (cf. *kaų́lá* 'little frog')
	/į-kálaango/ Cl. 8-frying pan	*į-kálaango*	'frying pans'
	/į-ų́lá/ Cl. 8-frog	*y-ųų́lá*	'frogs'

We must restrict GF so that a prevocalic long vowel does not desyllabify, to account for the forms in (10): in the first example, the underlying short vowel of the locative prefix *mų* is lengthened before dimoraic stems by an independently motivated rule. Vowel length which blocks GF may derive from the compensatory lengthening effect of GF itself, as the form *mwį̨įųté* shows, indicating that the rule iterates from left to right.

(10)	*mųų-até* Loc.-hand of bananas		'in the hands of bananas'
	/mų-aanjų́/ Loc.-firewood	*mwaanjų́*	'in the firewood'
	/mų-į-ųté/ 2pl.-them (Cl. 9)-pull	*mwįį-ųté*	'you should pull them (Cl. 9)'
	/ba-į-ųté/ 3pl.-them (Cl. 9)-pull	*bayųųté*	'they pulled them'

Three levels can be motivated in Kimatuumbi. Level 1 morphology constructs the stem from the root, derivational affixes such as the causative and benefactive, and the stem-final tense inflection. Level 2 verbal morphology includes addition of object prefixes, tense-aspect prefixes, and subject prefixes. Level 2 nominal morphology is addition of the noun class prefixes. At Level 3, the locative nominal prefixes *kų-, pa-,* and *mų-* are added, and in verbs the relative clause head agreement prefixes such as *pa-* and *cha-* are added.

The Glide Formation rule applies cyclically, in particular interstratal-cyclically but not stratum-internal–cyclically. This is seen in the contrasting derivations of *mwįįųté* in (11a), which has the Level 2 prefixes *mų* and *į,* versus *mųyųų́lá* in (11b), which has the level 3 prefix *mų* and the level 2 prefix *į*. The problem is that we have the same basic configuration of phonemes in both cases, but determining which of the vowels becomes a glide requires knowing the level at which each morpheme is made available to the phonology.

(11)	a.	[*mų-į-ųté*]	
		mų-į-ųté	Input to L_2
		mwįįųté	Glide Formation
		'you should pull it'	
	b.	[*mų* [*į-ų́lá*]]	
		į-ų́lá	Input to L_2
		yųų́la	Glide Formation
		mųyųų́lá	Input to L_3
		NA	Glide Formation
		'in the frogs'	

In the case of *mwįįųté,* the vowel sequence *ų+į* appears entirely within Level 2, so it is the first of the prevocalic high vowels which glides, giving the phonetic form. In the case of *mųyųų́lá,* the locative prefix *mų* is only available at Level 3, but *į* is available at Level 2, so *į* undergoes GF since it is the only vowel encountered at this stage of the derivation. Therefore GF must be lexical.

Now consider the ordering of Shortening and GF. Shortening precedes GF, as shown by the fact that Shortening does not apply to the long vowel which arises as a result of applying GF, at least at Level 2. This is shown by the forms in (12).

(12) /mų-aké lį́/ *mwaaké lį́* 'you should not hunt'
2sSub-hunt not
(**mwaké lį́*)
/kį-ų́la chaángu/ *kyųų́la chaángu* 'my frog'
Cl. 7-frog my
(**kyų́la chaángu*)

The underlying prefix plus stem vowel combination undergoes GF, which lengthens the stem vowel, but the derived long vowel is not shortened in the presence of a modifier. This requires ordering the lexical rule GF after the supposedly post-lexical rule Shortening.

Further data show that Shortening is a Level 1 rule and actually follows GF on that level. GF also applies at Level 1, the stem level, as we see in (13), where the short vowel of the reciprocal suffix *-an-* lengthens as a result of desyllabifying the suffix *-į-*.

(13) *ák-a* 'to net-hunt'
hunt-tense
ák-an-a 'to net-hunt each other
hunt-recip.-tense
/ak-į-an-a/ *ák-y-aan-a* 'to net-hunt for each other'
hunt-benefact.-recip.-tense

Interestingly, long vowels which arise by applying GF at Level 1 do undergo Shortening, in contrast to long vowels which derive by applying GF at Levels 2 and 3. As can be seen in (14), GF is applicable on two levels in underlying *tų-ak-į-an-a įtúumbili,* namely on Level 1 to *į+a,* and on Level 2 to *ų+a.* As shown by the surface form *twaakyana įtúumbili,* the long vowel derived by GF at Level 1 shortens, but the long vowel derived at Level 2 does not.

(14) [*tų*-[*ak-į-an-a*]] *įtúumbili* →
we-hunt-benefact.-recip.-tense monkeys
twaakyana įtúumbili
'we net-hunt monkeys for each other'

Thus, Shortening is ordered after GF, and only applies at Level 1.

(15) *ak-į-an-a įtúumbili* Input to Level 1
akyaana įtúumbili Glide Formation

akyana įtúumbili Shortening
tų-akyana įtúumbili Input to Level 2
twaakyana įtúumbili Glide Formation

For this derivation to be possible, Shortening must be lexical, which means that it is necessary to allow rules of the lexical component access to the output of syntax. This is impossible in LP but is allowed in NLP.

Other rules exhibit similar properties. One of these, Initial Tone Insertion (ITI), is also relevant in Section 3. This rule, illustrated in (16), assigns an H tone to the initial vowel of a lexical class of morphemes, as long as the morpheme is preceded by a word bearing no stem H.

(16) *kįndoló* ***cha*** *Mambóondo* 'sweet potato of Mamboondo'
kįwikilyo ***chá*** *Mambóondo* 'cover of Mamboondo'
mabígiį ***ga****-bíli* 'two beer brewing areas'
matanga ***gá****-bili* 'two cucumbers'
aatį́belekwá ***kų****-Kįpoóį* 'he was BORN in Kipooi'
abelekįlwe ***kų́****-Kįpoóį* 'he was born in Kipooi'

The full list of morphemes which undergo ITI is given in (17).

(17) *a-* demonstrative prefix
na 'with, and'
ṇ(cheche) initial syllabic nasal of 'four'
ṇ(tupú) initial syllabic nasal of 'is not'
ka- subord. verb prefix
malaáu 'tomorrow'
kįtįwį 'how'
namanį 'what'
ñaį 'who'
ganį 'which'
bųlį 'how'
kili 'what'
gaaku 'what kind'
gu- et al. demonstrative prefix
wa- et al. associative prefix
gų- et al. numeral prefix
mų-, pa-, kų- locative prefixes

An important condition on the triggering element seen in (18) is that, while a stem H in the preceding noun blocks the rule, a prefixal H does not.

(18) *kį-wikilyo* ***gánį*** 'what type cover?'
kį-túmbili ***ganį*** 'what type monkey?'
kį́-n'ombe ***gánį*** 'what type cows?'

Thus the stem H in *kį-túumbili* blocks assignment of H to *ganį,* but the prefix H in *kį́-ng'ombe* does not.

The fact that the rule only applies to a lexically specified set of morphemes and is sensitive to the stem–prefix distinction argues that the rule should be lexical. An ordering argument cinches this conclusion. There is a further restriction on Glide Formation in Kimatuumbi, which is that an H-tone vowel cannot undergo GF before a long vowel, although an L-tone vowel can. Word-internal examples of this condition are seen in (19), where the prevocalic vowels *į́* and *ų́* cannot glide before a long vowel because of this constraint.

(19)	*chatų́oóndįté*	'what we peeled'
	panį́aándįįké	'when I wrote'

Now consider the data in (20), with the prefix *kų-* before a long vowel.

(20)	*ųtįlį́ kųaanjų́*	→	*ųtįlį́ kwaanjų́*	'you should run to the firewood'
	ųtįlį kųaanjų́	→	*ųtįlį kų́aanjų́*	'you ran to the firewood'

An H can be assigned to *kų-* by ITI, and this derived tone affects whether GF can apply before a long vowel—if the prefix has a derived H, as in the second example, then it cannot undergo GF. This shows that ITI applies before GF. Since GF is lexical, ITI must also be lexical. This creates another paradox for the standard model of LP. The sandhi rule ITI has to apply before a lexical rule, so it MUST be lexical, but the rule refers to phonological and morphological properties of the preceding word, so the rule CANNOT be lexical.

2.2. Precompilation

NLP has no problems with this state of affairs, since in that theory the output of the syntax is fully available to lexical phonology, and therefore these sandhi rules can be lexical. The question remains whether one can handle these data, retaining the supposed ordering between syntax and lexical phonology, by modifying LP in some way. Hayes (1990), discussing similar problems, including the Shortening–Glide Formation paradox of Kimatuumbi, proposes a different modification of phonology, namely precompilation theory. In precompilation theory a word may have multiple lexical derivations; hence multiple outputs emerge from the lexicon for each word. Each of these derivations is tagged for a property referred to as a lexical instantiation frame. Languages may define sets of instantiation frames which serve as context for lexical phonological rules. Upon entering the postlexical phonology, the frame definitions of the language are consulted, and the syntactic, morphological, and phonological properties of the word in its sentence are checked; out of the various derivations generated in the lexicon, the correct form is then inserted into the sentence, and the string is submitted to the postlexical phonology. Thus, the precompiled version of Kimatuumbi Shortening is formulated as in (21).

(21) $\mathrm{VV} \rightarrow \mathrm{V} / [\,\ldots \_\_\_ \ldots\,]_{[\mathrm{Frame}\ 1]}$

The definition of Frame 1 is given as (22).

(22) FRAME 1: $[_{X'} \ldots [_{X} \_\_\_]\ Y] \qquad Y \neq \emptyset$

The two derivations in (23) are then generated. The derivation where Frame 1 rules apply generates the Frame 1 allomorph, and the other, where these rules do not apply, generates the elsewhere form.

(23) [*kyaandangyo chaángu*] 'my forest farm'

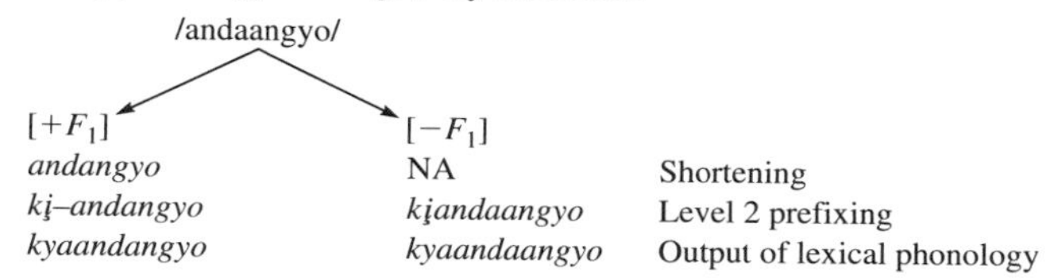

Later, the appropriate allomorph is selected. If the word in question appears in the syntactic context defined in (22), the Frame 1 allomorph is inserted; otherwise the elsewhere allomorph is inserted.

Frame definitions may include phonological information from neighboring words. Kimatuumbi Initial Tone Insertion could be stated to apply in the context of Frame 2.

(24) INITIAL TONE INSERTION:

$$\mathrm{V} \rightarrow \underset{\mathrm{H}}{\overset{|}{\mathrm{V}}} / [\underset{[+\mathrm{D}]}{\_\_\_}\ _{[\mathrm{Frame}\ 2]}$$

Frame 2 is defined as in (25).[1]

(25) FRAME 2: $[_{\mathrm{stem}} \sim \mathrm{H}]\ X \_\_\_ \qquad$ (X does not contain $_{S}$)

Precompilation thus allows lexical rules to indirectly see into surrounding words without directly looking at them. That is, the rule system freely generates all sorts of possibilities, then filters out the incorrect ones at a later stage. An observation can thus be made about the predictions of LP. Although standard LP does not include precompilation, this machinery is basically consistent with the architecture of the theory. Since LP alone cannot handle Kimatuumbi, it must adopt the subtheory of precompilation to achieve observational adequacy. However, since both Extended LP and NLP can generate the correct forms, and since the device of precompilation allows precompiling any information about the syntax, morphology, and phonology of surrounding words, then ELP makes no prediction about information relations between syntax and phonology; rather, it describes these relations by different means from NLP, but the forms generable in both theories are the same.

If the theories are weakly equivalent, then we must turn to secondary considerations such as elegance and computational complexity to evaluate the theories. There is a computational advantage to allowing lexical rules to directly see the output of syntax. In precompilation theory, there can be multiple frames, and frames can overlap, so each frame definition doubles the number of derivations necessary for a form. For instance, if there are two frames defined in a language, then four derivations are required for a word, one for Frame 1, one for Frame 2, one for Frames 1 and 2, and one for the elsewhere form. In general, when there are *n* frames, we need 2^n derivations. In the case of Kimatuumbi (as discussed in Odden, 1992), there are eight external sandhi rules which are part of the lexical phonology, so 256 parallel derivations are needed for each word. On the other hand, in the theory ordering lexical phonology after syntax, only one derivation is required, since the rules simply inspect the word-external context to determine whether their conditions for application are satisfied. Precompilation theory thus entails more complex computations.

3. MORPHOLOGY AND PHONOLOGY

I now turn to the second question of information access, namely the fundamental question in morphology–phonology interaction, which is whether morphology can be sensitive to the output of phonology. Since my thesis is that morphology exclusively PRECEDES phonology, I start with an investigation of a new case where morphology seems to FOLLOW phonology.

3.1. 1-Singular Allomorphy in Arabic

The problem discussed here involves the phonology of glides in Classical Arabic, and an allomorph of the 1-singular possessive suffix. An excellent analysis of Arabic glides is available in Brame (1970). A basic fact about glides in Classical Arabic is that they are phonologically "weak" and often elide. The important generalization for our purposes is that intervocalic glides delete, and the resulting vowel cluster fuses into a single long vowel. Since Classical Arabic does not allow long vowels in closed syllables, this long vowel may then shorten. These rules are seen in the paradigm of the perfective verb in (26). The left column shows the paradigm of a verb which suffers no alternations. The other two columns illustrate stems with final *y* and *w* which delete intervocalically.

(26)

SOUND VERB	FINAL *y*	FINAL *w*	
qatal-tu	*ramay-tu*	*daʕaw-tu*	1 sg.
qatal-nā	*ramay-nā*	*daʕaw-nā*	1 pl.
qatal-a	*ram-ā*	*daʕ-ā*	3 sg. masc.
qatal-at	*ram-at*	*daʕ-at*	3 sg. fem.
'kill'	'throw'	'call'	

Three rules are responsible for these alternation, namely, Glide Elision, which deletes intervocalic glides; Vowel Fusion, which fuses vowel clusters into one long vowel; and Closed Syllable Shortening.

(27) GLIDE ELISION:

$$\begin{matrix} C \\ \begin{bmatrix} -\text{con} \\ +\text{son} \end{bmatrix} \end{matrix} \rightarrow \emptyset \,/\, V \_\_\_ V$$

VOWEL FUSION:

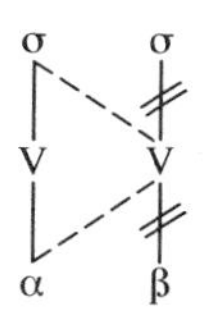

CLOSED SYLLABLE SHORTENING:

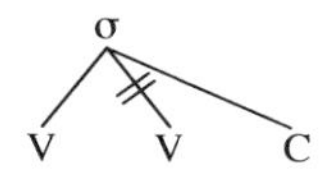

Derivations of illustrative forms are given in (28).

(28)

ramay-a	*ramay-at*	underlying
rama-a	*rama-at*	Glide Elision
ramā	*ramāt*	Vowel Fusion
NA	*ramat*	Shortening

The rules Glide Elision and Vowel Fusion are the two crucial rules involved in this case of phonology supposedly preceding morphology.

The allomorphy we are concerned with is that of the 1-singular pronominal suffix on nouns. As we see in (29), nouns are composed of a stem plus an obligatory case ending, *u* (nom.), *i* (gen.), or *a* (acc.).

(29) *ʔal-kitāb-u* 'the book (nom.)'
def-book-nom.
ʔal-kitāb-i 'the book (gen.)'
def-book-gen.

ʔal-kitāb-a	'the book (acc.)'
def-book-acc.	

A pronominal suffix such as *hā, ka,* or *nā* may be added, and it stands after the case ending, as (30) shows.

(30)	*kitāb-u-hā*	'her book (nom.)'
	kitāb-u-ka	'your (masc. sg.) book (nom.)'
	kitāb-i-ka	'your (masc. sg.) book (gen.)'
	kitāb-a-nā	'our book (acc.)'

In (31) we find examples of nouns with the 1-singular suffix *-ī-*. This suffix is vowel-initial and combines with the case marker in such a way that the case marker is completely lost.

(31)	/kitāb-u-ī/	*kitāb-ī*	'my book (nom.)'
	/kitāb-i-ī/	*kitāb-ī*	'my book (gen.)'
	/kitāb-a-ī/	*kitāb-ī*	'my book (acc.)'

Vowel Fusion (27) cannot apply when the second vowel in a sequence of vowels is long, but Arabic does not tolerate vowel–vowel sequences, so the first vowel of the underlying vowel sequence is therefore deleted; this can be handled by making Vowel Fusion a mirror image rule.

The 1-singular suffix is subject to phonologically conditioned allomorphy, illustrated in (32); if it stands immediately after a long vowel or diphthong, it takes the form *ya*. By a regular morphological principle, the indefinite suffix *na* or its variant *ni* is not used when followed by a pronoun suffix.

(32)	Noun		Noun + 1sg. poss.
	γulām-ā-ni	'slaves (nom. dual)'	*γulām-ā-ya*
	slave-nom. dual-indef		slave-nom. dual-my
	γulām-ay-ni	'slaves (oblique dual)'	*γulām-ay-ya*
	slave-obl. dual-indef		slave-obl. dual-my
	muʕallim-ū-na	'teachers (nom. pl.)'	*muʕallim-ū-ya*
	teacher-nom. pl.-indef		teacher-nom. pl.-my
	muʕallim-ī-na	'teachers (oblique pl.)'	*muʕallim-ī-ya*
	teacher-obl. pl.-indef		teacher-obl. pl.-my

In these examples, the long vowel or diphthong which conditions the *ya* variant is present in underlying representation. Other examples, seen in (33), show that long vowels which derive by phonological rule, in particular by Glide Elision and Vowel Fusion, also trigger the *ya* allomorph.

(33)	*ʔal-qahw-at-u*		'the coffee (nom.)'
	/ma-qhaw-un/	*ma-qha-n*	'a coffee house (nom.)'
	/ʔal-ma-qhaw-u/	*ʔal-ma-qhā*	'the coffee house (nom.)'
	/ma-qhaw-u-1sg./	*ma-qhā-ya*	'my coffee house'

ʔal-hawāy-at-u		'the hobby (nom.)'
/ʔal-haway-u/	*ʔal-hawā*	'the desire (nom.)'
/haway-u-1sg./	*hawā-ya*	'my love'
qaḍay-tu		'I settled'
/qāḍiy-un/	*qāḍin*	'a judge (nom.)'
/ʔal-qāḍiy-un/	*ʔal-qāḍī*	'the judge (nom.)'
qāḍiy-u-1sg./	*qāḍī-ya*	'my judge'

Thus the stem for 'coffee' ends in the glide *w,* which surfaces postconsonantally in *ʔalqáhwatu.* Intervocalically, in *ʔalmáqhā,* the glide deletes before the case ending and the vowel cluster fuses into a long vowel. This derived long vowel then conditions the *ya* allomorph. As (34) indicates, this suggests that the 1-singular allomorph is determined after Glide Elision and Syllable Fusion.

(34)	/maqhaw-u/	underlying
	maqhau	Glide Elision
	maqhā	Vowel Fusion
	maqhāya	affixation of 1-singular

This is what LP predicts could happen, but it would seem to be a problem for NLP, which requires all morphemes to be concatenated before any phonological rules apply. However, it is shown below that this case CAN be handled in the noninteractive theory.

3.2. Morphological and Phonological Operations

This section presents a reanalysis of this and similar cases where morphology has been claimed to follows phonology. A search of the literature reveals a number of putative cases of phonological rules applying before morphology; Hargus (this volume) provides an extensive list of such cases. The largest class is typified by the examples in (35).

(35) Overapplication of phonological rules under reduplication (Kihehe, Tagalog, Javanese). In Kihehe, the stem, excluding prefixes, reduplicates (*kúte-lekateléka*). Phonological rules of syllable fusion draw prefix material into the stem, causing them to be reduplicated (*kwíitakwiíta*). (Odden and Odden, 1986)

The imperative in Danish is formed by deleting the infinitive -ə suffix. Deletion follows a vowel lengthening rule, so /bæðə/ becomes *bæ:ðə* (which is the infinitive), then the infinitive ending is deleted in the imperative, giving [bæ:ð]. Similar rules deleting the agreement morpheme *y* in Abkhaz, and the verb suffix *a* in Icelandic, have been found. (Anderson, 1975)

One large class includes overapplication of phonological rules under reduplication, as in Kihehe. Another large class is typified by imperative formation in Danish, which deletes the -ə suffix of the infinitive. Imperative Deletion has to be ordered after a phonological rule of open-syllable vowel lengthening.

There seems to be little doubt that the phonological rules which supposedly precede morphology in these cases are indeed phonological rules. What is not at all clear is that the supposedly morphological operations are part of morphology. Consider the class of post-phonological subtractions, such as the Danish imperative: other cases like this are considered in Section 3.2.2. In light of the rule ordering fact that truncation follows a phonological rule, the only possible analysis in NLP is to treat the deletion as part of phonology, as (36).

(36) DANISH IMPERATIVE TRUNCATION
$ə \rightarrow \emptyset \,/\, \underline{\quad}\, _{\omega}]$
[Imper]

I thus adopt the analysis proposed by Anderson (1975) that the imperative is based on a form identical to the infinitive.

There is nothing in the generally accepted and motivated theory of phonology, be it LP or nonlexical theories, which precludes having a rule like (36) in the phonology, since no principle of phonological theory prohibits rules from referring to morphological properties. Therefore the analysis (36) is possible in all theories. In LP, it could also be treated as a morpheme-deletion rule and be part of the morphological component, as in (37).

(37) $[\text{Infin}] \rightarrow \emptyset \,/\, \underline{\quad}\, _{\omega}]$
[Imper]

For that matter, if one allows deletion of phonological units in the morphology, not just deletion of morphemes, then one could assume a rule with the formal statement (36) but place that rule in the morphological component. In other words, with no further conditions on phonology or morphology, three analyses are possible and cannot be distinguished empirically or on the basis of rule elegance. If one adopts the position that rules such as Danish Imperative Truncation are phonological rules with morphological conditions and are not rules of the morphological component, then they clearly do not show that the output of phonology can serve as the input to morphology.

One of the basic stumbling blocks in resolving issues regarding the relation between phonology and morphology is this analytic ambiguity, and in particular the fact that many theories allow one to consign phonological processes either to the phonology or to the morphology rather freely. We must make clear what we mean by "rule of morphology"; the claim made here, and the claim which must be made in LP if there is content to the claim for the interleaving of phonology and morphology, is that a "rule of morphology" is a rule in the morphological component. Putting Danish Imperative Truncation in the phonology but calling it a "rule of morphology" simply because it applies in a morphologically defined context trivializes the difference between phonology and morphology. By analogous reasoning, we should call the Kimatuumbi rule Shortening a rule of syntax because it applies in a syntactically defined context.

The systematic uncertainty about what constitutes a possible morphological rule surely needs a principled resolution, so to attack the problem from the side of morphology, (38) is adopted to restrict morphology to concatenation.

(38) PRINCIPLE OF MORPHOLOGY–PHONOLOGY SEGREGATION: The only operation allowed in morphology is concatenation.

Of course, in thinking about this restriction to concatenation, one should keep in mind that nonlinear representations may make it LOOK like a morphological process is doing metathesis or infixing, or geminating consonants. As McCarthy (1979) shows, this is just an illusion.

The complete segregation of morphological and phonological operations makes strong claims about morphology. A consequence of this principle is that we rule out on theoretical grounds supposed cases of "Process Morphology" (Matthews, 1974, inter alia), where morphological rules perform phonological changes. Examples of process morphology must be reanalyzed as two processes, namely purely morphological concatenation, plus a phonological operation. For instance, the morphological part of German Umlaut is simply stating the conditions for adding an affix or set of affixes. It happens that the phonological content of this suffix is or contains a floating vowel feature [−back]. The phonology is then responsible for linking that feature to the appropriate vowel.

3.2.1. REDUPLICATION

Such a division of labor removes the Kihehe kind of reduplication from the pool of support for the interactive model. The problem of Kihehe is that the entity which reduplicates is the stem, which is the output of Level 1 morphology and thus generally excludes the object prefix or the infinitive prefix, which are at Level 2. However, in case some prefixal element has fused syllabically with the initial stem syllable, the prefix segments get copied as well.

(39)		
	ku-teleka	'to cook'
	ku-teleka-teleka	'to cook a bit'
	ku-lu-teleka	'to cook it'
	ku-lu-teleka-teleka	'to cook it a bit'
	kw-iita	'to spill'
	kw-iita-kw-iita (/ku-ita/)	'to spill a bit'
	ku-lw-iita	'to spill it'
	ku-lw-iit-lw-iita (/ku-lu-ita/)	'to spill it a bit'

It thus seems that Glide Formation must precede reduplication, in order to explain why copying includes material from a prefix.

As numerous researchers (e.g., Marantz, 1982), have observed, reduplication is not a single complex operation but is a set of interrelated phenomena implemented by a number of restricted rules. Under such views of reduplication, the purely morphological operation is the affixation process—a degenerate element such as a syllable template is added. In the case of Kihehe it is not trivially obvious what element is affixed, since multiple syllables and morphemes are copied. I assume that the root plus following suffixes form a prosodic word ω, and that the empty affix is ω. Reduplication is the prefixing of an empty ω on Level 2 to the Level 1 constituent, the stem. The phonological copy operation involves mapping the empty ω onto the ω created at Level 1—there are numerous models of how this procedure works, but for the sake of exposition I adopt the parafixation model of Clements (1986). The empty ω then receives a copy of the prosodic and segmental material subordinate to the original ω and is sequenced to the left of that ω. The derivation of the reduplicated form *kutelekateleka* is provided below.

(40)

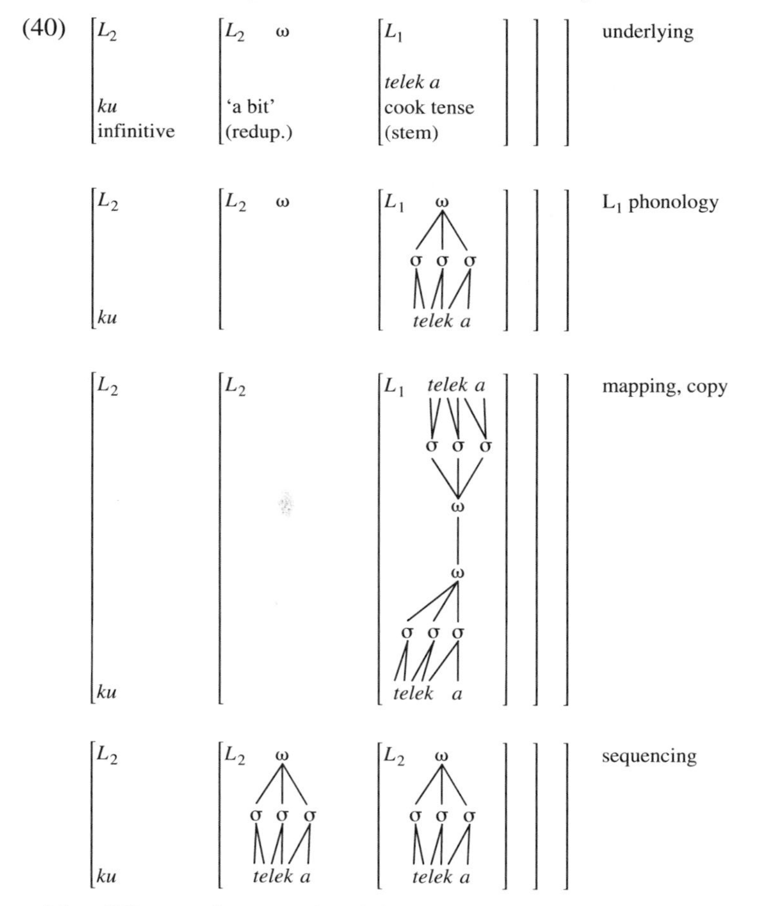

The difference between *kutelekateleka* and *kwiitakwiita* is simply that in the latter case, where the infinitive prefix is copied contrary to the general pattern, the rule Glide Formation applies before the copying rule, so segmental material which has accidentally become dominated by the base ω—in general, the output of any syllable reorganization—get copied along with the segments whose membership in the base ω is motivated on purely morphological grounds.

(41)

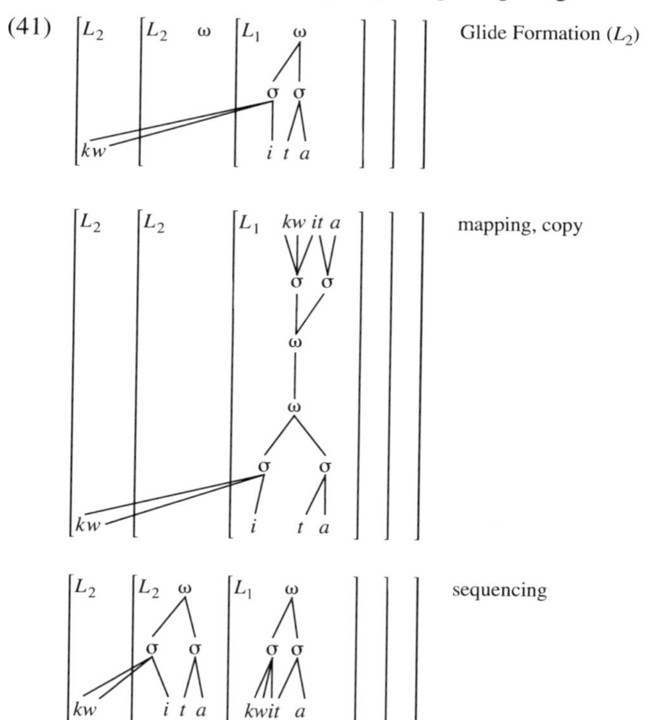

Adding the prosodic affix ω constitutes the entire morphology of reduplication; the ability to add this affix or the selection of a specific reduplication morpheme as the realization of a morphological category is not in any way affected by prior application of phonological rules in Kihehe, nor is it in any other language. The interesting and characteristic work involved in reduplication is largely done by the phonology, which receives this degenerate representation, namely a sequence of real segments plus some segmentally empty prosodic template, and the phonology has the responsibility for filling in that template. In Kihehe and cases like it, this takes place after certain phonological rules.[2]

3.2.2. Truncation

Returning to cases like Danish, other cases of so-called subtractive morphology have been brought out in the literature. Martin (1988) shows that pluralization in Koasati, seen in (42), may delete the stem-final rhyme.

(42)

SINGULAR	PLURAL	GLOSS
pitáf-fi-n	*pít-li-n*	'to slice up the middle'
tiwáp-li-n	*tíw-wi-n*	'to open something'
ataká:-li-n	*aták-li-n*	'to hang something'
misíp-li-n	*mís-li-n*	'to wink'
koyóf-fi-n	*kóy-li-n*	'to cut something'

In NLP, this process must result from a morphologically conditioned phonological rule, since all deletions must be part of phonology.

(43) KOASATI RIME DELETION:
$R \rightarrow \varnothing$ / ___ $_{stem}]$
[+Plural]

This case is similar to what we find in Danish, except that deletion affects a higher level prosodic unit, namely a rime, and therefore indirectly affects multiple segments.

Koasati constitutes a neutral territory, where both the LP and NLP accounts are plausible and consistent with the internal structure of the respective theories. There is a similar deletion process in Kimatuumbi which must be analysed as resulting from a deletion rule—and since this deletion is postlexical, the deletion must be phonological.[3] This rule deletes the segmental material of one of the locative prefixes, *kų-*, after a vowel; this rule, illustrated in (44), is optional, so there are two variants for each sentence.

(44)

nįyenda kų́Kįpoóį	'I am going to Kipooi.'
nįyendaá Kįpoóį	id.
eendábųtųká kųKįpátįmų	'He is running to Kipatimu.'
eendábųtųkáa Kįpátįmų	id.

It is apparent that the locative prefix *kų-* is present in underlying representations, but is in part deleted—the evidence for its underlying presence even when deleted is that its tone and mora are preserved. The rule deletes the segmental material of the syllable *kų-* but preserves tone and moraic structure.[4]

(45) LOCATIVE TRUNCATION (optional):
σ $[_{\omega}\sigma \rightarrow \varnothing$ (prosodic structure preserved)
[*kų*]

The syllable preceding *kų-* takes the tone and mora originally part of the syllable of *kų-*, so for this reason, the locative truncation rule is stated to affect only the segmental representation. As seen in the derivation (46), the H tone on *kų-* comes from applying Initial Tone Insertion.

(46)

nįyenda kų-kįpoóį	underlying
nįyenda kų́-kįpoóį	ITI

nį̧yenda μ́ kį̧poóį̧	Locative Truncation
nį̧yendaá kį̧poóį̧	reaffiliation of stranded mora

Finally, *kų-* deletion is possible only if the prefix syllable is monomoraic; various regular syllable fusions can make the prefix bimoraic, thus blocking deletion, as in (47).

(47)	*nį̧yenda kwį̧́į̧sį̧́wá*	'I am going to the islands'
	nį̧yenda kų́ųnkóon go	'I am going to Mkongo'
	nį̧yenda kų-mų-kóongo	underlying
	nį̧yenda kų-m̩-kóongo	U-deletion
	nį̧yenda kų́-m̩-kóongo	ITI
	nį̧yenda kų́ų-nkóo ngo	Nasal desyllabification
	NA	Locative Truncation

The second example involves lengthening of the locative prefix syllable as a consequence of postlexical desyllabification of the derived syllabic nasal in *nkóongo;* this then argues that Locative Truncation is postlexical. Locative Truncation applies after phonological rules, so it must itself be a phonological rule, specifically the dissociation of the segments of this morpheme, with retention of prosodic structure.

3.2.3. Truncation and Defaults

These deletions and prosodic restructurings bring us closer to the apparent case of postphonological allomorphy in Arabic which I started with. Before getting to that case, I consider another example which is often treated as phonologically conditioned allomorphy, but which has another interpretation, as a morphologically conditioned phonological rule, one with a similarity to Kimatuumbi Locative Truncation. This is the case of Korean *i* ~ *ka* allomorphy.

The relevant facts are as follows. Case markers suffer certain variations, determined by whether they are added to a consonant-final base or a vowel-final base. Thus the accusative is *rɨl* after a vowel but *ɨl* after a consonant, the topic marker is *nɨn* after a vowel but *ɨn* after a consonant, and the nominative is *i* after a consonant and *ka* after a vowel.

(48)	citation:	*param*	*pori*
	nominative:	*param-i*	*pori-ka*
	accusative:	*param-ɨl*	*pori-rɨl*
	topic:	*param-ɨn*	*pori-nɨn*
		'wind'	'barley'

Writing rules to delete *l* or *n* after a consonant is unproblematic, and in fact treating the *ɨl* ~ *rɨl* alternation with suppletion-style allomorphy fails to capture the phonological similarity between the allomorphs. The problem really is in the nominative; can we handle this alternation by a phonological rule? It turns out that there is a very simple way to account for this allomorphy by an operation entirely analogous to the Kimatuumbi Locative Truncation and Koasati Rime Deletion rules. Specifically, we assume the underlying affix *ka* and invoke a rule to delete the segmental content of this syllable after a consonant.

(49) KOREAN NOMINATIVE DESTRUCTURING:

σ	σ → Ø	(prosodic structure preserved)
|	[+Nom]	
C		

This will leave behind a segmentless mora. Default rules then assign the necessary features, and we end up with *i*.[5]

(50)

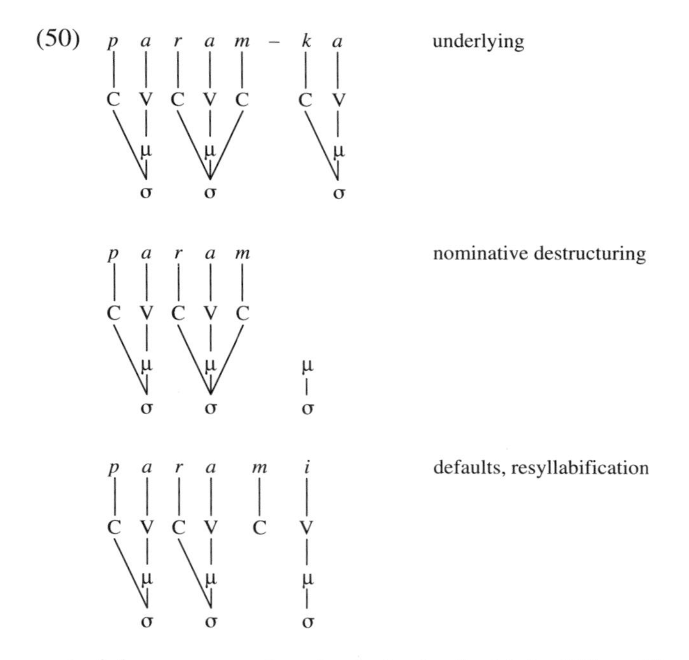

As it happens, no phonological rules feed into (49), so Korean is not crucial for distinguishing the theories. Nevertheless, it suggests a direction for reanalysis of other supposed cases of phonologically conditioned allomorphy: such rules might be slightly bizarre morphologically conditioned rules in the phonology. This then brings us to the Classical Arabic possessive allomorphy rule, where we find *ya* selected after long vowels. This will be handled as diphthongization arising from prosodic destruction. The syllable structure of underlying *i:* is reduced to a simple CV core syllable, with *i* assigned to the onset by rule (51).

(51) CLASSICAL ARABIC 1–SINGULAR DIPHTHONGIZATION

```
    σ              σ          σ
   / \            / \         |
  V   V   →      C   V   /    V ____
   \ /           |
    i            i
```

The syllable peak now has no segmental material, so default rules fill in the values for *a*.

(52)

```
maqha        i          output of Glide Elision, Vowel Fusion
 / \        / \
V   V      V   V

maqha      i            diphthongization
 / \       |
V   V      C   V

maqha      i   a        defaults
 / \       |   |
V   V      C   V
```

These examples show that deletion is needed in phonology, which is hardly surprising, and that deletion can affect multiple segments, as long as they form a higher level constituent. In this enterprise of reanalyzing putative feeding from phonology into morphology, it is important to know what limits are to be imposed. The limits are, of course, the limits imposed on phonological analysis: we do not propose that ANY well-motivated constraints on phonology be relaxed for the sake of reanalyzing supposed morphological operations. Consistent with the constraint that phonological operations apply to prosodic or (sub)segmental constituents, we predict that there is no so-called subtractive morphology affecting morphemes which are not phonological constituents. A specific case of this constraint on analysis can be seen in Chimwiini.

3.2.4. THE CHIMWIINI PASSIVE PERFECTIVE

Kisseberth and Abasheikh (1974) note that the passive suffix in Chimwiini is generally *o:w*, as we see in (53).

(53) *ku-l̪um-o:w-a* 'to be bitten'
na-kimb-il-o:w-a 'she is being sung to'
ku-d̪ar-o:w-a 'to be touched'

Before the passive suffix, dental *l̪* becomes alveolar, as the forms of (54) show.

(54) *ku-ya:l̪-a* 'to sow' *ku-yal-o:w-a* 'to be sown'
k-i:ngil̪-a 'to enter' *k-ingil-o:w-a* 'to be entered'
x-fu:ngul̪-a 'to open' *x-fungul-o:w-a* 'to be opened'

Kisseberth and Abasheikh suggest that this could be done by a phonological rule, as in (55).

(55) *l̪ → l* / ___ + *o:w*

The perfective tense passive is somewhat problematic, since the passive suffix *o:w* is not found on the surface. Furthermore, the perfective passive irregularly selects the final vowel *a* rather than *e*, as (56) shows.

(56) *l̪um-i:l̪-e* 'he bit' *l̪um-i:l-a* 'he was bitten'
som-e:l̪-e 'he read' *chi-som-e:l-a* 'it was read'
fungi:l̪-e 'he opened' *i-fungi:l-a* 'it was opened'

These examples also show that the rule changing dental *l̪* to alveolar still applies, even though the supposed conditioning factor, the passive morpheme, is not phonetically present.

In a model countenancing morpheme deletions and phonology feeding into morphology, we could handle this by applying the dental-to-alveolar rule first, then deleting *-o:w*.

(57) *l̪um-i:l̪-o:w-a* underlying
l̪um-i:l-o:w-a *l̪*-to-*l*
l̪um-i:l-a *o:w*-Deletion

This is not allowed in the model proposed here, since morpheme deletion is barred. In this case, the rule cannot be phonological deletion, since the sequence *-o:w* is not any kind of constituent; if it is unsyllabified, it is certainly not a rime. If it is syllabified, it straddles syllables.

Therefore, the only solution is to directly restrict the insertion of the passive affix, so that it is not insertable in [+PERFECTIVE] verbs. Then how about the dental-to-alveolar change? As Kisseberth and Abasheikh point out, this change need not be triggered by the phoneme sequence *-o:w* but could equally refer to the feature [+PASSIVE]. Certainly the change from dental to alveolar does not involve feature spreading from one of the suffix segments. (I assume that the rule deletes the feature [+distributed], with later default assignment of the feature [−distributed].)

(58) *l̪ → l* / ___ + [PASSIVE]

Therefore, NLP is forced to adopt the solution suggested by Kisseberth and Abasheikh that the mutation of *l̪* is triggered not by the passive suffix itself, but the morphological feature [PASSIVE].

Lack of space prevents actually reanalyzing other cases which could be cited—supposed examples from Javanese (Hargus, this volume), Shi, and Luganda (Hyman, 1990) are reanalyzed in Odden (1990b)—but it should be clear that it will take much stranger allomorphy than is currently available to give unambiguous support to the claim that phonology can feed into morphology. Allomorphy like English *go* ~ *went* or *be* ~ *am* ~ *is* ~ *were* certainly would qualify, but none of this variation is phonologically conditioned, much less conditioned by derived phonological information.

3.3. Apparent Problems

There are still untouched cases where phonological reanalysis is not possible. The best known case is the verb-to-noun derivational suffix *-al* in English, which, it is often said, can attach only to final-stressed stems.

(59)					
	arrival	*disposal*	*acquittal*	*refusal*	*reversal*
	survival	*bestowal*	*withdrawal*	*betrothal*	*avowal*
	renewal	*revival*	*approval*	*transferral*	*betrayal*
	appraisal	*deferral*	*referral*	*perusal*	*upheaval*
	burial	*denial*			

This stands as one of the stronger arguments available for phonology preceding morphology, since the putatively derived phonological condition is one of the factors determining whether the affix can be used at all; that is, we are not dealing with variations in the shape of a morpheme or with phonological deletion. This case is nevertheless not strong enough to force adoption of LP; given the nonproductivity of this affix and the small number of forms available, it is impossible to really test any hypothesis regarding this affix. Supposing that position of stress were the correct generalization, it is possible that stress in these words is present in underlying representation, so this would not be a case of morphology being sensitive to derived phonological information. Furthermore, there is a different generalization which covers the data, namely that *-al* only combines with Latinate bound prefix plus monosyllabic root.[6]

Booij (1981) and Booij and Rubach (1984, 1987) propose two other cases from Dutch; these yield to reanalysis. The first case involves the supposed interaction between schwa deletion and a rule of allomorphy. Supposedly, the final schwa of *ambassade* 'embassy' deletes before *eur*, giving *ambassadeur*.

(60) $ə \rightarrow \emptyset$ / ___ V

Then an allomorphy rule replaces *eur* with *ris* in the feminine, giving *ambassadrice*.

(61)	*ambasadə-ör*	affixation
	ambasad-ör	schwa deletion
	ambasad-ör-isə	affixation
	ambasad-r-isə	*rice*-allomorphy

The interleaving of phonology and morphology is motivated by the fact that the feminine allomorphy is consonant-initial, hence could not trigger Schwa Deletion, so if the feminine allomorph were added directly to *ambassade,* we would generate incorrect **ambassaderice.*

There are a number of possibilities for reanalysis, all of which are consistent with the data cited by Booij and Rubach. One possibility is that schwa deletes before *rice.* Or, the allomorphy rule could be a morphologically conditioned phonological rule, like the cases we have seen earlier. Another possibility is to derive *ambassadrice* from the root *ambassad,* not the noun *ambassade.* A fourth possibility is simply to not derive *ambassadrice* from anything, except French.

The second example, in many ways similar to English *-al,* is the case of the suffix *-ief* which only productively attaches to nouns ending in unstressed *i.*

(62)	*psychologíe*	'psychology'	*psychologisch*	'psychological'
	hysteríe	'hysteria'	*hysterisch*	'hysterical'
	agréssie	'aggression'	*agressief*	'agressive'
	áctie	'action'	*actief*	'active'

Dutch stress is certainly not transparently predictable like Latin or Arabic stress, so an obvious direction to look for reanalysis is to assume that stress is present in underlying representations, in which case we are no longer dealing with derived phonological information. Booij (personal communication) informs me that the default position for stress assignment is on the penult, and van der Hulst (1984: 235) confirms this generalization: this fits with our hypothesis. Words with irregular stress, especially final stress, will be entered in the lexicon with stress preassigned, whereas words with penultimate stress will have no underlying stress. The condition for affixation of *-ief* is then simply, as Booij and Rubach assume, that it only attaches to words ending with unstressed *i.* Words such as *psychologíe* with final lexical stress do not satisfy this condition, so cannot take the affix *-ief.*

3.4. Precyclicity or Precompilation?

To close this investigation, I look at a problem where LP and NLP seem to make different predictions. This is a case in Maltese Arabic where Level 1 phonology needs to access Level 2 information. This would seem to refute the interactive theory, since Level 2 morphology has not even been done at the stage of Level 1 phonology. However, there is a way out for LP.

The cyclic Stress rule of Maltese is involved, which Brame (1974) formulates as in (63) (additional data come from Aquilina, 1965; Aquilina and Isserlin, 1981).

(63) STRESS:
$V \rightarrow [+\text{stress}] \,/\, \_\_\_\_ \; C_0((VC)\; VC^1)]$

Applying after stress is an Apocope rule which deletes an unstressed vowel in an open syllable.

(64) APOCOPE:
$\breve{V} \rightarrow \emptyset \,/\, \_\_\_\_ \; CV$

These rules interact to account for the paradigm of *ḥataf* in (65).

(65)

/ḥataf-t/	*ḥtáft*	'I snatched'
/ḥataf-na/	*ḥtáfna*	'we snatched'
/ḥataf/	*ḥátaf*	'he snatched'
/ḥataf-u/	*ḥátfu*	'she snatched'
/ḥataf-it/	*ḥátfet*	'she snatched'

Stress and Apocope apply to underlying *ḥataf+u* to yield *ḥátfu,* and apply to *ḥataf+na* to yield *ḥtáfna.*

(66)

ḥataf	*ḥataf-u*	*ḥataf-na*	underlying
ḥátaf	*ḥátaf-u*	*ḥatáf-na*	Stress
NA	*ḥátf-u*	*ḥtáf-na*	Apocope

Other morphemes which are Level 2 suffixes, seen in (67), can be added to the verb after affixation of subject agreement, including the object suffixes *-kum* 'you (pl.)' and *-ik* 'you (sg.)', and the negative suffix *-š.*

(67)

hatáf-š	'he didn't snatch'
hatf-ít-kom	'she snatched you (pl.)'
hátf-ek	'he snatched you (sg.)'

The argument that these affixes are at a different level is the cyclic pattern of stress assignment. One fact which cyclic stress explains is the surface contrast in (68) between bistratal [ḥatáfna] 'he snatched us' and monostratal [ḥtáfna] 'we snatched'. On Level 1, Stress and Apocope apply to the form [ḥataf] 'he snatched' and to [ḥataf+na] 'we snatched'. The second form is directly mapped onto the phonetic output [ḥtáfna]. The first form *ḥataf* contains a Level 2 suffix, so Stress and Apocope reapply on the L_2 cycle. The stress is reassigned to the penult, but due to the previously assigned stress on the first syllable, Apocope is blocked and the phonetic form is [ḥatáfna].

(68)

[ḥatáfna]	[ḥtáfna]	
'he snatched us'	'we snatched'	
ḥataf	*ḥataf-na*	input to L_1
ḥátaf	*ḥatáf-na*	Stress
NA	*ḥtáf-na*	Apocope

ḥátaf-na	input to L_2
ḥàtáf-na	Stress
NA	Apocope

Therefore the object suffixes and negative *š* must only be available on Level 2, and Stress and Apocope are cyclic rules.

Now we turn to the other rule. The Level 2 affixes have a further peculiarity seen in (69); namely, they lengthen a preceding vowel. Thus *ḥtáftu+na* becomes *ḥtaftúuna* and *ḥtáfna+kom* becomes *ḥtafníekom.* The negative suffix *-š* also induces Boundary Lengthening, so *ma ḥátfu+š* become *ma ḥatfúuš.*

(69) *ḥtaftúuna* 'you (pl.) snatched us' (*ḥtáftu* 'you (pl.) snatched')
ḥtafníekom 'we snatched you (pl.)' (*ḥtáfna* 'we snatched')
ma ḥatfúuš 'they didn't snatch' (*hátfu* 'they snatched')

A straightforward formulation of this lengthening is possible within any theory: any Level 2 suffix induces Lengthening.

(70) BOUNDARY LENGTHENING (Level 2):
$V \rightarrow VV\ /\ \_\_\_\ ]\ X$

Note that this derived length attracts stress, so we get *ḥatfúuš,* not **ḥátfuuš.* Therefore, Boundary Lengthening precedes Stress on Level 2.

Now we arrive at the paradox in (71). The problem is that verb stems which end with a vowel, such as *ʔára,* must lengthen their final vowel before a Level 2 suffix as predicted, and this lengthening must take place on Level 1 before L_1 stress is assigned so that the initial vowel remains unstressed and therefore undergoes Apocope.

(71) /ʔara-Ø/ *ʔára* 'he read'
/ʔara-Ø + na/ *ʔráana* 'he read us'
/jara-Ø/ *jára* 'it happened'
/jara-Ø + l-i/ *jráa-li* 'it happened to me'

In LP, Lengthening would have to be assigned to Level 2, since it is triggered only by Level 2 suffixes. Therefore assignment of Stress on Level 1 must precede Lengthening and should not be sensitive to the output of Lengthening. But this prediction is incorrect, as seen in the derivation (72).

(72)

ʔara+Ø	subject affixing
ʔára+Ø	Stress
NA	Apocope
———	[L_2]
ʔára+na	object affixing
ʔáraa+na	Lengthening

ʔàráa+na	Stress
NA	Apocope
*[ʔaráana]	

On the Level 1 cycle, stress should be assigned to the first vowel, just as it is in the unsuffixed form; on Level 2, the final vowel is lengthened and that vowel then gets the stress, but the subordinated stress on the initial vowel would incorrectly block Apocope. The correct derivation requires that Lengthening apply prior to Level 1 Stress, giving *ʔaraa+na* as the input to Stress, so that the penultimate vowel is stressed and the initial vowel is never stressed.

(73)

ʔara-na	output of morphology
ʔaraa-na	(precyclic) Boundary Lengthening
ʔaráa-	Level 1 Stress
ʔráa-	Level 1 Apocope
ʔráana	Level 2 (nothing applies)

These facts can be accommodated in any theory where all morphemes are concatenated before any phonological rules apply, providing that we allow some rules, and in particular, Boundary Lengthening, to apply precyclically, so that Level 2 suffixes can be seen and thus trigger lengthening before Level 1 phonological rules apply. In fact, we can also account for this problem if we treat Lengthening as a precompiled rule, which would be written as (74).

(74) LENGTHENING (precompiled);
$V \rightarrow V: / \_\_\_]_{[\text{FRAME } 1]}$

The Level 1 phonology will generate both *ʔara* and *ʔaraa*. The former leaves Level 1 as *ʔára* and the latter leaves Level 1 as *ʔráa*.

(75)

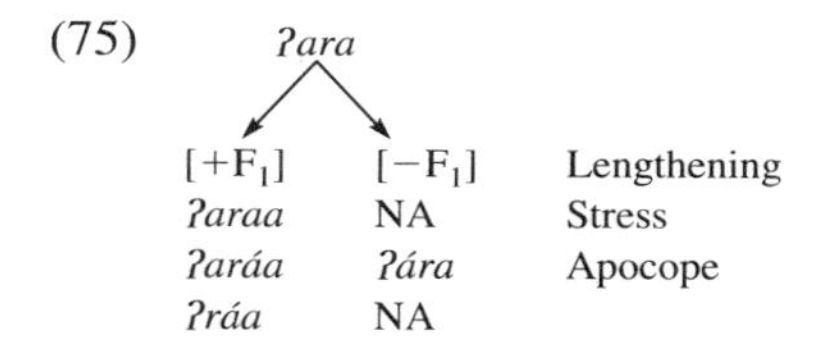

Frame 1 is defined as in (76).

(76) Frame 1: $[_{\text{VERB}} \_\_\_] \left\{ \begin{array}{l} \text{Object} \\ \text{Negative} \end{array} \right\}$

So when a negative or object affix is encountered in Level 2, the variant *ʔráa* is selected.

4. SUMMARY

To conclude, I have investigated two manifestations of the question of what information is available to each component in the grammar and considered how LP and NLP explain the behavior of linguistic systems. It was shown that plain LP cannot explain the behavior of sandhi rules in Kimatuumbi or precyclic Boundary Lengthening in Maltese, but extending the theory with precompilation puts the theories on an equal footing descriptively. Arguments have been given against the claim that morphology and phonology interact in the way implied by the model (1). This certainly does not refute LP, since the model (1) might still be right, even if there is no evidence for it in the realm of information access. At this stage, though, it is not obvious where else we could derive support for the interactive model.

NOTES

[1] Sharon Hargus has suggested the possibility of eliminating the negative condition "not preceded by H" in this rule by giving the morphemes in question an underlying initial H, which deletes after a stem H. This possibility can be ruled out on two grounds. First, the citation form of the relevant morphemes lacks the H, cf. *mų-kįkálaango* 'in the frying pan': in the citation form, there is no preceding H, so no reason to delete the putative underlying H of /mų́-kįkálaango/. Second, ITI is subject to a syntactic condition that the toneless stem which conditions ITI and the morpheme which undergoes the rule cannot be separated by a righthand S-bracket. So, despite the fact that *mųųndų* 'person' has no H tones and the following morpheme *mų* is one of the morphemes undergoing ITI, ITI does not apply in the sentence *naabíkįtee ñama* [*yayáapimįlwé na mųųndų*] *mų-kįkálaango* 'I put the meat which was bought by the person in the frying pan' because the determinant and focus are in different clauses. If we construe ITI as deletion of an underlying H, we must further expand the environment for that rule, so that if the H is separated from the preceding word by $_S]$, then the initial H tone must also be deleted, even if there is no preceding H.

[2] An analysis of reduplication in LP, viewed as an operation in the morphology, would most likely have the same form as the NLP analysis. Since reduplication may (under resyllabification, as in reduplication of *kwiita* or *kulwiita*) copy an object prefix or the infinitive prefix *ku,* reduplication follows prefixation of these morphemes. The problem is identifying the substring subject to reduplication. Given inputs such as REDUP+*ku*[*teleka*] and REDUP+*ku*[*lu*[*teleka*]] which reduplicate as *kutelekateleka* and *kulutelekateleka,* the morphological constituent which copies is the stem. But by the assumptions of LP, the internal morphological structure of the verb is not recoverable. Morphological structure simply does not suffice to identify the correct substring which reduplicates in the case of *kulwiitalwiita,* where the structure which is copied includes nonstem material (*lw,* the object prefix). Therefore, in the LP account, some prosodic structure must form the basis for

identifying the structures subject to reduplication, and this structure must include the stem syllables but may not include prefix syllables except when prefix syllables fuse with stem syllables by phonological rules.

[3]The reason that postlexical deletion, especially any deletion applying after phonological rules, should be phonological is that the morphological component is, in the theory of LP, part of the lexicon. Of course, one could expand LP in such a way that "postlexical morphology" is not a theoretical anomaly, but such a move would seriously undermine the motivation for distinguishing between the lexical and postlexical components.

[4]It is beyond the scope of this article to present a complete theory of rules of this type, but it is important to know something about how such rules are constrained. It is assumed here that rules may either delete the segmental and prosodic material under a specified prosodic constituent, or may delete the segmental material under the constituent leaving prosodic structure intact. Rules of the former type are written as simply deleting the relevant prosodic constituent. Rules of the latter type are written as deletion of the prosodic element, with the additional annotation that "prosodic structure is preserved."

[5]It is often assumed that *ɨ*, not *i*, is the vowel which arises from default rules in Korean. However, *ɨ* has a restricted distribution in Korean: no morphemes ends in *ɨ* except for the demonstratives *kɨ* and *nɨ*. The relevant generalization is that *ɨ* cannot be prepausal—the demonstratives can never be prepausal. A similar constraint on *ɨ* appears in Tigrinya; epenthesis inserts *ɨ* in word-final position, but the vowel is realized phonetically as *i* in that position. Chung (1991) provides other arguments that word-finally, *i* and not *ɨ* arises by default.

[6]The forms *denial* and *trial* do not conform to this generalization; note, however, that the stress-final generalization is falsified by *burial.*

REFERENCES

Aquilina, J. (1965). *Teach Yourself Maltese.* English Universities Press, London.

Aquilina, J., and Isserlin, B. (1981). *A Survey of Contemporary Dialectal Maltese.* B. S. J. Isserlin, Leeds.

Anderson, S. (1975). On the interaction of phonological rules of various types. *Journal of Linguistics* **11,** 39–62.

Booij, G. (1981). Rule ordering, rule application, and the organization of grammars. In *Phonologica 1980* (W. U. Dressler, ed.), pp. 45–56. Institut für Sprachwissenschaft, Innsbruck.

Booij, G., and Rubach, J. (1984). Morphological and prosodic domains in lexical phonology. *Phonology Yearbook* **1,** 181–207.

Booij, G., and Rubach, J. (1987). Postcyclic versus postlexical rules in lexical phonology. *Linguistic Inquiry* **18,** 1–44.

Brame, M. (1970). *Arabic Phonology.* Doctoral dissertation, Massachusetts Institute of Technology, Cambridge.

Brame, M. (1974). The cycle in phonology: Stress in Palestinian, Maltese, and Spanish. *Linguistic Inquiry* **5,** 39–60.

Chung, Y. H. (1991). *The Lexical Tone System of North Kyungsang Korean.* Doctoral dissertation, Ohio State University, Columbus.

Clements, G. N. (1986). The problem of transfer in non-linear phonology. *Cornell Working Papers in Linguistics* **7,** 1–36.

Halle, M., and Vergnaud, J.-R. (1987). *An Essay on Stress.* MIT Press, Cambridge, Mass.

Hayes, B. (1990). Precompiled phrasal phonology. In *The Phonology–Syntax Connection* (S. Inkelas and D. Zec, eds.), pp. 85–108. CSLI Publications and University of Chicago Press, Chicago.

Hulst, H. van der (1984). *Syllable Structure and Stress in Dutch.* Foris, Dordrecht.

Hyman, L. (1990). *Conceptual Issues in the Comparative Study of the Bantu Verb Stem.* Paper presented at the 21st Conference on African Linguistics, University of Georgia, Athens.

Inkelas, S. (1989). *Prosodic Constituency in the Lexicon.* Doctoral dissertation, Stanford University, Stanford, Calif.

Kaisse, E., and Shaw, P. (1985). On the theory of lexical phonology. *Phonology Yearbook* **2,** 1–30.

Kiparsky, P. (1982). Lexical phonology and morphology. In *Linguistics in the Morning Calm* (I. S. Yang, ed.), pp. 3–91. Hanshin, Seoul.

Kisseberth, C., and Abasheikh, M. (1976). On the interaction of phonology and morphology: a Chi-mwi:ni example. *Studies in African Linguistics* **7,** 31–110.

Marantz, A. (1982). Re reduplication. *Linguistic Inquiry* **13,** 435–482.

Martin, J. (1988). Subtractive morphology as dissociation. *Proceedings of the West Coast Conference on Formal Linguistics* **8,** 229–240.

Matthews, P. (1974). *Morphology: An Introduction to the Theory of Word Formation.* Cambridge University Press, Cambridge.

McCarthy, J. (1979). *Formal Problems in Semitic Phonology and Morphology.* Doctoral dissertation, Massachusetts Institute of Technology, Cambridge.

Mohanan, K. P. (1986). *The Theory of Lexical Phonology.* Reidel, Dordrecht.

Odden, D. (1987). Kimatuumbi phrasal phonology. *Phonology Yearbook* **4,** 13–36.

Odden, D. (1990a). Syntax, lexical rules and postlexical rules in Kimatuumbi. In *The Phonology–syntax Connection* (S. Inkelas and D. Zec, eds.), pp. 259–277. CSLI Publications and University of Chicago Press, Chicago.

Odden, D. (1990b). Phonology and its interaction with syntax and morphology. *Studies in the Linguistic Sciences* **20,** 69–108.

Odden, D. (1992). *Kimatuumbi Phonology and Morphology.* Unpublished manuscript, Ohio State University, Columbus.

Odden, D., and Odden, M. (1986). Ordered reduplication in Kíhehe. *Linguistic Inquiry* **16,** 497–503.

THE STRUCTURE OF THE SLAVE (NORTHERN ATHABASKAN) VERB

KEREN D. RICE

Department of Linguistics
University of Toronto
Toronto, Ontario, Canada M5S 1A1

1. INTRODUCTION

The Athabaskan verb is commonly described as consisting of a stem and a number of prefixes, both inflectional and derivational in nature, whose ordering is unpredictable and requires a slot-and-filler, or template, analysis. The verb in Athabaskan languages is unusual in several ways, posing problems for universal theories of word formation. First, it is generally observed that inflection stands outside of derivation rather than inside of or interspersed with derivation (e.g. Anderson, 1982, 1988; Williams, 1981). In Athabaskan languages, inflectional and derivational elements are intermingled within the word. Second, languages requiring slot-and-filler morphology appear to be unusual (e.g., Myers, 1987; Speas, 1984), creating a third type of morphology distinct from concatenative and nonconcatenative morphology. Athabaskan languages appear to require such morphology to describe the order of verbal morphemes. Third, morphological co-occurrence restrictions in languages have been argued to operate on a principle of adjacency which requires that morphological subcategorization frames refer only to adjacent elements (e.g., Allen, 1978; Lieber, 1981; Siegel, 1978). Athabaskan languages show cooccurrence restrictions between nonadjacent morphemes that are not explained given a theory of slot-and-filler morphology (e.g., Randoja, 1989; Speas, 1986, 1989; Thomas-Flinders, 1983). And fourth, domains defined by the morphology and those required by the phonology have been argued to be

Phonetics and Phonology, Volume 4
Studies in Lexical Phonology

isomorphic (e.g., Kiparsky, 1982; Mohanan, 1982, 1986). In Athabaskan languages the domains required for the phonology are nonisomorphic with those required by the morphology.[1] In most accounts of the Athabaskan verb (e.g., Hargus, 1988; Kari, 1976; Randoja, 1989; Rice, 1989; Speas, 1986) it is assumed that affixes are diacritically marked for phonological domain in order to account for this discrepancy.

In this article, I would like to examine the Athabaskan verb afresh. The main goal is to set forth a new proposal regarding the verb that will account for the properties noted above. I first give some background on the structure of what is traditionally called the verb word and on the treatment of the verb in the literature. I then turn to three questions about the verb: Is it a morphological or a syntactic construct; Is the order of morphemes stipulated or predictable; and Are the phonological rule domains stipulated or derived? I end with a comparison of the theory that I propose with a model of lexical phonology and morphology, concluding that while I have argued against lexical phonology and morphology for the verb structure, the verb nevertheless provides support for a number of principles of the theory.

2. THE STRUCTURE OF THE SLAVE VERB

The verb in an Athabaskan language is generally characterized as a template, consisting of a string of fixed-order position classes and morphemes that are marked lexically for the position that they fill in the template. In addition, boundary types are associated with the different morpheme positions to account for their phonological properties. The template proposed for Slave ([slevi]), an Athabaskan language of Canada, in (1) is slightly adapted from that proposed by Rice (1989).

(1) preverb # distributive # iterative # incorporate # direct object %
D D D D I
deictic subject % theme-derivation-aspect + conjugation/mode + subject
I D/I D I I
= voice + stem

Several observations about the verb are in order concerning the content of the slots, the identification of morphemes as inflectional (I) or derivational (D), the cooccurrence restrictions between positions in the verb, and the use of phonological boundaries.

2.1. The Content of the Templatic Positions

In this section I identify briefly each of the morpheme positions, starting at the left of the verb, with the preverbs.

PREVERBS, traditionally called incorporated postpositions and adverbs, represent oblique relations or manner. See Kari (1989, 1990) and Rice (1991b) for details. Typical meanings of preverbs include 'around, away, up onto, out of, across, to a point, into fire, into air, in half, to pieces, excess'. While the meanings of many of the morphemes in this position are transparent, with some the meaning is defined only in combination with the stem.

The DISTRIBUTIVE morpheme is aspectual, marking distributivity: each one separately. It can have scope over the agent, theme, action, or location.

The ITERATIVE morpheme, another aspectual marker, indicates that an action is habitual or repeated, depending on other morphemes present within the verb.

INCORPORATES are of two types, nouns that are internal arguments (Rice, 1991c) and stems with an adverbial function. The meaning of the verb with an incorporate differs in systematic ways from the meaning of the verb without the incorporate. See Rice (1989) and Axelrod (1990) for discussion.

DIRECT OBJECT morphemes mark the person and number of the direct object.

DEICTIC SUBJECT, or third person subject, position includes two morphemes, *k*- 'third person plural human subject' and *ts'*- 'unspecified subject'. It has been argued for Navajo, another Athabaskan language, that the cognate morphemes represent a type of object marking and can be collapsed with the object markers (Speas, 1991). I assume that such an analysis is possible for Slave; this question requires further close attention.

THEME-DERIVATION-ASPECT is a grab-bag position in which three types of elements can be identified. First, productive aspectual morphemes are found. These include *d* 'inceptive', *n* 'terminative, completive', *í* 'transitional', and *u* 'conative'.[2] I will call these morphemes SECONDARY ASPECT. Second, there are GENDER morphemes, generally called derivational prefixes. These include *d* 'fire', *d* 'benefactive', *d* 'by mouth', *n* 'mind, feeling', *n* 'water', *y* 'dual subject'. These morphemes certainly mark gender historically. Some are extremely productive; for instance, the morpheme *d* 'by mouth' occurs in a wide range of verbs having to do with noise; examples include 'whistle', 'snore', 'burp', 'sit', 'bark', 'cough', 'squeak', 'ask', 'honk' (goose call), 'whine, fuss', 'argue', 'defend (help with words)', 'walk laughing, crying, etc.', 'joke (tease with words)', 'win with words'. Others occur only in restricted cases. For example, the morpheme *n* occurs in verbs meaning 'handle unspecified object (water) on object, or wash' and 'handle in water'. Without *n,* the meaning of the verb would not include the concept of water. The prefix *y* must occur in certain verbs with a dual subject (e.g. 'dual arrive'); however, it is not generally found even when the stem requires a dual subject. Third, there are morphemes which always occur with a particular verb stem; these morphemes are generally termed THEMATIC in the Athabaskan literature. They are part of the underlying representation of the lexical item. For instance, the basic lexical entry for the verb 'handle singular object (uncontrolled)' includes the prefix *y,* with every derivative based on this lexical entry requiring this morpheme. I call both the gender and the thematic morphemes GENDER in this article. While in general gender precedes secondary aspect, the ordering may be overridden by phonological constraints. In Slave, the ordering of these morphemes is: *u, y* gender, *d, n, y* secondary aspect, *í*. See Rice (1989) on Slave; Hargus (1988) on Sekani; Kari (1989) on Ahtna; and Speas (1986), Wright (1986), and McDonough (1990) on Navajo.

CONJUGATION and MODE will be considered together. Mode is a misnomer which is used for convenience in Athabaskan literature. Three morphemes are found in this position in Slave, ∅ imperfective, *ñ* perfective, and *ghu* optative.[3] The first two mark aspect and the third indicates mode, or in some cases a remote future tense. A morpheme in this position must occur in every verb. I call these morphemes PRIMARY ASPECT. The morphemes called conjugation have the forms ∅, *n, w,* and *y* in Slave.[4] Each verb requires a particular conjugation pattern or set of conjugation markers for the imperfective, perfective, and optative. The conjugation pattern is determined in two different ways. First, an underlying lexical entry has a conjugation pattern associated with it, largely determinable by semantics. For instance, verbs of motion require the conjugation pattern *n* imperfective, *n* perfective, *n* optative, while those involving sustained actions over time require ∅ imperfective, *y* perfective, ∅ optative. Second, preverb and aspectual morphemes are conjugation choosers and determine the choice of conjugation pattern for a particular verb. For example, the adverb *dah* 'up onto a horizontal surface' requires *w* imperfective, *w* perfective, *w* optative conjugation marking; the adverb *ká* 'out from inside' requires ∅ imperfective, *y* perfective, ∅ optative conjugation marking; and the secondary aspectual marker *d* 'inceptive' requires ∅ imperfective, *w* perfective, ∅ optative conjugation marking. The customary and distributive also select conjugation patterns.

The SUBJECT markers indicate the person and number of the subject. These include first person singular, second person singular, first person plural, second person plural, and third person (number is not determined in this position).

The conjugation–primary aspect–subject portions of the verb combine in ways that are not always predictable. For instance, the first person singular subject has the form *h* except in the perfective of ∅ and *h* voice element verbs, where it is *i*. While it is possible to assign the morpheme *h* the meaning 'first person singular subject', the morpheme *i* includes more than one meaning, namely first person singular subject and perfective primary aspect. The optative is predictably *u* or *wo-* except when the conjugation marker is *n* or *w,* when it is *´wo* or *wo* (the acute accent indicates that a high tone falls on the vowel of the preceding syllable). Other morphemes show similar patterns. While the second person singular is regularly nasalization in certain environments, in ∅ and *h* voice element perfectives it has the form *ne* in these environments. The third person exhibits similar allomorphy, with an unusual form in the perfective of ∅ and *h* voice element verbs. *n* and *w* conjugation optatives also display unexpected patterns. The nonsystematic combinations of conjugation–primary aspect–subject suggest that in at least some cases this stretch of the verb should be treated as a single unit, or portmanteau morph, with complex meaning, as proposed, for instance, by Anderson (1982) for Georgian and by Williams (1981) for Latin.

The so-called classifiers, here labeled 'voice', mark valence/voice and transitivity, changing the argument structure required by a verb. For instance, the *h* (*ɬ) voice element adds an agent argument, creating a transitive/causative, and the *d* voice element causes the loss of the agent argument, creating a passive. In addition, a voice element may be part of the lexical entry of a verb as the form of the voice element is not always predictable from the argument structure of the verb.

Finally, the stem itself is actually complex, consisting of a root and an aspectual suffix.

In (2), the verb template, as redefined based on the above discussion, is shown.

(2) preverb # distributive # iterative # incorporate # object agreement % third person subject % gender + secondary aspect + primary aspect + subject agreement = voice + verb root + aspect

2.2. Inflection or Derivation?

I look at the inflection/derivation distinction briefly here and return to it in more depth later. I have labeled most morphemes in (1) as inflectional (I) or derivational (D) following traditional Athabaskan practice (e.g., Kari, 1979, 1990; Sapir and Hoijer, 1969). The pronominal agreement markers (object of postposition, direct object, deictic subject, subject) are treated as inflectional in the literature. The status of aspectual and gender material is not clear; I return to this question below. On the surface at least, the Athabaskan verb is highly marked, with inflectional affixation appearing linearly inside of derivational affixation.[5]

2.3. Cooccurrence Restrictions

Cooccurrence restrictions between positions within the Athabaskan verb are frequently found. I mention some briefly; see Hargus (1988) on Sekani, Rice (1989) on Slave, Speas (1986) on Navajo, and Randoja (1989) on Beaver for more extensive discussion.

As discussed earlier, conjugation morphemes do not occur freely but are dependent on other information. They can be determined by the underlying semantics of the verb or by preverbs, secondary aspect morphemes, the distributive, and the iterative. Some cooccurrence restrictions hold between the voice elements and anaphoric pronouns, with the reflexive and reciprocal generally requiring the *d* voice element. In addition, the iterative usually must occur with the *d* voice element, at least in intransitive verbs.

Other morphemes are discontinuous; for instance, certain preverbs require a gender morpheme. The preverb *di* 'fire' occurs only with the gender morpheme *d* 'fire'.

2.4. Phonological Boundaries

Phonological rule domains are indicated by boundary symbols in (1) and (2). The verb divides into four major domains with respect to phonological rules (e.g., Hargus, 1988; Kari, 1975, 1976; Li, 1946; Randoja, 1989; Rice, 1989). The symbols #, %, +, and = delineate these domains. # separates the so-called disjunct morphemes, which interact little with each other or with the rest of the verb. It is generally regarded as the strongest of the word-internal boundaries. + separates the morphemes called conjunct prefixes, which enter closely into phonological combination. The % boundary is used for the direct objects and deictic subjects. While these morphemes often pattern with the conjunct morphemes, in some ways they pattern with the disjunct morphemes, thus being intermediate between the two. Finally, the symbol = separates the voice element and stem from the conjunct morphemes (Hargus, 1988; Kari, 1976; McDonough, 1990; Rice, 1989). The boundaries thus define phonological rule domains, with the conjunct morphemes more closely bound to the verb stem than the disjunct morphemes.

2.5. The Derivation of the Verb Word

While (1) represents the linear ordering of morphemes, the verb has often been treated as composed of several distinct levels morphologically (e.g., Hargus, 1988; Kari, 1976, 1990; Li, 1946; Randoja, 1989; Rice, 1989; Sapir and Hoijer, 1969). The basic lexical entry, known as the VERB THEME, is the structure that is entered in the lexicon. It obligatorily includes a root and a voice element, which may be null. In addition, the theme includes any morphemes that must be present in all forms of the verb. These include preverbs and thematic (gender) morphemes. Some examples of themes are given in (3).

(3) a. *d-dǫ* 'drink'
voice-stem
b. *ya-h-ti* 'preach, bark'
preverb-voice-stem
c. *d-l-wé* 'sg. fall'
gender-voice-stem

In the first stage of word formation, a level called the verb base is formed. At this level, derivational affixes are added to the verb theme. These include preverbal, gender, and secondary aspectual items. Some sample bases formed on the themes in (3) are given in (4). Verb words are also shown; see the discussion below.

(4) a. verb theme: *d-dǫ* 'drink (object)'
verb word: *hedǫ* 's/he drinks (object)'

	verb base:	*te-d-d-dǫ*	'drink to excess'
		preverb-sec asp-voice-stem	
	verb word:	*tedéhdǫ*	's/he drank to excess'
b.	verb theme:	*ya-h-ti*	'preach, bark'
		preverb-voice-stem	
	verb word:	*yahti*	's/he preaches, barks'
	verb base:	*xa-ya-d-d-h-ti*	*'pray'*
		preverb-preverb-gender-voice-voice-stem	
	verb word:	*xayadeti*	's/he prays'
	verb base:	*k'a-ya-ʔe-h-ti*	'interpret'
		preverb-preverb-DO-voice-stem	
	verb word:	*k'ayaʔehti*	's/he interprets'
c.	verb theme:	*d-l-wé*	'fall'
		gender-voice-stem	
	verb base:	*ká-d-d-l-wé*	'fall out'
		preverb-gender-asp-voice-stem	
	verb word:	*kádedéhwé*	'she/he/it fell out'
	verb base:	*teh-d-l-wé*	'fall into water'
		preverb-gender-voice-stem	
	verb word:	*tedę́wé*	's/he fell into water'

At the final stage of word formation, the verb word is produced. At this level, inflectional affixes are added (e.g., subject, object markers, perhaps conjugation and primary aspect) and the formation of the verb word is complete. (See Kari, 1979, 1990, 1992, for a far more highly articulated model of word formation in Ahtna.)

This model of word formation includes three levels: verb theme (basic lexical entry), verb base (verb minus inflection), and verb word (inflected verb). Such a model of word formation is proposed in order to account for paradigmatic properties of the Athabaskan verb. It results in making the Athabaskan verb far more like verbs in other languages as well, with derivational morphology preceding inflectional morphology derivationally.

Given this model of word formation and the phonological boundaries discussed in Section 2.4, it is obvious that word formation and phonology do not take place in tandem, as the phonological domains are not defined until the verb word is formed (see Hargus, 1986, for some comments). Because of this lack of isomorphism between word formation and phonology, the Athabaskan literature recognizes two models of the verb. One (verb theme, verb base, verb word) accounts for the morphological structure of the verb, allowing for derivation to precede inflection. The second (disjunct, conjunct prefixes, stem) accounts for the phonological structure of the verb. This second type of structure is coded as boundary symbols (or some other diacritic) on the lexical entry of the affixes.

3. PREVIOUS TREATMENTS OF WORD FORMATION

Many accounts of the Athabaskan verb have been proposed, falling into two basic categories. One, represented best by the work of Hargus (1988, etc.), assumes the lexical phonology framework, arguing that a templatic structure such as that in (1) represents the structure of the verb morphosyntactically as well as phonologically. The level at which a particular morpheme is added to the verb and the order in which the morphemes are added is stipulated in the grammar of the language. Cooccurrence restrictions are represented through complex lexical entries. In a model where phonology and morphology proceed in tandem, the fact that inflection is normally outside of derivation is accidental. Nonadjacent cooccurrence restrictions within the verb are met by diacritic markings on affixes. Morphosyntactically, then, the Athabaskan verb must be regarded as unusual. This model leaves unexplained certain facts about the phonology; for instance, the phonology of stems and of disjunct morphemes is similar while that of the conjunct morphemes is different. Since stems and disjunct morphemes appear on nonadjacent levels of the lexical phonology, this similarity in their phonology is surprising.

The second type of analysis is represented by work of authors such as Kari, Speas, Wright, and Randoja. These authors propose models in many ways similar to that described in Section 2.5, arguing that the morphosyntactic structure of the verb is not isomorphic to the linear ordering of affixes. Speas (1984, 1986, 1990), echoed by Randoja (1989), points out that in the interest of maintaining a restrictive theory of morphology and word formation, no alternative solution to the morphology problem is available.

Speas, Kari, Wright, and Randoja implement this basic model in very different ways. While Speas (1990) and Kari (1979) account elegantly for the morphosyntactic side of verb structure, they offer no systematic account of the phonology (but see Kari, 1990, for discussion of Ahtna phonology).

Wright (1983, 1986) and, particularly, Randoja (1989) attempt to integrate the phonology and the morphology sides into a coherent model. Randoja, in an examination of verb structure in Beaver, proposes that the basic structure of the verb is encoded in a thematic template which represents both the lexical entry of the verb and the division of the verb into phonological rule domains. She argues that derivational affixation precedes inflectional affixation, with morphemes achieving their surface position by mapping to the thematic template. The order of mapping follows from universal principles (inflection outside derivation, adjacency), with the slot in the template to which the affix maps being stipulated in the lexical entry of the affix. Thus, each affix is marked for the domain to which it is mapped. It is this basic type of model that I would like to pursue in this article. My model differs from that proposed by Randoja in that I argue, following Speas (1990, 1991), that the basic verb structure is phrasal in nature and the wordlike nature of the verb is a phonological characteristic only. I propose to eliminate the language-particular template in favor of a structure where the ordering of morphemes within the verb word follows from properties of universal grammar. Finally, I propose to eliminate diacritic marking of phonological levels, proposing that the phonological levels are derived by algorithm.

Before turning to my proposal, I summarize some of the problems that must be dealt with in accounting for the structure of the Slave verb.

1. While inflection generally occurs outside of derivation, in Slave inflection is linearly inside of derivation.
2. While the order of verbal affixes generally reflects scopal properties or relevance to the verb (Bybee, 1985), in the Slave verb the order of morphemes appears to be random.
3. While morphological subcategorization frames generally do not state dependencies between nonadjacent items, in Slave dependencies exist between nonadjacent items.
4. While lexical phonology proposes that word formation and phonology proceed in tandem, in Slave the linear ordering of affixes represents phonological rule domains but does not readily account for word formation.

The model that I propose accounts for these properties as follows.

1. The conjunct morphemes are functional items which head phrasal projections. Following work by Pollock (1989), Chomsky (1988), Speas (1990, 1991), and others, they occur as syntactic objects outside of the verb phrase, and thus outside of any elements that might be construed to be derivational. Inflection thus is outside of derivation.[6]
2. The ordering of morphemes within the conjunct portion of the verb reflects the ordering expected based on scopal properties or relevance to the verb. Position classes are unnecessary as ordering is based on general principles related to scope.
3. Nonadjacent dependencies are accounted for by treating discontinuous constituents as syntactic objects, in the sense of DiSciullo and Williams (1988): they are phrasal units that are listed in the lexicon. Morphological violations of adjacency thus are only superficial.
4. Phonological domains are determined by mapping of syntactic structure onto prosodic structure. Phonological structure is thus directly related to syntactic structure.

4. THE SYNTAX OF THE SLAVE VERB

Convention has it that in polysynthetic languages the word takes over the function of the sentence. In generative grammar, one approach to the problem of polysynthetic languages is to claim that a word in such languages actually is a sentence (e.g., Anderson, 1982, 1988; Baker, 1988; Chomsky, 1988; DiSciullo and Williams, 1988; Speas, 1990). In this section, I explore the possibility that the Athabaskan verb is phrasally rather than lexically formed. I argue that the traditionally termed disjunct morphemes are lexical items and the conjunct morphemes functional items. Following Pollock (1989) and Chomsky (1988) among others, I suggest that the functional items project independent positions in the syntax, heading phrasal projections.[7]

4.1. The Functional Nature of the Conjunct Morphemes

As discussed in Section 2.2, determining which morphemes are inflectional or functional in Slave is not entirely straightforward. In this section, I argue that the traditional disjunct morphemes are lexical items and the conjunct morphemes functional items. In making this argument, I assume that the lexical/functional contrast can be established in several ways. First, functional items are syntactically active while lexical items are not.[8] In determining which items are syntactically active, I follow Anderson (1982, 1988), who argues that syntactically active items show configurational, agreement, inherent (e.g., gender), and phrasal properties. Second, functional items are obligatory, being marked each time a category to which they apply appears (Anderson, 1982; Bybee, 1985: 27). Lexical items, on the other hand, are not obligatory in this sense. Third, functional items can combine to form portmanteau morphemes with more than one element of meaning in a single entry. Lexical items do not combine with each other or with functional items. See Anderson (1988) for discussion. Finally, functional classes are generally closed classes while lexical classes tend to be open.

Given these criteria, the following morphemes in Slave can be considered to be functional.

1. Pronominal agreement. Saxon (1986) argues that the pronominal elements of Dogrib, a language closely related to Slave, represent agreement between a noun phrase and the clausal element on which it depends syntactically. She additionally argues that pronominal inflection is obligatory, even when a specified noun is present, and that nouns are arguments rather than adjuncts. Given these characteristics, she concludes that the pronominal elements represent agreement and thus are functional. A similar argument is made by Speas (1989) for most pronominal elements in Navajo. Given the similarities between Dogrib and Slave, I believe that Saxon's arguments based on relevance to the syntax and obligatori-

ness can be extended to Slave as well. In addition, as discussed in Section 2.1, the subject markers at least conflate with aspect morphemes to yield portmanteau forms, another diagnostic of their functional nature.

2. PRIMARY ASPECT. Anderson (1982) points out that tense/aspect play an important role syntactically, so one might expect these morphemes to be of syntactic relevance. There are positive reasons in Slave to consider the primary aspect morphemes as inflectional. First, cooccurrence restrictions are found between primary aspect and aspectual category-assigning morphemes which follow the verb root: if the verb stem is optative, then the morpheme optative must be present in primary aspect position, and so on. Second, cooccurrence restrictions are found with other postverbal material. For instance, the imperfective verb combines with the postverbal particle *gha* to yield a future. The optative combines with the postverbal *sáná* to give a prohibitive meaning. If the postverbal particles are regarded as higher predicates (see Rice, 1989), it is possible to view this as selection of primary aspect by a higher verb, a configurational property. Third, primary aspect is an obligatory part of the verb, again an indication that it is functional. Finally, the subject and primary aspect morphemes combine to form portmanteau morphs, suggesting that each of the components is functional.

3. CONJUGATION. Two facts suggest the functional nature of the conjugation morphemes. First, these morphemes are obligatory. Second, they combine with primary aspect and subject in unpredictable ways, suggesting that a single morpheme may include the meaning conjugation, primary aspect, and subject. Again, since functional morphemes form portmanteaus only with other functional items, this suggests that these morphemes must be functional.

4. SECONDARY ASPECT. These morphemes show cooccurrence restrictions with temporal adverbs that are clearly outside of the verb, and they are required in order to yield the particular meaning. For instance, the inceptive, which marks a point in time, does not occur with an adverb indicating a span of time. In addition, some of these morphemes combine in unexpected ways phonologically with the conjugation markers and subject pronouns. These combinations can be treated as portmanteau morphemes, providing evidence for their inflectional nature.

5. GENDER. The morphemes that I have labeled gender (those normally termed derivational) have some nonlocal correlates, as discussed in Section 2.1. Given this, these morphemes appear to be functional. In addition, they show the same patterns of combination with conjugation and primary aspect as the secondary aspect morphemes. While these morphemes have nonlocal properties, they are not found with every verb that has a particular item as an argument (e.g., 'go into water' does not occur with the *n*). The gender morphemes appear to have been productively inflectional historically, showing regular agreement with an argument of the verb; however, it is not clear that this is the case synchronically. Finally, the gender morphemes, like the secondary aspect morphemes, can combine in unpredictable ways with the conjugation markers and subject pronouns, form-

ing portmanteau morphs. I consider gender morphemes to be functional, understanding that problems exist with this definition. See also Section 5 for discussion.

The other primary candidates for functional status are the distributive and iterative morphemes. These morphemes are aspectual in meaning and thus might be expected to be inflectional. However, unlike the primary and secondary aspect morphemes, these morphemes are not obligatory with a particular meaning, a criterion identified by Anderson and Bybee as important for inflection. For instance, the iterative meaning can be expressed simply by stem choice, and the iterative morpheme need not be present in the verb word. This can be seen in (5).

(5) *nidį́dhah* ' s/he picked up plural objects'
ninadį́dheh, nidį́dheh 's/he picked up plural objects repeatedly'

The first line is not an iterative form. In the second line, the first word includes the iterative morpheme *na,* while this morpheme is absent in the second word, with iterative meaning contributed solely by the verb stem. In the case of imperfective, perfective, and optative, or primary aspect morphemes, these morphemes are obligatory and aspect is not determinable by stem form alone. By the criterion of obligatoriness, then, the iterative does not qualify as functional.

The distributive morpheme is like the iterative morpheme in that the meaning of distributivity can be given solely by stem form or by choice of conjugation.

(6) *náneyihkwa* 'I whipped it' (*y* conjugation)
náyánehkwa, nánehkwa 'I whipped it repeatedly' (*w* conjugation)

In the distributive examples on the second line, the distributive meaning can be expressed only through the choice of the *w* conjugation marker, as in the second form; the nondistributive reading is assigned to the form with the *y* conjugation marker given on the first line. Thus, while the iterative and distributive morphemes are aspectual semantically, the fact that they are optional suggests that they are not functional.

In order to complete this survey of the verb, I will comment on the status of the voice elements. These morphemes do not appear to be functional. Voice and transitivity markings are not obligatory in that, while every verb must contain a voice element, this element does not always have a grammatical function. While the *h* voice element marks transitives and the *d* passives, *h* need not be present in transitives and *d* need not be present in passives. Furthermore, *h* can be present in intransitives and *d* in nonpassives. For instance, the transitive verb 'kick' (stem *ta*) has a ∅ voice element while the intransitive verb 'dual go' (stem *the*) has an *h* voice element. These morphemes show the types of idiosyncrasies associated with derivational morphology rather than with inflection.[9] I thus assume that the voice element combines with the verb stem lexically, with voice and transitivity alternations determined in the lexicon. See also McDonough (1990), Speas (1991).

So far, I have proposed that the pronominal agreement markers, primary and secondary aspect, conjugation, and gender are functional. When the verb structure as a whole is examined, a striking property is evident: these are exactly the morphemes that fall in the conjunct portion of the verb word. The disjunct/conjunct distinction thus can be seen as reducing to a distinction between lexical categories (disjunct morphemes, stems) and functional categories (conjunct morphemes).

4.2. The Ordering of the Functional Items

So far I have argued that the conjunct morphemes can be viewed as functional. I now address the ordering of these elements, examining whether their ordering is a language-particular property or follows from more general principles.

An assumption may be made that the order of morphemes at the level of logical form is a reflection of scopal properties (e.g., Baker, 1988; Speas, 1991). The order of morphemes must directly reflect scopal relations or must be mappable to the scopal ordering. If a language does not have movement at logical form, one might expect the syntactic ordering of morphemes to be a direct reflection of scope. With this hypothesis in mind, I turn to an examination of the ordering of the functional elements in Slave. I use the term SCOPE in the following discussion; by this I mean something similar in nature to Bybee's (1985) term RELEVANCE TO THE VERB.

When the position of the verb stem is ignored, the following order of morphemes is found.

(7) DO–gender–secondary aspect–conjugation/primary aspect–subject

The subject morpheme, which occurs on the right edge of the inflectional complex in Slave, can be viewed as being relevant to an entire sentence (e.g., Speas, 1991); if ordering is a consequence of scope, one might expect to find it appearing on an edge. Aspect may be seen as having scope over the verb and the direct object. In Slave, primary aspect is required in every verb while secondary aspect is not, and some secondary aspects occur with a restricted range of primary aspects; it thus appears that primary aspect may have scope over secondary aspect. Gender in Slave generally represents concord with nonagentive thematic roles, or nonsubjects, so it is not unreasonable to think of this morpheme as having scope over the direct object, but not over other functional material. Finally, the direct object has scope only over the verb itself.

Based on these criteria, the ordering of the Slave functional morphemes appears to be a consequence of their scopal properties. Strikingly, the order found in Slave does not appear to be unique to Slave. In recent work on the ordering of functional elements, Speas (1991) examines six languages (English, French, Modern Greek, Finnish, Basque, Navajo), finding the morpheme order in (8) to be constant across languages.[10]

(8) subject agreement–tense–aspect–object agreement–voice–verb

The languages discussed by Speas do not have gender within the verb, so the models are not directly comparable. However, it is notable that the order of functional elements in Slave may not be unique to this language but may be found cross-linguistically. If this is true, a language-particular statement of scopal relationships is unnecessary and the order of functional items in Slave can be seen to follow from a theory of scopal ordering that is part of universal grammar.

4.3. The Structure of the Functional Complex

Assuming that the functional morphemes project phrasally, I propose the structure in (9) for the Slave verb.

(9)

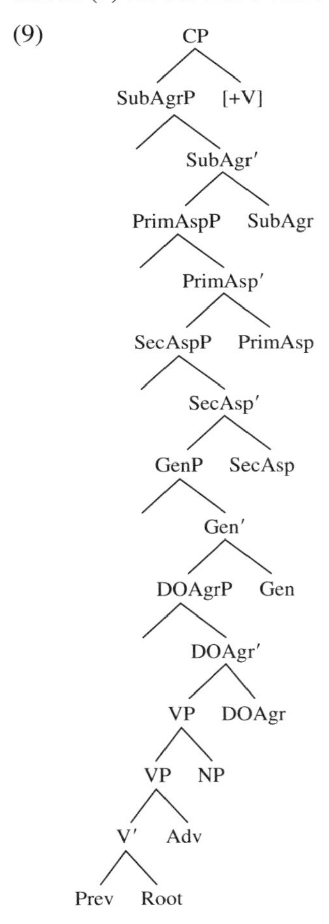

Certain aspects of this structure require comment. First, the functional categories are hierarchically arrayed above the verb phrase, with morphemes of greater scope being higher than morphemes within their scope. Scope relationships are thus structurally encoded. The ordering of Subject Agreement at the top of the tree follows from this assumption. The verb phrase, as required by the scopal ordering principle, is subordinate to the functional categories, appearing at the bottom of the tree. Second, within the verb phrase, the head of the verb phrase is indicated as a root, without category. Evidence for this comes from the fact that many nouns and verbs share a root, with category status achieved through suffixation. This root has syntactic properties in that it specifies an argument structure, but is also a morphological entity in that it lacks category features. The category features are present as the head of CP.[11] This element is a syntactic head but is morphologically subcategorized for by the root. In order for the root to receive its category features, it must raise into head position, or to CP, by X^0 movement. Following Baker and Hale (1990), I assume that functional heads do not serve as barriers for movement, and the root stops when it reaches an element marked [+V]; in other words, it stops when it receives category features, satisfying its morphological subcategorization frame. In this way, the discrepancy between (1) and (9) is accounted for: the root moves from its syntactic position in the verb phrase to its surface position in CP in order to receive a category. The output of X^0 movement is shown in (10). Traces of moved items and material in specifier positions are omitted.

(10)

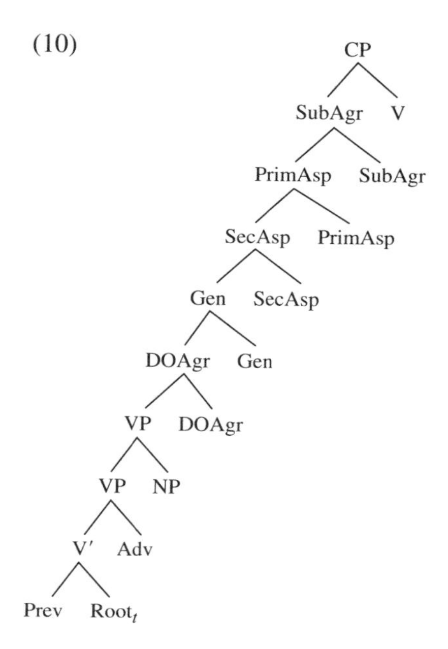

A consequence of raising is that the functional heads and the verb achieve single word status, forming a complex word (notice the absence of phrasal levels in the derived structure for the functional categories); the linear string resembles that in the template in (1).

4.4. The Structure of the VP

So far I have largely ignored the internal structure of the verb phrase. The lowest functional category takes as its complement the verb phrase. The morphemes that are within the verb phrase in Slave are the root and the disjunct morphemes (preverbs, distributive and iterative adverb, incorporates). The structure of this part of the verb is included in (9); see Rice (1991b) for details. I assume that each of the elements of the VP is itself a word, that is, these elements do not form a single lexical item.

The noun phrase that is daughter of VP is the direct object. I assume that this noun phrase generally moves into Specifier of Object Agreement position. In certain cases, which I will not attempt to account for here, it remains within the verb phrase, giving the effect of noun incorporation. I posit a single VP-internal adverb position for the iterative and distributive morphemes; see Rice (1991b) for details. I treat these adverbs as daughters of a phrasal rather than an X^0 projection: they are involved in the selection of functional items which are not strictly adjacent. If they were part of the verb root (i.e., X^0), they would be expected to select only strictly locally within the word. The preverbs also appear to be lexical categories which are not part of the root. They do not have syntactic correlates in the way the functional items do. Some preverbs may occur as separate lexical items independent of the verb word. For instance, the preverb *dah* 'above, located on top' can occur as an independent postposition, as in the phrase *shíh dage* 'on top of the mountain, located on top of the mountain'. The preverb *ʔóné* 'away from' occurs as a postposition, as in the postpositional phrases *shíh ʔóné* 'beyond the mountain' or *yahʔóné* 'over there'. I treat the preverbs as daughters of V′.

The ordering of morphemes within the VP can perhaps be seen as following from universal properties of scope, just as the ordering of the functional items can be. See Rice (1991b) for discussion. Thus templatic ordering becomes unnecessary for the verb overall, as an overarching principle exists that determines the order in which the morphemes come.

Restrictions exist on the content of incorporates within the verb phrase. Stems can be incorporated (i.e., need not move into Specifier of Direct Object Agreement position), even possessed nouns with an agreement pronoun as possessor; however, heavier noun phrases are not possible, and must occur in Spec of DOAgr. A similar restriction holds of preverbs: a modified preverb is not allowed within the verb phrase. The reasons for such restrictions are beyond the scope of this article.

4.5. Summary

In this section, I have developed a proposal of Speas (1990) for the structure of the verb. I have suggested that the ordering of inflection inside of derivation is a surface phenomenon only; Slave is not highly marked in requiring that inflection not be syntactically accessible. This result is achieved by treating the verb complex as syntactic, as follows from the assumption that morphemes with syntactic properties are syntactically accessible. The Athabaskan verb need not be templatic, as the ordering of morphemes results from scope relationships. Thus, this treatment allows for the elimination of a number of problematic areas that make the verb highly marked among languages.

A major problem that remains to be accounted for is that of phonological domains. Before turning to this problem, I would like to remark briefly on the underlying representation of verbs.

5. THE UNDERLYING REPRESENTATION OF THE VERB

As discussed in Section 2.5, the basic lexical entry of a verb obligatorily includes a voice element and a root. I assume that the voice element is combined with the root lexically, with voice and transitivity alternations determined in the lexicon; see Section 4.1 for discussion. The minimal lexical entry of a verb is thus as shown in (11).

(11) voice–root$]_{\text{Root}}$

More complex lexical entries exist, as illustrated in Section 2.5. Preverbs and other morphemes can occur within the verb theme. In such cases, the meaning is defined on the entry as a whole, not on individual morphemes. For instance, in the verb theme *n-h-ji* 'scare' it is not possible to assign meanings to the individual elements of the theme. In such structures, the assumption made in the Athabaskan literature has been that these are single words (see, e.g., Kari, Randoja, Rice, Speas, Wright, and many others). However, an alternative solution is available. DiSciullo and Williams (1988), in a study of English phrasal idioms, suggest that these idioms are syntactic objects that are listed in the lexicon. The idioms are like words in that their meanings are noncompositional but differ from words in being phrasal. I propose that the discontinuous verb themes in Slave entries should be considered as comparable to English phrasal idioms. (12) gives an example.

(12) $[h]_{\text{voice}}\,[ti]_{\text{Root}}\,[ya]_{\text{Preverb}}$ 'preach, bark'

Each morpheme is labeled for category. When this phrasal unit is inserted into the larger syntactic structure, the morphemes are correctly placed. No further stipulation of position is required, as it is a direct consequence of the phrasal structure, which in turn is predicted from scopal properties.

Lexical entries can also include gender material and direct objects. For instance, the verb 'scare' has a gender morpheme and 'tell a lie' a direct object that must occur with the verb stem.[12]

(13) $[h]_{\text{voice}}\ [ji]_{\text{Root}}\ [n]_{\text{gender}}$ 'scare'
$[ts'i]_{\text{Root}}\ [go]_{\text{DO}}$ '(tell a) lie'

By treating discontinuous verb themes as idiomatic, the benefits achieved by the analysis proposed here can be maintained. Slave may be unusual in the number of phrasal idioms it has, but the construct is not in and of itself unexpected.

6. THE PHONOLOGICAL STRUCTURE OF THE SLAVE VERB

So far, I have suggested that the Slave verb is phrasal in origin and is not a lexical construct. However, the verb is a single unit phonologically, as has long been recognized in the Athabaskan literature. This status is achieved partly through raising, which creates an X^0 level of the functional complex and stem. I suggest in this section that word status is also achieved through mapping to prosodic domains.

6.1. Evidence for Domains of Rule Application

As discussed in Section 2.4, the verb in Slave (and in Athabaskan languages in general) is generally conceived as being divided into a number of phonological domains (e.g., Hargus, 1988; Kari, 1976; Randoja, 1989; Rice, 1989). The major domains are the disjunct (lexical) morphemes, the conjunct (functional) morphemes, and the stems; the functional items themselves divide into two domains. In this section I briefly outline the types of phonological evidence that distinguish these domains; more extensive discussion of evidence for domains in Slave is found in Rice (1992).

The functional and lexical domains differ in several ways, with lexical items sharing properties with stems and functional items having unique properties. One difference between these morphemes is in canonical phonological form. The lexical morphemes and stems have the following properties.

(14) a. They can begin with any consonant in the underlying inventory.
b. They can contain any vowel.
c. These morphemes can have the form CV(C) and CVCV(C). Generalizing, they each constitute a prosodic foot.

The functional items, on the other hand, show a more limited range of properties.

(15) a. They can begin with only a subset of the underlying consonants.
b. They generally contain the vowel [e], although [i], [a], [u] are possible. [e] can be treated as epenthetic, and thus most conjunct morphemes can be viewed as having the canonical shape C. (See Randoja, 1989, for detailed discussion.)

A second major difference between lexical and functional morphemes is in their conditioning of prefixal alternants. Functional items combine freely with each other but show little combination with lexical morphemes. Lexical items, on the other hand, generally pattern as independent words, only rarely combining with functional items or with each other. To give but one example, the second person singular subject can be viewed as having the underlying representation /n/. When it follows a functional element, it surfaces as nasalization on the preceding vowel; when it is word-initial or follows a lexical element, it surfaces in the form /ne/. The process accounting for this surface allomorphy is generally described as epenthesis if no syllable is present on the functional domain.[13] Numerous other phonological processes define these domains. A third type of evidence for phonological domains comes from edges. For instance, closed syllables are found only in certain locations in the Slave verb: at the edge of a lexical item, at the edge of an agreement morpheme, or word finally, defining the same domains as defined by phonological rules. I assume the correctness of these domains (see Rice, 1992 for details) and consider the question of how they are determined.

6.2. Deriving the Domains

Rule domains in the verb have been accounted for with boundaries (1) or diacritics marking the level at which a morpheme is attached (e.g., Hargus, 1988; Randoja, 1989; Rice, 1989). In all cases, the entry of each nonstem morpheme includes, in addition to phonological and semantic information, a statement of its level of affixation. In this section, I propose a rather different account of the phonological domains, one in which the domains are derived by inspection of the syntactic structure. The domains thus are not primitive, as in the other theories, but are derived.

Different types of phonological domains must be derived from the structure in (10). First, the traditional verb word is a single domain phonologically. Second, lexical morphemes each pattern phonologically as separate items and must be defined as such within the larger verb word. Third, functional morphemes and the stem pattern as a single item, and finally agreement morphemes, both subject and direct object, form the edges of domains.

In order to derive the phonological domains, I appeal to the literature on the derivation of phonological domains from syntactic structures. It has been argued that phonological rules operate in prosodically rather than morphologically or syntactically defined domains. See, for instance, Selkirk (1986), Nespor and Vogel (1986), Hayes (1989), and many of the papers in Inkelas and Zec (1990). Selkirk (1986) proposes that syntactic domains are mapped onto phonological domains by an algorithm that refers to edges of syntactic constituents. She argues that a phonological domain may be determined by seeking out an edge, right or left, of a category of the X-bar hierarchy, X or X^{max}. Hale and Selkirk (1986) add a further parameter, arguing that languages may refer to functional and lexical categories as well as to edge and level.

I propose that phonological domains in Slave are read off the derived syntactic structures as follows. The verb word, which I refer to as the PHONOLOGICAL PHRASE, is defined by marking the right edge of X^{max}, where X is a functional category. This defines the right edge of CP as a single word. Items preceding the verb word are in their own functional projections (e.g., DP) and form their own phonological phrases. Since the surface structure of the verb contains no other maximal functional projections, the entire verb word is included in the phonological phrase. Within the phonological phrase, words are determined by marking the right edge of X^0, where X is lexical. Lexical categories include preverb, adverb, noun, verb, and postposition. Noun, verb, and preverb are likely lexical categories universally; for the others it may be necessary to list as part of the basic lexical entry that they are lexical. This information is needed for the morphosyntax and is available to the phonology. Marking the right edge of lexical X^0 defines each disjunct item as a word, as accords with traditional treatments. The functional items plus the verb stem form a word on their own. Finally, what I call SMALL WORDS are defined by marking the right edge of agreement. Thus the direct objects and the span of morphemes from gender through subject form small words within a word. The isolation of agreement is an unusual feature of this analysis. The treatment of agreement as distinct from other inflection is not a characteristic of just Slave; Dresher (this volume) argues that Old English agreement is distinct from inflection such as number, gender, and person marking, and he defines a level which includes all inflection except for agreement.

The settings for the derivation of phonological domains are summarized in (16).

(16) a. right edge of X^{max}, X is functional—phonological phrase
b. right edge of X^0, X is lexical (noun, verb, adverb, postposition)—word
c. right edge of agreement—small word

In (17), a sample bracketed S-structure is given, with the derived phonological domains indicated beneath it.

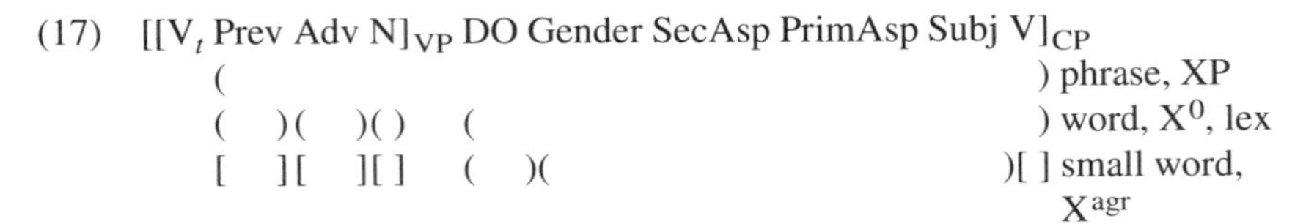

(17) [[V_t Prev Adv N]_VP DO Gender SecAsp PrimAsp Subj V]_CP
( ) phrase, XP
( )( )( ) ( ) word, X0, lex
[ ][ ][ ] ( )( )[ ] small word, Xagr

Assuming the strict layer hypothesis (e.g., Hayes, 1989; Nespor and Vogel, 1986; Selkirk, 1980), each word constitutes a small word (marked with square brackets). This hypothesis requires that (1) a given nonterminal unit of the prosodic hierarchy, X^p, is composed of one or more units of the immediately lower category, X^{p-1}, and (2) a unit of a given level of the prosodic hierarchy is exhaustively contained in the superordinate unit of which it is a part (Nespor and Vogel, 1986: 7). If the words do not contain small words, then the first condition of the strict layer hypothesis is not met. Small words cannot span words by the second condition of hypothesis.

Many processes reveal the need for these domains; I mention only a few. The small word is motivated by restrictions on the distribution of closed syllables.[14] Preverbs and incorporated stems can end in a consonant; the reciprocal morpheme, a direct object, is consonant-final, *ʔeɬéh*; and in subject agreement position the first person singular *h* and the second person plural *ah* are consonant-final. Stems can also be consonant-final. Consonant-final morphemes thus occur only at the edge of a small word. The small word is also the domain of syllabification. It is also necessary to account for the fact that certain phonological processes occur only within the small word and not between small words; specifically, direct objects pattern with the lexical morphemes in certain ways. The word is required to account for numerous phonological processes that happen within the conjunct domain. The word forms the domain of foot formation (the minimum prosodic word) and of the numerous rules of Slave that make reference to the foot, including extra-high tone formation, conjugation tone mapping, voicing assimilation, vowel assimilation, and others (Rice, 1991a). Finally, various processes occur within the phonological phrase. For instance, the edge of the phonological phrase defines the environment for insertion of a glottal stop after a high-tone vowel; tone displacement in Hare (Rice, 1991a) has the phonological phrase as its domain. Some of these processes are summarized in (18).

(18) PHONOLOGICAL PHRASE: domain of syllabification, minimal word constraints, glottal epenthesis, assimilation to quality of a vowel
WORD: /a/ raising, foot-based processes, assimilation to nasality of a vowel
SMALL WORD: rhymal constraints

The Slave phonological domains follow from independently required structural properties of morphemes (category) coupled with the end-based theory and need not be encoded independently in the representation of each morpheme.

7. SUMMARY

I have argued, contrary to the usual hypothesis that the verb in Slave is a lexical construct, that the verb "word" in Slave is phrasal, with its single word status being a consequence of raising and mapping to prosodic structure. A lexical entry can be a single word or a phrasal idiom, consisting of more than one word. The ordering of morphemes is predictable based on scope relations, or relevance to the verb, with the actual ordering differing from the underlying order largely in the position of the verb root. In order to derive the surface position of the root, I suggested that raising moves it from its position within the verb phrase in order to assign it category status.

The traditional single 'word' status of the verb in Slave is in this account a derived property. The end-based algorithm defines the verb as a single unit by seeking out the right edge of phrasal projections of functional categories. The phonological domains within the word are determined by first marking the right edge of major category lexical items and second marking the right edge of agreement morphemes. The verb "word" is thus not a lexical construct but a phonological one, and verb affixes are syntactically words.

8. COMPARISON WITH LEXICAL PHONOLOGY

How does this model compare with lexical phonology? Different assumptions are made in the theories, so in some sense they are not comparable. For instance, in many versions of the theory of lexical phonology, word formation takes place entirely in the lexicon, so given the status of the verb as a single word phonologically, the hypothesis in lexical phonology is that it is formed in the lexicon (Hargus, 1988). Second, some of the characteristics of the verb that I have identified as unusual are not issues in lexical phonology; for instance, it is not claimed that there is a relationship between the ordering of levels and the position of derivational and inflectional morphology. The need for a template is not necessarily marked within lexical phonology as the template can simply be viewed as an extension of the notion of ordering of levels to ordering within levels. Despite the fact that the two theories are in many ways incommensurate, I believe that the model proposed in this article enjoys some advantages. First, it allows for an account of the ordering of morphemes, with functional items outside of lexical items and perhaps with ordering within these categories itself being a consequence of scope or relevance to the verb. In the lexical phonology model, the ordering of morphemes both on and within levels must be stated in the grammar. Second, it makes Slave look more like other languages where inflection is syntactically accessible in an outer layer of the word. While this is not particularly a concern of lexical phonology, it still might be viewed as an advantage that such an account is possible. Third, the rule domains are derived and need not be stipulated as part of the lexical entry of each morpheme. The marking of morphemes as belonging to a particular level has been an issue of controversy in lexical phonology (see Goldsmith, 1990, for an overview), and the issue disappears if rule domains are derived. Fourth, something I have not dealt with in depth, the phonological rules apply on the derived prosodic domains; the same rules are available everywhere and it is the segmental and metrical makeup of the domain that makes the results different in the different domains. Thus the fact that the stem and the disjunct prefixes share similar rules is not surprising [as it is in lexical phonology, as this appears to be a violation of either the strong domain hypothesis (Kiparsky, 1984) or the continuous stratum hypothesis (Mohanan, 1986)]—they share properties because their segmental and metrical properties are similar, and these properties are similar because they are major-category lexical items as opposed to functional items. In a lexical phonology model, some of the basic tenets of lexical phonology must be rejected since rules apply to discontinuous domains.

What general conclusions can be drawn with respect to lexical phonology? This is a difficult question to answer, as I have suggested that a language that appears to have complex morphology, and thus appears to be a good test case for lexical phonology, does not in fact have complex morphology. The surface complexities in the morphology result from derived rather than underlying properties. Thus, any conclusions regarding the interaction of phonology and morphology in word formation say nothing at all about lexical phonology. However, the Slave findings perhaps force a reevaluation of other languages that look particularly troublesome for lexical phonology. If they receive similar reanalyses, it may be that languages in which word formation is truly morphological rather than resulting from phonological domain assignment are in fact well accounted for by the model.

The phonological model that is briefly described in this paper also can be viewed as providing support for some of the tenets of lexical phonology. Kiparsky (1984) proposes the strong domain hypothesis, which allows the grammar of a language to stipulate where a rule ceases to apply, but not to turn a rule on. All rules are thus potentially applicable at the first level and apply there if permitted by other principles such as the strict cycle condition and structure preservation. In the model that I have proposed, this is precisely the case: all rules are applicable at the small word and fail to apply there if their structural description is not met (i.e., the foot is not present yet) or if they violate structure preservation (e.g., insertion of glottal stop at the edge of a phonological phrase). Thus, in a sense this model supports many of the principles of lexical phonology.

9. CONCLUSION

The model of verb structure that I have developed in this article is meant to set out a research program, and as such it inevitably raises more questions than it answers. First, certain problems particular to Slave (and to the Athabaskan family) have not been discussed. For instance, I have ignored the deictic subjects, and restrictions on incorporates have not been accounted for. The phonological mechanism required for ordering some of the morphemes within the small word is not discussed. The model forces noun phrases to be analyzed as determiner phrases; the evidence for this must be explored. Details of domain phonology need to be worked out: while much of the phonology operates quite straightforwardly off metrical structure built within the words defined by the prosodic algorithm, some problems are found. In addition to these kinds of language-particular problems, many other problems with the account remain. Much of what I have proposed about the syntactic structure is highly speculative, and far more detailed arguments must be developed for the position outlined here. I have made use of scope for the ordering of morphemes; just what is meant by scope remains to be worked out. The claim that scopal ordering is a universal property also requires considerable investigation. I have argued for a syntactic model; however, much of what I have said about the phonology could also follow from a lexical treatment of word formation where the verb had a lexical structure similar to the syntactic structure that I have proposed, so the account of verb formation is quite independent of the account offered of the phonology. The treatment of agreement as special by the phonology requires explanation; at this point it serves only to describe the observable facts.

Despite these problems, the approach taken in this article seems highly promising. It makes the Athabaskan languages less bizarre in their formal properties and more like better understood languages. It also lends some strength to many tenets of the theory of lexical phonology. This conclusion is promising and is definitely worthy of further exploration.

ACKNOWLEDGMENTS

I have several people to thank for their helpful discussion of this article: Leslie Saxon, Peggy Speas, Eloise Jelinek, Sharon Hargus, Elizabeth Cowper, Diane Massam, Aryeh Faltz, the participants in the lexical phonology conference, and the reviewer of an earlier version of the article.

NOTES

[1] Inkelas (1989) proposes a version of lexical phonology in which cases of lack of isomorphism receive an account.

[2] In Rice (1989) I identified a number of different aspectual morphemes of the form *í-* and two of the form *n-*. The *í-* morphemes include semelfactive (action performed a single time), seriative (segmented action), and transitional; the *n-* morphemes are completive and inchoative. Kari (1989) argues that the particular aspectual meaning carried by these morphemes is a property of the semantics of the verb as a whole and is not a result of the existence of numerous homophonous affixes. I adopt this position here.

[3]I use orthography in most cases. The following symbols should be noted. *gh* is voiced velar fricative, *dh* a voiced dental fricative, *th* a voiceless dental fricative, an acute accent represents a high tone, a hook under a vowel represents nasalization. The symbol *ñ*, a palatal nasal, is an abstract representation for a morpheme which may surface as a high front vowel, as nasalization on a vowel, or as voicing on a continuant, depending on phonological and morphological context.

[4]*w-* is the reflex in Hare, a Slave dialect, of **s*; and *y-* is the reflex of **gh*.

[5]It is interesting that inflectional and derivational affixes also appear in a marked order in the Slave noun. In particular, the inflectional morpheme indicating possessive agreement is phonologically closer to the stem than the derivational augmentative and diminutive morphemes. See Rice (1991a) for some discussion.

[6]The inflection/derivation question disappears in some ways since I treat the verb as phrasal rather than lexical in nature. The so-called derivational items are treated as lexical categories and the inflectional items as functional categories.

[7]This position thus represents an abandonment of the strong version of the lexicalist hypothesis, which requires that all word formation take place in the lexicon. Instead, inflectional morphology is part of syntax proper and lexical operations are restricted to derivational morphology. This assumption alone rules out the type of lexical phonology model proposed by Hargus (1988), as in that model the verb word is formed in its entirety in the lexicon.

[8]I use the term FUNCTIONAL where Anderson (1982, 1988) uses the term INFLECTIONAL.

[9]In addition, the classifiers have unique phonological properties.

[10]This ordering is similar to that found by Bybee (1985) in her survey of morpheme ordering in fifty languages; however, Bybee's survey is based on surface morpheme order and Speas's on a more abstract underlying order, so they are not directly comparable.

[11]The rudiments of this analysis come from work by Palma dos Santos (1991).

[12]It is useful to summarize the types of word formation found in the Slave verb. First, voice elements can be added to the root in the lexicon. Otherwise no lexical word formation is found. Syntactic "word formation" arises from the operation of Raising. Finally, as discussed in Section 6, phonological "word formation" results from the imposition of prosodic structure on the syntactic structure.

[13]This process is also often thought of as deletion on the functional domain (e.g., Rice, 1989). Whether epenthesis or deletion is the preferred analysis does not affect the claim that the morpheme patterns differently depending on its position in the word.

[14]Similar restrictions are found within nouns and postpositions, which also constitute small words by the definition given.

REFERENCES

Allen, M. (1978). *Morphological Investigations.* Ph.D. dissertation, University of Connecticut, Storrs.

Anderson, S. R. (1982). Where's morphology. *Linguistic Inquiry* **13,** 571–612.

Anderson, S. R. (1988). Morphological theory. In *Linguistics: The Cambridge Survey,* vol. 1, *Linguistic Theory: Foundations* (F. J. Newmeyer, ed.), 146–191.

Axelrod, M. (1990). Incorporation in Koyukon Athapaskan. *International Journal of American Linguistics* **56,** 179–195.

Baker, M. (1988). *Incorporation: A Theory of Grammatical Function Changing.* University of Chicago Press, Chicago.

Baker, M., and Hale, K. (1990). Relativized minimality and pronoun incorporation. *Linguistic Inquiry* **21,** 289–297.

Bybee, J. L. (1985). *Morphology, A Study of the Relation between Meaning and Form.* Benjamins, Philadelphia.

Chomsky, N. (1988). Some notes on economy of derivation and representation. *MIT Working Papers in Linguistics* **10,** 43–74.

DiSciullo, A.-M., and Williams, E. (1988). *On the Definition of Word* (Linguistic Inquiry Monograph 14). MIT Press, Cambridge, Mass.

Goldsmith, J. 1990. *Autosegmental and Metrical Phonology.* Blackwell, Oxford.

Hale, K., and Selkirk, E. O. (1987). Government and tonal phrasing in Papago. *Phonology Yearbook* **4,** 151–183.

Hargus, S. (1986). Phonological evidence for prefixation in Navajo verbal morphology. *Proceedings of West Coast Conference on Formal Linguistics* **5,** 53–67.

Hargus, S. (1988). *The Lexical Phonology of Sekani.* Garland, New York.

Hayes, B. (1989). The prosodic hierarchy in meter. In *Rhythm and Meter* (P. Kiparsky and G. Youmans, eds.), pp. 201–260. Academic Press, Orlando.

Inkelas, S. (1989). *Prosodic Constituency in the Lexicon.* Doctoral dissertation, Stanford University, Stanford, Calif.

Inkelas, S., and Zec, D. (1990). *The Phonology–Syntax Connection.* CSLI Publications and University of Chicago Press, Chicago.

Kari, J. (1975). The disjunct boundary in the Navajo and Tanaina verb prefix complexes. *International Journal of American Linguistics* **41,** 330–345.

Kari, J. (1976). *Navajo Verb Prefix Phonology.* Garland, New York.

Kari, J. (1979). *Athabaskan Verb Theme Categories: Ahtna* (Alaska Native Language Center Research Papers 2). Alaska Native Language Center, Fairbanks.

Kari, J. (1989). Affix positions and zones in the Athapaskan verb complex: Ahtna and Navajo. *International Journal of American Linguistics* **55,** 424–454.

Kari, J. (1990). *Ahtna Dictionary.* University of Alaska Press, Fairbanks.

Kari, J. (1992). Some concepts in Ahtna Athabaskan word formation. In *Morphology Now* (M. Aronoff, ed.), pp. 107–131. State University of New York Press, Albany.

Kiparsky, P. (1982). Lexical morphology and phonology, In *Linguistics in the Morning Calm* (I.-S. Yang, ed.), pp. 3–91. Hanshin, Seoul.

Kiparsky, P. (1984). On the lexical phonology of Icelandic. In *Nordic Prosody III* (C.-C. Elert et al., eds.), pp. 135–162. University of Umea, Umea, Sweden.

Li, F.-K. (1946). Chipewyan. In *Linguistic Structures of Native America* (H. Hoijer, ed.), pp. 398–423. Viking Fund Publications in Anthropology, New York.

Lieber, R. (1981). *On the Organization of the Lexicon.* Doctoral dissertation, Massachusetts Institute of Technology, Cambridge.

McDonough, J. (1990). *Topics in the Phonology and Morphology of Navajo Verbs.* Doctoral dissertation, University of Massachusetts, Amherst.

Mohanan, K. P. (1982). *Lexical Phonology.* Doctoral dissertation, Massachusetts Institute of Technology, Cambridge.

Mohanan, K. P. (1986). *The Theory of Lexical Phonology.* Reidel, Dordrecht.

Myers, S. (1987). *Tone and the Structure of Words in Shona.* Doctoral dissertation, University of Massachusetts, Amherst.

Nespor, M., and Vogel, I. (1986). *Prosodic Phonology.* Foris, Dordrecht.

Palma dos Santos, A. (1991). *Negative Inflection in the Athapaskan Verb.* Unpublished manuscript, University of Toronto.

Pollock, J-Y. (1989). Verb movement, universal grammar, and the structure of IP. *Linguistic Inquiry* **20,** 365–424.

Randoja, T. (1989). *The Phonology and Morphology of Halfway River Beaver.* Doctoral dissertation, University of Ottawa.

Rice, K. (1989). *A Grammar of Slave.* Mouton de Gruyter, Berlin.

Rice, K. (1991a). Prosodic constituency in Hare (Athapaskan): Evidence for the foot. *Lingua* **82,** 201–245.

Rice, K. (1991b). Predicting the order of the disjunct morphemes in the Athapaskan languages. *Toronto Working Papers in Linguistics* **10,** 99–121.

Rice, K. (1991c). Intransitives in Slave (Northern Athapaskan): Arguments for unaccusatives. *International Journal of American Linguistics* **57,** 51–69.

Rice, K. (1992). *On deriving rule domains: The Athapaskan case. Proceedings of West Coast Conference on Formal Linguistics* **10,** 417–430.

Sapir, E., and Hoijer, H. (1969). *The Phonology and Morphology of the Navaho Language* (University of California Publications in Linguistics 50). University of California Press, Berkeley and Los Angeles.

Saxon, L. (1986). *The Syntax of Pronouns in Dogrib (Athapaskan): Some Theoretical Consequences.* Doctoral dissertation, University of California, San Diego.

Selkirk, E. O. (1980). Prosodic domains in phonology: Sanskrit revisited. In *Juncture* (M. Aronoff and M.-L. Kean, eds.), pp. 107–129. Anma Libri, Saratoga.

Selkirk, E. O. (1986). On derived domains in sentence phonology. *Phonology Yearbook* **3,** 371–405.

Siegel, D. (1978). The adjacency constraint and the theory of morphology. *Proceedings of the North Eastern Linguistics Society* **8,** 189–197.

Speas, M. (1984). Navajo prefixes and word structure typology. *MIT Working Papers in Linguistics* **7,** 86–109.

Speas, M. (1986). *Adjunctions and Projections in Syntax.* Doctoral dissertation, MIT, Cambridge, Mass.

Speas, M. (1990). *Phrase Structure in Natural Language.* Kluwer, Dordrecht.

Speas, M. (1991). Functional heads and the Mirror Principle. *Lingua* **84,** 181–214.

Thomas-Flinders, T. (1983). *Morphological Structures.* Doctoral dissertation, University of California, Los Angeles.

Williams, E. (1981). On the notions "lexically related" and "head of a word." *Linguistic Inquiry* **12,** 245–274.

Wright, M. (1983). The CV skeleton and verb prefix phonology in Navajo. *Proceedings of the North Eastern Linguistics Society* **14,** 461–477.

Wright, M. (1986). Mapping and movement of partial matrices in Navajo. *Proceedings of the North Eastern Linguistics Society* **17,** 685–699.

LOOKING INTO WORDS

RICHARD SPROAT

Linguistics Research Department
AT&T Bell Laboratories
Murray Hill, New Jersey 07974

1. INTRODUCTION

Lexicalist theories of morphology have generally assumed some version of the notion of LEXICAL INTEGRITY, originating in Chomsky (1970). While there has been a substantial amount of disagreement about what precise range of data the principle is intended to cover and how best to handle data which appear to involve flagrant violations of it, there has been a general assumption that postlexical processes are barred from making use of information about the internal properties of words. Among the more specific views on lexical integrity is the implementation of the principle, within the theory of lexical phonology and morphology, as a special case of the more general principle of BRACKETING ERASURE (BE) (Kiparsky, 1982a; Mohanan, 1986; Pesetsky, 1979) or OPACITY (Mohanan, 1982). While various views have been expressed on how BE applies within the morphological component (see Mohanan, 1982, 1986, for descriptions of two of the differing views, and see Kiparsky, 1982b, and Hargus, 1985, for some views on how BE may fail to apply within the lexicon in some cases), it is generally agreed that it at least applies at the output of the morphological component, erasing internal brackets and thus obliterating information about the internal structure of words. Lexical integrity thus follows from BE. For example, Mohanan (1986:24–25) argues:

> Another consequence of BE, as pointed out in Pesetsky (1979), is that it derives the principle of Lexical Integrity, first proposed in Chomsky (1970). The Lexical Integrity Hypothesis says that syntactic rules cannot have access to the internal structure of words. It

Phonetics and Phonology, Volume 4
Studies in Lexical Phonology

> prevents, for example, a pronoun taking *father* in *fatherless* as its antecedent, exempts the *self* in *self-destruction* from the syntactic conditions governing anaphor binding, and prevents *-al* and *-ion* from being attached to *refuse* and *destroy* in the syntax. Given that morphological operations take place in the lexicon, and that internal brackets are erased by BE in the output of the lexicon, it follows that syntactic operations will be blind to the internal structure created by morphological operations.

In fact, given BE, not only are syntactic operations supposedly blind to morphological structure, but *all* postlexical operations are supposedly blind to such structure (Mohanan, 1986:24). I term this view the STRONG INTERPRETATION of bracketing erasure.

My purpose in this article is to tie together two rather different recent pieces of research on which I have been collaborating and to bring the data and conclusions of each to bear on the question of the status of lexical integrity and its implementation via BE. The two pieces of research concern on the one hand the sensitivity of rules of phonetic implementation to some aspects of morphological structure, and on the other the relationship between morphology and pragmatics. In both cases it will be argued that there must be some sensitivity of INTERPRETIVE COMPONENTS, such as phonetics and pragmatics, to the internal structure of words. I take what I believe to be the uncontroversial view that phonetic implementation reads off (postlexical) phonological structure, and that pragmatics—at least the part of pragmatics that deals with anaphora resolution—reads directly off semantic structure (and ultimately off syntactic structure). In particular, no "back doors" into lexical structure are assumed to exist for these components. Under that view, the sensitivity to word structure of the interpretive components in question is therefore potentially problematic for the strong interpretation of BE. I conclude the article by pointing out that the data presented are not incompatible with some recent views of the nature of BE, but that they are incompatible at least with the strong interpretation.

One point which will be clear is that the most extensive and hence persuasive evidence that interpretive components must be able to "see" inside words comes from compounding. Some authors, such as Fabb (1984), have argued that (at least some) compounding should be handled in the syntax. Indeed, the even stronger position that there is no separate morphological component, and that all morphology must therefore be done "in the syntax," has been taken in Sproat (1985) and Lieber (1991). Needless to say, under either of these approaches the most persuasive of the evidence discussed here is unproblematic. Indeed, it is consistent with any of the following possible theories.

(1) a. Compounding is done in the syntax.
    b. All morphology is done in the syntax.
    c. Morphology is done in the lexicon, but there is no BE, at least on the strong interpretation.

I turn now to a description of the data.

2. SENSITIVITY OF PHONETIC IMPLEMENTATION RULES TO LEXICAL BOUNDARIES

As part of a study of the articulatory phonetics of allophonic variation of the phoneme /l/ in English, Sproat and Fujimura (1989, 1993) investigated the effects of boundary strength on intervocalic preboundary /l/s. Specifically, we elicited a number of utterances from five speakers (four American Midwestern, one "British") in which /l/s were produced in the environment /il]ɩ/, where the first vowel was always a stressed /i/, the second vowel was always an unstressed /ɩ/ (hence the /l/s were contained within trochaic stress context), and the only variable was the linguistic boundary denoted by the left bracket. This boundary was varied over the following possibilities, where each boundary case is followed by the sentence(s) used as stimuli.

(2) a. 0 (no boundary) *Mr. Beelik wants actors/Mr. Beelik's from Madison.* (2 speakers only)
  b. + (stratum I boundary) *The beelic men are actors.*
  c. # (stratum II boundary) *The beeling men are actors.*
  d. C (compound, stratum III boundary) *The beel equator's amazing.*
  e. P (phrasal boundary separating VP internal constituents): *I gave Beel equated actors.*
  f. V (phrasal boundary separating subject from VP): *Beel equates the actors.*
  g. | (Major intonation break between an utterance-initial vocative and the remainder of the utterance): *Beel, equate the actors.*

The utterances were performed at a moderate reading rate, and all the utterances investigated were fluent productions of this type. The major conclusion of the study—which included syllable (morpheme)-initial as well as the syllable (morpheme)-final contexts mentioned above—was that the allophonic variation between syllable-initial (light) /l/s and syllable-final (dark) /l/s is not categorical. Rather the variation is continuous and is produced by a phonetic implementation function[1] whose parameters are both discrete variables—referring directly to whether the /l/ is syllable-initial or syllable-final—and continuous variables. One such continuous variable, and one which explains a great deal of the variation in preboundary /l/s, is the duration of the preboundary rime; /l/s in shorter rimes are lighter along a number of different acoustic, articulatory, and physiological dimensions than /l/s in longer rimes.

One of the findings of this investigation was that there was a good correlation between the measured acoustic duration of the preboundary rime—where this was defined as the sequence /il/, the tacit assumption being made that there was no resyllabification of the /l/ across the weaker boundaries—and an a priori linguistic notion of boundary strength; in particular, preboundary rimes before weaker

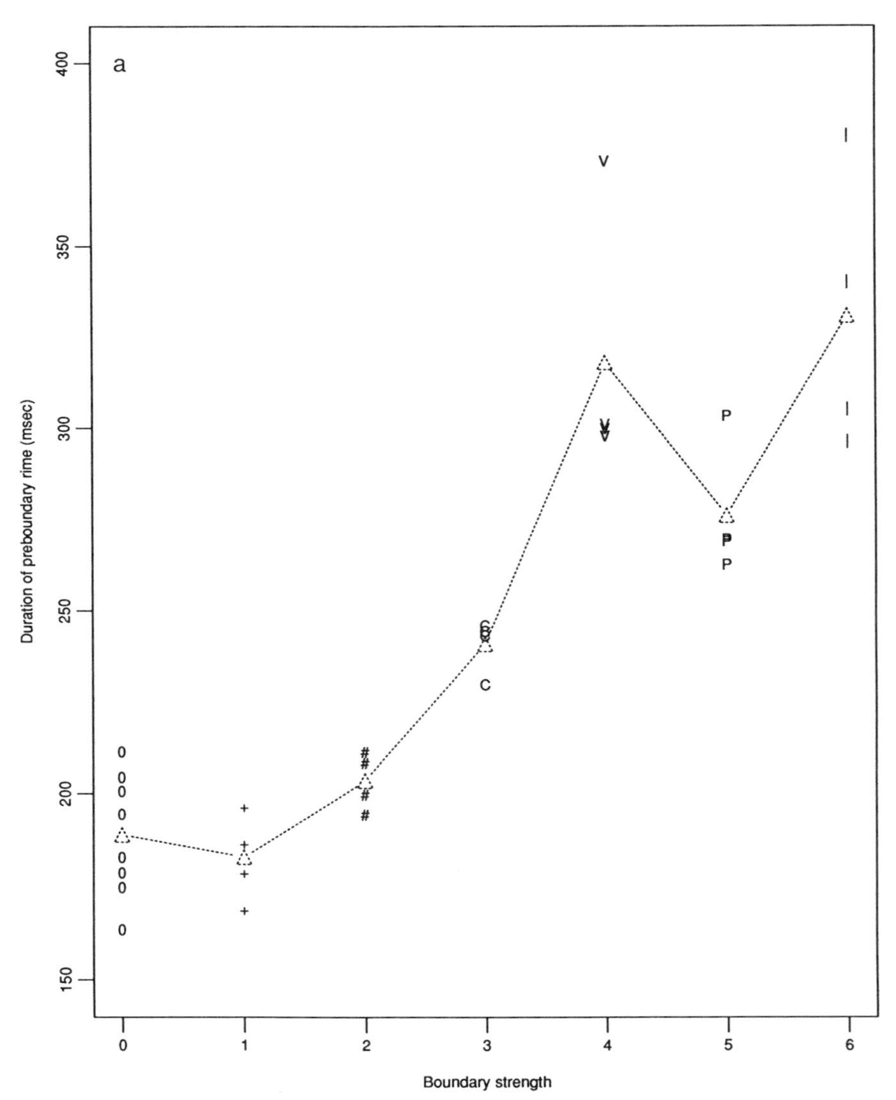

Figure 1. Sensitivity of phonetic implementation rules to boundary strength. (a), speaker CS; (b), speaker CC.

boundaries were shorter. A typical example of the variation is plotted in Figure 1a for one of the American speakers. In this figure, the *x* axis gives ad hoc numerical values for the boundaries according to an a priori sense of their relative strength. The *y* axis gives the duration of the preboundary rime as defined above, in milliseconds.

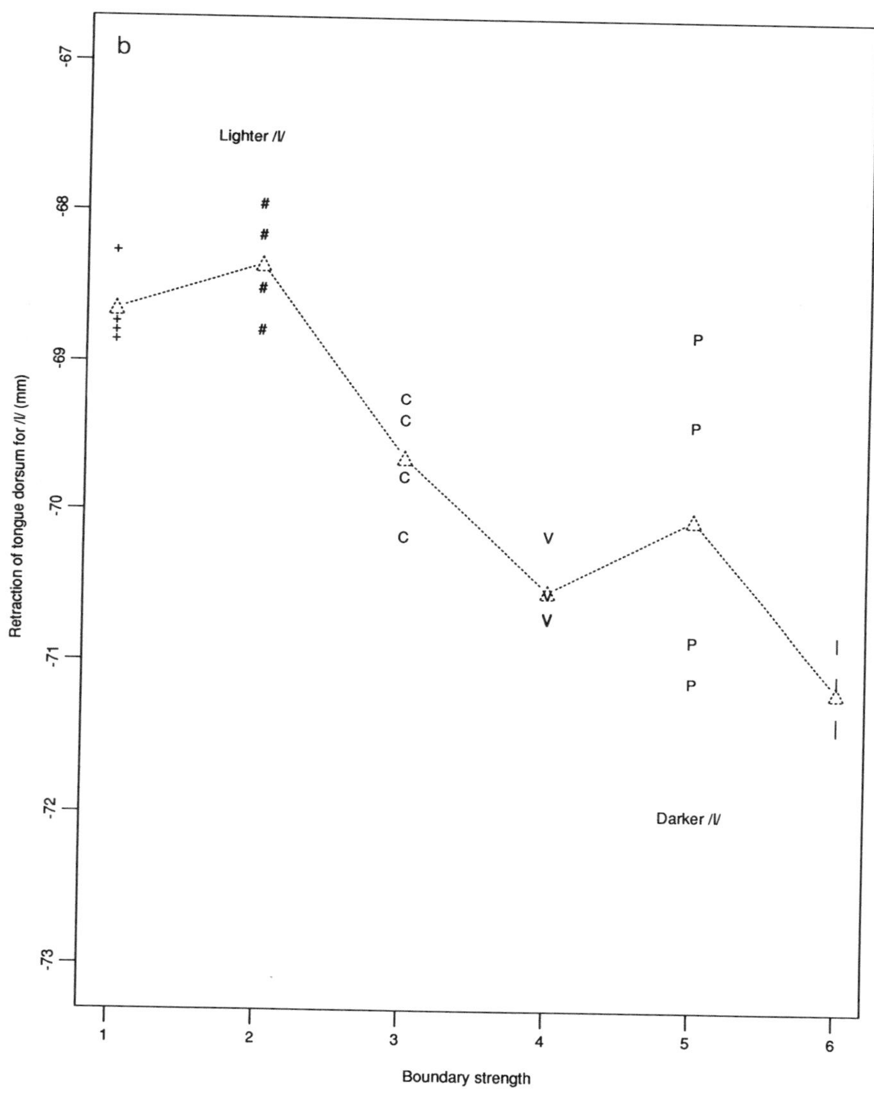

Figure 1. *Continued.*

All speakers showed similar trends, the only notable difference being in the implementation of the V and P boundary contexts, where some speakers reversed the trend shown for speaker CS, presumably because of differing intonational implementation strategies. I have, however, not done a systematic study of the intonational implementation of the phrasal cases: my primary interest for the current purposes is to discuss the lexical cases involving the boundary contexts labeled +, #, and C. There should, of course, be nothing surprising in the conclusion that phonetic implementation rules, such as those responsible for assigning duration, should be sensitive to different kinds of boundaries; see, inter alia, Lehiste (1980), Pierrehumbert and Beckman (1988), and Silverman (1988), who discuss the sensitivity of phonological implementation rules to various kinds of phrasal boundaries. However, the evidence that there is some sensitivity to word-internal contexts is perhaps somewhat novel; it is also problematic if the view is taken that word-internal boundaries are invisible to postlexical processes, assuming that phonetic implementation rules are considered to be postlexical processes (see Kiparsky, 1985, for discussion of that issue, as well as Mohanan, 1986, etc.). Nonetheless, it is clear from an examination of Figure 1a that while on the one hand rimes preceding the supposed lexical compound (C) boundary are shorter in duration than rimes preceding phrasal boundaries, they are also longer than rimes preceding other lexical boundaries. Now, for no speaker is it the case that the + or # boundary contexts show a significant difference from each other or from the no-boundary context (0). On the other hand, for every speaker (except speaker RS, whose trend is nonetheless in the required direction) the difference between the compound boundary cases and the other lexical cases is significant, as the results of a *t* test confirm, for the distinction between + and C boundary contexts.[2]

(3)

Speaker	t	p
CS	$t_6 = -8.33$	<0.0005
CC	$t_6 = -6.19$	<0.001
AD	$t_6 = -2.87$	<0.05
DB	$t_6 = -5.27$	<0.005
RS	$t_6 = -1.25$	0.26

All speakers show a 27–69 msec difference in the mean preboundary rime durations of the + and C contexts. One interpretation of these data, then, is that while there is no evidence of sensitivity to weaker lexical boundaries (+ and #), duration rules are sensitive to the edges of other domains, including compound boundaries.

Note that one could also relate the above data to the observations discussed in Lehiste (1972, 1980, etc.) that there is an inverse relationship between a syllable's duration and the number of syllables in the word containing that syllable. Lehiste (1980:5) notes, for example, that the length of the syllable *speed* as an isolated word was systematically longer than the same syllable in the word *speedy.* It should be borne in mind that in the work reported in Lehiste (1972) many of the test examples were words produced in isolation; it is not clear that, with words produced in a phrasal context, the effect that Lehiste reports is nearly so strong (J. van Santen, personal communication, 1989). Nonetheless, one might suppose that the rime in *beel* in the compound case is longer than the corresponding rime in the # and + cases simply because of the effect of Lehiste's observed tendencies. While this might account for the difference, note that in order for the explanation to work, the word boundary after *beel* in *beel equator* must be visible qua word boundary.[3] This may seem painfully obvious and unproblematic and probably would seem so to the majority of phoneticians who have investigated duration. But again, given the strong interpretation of BE, it is not at all obvious that the required word boundary information would be available to phonetic implementation.

It should also be pointed out that duration is not the only phonetic property which shows itself sensitive to at least some lexical boundaries in our work on /l/. The allophonic variation in /l/ itself is also sensitive to boundary strength. For example, the degree of tongue dorsum retraction also shows a significant difference in behavior between compound and other lexical boundaries, as suggested by Figure 1b, and also the following results of a t test for the comparison between tongue dorsum retraction in the + and C environments.

(4)

Speaker	t	p
CS	$t_6 = 6.67$	<0.001
CC	$t_6 = 4.00$	<0.01
AD	$t_6 = 2.52$	<0.05
DB	$t_6 = 1.74$	0.13
RS	$t_6 = 2.14$	0.076

Tongue dorsum retraction is one determinant of lightness of /l/: a more retracted tongue dorsum—that is, a more strongly negative y value in Figure 1b—yields a darker /l/. Now, as noted above, a major determinant of lightness of preboundary /l/s was found to be the duration of the preboundary rime, and so the data in Figure 1b can at the very least be viewed as an independent check on the same sensitivity to boundary strength as discussed above. On the other hand, Sproat and Fujimura (1989) note that duration cannot explain all of the observed variation, and it is at least possible that segments adjacent to boundaries may be more directly sensitive to the boundary in question (much as tones are sensitive, following Pierrehumbert and Beckman, 1988, etc.). Therefore, the sensitivity of the quality of /l/ to the strength of the boundary shown in Figure 1b may be partly indicative of an independent sensitivity of phonetic implementation to within-word boundary strength.

I turn now to the question of how to refer to boundaries in phonetic implementation. One of the positive contributions of the work on level-ordered morphology dating back to Siegel (1974) and culminating in lexical phonology and morphology is the observation that boundary symbols in the sense of Chomsky and Halle (1968) are both undesirable and unnecessary. The work done by boundaries in the older theory is taken over by lexical strata in the newer approach. The problem for the current discussion is that information about the strata at which lexical constructions, including compounds, are derived is supposed to be invisible to postlexical processes. So, unlike the boundary symbols of Chomsky and Halle (1968), which might conceivably have struck around until phonetic implementation, no such information is available under the later theories.

There are two ways out of this problem, both of which appear to compromise the strictest assumptions about BE. Let us concentrate on the case of compounds, where there is clear evidence that the word-internal boundary must be visible. The first solution would make use of the idea that, from a metrical phonological point of view, English compounds consist of two phonological words ω, in the sense of Selkirk (1980) and subsequent research, including Booij (1983) and Booij and Lieber (this volume). The representation of *beel equator* would thus be metrically as in (5a). If we assume that the metrical structure is available to phonetic implementation, then we could account at least for the facts of preboundary lengthening by allowing phonetic implementation rules to refer to the metrical phonological word.

(5)

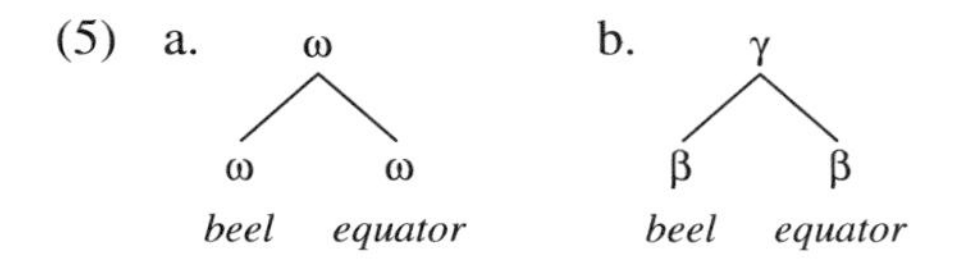

A slightly different interpretation is available under the theory proposed in Inkelas (1989, this volume). Inkelas suggests that the lexical strata of lexical phonology should be reinterpreted as being prosodic domains on a par with the prosodic domains discussed for phrasal phonology in various work including Nespor and Vogel (1986) and Pierrehumbert and Beckman (1988). Under her analysis (1989:94–96), a compound in English would be considered, phonologically, to consist of a combination of two β (= stratum II) domains into a γ domain, as indicated in (5b). This view is particularly interesting since it is known (Pierrehumbert and Beckman, 1988) that phonetic implementation rules are sensitive to phrasal prosodic domains, and it seems a natural extension to assume some sensitivity to lexical prosodic domains also.

On either of these views, however, the strong interpretation of BE is compromised. In the second view, the compromise is rather direct, since in Inkelas's theory, bracketing erasure is implemented as erasure of information about word-internal prosodic boundaries. There is a complication here: Inkelas's model of prosodic bracket erasure (1989:57) does not erase internal brackets if the two daughters of a node are of a different prosodic type from the mother node; in (5b), then, the two β nodes would remain visible, so one might explain the above data on that basis. However, if the whole compound *beel equator* were embedded in a larger compound, the two β nodes would be erased under Inkelas's theory, and so one would expect the rime of *beel* in this larger compound to have a categorically different duration from that in *beel equator.* This seems highly unlikely, so it would still seem necessary to compromise BE. Inkelas does, however, suggest an alternative interpretation of bracketing erasure which does not involve actual erasure of prosodic information, and I return to that alternative below.

In the first view, the compromise is more indirect, in that internal morphological structure becomes visible to postlexical processes by encoding at least part of that structure in metrical representation, which is not generally subject to erasure of its internal structure.[4] At the very least this weakens the predictive power of BE, since some of morphological structure becomes visible via smuggling through metrical structure.[5]

I now turn to the other set of data which suggest that word-internal structure may be visible to interpretive components.

3. PRAGMATICS AND WORD-INTERNAL STRUCTURE

In Sproat and Ward (1987); Ward, Sproat, and McKoon (1991); McKoon, Ratcliff, Ward, and Sproat (1990); and McKoon, Ward, Sproat, and Ratcliff (1993), we have investigated the status of so-called anaphoric islands. It will be recalled that Postal's (1969) original study concluded that there was a grammatical (i.e., morphosyntactic) constraint prohibiting anaphoric reference into and out of words.[6] While various researchers, including Lakoff and Ross (1972), Corum (1973), and Watt (1975), have noted the fact that some constructions which ought to be infelicitous according to the anaphoric island condition are in fact quite felicitous, it has nonetheless generally been assumed that pronouns may not take as their antecedents elements which are inside words. Those cases where examples seem fully felicitous have been suggested to be derived by "pragmatic inference" (cf. Shibatani and Kageyama, 1988), though what form this "inference" takes and how such "inference" differs from "real" anaphora has never been defined. The supposed categorical prohibition on reference by pronouns into words has been taken to be derivable from lexical integrity and therefore from BE by Simpson (1983) and Mohanan (1986)—see, e.g., the quote from Mohanan in Section 1.

There is a problem with this view: it appears to be the case, as argued by Sproat and Ward (1987), Ward et al. (1991), McKoon et al. (1990, 1993), that there is no specifically morphological constraint which prohibits pronouns from taking their antecedents within words. As is argued in detail in those references, as well as in the work of several authors cited above, fully felicitous examples of apparent violations of the so-called anaphoric island condition can readily be found. The following naturally occurring examples should suffice to make the point (in these examples, boldface marks intended coreferents and brackets delimit the lexical item containing the antecedent).

(6) a. *Patty is a definite* [***Kal Kan*** *cat*]. *Every day she waits for* ***it.***
Television advertisement for Kal Kan, January 28, 1987)

b. *There's a* [***Thurber*** *story*] *about* ***his*** *maid. . .*
Heard in conversation, September 7, 1988

c. *We went up to* [***Constable*** *country*]; *we stayed in the village* **he** *was born in.*
Heard in conversation, October 11, 1988

d. *I refer you to the* [***Schachter*** *paper*]; ***he's*** *very proud of it . . .*
Speaker in response to a question at North Eastern Linguistics Society, November 12, 1988

e. *Well, action is still needed. If we're to finish the job, Reagan's Regiments will have to become the* [***Bush*** *Brigades*]. *Soon* ***he****'ll be the chief, and he'll need you every bit as much as I did.*
R. Reagan, farewell speech, January 11, 1989, reported in Associated Press Newswire

f. *Millions of* [***Oprah Winfrey*** *fans*] *were thoroughly confused last week when, during* **her** *show, she emotionally denied and denounced a vile rumor about herself.*
Mike Royko, May 22, 1989, cited by McCawley, 1989, as an example of reflexive usage—i.e., not as an example of an anaphoric island

g. *I had a* [***paper****route*] *once but my boss said I took too long deliverin'* ***'em.***
"L.A. Law," 1987

h. *I'm a* [***mystery-story*** *buff*] *and read (and watch on PBS) a lot of* ***them.***
Northwestern University electronic bulletin board, January, 1989

i. *We asked* [***Saab 9000-CD*** *owners*] *about* ***its*** *road-handling . . .*
Television ad for Saab, March 12, 1989

j. *For a* [***SYNTAX*** *slot*], *I'd rather see someone with more extensive coursework in* ***it.***
Heard during a discussion of various subdisciplines of linguistics, where the speaker was contrasting syntax with other subdisciplines, January 18, 1987

k. *At the same time as coffee beans were introduced, the Arabs made changes in* [***coffee*** *preparation*] *that greatly improved* ***its*** *flavor.*
Schapira, J., Schapira, D., and Schapira, K., *The book of coffee and tea,* 1982, p. 7

l. A: *Are we ciderless?* B: *Yes we're* [***cider****less*]. *You should have told me—I would have brought* ***some.***
In conversation, January 23, 1987

m. *Do* [***parent****al*] *reactions affect* ***their*** *children?*
Heard in conversation by Jill Burstein, March 15, 1990

n. *"I heard someone say," he began, "that you are a [**New Zealand**er]. I was out **there** as a small boy."*
Marsh, N., *Night at the Vulcan,* 1951, p. 207

o. *Our neighbors, who are sort of [**New York City**–ites], they have jobs **there** . . .*
Heard in conversation, December 30, 1990

In Ward et al. (1991), we suggest that it is wrong to claim that apparently felicitous examples like the above are really ungrammatical and are somehow amnestied by pragmatic factors. Note that examples of the other half of the anaphoric island constraint, namely the prohibition in English on pronouns occurring within words, are never amnestied by pragmatic factors.

(7) **I don't eat **bananas** because I'm a **them**-hater.*

(7) is not acceptable under any conditions.[7] Thus, if the examples in (6) are considered ungrammatical, we would have to explain why their ungrammaticality can be amnestied, whereas that of (7) cannot.

Still, we must account for the phenomenon that Postal (1969) originally described: clearly not all cases where an anaphor finds its antecedent within a word are felicitous. And we must also provide an account of which factors render some examples felicitous.

3.1. Why Reference into Words Is Often Infelicitous

Various considerations lead one to expect that reference into words will often be infelicitous. For one thing, words often have idiosyncratic semantics and it is a precondition for felicity of reference into words that the word in which the intended antecedent is found be sufficiently transparent semantically. Consider the following examples.

(8) a. *Fred is a **cow**boy. #He says **they** can be difficult to look after.*
b. *#John wants to be a **fire**man because he likes putting **them** out.*

Words like *cowboy* and *fireman* are lexicalized (institutionalized, opaque) compounds. What this means is that although the words morphologically contain *cow* and *fire* respectively, and although (in the real world) cowboys are somehow related to cows and firemen to fires, it is very clear that one does not get the semantic referent of either word by any decompositional strategy. Since interpreting the meaning of *cowboy* and *fireman* does not require the semantic interpretation of the morphological parts, we would not expect reference to those parts (more correctly, to the discourse entities they might evoke) to be felicitous.

In cases where the semantics of a word are sufficiently transparent, reference into words is often quite felicitous. Consider some of the examples of naturally occurring data from above. In synthetic compounds of the type found in (6i), for example, there is no question that by and large such constructions are interpreted compositionally, since it is derivable from the meaning of *own* and *-er* that a *Saab 9000-CD owner* is glossed 'someone who owns a Saab 9000-CD'. In completely nonce formations such as *Kal Kan cat* in (6a), we can appeal to the fact (cf. Downing, 1977) that hearers are able to compute an interpretation (appropriate to the discourse context) for such cases by considering appropriate relations between the parts of the compound; the hearer in this case would need to figure out what relation between the substance Kal Kan and cats is being communicated. This crucially involves accessing the referents of the terms *Kal Kan* and *cat,* unlike the situation with *cowboy* and *fireman.*

A second consideration revolves around the syntactic function, position, or type of items which are contained within words. Here I just consider the case of the left-hand member of a compound. It is generally assumed that the left-hand member of a compound functions as a modifier of the right-hand member; see Levi (1978), inter alia. So, if it turns out that there is reason to assume that prenominal modifiers are generally less accessible—in a sense to be clarified below—than other syntactic positions, we have another part of the explanation for why reference into compounds is often infelicitous. With this in mind, consider the following discourse, where either (9a) or (9b) can be the second sentence.

(9) *John doesn't like to visit his relatives very much.*
  a. *His intolerable aunt is hostile.*
  b. *His hostile aunt is intolerable.*
  He never has a very good time.

In an experiment reported in McKoon et al. (1990) and Ward et al. (1991), subjects read blocks of example discourses such as the two represented in (9) and were subsequently presented with lists of test words where they were required to indicate as rapidly and accurately as possible whether or not the test word was in one of the preceding discourses. In cases where a word was a modifier, such as *hostile* in (9b), subjects responded significantly more slowly to the test item *hostile* than when that word had appeared in a predicate as in (9a); in the two discourses in (9), the complementary results were found for *intolerable.* So there is good psycholinguistic evidence that modifier position is indeed less accessible than at least one other syntactic position, and we suggest in Ward et al. (1991) that this fact is another factor in determining the relative infelicity of reference into words.

Note that the above factors—semantic opacity and the effect of the type of syntactic function (or position) of some word-internal elements—do hinge on properties of the morphological constructions involved. But there is no morphosyntactic PROHIBITION against reference into words. Rather, various properties of words conspire to render such reference infelicitous (or not fully felicitous) in many cases.

3.2. Increasing the Felicity of Reference into Words

Various semantic and pragmatic factors may make reference into words felicitous. One precondition I have already discussed is that the word which contains the intended antecedent be semantically transparent. Other factors that are relevant are contrast and topicality. For example, in (6j), contrast between *syntax* and other subdisciplines of linguistics helps render the discourse entity evoked by *syntax* in the compound *syntax slot* more accessible for subsequent reference by the pronoun *it.* Also, psycholinguistic studies reported in McKoon et al. (1993) and Ward et al. (1993) show that discourses in which the intended word-internal antecedent is topical felicitate subsequent reference to the discourse entity evoked by that antecedent. For example, a discourse concerning animals and nature but with no prior explicit mention of the word *deer* will render reference to deer, as evoked by the appearance of the morpheme *deer* within a compound such as *deer hunter,* more accessible for subsequent reference than a discourse in which deer are not topical.

(10) a. TOPICAL: *Sam likes the outdoor life. Having grown up in rural Kentucky, he knows a lot about nature and is an expert at fishing and shooting. He goes on hunting trips as often as he can. He used to hunt just small game, like rabbit and quail. However, lately he's taken up* ***deer*** *hunting. He thinks that* ***they*** *are really exciting to track.*

b. NONTOPICAL: *Sam has many interests in the outdoors. He's an avid skier, and each winter he takes about a month off from work to ski in Colorado. In the summertime, he visits his parents in Montana where he has a chance to do some mountain climbing. Lately, he's taken up* ***deer*** *hunting. He thinks that* ***they*** *are really exciting to track.*

This accessibility-raising effect can be verified by measuring subjects' reading time for the (final) sentence containing an anaphor (*they*) referring to deer; reading time is significantly faster in the topical context than in the nontopical context. We argue that this is because in the nontopical context, it is harder for the subject to resolve the reference of the pronoun (*they*) than in the topical context.[8]

3.3. Summary

So, under appropriate discourse conditions reference into words is possible, apparently contradicting claims that such reference is morphosyntactically ruled out. Indeed, Mohanan's own examples, *fatherless* and *self-destruction,* have no special properties in this regard.[9] For the first case, the following seems perfectly felicitous [cf. (6,l)].

(11) *Mary has been* ***father****less for years;* ***he*** *died when she was five.*

So reference to *father* in *fatherless* is not in general ruled out. With regard to the second example, *self-destruction,* the issue arises as to whether *self-* should be considered to be an anaphor or merely an operator which binds two arguments in the argument structure of its base, as suggested by Di Sciullo and Williams (1987). If *self-* is just a lexical operator and not an anaphor, then no special statement is needed to exempt *self-* from anaphor binding principles, which would not apply to it anyway. For those who have argued that *self-* is an anaphor (e.g., Lieber, 1984, 1991; Sproat, 1985), it is not difficult to find examples which seem to suggest that *self-* can be bound by an element outside its containing word.

(12) ***John****'s gradual* ***self****-destruction by drug use was heartrending to his family.*

What is the relevance of these observations to the issue of BE? Clearly we want to say that the reason the examples in (3) are felicitous is that the antecedents in question evoke the relevant discourse entities by being MORPHOLOGICALLY present. To be sure—and to allay any possible misunderstandings—there are cases which seem to require a different analysis.

(13) A: *You're not* **English,** *are you?* B: *No, I was brought up* ***there*** . . . (*Gaslight*)

Here, it seems unlikely that *England*—the antecedent of *there*—is morphologically present in *English.* Rather, there seems to be some sort of lexical inference going on, in the sense that *English* functions as the PROVENANCE adjective related to *England,* and it is this well-instantiated LEXICAL relationship[10] which renders the example felicitous. The analysis of this particular case is reminiscent of the analysis of the RELATEDNESS PARADOX *theoretical linguist* in Mohanan (1986:25); recall that in that case *theoretical* is normally interpreted as modifying *linguistics,* not *linguist,* since the meaning is 'one who practices theoretical linguistics'. Mohanan suggests, correctly I believe, that *theoretical* can modify *linguistics,* not because the latter is morphologically contained within *linguist*—it patently isn't—but rather because *linguist* is known to mean 'one who practices linguistics'. The modification of *linguistics* is thus at some semantic level and not at the morphological level; see also Spencer (1988) for discussion of this kind of relatedness paradox. It seems to be true, in fact, that cases like *linguist* which allow for these kinds of relatedness paradoxes also typically allow for the kind of reference exhibited in (13). Compare the relatedness paradoxes in (14a,c) with (14b,d), where the pronoun corefers with part of the meaning of the containing word.

(14) a. *John's an East German.* (cf. *East Germany*)
  b. *John's a* ***German*** *though he hasn't lived* ***there*** *for many years.*
  c. *John's a transformational linguist.*
  d. *John's a* ***linguist;*** *he says* ***it****'s an exciting field.*

Plausibly, similar mechanisms for extracting *Germany* from *German* and *linguistics* from *linguist* are involved in all cases.

One might attempt an analysis along the lines of that required for (13) or *theoretical linguist* by suggesting that the compound *Kal Kan cat* is lexically related to *Kal Kan* by some relation—say the CAT-WHICH-LIKES-X relation—and that it is because of this semantic relationship that reference to Kal Kan is felicitous in (6a). The problem with this view is that, as Ward et al. (1991) argue for examples like (13), and as Spencer (1988) argues for examples like *theoretical linguist,* such semantic inference seems to require minimally that the containing words—that is, *English* contains *England,* and *linguist* contains *linguistics*—be listed lexical items or that there at least be a well-instantiated conventional relationship between the containing word and the word which it notionally contains. Presumably *Kal Kan cat* has neither of these characteristics; it is a completely nonce formation. Clearly then, the most straightforward analysis of an example like (6a) is that reference to Kal Kan is possible because of the morphological presence of *Kal Kan* within *Kal Kan cat.* Precisely put, *Kal Kan* evokes a discourse entity which corresponds to the substance Kal Kan, and which is sufficiently accessible in the discourse for subsequent anaphoric reference. Only a prejudice that components of words cannot be visible at postlexical levels would prevent one from adopting this most straightforward analysis.

If, as I have suggested, there is no morphosyntactic restriction preventing anaphors from referring into words, then two things would appear to follow. First of all, evidence for lexical integrity, or its implementation via BE, cannot be sought in that domain, contra Simpson (1983) and Mohanan (1986); the data on which Simpson's and Mohanan's arguments rest are simply incorrect. Second, the conclusion would actually seem to be problematic for BE, at least on its strongest interpretation. It is true that the grammar itself does not need to be able to see inside *Kal Kan cat* in order to allow reference to the discourse entity evoked by *Kal Kan* to serve as a felicitous antecedent for an anaphor.[11] Indeed, in Ward et al. (1991), we followed Reinhart (1983) in suggesting that the grammar need make no statement about the referential possibilities of pronouns; under this approach, word-internal antecedents such as *Kal Kan* are in no way special and are governed by the same kinds of pragmatic constraints as govern other instances of pronominal anaphora. But the pragmatics must still be able to see *Kal Kan,* and if we take seriously Mohanan's suggestion that all postlexical processes are barred from having access to the internals of words, then one would think that such visibility would not be available.

4. SOME CONCLUSIONS

The data presented in the preceding two sections is at worst problematic for the strong interpretation of BE, and at the very least—if word-internal structure is allowed to be smuggled through in ways other than morphological bracketing—suggests that the strong interpretation of BE might not be doing as much work as initially appears.

The strong interpretation of BE expounded in Mohanan (1986) was cast in terms of a theory of morphology where words have a single structure. Similarly, Mohanan's view of lexical insertion into syntactic structure appears to be that phonetic strings are inserted into syntactic frames (see pp. 145ff., for example); one consequence of this view is that Mohanan extends the domain of BE into the postlexical component, where it erases information about syntactic constituency with the result that the later phonetic implementation rules have no access to such structure. One reasonable interpretation of recent work on phrasal phonology is that syntactic structures on the one hand and prosodic or phonological structures on the other exist in parallel and that phonetic implementation accesses only prosodic/phonological structure.[12] If phonetic implementation accesses only prosodic structure, however, it follows (trivially) that it cannot access syntactic structure, and thus BE seems to be unnecessary at the postlexical level.

Related to this view of the relationship between syntax and phrasal phonology are theories of word structure where real morphological (or morphosyntactic) structure is parallel to but separate from phonological (or morphophonological) structure. Sproat (1985) argued for such a view, and more recently Inkelas (1989) has adopted the same position, recasting morphophonological structure in terms of prosodic structure in the lexicon, as discussed above. An obvious next step is to assume that phonetic implementation rules only have access to lexical prosodic information and not to morphosyntactic structure. On the other hand, the evocation of discourse entities in the pragmatics would have access to morphosyntactic structure. Given that morphosyntactic and morphophonological (lexical prosodic) structures are separate, one could, of course, imagine a scenario where BE applies, say, in prosodic structure but not in morphosyntactic structure, and under such a scenario one or the other set of data presented in this paper would then be unproblematic. With that in mind, let us consider the status of BE at each of the levels separately.

First of all, theories of BE in phonological structure have been proposed which are unproblematic from the point of view of the phonetic implementation data discussed in this paper. One such idea is the suggestion of Inkelas (1989:58) that BE may be reinterpreted "as a constraint on what phonological rules may refer to" and that "instead of forcing internal brackets to be erased, we need only impose the requirement on rules that they look only at the highest node [i.e., highest relative to the current analysis] in prosodic structure." Thus, BE is simply a PHONOLOGICAL locality condition. Obviously this view is completely compatible with the data described in this paper. If we assume that phonetic implementation applies to annotated prosodic structures such as those in (5), then it seems reasonable to assume that phonetic implementation will have access to all domains represented in such structures. Of course, it will be up to phonetic implementation to decide whether and how it makes use of such information. For example, it would be consistent with the data in this paper to assume that preboundary lengthening may in principle have access to all levels of prosodic boundary but in fact is only sensitive to boundaries at or above the compound level. We do not currently understand enough about phonetic phenomena such as preboundary lengthening to say what range of sublexical prosodic boundaries may be visible to these phenomena cross-linguistically, though it is clear that at least some sensitivity to such boundaries is required. It may in any event be assumed that phonetic implementation is not constrained by phonological locality.[13]

Turning now to BE in the morphosyntactic representation, note again that the original content of lexical integrity was specifically concerned with the relation of morphology to syntax, so in the parallel structures view of morphology, it is BE at the morphosyntactic level of representation which is relevant for lexical integrity as originally construed. Lexical integrity has always been a problematic principle. For one thing, as argued in Sproat (1988), it is not clear to what extent it is an empirical claim that syntax cannot affect the internal structure of words; theories such as that of Baker (1988) would appear to violate it massively on at least the most simplistic view.[14] In any event, it seems clear that, if my interpretation of the data from so-called anaphoric islands is correct, pragmatics at least must be able to look inside words, suggesting that real morphological content may be visible.

Of course, morphosyntactic BE has been appealed to to perform other services besides deriving lexical integrity. So, as Pesetsky (1979) pointed out,[15] BE subsumes the adjacency condition of Allen (1978). Recall that under the adjacency condition, a morphological rule attaching X to [[Y]Z] may make reference to properties of the morpheme Z, but it may make no reference to any properties of Y. As Pesetsky argued, BE is even stronger than the adjacency condition and thus properly subsumes it: since all brackets except the outermost pair in [YZ] have been erased,[16] the rule attaching X can only refer to the outermost brackets and their labels and is blocked from referring even to Z, and a fortiori to Y. Thus, an affix like *-ment* can attach to a word like *enjoy* because the brackets surrounding *enjoy* are labeled V and *-ment* is subcategorized to attach to V. It is irrelevant that the morpheme adjacent to *-ment,* namely *joy,* is labeled N; indeed, properties of more deeply embedded morphemes which are not themselves percolated to higher nodes are systematically irrelevant to the attachment of morphemes later on in the derivation. BE predicts this systematic myopia in that it requires that morphological derivations only look at features of the topmost node.

The problem with adducing these considerations as evidence for the necessity of BE in morphology is that there are all sorts of places in grammar where only the topmost node is relevant. In syntax, for example, if one is checking to see that a verb's subcategorization requirements are satisfied, one only needs to look at the topmost node of the verb's sister(s) to establish that those nodes meet the subcategorization requirements; alternatively, one may want to say that one looks at the head of the sister(s), but that can apparently always be recast as an instance of looking at the topmost node under the assumption that the head's features are inherited by all phrases which it heads. Verbs may specify a subcategorization for an NP, but they apparently may not specify a subcategorization for an NP which is modified by at least one adjective, or an NP which is followed by a relative clause. Such information is presumably available—no one to my knowledge has proposed the application of BE in the syntax to render it unavailable[17]—and yet information about anything other than the topmost nodes of sisters, and whatever information is inherited by them from their heads, is systematically irrelevant to subcategorization considerations. Presumably this is because subcategorization frames are restricted to specifying a set of slots and the features of, but no structural information about, the fillers of those slots. However this is to be stated exactly, it would seem to subsume the adjacency condition every bit as well as BE.

Although I have called into question the usefulness and correctness of what I have termed the strong interpretation of BE, the ultimate conclusion of this paper is, I think, a positive one. The data presented here give a better sense of the kinds of ways in which postlexical components may make reference to word structure, and they suggest how the correct versions of BE—and lexical integrity more generally—should look. I would like to end by suggesting that a fruitful area of future research on morphology would be a systematic investigation of the relevance of morphological structure to phonetic implementation and pragmatics. As far as I know, although phonetic implementation is at least discussed in the lexical phonology literature, what discussion there has been has usually been at a rather high level, and even when it does treat the issue in some detail, it has focused on the phonetic implementation of purely phonological information, with no attention to the possible relevance of word structure itself to phonetics. There are few if any studies from the lexical morphology tradition that address the relationship between morphology and pragmatics. Words do not exist in a vacuum, yet researchers have on the whole tended to take a rather narrow view of the kinds of data that are relevant to theories of morphology, usually limiting themselves to at most discussing the relation between morphology and phonology or morphology and syntax. The field is ready to become more cosmopolitan.

ACKNOWLEDGMENTS

I thank Sharon Hargus and an anonymous reviewer for helpful comments on this article.

NOTES

[1]Not a low-level phonological rule, contra the analysis of /l/ variation in Halle and Mohanan (1985) and Mohanan (1986). We make the common assumption (cf. Liberman and Pierrehumbert, 1984) that phonetic implementation rules introduce continuous variation whereas phonological rules of any kind, including low-level ones, introduce categorical variation.

[2]Note that all speakers pronounced *beel equator* as a compound—i.e., deaccenting *equator*—except speaker AD, who did place some prominence on *equator* in some of the examples; this accenting difference did not appear to show up in the form of a different trend for speaker AD.

[3]If it is not visible, then the whole compound *beel equator* should count as a tetrasyllabic word, and the rime of *beel* should be shorter in this case than in the disyllabic *beeling*, by Lehiste's argument.

[4]On the interpretation of Booij and Lieber (this volume) and apparently also Cohn (1989), metrical structure—prosodic structure, in their terms (see Inkelas, 1989, for a discussion of the terms *prosodic* and *metrical*)—is the only structure to which lexical phonological rules can refer. On that view, then, the only representation of morphological structure that the phonology sees is the metrical structure, so if BE were to apply so as to render morphological information invisible to phonological structure, it would have to erase metrical structure. Of course, metrically weak morphemes such as affixes might be incorporated into whatever metrical structure they attach to, so that the resulting structure is indistinguishable from a metrical structure derived from a monomorphemic input. So BE might in such cases follow from metrical considerations alone. On the other hand, there is no reason to assume on purely metrical grounds that the phonological wordhood of the components of a compound should be erased.

[5]I note in passing that Booij (1983) uses metrical structure to account for some Dutch data which appear to compromise lexical integrity. Also Mohanan (1986:60 n. 10) intimates that such a compromise might be possible since "postlexical phonological operations have access to the phonological structures exiting from the lexicon (e.g. stress trees, syllable trees)."

[6]I continue to use Postal's original terminology and talk of reference into words. However, in doing so I am being rather terminologically loose: the correct way to describe the situation is to say that an anaphor is used to refer to a discourse entity evoked by a morpheme which is morphologically contained within another word.

[7]There are a number of possible reasons for this: as Paul Kiparsky has noted (personal communication) pronouns are closed-class items and as such are generally barred from undergoing morphological derivation. Of course, as an anonymous reviewer points out, there are derived forms of prepositions such as *thereto, thereabout*. However, it is fair to say that such formations are not productive in present-day English.

A somewhat related possibility is the more general statement that functional categories and their projections cannot serve as the basis of morphological derivation in English. This would link the unavailability of **them*-hater with the unacceptability of **the The Bronx hater* (Fabb, 1984); note that on recent views of phrase structure, in particular Abney (1987), a fully specified NP is considered to be a projection of a functional category (in this case the determiner *the*), and therefore the full DP *The Bronx* could not be morphologically contained within the compound by the proposed prohibition. See Sproat (1985, 1988) for a third possible account.

Finally, note that if a language lacks whatever grammatical constraint of English prevents pronouns from occurring within words, then we would expect pronouns which do occur, say as the lefthand member of a compound, to be able to corefer with antecedents outside the word. This is exactly what we find in Sanskrit (Gillon, 1990).

(i) ***rāgasya****-an-upayoge* *katham* [***tat****-śaktiḥ*] *upayujyate*
passion-non-use how it-potentiality use
If there is no causal role for **passion,** in what way does **its** potentiality have a causal role?'

[8] Of course, it is necessary to check that the subject is resolving the reference correctly; see McKoon et al. (1993) and Ward et al. (1991) for details of the methods used for verifying that reference was resolved. Note also that topicality was shown in the cited work to have a significant (though reduced) effect on reference to full noun phrases in discourses similar to (10) (e.g., *lately he's taken up hunting deer*).

[9] The fact that BE prevents *-al* and *-ion* from attaching to *refuse* and *destroy* in the syntax—as noted by Mohanan in the above-quoted passage—has, of course, nothing to do with anaphoric islandhood, and is therefore largely irrelevant to the points discussed in this article. Still, it is worth pointing out that as far as one can tell, the prohibition on attachment of derivational affixes in the syntax has essentially zero empirical content. What would go wrong if such affixes WERE attached in the syntax?

[10] I.e., a lexical relationship for which one can find many instances: for any country, one can find (or construct) a provenance term related to that country.

[11] Thanks to an anonymous reviewer for pointing out some unclarities in an earlier version of this discussion.

[12] Note that data discussed in Pierrehumbert and Beckman (1988), among others, suggest that phonetic implementation MUST access prosodic structure—apparently contra Mohanan (1986: 175) who suggests, "Thus phonological structures at all levels exist only in the lexical and syntactic modules, and are dissolved in the implementational module."

[13] Another view possibly compatible with the phonetic data presented in this paper is the view intimated in Booij and Rubach (1987) that bracketings constructed at stratum II are not erased by BE, since BE only applies at cyclic strata and stratum II is a noncyclic stratum. A further compatible view is that of Hammond (1984). Hammond argues that BE does not apply to compounds, although it applies to other morphological constructions. In general, any version of lexical phonology and morphology which assumes a sufficiently weak interpretation of BE will be compatible with more or fewer of the data presented here.

[14] For a particularly lucid discussion of the various arguments for and against lexical integrity, see LeRoux (1988).

[15] Thanks to Sharon Hargus for reminding me of this point.

[16] In Pesetsky's theory, BE applied at the end of each cycle.

[17] Again, Mohanan's proposal that BE apply in the syntax was intended to rule out phonetic implementation rules from accessing syntactic information.

REFERENCES

Abney, S. (1987). *The English Noun Phrase in its Sentential Aspect.* Doctoral dissertation, Massachusetts Institute of Technology, Cambridge.

Allen, M. (1978). *Morphological Investigations.* Doctoral dissertation, University of Connecticut, Storrs.

Baker, M. (1988). *Incorporation: A Theory of Grammatical Function Changing.* University of Chicago Press, Chicago.

Booij, G. (1983). Coordination and reduction in complex words: A case for prosodic phonology. *Vrije Universiteit Working Papers in Linguistics 3,* Vrije Universiteit, Amsterdam.

Booij, G. and Rubach, J. (1987). Postcyclic versus postlexical rules in lexical phonology. *Linguistic Inquiry* **18,** 1–44.

Chomsky, N. (1970). Remarks on nominalization. In *Readings in English Transformational Grammar* (R. Jacobs and P. Rosenbaum, eds.), pp. 184–221. Ginn, Waltham, Mass.

Chomsky, N., and Halle, M. (1968). *The Sound Pattern of English.* Harper and Row, New York.

Cohn, A. (1989). Stress in Indonesian and bracketing paradoxes. *Natural Language and Linguistic Theory* **7,** 167–216.

Corum, C. (1973). Anaphoric peninsulas. In *Papers from the Regional Meeting of the Chicago Linguistic Society* **9,** 89–97.

Di Sciullo, A. M., and Williams, E. (1987). *On the Definition of Word.* MIT Press, Cambridge, Mass.

Downing, P. (1977). On the creation and use of English compound nouns. *Language* **53,** 810–842.

Fabb, N. (1984). *Syntactic Affixation.* Doctoral dissertation, Massachusetts Institute of Technology, Cambridge.

Gillon, B. (1990). Sanskrit word formation and context free rules. *Toronto Working Papers in Linguistics* **11**(2).

Halle, M., and Mohanan, K. P. (1985). Segmental phonology of Modern English. *Linguistic Inquiry* **16,** 57–116.

Hammond, M. (1984). Level ordering, inflection, and the righthand head rule. *MIT Working Papers in Linguistics* **7,** 33–52.

Hargus, S. (1985). *The Lexical Phonology of Sekani.* Doctoral dissertation, University of California, Berkeley.

Inkelas, S. (1989). *Prosodic Constituency in the Lexicon.* Doctoral dissertation, Stanford University, Stanford, Calif.

Kiparsky, P. (1982a). Lexical morphology and phonology. In *Linguistics in the Morning Calm,* (I.-S. Yang, ed.), pp. 3–91. Hanshin, Seoul.

Kiparsky, P. (1982b). Word formation and the lexicon. *Mid-America Linguistics Conference* 3–29.

Kiparsky, P. (1985). Some consequences of lexical phonology. *Phonology Yearbook* **2,** 85–138.

Lakoff, G., and Ross, J. (1972). A note on anaphoric islands and causatives. *Linguistic Inquiry* **3,** 121–125.

Le Roux, C. (1988). *On the Interface of Morphology and Syntax: Evidence from Verb–Particle Combinations in Afrikaans.* Master's thesis, University of Stellenbosch, Stellenbosch, South Africa.

Lehiste, I. (1972). The timing of utterances and linguistic boundaries. *Journal of the Acoustical Society of America* **51,** 2018–2024.

Lehiste, I. (1980). Phonetic manifestation of syntactic structure in English. *Annual Bulletin of the Research Institute of Logopaedics and Phoniatrics* **14,** 1–27.

Levi, J. (1978). *The Syntax and Semantics of Complex Nominals.* Academic Press, New York.

Liberman, M., and Pierrehumbert, J. (1984). Intonational invariants under changes in pitch range and length. In *Language Sound Structure.* (M. Aronoff and R. Oehrle, eds.), pp. 157–233. MIT Press, Cambridge, Mass.

Lieber, R. (1984). Grammatical rules and sublexical elements. In *Papers from the Parasession on Lexical Semantics,* pp. 187–199. Chicago Linguistic Society, Chicago.

Lieber, R. (1991). *Deconstructing Morphology: Word Formation in a Government-Binding Syntax.* The University of Chicago Press, Chicago.

McCawley, J. (1989). *1989 Linguistic Flea Circus.* Unpublished manuscript, University of Chicago.

McKoon, G., Ratcliff, R., Ward, G., and Sproat, R. (1990). *Structural and Discourse Manipulations of Salience in the Interpretations on Anaphora.* Paper presented at the Third Annual CUNY Conference on Human Sentence Processing, New York, N.Y.

McKoon, G., Ward, G., Sproat, R., and Ratcliff, R. (1993). Morphosyntactic and pragmatic factors affecting the accessibility of discourse entities. *Journal of Memory and Language* **32,** 1–20.

Mohanan, K. P. (1982). *Lexical Phonology.* Doctoral dissertation, Massachusetts Institute of Technology, Cambridge.

Mohanan, K. P. (1986). *The Theory of Lexical Phonology.* Reidel, Dordrecht.

Nespor, M., and Vogel, I. (1986). *Prosodic Phonology.* Foris, Dordrecht.

Pesetsky, D. (1979). *Russian Morphology and Lexical Theory.* Unpublished manuscript, Massachusetts Institute of Technology, Cambridge.

Pierrehumbert, J., and Beckman, M. (1988). *Japanese Tone Structure.* MIT Press, Cambridge, Mass.

Postal, P. (1969). Anaphoric islands. *Papers from the Regional Meeting of the Chicago Linguistic Society* **5,** 205–239.

Reinhart, T. (1983). *Anaphora and Semantic Interpretation.* University of Chicago Press, Chicago.

Selkirk, E. (1980). The role of prosodic categories in English word stress. *Linguistic Inquiry* **11,** 563–606.

Shibatani, M., and Kageyama, T. (1988). Word formation in a modular theory of grammar. *Language* **64,** 451–484.

Siegel, D. (1974). *Topics in English Morphology.* Doctoral dissertation, Massachusetts Institute of Technology, Cambridge.

Silverman, K. (1988). Utterance-internal prosodic boundaries. *Proceedings of the Australian International Conference on Speech Science and Technology* **2,** 86–91.

Simpson, J. (1983). *Aspects of Warlpiri Morphology and Syntax.* Doctoral dissertation, Massachusetts Institute of Technology, Cambridge.

Spencer, A. (1988). Bracketing paradoxes and the English lexicon. *Language* **64,** 663–682.

Sproat, R. (1985). *On Deriving the Lexicon.* Doctoral dissertation. Massachusetts Institute of Technology, Cambridge.

Sproat, R. (1988). On anaphoric islandhood. In *Theoretical Morphology* (M. Hammond and M. Noonan, eds.), pp. 291–301. Academic Press, San Diego.

Sproat, R., and Fujimura, O. (1989). *Articulatory Evidence for the Non-categoricalness of English /l/ allophones.* Paper presented at the winter meeting of the Linguistic Society of America, Washington, D.C.

Sproat, R., and Fujimura, O. (1993). Allophonic Variation in English /l/ and its implications for phonetic implementation. *Journal of Phonetics* **21.**

Sproat, R., and Ward, G. (1987). Pragmatic considerations in anaphoric island phenomena. *Papers from the Regional Meeting of the Chicago Linguistic Society* **23,** 321–335.

van Santen, J. (1989). *Modeling Contextual Effects on Vowel Duration.* I. *Description of Individual Factors.* Unpublished manuscript, AT&T Bell Laboratories.

Ward, G., Sproat, R., and McKoon, G. (1991). A pragmatic analysis of so-called anaphoric islands. *Language* **67,** 439–474.

Watt, W. (1975). The indiscreetness with which impenetrables are penetrated. *Lingua* **37,** 95–128.

II

On Some Basic Tenets of the Theory

ON THE WORD LEVEL

TONI BOROWSKY

Department of Linguistics
University of Sydney
Sydney, New South Wales 2006, Australia

1. INTRODUCTION

In this article I put forward a model of lexical phonology in which the properties of the two major levels follow from the fact that at the Word level all the phonological processes precede, rather than follow, all morphological operations. At the Stem level, the morphology precedes and feeds phonology in a cyclic fashion, as is usual in any standard lexical phonology.

The theory I propose challenges two basic assumptions in lexical phonology: First, most work in lexical phonology is characterized—if not explicitly, then implicitly—by the idea that where there is interaction between the morphological and the phonological modules,[1] the phonology follows the morphology. I offer instead a model in which this ordering is reversed on the Word level. Second, I consider the idea that the two classes of affixes can be diagnosed on purely phonological grounds. Affixes at the Word level are generally defined negatively, in terms of the phonological rules (usually those of the first level) which do not apply at this level.[2] This alone is offered as an explanation for the fact that these affixes display what is known as "open juncture" while the affixes of the first level display "close juncture." Yet in most lexical phonologies, even though it is, implicitly at least, recognized that the two levels have quite distinct properties, they are assumed to be the same. In this article I show that the differences in the phonology of the two lexical levels are much more than the differences in the sets of rules which apply or do not apply at each level. I claim that the two levels are characterized by distinct interfacing between the morphology and the phonology. The phonological properties which characterise each level are derived from the interaction between the two modules.

In (1) is shown a diagram of the proposed model. In relevant morphological respects, it can be construed as identical with the model proposed in Selkirk (1982). There are two lexical domains, and only two, corresponding to Stem level (= Level 1) and Word level (= Level 2). (See also Aronoff and Sridhar, 1983; Sproat, 1985).

(1)

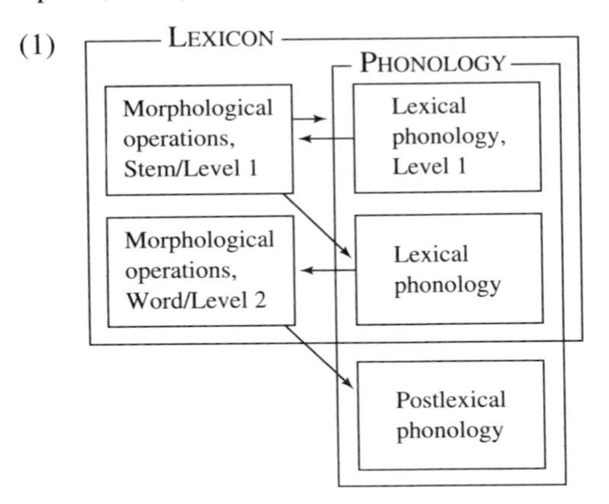

This model is dramatically different from the available alternate models in which it is assumed that the Word level is either cyclic like the Stem level (e.g., Borowsky, 1986; Kiparsky, 1982) or non- or postcyclic (e.g., Booij and Rubach, 1987; Halle and Mohanan, 1985). I present a schematized version of these models in (2). In the course of this article we shall see many reasons to reject this sort of model.

(2)

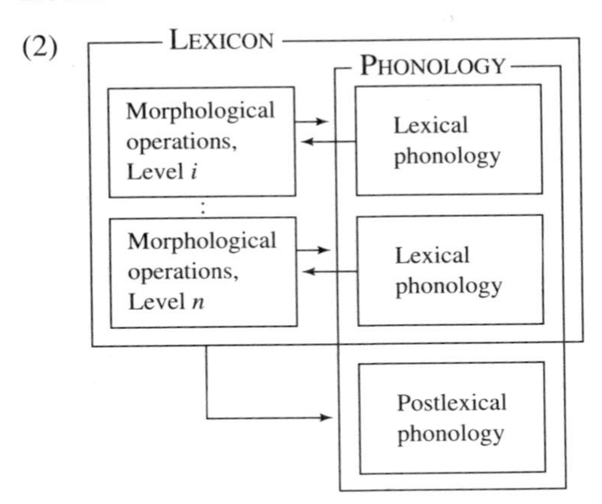

The two lexical domains exhibit many differences which are, in the theory in (1), a direct result of the different type of interaction between the phonological and morphological systems of each domain. On the first domain, the Stem level, the morphology and phonology interact as usual in standard lexical phonology. Every morphological operation feeds into the phonological system, and the result is returned to the morphological system. The phonology of this level exhibits the collection of properties considered to be diagnostic of lexical phonology: that is, the rules are structure-preserving, are cyclic, and obey the strict cycle condition. After all Level 1 operations are completed, the resulting forms complete another circuit through the phonological system before any Level 2 affixation takes place. This, the word cycle, is the last phonological domain in the lexicon and constitutes what I call the Word level. Rules of this level may be non–structure-preserving.[3] The Word level is not cyclic in the usual sense: it does not show evidence of strict-cyclic effects. Since I will show that, at least for English, there is no evidence that there is any lexical phonology beyond this one cycle at the Word level, there is also no evidence to determine whether or not it is cyclic. Word-level affixes may be attached, but no further lexical phonology takes place. It thus appears that on this level phonology precedes but does not follow morphology. The next cycle through the phonology, after Word-level morphology, is the first domain of the postlexical phonology—the phonological word.

The article is structured as follows: I begin by showing, on the basis of data from English and German, that there exists a single cycle at which the rules which apply at the Word level must apply. This cycle must precede any affixation at this level. I then go on to suggest that there is no other phonological domain at the Word level on the basis of a consideration of the nature of Level 2 phonological processes as well as the structure of forms derived at this level.

My proposal, therefore, has two parts. I make an empirical point: that the Word is a phonological domain. There must be a Word cycle at Level 2 before any morphology, and this cycle appears to be the only phonological cycle for which there is any evidence at this level. Based on this observation, I make a theoretical proposal about the interplay between the two modules that comprise the lexicon which bears crucially on how the lexical phonology is to be structured and interpreted. In the course of the discussion I show that noncyclicity (as suggested by Booij and Rubach, 1985; Halle and Mohanan, 1985; Kiparsky, 1985; and others) is not an adequate explanation of the properties of the Word level and is incompatible with the facts discussed in this paper. I then consider an alternative analysis of the facts which has been suggested to me and show it to be inadequate. The Appendix provides further examples of rules of the type discussed in the body of the article.

2. THE WORD CYCLE

In Borowsky (1986) I argue, on the basis of the morphophonemic alternations exemplified in (3), that there must be a single cycle through the phonology after all Level 1 processes, but before any Level 2 morphology. This cycle corresponds to the morphological operation in Selkirk (1982) which changes a Stem form to a Word form. It is on this cycle that the process which accounts for these alternations take place.

(3) a. [+son] → [+syll] / C ____]

____]	____] aff 2	____] aff 1
wonder	*wondering*	*wondrous*
cycle	*cycling*	*cyclic*
theater	*theatergoer*	*theatrical*
meter	*metering*	*metric, metrical*
rhythm	*rhythm-and-blues*	*rhythmic*
anger		*angry*
center	*centering*	*central centrality*
[saykl̩]	[saykl̩iŋ][4]	[siklik]
	[sayklіŋ]	*[sikl̩ik]

b. *b*/*g* → ø/N ____ $]_\sigma$ (where N = homorganic nasal)

____]	____] aff 2	____] aff 1
long	*longing*	*elongate, longitude, longest*
strong	*strongly*	*strongest*
bomb	*bombing*	*bombard*
crumb	*crumby*	*crumble*
thumb	*thumbing*	*thimble*
[lɔŋ]	[lɔŋiŋ]	[ilɔŋget]

c. *n* → ø / *m* ____]

____]	____] aff 2	____] aff 1
condemn	*condemning*	*condemnation*
autumn	*autumning*	*autumnal*
hymn	*hymning*	*hymnal*
[him]	[himiŋ]	[himnəl]
	*[himniŋ]	*[himal]

d. *g* → ø / ____ [+nasal]]

____]	____] aff 2	____] aff 1
resign	*resigning*	*resignation*
sign	*signer*	*signature*
paradigm		*paradigmatic*
[sayn]	[saynər]	[signəčur]
*[saygn]	*[saygner]	*[sinəčur]

Note that though the details of the changes induced in each set of alternations are different, the patterns of changes are identical; all are found in the word-final environment, as shown in the first column; they appear too before all Level 2 suffixes, second column. Before Level 1 suffixes, as shown by the examples in the third column, none of these phenomena take place.

These facts are most adequately explained as due to prosodic licensing (Itô, 1986). Each change is a syllabification-induced change which occurs to license, or eliminate, material left unlicensed by the Level 1 phonology. That is, at Level 2 when the final consonants of Level 1, previously licensed by extrametricality, become visible to the phonology, these changes are induced. Thus though the facts in (3) are set out as if illustrating different rules, I assume that they are actually the result of a single process: prosodic licensing. Bearing this in mind, I concentrate my discussion on the first of these examples, Sonorant Syllabification, drawing attention throughout to the similarities with the other alternations.

Final sonorants become syllabic at the word edge. In the examples given in (3a) we see that though these sonorants are consistently nonsyllabic where followed by Level 1 suffixes, as in *metric,* they are always syllabic word finally, as in *meter,* and they may optionally be syllabic before all Level 2 affixes, as in *metering.* Notice that this alternation is not pandialectal; some speakers do not pronounce these forms with a syllabic sonorant if followed by a vowel-initial Level 2 affix. This is the result of a postlexical desyllabification rule which is optional in the dialects under discussion. The crucial thing to explain here is the fact that there is never a syllabic sonorant before a Level 1 affix or a nonsyllabic sonorant word finally. The only place optionality arises is before Word level affixes. That is, though both alternatives are available in some dialects before Level 2 affixes, thus [miytr̩iŋ] or miytriŋ], no dialect ever has a syllabic sonorant in any Level 1 derivative *[mɛtərik]. (Note also that the optionality of syllabicity or nonsyllabicity of sonorants does not extend to any of the other processes: the forms *hymning* or *signing* are never available as *[himniŋ] or *[signiŋ].) This arrangement of facts suggests that the process by which sonorants become syllabic does not take place at the first level of the lexicon. At the Stem level, final sonorants become onsets of vowel initial suffixes, as in (4).

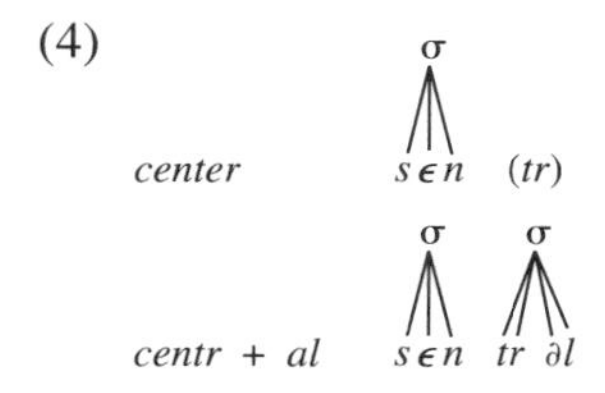

In the same way the consonants participating in the other alternations are licensed at Level 1 by regular syllabification: the consonants, shown in boldface, in *elon**g**ate, solem**n**ity,* and *autum**n**al* turn up as onsets, while the *g* in *si**g**nature* is licensed in the coda by the syllabification of the following *n* into the suffix onset.

At Level 2 the final sonorant is syllabic even before vowel-initial suffixes attached at this level. The process which makes final sonorants syllabic makes no reference to the following suffix; it appears to see only the word as it emerges from the Level 1 phonology. The final consonant is not licensed as the onset of the suffix syllable. The other consonants delete in precisely the same circumstances.

All these alternations are easily accounted for if prosodic licensing is enforced before the Level 2 affixes are adjoined—that is, on the Word cycle. Then the two different surface environments, word-final and preceding Level 2 affixes, are in fact the same when the processes occur, as shown in (5).

(5)

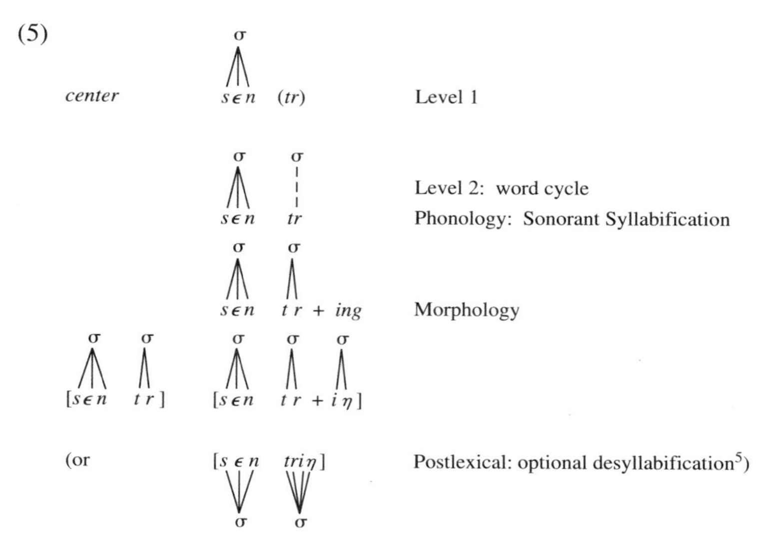

Since prosodic licensing takes place before any Level 2 affixation, the option of incorporating final stray consonants as onsets of following suffixal syllables is simply not available.

Before introducing additional evidence found in English for the word cycle, let me turn to some similar facts from German.

2.1. German Morphophonemics

Counterparts of two of the English processes shown above exist as well in German. The German facts present the same problems as the English ones do and must be analysed in the same way.

In German, syllabic and nonsyllabic sonorants alternate, and *g* deletes after [ŋ] in processes similar to the English ones. Before Level 1 affixes, sonorants are always nonsyllabic. Word-final sonorants are obligatorily syllabic when absolute final and optionally syllabic when followed by Level 2 affixes.[6] Compare the two patterns in (6).

(6) LEVEL 1: obligatorily nonsyllabic
filtr + ieren 'to filter'
registr + ieren 'to register'

metr + isch	'metrical'
(Gelt)wechsl + er	'changer'
Verdunklung	'blackout'

LEVEL 2: syllabic finally, else optional

silber + ig (silbr + ig)	'silvery'
zucker + ig (zuckr + ig)	'sugary'
schmuddle + ig (etc.)	'grimy'
Verwechselung	'mixup'
Verdunkelung	'darkening'

Similarly, in word-final position, and before Level 2 affixes, [g] deletes after [ŋ], as well as when it cannot be syllabified (Hall, 1989b).

(7) LEVEL 1:

diphthong + ier + en	'to diphthongize'
tang + ier + en	'to affect'
laryng + al	'laryngeal'

versus

LEVEL 2:

Spreng + ung	'explosion'
sing + e	'(I) sing'
Jung + en	'boys (nom.)'
Jung + ling	'(a) youth'

The analysis of both sets of facts is identical to the one I have given for the English alternations. Prosodic licensing takes place before affixation at Level 2. Thus the relevant consonants are not syllabified into the onset of one of these affixes and are licensed by Sonorant Syllabification for final sonorants, or deleted, as for final *g*s after [ŋ]. The optional pronunciation with desyllabified sonorants arise by a postlexical reduction process. Thus, I conclude that German has a word cycle at Level 2 just as does English.

Another extremely interesting example of a word-cycle rule in German is the [ç, x] alternation. Briefly, the segments [ç] and [x] are in complementary distribution. The velar fricative occurs after [+back] vowels while the palatal fricative occurs after [−back] vowels and elsewhere. Examples are given in (8).

(8)

[ç]		[x]	
ich	'I'	*Buch*	'books'
höchlich	'highly'	*hoch*	'highly'
Küche	'kitchen'	*Koch*	'cook'
riechen	'to smell'	*rauchen*	'to smoke'
sicher	'sure'	*Sprache*	'language'

This distribution can be stated informally as in (9).[7] The analysis I present below is taken from Hall (1989a) after Bloomfield (1930).

(9) $ç \rightarrow x$ / [+back] ____

The minimal pairs in (10) appear to be counterexamples to this rule. In (10a) the palatal fricative occurs after [+back] vowels where the [x] is expected. In (10b) the [x] occurs as it should.

(10)				
	a.		[ç]	
		Kuhchen	[ku:çən]	'little cow'
		Pfauchen	[p^{f} aoçən]	'little peacock'
		Tauchen	[taoçən]	'little rope'
	b.		[x]	
		Kuchen	[ku:xən]	'cake'
		pfauchen	[p^{f} aoxən]	*'to hiss'*
		tauchen	[taoxən]	'to dive'

The distinguishing factor in these examples is that the forms in which *ç* appears after a [+back] vowel are morphologically complex forms derived at Level 2. (I follow here Hall's, 1989a, analysis and refer the reader to that article for argumentation supporting the assignment of this rule to Level 2.) Thus although the phonological environments appear to be identical, the examples in (10a) have a Word-level morpheme boundary between the vowel and the fricative, while those in (10b) are monomorphemic: [[*Kuh*]*chen*] vs. [*kuchen*].

In order to account for this, Hall (1989a) builds into his rule (11) the stipulation that the relevant segments must be tautomorphemic.

(11)

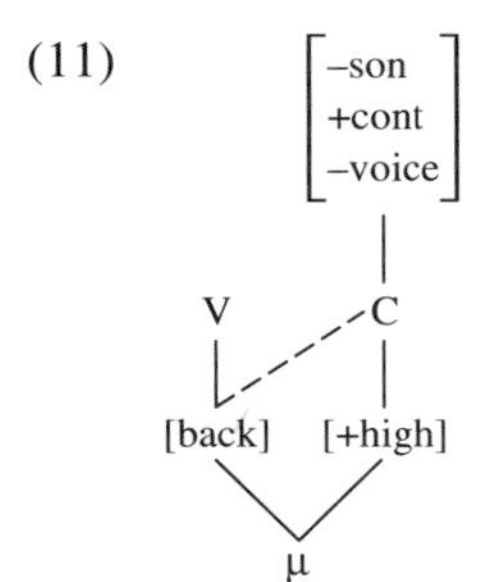

Backness spreads from a vowel onto a following consonant so long as both segments are inside the same morpheme—are tautomorphemic.[8] (Note that this is the equivalent of saying that the rule is blocked across the Word/Level 2 boundary.)

Clearly this rule is another candidate for application at word cycle. If rule (9) applies on the Word cycle, before affixation of the diminutive morpheme, the fact that this [ç] is not affected by Fricative Assimilation is unsurprising.

What is perhaps surprising and makes this rule of particular interest to us is the fact that it does not apply after the affix has been attached. This is certainly what we would normally expect if phonology follows morphology—whether cyclically or noncyclically—since the target and the trigger cooccur only after the morphology. However, the rule must be blocked from applying in precisely this environment. Hall accomplishes this with his tautomorphemic condition.

(Hall's term "tautomorphemic" is slightly misleading since it must exclude all morphological complexity arising before the Word level. Let us instead use the word TAUTOLEXICAL with the specific interpretation, in the same Word. Word-level rules are limited to applying within the domain of a Word, or morpheme, as it is available at Level 2. That is, any form at Level 2, even if derived at Level 1, is a Word and is treated in the same way as an underived word. All internal morphological information from Level 1 is gone at Level 2. Thus it is only Word-level/Level 2 morpheme boundaries which make two morphemes not tautolexical.)

Restricting a rule to tautolexical application is, at first glance, an unusual and probably highly undesirable condition on a rule. In the proposed model this apparently baroque condition on Hall's rule is derived. In fact, tautolexicality is a characteristic property of rule application at the Word level and not at all baroque. All Word level rules, including the German Fricative Assimilation rule, apply on the cycle before morphology. There is therefore no need for a stipulation to ensure that a rule applies tautolexically. On the Word cycle, only one morpheme can be seen by the phonology; all internal morphological structure from Level 1 has been erased, and no additional morphemes have yet been added. The next cycle through the phonological system will be postlexical, where the rule is not available.[9] Consider the following derivation.

(12)

Stem/Level 1:	*hoch*		*kuh*	*kuchen*	
	hoch	*höch*	—	—	Umlaut (Lieber, 1989)
Word/Level 2:	*hoch*	*höch*	*kuh*	*kuchen*	
	[x]	[ç]	—	[x]	Fricative Assimilation
Morphology:		*höch+lich*	*kuh+chen*	—	
	[hox]	[höçliç]	[ku:çən]	[ku:xən]	

At level 2, if the umlauted allomorph is selected, the fricative is a palatal; if not, the fricative is velar. On the word cycle of *Kuh,* the rule does not apply. Thereafter the rule does not get another opportunity to apply. As a Word-level rule, its time has come and gone—before the morphology creates the sequence meeting its structural description.

2.2. Summary

To conclude this section, I recapitulate: we have seen further evidence of the need for the Word cycle in German. In addition, and more importantly, we have seen a property of Word-level rules which I have argued is characteristic: they apply only tautolexically. The German facts show that a Word-cycle rule, in this case Fricative Assimilation, does not apply after the Word cycle even if its structural description is met. The picture of the Word level we see emerging from these facts is one in which there is a single domain of phonological rule application prior to any morphology. No evidence has been adduced so far for another cycle through phonology after morphology. However, we count as evidence against the claim that there may be another cycle the fact that Word-cycle rules must be stipulated to apply only tautolexically.

3. ENGLISH ALLOPHONIC RULES

I now introduce a series of allophonic rules drawn from various dialects of English. These rules exhibit the same properties as the processes discussed in the previous sections. Although these rules are allophonic and perhaps the sort of rules we might intuitively expect to be postlexical rather than lexical, we will see that they have clear lexical properties. All of them are sensitive to morphological structure in a way that is quite uncharacteristic of postlexical rules. Some of them can be shown not to be postlexical quite directly. While some of the rules have general postlexical counterparts in other dialects, in the dialects concerned they are clearly contextually determined and have taken on the characteristics of Word-level rules. Note again that all of these rules violate structure preservation because they create new segments—allophones. Since these rules behave in precisely the same way as the rules discussed so far, they provide strong support for the domain and mode of rule application proposed herein.

All data and some analyses are taken from Wells (1982) and Harris (1989, 1991). I have confined my discussion in the text to four of these rules. Further examples of this kind of rule, with brief descriptions of each, can be found in the Appendix. In each case, in the alternations discussed, the allophone found in the unaffixed word occurs also if followed by a Level 2 affix. In monomorphemic forms, or those derived at Level 1, a different allophone is found. In other words, these alternations show the same patterns of distribution as the morphophonemic rules discussed above.

3.1. Belfast Dentalization

There is a rule of dentalization found in the dialect of English spoken in Belfast which causes alveolar consonants to become dental when followed by tautosyllabic *r*.

(13) *t, d, n, l* → *t̪, d̪, n̪, l̪* / ___ (ə)*r*

(Note that some dialects of English have a general and unrestricted dentalization process; however the dialect we are concerned with is not one of these.)

In Belfast the dental realization of alveolars before *r* occurs in monomorphemic forms as well as in forms derived at Level 1. Examples are given illustrating the alternation in these environments in (14).

(14)	Dental	Nondental
a.	*train, drain*	*bedroom, hard rain*
b.	*elementary, sanitary*[10]	*element row*

Compare the two sets of examples in (15). In these we see the dentalized forms in the monomorphemic words in the first column while the words in the second column show no dentalization even though they appear to be in almost identical environments.

(15) Dental	Nondental
*spi**d**er*	*wider*
*la**dd**er*	*louder*
*spa**nn**er*	*finer*
*pi**ll**ar*	*filler*
*ma**tt**er*	*fatter*

The word *spider* with a dental contrasts with *wider* with an alveolar *d.* The difference between the forms in (15) is the fact that the forms in the first column are monomorphemic, while those in the second are derived at Level 2. The rule does not apply in any of the forms in which the conditioning (ə) *r* is in a Level 2 affix and therefore not in the same morpheme as the dentalizing consonant. Thus we see the same pattern emerging as we found with the German Fricative Assimilation rule: if the trigger of the rule is in a Word-level suffix, while the target is in the preceding morpheme, the rule does not apply. Where the rule does apply, it applies when both trigger and target are tautolexical: that is, ON THE WORD CYCLE. Note that the rule cannot be a postlexical rule in Belfast English because postlexically there is no way to distinguish a monomorphemic word like *spider* [d̪ər] from a bimorphemic word like *wider* [dər].

In order to account for these facts, Harris (1989) analyses this rule as restricted to Level 1 in spite of the fact that it violates both structure preservation and the strict cycle constraint (SCC).[11] As pointed out above, it is clearly not postlexical.

On the basis of these properties, as well as the fact that its pattern is exactly that of the clearcut Word-level rules, I assign it to the Word level instead, pace Hall.

Let us then compare the derivations of the forms in (16). At Level 1, the rule does not apply at all—it is blocked by structure preservation as well as the SCC. At Level 2 it applies on the word cycle to generate the correct forms in the first and last case. Since morphology follows phonology, the rule does not get an opportunity to apply on the Word cycle in the middle case. After the affix *-er* is attached to *wide,* the rule does not apply. Thus *wider* has a nondental *d.*

(16)					
		spider	*wide*	*element + ary*	
	Stem/Level 1:	—	—	—	Dentalization
	Word/Level 2:		*wide*		
	Word cycle	*spi* ***d̪*****ər*	—	*elemen***t̪ry*	Dentalization
	Morphology:		*wide + r*		
		[spay**d̪r̩̪**]	[waydr̩]	[ɛləmɛ**n̪t̪**ri]	

Once again, this case shows that a Word-level rule must apply on the word cycle, and further, must not get another opportunity to apply at all thereafter. The rule only applies tautolexically. In my terms, the domain of this rule is the Word cycle. After the morphology has taken place, the rule is no longer active. Thus even when a suffix is added which results in a string which meets the structural description of the rule, the rule does not apply.

Note that if we were to assume, following Halle (1988), Halle and Mohanan (1985), or Booij and Rubach (1987) or others, that the rule is applying on a noncyclic domain, we would be forced to stipulate that the rule can apply only tautolexically. The rule would have to be blocked by the intervening bracket. Yet it is not blocked by the Level 1 bracket in [[*element*]*ary*] because by the time it gets to apply—that is, at the Word level—all Level 1 brackets have been erased. So only the Level 2 bracket is a blocker. However, if the rule applies before any affixation at the Word level, nothing special needs to be said. The correct result is derived quite simply.

3.2. Aitken's Law

In various Scottish and Irish English dialects, reported in Wells (1982) and Harris (1987, 1989, 1990), among others, there is a rule which lengthens stressed vowels when they are followed by voiced fricatives or *r,* or when word final. In these dialects, unlike most other varieties of English, there is no phonemic length distinction in vowels. Length is determined by this rule, known as Aitken's Law (Wells, 1982). The rule is therefore clearly not structure-preserving in these dialects and thus cannot apply at the stem level. Harris (1991 : 101) gives an informal statement of the rule which I adapt as follows.

(17) AITKEN'S LAW: Stressed vowels[12] are long before a [+voice, +continuant] segment or before]. Elsewhere they are short.

Accordingly, as pointed out by Wells (p. 400), a word such as *mood* [mud] rhymes with *good,* and *bead* has a vowel which is the same length as the vowel in *bid.* Long vowels are found only in the Aitken's law environments: *agree, seize, beer, breathe, Seery,* versus short vowels in *feet, feed, cease, feel, Sheedy,* and so on. In these examples we see the rule violating the SCC as well.

Once again we might assume that this rule is a postlexical rule, were it not for the fact that length derived by Aitken's Law in the word-final environment is retained even when the syllable is closed by a word-level suffixal consonant. So, one finds minimal pairs like those below where a morpheme-final vowel is followed by a suffixal *-d.* The morphologically complex forms are vowel final for the purposes of Aitken's law.

(18)

___]*d*		___ *d*]	
agreed	[əgri:d]	*greed*	[grid]
kneed	[i:]	*need*	[nid]
brewed	[u:]	*brood*	[brud]
stayed	[e:]	*staid*	[sted]
toed	[o:]	*toad*	[tod]
gnawed	[ɔ:]	*node*	[nod]

The sole difference between a form like [bru:d] *brewed* and [brud] *brood* is the morpheme boundary which intervenes between the vowel and the consonant. The lengthening found on word-final vowels is carried over to the suffixed forms. So the lengthening of the vowels must take place before the syllable is closed by the past-tense affix, which should otherwise bleed the application of the rule. In the monomorphemic words there is no lengthening because the vowel is never final.

Aitken's law must apply at the word-level (see also Harris, 1990). It cannot be postlexical because the boundary between the two morphemes would be erased by the postlexical phonology and there would be no way to distinguish the monomorphemic words from the bimorphemic words. This pattern is unmistakably the Word-level pattern we have observed so far.

(19)

Level 2:	*agreed*	vs.	*greed*	
Word cycle:	*gri*		*grid*	
	gri:		DNA	Aitken's law
Morphology:	*gri: + d*			

In some Scottish English dialects, there is a related diphthongization. The word-final context of Aitken's law generalizes to become a syllable-final environment. The two variants are distinguished in quality: thus [ʌi] alternates with [a˙e]. *fire* [fa˙e.ir], *high, alive, prize,* all with [a˙e], versus *wipe, tribe, wide* with [ʌi] (Wells,

1982:405). The long variant [a'e] appears in word-final position even when followed by an apparently tautosyllabic consonant, as shown in (20). Again the word-final environment is unchanged for the purposes of this rule by the following suffix. Thus the rule accounting for this allophony must apply before the suffixes are incorporated. Monomorphemic *viper* contrasts with bimorphemic *wipe+r* exactly as predicted if the rule applies on the word cycle and morphology only takes place afterwards.

(20)	[a'e]	[ʌi]
	tied	*tide*
	sighed	*side*
	shyness	*shining*
	viper	*wiper*
	spider	*wider*

3.3. London [ʌu] ~ [ɒu]

In London Vernacular English, syllable-final /l/s are sometimes vocalized. Harris (1989) shows, based again on the description of these facts in Wells (1982: 312), that in this environment vowels preceding this *l* show certain coarticulatory effects. For example, the length distinction in high vowels is neutralized so that *pull* and *pool* are both pronounced [pʊu] and *fill, feel* are [fɪʊ]. Important to my discussion is the fact that the vowel of *cola, Roland,* [ʌu], becomes [ɒu] when followed by tautosyllabic *l*. The rule is given informally in (21).

(21) [ʌu] → [ɒu] / ___ l $]_\sigma$[13]

The vowel of an unaffixed word is maintained in words derived by affixation at Level 2 even though the *l* has apparently become the onset of the affix syllable. Thus once again we find contrasts such as those shown in (22).

(22)	[ʌu]	[ɒu]
	Roland	*rolling*
	slowly	*goalie*
	polar	*roller*

On the other hand, forms derived at Level 1 behave as if they are monomorphemic at Level 2; thus *polar,* from [[*pole*]*ar*], has the vowel [ʌu], showing that the rule did not apply to this form on the first Stem-level cycle. Thus yet again, we have a non–structure-preserving rule applying before morphology at Level 2. Compare the derivation of *polar* with that of *roller.* The rule must apply to *roll,* but not to *pole,* before the final *l* is syllabified into the onset of the suffix syllable. That is, it must apply on the word cycle—at the Word level.

(23)

	polar	*roller*	
Level 1/stem:	*po(le)*	*ro(ll)*	Rule (21) DNA
Morphology:	*pol + ar*	—	
Phonology:			Rule (21) DNA
Level 2/word:			
Word cycle:	*polar*	*roll*	
	NA	[rɒu]	Rule 21
Morphology:		*roll + er*	
Postlexical:	[pʌulər]	[rɒulər]	

3.4. Northern Irish *daze* versus *days*

In Northern Irish English (Wells, 1982; Harris, 1990), there is an allophonic alternation between the vowel found word finally in words like *stay, day, lay,* with [ɛ:], and the same vowel when nonfinal: *fade, fate, station, cater, fail,* with [ɪə]. Note that the rule does not apply in the syllable-final environment—consider *station* as compared with *stay.*

(24) [ɪə] → [ɛ:] / ____#

We can see from the above examples that the rule is non–structure-preserving and violates the SCC and therefore cannot be a Stem-level rule. Yet nevertheless we again find that a contrast arises between the two allophones when we look at forms derived at the Word level, so the rule cannot be postlexical, either.

(25)

[ɪə]	[ɛ:]
Daly	*daily*
Reagan	*ray gun*
daze	*days*
staid	*stayed*
grains	*greyness*

Thus we fix this rule on the Word level. In order to derive the forms in (25), the rule must apply on the Word cycle before any Word-level affixation, as follows.

(26)

Level 2:	*Daly*	versus	*daily*	
Word cycle:	—		*day*	
			[ɛ:]	Rule (24)
Affixation:	—		*day + ly*	
Output:	[dɪəliy]		[dɛ:liy]	

So far we have seen a very distinctive set of rules, all supporting the claim that there is a single cycle through the phonology before any morphology takes place at Level 2, that is, at the Word level. (More such rules appear in the Appendix.) Each of the rules we have seen is oblivious to material introduced by the morphology of Level 2; this is evidenced by two things: each rule appears to apply only inside the morpheme concerned—the rules apply only tautolexically; and at least two of them are clearly blocked from applying when their structural description is satisfied by a string which spans two Word-level morphemes.

4. THE WORD LEVEL

I concluded the previous section with the claim that there exists a cycle—the Word cycle—which takes place after Level 1 but before any Level 2 morphology. It should be clear at this point that unless we assume the existence of such a cycle, we cannot adequately explain the array of facts we have seen. In this section I take this argument one step further and argue that this cycle is the only phonological cycle at Level 2. I suggest also that this cycle is extended to all the formatives at this level. That is, I argue that all Word-level affixes also go through the phonology on the word cycle in English, and only thereafter are they joined together by morphological processes. There is no further lexical phonology after Level 2 morphology.

This study of the phonological processes associated with the Word level in English has revealed a surprising fact given standard assumptions about lexical phonology. It turns out that every phonological rule at this level is a word-cycle rule. I have found no Level 2/Word-level phonological rules which are not Word-cycle rules. Quite simply, although we may for theoretical reasons want to argue that the results of morphological operations at this level must cycle again through the lexical phonology (whether just once, as in a noncyclic theory, or more than once, as for a cyclic model), there is no evidence for this. Given this, there is no empirical reason to assume any further cycle through the phonology at this level. All the known facts are compatible with the view that the next domain of phonological rule application is the domain of the phonological word—in the postlexical phonology.[14]

Now note that it does not follow that, because there is no evidence of phonology after the word-cycle,[15] that all the AFFIXES should have undergone phonology at the word cycle prior to morphological concatenation. It is entirely possible that the fact that phonology precedes morphology is only apparent. That is, because all the rules are word-cycle rules, they precede morphology. Then there simply is no more lexical phonology in English—though it is entirely possible that there might have been.

In the following sections I consider a number of phenomena in support of the claim that there is no further lexical phonology after the Word cycle and that therefore the affixes must have undergone their phonology on this cycle. First I discuss the affix /ing/, which is an affix that undoubtedly undergoes a Word-cycle phonological rule. Then I consider some lexical rules which mysteriously seem to skip over Level 2. These two sections together provide evidence that some Word-level affixes are independent phonological domains on the Word level and that there is no phonology beyond the Word cycle. Last I look at the general properties of forms derived by affixation at the Word level and show that these properties are only explained if the above conclusions are drawn.

4.1. Rules Which Apply to Affixes: /-ing/

There is one Level 2 affix in English which shows unequivocally the application of a phonological rule which is itself a word-cycle rule. That is, the affix /-ing/ requires the operation of the rule which deletes the final *g* in the same way as a word like *long* does.[16] Thus we know that this affix undergoes word-level phonology.

The usual assumption about the phonological behavior of bound morphemes like /-ing/ is that phonology should take place only after they are attached to the word. Given this, we have no reason to expect that the *g* should not behave like any final *g* at Level 1—that is, it should be extrametrical on its own cycle and rescued by syllabification into the onset of the following syllable [[[*swinø*] *iN***g**] *est*] on the next. Of course it is not. The form *[*swiŋiŋ***g***ə***st**] is ungrammatical. Given this, let us suppose instead that the *g* is not extrametrical. Then we can derive the correct result if we ensure the derivation is cyclic, as suggested in Borowsky (1986)—that is, the *g* will disappear on the /*swiŋ+ing*/ cycle. This is directly counter to all other claims about the Word level in the literature (Booij and Rubach, 1987; Halle and Kenstowicz, 1989; Halle and Mohanan, 1985; Halle and Vergnaud, 1987), where it is argues that the Word level is noncyclic.

However, if the derivation is cyclic, there are still problems. We have seen that one of the properties of these word-cycle rules is the fact that if their structural description is met on a cycle created after affixation at Level 2, the rule does not apply. That is, in those cases, German Fricative Assimilation and Belfast Dentalization, in which the trigger and the target of the rule appeared in different morphemes, the rule never applied. The rules only applied tautolexically. If the derivation were cyclic, then the rule should get another chance to apply on the cycle at which the trigger and target both occur. But this is not the case; neither of these two rules applies after the word cycle.[17] Note that the same situation arises if the derivation is noncyclic and all morphology precedes all phonology. There is still a difficulty explaining the behavior of these rules without resorting to the use of brackets as a blocking device. (Interestingly, there do not seem to be any parallel examples, that I know of, of rules which are crucially blocked by the Stem-level boundary.) In the case of /ing/, the *g* would have to delete sensitive to the Word boundary]. Yet the proper characterization of this deletion is in terms of syllable structure: the *g* deletes if not syllabifiable, at the Word level. It must be syllabifiable in the same Word—that is, tautolexically.

The tautolexical property of these rules is unproblematic if all Word-level phonology applies to all formatives on the Word cycle, before any morphology. Indeed, it is predicted. Then the final *g* of /ing/ is prosodically licensed at the same time that the final *g* of *long* is—on the word cycle. Since neither *g* can be licensed, they delete.

Thus while German Fricative Assimilation and Belfast Dentalization gave evidence that Word-level rules do not apply across the Word affix boundary, the affix /-ing/ provides evidence that there is at least one word-cycle affix which undergoes a Word-cycle rule, independent of anything it may be adjoined to. An affix undergoes a tautolexical Word-cycle rule.

4.2. Rules Which Seem Not to Apply at Level 2: Nasal Assimilation and Stress

There are rules which are apparently available at domains both preceding and following the Word level but do not apply at the Word domain itself. Standard lexical phonological solutions must stipulate that the rule is blocked at this level. Consider, for example, the rules responsible for Nasal Assimilation and Stress Assignment in English.

Nasal Assimilation applies regularly at Level 1 as well as postlexically, but it appears to skip Level 2. At Level 1, Nasal Assimilation applies to derive forms like *impress, compel* from /iN+press/ and /coN+pel/, and so on. It also clearly applies postlexically: *pu*[ŋ]*kin 'pumpkin', Va*[ŋ]*couver, i*[m] *Bolivia,* and so on. It does not apply at Level 2 between the prefix *un-* and a following word: there is no obligatory nasal assimilation—*unbelievable* is [ʌnbiliːvəbl̩]. However, postlexical application of this rule will give us the optional [ʌm]*believable,* showing that the rule has not turned off.

Halle and Mohanan (1985) as well as Borowsky (1986) have argued independently that in fact Nasal Assimilation does apply at Level 2 to generate forms like *long* before the *g* deletes. Why, then, does it not apply in *unbelievable* and others?

It has been proposed (Booij and Rubach, 1987) that some prefixes must remain separate from the rest of the form in order to block certain rules from applying to them. That is, they maintain some sort of phonological integrity even after affixation. In Booij and Rubach's system, these affixes form a PROSODIC WORD OF MOT and as such are treated by the phonology as a separate domain for phonological rules. According to Booij and Rubach, the abovementioned facts about *un-* fall out because the prefix is a prosodic constituent on its own. *un-* is a mot which is separate from the second mot: *-able.* First prosodic structure is assigned and then other phonological rules take place.

The notion mot or prosodic word is, in principle, similar to my claim that at the word level, affixes cycle independently through the phonology. Booij and Rubach are unclear about how, or indeed when, their mot is derived. For them it must be stipulated that certain forms have this prosodic structure so that their phonological behavior follows. In the model of the phonology proposed herein, the mot is derived on the Word cycle. Mot is word. The theory predicts that all affixes at the Word level should retain their phonological integrity in this way, with respect to lexical rules. They do this because phonology precedes morphology and does not interact with it at this level. Since each affix is organized by the phonology as an independent form on the Word cycle, the affix has a separate identity.

No assimilation takes place between /un-/ and a following consonant in the adjacent morpheme at the Word level because the morphemes are not adjacent when they cycle through the phonological system. The prefix goes through the phonology, and the stem to which it attaches goes through the phonology, and the rules which are applicable apply to both forms independently. Nasal Assimilation is not applicable, since the *n* is not adjacent to an assimilator. This is different from the claim of Booij and Rubach. For them, the affixes and stem are morphologically adjacent but in distinct prosodic/phonological constituents, while in my system they are not morphologically adjacent while the Word-level phonological rules are applying.

Thus the state of being a mot is derived from the order of events in my system. The property of being a prosodic unit is derived quite simply via the phonology; every form that cycles through the phonology at some point in the derivation is a prosodic unit in that domain. At the Stem level, the morphology creates complex forms which cycle through the phonology. Each such unit is a prosodic unit. At the Word level, no complex forms arise until after the phonology has taken place on all formatives. All the affixes attached at the Word level, as well as all forms which have come from Level 1 into this level, are prosodic units. No Level 1 affix could ever be a mot because at Level 1 no affix can constitute, by itself, a domain for phonological rule application. On the other hand, all morphemes are prosodic units at the Word level. In other words, it is not the case that Nasal Assimilation skips Level 2. The rule may apply at every level—cyclically at the first level, noncyclically when postlexical, and tautolexically at the Word level. Its tautolexical application at the Word level—(it applies in *long* but not in *un+believable*)—is entirely consistent with the architecture of the system proposed herein.

Further evidence that forms at the Word level constitute independent prosodic domains comes from the stress rules. Most work in lexical phonology makes the assumption that the general stress rules do not apply at the Word level in the way they do at the first level. The Word affixes never affect previously assigned stresses. To account for this it is said either that each of the affix classes is marked as stress-neutral or stress-sensitive; or that the block of stress-neutral affixes is attached after the stress rules apply.[18] That is, the failure of certain stress rules to apply at the Word level is stipulated.

It cannot be the case that the regular stress rules have turned off altogether after Level 1, since they apply to compounds, and some of the so-called stress-neutral affixes are themselves stressed—some of the prefixes for example, as well as /-hood/.[19] The grammar must surely do more than merely stipulate, to account for the fact that the one class of affixes never has any effect on previously assigned stresses while the other does. It does not follow from cyclicity. It is just as possible that earlier stresses could be wiped out on a noncyclic domain as on a cyclic domain. Note too that the fact that it is always the second-level affixes which are stress neutral and the first-level affixes stress sensitive is unexplained so long as some stress rules can apply at the second level. It could in principle be the other way round given any other lexical phonology model—but it is not.

If we assume that the stress rules apply to each morpheme individually on the word cycle,[20] it follows that these affixes will always be stress-neutral with respect to the rest of the morphological structure derived at the same level. On the other hand, Level 1 affixes attach prior to phonology—the output of every morphological operation creates a word which must be input to a phonological cycle. Thus it follows that these affixes will add to the syllable count of the whole form and thus affect the overall stress pattern. In other words, the phonological behavior of the classes of affixes stems from the architecture of the model, and it is not merely a stipulation about each class of affixes or about the stress rules.

4.3. The Characteristics of Stem and Word

There is a clear difference between the way derived forms at the Stem and Word levels look on the surface. These differences are visibly manifest in the surface shapes of the forms associated with each level. Rules of the Stem level typically knit the morphemes together, erasing the internal edges and redoing the prosodic organization every time a morpheme is added. The output is a form which looks like an underived form—a form showing close juncture. For example, there are no underlying geminate consonants in English. There are no geminates in any underived words in English. If two identical consonants arise through the concatenation of two morphemes, the resulting sequence is degeminated, making the resulting word look like an underived word; for example, /in + numerable/ → [inumərəbl].

On the other hand, forms derived at the Word level have sharp internal edges which exhibit all sorts of word-edge characteristics.[21] For example, the syllable appendix, which appears only in absolute final position of monomorphemic words, appears regularly followed by Word-level suffixes: the sequence of consonants ending the first syllable of the word *worldly* is a sequence not permitted internally in monomorphemic forms or in words derived at Level 1 (see Borowsky, 1989). Word-level rules do not knit edges together but are instead characteristically sensitive to the edges in a manner never found with rules of the first level. Word-level forms look like concatenations of morphemes and not like underived words. Thus there is no obligatory degemination if the adjunction of two morphemes creates a geminate. The geminate may remain, depending on speech rate; for instance, *unnatural, pine needle, rat trap, bus stop.* At the Word level the previously assigned prosodic organization is maintained no matter how many Word-level affixes are attached; *cónsciencelessness.*

Most work in lexical phonology makes little of these observations,[22] merely attributing the differences between the two levels to the fact that the levels are characterized by distinct sets of rules and, more recently, to the claim that the Word level is noncyclic. However, neither of these ideas gives a satisfactory explanation of the observed differences in Stem forms and Word forms. The hypothesis that certain rules are restricted to certain levels does not explain why the forms should be superficially so different. To say that the degemination rule, or the stress rule, or constraints on the structure of a well-formed syllable turn off after the first level is to explain none of these things. It leaves aside as well the fact that those rules which do apply at the second level are still not accomplishing the same sort of edge-erasing function as the rules of the first level. The output of the Word-level phonology and morphology never looks like an underived word.

Neither can the claim that the word level is noncyclic, as has been suggested by Halle and Mohanan (1985), Booij and Rubach (1987), or Kiparsky (1985) provide an adequate explanation. In fact, as we will see below, the claim is descriptively inadequate. If the Word level is noncyclic, rules should take place across the board within the proscribed domain, as in the postlexical phonology, and not be restricted to smaller domains internal to the proscribed domain, as it seems to be at the Word level.

Although it may apply cyclically inside nested prosodic domains, postlexical phonology is reputed to have the property of applying the rules across the board within each of these domains, ignoring constituency information internal to that prosodic domain. Thus, for example, the Flapping rule changes /t,d/ to [D] in foot-medial position wherever its structural description is met within some larger prosodic domain. Thus it applies inside words, as well as inside some phrasal structures: *repe*[D]*i*[D]*iveness, mor*[D]*ality, go* [D]*omorrow, ge*[D] *Anne.* Word-level phonology shows nothing like this taking place. What we have seen instead is that morphological boundaries at the Word level create independent phonological domains internal to the domain of the whole word and that rules respect those internal domains—they apply tautolexically.

Let us assume that the first or stem level of the lexicon contains, inter alia, a list of stems and a list of affixes, as well as the rules which relate each stem to the others in the list (or, alternately viewed, the rules derive each stem from another). What this means is that each form derived at Level 1 exists as an independent form in the list.[23] Assume as well that the Word level is distinguished by the fact that every possible derived form is actively derived, and these lexical entries are not independently listed. So, in this lexicon, all the stems, as well as both classes of affixes, are listed, but no derived Word-level forms occur in the list. If we assume all this to be the case, the set of affixes which select for Stems (i.e., the Level 1 affixes) can be identified without explicit marking. These affixes are the ones which occur in the listed forms. The Word-level affixes occur in the lexical lists only as separate bound morphemes. They do not also appear in the listed words. The two classes of affixes can be differentiated by structure preservation, as it were. The set of affixes which also occur as components of listed words will be the Level 1/Stem-level affixes.

The fact that the Stem level is cyclic is due to the fact that the existing lexical items are derived from one another. Thus *presidential* is derived from /president + ial/, and *presidentiality* is derived from /presidential + ity/. Similarly, the fact that the level is structure-preserving follows: relating forms in existing items allows no room for innovation in the derivations. Clearly, no new segments or structures could be introduced. (I refer the reader to Sproat, 1985, who makes the same observations.) Note, lastly, that the SCC, by which structure-changing rules are blocked in nonderived environments, is also derived: listed entries will block any internal changes due to the elsewhere condition (see Kiparsky, 1982), and thus the only permissible changes are ones at edges where new material is being incorporated.

None of these characteristics carry over to the Word level. We do not readily assume that morphologically complex words at this level must be listed—at least not in the way that *conjoin, conjunctive, conjunction,* for example, are listed. The first level of the lexicon is not considered to be "productive"[24] because it is mainly concerned with existing words. (For example, a word like *enjunctive* is a possible, but nonexisting, word because it is not in the list even though it can be derived by the rules.) Word-level forms like *swingingest, unchocolatyest,* or *neighbourhoodlessness* are not independently listed; they are actively derived by the morphology—this level IS productive. There is no cyclic or structure-preserving phonology because existing forms are not being related to each other. So, truly productive affixes seem to attach to fully processed words.[25]

In conclusion, I have argued that the interaction of phonology and morphology in the lexicon differs on the two levels of the lexicon. I have shown that the phonological properties of each level are derived not from cyclicity/noncyclicity, but from the fact that there is no lexical phonology after affixation at the Word level since the phonology precedes the morphology on this level.

The argument can be summarized as follows: the attested rules which can be fixed to apply at the Word level must all apply on a phonological cycle which takes place before any morphology—the word cycle. These rules do not apply after the word cycle. There is no phonological evidence of interaction with the morphology at the Word level. In fact, the phonological characteristics of the Word level suggest that there is none. From this I conclude that the lexicon has two domains at which phonology takes place. This is structured so that at the Stem level the phonology and morphology interfeed in the way usually assumed in most standard lexical phonologies. On exiting the Stem level, all forms cycle through the phonology on their way to the morphology of the Word level. This is the Word-cycle and constitutes the second and final lexical phonological domain. It is the only phonological cycle at this level and links the two domains. The output of the Word-level morphology enters the phonology again on its way into the syntax; this is the first postlexical domain, the phonological word. It is this domain which corresponds with the domain identified as the word level in Booij and Rubach (1987), Kiparsky (1985), and so on. This is the so-called "postcyclic" or "non-cyclic" domain, not the word level, and it is not a lexical domain.

5. AN ALTERNATIVE PROPOSAL

An alternative way of describing some of the facts I have considered has been suggested to me by Paul Kiparsky.[26] Although the analysis is, I believe, incorrect, I take it seriously because it reflects a very interesting observation about the nature of many of the word-level rules. Since my claim is somewhat innovative, I do not want to discount any alternatives which would allow these facts to be accommodated within a traditional view of lexical phonology. I believe that the view I present accounts for the peculiar properties of word-level phonology, but it is entirely possible that further research will provide the crucial evidence to support one or the other of these two views.

The crux of the alternative idea is the observation that many of the word-cycle rules we have seen are sensitive to syllable structure as it is defined at the word cycle. If we make a single assumption about syllabification processes in the lexicon, we can account for many of the facts we have seen within a theory in which the phonology, after the word cycle, is cyclic. Assume that all lexical syllabification is purely structure-building. Postlexically, syllabification may be structure-changing. Thus syllabification affects only unsyllabified segments—at both levels of the lexicon. At the first level, final consonant extrametricality (Hayes, 1982) blocks the syllabification of final consonants until the following cycle (Borowsky, 1986; Itô, 1986), when the C loses its extrametrical status and is incorporated into the suffix syllable. Assume, in addition, that there is no such final consonant extrametricality at the Word level. Then, by general principles of prosodic licensing, each morphological constituent will be an independent syllabic domain if the morphemes are attached cyclically.

It follows that there will be no resyllabification of any previously organized segments when suffixes are attached, since such an operation would be structure-changing. Any consonant still left unsyllabified by the time a form reaches Level 2 will be dealt with on the word cycle, since it cannot remain extrametrical any longer. On the word cycle, all stray material is syllabified (or deleted). When an affix is attached, the new material is syllabified, but the previous cycle's syllabification is left intact because there is no resyllabification of material organized earlier. As an example illustrating the difference between syllabification strategies at the two levels, compare the derivations of *longer* and *longish.*

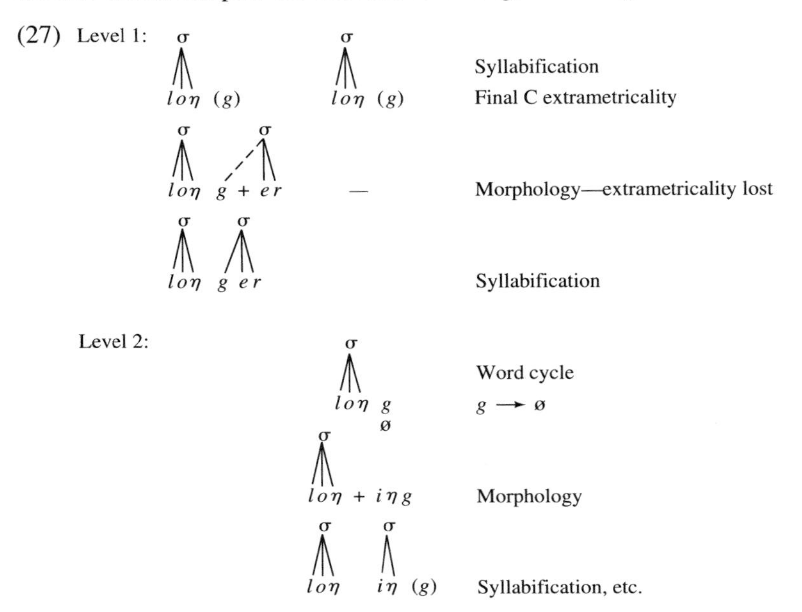

How does this idea explain the facts I have been discussing? If syllabification from the word cycle is maintained throughout the Word level, then any rule which is sensitive to syllabification will apply in syllables which have not been restructured. For example, a rule which I have claimed must apply on the word cycle could in fact apply at any time at the word level because the syllable structure at this level will not be changed even after suffixation. Thus, so long as we allow syllabification to take place either before or at the word cycle, the other rules will apply without problem.

(28)

	σ	σ σ	σ	
Level 1:	*po (l)*	*po l + ar*	*ro (ll)*	Syllabification
	σ	σ σ	σ	
Level 2:	*pole*	*polar*	*roll*	Syllabification
			σ σ	
			roll + er	Syllabification Rule (21)

Recall that the most serious argument against the idea that the Word level was cyclic after the word cycle were those cases in which the addition of an affix produced a sequence which met the structural description of a word-cycle rule. In these cases the rule was blocked in a way which runs counter to our usual expectations about cyclic rule application. There were two examples of this—one was Belfast Dentalization, and the other was German Fricative Assimilation. Belfast Dentalization applied only when the target and the trigger of the rule are tautomorphemic. If syllabification of the word is left undisturbed after the word cycle, the structural description of a syllable-sensitive rule like this will not be met after an affix is adjoined. Thus, even if the rule does apply cyclically, its structural description would not be met at the Word level. Consider as an example the derivation of *wider.*

(29)

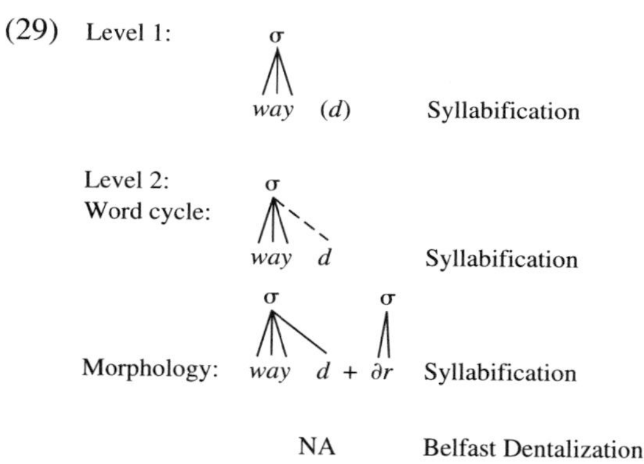

(*d* and *r* are not tautosyllabic)

In this derivation we see that at Level 1 the final consonant is extrametrical. Since no affix is adjoined, the form goes through to the Word level, where at the word cycle the final consonants are licensed—in this case by syllabification. Morphology then adjoins an affix. Belfast Dentalization is blocked at this point because the two relevant segments are not tautosyllabic. As long as this syllabification is maintained through this level, the rule will not apply here. Thus this alone can account for the fact that even when the two segments occur across a boundary the relevant rule does not apply, and it is therefore entirely possible that the Word level is, after all, cyclic.

Unfortunately, however attractive this proposal may seem, given the present state of our knowledge it remains incompatible with many of the facts. In addition it does not suffice as an explanation of the observed properties of the Word level.

The analysis proposed above explains the cases in which the desired effect is to block resyllabification of word-final consonants into suffixal onsets.

(30)

* σ		σ		
V	C]	V		
w i	*d*	*e r*		Belfast Dentalization
r o	*ll*	*i ng*		London [^u] / [ν u]

However, it is more difficult to explain those cases in which the syllabification of suffixal material is to be incorporated into the word-final syllable, or in the case of prefixes, the word-initial syllable.

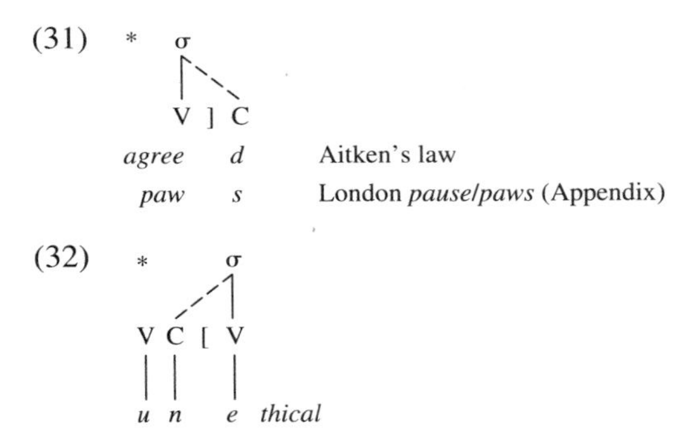

In (31) the suffix consonant is stray and therefore free to be syllabified and incorporated into the previous syllable. The same should be the case in (32). This means that there is a potential difference between these two environments and the one in (30), for the purposes of phonological rule application. I do not know whether this difference is ever exploited. The attested cases do not distinguish between the two types of environment—all the given data make no distinction between the various types of suffixes attached at Level 2; the form *day*]*s* has an open syllable equivalent in every way to that in *dai*]*ly,* for the purposes of the rule accounting for the distribution of the [ɛ:] ~ [ɪə] allophones in Northern Irish.

None of the assumptions about syllabification, which we have made in order to make this proposal work, can block the incorporation of unsyllabified material into an already structured syllable—this is certainly not covered by the usual interpretation of what it means to be structure-changing. Besides, we have already allowed for the syllabification procedures on the Word cycle: stray consonants on the word cycle may be incorporated—final syllabic sonorants—or deleted, if unsyllabified by the first level syllabification processes.

As John McCarthy (personal communication) has pointed out to me, the syllabification explanation makes another prediction. In the known dialects, on this view, the onsetless syllables which arise at Level 2 would persist till the postlexical phonology, where they would be given onsets by resyllabification. For example, in an *r*-less dialect like my own,[27] the word *wondering* is pronounced with an *r* as the onset of the final syllable: [wʌndəriŋ], and not *[wʌndəiŋ]. This shows clearly that resyllabification took place, since syllable-final *r*s are never pronounced; compare *wonder,* which I pronounce [wʌndə]. One might therefore expect a dialect somewhere in which the empty onsets of vowel-initial Word-level affixes are filled by some sort of consonant insertion, say. Yet there are no such cases that I know of. No English dialect has forms like [[*roll*]*ʔer*], [[*roll*]*ʔing*] with a glottal stop filling the onset of the second syllable.

In addition to making incorrect predictions about the kinds of phenomena we may find, the proposal is observationally wrong. Consider, for example, the fact that German Fricative Assimilation is not, as far as I can tell, sensitive to syllable structure. Manipulating the rule in different ways does not make any difference. Even if we assume that German has a phonemic distinction between /x/ and /ç/, it is not clear how to describe the generalization about their distribution in syllabic terms. Although neither the reviewer nor Paul Kiparsky actually made any attempt to explain this particular phenomenon in terms of syllable structure, a fairly plausible analysis might be given along this line: the feature [+back] is spread from vowels to tautosyllabic fricatives; the other alternant, [ç], occurs elsewhere. It is difficult to reconcile such an analysis with monomorphemic forms like: *Buche* 'beech tree', *Knochen* 'bone', *Kuchen* 'cake', *Sprache* 'language', and so on (all with [x]). Ambisyllabicity must be ruled out as a possible explanatory factor because not only are there minimal pairs—compare *sicher* with [ç] versus *kachel* [x], but we will then be stuck again with no explanation for the crucial *-chen* cases. Besides, ambisyllabicity, aside from being a postlexical phenomenon, must be the result of a structure-changing syllabification procedure and thus is not within the spirit of the proposal I am considering here.

Similarly, Aitken's law is also not clearly syllable-sensitive. From the discussion in Wells (1982), one might get the idea that Aitken's law is some kind of open-syllable lengthening. John Harris and Norval Smith have pointed out to me (personal communication) that this is not the case. There are minimal pairs such as *Seery* [si:ri] (long vowel before *r*) versus *Sheedy* [šidi] (short vowel) which illustrate that the rule applies even when the conditioning consonant is not tautosyllabic; and it does not apply if the vowel is merely in an open syllable (see also *ready* and *booty* which have short vowels and are not *[rɛ:di] or *[bu:ti]). The stress requirement on the rule makes it an interesting candidate for a prosodically conditioned rule—which may reintroduce some syllabic conditioning; however, further research would have to be done to take this remark out of the bounds of pure speculation. I therefore assume that the rule is not sensitive to syllable structure in any crucial way; Nor is the Northern Irish alternation:[28] [ɛ:] is word-final, as in *stay,* while the other allophone is found syllable finally, as in *state, station* with [ɪə].

Given that many of the Word-level rules are not syllable-sensitive, the proposal outlined in this section can be rejected, but it brings up a number of related questions which proponents of this idea have not attempted to answer. Why should it be the case that syllabification at the two lexical levels is different? Why do so many rules appear to be sensitive to the syllable structure assigned at the word cycle? Why does it appear that syllable structure is retained at this level? The analysis outlined in this section simply states that it is, without offering any explanation. This view predicts as well that there should be Level 2 rules which apply across the boundaries between morphemes. I have not yet uncovered any such rules.

However, if all phonology takes place before morphology in the word domain, these observations follow. It could only be the syllable structure assigned on the word cycle that will be relevant for rules at the Word level. The system predicts that all Word-level rules which are sensitive to syllable structure will refer to the syllable structure assigned on this cycle. Second, since no rules apply after the morphology of the Word level, no phonology across the morpheme edges will be found at this level. All edge-erasing phonology other than automatic resyllabification will be postlexical. Thus, uniform continuous syllabification processes may be maintained through all levels if the distinction between levels is seen to be a consequence of the way the morphology and phonology feed each other at each level rather than a consequence of stipulations about how individual rules apply at each level.

6. APPENDIX: FURTHER EXAMPLES OF WORD-LEVEL RULES

In this Appendix I list, with brief descriptions, some further examples of rules of English[29] which I consider to be Word-level rules.

6.1. *æ*-Tensing

The rule of *æ*-Tensing is found in many dialects of English. In most of these it applies generally and unconditionally but in others—New York City, Philadelphia, Belfast (Irish English)—the rule is contextually determined. The vowel *æ* tenses when followed by a tautosyllabic nasal fricative or voiced obstruent (though not *d* in Philadelphia).

The data and analysis presented here are taken from Dunlap (1988) on Philadelphia English and Harris (1989) on Belfast English.

(33) *æ* Tensing:

$$æ \rightarrow \text{E} / \underline{\quad\quad} \begin{Bmatrix} \text{nasals} \\ \text{fricatives} \\ \text{voiced stops} \end{Bmatrix}$$

[E]	[æ]
graph	*graphic*
psychopath	*psychopathic*
mass, massive	*massive*
class, classy	*classical, classify*
classing	

The form *gr*[æ]*phic* shows that the rule cannot apply cyclically at Level 1 because that would generate *gr*[[E]*phic*. The rule must apply at the Word-level because we get tense [E] in both affixes and unaffixed forms. Since the rule is sensitive to a tautosyllabic consonant, it must apply before affixation, and subsequent syllabification at Level 2 takes the final consonant out of the syllable to make the onset of the suffix.

(34)

Level 1:	Cycle 1	Cycle 2	
	class	*class + ify*	
	NA	NA	*æ*-Tensing
Level 2:			
Word cycle	*cl*[E]*ss*		*æ*-Tensing
Cycle 2	*cl*[E]*ss + y*		

The unaffixed *class* undergoes the rule, becoming *cl*[E]*ss*. Then the affix is incorporated, rendering the correct output *cl*[E]*ssy*.

6.2. Vowel Rounding in Adelaide English

In the Adelaide dialect of Australian English as described by Simpson (1980), there is a rule similar to the London rule in (28). Certain vowels are rounded in the environment of a tautosyllabic *l*.

(35) $[+\text{back}, \alpha\text{high}] \rightarrow [+\text{round}] / \_\_\_]$

Thus there is a contrast between unrounded V in *holy, lowly, Julie* versus rounded V in *goal, fool, pole.* Again this rounding is carried over from the unaffixed forms to those forms affixed at Level 2, even though the conditioning *l* has been moved to the onset of the affix syllable. That is, the syllable-final *l* in *goal* conditions rounding before affixation to create a contrast between monomorphemic *holy* and bimorphemic *goalie.*

(36)

[−round]	[+round]
holy	*goal*
bowler (hat)	*bowler* 'one who bowls'
Julie	*fooling*

6.3. London *pause~paws*

In London English (data from Wells, 1982:310–313 and Harris, 1991), the vowel *o* has two allophones: [ɔə] and [oʊ]. The [ɔə] variant occurs in final open syllables, the other variant [oʊ] occurs elsewhere.

(37)

[ɔə]	[oʊ]
saw, soar[30]	*sauce*
law, lore	*lord*
paw, pore	*thought*

Once again, the complementary distribution seen in the monomorphemic examples does not carry over to forms derived at Level 2. Whichever variant is found in unaffixed forms is found as well before suffixes.

(38)

[ɔə]	[oʊ]
bored	*board*
paws	*pause*
poorly	*Crawley*
law term	*Lawton*

The affixes do not close the syllables for the rule. Instead the rule applies as if the final vowel of the stem was in an open syllable, itself final. The rule thus applies on the word cycle before any Level 2 morphology.

There are a few other rules which appear to me to be examples of word-cycle rules; however, I do not have enough information about them to be absolutely sure. These rules exhibit the same sort of patterning shown by all the previous examples.

Pre-*l* Breaking (Wells, 1982) makes a monosyllabic word disyllabic before *l*. As usual, the effects of this rule carry over to affixed forms in which the *l* appears now to be in the onset of the affix syllable.

(39)

feel	[fiəl/fiyəl]	*rule*	[ruəl/ruwəl]
feeling	[fiəliŋ/fiyəliŋ]	*ruling*	[ruəliŋ/ruwəliŋ]

Sledd (1958) mentions an allophonic alternation found in dialects of Southern American which again shows similar distribution patterns. There are two allophones of the /i/ vowel. One is found followed by tautosyllabic *r* as well as when the *r* is followed by Level 2 affixes. The other is found elsewhere.

(40)

[ɪə]	[i:]
beer	
beery	*Erie*
jeer	
jeering	*hero*

ACKNOWLEDGMENTS

I thank Geert Booij, Allan James, John Harris, Harry van der Hulst, John McCarthy, Norval Smith, and three anonymous reviewers for their comments on earlier versions of this paper. John Harris, Paul Kiparsky, and John McCarthy also provided me with additional examples of word-level rules. I am also grateful to students in my seminars at the University of Delaware and Rijksuniversiteit te Leiden, in particular Barbara Bullock and

Mark Verhijde, as well as to audiences at the Lexical Phonology Workshop, Seattle; the University of Texas, Austin; and the University of Massachusetts, Amherst. The article was completed while I had the honor of being a fellow at the Netherlands Institute for Advanced Study (NIAS), and I am grateful indeed to the Institute for providing me with such a pleasant and wonderful environment.

NOTES

[1] Three general types are distinguishable:

1. The interactive model: Each morphological operation is input to a phonological cycle (e.g., Kiparsky, 1982; Mohanan, 1986; Pesetsky, 1979).
2. The noninteractive model: All morphology precedes all phonology (e.g., Halle and Kenstowicz, 1989; Halle and Vergnaud, 1987; Odden, this volume; Sproat, 1985).
3. The combination model: Morphology feeds phonology cyclically at some levels and applies in a block before phonological rules at another (Booij and Rubach, 1985; Halle and Mohanan, 1985; Kiparsky, 1985).

[2] There has been very little in-depth study of the phonology associated with the stress-neutral affixes, as far as I know. The processes discussed in Section 2, which have been widely discussed, and more recently the phenomena discussed by Dunlap (1987), Hall (1989a), and Harris (1989, 1991) are the only ones to have received much attention.

[3] In Borowsky (1986, 1989) I showed that the pattern of so-called lexical properties only holds at the first level. Halle and Mohanan (1985) argue that the second level violates the strict cycle condition; the cyclicity of this level has been called into question by Booij and Rubach (1987), Halle and Mohanan (1985), and Halle and Vergnaud (1987), for example.

[4] See note 5.

[5] A reviewer has suggested that the optional desyllabification I propose may not be an optional postlexical rule. The reviewer cites examples like: *whistling, wrestling, hustling, crippling, enabling,* and *troubling,* all of which s/he finds acceptable with nonsyllabic /l/, while examples like *Sicily, Esalen, oscillatory, insolent,* and *sibilant* are rather better with syllabic /l/. I suggest that the latter cases are different in that they all have underlying vowels (either full vowels or schwa). These vowels, even when they are destressed, are different from the syllabic sonorant cases where there is never a vowel. The two cases merge very late—possibly in the phonetic implementation—and we can assume that any desyllabification that takes place must take place before this. No doubt word frequency also has some effect, as suggested by the same reviewer.

[6] I have taken most of the data from Rubach (1990). The interpretation of the facts is mine, however. An anonymous reviewer argues that the proper treatment of sonorants is to desyllabify them in certain environments, as suggested by Rubach. This solution misses the generalization. The crucial fact here is that sonorants are never syllabic before Level 1 affixes even though they are optionally syllabic before those that are found at Level 2. Desyllabification leaves this unexplained. Note that this is the same pattern found with the English cases. The same reviewer goes on to suggest that the array of facts found for *g*

deletion is unconvincing because it is so small: that the relevant words should simply be marked as exceptions to *g*-deletion. Yet the observation that the facts pattern in one direction and not in the opposite direction is a valid one. *g* does not delete before the Level 1 affixes. This is significant. Marking forms as exceptions when their pattern is predictable, even if there are only a few such forms, misses the point. True exceptions would not fall into a pattern and we would get a random set of variations.

[7] The formulation of the rule is not crucial and does not affect my point, since it is the pattern of distribution I am concerned with. The correct analysis seems to me to be one similar to Hall's, in which the fricative is unspecified and gets [back] by rule and is otherwise nonback.

[8] If you think about it, all the rules seen so far—English as well as German—have a similar property. The crucial factor for all these rules is the fact that they are blind to any material outside their immediate domain. Most of the rules I have discussed so far have the property of applying only within the Word built in, by dint of the] in their conditioning environment. (Note it may equally well be [.) This seems to be similar to saying these processes only apply tautomorphemically. The sole difference is that in these rules the word edge IS the conditioning environment.

[9] In some dialects of German the rule is postlexical and in fact the forms in (10) are all pronounced with [x] as expected.

[10] Note that in these dialects these words are pronounced without a vowel in the suffix: [ɛləmɛn̪t̪r̪iy], [saenɪt̪r̪iy].

[11] Harris formulates the rule as a blank-filling rule, which gets him around the SCC violation. However, on his analysis it remains an odd rule since it applies ONLY at Level 1, which is peculiar by virtue of the fact that it is clearly not structure-preserving, as he himself notes. I think this is dubious since it is quite unlike any of the other rules of English which are restricted to Level 1. These are a small set of highly morphologized rules, e.g., Trisyllabic Laxing, Velar Softening, and Spirantization. Belfast Dentalization is quite unlike any of these rules.

[12] It is not entirely clear what the effect of stress on Aitken's law is. The stress condition is perhaps more complicated than is presented. As John McCarthy has pointed out to me, the only unstressed vowels in English are schwas, which would not undergo the rule. The only cases of nonschwa unstressed vowels occur word finally. He notes as well that there is no interaction of cyclic stress assignment with the rule which supports the claim that it is a Word-level rule.

[13] See Harris (1990) for arguments leading to his assigning this rule to Level 2.

[14] Booij and Rubach (1987) discuss Dutch Syllable Final devoicing ($[-\text{son}] \rightarrow [-\text{voice}]$ / ____ $) as an example of what they refer to as a word-level rule which applies non(post)cyclically. That this rule is not cyclic is illustrated by alternations like *held* [t] 'hero' vs. *heldin* [d] 'heroine'. They argue further that the rule is lexical on the grounds that it precedes two other clearly postlexical processes, Voicing Assimilation and Resyllabification. This argument, based on ordering of rules, does not conclusively place Dutch Final Devoicing in the lexicon, however, and I assume that this rule and others like it (e.g., English *r*-deletion) are very early postlexical rules which apply in the first postlexical domain of phonological word.

[15] A study of the few rules associated with the rest of the Level 2 affixes reveals only

one possible candidate which could show some phonological interaction between affix and stem or affix and affix. That is the cluster of rules, Voicing Assimilation and epenthesis/deletion, found with the inflectional affixes *-ed* and *-es*. I suggest, however, that these processes are postlexical and do not take place at Level 2 at all. We know that they must apply postlexically in certain syntactic structures: *the dog's bone, the cat's milk, the horse's mouth;* as well as after postlexical reduction processes: *the cat's gonna bite, the dog's gonna scratch, the horse's gonna snort,* etc. There is no evidence to force us to apply the rules at Level 2 when the affixes are attached.

[16]The same observation holds for the /*-ung*/ affix in German. Bloomfield (1930) suggested that the German affix /-chen/ should be treated as an independent form for the purposes of the rule which determines the distribution of [x] and [ç] exactly as I suggest in this system. The affix must cycle independently through the phonology in order to derive the [ç] from some underlying underspecified fricative.

[17]Another possibility which has been suggested to me is the one to be discussed in Section 5.

[18]Note that I exclude the compound stress rule or the nuclear stress rule. When I refer to the regular stress rules I mean the word-stress rules. For an account of the different compound stress phenomena compatible with my view, see, e.g., Sproat (1985), Selkirk (1982).

[19]Perhaps also /-ly/, /-y/ and /-ish/—all of which retain their full vowels. It could be that these affixes have tense vowels but are not stressed. *-ize* is another affix which seems stressed to me. This affix is generally problematic, and it is sometimes claimed that it has a dual class membership (Kiparsky, 1982; Selkirk, 1982). I personally believe this affix is really a Level 1 affix and not stress-neutral at all—as evidenced by words like *demócratize, autómatize, cathólicize,* and others. I suggest that the affix is itself stressed and thus shifts stress off adjacent stressed syllables. It does not have any effect on stress in a word like *standardization* because there is no stress adjacent to its own stress. Stress cannot shift to the last syllable of *standard* because that would cause a clash.

[20]Note that it does not follow that all Level 2 affixes should be stressed just because each of them has been cycled on. For example, suffixes like *-ness, -less,* and even *-dom* with internal [ə]s do not get stressed (e.g., *stresslessness, mercilessness* have only one stress per word). On the other hand, affixes like *un-, re-,* and *-hood* are stressed even though their stresses do not appear to affect the rest of the stresses of the word—e.g., *rèróute, ùnfórtunate, bóyhòod.* Similarly, affixes consisting of one consonant, say, either would be repaired by syllabification by the insertion of a [ə], or they could escape syllabification till later. Repairing them by means of epenthesis would have the effect of making the English inflectional affixes /-d/ and /-z/ into /-əd/ and /-əz/. This could be why we cannot decide which is the correct underlying representation for these affixes.

[21]The only potential edge-erasing phonology we find is CV syllabification, which we assume takes place automatically and continuously throughout the derivation (Itô, 1986). However, even if syllabification were to be suspended, there is no evidence which would force the syllabification of stem final Cs to apply at the word level. It could be done on the first postlexical phonological domain, as the Dutch final devoicing facts mentioned in note 14 suggest.

[22]With the exception of Sproat (1985), who makes most of these observations.

[23] Following Kiparsky (1982) we could assume that the output of every cycle is a "lexical entry." This could be interpreted to mean that each form derived at Level 1 is "listed" in a strange sense (not exactly that of Jackendoff): the lexical identity rule for each form.

[24] Of course this is not true. We CAN produce new words by means of the morphological and phonological rules at the first level. The lexicon is not merely a list of existing words. But it does seem that by some measure of productivity the Word level is more so than the Stem level.

[25] Suppose that to be productive in the sense of Word-level productive means that the affix is used on line in the actual creation of complex words. That is, Stem-level forms may be analyzable but when you use them in production you just do a lexical look-up of the whole word. It is lexically listed. On the other hand, when you use a Word-level affixed form, you actually put it together during production. It is not available as a prepackaged form. Psycholinguistic data, as far as I know, have shown that Level 1 phonological and morphological processes are never affected in speech errors and so on, while Level 2 processes are. We could suppose therefore that the base of affixation in these forms is not an underlying representation but an actually occurring word. This would support my picture of the lexicon. I am grateful to Donca Steriade for making these points to me.

[26] A similar suggestion was made by an anonymous reviewer.

[27] Conservative South African English.

[28] It may be possible to redefine these rules as foot rules, similar to English Flapping. Even on this assumption, though, we cannot maintain the idea that lexical syllabification is limited to structure-building processes only. However, until more is known about the rules in question, I leave these speculations for future research.

[29] English and German are not the only languages which have a word cycle. For some word-level rules in Arabic dialects see Dunlap (1987), who discusses two rules: Palestinian Backing (from Younes, 1984) and Bedouin Hijazi Liquid Emphaticization (from Al-Mozaini, 1982). Booij and Rubach (1987) refer to Rochet's (1973) discussion of *Loi de position* and other examples from French dialects. Danish Grave Assimilation appears to me to be a similar type of rule (see Borowsky, Itô, and Mester, 1984, and references cited therein). Most of the well-known word-final cluster simplification rules, especially in Indo-European languages (Catalan: see, e.g., Kiparsky, 1985; Danish: Itô, 1984; Icelandic: e.g., Kiparsky, 1985; Itô, 1986; etc.), appear to be examples of the same Word-level prosodic licensing phenomena as the English cases in (3).

[30] Recall that London English is a nonrhotic dialect: *lore* and *law* are homophonous.

REFERENCES

Al-Mozainy, (1981). *Vowel Alternations in a Bedouin Hijazi Arabic Dialect: Abstractness and Stress.* Doctoral dissertation, University of Texas, Austin.

Aronoff, M., and Sridhar, S. N. (1983). Morphological Levels in English and Kannada; or Atarizing Reagan. *Papers from the Parasession on the Interplay of Phonology, Morphology and Syntax,* pp. 3–16. Chicago Linguistic Society, Chicago.

Bloomfield, L. (1930). German ç and x. *Le Maître Phonétique 3* **20,** 27–28.

Booij, G., and Rubach, J. (1987). Postcyclic versus postlexical rules in lexical phonology. *Linguistic Inquiry* **18,** 1–44.

Borowsky, T. (1986). *Topics in the Lexical Phonology of English.* Doctoral dissertation, University of Massachusetts, Amherst.

Borowsky, T. (1989). Syllable Codas in English and Structure-Preservation. *Natural Language and Linguistic Theory* **7,** 146–166.

Borowsky, T., Itô, J., and Mester, A. (1984). The formal representation of ambisyllabicity: Evidence from Danish. *Proceedings of the North Eastern Linguistic Society* **14,** 38–48.

Dunlap, E. (1987). *æ Tensing in New York English.* Unpublished manuscript, University of Massachusetts, Amherst.

Hall, T.-A. (1989a). Lexical Phonology and the distribution of German [ç] and [x]. *Phonology* **6,** 1–17.

Hall, T.-A. (1989b). German syllabification, the velar nasal, and the representation of schwa. *Linguistics* **27,** 807–842.

Halle, M. (1988). *Why Phonological Strata Should Not Include Affixation.* Unpublished manuscript, Massachusetts Institute of Technology, Cambridge.

Halle, M., and Kenstowicz, M. (1989). *On Cyclic and Noncyclic Stress.* Unpublished manuscript, Massachusetts Institute of Technology, Cambridge.

Halle, M., and Mohanan, K. P. (1985). Segmental Phonology of Modern English. *Linguistic Inquiry* **16,** 15–116.

Halle, M., and Vergnaud, J.-R. (1987). *An Essay on Stress.* MIT Press, Cambridge, Mass.

Harris, J. (1989). Toward a lexical analysis of sound change in progress. *Journal of Linguistics* **25,** 35–56.

Harris, J. (1991). Derived phonological contrasts. In *Studies in the Pronunciation of English; A Commemorative Volume in Honour of A. C. Gimson* (S. Ramsavan, ed.), pp. 87–105. Croom Helm, London.

Hayes, B. (1982). Extrametricality and English stress. *Linguistic Inquiry* **13,** 227–276.

Itô, J. (1984). *Consonant Loss in Danish and Phonological Theory.* Paper presented at ICU Summer Institute in Linguistics, Tokyo.

Itô, J. (1986). *Syllable Theory in Prosodic Phonology.* Doctoral dissertation, University of Massachusetts, Amherst.

Itô, J. (1989). A prosodic theory of epenthesis. *Natural Language and Linguistic Theory* **7,** 217–259.

Kahn, D. (1976). *Syllable Based Generalizations in English Phonology.* Doctoral dissertation, Massachusetts Institute of Technology, Cambridge.

Kiparsky, P. (1982). From cyclic phonology to lexical phonology. In *The Structure of Phonological Representations. Part I* (H. van der Hulst and N. Smith, eds.), pp. 131–175. Foris, Dordrecht.

Kiparsky, P. (1985). Some consequences of lexical phonology. *Phonology Yearbook* **2,** 85–138.

Lieber, R. (1979). *On the Organization of the Lexicon.* Doctoral dissertation, Massachusetts Institute of Technology, Cambridge.

Mohanan, K. P. (1986). *The Theory of Lexical Phonology.* Reidel, Dordrecht.

Rochet, B. (1973). On the Status of the Word in French Phonology. *International Review of Applied Linguistics in Language Teaching* **25,** 187–196.
Rubach, J. (1990). Final devoicing and cyclic syllabification in German. *Linguistic Inquiry* **21,** 79–94.
Selkirk, E. O. (1982). *The Syntax of Words.* MIT Press, Cambridge, Mass.
Simpson, J. (1980 *Cyclic Syllabification and a First Cycle Rule of Vowel-rounding in Some Dialects of Australian English.* Unpublished manuscript, Massachusetts Institute of Technology, Cambridge.
Sledd, J. (1958). Some questions of English phonology. *Language* **34,** 252–258.
Sproat, R. (1985). *On Deriving the Lexicon.* Doctoral dissertation, Massachusetts Institute of Technology, Cambridge.
Wells, J. (1982). *Accents of English,* 3 vols. Cambridge University Press, Cambridge.
Younes, M. (1984). Emphasis and the low vowels in Palestinian Arabic. In *Working Papers in Cognitive Science* (J. McCarthy and A. Woodbury, eds.).

STRUCTURE PRESERVATION AND POSTLEXICAL TONOLOGY IN DAGBANI

LARRY M. HYMAN

Department of Linguistics
University of California
Berkeley, California 94720

1. INTRODUCTION

Among the most attractive ideas motivating the framework of lexical phonology is the view that a single rule may apply in different places within the phonology but show different effects, depending on where it applies. For instance, it has been hypothesized that a structure-changing rule applying lexically can apply only to derived domains, must be structure-preserving, and may have lexical exceptions. On the other hand, the same rule applying postlexically may have just the opposite properties. That is, it may apply across the board (i.e., also to non-derived domains), it may introduce new segments, and it is not expected to have lexical exceptions. While these purported differences are still being tested (and have sometimes been challenged in the literature),[1] there can be no doubt about the general tendency for lexical rule application to be of a different character from its postlexical counterpart.

In this article I examine the issue of structure preservation (SP) as it pertains to the tonology of Dagbani, a Gur language spoken in Ghana. The issue of interest is that Dagbani has a pervasive constraint forbidding contour tones throughout most of the tonology. By SP, a rule whereby a high tone (H) spreads onto a following low-tone (L) syllable automatically delinks that L, so as to avoid the unacceptable contour. At a later stage in the derivation, however, the same H-spreading rule reapplies, this time WITHOUT L-delinking. As a result, HL contour tones

Phonetics and Phonology, Volume 4
Studies in Lexical Phonology

ultimately surface in violation of SP. The key issue here concerns the place in Dagbani phonology at which SP has apparently turned off. As we shall see, this level does not correspond to the lexical/postlexical distinction postulated by the theory. Finally, since multiple application of tone-spreading has a cumulative effect, the strong domain hypothesis (SDH) of Kiparsky (1984) predicts that a H tone could potentially spread as many syllables away from its underlying position as there are strata or levels within the language-particular phonology. Thus, a second issue in this study concerns the appropriateness of the SDH in predicting the observed tonal facts in Dagbani.

The paper is organized as follows. In Section 2 I present the morphological and phonological structure of nouns in Dagbani, including their lexical tonal representation. In Section 3 I establish that the rule of H-tone Spreading alluded to above applies at the postlexical level but has two different effects: one supporting versus one violating SP. In Section 4 I consider different interpretations of these facts, arguing finally in the conclusion in Section 5 for a modification both of SP and of the SDH.

2. LEXICAL TONOLOGY

For expository reasons, most of the discussion in this article concerns the realization of tone on nouns or on words that follow nouns.[2] Before addressing the specific tonal properties of nouns in Dagbani, a few general observations concerning the overall system are in order. First, the tone-bearing unit (TBU) in this language is the syllable (or, perhaps more appropriately, the head mora of the syllable).[3] Second, a surface TBU may be realized on either a H or a L pitch level, or it can be realized with a HL falling contour. The corresponding LH rising contour does not exist in Dagbani. Finally, as will be seen in many of the examples, the language possesses a surface phonemic downstep, contrasting the sequences H–H and H–ꜜH.[4]

As a preliminary to understanding the nominal tonology of Dagbani, the examples in (1) are designed to illustrate that the vast majority of nouns end with an overt (noun class) suffix.[5]

(1) a. *bí-á* 'child' pl. *bí-hí*
b. *pág-á* 'woman' pl. *pág-bá*
c. *tìb-lí* 'ear' pl. *tìb-á*
d. *wáb-gú* 'elephant' pl. *wáb-rí*
e. *bìh-ɨ́m* 'milk'

On the other hand, as seen in (2), a limited of nouns do not show an overt suffix.[6]

(2) a. *bá* 'father' *mà* 'mother'
zá 'starch' *zò* 'friend' (~*zòrí*)

b.	*kòdú*	'banana'	*kúrcú*	'pig'
	kúrwà	'pot'	*báají*	'bag'
c.	*àbòbòí*	'plantain'	*àkàrmá*	'drummer'

While those in (2a) are native, the nouns in (2b) and (2c) are all borrowings (the latter set showing an initial [a], the only vowel that can begin a Dagbani noun—and only in borrowings). While the majority of nouns form their plural by substituting a different noun class suffix, as seen above in (1a–d), the nouns in (2) all form their plural by adding the self-standing form *nɨ̀má,* as in *bá nɨ̂má* 'fathers', *kòdù nɨ́mà* 'bananas'.

I now show that bisyllabic nouns consisting of a monosyllabic stem plus an overt suffix fall into one of four general tone classes, as distinguished in (3a–d).

(3)	CVC.CV		CV.CV		CV.V	
a.	*ɲéb-gá*	'crocodile'	*pág-á*	'woman'	*dó-ó*	'man'
b.	*wáb-gú*	'elephant'	*sán-á*	'stranger'	*nó-ó*	'chicken'
c.	*dàb-lí*	'slave'	*wà-hú*	'horse'	*nà-á*	'chief'
d.	*záb-gù*	'hair'	*kpáŋ-à*	'guineafowl'		

The three columns in (3) represent the three different bisyllabic structures that are attested: CVC.CV, CV.CV, and CV.V. While the nouns in (3a) and (3b) have the same surface realization in isolation, it happens that their tonal properties are quite different in context. Finally, only three tone patterns were noted on CV.V nouns, whose vocalic suffix is underlying /-á/.

I now argue that noun class suffixes are all underlyingly H, and that the tonal classes in (3a–d) can be distinguished by representing the underlying stem tones as follows (cf. Goad, 1988).[7]

(4) a. /pag/ 'woman' c. /war/ 'horse'
        L

b. /san/ 'stranger' d. /kpaŋ/ 'guineafowl'
    H HL

As indicated in (4), it is proposed that stems such as in (3a) are underlyingly toneless, those in (3b) are H, those in (3c) are L, and those in (3d) are HL.

To justify this position, consider first the noun + adjective sequences in (5).

(5) a. /pag + tɨta-li/ → *pàg tɨ́tá-lɨ́* 'big woman'
    H H

b. /san + tɨta-li/ → *sá:n tɨ́tá-lɨ́* 'big stranger'
    H H H

c. /war + tɨta-li/ → *wàr tɨ́tá-lɨ́* 'big horse'
    L H H

d. /kpaŋ + tɨta-li/ → *kpá:n ꜝtɨ́tá-lɨ́* 'big guineafowl'
    HL H H

As seen, when followed by an adjectival noun such as *tɨ́tá-lɨ́* 'big' (which consists of a H stem + H noun class suffix), a modified noun appears without its suffix.[8]

The surface tones of (5b,c) follow directly from the underlying representations without modification. The H of the underlying HL of /kpaŋ/ 'guineafowl' is realized on the noun stem in (5d), while the L causes the following H's of the adjective to be lowered to a downstep. In (6a) the toneless noun stem /pag/ 'woman' receives a L tone by default.

Turning to a more complex set of alternations, consider the realization of these same nouns when followed by a H tone noun in (6).

(6)	a.	*pág-á yí-lí*	'woman's house'	[páɣ yílí]
	b.	*sán-á ꜝyí-lí*	'stranger's house'	[sán ꜝyílí]
	c.	*wà-hù yí-lí*	'horse's house'	[wàh yílí]
	d.	*kpáŋ-ꜝá yí-lí*	'guineafowl's house'	[kpáŋ ꜝyílí]

In (6) these nouns appear within the genitive construction, which in Dagbani consists of a simple juxtaposition of possessor + possessed.[9] As seen in the phonetic transcriptions to the right, the final vowel of the possessor is generally elided when not phrase final, a phenomenon that is quite widespread in Gur languages (see, e.g., Rialland, 1980). As seen in (6a,b), the two H–H tone patterns in (3a,b) again show a difference in context: nouns such as *sán-á* 'stranger' condition a following downstep, while nouns such as *pág-á* 'woman' do not. In (6c), the L–H of *wà-hú* has become L–L, while in (4d), the H–L of *kpáŋ-à* 'guineafowl' is realized as H–ꜝH.

The realizations in (6) are those found quite generally when full nouns are followed by any word beginning with a H tone. By "full nouns" I mean nouns that consist of a stem + suffix, as we have seen. In (6c) the underlying L–H sequence of /wàr-hú/ 'horse' becomes L–L by the postlexical L-tone Spreading rule in (7a).[10]

(7) a. b.

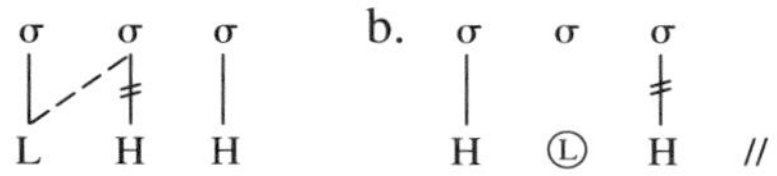

The H–ꜝH sequence on *kpáŋ-ꜝá* in (6d) is directly attributable to the fact that the noun stem /kpaŋ/ is underlyingly HL and the following suffix *-a* is underlyingly H. In isolation such nouns are realized H–L as the result of the late rule in (7b), which lowers a single ꜝH to L before pause.

This leaves the problem of accounting for the difference between (6a) and (6b). Though both are realized H–H in isolation, nouns such as *sán-á* 'stranger' condition a downstep on a following H, while nouns such as *pág-á* 'woman' do not. In this proposal, the underlying representations are as in (8).

(8) a. [[pag] a] 'woman'
       H

   b. [[san] a] 'stranger'
       H H

   c. [[war] hu] 'horse'
       L H

   d. [[kpaŋ] a] 'guineafowl'
       HL H

The lexical tone rules that are needed to derive the surface forms of these nouns are formalized in (9).

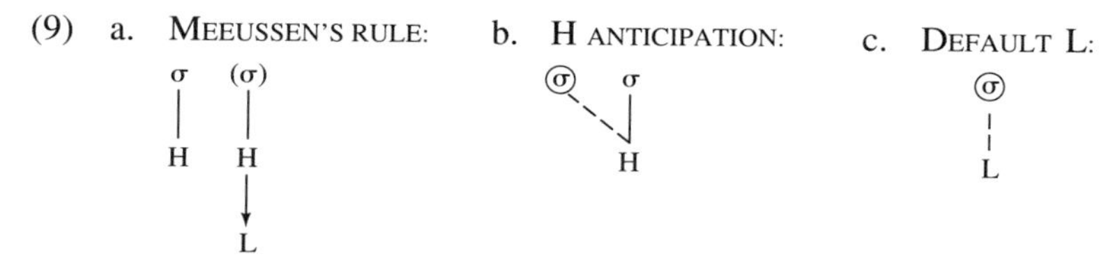

The rule in (9a) dissimilates a H to L when immediately preceded by a H (as happens with "Meeussen's Rule" in Bantu). By a rule of H-tone Anticipation, (9b) spreads the H of the suffix onto a preceding toneless noun stem [thereby accounting for the H tone that appears on (a) nouns when suffixed].[11] Finally, (9c) shows that after (9a) and (9b) have applied, any TBU that is still toneless receives a L tone by default. The output of the three rules in (9) provides the lexical representation of each noun. Finally, in the case of H–L nouns derived by (9a), a postlexical rule of rightward H-tone Spreading (HTS_1) applies, which also delinks the L, as formalized in (10).

(10) (σ) σ

H L

The two H–H noun patterns can be now derived as follows.

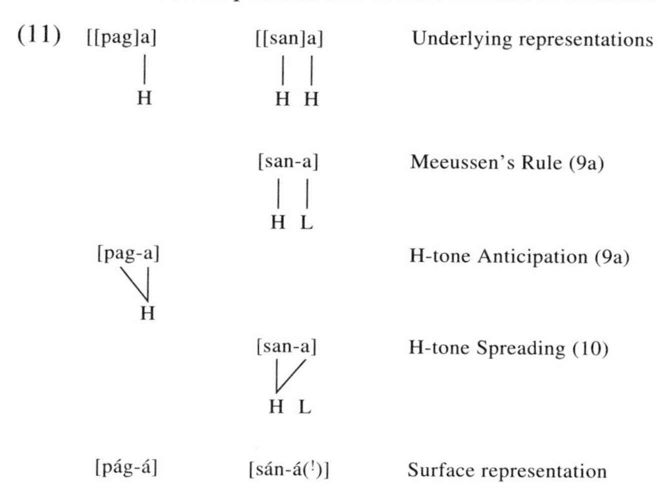

As seen in the left column, the H–H of *pág-á* 'woman' is derived by anticipating the H of the suffix *-á* onto the preceding toneless stem /pag/.[12] The H–H of *sán-á* 'stranger' is derived in quite a different way. First, Meeussen's Rule converts the underlying H–H sequence to H–L. Then H-tone Spreading (a postlexical rule) spreads the H, delinking the L. The configuration in (12a) of an unlinked L tone wedged between H's is realized as a H followed by a downstepped ꜝH. Thus, (6b) would be represented as in (12b).

(12) a. σ σ
| |
H L H

b. *sáná ꜝyí-lí* 'stranger's house'
H L H

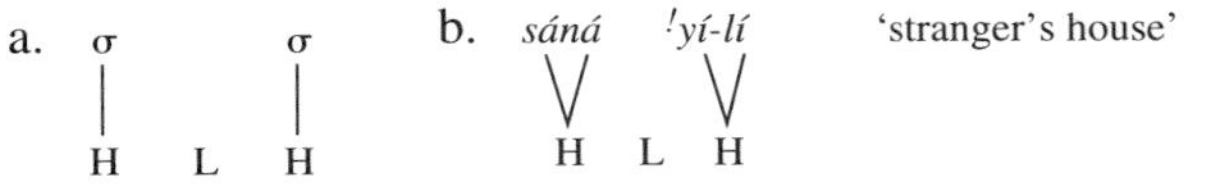

The floating L following such nouns as *sán-á* 'stranger' has no effect before pause. However, as pointed out by Wilson (1970:409), nouns such as *pág-á* and *sán-á* have different surface realizations when accompanied by the vocative intonation which involves a lengthened final vowel.

(13) a. *pág-áá* 'Woman!' b. *sán-áà* 'Stranger!'

As seen in (13b), the floating L is, in this case, allowed to link onto the lengthened final vowel, suggesting that the extra length constitutes an additional TBU (syllable?). With these derivations and additional observations established, we can now turn to the theoretical problems posed by the rule(s) of H-tone Spreading.

3. POSTLEXICAL TONOLOGY

In Section 2 I presented full nouns followed by a possessed noun with initial H tone [cf. (4)] and noun stems followed by adjectives with both initial H [cf. (5)] and initial L [cf. (7)]. What was not shown was the realization of the four full noun forms followed by a possessed noun with initial L. This gap is now filled by the data in (14).

(14) a. *pag-a kodu* ⟶ *pág(-á) kódù* 'woman's banana'
H L H

b. *san-a kodu* ⟶ *sán(-á) kôdú* 'stranger's banana'
H L L H

c. *wa-hu kodu* ⟶ *wà-h(ù) kódù* 'horse's banana'
L H L H

d. *kpaŋ-a kodu* ⟶ *kpáŋ-ꜝ(á) kódù* 'guineafowl's banana'
HL H L H

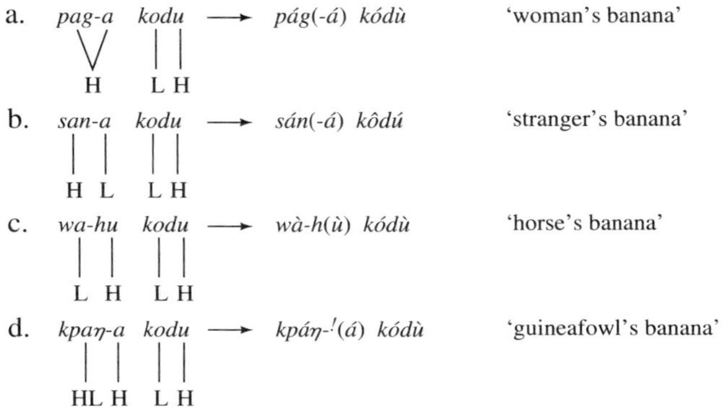

The input tones indicated on *pág-á* and *sán-á* in (14a,b) are those lexically derived in (11). In the outputs in (14), the final vowel of the possessor noun is shown in parentheses since, as was already said, it is subject to reduction, even deletion.

The derivations of (14c,d) are straightforward, involving the spreading of the H of the first suffix onto the L syllable of kòdú 'banana'. The postlexical application of HTS_1 [rule (10)] causes this L to delink, which derives intermediate *kó'dú*. However, as already pointed out, since there is only one 'H TBU before pause, *'dú* becomes L. Finally, the H on the *-hú* suffix in (14c) is lost, either as a result of the vowel reduction process or by the rule of L-tone Spreading in (7a).

The intrigue of the above comes from the comparison of (14a) and (14b). Whereas HTS_1 will derive the correct output in (15a), it will not produce the correct output in (15b).

(15) a. *pag(-a) kodu* [páɣ kódù] (<*pág kó'dú*)

H LH

b. *san(-a) kodu* *[sán kòdú] (cf. [sán kôdú])

H L LH

HTS_1 applies between the two nouns in (15a) to derive the intermediate form shown in the right column, which then undergoes final lowering of 'H to L. In (15b), HTS_1 spreads the stem H of first noun onto the following suffix L, which then delinks. As shown, this should produce a H–L–H sequence in the output. What is observed in (14b), however, is a HL falling tone on [kôdú]. But where does the H of this fall come from?[13] And crucially, regarding the issue of SP, why doesn't the L of the falling tone delink in accordance with the pervasive constraint against HL tones?

The data in (14a,b) show that when a H tone spreads onto a L–H sequence postlexically, two contrasting realizations are obtained: H–'H (simplified to H–L) and HL–H. In (16) we observe a similar opposition when the L tone adjective /kàr-lí/ 'big' follows these nouns.

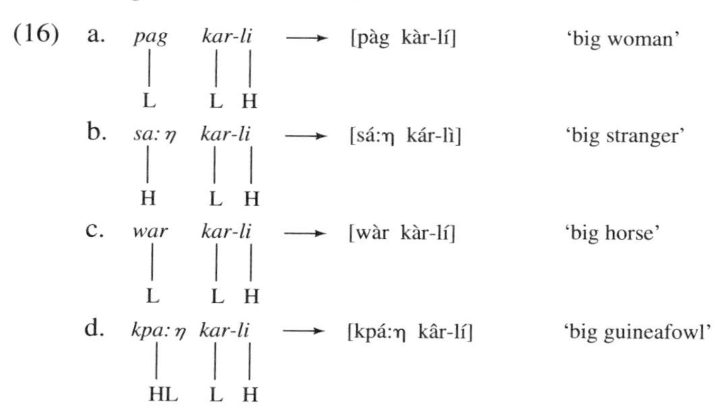

Again, the tonal inputs are those obtained at the end of the lexical phonology. These tones combine to produce the postlexical outputs in (16a) and (16c) without further modification. In (16b), a postlexical application of HTS_1 correctly derives the output (through an intermediate *kár-ꜜlí,* which simplifies to *kár-lì* before pause). In (16d), however, we obtain [kpá:ŋ kâr-lí], with a HL falling tone on [kâr], apparently derived by a H-tone Spreading rule of some sort.

From the forms in (14a,b) and (16b,d), we tentatively arrive at the following descriptive generalizations in (17).

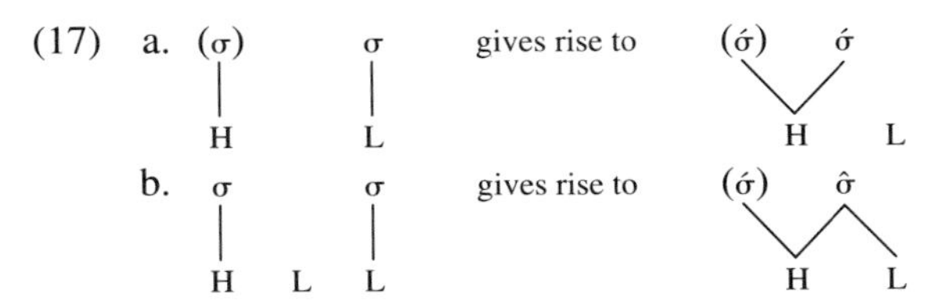

In (17a) a H–L sequence becomes H–H followed by an unlinked L (which can condition downstep on a following H), while in (17b), where there is an unlinked L between the linked H and L tones, the surface instead is a H–HL sequence. As final evidence for these "generalizations," consider the realization of the nouns in (18), first seen in (2a), which do not have an overt (i.e., segmental) noun class suffix.

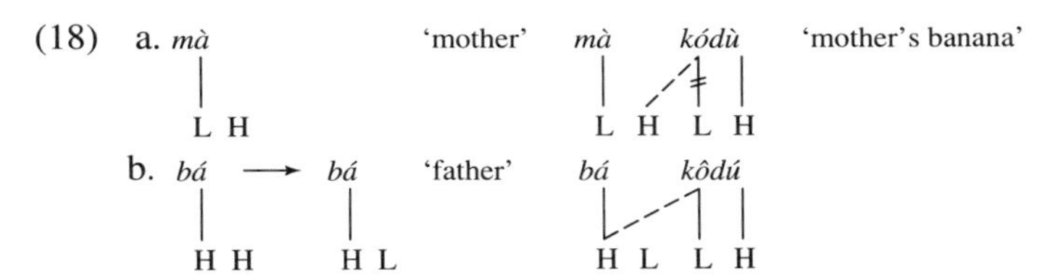

While these two nouns show a single tone in isolation, L versus H respectively, it is clear from the genitive forms to the right that they actually have a H-tone suffix. In (18a) this H is anchored onto the L of *kòdú* 'banana', which is then delinked, creating intermediate *kóꜜdú,* whose ꜜH then is lowered to *kódù* before pause. In (18b), the H suffix first dissimilates by (9a) to become L. Then, as shown, somehow the H of *bá* spreads over the unlinked L onto the linked L of *kòdú* to create the HL falling tone. The question is how to bring this result about.

Let us refer to the H-tone Spreading rule that results in a HL falling tone as HTS_2. There are at least two problems associated with HTS_2. The first has already been mentioned, namely, Why doesn't it cause delinking of the L? The second problem is perhaps even more basic: How can any rule of HTS apply across an unlinked L? The normal expectation is that a free L in a sequence such as we have to the right in (18b) would BLOCK HTS, as the earliest studies on floating tones showed. If, as I believe, floating L's should universally block HTS, then one possibility is to delete them, as needed. Thus, a "natural" solution to this problem would be to recognize the following three rules.

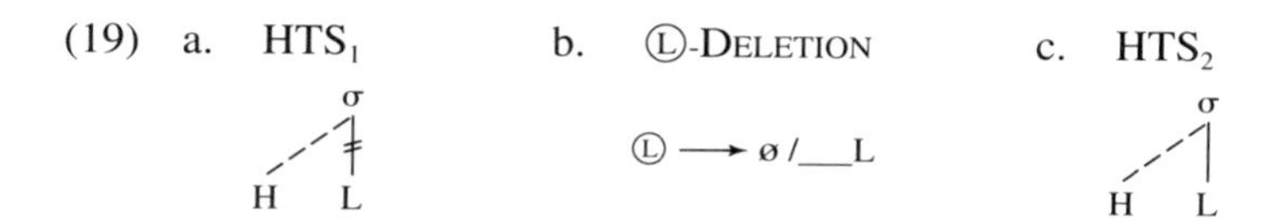

First, HTS_1 applies in (19a), automatically delinking the L (by SP). This free L tone (indicated by Ⓛ) is then deleted when followed by another L tone.[14] At this point HTS_2 can apply, as in (19c). As seen, this rule of H-tone Spreading does not delink the L and thus does not respect SP.

On the other hand, it might be suggested that Ⓛ-deletion is not needed, and in fact, that HTS_2 REQUIRES a free L tone in order to apply, as in (20a).

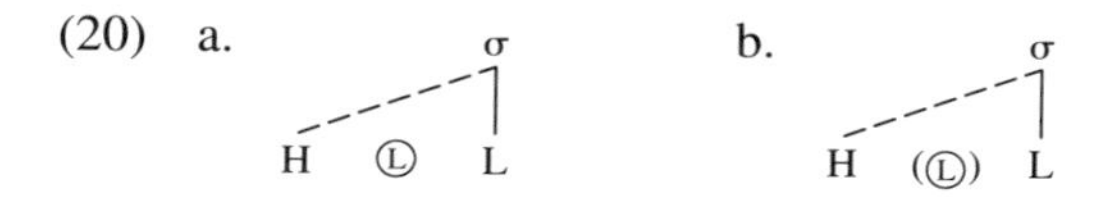

The derivation in (21a), however, shows that HTS_2 does not require a free L.

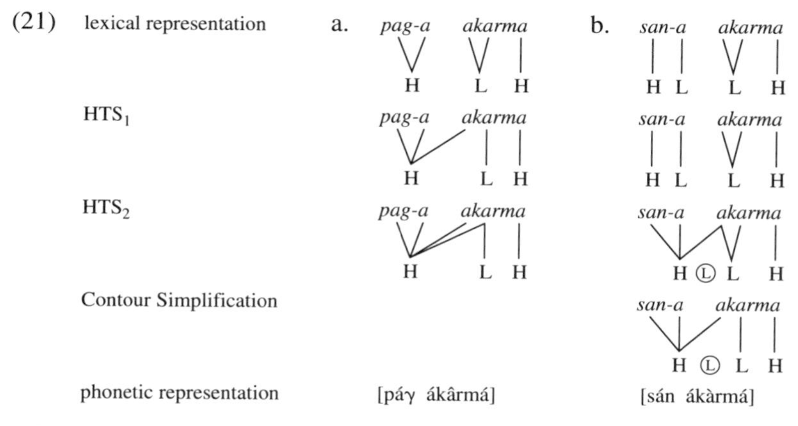

In this example, the noun [àkàrmá] 'drummer' has a single L tone lexically linked to its first two syllables. HTS_1 first applies, delinking this L from the first syllable of the noun, followed by HTS_2, which forms a HL contour on the second syllable. Thus, if there is no Ⓛ-deletion, HTS_2 would have to be formulated as in (20b), that is, with an optional free L. Finally, a rule of L absorption applies, as in (22), removing the L of a HL contour when followed directly by another L or by pause.[15]

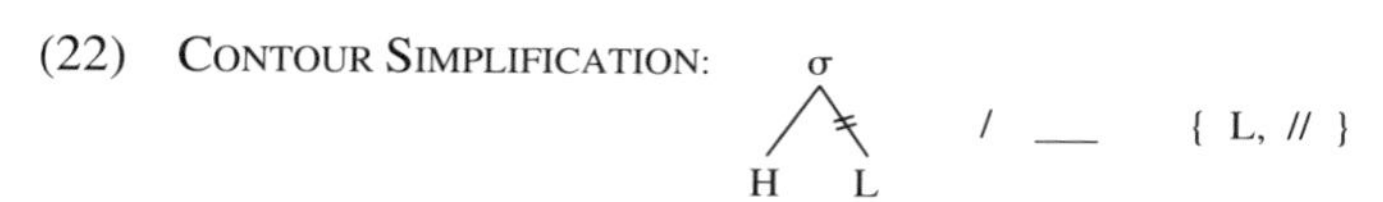

The need for this rule is seen in the last stage of the derivation in (21b), since the output is not *[sán âkàrmá].

This, then, completes the presentation of the two postlexical phenomena dubbed HTS_1 and HTS_2. In the next section I consider different interpretations of these facts.

4. DISCUSSION

In order to account for the two H-tone Spreading phenomena, HTS_1 and HTS_2, we must first raise the question of whether they should be viewed as one or two rules. As a first argument in favor of viewing both HTS processes as a single rule, there is the obvious formal similarity between them: both spread a H onto a following L-tone syllable. As a second argument, there is the fact that only the putative rule of Ⓛ-Deletion (19b) is possibly ordered between them. If there is no rule of Ⓛ-Deletion, the two "rules" can be ordered consecutively in the phonology. As we shall see shortly, HTS_1 and HTS_2 apply in exactly the same domain. Thus, according to the practices of standard generative phonology, HTS_1 and HTS_2 should be collapsed, if a formalism can be found.

However, standing in the way of this single-rule analysis is the fact that HTS_1 and HTS_2 have slightly different properties. First, HTS_1 cannot apply across a free L, while HTS_2 can—alternatively, as seen in (19b), Ⓛ-Deletion can intervene between HTS_1 and HTS_2, in which case the two processes cannot in any case be collapsed.[16] As a second difference, HTS_1 causes the L to delink, while HTS_2 does not, thereby forming a HL contour otherwise unattested in the language.

To slightly restate these findings, there are three logical analyses, as summarized below in (23).

(23) a. HTS_1 and HTS_2 are two separate rules with an accidental resemblance; the fact that the properties of these two rules differ slightly must simply be stipulated.

b. HTS_1 and HTS_2 constitute a single rule which has two separate applications; the properties of the two applications differ because of the place in the phonology where each application takes place.

c. HTS_1 and HTS_2 constitute a single (complex) rule, which applies only once in the postlexical tonology.

We have already considered (23a) in connection with the discussion of the rules in (19) and (20). It clearly is not appealing to set up two such similar rules, and I thus view the solution in (23a) as a last resort. The solution in (23b) is the one I would like to support. In order for it to go through, however, it is necessary to show that the first application of HTS (i.e., HTS$_1$) occurs in one place in the phonology, while the second application (HTS$_2$) occurs later in another place. Unfortunately for this analysis, HTS$_1$ and HTS$_2$ apply in exactly the SAME place in the phonology.

As a first demonstration of this fact, consider the derivations in (24).

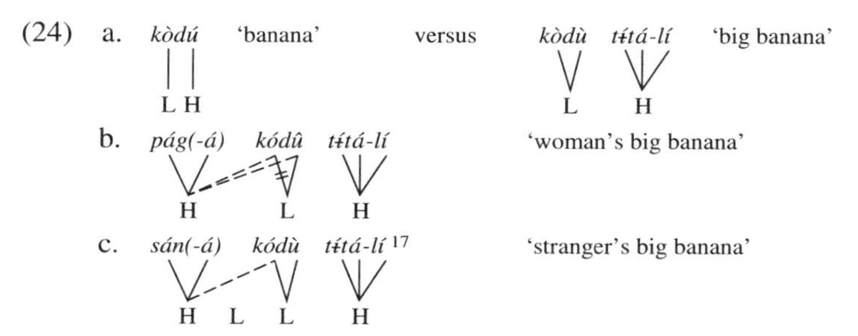

In (24a) we see that when a L–H noun such as *kòdú* 'banana' is followed by a H tone, it flattens to *kòdù,* which consists of a single L tone linked to both syllables.[18] In (24b) the H of *pág-á* 'woman' spreads twice onto this same word *kòdù,* first yielding *kódù,* then *kódû.* In (24c), the lexical H of the noun stem *sán* 'stranger' first spreads onto the suffixal *-à,* delinking its L, and then spreads again onto the first syllable of *kòdù* (producing *kôdù,* which then simplifies by L-absorption to *kódù,* as seen).

The derivation in (24b) shows that the same word may be affected by both HTS$_1$ and HTS$_2$. Now compare (25a), where HTS$_1$ and HTS$_2$ both cross a word boundary, thus involving the three-word sequence in the derivation.

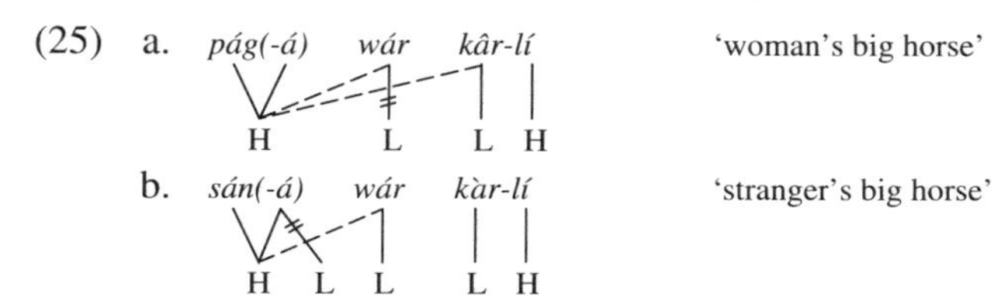

The derivation in (25b) shows the lexical H of the noun stem *sán* spreading onto the suffix *-à,* followed by a second spreading of this H onto the following noun stem *wár* 'horse'. Combining these observations, we arrive at the conclusion that both HTS$_1$ and HTS$_2$ are free to apply either within or across words.

Perhaps we might still maintain that the two applications of HTS occur at different levels in the postlexical phonology. Assuming the distinction made by Kaisse (1985), HTS$_1$ might apply at P_1 and HTS$_2$ at P_2. In this case we could, following Kaisse (1990) and Rice (1990), say that SP is respected at P_1 (and hence HTS$_1$ requires L delinking), while SP is not respected at P_2 (and hence HTS$_2$ is allowed to create a HL contour tone). Unfortunately, it has been impossible to find any confirming evidence since, for instance, both HTS_1 and HTS_2 are obligatory and not subject to tempo, stylistic, or other variables affecting their application differentially. In addition, prosodic domains are totally irrelevant: HTS_1 and HTS_2 will apply anywhere in an utterance unless the respective H and L tones are separated by pause. The data in (26)–(30) show that both rules apply within a number of constructions which in other languages would have divided up into two or more phonological phrases.

(26) (Nonbranching) subject + verb:

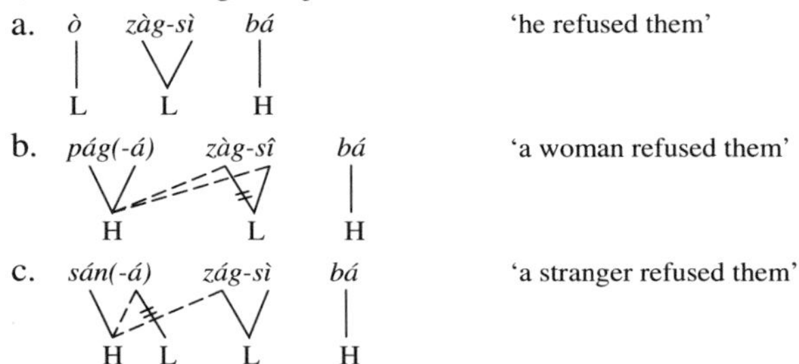

(27) (Branching) subject + verb:

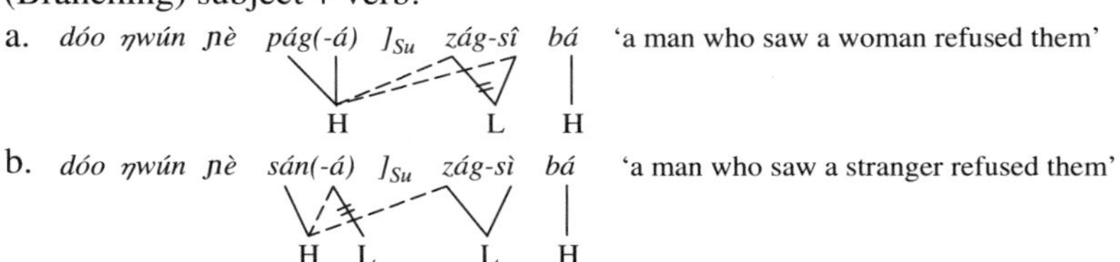

(28) $Object_1$ + $object_2$:

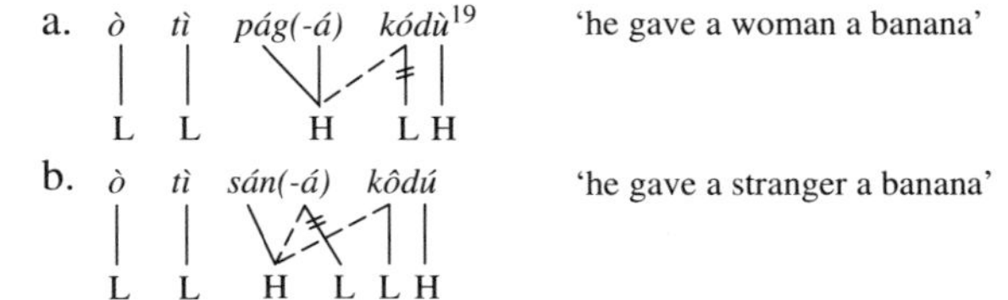

(29) Object + adverb (*sòhlá* 'yesterday'):

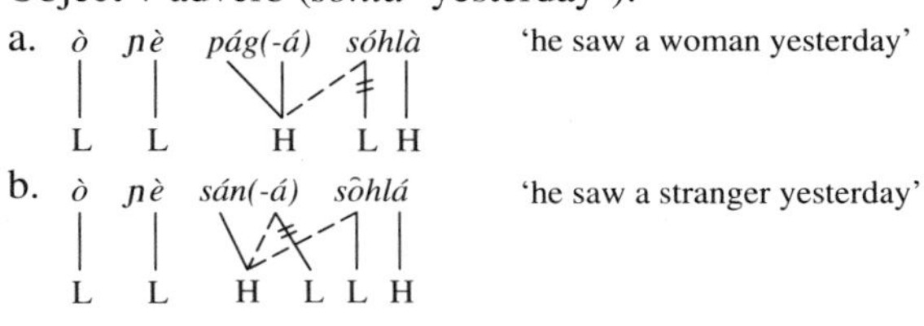

(30) Object + branching object [*à kòdú* 'your (sg) banana']:

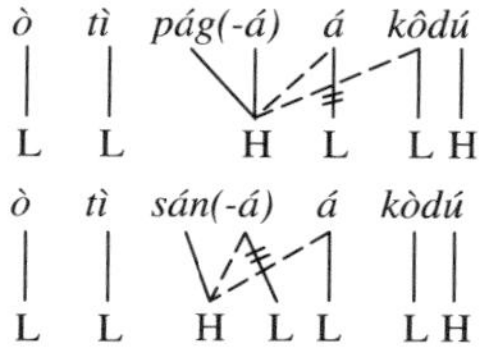

a. 'he gave a woman your banana'

b. 'he gave a woman your banana'

Since both HTS_1 and HTS_2 apply anywhere within the utterance domain, it is clear that we cannot assign them to different postlexical strata or prosodic domains—and hence that we cannot account for their different behavior vis-à-vis SP in this way. However, there is another possibility that needs to be considered: perhaps HTS_1 is a normal postlexical rule (applying anywhere within the utterance), and HTS_2 is a so-called phonetic implementation (PI) rule (Liberman and Pierrehumbert, 1984). In this case, we would say that the whole of Dagbani phonology respects the one-tone-per-TBU constraint, whereas the phonetics does not. As Liberman and Pierrehumbert point out, the dividing line between domain-free postlexical phonology and PI rules is not a clear one. Both are allowed to have optional and gradual effects (cf. Kiparsky, 1985), and both of course occur late in the derivation. In Dagbani, we note that if HTS_2 is a PI rule, then at least three rules must follow it. The first is Contour Simplification, formulated in (22), which, applying after HTS_2, would also have to be a PI rule. The second rule, interrogative H-Lowering, is summarized in (31a).

(31) Interrogative intonation:

a. H-LOWERING: $H^n]_{CG}\,]_U \rightarrow L^n$ (i.e. $H^n]_{CG}\,]_U$ ↓ L^n)

b. FINAL LENGTHENING: $V]_U$ ↓ V:

According to (31a), the final H or sequence of H's occurring within the last clitic group (CG) of an interrogative utterance becomes L.[20] In addition, the final vowel is lengthened, as seen in a comparison of the declarative and interrogative sentences in (32).

(32)	a.	*ò ɲè sán-á*	→	*ò ɲè sàn-à:*	'did he see a stranger?'
	b.	*ò ɲè sán-á=ŋóʔ*	→	*ò ɲè sàn-à=ŋò:*[21]	'did he see this stranger?'
	c.	*ò ɲè bɨ́=sán-á*	→	*ò ɲè bɨ̀=sàn-à:*	'did he see their stranger?'
	d.	*ò ɲè sá:n tɨ́tá-lí*	→	*ò ɲè sá:n tɨtà-lì:*	'did he see a big stranger?'

(32b) shows that the demonstrative =*ŋóʔ* 'this' is an enclitic, while (32c) shows that possessive pronouns such as *bɨ́=* 'their' are proclitics. On the other hand, a noun (stem) + adjective sequence constitutes TWO CGs, as seen in (32d). That interrogative H-Lowering is a lowering rule, rather than some kind of spreading rule, is seen from the tonal minimal pair in (33).

(33) a. *ò ɲè wáb tɨ́tá-lí* → *ò ɲè wáb tɨ̀tà-lì:* 'did he see a big elephant?'
L L H H → L L H L (*wáb-gú* 'elephant')

b. *ò ɲè záb ꜜtɨ́tá-lí* → *ò ɲè záb ꜜtɨ̀tà-lì:* 'did he see a big hair?'
L L H L H → L L H L L (*záb-gù* 'hair')

In each case it is the last H tone that has lowered to L, producing a surface pitch height contrast between L and ꜜL in just this one construction.[22]

The relevance of interrogative H-Lowering is seen in (34).

(34) a. *ò ɲè sán(-á) kôdú* → *ò ɲè sán(-á) kôdù:* 'did he see the stranger's banana?'
L L H L L H → L L H L L L

After lowering has occurred, we obtain a HL–L sequence on *kôdù:*. Hence it must be the case that H-Lowering follows L-absorption. Thus, if HTS_2 is a PI rule, then so is Contour Specification and so is H-Lowering! Finally, the derivation in (35a) shows that ꜜH-Lowering, which affects a single TBU before pause, is a THIRD rule that must follow HTS_2.

(35) a. /zab-gu/ 'hair' → *záb-ꜜgú* → *záb-gù*
HL H

b. /zab-gu/ 'hair' → *záb-gù* → **záb-gû*
HL H

In (35b), if ꜜH lowering applies first to this form, then HTS_2 will incorrectly derive a final HL falling tone. While it is conceivable that PI rules might be ordered like true phonological rules, the result just obtained further blurs the distinction. I thus conclude that there is no reason to attribute HTS_2 to phonetic implementation.

Returning to the three logical analyses listed in (23), it has been hard to substantiate the view in (23b), since we have found no compelling reason to assign HTS_1 and HTS_2 to two different strata or components. We have yet to consider the possibility in (23c), that both processes be stated as a single (complex) rule applying once in the phonology. Certainly this is consistent with the facts: wherever both HTS_1 and HTS_2 can apply, they both do apply. What we need is a complex rule that says: Spread a H onto a following L TBU, delinking this L, and if there is a second L TBU, the H spreads also onto it, forming a HL contour.

If tones link directly to TBUs (here, syllables), then the rule is formulated as in (36a).

(36) a. σ (σ) σ — H L L   b. o o o — H L L

As seen, the middle TBU must be optional, because HTS_2 will also apply across a free L tone, as we have seen. The rule can be slightly simplified if we instead assume that tones link directly to some kind of tonal node, as in (36b), in which case the middle node can be either linked or free.[23] In both formulations, I ignore the problem of distinguishing between two L tone features, as indicated, versus one L linked to two syllables or tonal nodes. Another problem not addressed is what to do about H–L–H sequences, where HTS_1 obligatorily applies but HTS_2 cannot apply (since there is no second L tone), since one interpretation of the rules in (36) is that either both H-spreading processes apply—or else neither. Even assuming that these difficulties can be overcome, there is reason to reject this approach. One obvious objection is that a phonological rule should in general be restricted to affecting only one target (though perhaps applying iteratively to a string of targets). If contrary formulations such as in (36) are allowed, then there is no reason why we could not add one more syllable (or tonal node) with L tone and have HTS potentially apply THREE times, and so on. In other words, despite any temptation one might have to say that there is one postlexical process of HTS that affects up to two L-tone syllables, it is formally undesirable to conceptualize the change of H–L–L to H–H–HL as a single rule application. In the following section I therefore return to the idea that there is a single HTS process that applies more than once in the phonology.

5. CONCLUSION

The position arrived at in the preceding section is that HTS_1 applies at the postlexical level, followed by the application of HTS_2 at the very same level. Since postlexical HTS_1 respects the "one-tone-per-TBU" lexical constraint, I am in agreement with Kaisse (1990) and Rice (1990) that SP may persist into the postlexical phonology. What is curious, however, is that the constraint against HL contours is *arbitrarily* abandoned, since HTS_2 applies immediately following HTS_1. If this represents, as I have suggested, the point at which SP becomes inoperative, then it appears that SP not only need not turn off at the end of the lexical phonology, but also may turn off at any designated point in the postlexical derivation.[24]

With SP somewhat in doubt, I would like to conclude with a brief consideration of Kiparsky's (1984) SDH. According to the SDH, all phonological rules potentially apply from the beginning of the phonology and continue to apply at each stratum until/unless they are specifically turned off. While a rule can cease to apply at a given level (e.g., be restricted to lexical stratum 1), a rule cannot be turned *on* in the middle of the phonology. An exclusively postlexical application would be achieved in cases where a lexical application would violate a specific principle such as SP. In the case of HTS, there is no a priori reason why it could not first apply lexically. With this in mind, we can reinterpret the derivation of *pág-á* 'woman' of (11) along the lines of Kenstowicz et al.'s (1988) analysis of Moore. Instead of viewing the H of the suffix as prelinked, as in (37a), where the H spreads leftwards onto the toneless noun stem, in (37b) we start with the suffixal H as unlinked.

```
(37)  a. /pag-a/  →  pag-a        b. /pag-a/  →  pag-a  →  pag-a
             |         \/                          |          \/
             H          H               H          H           H
```

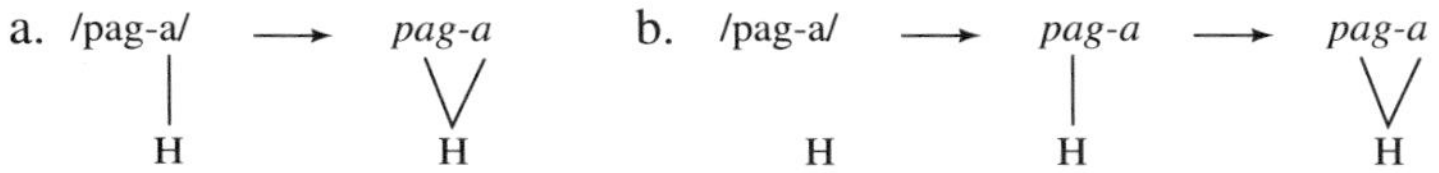

After this unlinked H associates to the leftmost TBU, HTS applies lexically to derive the H–H sequence. With a lexical application we see that a H may migrate three syllables to the right of its initial link, spreading once lexically, a second time by HTS$_1$, and a third time by HTS$_2$ [recall (24b)]. The lexical application is needed only in cases such as (37b), where I have supposed that an initial H is followed by a toneless TBU. In case the H is followed by a L, such as in the derivation in (38), it is not possible to tell whether the word-initial H-tone spreading is from putative lexical HTS or from HTS$_1$.

```
(38)  /san-a/  →  san-a  →  sán-á      'stranger'
       |  |        |  |       \/
       H  H        H  L       H  L
```

What is clear is that if it is from lexical HTS, then this form cannot then trigger HTS$_1$ postlexically, because of the floating L tone that blocks HTS$_1$. Instead, it can only trigger HTS$_2$, which is not blocked by floating L.

I will not resolve this ambiguity except to note that a simpler (and nonambiguous) solution would be reached if lexical HTS were restricted to applying to cases where the H is followed by a toneless TBU—unlike either HTS$_1$ or HTS$_2$. What is interesting from the point of view of the SDH is the prediction that if HTS applies at every stratum (lexically and postlexically), then one should observe the H spreading as many TBUs to the right as there are strata. In a language where, say, HTS applies at lexical stratum 1, lexical stratum 2, and postlexical stratum 1, the H should spread a maximum of three TBUs to the right. Rather than counting to the number 3 (or some higher number if a language has more than three strata), the lexical model predicts that the rule counts only one TBU, but three times! Is there then such a language which confirms this prediction? It was hoped that Dagbani would be this language. However, as I have shown, the multiple versions of HTS show differences (e.g., with respect to SP) that cannot be neatly attributed to strata.

ACKNOWLEDGMENTS

Materials for this article were gathered in the field methods course given in the Spring of 1988 at the University of Southern California. I am indebted to Mr. Abdul Saedu, who served as informant, and to the members of that course for their participation in the discovery of the tone system of Dagbani. I would like to thank Drs. W. A. A. Wilson and A. Naden for sending me their work on Dagbani and related Gur languages and for their comments and general help during our initial analysis of these materials. For previous work on Dagbani tonology, see especially Wilson (1970). Finally, thanks to Ellen Kaisse and an anonymous Academic Press referee for comments.

NOTES

[1]For example, Harris (1987) argues that structure preservation is not respected in the lexical phonology in Southeastern Bantu, while Kaisse (1990) and Rice (1990) give examples where structure preservation persists into the postlexical phonology. Given the conclusion I reach in this study, it may be that some of the claimed lexical/postlexical distinctions are simply "tendencies" that are reflected in many, but not all, languages.

[2]The verbal tonology has also been studied and analyzed and supports the conclusions reached on the basis of the nominal tonology.

[3]The following tone marks are written over the *first* (or only) V of each syllable: ´ = H(igh) tone, ` = L(ow) tone, ˆ = HL (falling) tone; ꜝ marks downstep tone.

[4]I might note that the drop from H to ꜝH is considerably greater in interval than in other languages I have studied. As we shall see, if only one TBU occurs with the ꜝH tone before pause, it is actually realized L.

[5]Of 148 "basic nouns," 139 (or 94%) occur with a noun class suffix.

[6]We shall see below that these nouns may actually have a floating H suffix, however; see (18).

[7]This analysis was greatly facilitated by a talk given by Michael Kenstowicz in April 1988 at the University of Southern California, which has since appeared as Kenstowicz, Nikiema, and Ourso (1988).

[8]These forms show a number of segmental alternations which are irrelevant to the tonal phonology, e.g., the length of the vowel in *sá:n* in (5b) and *kpá:n* 'guineafowl' in (5d) and the surface [r] in *wàr* 'horse' in (5c), etc. The forms that are shown should not be confused with the similar but not identical phonetic transcriptions in (4), where the suffix

is present but is subject to final vowel reduction. To underscore this point, consider the corresponding genitive and pre-adjective realizations of *ɲéb-gá* 'crocodile' and *wáb-gú* 'elephant', whose isolation forms were originally cited in (3a,b):

(i)	*ɲéb-g*$^{ɨ́}$ *yí-lí*	'crocodile's house'
	wáb-g$^{ɨ́}$ *$^{!}$yí-lí*	'elephant's house'
(ii)	*ɲèb tɨ́tá-lí*	'big crocodile'
	wáb tɨ́tá-lí	'big elephant'

In (i) the vowel of the suffixes *-gá* and *-gú* is replaced by a very short, perhaps epenthetic centralized vowel following the /g/ of the suffix. In (ii), on the other hand, both this vowel and the /g/ are missing, again illustrating that a noun appears bare (without suffix) when modified by an adjective.

[9] This contrasts with the situation in other Gur languages such as Moore and Lama, where Kenstowicz et al. (1988) have shown the need for a L tone genitive particle.

[10] Though irrelevant to the analysis, it is possible that at this postlexical level the two H's would have already conflated as a single H linked to the two syllables.

[11] In Section 5 I shall consider an alternative whereby the H of the suffix comes in unlinked, associates first to the noun stem, and then spreads rightward.

[12] According to the common practice of filling a gap in the pattern, one might propose that nouns such as /pag/ are actually underlyingly LH. Though not an insurmountable problem, there are at least two reasons for not doing this. First, there is the question of why a H-tone suffix should cause a LH contour to become H, rather than simplifying to L [as in fact happens elsewhere in the language by the rule of contour simplification in (22)]. Second, there is the problem that this H does not surface when followed directly by a L tone—cf. (16a).

[13] It cannot literally be from HTS$_1$, as conceived up to this point, since the L of *kòdú* would then be expected to delink, ultimately yielding **sán kódù*.

[14] (19b) could also apply to delete the free L tone before pause, since in that position it also has no surface effect. On the other hand, free L's are not deleted before H tone, since they are needed to condition downstep.

[15] Cf. Wilson (1970:414): "A sequence HL other than V́(C)CV̀ becomes HH before L." The effect of this rule is to guarantee that a HL falling tone will surface only if it is followed by a H tone, a constraint that is found in a number of other tone languages, e.g., Kinande, Luganda, etc. There is an (intonational) exception to this, however; see (34).

[16] If HTS$_1$ did apply across the free L tone in (15b) and (16d), for instance, we would obtain the incorrect outputs *[sán kódù] (from intermediate **sán kó*$^{!}$*dú*) and *[kpáŋ kár-lì] (from intermediate **kpáŋ kár-*$^{!}$*lí*), respectively.

[17] After HTS$_2$ applies to this form and others cited below, a H–HL sequence is obtained, e.g., intermediate *kôdù* in (24c). As transcribed, this fall is simplified by contour simplification (22).

[18] This rule of L-tone Spreading (LTS) spreads rightwards onto a H TBU if the latter is in turn also followed by a H TBU, i.e., L–H–H becomes L–L–H. The H–H sequence either may be a single H that has spread by HTS$_1$, or it may be a separate H feature from the next morpheme. In either case the rule applies. (For discussion of the relevance of such ex-

amples to the feature geometry of tone within a parametric framework, see Hyman and Pulleyblank, 1988.)

[19] In this example [and also in (29a)], only HTS_1 can apply, since after the initial spreading of H, the intermediate output of 'banana' (*kó'dú*) does not have a following L TBU For HTS_2 to apply. (Recall that this intermediate representation becomes *kódù* before pause.)

[20] This differs slightly from Wilson's (1970:414) statement of the rule ["Before the ? [interrogative] marker a final H tone or H tone sequence is lowered to L back as far as the last Downstep of the utterance (if any)"] because of the data in (32d).

[21] (32b) also shows that when a form would normally take a glottal stop prepausally in a declarative utterance (cf. Hyman, 1989), the glottal stop is not observed within the corresponding interrogative.

[22] There is an alternative to H-Lowering whereby a boundary interrogative L delinks the H('s) on the appropriate TBU(s). Assuming that the affected sequences of H's have all been fused into a single H-tone feature at the CG level, the rule of H-Lowering simply targets the last H of the domain. In this alternative, this H would have to link to single tonal node, or else it is not clear how a boundary L can dislodge it from a sequence of TBUs. For this reason, and also for the reason that we know we need intonational rules that modify lexical tones (see, e.g., Hyman, 1990), I stick with the analysis given above.

[23] This seems to be what Wilson's (1970:413) rule is intended to do, which changes a [+h] [−h] [−h] sequence into [+h] [+h] [+h], independent of whether the second [−h] is linked or not.

[24] Since the discussion of SP centers around a single tonal constraint, what is needed is a demonstration that more than one such constraint turns off at the same arbitrary point in the postlexical phonology. Unfortunately, this is hard to demonstrate. It can be pointed out that the constraint against LH contours is never violated in Dagbani. However, none of the three rules that were said to follow HTS_2 (L-absorption, interrogative H-Lowering, 'H-Lowering) would in any case produce a LH contour—which COULD conceivably surface if the above analysis is correct.

REFERENCES

Goad, H. (1988). *Tone in the Dagbani Noun Phrase.* Unpublished manuscript, University of Southern California, Los Angeles.

Harris, J. (1987). Non-structure-preserving rules in lexical phonology: Southeastern Bantu harmony. *Lingua* **73,** 255–292.

Hyman, L. M. (1989). The phonology of final glottal stops. In *Proceedings of the West Coast Conference on Linguistics* **18,** 113–130.

Hyman, L. M. (1990). Boundary tonology and the prosodic hierarchy. In *The Phonology–Syntax Connection* (S. Inkelas and D. Zec, eds.), pp. 109–125. CSLI Publications and University of Chicago Press, Chicago.

Hyman, L. M., and Pulleyblank, D. (1988). On feature copying: parameters of tone rules. In *Language, Speech and Mind* (L. M. Hyman and C. N. Li, eds.), pp. 38–48. Routledge, London.

Kaisse, E. M. (1985). *Connected Speech: The Interaction of Syntax and Phonology.* Academic Press, Orlando.

Kaisse, E. M. (1990). Toward a typology of postlexical rules. In *The Phonology–Syntax Connection* (S. Inkelas and D. Zec, eds.), pp. 127–143. CSLI Publications and University of Chicago Press, Chicago.

Kenstowicz, M., Nikiema, E., and Ourso, M. (1988). Tonal polarity in two Gur languages. *Studies in the Linguistic Sciences* **18,** 77–103.

Kiparsky, P. (1984). On the lexical phonology of Icelandic. In *Nordic Prosody III* (C.-C. Elert et al., eds.), pp. 135–162. University of Umea, Umea, Sweden.

Kiparsky, P. (1985). Some consequences of lexical phonology. *Phonology Yearbook* **2,** 85–138.

Lieberman, M., and Pierrehumbert, J. (1984). Intonational invariance under changes in pitch range and length. In *Language Sound Structure* (M. Aronoff and R. T. Oehrle, eds.), pp. 157–233. MIT Press, Cambridge, Mass.

Rialland, A. (1980). Marques de ponctuation et d'intégration dans l'énoncé en gurma. *Bulletin de la Société de Linguistique de Paris* **75,** 415–432.

Rice, K. D. (1990). Predicting rule domains in the phrasal phonology. In *The Phonology–Syntax Connection* (S. Inkelas and D. Zec, eds.), pp. 289–312.

Wilson, W. A. A. 1970. External tonal sandhi in Dagbani. *African Language Studies* **11,** 405–416.

(POST) LEXICAL RULE APPLICATION

GREGORY K. IVERSON

Department of Linguistics
University of Wisconsin—Milwaukee
Milwaukee, Wisconsin 53201

1. INTRODUCTION

The theory of lexical phonology developed by Kiparsky (1982) proposes a fundamental distinction between LEXICAL and POSTLEXICAL rules—the latter but not the former apply across the board, that is, without regard for derivational history or morphological composition; are typically exceptionless; and commonly present only nonneutralizing or "allophonic" effects. A major descriptive feature of the theory as originally conceived is that a given phonological rule has membership in one or the other of these two categories, but not both. Kiparsky (1985) argues that in certain cases, however, specifically nasal consonant assimilation in Catalan and obstruent voice assimilation in Russian, a single rule must be accorded postlexical as well as lexical status. This relaxation of the theory is necessitated for Catalan, he maintains, by the apparent ordering paradox that in some derivations nasal assimilation must both precede and follow another, presumably lexical, rule. In the present article it is shown that the Catalan ordering paradox falls aside under more general conceptions of rule interaction and feature representation, and that the two rules actually both apply only within the postlexical domain. This result in turn has important implications in lexical phonology for implementation of the derived environment constraint on phonological processes such as palatalization in Korean, whose effects are sometimes derivationally restricted, sometimes not. Despite appearances to the contrary, rules like these may also apply within a single component of the phonology if it is only structure-preserving applications of rules

Phonetics and Phonology, Volume 4
Studies in Lexical Phonology

which must observe the derived environment constraint, and not, as conventional lexical phonology conversely has it, that any rule restricted to derived environments must also be structure-preserving. A further consequence of this association between structure preservation and the derived environment constraint is that phonological feature underspecification will be determined within the lexicon, independent of the contextual requirements of particular phonological rules.

2. CATALAN

As described by Mascaró (1976), the nasal /n/ in Catalan regularly assimilates in place of articulation to an immediately following consonant. Kiparsky (1985:95) illustrates with the following alternations in the pronunciation of *son* '(they) are'.

(1)			
	unassimilated:	*so*[n] *amics*	'they are friends'
	labial:	*so*[m] *pocs*	'they are few'
	labiodental:	*so*[ɱ] *feliços*	'they are happy'
	dental:	*so*[n̪] *dos*	'they are two'
	alveolar:	*so*[n] *sincers*	'they are sincere'
	postalveolar:	*so*[ṇ] *rics*	'they are rich'
	laminopalatal:	*so*[ṇ̡] [ǯ]*ermans*	'they are brothers'
	palatal:[1]	*so*[ṇ̡] [λ]*iures*	'they are free'
	velar:	*so*[ŋ] *grans*	'they are big'

The other phonemic nasals in the system, bilabial /m/ and palatal /ɲ/, do not assimilate at all, except that /m/ becomes labiodental before another labiodental: compare *so*[m] *dos* 'we are two' with *so*[ɱ] *feliços* 'we are happy'. But the palatal remains palatal in *a*[ɲ] *feliç* 'happy year', and so on, and the velar nasal, which derives as in other Indo-European languages from a nasal plus stop cluster, always remains velar: *ti*[ŋ] *pa* 'I have bread', and so on.

The ordering paradox in Catalan concerns the interaction of Nasal Assimilation with another general rule that deletes a stop homorganic with a preceding consonant when the cluster is tautosyllabic, that is, not immediately followed by a vowel in the same word. Hence, Cluster Simplification reduces /mp/ to /m/ in /kamp/ *camp* 'field' word finally ([kám] 'the field', [kám es] 'the field is') and in consonantally suffixed constructions ([káms] 'fields'), but it does not apply in forms where the suffix is vowel-initial: [kamp ɛ́t] 'little field'. Since the nasal's place of articulation is predictable from the following underlying stop before it deletes, the least redundant lexical representation of [kám] would be as /kaNp/, with the nasal unspecified for place of articulation. Similarly, the velar nasal in [bɛ́ŋ] *venc* 'I sell' would derive from an underspecified representation /bɛNk/, as would the alveolar in [bín] *vint* 'twenty', presumably from /biNt/.

As Kiparsky illustrates in his derivation of Mascaró's example *venc vint pans* [bέŋ bím páns] 'I sell twenty loaves of bread', accordingly, two results must be assured. First, once underspecified /N/ becomes either labial or velar in assimilation to its following consonant, it must not undergo assimilation again after cluster reduction has applied, for [bέŋ bím] does not become *[bέm bím]. But, second, the coronal realization of underspecified /N/ ɪs subject to assimilation a second time, because intermediate [bín páns] (< /biNt pan+s/) becomes [bím páns].

(2)	/bɛNk	biNt	pan+s/	
	bɛŋk	*bint*		Nasal Assimilation
	bɛŋ	*bin*		Cluster Simplification
		bim		Nasal Assimilation
	[bέŋ	bím	páns]	

The ordering of the rules in this fashion—putting aside for the moment the question of how to prevent reapplication of Nasal Assimilation in the sequence [bέŋ bím]—violates the irreflexivity assumption of standard generative practice (a rule may not precede itself) because Nasal Assimilation is applied both before and after Cluster Simplification. Kiparsky removes this part of the problem for the theory first by ordering Nasal Assimilation before Cluster Simplification in the lexical phonology per se, then by assigning Nasal Assimilation to the postlexical phonology as well. As Nasal Assimilation thus appears in two separate, independently sequenced components of the phonology, its application both before and after Cluster Simplification in the derivation of the [m] in [bím páns] turns out to be simply a derivative property of the rule's multiple componential assignment rather than a stipulation contradicting the precepts of extrinsic ordering.

The other part of the problem in a derivation like (2), however, is that postlexical application of nasal assimilation must be restricted just to /n/, because labials, palatals, and velars do not assimilate in place of articulation.[2] Kiparsky here proposes to characterize the nasal which does assimilate as underlyingly completely unspecified for place of articulation features, as /N/. On this implementation of radical underspecification, the assimilating nasal will be represented without place features not just when it appears before a tautomorphemic consonant, as in *vint,* but even when it does not, as in *son.* In fact, as he later points out, this idea can be extended (and arguably should be—cf., e.g., Yip, 1991, for English; Iverson, 1989, for Korean; Paradis and Prunet, 1989, for numerous other languages) to all the anterior coronals because place of articulation in general need be specified only for labials, palatals, and velars; that is, place features should be unmarked for the dental or alveolar obstruents /t d s/, too. For this class of consonants now with no inherent place of articulation specifications at all, appropriate coronal place features will be filled in later in the derivation by default rules whenever assimilation (in the case of nasals) has not applied instead.

Characterizing all the anterior coronals as unspecified for place of articulation features means that the problematic derivation in (2), which motivated assignment of Nasal Assimilation to both the lexical and postlexical components in the first place, takes on a rather different character.

(3)	/bɛNk	biNT	paN+S/	
	bɛŋk			Nasal Assimilation
	bɛŋ	*biN*		Cluster Simplification
		bim		Nasal Assimilation
			pan+s	Default Place Features
	[bɛ́ŋ	bím	páns]	

In (3), even coronal obstruents are systematically underspecified for place of articulation features. But while Nasal Assimilation still applies before Cluster Simplification in the derivation of [bɛ́ŋ] and after it in the derivation of [bím], there is no violation of irreflexivity because it is not the case that Nasal Assimilation must apply twice in the SAME derivation. Here, rather, the rules interact freely (ordered locally in the sense of Anderson, 1974, or not ordered at all, per Koutsoudas, Sanders, and Noll, 1974). Nasal Assimilation simply applies whenever its structural description is met: before Cluster Simplification in /bɛNk/, where velar place features are present; but not at all in /biNT/, where place features are not available until the underspecified /N/ comes into juxtaposition with labially specified /p/ in the following word via the application of Cluster Simplification. Consistent radical underspecification of place of articulation features thus naturally removes the apparent ordering paradox in Catalan, provided that the mode of rule interaction permits Nasal Assimilation to apply to any representations that satisfy its structural description.

With no ordering paradox, Cluster Simplification and Nasal Assimilation may both apply exclusively within the same component of the phonology. Kiparsky maintains that Cluster Simplification must be a lexical rule because it appears not to interact with, that is, not be bled by, the postlexical resyllabification that takes place between words (/kaNp es/ → /kamp es/ → [ká.mes], not *[kám.pes]; cf. /kaNp+ɛ́t/ → /kamp+ɛ́t/ → [kam.pɛ́t]). But there are good reasons to suppose that the rule is postlexical instead. First, if removal of the constituent-final stop is accomplished through stray erasure of a consonant not having satisfied the template for syllabification, as deletion phenomena in general are characterized under the prosodic theory of the syllable (Itô, 1986, 1989), then Catalan emerges as just the reverse of other languages with place of articulation constraints on the syllabic incorporation of consonant clusters. For example, in Diola Fogny (Sapir, 1965), clusters may occur at the end of the word just in case they are homorganic, but in heterorganic clusters the second consonant is deleted. Catalan is quite the opposite of this since it freely tolerates heterorganic clusters word-finally (*serp* 'snake', *porc* 'pig', *bosc* 'forest'), reducing only the homorganic ones. If Itô (cf. also Goldsmith, 1990) is right that the relevant place of articulation constraint on consonant clusters has to do with the licensing of appropriate phonological features in the syllable coda, then any language which permits word-final heterorganic clusters (two place specifications) should also allow homorganic clusters (one place specification). The fact that Catalan contradicts this implication suggests that other factors are at play in the determination of its surface syllabification.

Those factors, Gonzàlez (1989) clarifies, concern how tightly bound the word containing the final consonant cluster is with the following vowel-initial word. At a major syntactic constituent break, as between NP and VP in *el camp* ([kám]) *es* . . . 'the field is . . .', cluster simplification indeed is essentially obligatory. But it is optional when the association between constituents is tighter, as within NPs like *el camp* ([kámp]/[kám]) *espanyol* 'the Spanish field', *el pont* ([pón̪t̪]/[pón]) *alt* 'the tall bridge', and so on. Word-final prevocalic clusters syllabify entirely within the coda when at the end of a major syntactic phrase, in other words, but optionally split between the coda of one syllable and the onset of another when they are internal to the phrase. This syllabification must be postlexical because it is sensitive to constituent categories larger than the word, the maximum domain of the purely lexical component. As it is defined on a sequence of homorganic consonants at the end of the syllable, which sometimes straddles the division between words, application of Cluster Simplification thus depends on postlexical syllabification after all, which is the reason it is more likely to apply at the end of an NP than at the end simply of a Noun.[3]

(4) 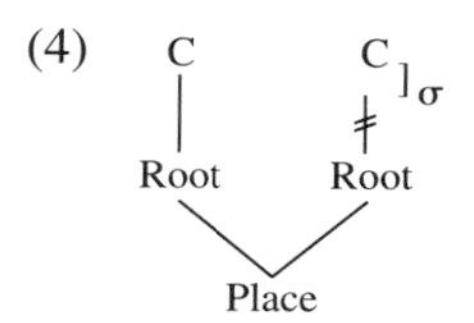

Like Cluster Simplification, Nasal Assimilation must also be a postlexical rule, since it too applies between words (cf. [bím páns]), and so the rules now interact as illustrated in (3).[4]

But another part of Kiparsky's reasoning that Nasal Assimilation must apply postlexically (besides, in his view, lexically) is that the underlyingly unspecified nasal takes on even the nondistinctive place features of a following consonant, as exemplified in (1). The anterior coronal obstruent stops are dental rather than alveolar, for example, so before them /N/ assumes dental articulation too; before labiodental fricatives, similarly, /N/ (as well as /m/) is labiodental, and it is postalveolar before postalveolar /r/, and so on. By the principle of structure preservation ("lexical rules cannot introduce or refer to redundant features"), crucially, assimilation to noncontrastive place of articulation features like [±distributed]—which distinguishes bilabials from labiodentals, dentals from alveolars, and postalveolars from laminopalatals—is prohibited except in the postlexical phonology, where "allophonic" features are first made reference to. If the rule of Nasal Assimilation is to account for the occurrence of labiodental, dental, postalveolar, and laminopalatal nasals in Catalan under lexical phonology's assumption of structure preservation, therefore, it must be through the rule's postlexical application. This is consistent, of course, with the status of Nasal Assimilation (and Cluster Simplification) as strictly postlexical, but it turns out to be quite beside the point when various phonetic detail and default rules are taken into account.[5]

Thus, as noted too by Goldsmith (1990) in this connection, the assignment of particularly labiodental place of articulation to labial fricatives but bilabial place to labial stops in Catalan is itself a postlexical matter, because no potential contrast exists in this language between the two refinements of labial place specification: for them the feature [distributed] is entirely redundant here. A postlexical rule spelling out predictable labiodental articulation for labial fricatives, and bilabial for all other labials, would be as in (5).

(5) a.

$$\text{Labial} \quad \rightarrow \quad [-\text{distributed}] \quad / \quad \begin{bmatrix} -\text{sonorant} \\ +\text{continuant} \\ \underline{\qquad\qquad} \end{bmatrix}$$

b.

$$\text{Labial} \quad \rightarrow \quad [+\text{distributed}]$$

Following these requirements, /f/ is filled out as labiodental, /p/ and /m/ (by default) as bilabial.

Under the obligatory contour principle (OCP) (e.g., McCarthy, 1986), moreover, which holds that adjacent identical features are prohibited, a sequence of /m/ followed by /f/ in the same phonological domain will fall under one Labial articulator node (in the geometric sense of Sagey, 1986) rather than two separate ones. When rule (5a) applies to /f/, therefore, it provides the feature [-distributed] to the Labial node which /f/ shares with the preceding nasal in an /mf/ sequence, and so both segments simultaneously become labiodental.[6] When followed by /p/ (or by no consonant at all), on the other hand, the inapplicability of (5a) allows (5b) to complete the representation of /m/ as bilabial.

(6)

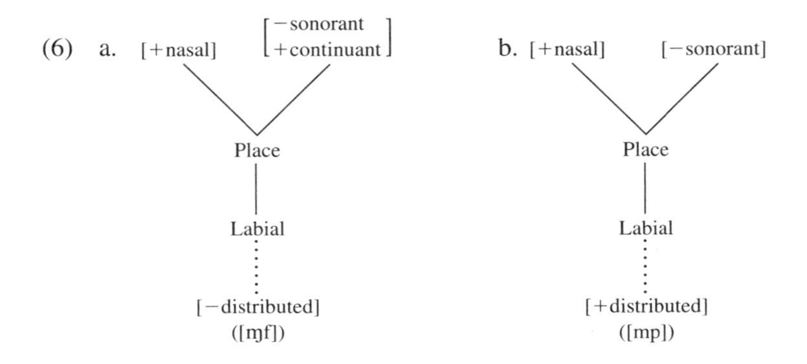

An analogous account accommodates the other subphonemic places of articulation. Since dental /t/ ([t̪]) and /d/ ([d̪]) are phonetically [+distributed], /n/ (< /N/) in /nt/ ([n̪t̪]) and /nd/ ([n̪d̪]) clusters acquires that feature too by virtue of the same redundancy rule which assigns [+distributed] to an anterior coronal stop sharing its Place node with the nasal. Before the nonanterior coronals, which comprise the [+distributed] laminopalatal fricatives /š, ž/ and the palatal sonorants /λ, ɲ/, the Place-sharing nasal also becomes [+distributed]; but elsewhere, such as when sharing Place with the remaining coronals /s, z, l, r/ or when independent of other segments (phrase finally, before a vowel), it is default-specified as [−distributed]. Finally, assuming with Kiparsky that postalveolar /r/ and the palatals are [+high], this feature too automatically accrues to the nasal when it shares its Place node with a following /r/;[7] otherwise, the nasal sharing Place with a coronal is given the default value of [−high].

Before these postlexical redundancies come into play, however, the unspecified nasal in a cluster will have acquired its basic place of articulation from a following labial, palatal, or velar via the phonological rule of Nasal Assimilation.

(7) [+nasal] ⋯⋯⋯ [+consonantal]
| Place

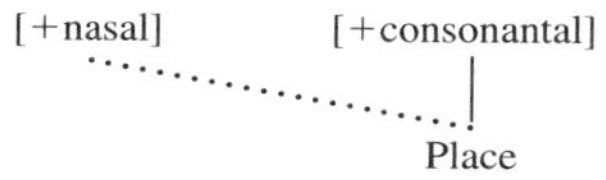

"Place" dominates one of the articulators Labial, Coronal, or Dorsal. The only nasal to acquire one of these specifications by the spreading effects of rule (7), as Kiparsky's account also has it, is the unspecified one, because that is the only nasal which does not already have an occupied Place node. Thus, the palatal (Coronal) nasal does not assimilate to a following dental (initially unspecified, later Coronal), nor the bilabial one (Labial) to a following velar (Dorsal), because these nasals already are specified for Place articulators; inherently unspecified /N/, though, does assimilate to the Labial, Coronal, or Dorsal Place of a following consonant because this fills the void in its own representation. The reason why /m/ assimilates only to a following labiodental is that /m/ shares its Place specification with following labials, but not with other kinds of segments, and phonetic detail rules like (5a) spelling out the labiodental quality of /f/ also affect Place-shared /m/.

Under this geometric system of feature representation, to recapitulate, the labial nasal is identified by presence of the Labial articulator, the palatal nasal by presence of the Coronal articulator dominating the feature [-anterior], and the velar nasal by presence of the Dorsal articulator [which it only acquires via (7) from a following stop]. When (7) does not come into play to provide features to the lexically unspecified nasal /N/, its empty Place node is filled out by default, and the segment emerges as alveolar [n].

(8)

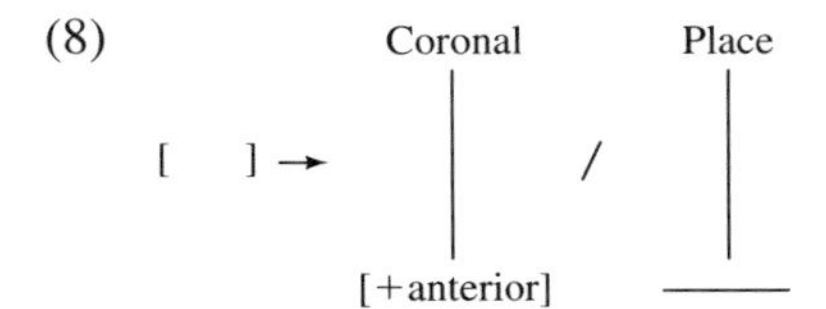

Rules like (5) defined on either anterior or nonanterior coronals would not affect palatals adjacent to dentals since, although they have Coronal in common, their remaining specifications under Place are not identical and so could not be shared, just as Dorsal and Labial are independent with respect to a velar preceding a bilabial. But in view of the operation of postlexical phonetic detail rules like (5) on linked as well as unlinked matrices, the precise homorganicity of clusters composed of nasals sharing basic place of articulation with a following consonant is due not to a rule of assimilation per se, but rather to the unifying effects of the OCP.

This circumstance limits the postlexical application of Catalan Nasal Assimilation following Cluster Simplification to sequences between words of the unspecified nasal followed by a consonant with an inherent articulator node, as in *vint pans* [bím páns]. Application of Nasal Assimilation prior to Cluster Simplification also affects only sequences consisting of the unspecified nasal followed by a consonant with an inherent Place specification. All other values of nasals are either underlying or filled in by phonetic detail cum default rules as exemplified in (5). As a consequence, there is no requirement for either of the Catalan rules discussed here to be accorded lexical as well as postlexical status; that is, both are interpretable as strictly postlexical.

The celebrated neutralizing/allophonic rule of Russian voice assimilation discussed at length by Kiparsky (1985) will also apply within a single component of the phonology if an idea put forward by Macfarland and Pierrehumbert (1991) is adopted (cf. Plapp, 1990), who consider structure preservation to be subject to the autosegmental linking condition that "association lines are interpreted as exhaustive" (Hayes, 1986). On this reading of structure preservation, novel segments may be introduced even into the lexical phonology proper if they are the products of assimilation, or feature spread, because the resulting shared feature configurations do not stand in violation of monosegmentally defined statements which exclude allophones from the phoneme inventory. For example, the voiced fricative [ɣ] could be introduced into the lexical component of Russian phonology, despite the fact that it is strictly an allophone of /x/, because its [+voice] feature is always shared with a neighboring voiced sound, never independently ascribed to [ɣ]. Under this (rather extensive) relaxation of structure preservation, both neutralizing and nonneutralizing applications of Russian voice assimilation can be directly accommodated within the lexical phonology per se—indeed, for that matter, within the postlexical component instead, since neutralizable inputs to the rule apparently always happen to be crucially derived. But there are other clear cases for which, in view of the standard theory's restriction of just lexical rules to derived environments, it would seem that dual lexical/postlexical status nonetheless is necessary. The following sections explore the significance of this sort of rule, which, when neutralizing, exhibits familiar derivationally restricted effects, but when not neutralizing applies without restriction. It will be argued that rules like these limit structure-preserving applications to derived environments as a matter of general principle, rather than of componential assignment, and as a result that the applications which fail to respect structure preservation are independent of considerations of autosegmental linking.

3. KOREAN

The palatalization of coronals in Korean is one such case, for in some forms it takes place only in derived environments; in others it applies across the board.[8] The language's obstruent system consists of the three-way stop contrasts, including one affricate series, and the two-way fricative contrasts illustrated in (9).

(9)						
	p	t	č	k	s	(Lax)
	p^{h}	t^{h}	č^{h}	k^{h}		(Aspirated)
	p′	t′	č′	k′	s′	(Tense)

Of these, the plosives /t t^{h}/ convert to the affricates /č č^{h}/ when in position before [i] or [y] in the next morpheme, in which position the fricatives /s s′/ also take on postalveolar articulation ([š š′]).[9] The palatalization process thus gives rise to alternations such as in (10) (with redundant voicing of the lax noncontinuants in intervocalic contexts).

(10)						
	/tat-/	'close'	[tat˺t′a]	(indic.)	[taǰi]	(noun)
	/tot-/	'rise'	[tot˺t′a]	(indic.)	[toǰi]	(noun)
	/pat^{h}-/	'field'	[pat^{h}ɨl]	(obj.)	[pač^{h}i]	(subj.)
	/os-/	'cloth'	[osɨl]	(obj.)	[oši]	(subj.)

Under the obstruent system of (9), the effect of palatalization in the first three of these forms is neutralizing, but in the fourth it is not. There are many apparent exceptions to the rule, however, because not only do the affricates appear morpheme-internally before [i], as in (11b), but so do the coronal stops, as exemplified in (11a).

(11)						
	a.	[madi]	'knot' (< /mati/)	b.	[čip˺]	'house'
		[pət^{h}i]	'endure'		[č′iǰə]	'tear' (imp.)
		[t^{h}i]	'dust'		[čiǰə]	'bark' (imp.)[10]

Unlike the stops, the two fricatives undergo palatalization even in morpheme-internal environments.[11]

(12) [ši] 'poem' (*[si])
[šikan] 'time' (*[sikan])
[š'i] 'seed' (*[s'i]).[12]

There would clearly seem to be a single generalization here, namely that coronals palatalize before [i] (and [y]), except that, if it would merge an underlying contrast, the process is blocked in intramorphemic contexts. This classic derived environment restriction means that Korean palatalization under present theoretical assumptions must be a lexical rule, for it is not free to apply across the board when it affects the stops. Yet the rule would also seem to be postlexical with respect to the fricatives, because these undergo palatalization irrespective of any morphological considerations; that is, for them the derived environment restriction plays no role and the rule does apply across the board. If palatalization is postlexical as well as lexical, however, then what prevents it from applying, incorrectly, to obstruent stops in morpheme-internal environments too?

Short of resorting to the null hypothesis that fricative palatalization is a different rule from stop palatalization (Ahn, 1988; Cho and Sells, 1991),[13] the alternative suggested by Iverson (1987; also Iverson and Wheeler, 1988) lies in reaffirmation of Kiparsky's (1973) revised alternation condition, which restricts just neutralizing rules to crucially derived forms. Kaisse (1986) reaches fundamentally the same conclusion in her analysis of consonant devoicing phenomena in Turkish, and Hualde (1989), in consideration of an apparently noncyclic lexical rule operating in the phonology of Basque, similarly advocates factoring the derived environment constraint out of the strict cycle condition as an independent restriction.[14] Kiparsky's (1973) proposal, to recapitulate here, holds that phonological rules observe the derived environment constraint only if they effect neutralizations, or "preserve structure."[15] Construed as a constraint on rule applications rather than on rules per se, this principle permits the various manifestations of Korean palatalization to fall directly under a single generalization, because palatalization of /ti/ to [či] is neutralizing (/ . . . či . . ./ sequences occur among the rule's inputs) and thus restricted to derived environments, but palatalization of /si/ to [ši] is not (the exclusive source of [š] is palatalization itself). Under the interpretation that the derived environment constraint is valid just for neutralizing rule applications, therefore, all the occurrences of Korean palatalization will be implemented by a single lexical rule whose apparent postlexical effects are due to the general invalidation of the derived environment constraint whenever the rule is not neutralizing.

The effect of limiting the derived environment constraint just to neutralizing applications of rules is to incorporate into that constraint the otherwise independent requirement of structure preservation. The function of this principle is to block lexical rules from creating or referring to any segments not found in the underlying inventory, that is, to force lexical rules to be strictly neutralizing. Since lexical rules are defined to be just those which must obey the derived environment constraint, the conventional theory's further attribution to them of structure preservation encodes their limitation to neutralization as a distinctly separate restriction. Under the assumptions here, though, where the derived environment constraint itself is sensitive to neutralization, lexical rules preserve structure because their application typically is restricted to derived environments; atypically—precisely when it would not be structure-preserving—even a lexical rule may apply across the board. In this way, structure preservation integrates with a major principle of the theory, the derived environment constraint, and so makes possible the unified description of derivationally sensitive neutralizations with across-the-board rule applications that fail to preserve structure or appear to be postlexical.

The fact that lexically restricted rules usually do preserve structure derives from the basic lexical/postlexical dichotomy inherent in the theory, wherein just those rules are defined as lexical which must observe the derived environment constraint; these, in turn, constitute the class of rules limited by the property of structure preservation. The innovation suggested here is to reverse this implication between structure preservation and the derived environment constraint, from the conventional relationship expressed in (13a) to the alternative in (13b).

(13) a. If a rule is lexical (observes the derived environment constraint), then it is also structure-preserving (neutralizing).
b. If a rule application is neutralizing (structure-preserving), then it also observes the derived environment constraint.

In distinguishing between a rule per se and its individual applications, (13b) retains structure preservation, or neutralization, as definitive for implementation of the derived environment constraint, but it also accommodates within the lexical component certain rule applications which are not structure-preserving and hence not restricted to derived environments.[16] Structure preservation on this proposal thus remains a property of traditionally lexical rules, though not necessarily of all lexical rule applications. By reversing the association between structure preservation and the derived environment constraint, however, (13b) raises the more fundamental question of whether a strict functional boundary really should be drawn after all between lexical and postlexical rules in the phonology, and suggests as an answer that, as elsewhere in grammar, it is general conditions on rules which are determinative of their application rather than the architecture of modular componentry.

4. CONTEXT-SENSITIVITY IN UNDERSPECIFICATION

Besides conditions, however, the phonological representations themselves can be made to constrain the applicability of rules, a possibility which in principle offers an alternative account of how derivationally restricted rules may have unrestricted postlexical effects. Radical feature underspecification, when determined according to phonological context, plays a critical role in this connection, as it allows maximization of the feature fill-in function of phonological rules by making both values of a feature available in lexical representation. Though it will be suggested below that this is misguided, and that feature underspecification should instead be context-free, first the derivational consequences of underspecification defined on phonological context need to be explored.

Kiparsky (1984) illustrates the context-sensitive implementation of feature underspecification with English quantity alternations, where vowels before consonant clusters in the same morpheme may be either long (*paint*) or short (*tent*), but only short before Level 1 suffixes whose amalgamation with stems results in consonant clusters. The vowel in *mean* is therefore predictably short before the irregular inflectional suffix *-t* (*meant*), though it is long everywhere else (*meaning, means,* etc.); this elsewhere [+long] value can be supplied by default if only basically short vowels outside the domain of the precluster shortening rule are underlyingly specified, so that lexically the vowel in *pen* is [−long], while that in *mean* is unspecified. In apparently exceptional *paint,* however, where the vowel is long despite its precluster appearance, specification as [+long] blocks application of the shortening rule because the relevant environment is not crucially derived. And since the invariably short vowel in a word like *tent* always appears before a cluster of consonants, its length value, like that of *mean,* may be left lexically unspecified as well, to be later filled in as [−long] by the same rule of derivation which provides that feature to the vowel in *meant.* The result is that some vowels are specified as [+long] (*paint*), some as [−long] (*pen*), and some not at all (*tent, mean*); yet this mode of underspecification is still radical since the contexts where plus values occur (before clusters) never overlap with those where minus values occur (not before clusters); that is, only one feature value is specified in any given context found among underlying representations.[17]

(14) LONG V: [+long] before clusters, otherwise unspecified
SHORT V: unspecified before clusters, otherwise [−long]

A similar organization of the lexicon is possible with regard to the variably restricted rule of palatalization in Korean. The required derivational results would obtain if the segments for which palatalization is never neutralizing are lexically unspecified for the features that define palatal articulation, say, [+high] subordinated to a Coronal node (with certain other features to be filled in by segmental redundancy rules), but those which contrast in terms of the palatalization features are underlyingly specified either [+high] or [−high], depending on context. The basic rule of Palatalization can be given as in (15a), spreading the tongue body features of a high front vowel or glide (here characterized as coronal, following Hume, 1989, and Gorecka, 1989) to a preceding underspecified consonant; (15b) gives the default configuration for consonants without inherent place of articulation specifications.[18]

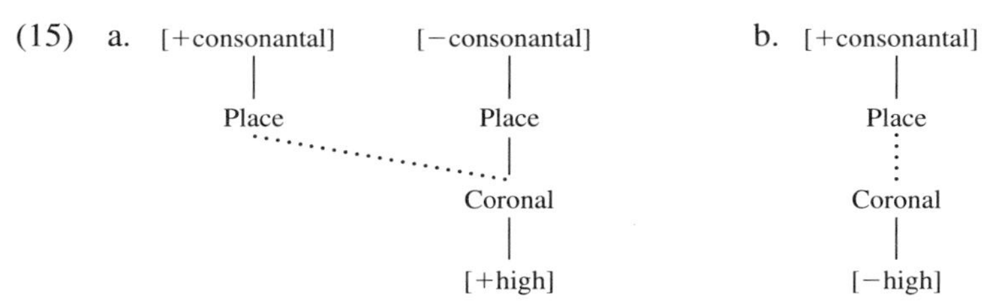

Assuming with Kiparsky that the derived environment constraint per the strict cycle condition restricts only structure-changing applications of lexical rules, the apparently postlexical effects of lexical palatalization with respect to the fricatives /s s′/ are merely the reflexes of structure-building—though not structure-preserving—rule application, because lexically these segments are always underspecified for place of articulation features. Parallel to the treatment of English long and short vowels before consonant clusters, then, the lexical representation of the segments for which palatalization is neutralizing will vary according to whether they are followed by /i/. The medial obstruent in monomorphemic [kačʰi] 'value', for example, is consistent with rule (15a), which means the rule itself could supply the appropriate Coronal configuration in the course of ordinary derivation to an underlying representation like /kaTʰi/, where T represents an obstruent stop unspecified for place of articulation. Alternating morphemes like [patʰ-]/[pačʰ-] 'field' could be represented similarly, /paTʰ-/, so that in supplying the Coronal articulator node rule (15) would also fill in [+high] when [i] follows ([pačʰi], by (15a)), [−high] otherwise ([patʰɯl], by (15b)). But affricates in other kinds of morphemes would have to be specified for at least part of this configuration, because [+high] articulation is not predictable in most environments (morpheme finally, before any vowel other than [i]); the many forms of this sort would have to be represented with specified /č čʰ c′/ ([+high]) rather than with underspecified /T Tʰ T′/. Finally, in order to prevent application of palatalization in monomorphemic structures containing any of [t tʰ t′] before [i], e.g., [madi] < /mati/ 'knot', coronal stops in this environment would need to be regularly specified as [−high], whereas in all other environments—again, morpheme finally and before vowels other than [i]—[t tʰ t′] could still be unspecified, later to be given the default value [−high] by rule (15b). What emerges from this is the following scheme of lexical specification for the feature [high] among coronal obstruents.[19]

(16) CONTEXT-SENSITIVE UNDERSPECIFICATION:

/t tʰ t′/	[−high] before /i/, otherwise unspecified (/T Tʰ T′/)
/č čʰ č′/:	unspecified (/T Tʰ T′/) before /i/, otherwise [+high]
/s s′/:	unspecified (/S S′/)

The reason that palatalization would have no effect on monomorphemic [. . . ti . . .] sequences under this system of representation is that, as a lexical rule, its feature-changing applications would be confined to derived representations. Structure-building applications of the rule predictably are not restricted in this way, though with respect to the fricatives the rule does create segments not found in the phoneme inventory and hence stands in violation of structure preservation. This aside, morpheme-internal blocking of just the neutralizing applications of Korean palatalization in terms of context-sensitive feature underspecification is a direct consequence of [−high] lexical marking for any [t tʰ t′] which happen to be followed by [i].

It is clear, however, that the only reason [t tʰ t′] in these environments are specified for [high] in the first place is to prevent them from undergoing palatalization; that is, [t tʰ t′] before [i] in the same morpheme are marked [−high] because they fail to undergo palatalization, and they fail to undergo palatalization because they are marked [−high].[20] At the same time, any gains in terms of simplicity relative to the lexical representation of [č čʰ č′] before [i] are only illusory, as these are offset by the complementary listing of [−high] for the plain stops in the palatalizing environment. If [t tʰ t′] were unspecified irrespective of context, on the other hand, as will be proposed presently, and [č čʰ č′] were as a consequence specified [+high] in all of their occurrences, then the derived environment restriction on rule (15a) could not be imposed by the strict cycle condition. If radically underspecified for the feature [high] everywhere, in other words, the coronal stops would incorrectly palatalize in morpheme-internal environments when it is assumed that just feature-changing rule applications observe the derived environment constraint.

Of course, palatalization of stops in Korean always would be feature-changing under the alternative of contrastive feature specification, which, though not advocated here, is exemplified for comparison in (17). But the derived environment constraint will properly affect even context-free radically underspecified representations, as in (18), if, following (13b), it is structure-preserving rather than simply structure-changing rule applications that are derivationally restricted.

(17) CONTRASTIVE SPECIFICATION:

/t tʰ t′/	[−high]
/č čʰ č′/	[+high]
/s s′/	unspecified

(18) CONTEXT-FREE UNDERSPECIFICATION:

/t tʰ t′/	unspecified
/č čʰ č′/	[+high]
/s s′/	unspecified

With respect to implementation of (13b), context-free radical underspecification provides sufficient information to establish that palatalization of stops would be neutralizing, or structure-preserving, but that of fricatives would not, because underspecification theory stipulates that at most one feature value may be present in underlying representation (in a given environment, anyway), the other being regularly supplied by rule. Any alternation between the sets in (18) of underspecified /t t^h t′/ (= /T T^h T′/) and specified /č $č^h$ č′/ is thus neutralizing because the value [+high] is present underlyingly among noncontinuant obstruents, the class of stops and affricates; but among fricatives, neither value of [high] occurs in underlying representations, so for them rule (15a) could have only a nonneutralizing effect.[21] For any binary feature subject to context-free underspecification, in fact, the paradigmatic environment in which overt values may be found in underlying representation constitutes a potential neutralization site; other environments do not. This point is important in meeting Kiparsky's (1982:40) objection that the property of neutralization cannot be determined from an inspection of the grammar alone, but rather requires checking all of the derivations. On the contrary, just as the property of structure preservation is determinable from comparison with the inventory of underlying representations, so too is the property of neutralization with respect to underlying contrasts.

The context-free approach to radical underspecification in (18) is confirmed over the context-sensitive characterization in (16) by two further aspects of Korean phonology, namely, syllable-final obstruent neutralization and aspiration coalescence, both of which are optimally described only if /t/ is the least specified consonant in this language, as it has also been characterized for English (e.g., Goldsmith, 1990; Yip, 1991), Maori (de Chene, 1988; Sanders, 1990), and several other languages. Thus the obstruents in (9) all reduce to one of three unreleased stops in syllable-final position: the labials to [p˺], the velars to [k˺], and all the others to [t˺]. Iverson and Kim (1987) characterize this process in geometric terms as the delinking of terminal features from obstruents in syllable-final position, removing all specified laryngeal features, the manner feature [continuant], and any secondary place of articulation features subordinate to the primary place nodes. Redundancy rules come into play to identify the unmarked laryngeal articulation as neither aspirated nor tense, and the unmarked manner of articulation as noncontinuant and nonaffricate, which accounts for why the ultimate output of the rule is a plain lax stop out of the set of [p˺ t˺ k˺], with primary place of articulation remaining intact. Surprisingly, however, syllable-final /h/ also undergoes this process, as shown particularly in careful pronunciations in which the /h/ also aspirates a following lax stop, as in /čoh+ko/ → [čot˺k^ho] 'good and', /tah+či/ → [tat˺$č^h$i] 'touch (susp.)'. The fact that /h/, a segment with no inherent place features of its own, regularly emerges as [t˺] too under syllable-final conditions lends considerable support to the lexical representation of /t/ with no specified features at all, because the same default redundancy rules that fill in the phonetic values for /t/ everywhere and for neutralized coronal obstruents syllable finally will also provide those values to /h/ in the syllable-final environment, producing [t˺].[22]

The identification of /t/ as completely unspecified in Korean phonology is at obvious odds with the diacritic blocking of palatalization in nonderived /. . . ti . . ./ sequences through lexical specification of just these /t/s as [− high] on the model of (16). To assert that /t/ is in general the unspecified Korean obstruent, but that in the many morphemes in which /i/ immediately follows it is not, is to cloud the generalization that all tautomorphemic /. . . ti . . ./ structures escape palatalization for the very same reason. The blocking of morpheme-internal palatalization through lexical specification of [− high] would instead characterize every underlying /. . . ti . . ./ sequence in the language as idiosyncratic, obscuring the generalization that it is all /t/s—rather than just certain morphemes which contain them—which fail to undergo palatalization when in a nonderived environment.[23] The restriction of just structure-preserving rule applications to derived forms, however, allows for consistent, context-free radical underspecification of unmarked Korean /t/ as in (18) while still accommodating appropriate applicational distinctions in the rule of palatalization, and reserving for genuinely exceptional, marked cases the blocking power of more complete lexical representation.[24]

5. CONCLUSION

To summarize, it would seem that the characterization of certain rules as both lexical and postlexical is not the optimal way to capture phonological generalizations which sometimes obey the derived environment constraint, sometimes not. Rather, the relevant restriction appears to be that all and only structure-preserving, or neutralizing, rule applications are constrained to derived environments, with the consequence that structure-building applications of lexical rules need not (though may) be structure-preserving. This rendering of the correlation, in turn, calls into question the utility of drawing a basic functional distinction between lexical and postlexical rule modules in the phonology, suggesting instead that the properties of structure preservation and derived environment restriction affiliate in predictable ways with the rules themselves rather than with the components in which they apply. With respect to radical feature underspecification, moreover, the limitation of structure-preserving rule applications to derived environments implies that the allocation of features to phonemes is consistently context-free, thus providing for a more direct association between the relative complexity of representation and any idiosyncrasies of derivation.

NOTES

[1] That the nasal assimilates only as far as laminopalatal place when before (palatal) [λ] is puzzling and presumably requires a special restriction. Catalan does have phonemic

/ɲ/, but simple avoidance of merger with this segment cannot be the whole story since the same nasal does merge with phonemic /m/ in *so*[m] *pocs* 'they are few'.

[2]Except that labial nasals do assimilate before labiodentals; see below.

[3]With no Root node, the melodically empty C will be stray-erased at the end of the derivation.

[4]The syntactic conditions on syllabification in Catalan would seem to be fully expressable in terms of parametric variation per the theory of syntax–phonology interaction developed in Kaisse (1985 : 186ff.).

[5]The postlexical derivation of velar nasals makes unnecessary the special lexical treatment of them Kiparsky (1985 : 101 – 103) proposes, because the velar nasal under present assumptions does not exist except at the postlexical level. Variation in the retention of postnasal [k] (as with [p] and [t]) is then due generally to the syntactic conditions on syllabification, though under the same stylistic conditions the velar stop is somewhat more likely to be retained than the labial or dental (Gonzàles, 1989).

[6]The blocking of rule (5b) in this case will follow from the elsewhere condition. This predictable precedence of the more specific rule (5a) over (5b) assures that the labiodental articulation specified for the fricative /f/ percolates onto the nasal /m/ in an /mf/ cluster, rather than the (default) bilabial articulation of /m/ onto /f/.

[7]Though not with a palatal (cf. note 1).

[8]Korean palatalization has been described from various perspectives by Kim-Renaud (1974), S.-G. Kim (1976), C.-W. Kim and Ahn (1983), Ahn (1985, 1988), Sohn (1987), Iverson (1987), Iverson and Wheeler (1988), and Cho and Sells (1991).

[9]Presumably /t′/ would undergo this process too, except that the only member of the tense stop series which occurs finally in stems is the velar /k′/ (Chung, 1980).

[10]Palatalization occasionally results in homophony, e.g., [maǰi] derives from either /mat+i/ 'the eldest' or /mači/ 'hempen paper', [kač^{h}i] from either /kat^h+i/ 'together' or /kač^{h}i/ 'value'.

[11]Besides /s s′/, the alveolar sonorants also evince allophonic palatalization between ([muɲi] < /mun+i/ 'door (subj.)') as well as within morphemes ([huʎʎuŋ] < /hullyuŋ/ 'magnificent'). Cho and Sells (1991) suggest that morpheme-internal instances of /t t^h t′/ "palatalize," too—but without affricating—so that the alveolar stops in (11a) would also reflect a degree of superficial coarticulation with /i/. But the effect here seems to be no more than is universally instantiated in such contexts, and in any case is not nearly as categorically salient as among the coronal sonorants and fricatives.

[12]As pointed out to me by Sang-Cheol Ahn, there is some variation among speakers as to the extent of palatalization with respect to tense /s′/, i.e., /s′i/ seems to vary individually between essentially unpalatalized ([s′i]) and sharply palatalized ([š′i]) articulations. Since the other potentially palatalizable tense obstruent, /t′/, happens not to occur in relevant derived environments (cf. note 9), palatalization for some speakers appears to exclude the tense obstruents in general.

[13]A variant of the Cho and Sells (1991) two-rule approach is outlined by Kiparsky (this volume) in which palatalization per se would always be allophonic, applying first in the derived environments of the lexical phonology, then without morphological restriction in the postlexical phonology. But before exiting the lexicon, the intermediate postalveolar stops (/ţ ţ^h ţ′/) produced by the rule in derived environments would merge with the phonemic affricates (/č č^h č′/) by a separate rule applying at the word level. The violations of

structure preservation entailed by this version of palatalization's application in the lexicon could then be sanctioned as per Macfarland and Pierrehumbert (1991), who invoke the autosegmental linking condition (Hayes, 1986) in order to grant lexical status to feature-spreading, allophonic assimilation rules. Irrespective of whether relaxation of structure preservation to this extent is ultimately well founded, however, Korean palatalization thus described still remains split between two rules, the neutralizing one of which applies context-free. Further, the attribution of postalveolar ([+anterior]) or palatalized ([+high]) articulation to nonaffricated coronal stops before [i] in forms like those in (11a) would represent a considerably greater degree of coarticulation than the phonetics warrants (cf. also note 11).

[14] The rule raises word-final /a/ to [e] after high vowels, as in /mutil+a/ → [mutiλe] 'the boy'. It must be noncyclic since the only constituent boundary before which it applies is at the level of the word; hence /a/ does not raise in /mutil+a+k/ → [mutiλak] 'the boy (erg.)'; yet the rule must be restricted to derived environments, since /a/ does not raise morpheme-internally, either: /ikas+i/ → [ikasi] 'to learn', /muga/ → [muγa] 'limit'. Cf. also Booij and Rubach (1987) for other instances of noncyclic lexical rules.

[15] As defined by Kiparsky (1973), a rule of the form A → B / C ___ D is neutralizing just in case there exist instances of CBD in the input to the rule.

[16] The property of structure preservation among lexical rules has been used to explain the neutrality of specific vowels in harmony systems, e.g., /i/ and /e/ in Finnish (Kiparsky, 1985). Precisely those vowels are neutral for which the effect of harmony would be allophonic (the simple backing of /i/ or /e/ in Finnish would create novel back unrounded vowels, but the backing of /y/ or /ö/ results in merger with underlying /u/ and /o/). If all applications of vowel harmony must be structure-preserving, which characterization of the rule as strictly lexical under the conventional theory would entail, then the neutrality of /i/ and /e/ would seem to fall out, although it begs the question of why neutral vowels then do not simply undergo rounding along with backing so as to merge with extant vowels in the system (the harmonic rounding of /i/ in Yawelmani Yokuts, for example, results in merger with underlying /u/ rather than in either nonapplication of the rule or in creation of the novel segment [y]). Under (13b), harmonic neutrality derives as per Steriade (1987), from the representational distinction between contrastive and redundant feature values.

[17] Of course, vowel length today would be represented not as a binary feature on the segmental or melodic tier, but as a timing unit on the skeletal or moraic tier (Clements and Keyser, 1983; Hayes, 1989), so that the structure of long vowels is VV, that of short vowels just V. Shortening then consists in the disassociation of the vowel's melodic features from one of its two timing elements, with the default interpretation that short segments in general are unmarked (if not strictly underspecified) relative to long or geminate ones. (Cf. also Myers, 1987; Yip, 1987.) Kiparsky's analysis varying the underlying specifications of a segmental feature [long] in English is nonetheless illustrative of the context-sensitive implementation of radical underspecification theory.

[18] Nothing crucial hinges here on spreading the vowel's presumed Coronal articulator to the underspecified consonant's Place node (as opposed to just spreading [+high] and always providing Coronal by default). The important point is that the output of Palatalization for stops is the same representation as underlies that of the affricates.

[19] When listed with either of its binary values, the feature [high] is ultimately dependent on there being an articulator node under Place, which, when not otherwise specified, is Coronal.

[20] This circularity is endemic as well to the class of traditional sequence redundancy

rules, which also predict features based on properties of segments found elsewhere in the morpheme (e.g., all the features of /s/ are redundant in initial triconsonantal clusters of English even though /s/ would otherwise be specified [+continuant]). Here, however, there is no interaction with derivation, since classical sequence redundancy rules apply strictly within morphemes; and neither does the representational savings they provide have to be undone by marking of the feature for blocking effect purposes in complementary environments (/t/ need not be specified [-continuant] in any environment even if /s/ in clusters is also unspecified for that feature because there are no lexical exceptions to the cluster generalization). Cf. Ao (1991) for a possible case in which a sequence redundancy rule nonetheless does appear to apply after a rule of phonological derivation, though the effect there is still inert, i.e., neither feeding nor bleeding.

[21] In terms of the definition in note 15, supplying the feature [+high] to underspecified /T/ is neutralizing because [+high] coronals (/č čʰ č′/, also underspecified for [continuant]) exist in the input to the rule. Supplying [+high] to /s s′/ (specified as [+continuant]), however, is not neutralizing because no [+high, +continuant] consonants exist in the input to the rule. A similar characterization of feature redundancy is outlined in Steriade (1987).

[22] This account is based on Iverson (1989), in which laryngeal segments are configured with specifications for laryngeal features and for [continuant], but without distinctive place of articulation features.

[23] The representation of /t/ as unspecified in all environments has the consequence that Korean morphemes with /. . . ti . . ./ are no more complex (in fact, one feature less so) than those with /. . . či . . ./. Similarly, invariant radical underspecification of vowel quantity in English does not distinguish the long vowels in *paint* and *pain* (both with /VV/), whereas the context-sensitive approach outlined in (14) would specify the vowel as long in *paint* but not in *pain.* In the absence of evidence showing Korean /. . . ti . . ./ to be more marked than /. . . či . . ./, or of any suggesting the vowel in *paint* is in some way more remarkable than that in *pain,* this consequence seems quite correct.

[24] This property also holds of underspecified segments for which rule application is blocked by virtue of exceptional marking elsewhere in the word. For example, the loanword in Hungarian *büró* [byro:] 'bureau' contravenes the regular front/back vowel harmony pattern of the language (Ringen, 1988); its exceptionality can be encoded by assigning the specification [−back] just to the word's leftmost vowel in underlying representation. In regular cases, [−back] is a property of either all the vowels in the morpheme (/OrOm, [−back]/ → [öröm] *öröm* 'joy') or none of them (/vArOs/ → [varos] *varos* 'city', with [+back] throughout by default). In irregular *büró,* however, the lexical attachment of [−back] just to the first vowel (or to the second in similarly disharmonic *sofőr* [šofø:r] 'chauffeur') causes the other vowel's backness value to be supplied by default rather than harmony since, in consequence of the morpheme's exceptional lexical marking, the spreading within it of [−back] would be neutralizing and so inapplicable in this nonderived context.

REFERENCES

Ahn, S.-C. (1985). *The Interplay of Phonology and Morphology in Korean.* Doctoral dissertation, University of Illinois, Urbana.

Ahn, S.-C. (1988). Lexicality vs. postlexicality in Korean palatalization. In *Linguistics in the Morning Calm 2* (The Linguistic Society of Korea, ed.), pp. 249–263. Hanshin, Seoul.

Anderson, S. R. (1974). *The Organization of Phonology.* Academic Press, New York.

Ao, B. (1991). Kikongo nasal harmony and context-sensitive underspecification. *Linguistic Inquiry* **22,** 193–196.

Booij, G., and Rubach, J. (1987). Postcyclic versus postlexical rules in lexical phonology. *Linguistic Inquiry* **18,** 1–44.

Cho, Y.-M., and Sells, P. (1991). *A Lexical Account of Phrasal Suffixes in Korean.* Unpublished manuscript, Stanford University, Stanford, Calif.

Chung, K. (1980). *Neutralization in Korean: A Functional View.* Doctoral dissertation, University of Texas, Austin.

Clements, G. N., and Keyser, S. J. (1983). *CV Phonology: A Generative Theory of the Syllable.* MIT Press, Cambridge, Mass.

de Chene, B. (1988). *Japanese* r-*epenthesis and Inflectional Boundary Buffer-Segments.* Paper presented at the winter meeting of the Linguistic Society of America, New Orleans.

Goldsmith, J. (1990). *Autosegmental and Metrical Phonology.* Blackwell, Oxford.

Gonzàlez, M. (1989). *Catalan Nasal Assimilation: Lexical or Postlexical?* Unpublished manuscript, University of Massachusetts, Amherst.

Gorecka, A. (1989). *Are Front Vowels Coronal?* Paper presented at the winter meeting of the Linguistic Society of America, Washington, D.C.

Hayes, B. (1986). Inalterability in CV phonology. *Language* **62,** 321–351.

Hayes, B. (1989). Compensatory lengthening in moraic phonology. *Linguistic Inquiry* **20,** 253–306.

Hualde, J. (1989). The strict cycle condition and noncyclic rules. *Linguistic Inquiry* **20,** 675–680.

Hume, E. (1989). *Blocking Effects in Korean Umlaut: Evidence for the Coronality of Front Vowels.* Paper presented at the winter meeting of the Linguistic Society of America, Washington, D.C.

Itô, J. (1986). *Syllable Theory in Prosodic Phonology.* Doctoral dissertation, University of Massachusetts, Amherst.

Itô, J. (1989). A prosodic theory of epenthesis. *Natural Language & Linguistic Theory* **7,** 217–259.

Iverson, G. (1987). The Revised Alternation Condition in lexical phonology. *Nordic Journal of Linguistics* **10,** 151–164.

Iverson, G. (1989). On the category Supralaryngeal. *Phonology* **6,** 285–303.

Iverson, G., and Kim, K.-H. (1987). Underspecification and hierarchical feature representation in Korean consonantal phonology. In *Papers From the Parasession on Autosegmental and Metrical Phonology,* pp. 182–198. Chicago Linguistic Society, Chicago.

Iverson, G., and Wheeler, D. (1988). Blocking and the elsewhere condition. In *Theoretical Morphology: Approaches in Modern Linguistics* (M. Hammond and M. Noonan, eds.), pp. 325–338. Academic Press, San Diego.

Kaisse, E. (1985). *Connected Speech: The Interaction of Syntax and Phonology.* Academic Press, Orlando.

Kaisse, E. (1986). Locating Turkish devoicing. *Proceedings of the West Coast Conference on Formal Linguistics* **5,** 119–128.

Kim, C.-W., and S.-C. Ahn. (1983). *Palatalization in Korean Revisited.* Paper presented at the winter meeting of the Linguistic Society of America, Minneapolis.

Kim, S.-G. (1976). *Palatalization in Korean.* Doctoral dissertation, University of Texas, Austin.

Kim-Renaud, Y.-K. (1974). *Korean Consonantal Phonology.* Doctoral dissertation, University of Hawaii, Manoa.

Kiparsky, P. (1973). Abstractness, opacity, and global rules. In *Three Dimensions of Linguistic Theory* (O. Fujimura, ed.), pp. 57–86. TEC, Tokyo.

Kiparsky, P. (1982). Lexical morphology and phonology. In *Linguistics in the Morning Calm* (I.-S. Yang, ed.), pp. 3–91. Hanshin, Seoul.

Kiparsky, P. (1984). On the lexical phonology of Icelandic. *Nordic Prosody III* (C.-C. Elert, ed.), pp. 135–164. Almqvist and Wiksell, Stockholm.

Kiparsky, P. (1985). Some consequences of lexical phonology. *Phonology Yearbook* **2,** 85–138.

Koutsoudas, A., Sanders, G., and Noll, C. (1974). The application of phonological rules. *Language* **50,** 1–28.

Macfarland, T., and Pierrehumbert, J. (1991). On ich-Laut, ach-Laut and structure preservation. *Phonology* **8,** 171–180.

Mascaró, J. (1976). *Catalan Phonology and the Phonological Cycle.* Doctoral dissertation, Massachusetts Institute of Technology, Cambridge.

McCarthy, J. (1986). OCP effects: gemination and antigemination. *Linguistic Inquiry* **17,** 207–264.

Myers, S. (1987). Vowel shortening in English. *Natural Language & Linguistic Theory* **5,** 485–518.

Paradis, C., and Prunet, J.-F. (1989). On coronal transparency. *Phonology* **6,** 317–348.

Plapp, R. (1990). *The Geometry of Russian Voice Assimilation.* Paper presented at the Minnesota Conference on Language and Linguistics, Minneapolis.

Ringen, C. (1988). Transparency in Hungarian vowel harmony. *Phonology* **5,** 327–342.

Sagey, E. (1986). *The Representation of Features and Relations in Non-linear Phonology.* Doctoral dissertation, Massachusetts Institute of Technology, Cambridge.

Sanders, G. (1990). On the analysis and implications of Maori verb alternations. *Lingua* **80,** 149–196.

Sapir, J. D. (1965). *A Grammar of Diola-Fogny* (West African Language Monographs 3). Cambridge University Press, London.

Sohn, H.-S. (1987). *Underspecification in Korean Phonology.* Doctoral dissertation, University of Illinois, Urbana.

Steriade, D. (1987). Redundant values. In *Papers from the Parasession on Autosegmental and Metrical Phonology,* pp. 339–362. Chicago Linguistics Society, Chicago.

Yip, M. (1987). English vowel epenthesis. *Natural Language & Linguistic Theory* **5,** 463–484.

Yip, M. (1991). Coronals, consonant clusters and the coda condition. In *The Special Status of Coronals: Internal and External Evidence* (C. Paradis and J.-F. Prunet, eds.), pp. 61–78. Academic Press, San Diego.

BLOCKING IN NONDERIVED ENVIRONMENTS

PAUL KIPARSKY

Department of Linguistics
Stanford University
Stanford, California 94305

1. THE PROBLEM

Some phonological rules apply freely across morpheme boundaries, and morpheme internally where fed by some earlier phonological rule, but are blocked elsewhere, in what are referred to as "nonderived environments." I will call this syndrome NONDERIVED ENVIRONMENT BLOCKING (NDEB). The theoretical basis for NDEB was sought first in constraints on underlying representations (the alternation condition) and later in constraints on rule application (e.g., the revised alternation condition, the strict cycle condition, the elsewhere condition). In this article, I propose to derive it from more general assumptions, namely (1) that lexical representations can be underspecified, (2) that phonological rules can apply in structure-building ("feature-filling") mode, and (3) that learners construct the simplest grammar. It will also be shown that these assumptions lead to predictions about the nature and scope of derived environment effects which are empirically more accurate than those which flow from any of the abovementioned approaches.

What rules are subject to NDEB? The best approximation so far seems to be that it is the class of obligatory neutralization rules. The revised alternation condition (RAC, Kiparsky, 1973; Iverson and Wheeler, 1988) expresses this directly by simply prohibiting obligatory neutralization rules from applying in nonderived environments. But the RAC is really no more than a descriptive generalization dressed up as a principle and is unstatable as a formal condition on phonological

Phonetics and Phonology, Volume 4
Studies in Lexical Phonology

rules. Notoriously, the class of neutralization rules cannot be formally specified, for whether a rule is neutralizing depends on the derivations of the grammar. The restriction to obligatory rules is likewise suspect, because everywhere else the principles governing the application of phonological rules apply equally to optional and obligatory rules. (There is no reason to believe that, when optional rules become obligatory in the course of language change, they suddenly become subject to different principles of rule application.) And the concept of "derived environment" itself plays no role elsewhere in the theory of grammar and indeed requires a peculiar disjunctive definition. Moreover, the RAC is probably inadequate on factual grounds as well, since it effectively bans ALL absolute neutralization, enforcing a degree of concreteness in underlying representations which throws out many well-motivated analyses (Dresher, 1981). Remedying this latter flaw by limiting the RAC to nonautomatic rules (Kiparsky, 1973) would make it theoretically even more objectionable, for determining whether a rule is automatic or not again involves looking at all the derivations.

The search for a more adequate account of NDEB effects led to two main alternatives. The more widely accepted of these invokes some version of the strict cycle condition (SCC) first proposed for phonology by Kean (1974). The restriction to obligatory neutralization rules was specified stipulatively in the version of Mascaró (1976) and received little attention in later work (Halle, 1978; Rubach, 1984). In Kiparsky (1982) it was further proposed to reduce the SCC itself to the elsewhere condition.[1] This allowed the remaining problematic predicate "derived" to be replaced by "distinct from a lexical item," a further improvement because distinctness is a basic predicate of the theory of grammar, and because it unifies the phonological and morphological kind of "derivedness." The SCC, then, made it possible to avoid all references to obligatoriness, to neutralization, to "derived environments," and to a rule's "automatic" status, and in addition had the virtue of permitting absolute neutralization, as long as this is effected by noncyclic (or postlexical) rules. These gains were, however, offset by a major degradation in empirical adequacy. The SCC defines the nature and scope of NDEB in ways which are not at all borne out by the evidence. In particular, it has become rather clear that NDEB is correlated with a rule's cyclicity and/or lexicality only approximately if at all. The RAC had struck much nearer the mark in connecting NDEB to a rule's obligatoriness and to its neutralizing status.

The second type of alternative account for the NDEB takes the derivational character of such notions as "obligatory neutralization rule" and "derived environment" as indications that the phenomenon should not be attributed to any constraints on grammars at all, but rather to the language acquisition process. In this vein, Anderson (1981) suggests that NDEB arises from the learner's lack of evidence for a rule's applicability in nonderived environments, and that nothing more than this need be said.[2] I concur with Anderson on the first point but not on the second. NDEB arises in situations where only derived environments provide positive positive evidence for the application of a rule, but it represents a generalization which grammars must be capable of expressing in a principled way. The alternatives are all unacceptable. Writing the "derived environments" expressly into the structural descriptions of rules as some combination of lexical and morphological conditions, aside from being ad hoc, would in some cases require global conditions otherwise unknown in phonological rules (Kiparsky, 1973). Listing the nonderived cases, or marking them as lexical exceptions, would miss the generalization that precisely nonderived environments are exempt—particularly unfortunate in the case of rules which otherwise have no lexical exceptions. Worse, it would be entirely out of the question for morphemes with two potential alternation sites, of which only the one in the derived environment undergoes the rule. For example, Finnish Consonant Gradation, which simplifies a geminate in the onset of a closed syllable, affects only the second geminate in such words as /attentaatti+n/ $\rightarrow$ *attentaati+n* 'assassination'.[3] Associating an exception feature with the first *tt* but not with the second would (beside missing the generalization that only geminates in nonderived environments are "exceptions" to the rule) contravene the robust generalization that exception features are associated with lexical items or at most with morphemes, but at any rate not with individual segments or syllables.

In this article I argue that in order for learners to arrive at the correct projections from the evidence accessible to them, the theory of grammar must make available rules and representations of a particular kind, namely structure-building rules and underspecified representations. Given such rules and representations, it will follow that the simplest grammars constructed by learners will project precisely the observed range of NDEB effects. In support of this position I show that NDEB effects are in many ways sharply constrained by structural principles. I provide a partial vindication for the claim behind the original RAC that obligatoriness and neutralization are a necessary condition for NDEB (though, I argue, not a sufficient condition), and that cyclicity and lexical status are only indirectly connected to it. Among the other consequences of my proposal for which I also give evidence are that NDEB is restricted to structure-building (feature-filling) rules and that the "derivedness" of an environment must be understood in a specific sense which differs from what has hitherto been supposed.

The next section of this article presents phonological evidence in support of the position that NDEB is independent of cyclicity and lexicality, and that it is associated only with obligatory neutralization rules. I then introduce my new account of NDEB and show how it works in the standard range of examples. Subsequent sections present some additional kinds of evidence supporting it and show how some apparently recalcitrant cases can be dealt with in a way that is consistent with it. I conclude by discussing NDEB in prosodic phonology, taking up first the possibility of unifying it with the free element condition proposed for rules of metrical structure assignment, then its role in syllable structure and quantity, and finally its relation to blocking of harmony and tonal spreading by opaque elements.

2. NDEB IS NOT SPECIFIC TO CYCLIC OR LEXICAL RULES

As its name indicates, the SCC was originally a condition on the application of cyclic rules. The reduction to the elsewhere condition would make it a condition on lexical rules, independently of their cyclic status. In this section I argue, contrary to both these views, that the NDEB phenomenon is independent both of cyclicity and of the lexical status of a rule.

2.1. There Are Cyclic Lexical Rules with No NDEB

First I demonstrate this independence in one direction by exhibiting a cyclic lexical rule which applies freely in nonderived environments. This is the vowel coalescence process in Finnish stated in (1).

(1) COALESCENCE:
ea, eä → *ee*
öä → *öö*
oa → *oo*

Coalescence is found in several regional dialects and applies as an optional rule in colloquial Helsinki speech (which the cited data represent). It is applicable to any unstressed vowel sequences of the form (1), whether underlying, as in (2a), or derived, as in (2b).

(2) a. /pimeä/ *pimeä* ~ *pimee* 'dark' (nom.sg.)
b. /nime+tä/ *nime+ä* ~ *nimee* 'name' (part.sg.)

The rule which feeds Coalescence in (2b) deletes *t* in an onset after a short vowel which does not bear primary stress (which is always on the initial syllable), as in /hattu+ta/ *hattua* 'hat', /jo+ta/ *jota* 'what', /veesee+tä/ *veeseetä* 'toilet'.[4]

(3) *t*-DELETION:

There is no *t*-Deletion after the long vowels created by Coalescence. For example, only the uncoalesced variant of (2a) allows *t*-Deletion after it. Because Coalescence is optional, this results in the variation seen in (4).

(4) /pimeä+tä/ *pimeää* ~ *pimee+tä* (**pimee+ä*) 'dark' (part.sg.)

So, since *t*-Deletion feeds Coalescence and Coalescence bleeds *t*-Deletion, Coalescence must apply both before and after *t*-Deletion. Specifically, the order is: (1) Coalescence within stems, (2) *t*-Deletion in stem+suffix combinations, (3) Coalescence in stem+suffix combinations. This order of application requires that *t*-Deletion and Coalescence apply cyclically, in that order, with "anywhere" resyllabification:

(5)

		/pimeä/	/nime/
FIRST	*t*-Deletion	—	—
CYCLE:	Coalescence (optional)	*pimee* ~ *pimeä*	—
SECOND	Morphology	*pimee+tä* ~ *pimeä+tä*	*nime+tä*
CYCLE:	*t*-Deletion	*pimee+tä* ~ *pimeä+ä*	*nime+ä*
	Coalescence (optional)	—	*nimee* ~ *nime+ä*

A second argument for the cyclic lexical status of both rules comes from their interaction with the morphology. Both rules must apply to stems before the allomorphs of lexical suffixes added to them are selected by the phonologically conditioned allomorphy rules in (6).

(6) a. ILLATIVE SINGULAR: The ending is *-seen* after a "contracted" (underlyingly disyllabic) long vowel, and -(*h*)V*n* elsewhere. E.g., *altaa+seen* (stem /altasV/) 'into the pool', *talo+*(*h*)*on* (not **talo+seen*) 'into the house'.[5]

b. POSSESSIVE SUFFIX: After a case suffix ending in short vowel, the 3-sg. possessive suffix has an optional allomorph -V*n*. E.g., *talo+ssa+an* ~ *talo+ssa+nsa* 'in his/her/its/their house', but only *kala+t+nsa* [→ *kala+nsa,* by (8)], 'his/her/its/their fishes' (not **kala+t+an*).

The examples in (7) show how the right forms are derived only if the allomorphs are chosen AFTER the application of Coalescence and *t*-Deletion to the stem.

(7) a. /pimeä/ 'dark': (ill.sg.) *pimeä+*(*h*)*än* ~ *pimee+seen* (**pimeä+seen*) [(6a) fed by Coalescence]

b. /nime+tä/ 'name' (part.sg.): 3poss. *nime+ä+än* ~ *nimee+nsä* (~ **nimee+än*) [(6b) bled by Coalescence]

c. /kala+ta/ 'fish' (part.sg.): 3poss. **kala+a+an* (*kala+a+nsa*) [(6b) bled by *t*-Deletion; this derivation requires that resyllabification is a cyclic rule or an everywhere rule]

On the assumption that cyclic phonological rules are interspersed with the morphology, the correct distribution of allomorphs follows directly from the cyclic status of Coalescence and *t*-Deletion. The choice of allomorphs is simply determined by the stem's phonological shape at the point when the suffixes are added.

For theories which do not allow cyclic phonology to interact with morphology (e.g., Odden, this volume), it is not so clear how to approach these facts. One move would be to stipulate that *-seen* and -V*n* allomorphs are licensed by a filter, or introduced by a replacement process in place of the "basic" allomorphs, AFTER the phonological rules have applied. This fails because rule (8), which deletes a consonant before a possessive suffix, such as the suffix-final *-n* in (9), does not license the possessive suffix allomorphy stated in (6), as seen from the ungrammaticality of the -V*n* allomorph of the possessive suffix in (10a).

(8) C → ∅ / ____ +Poss

(9) /huonee+seen+ni/ → *huoneeseeni* 'my room' (ill.sg.)
/hattu+hun+si/ → *hattu(h)usi* 'your hat' (ill.sg.)

(10) a. */hattu+hun+Vn/ → *hattu+(h)u+Vn → *hattu+(h)u+un
b. /hattu+hun+nsa/ → hattu+(h)u+nsa

Indeed, as the analysis of Kanerva (1987) makes clear, the conditions on the -V*n* allomorph of the 3.p. possessive suffix would on these assumptions have to be checked by filters at *two* separate stages of the phonological derivation. This would obviously require a still more drastic weakening of morphological theory.

In sum, I have presented two arguments that *t*-Deletion and Coalescence are lexical rules which apply cyclically in that order. The first argument is that this resolves the ordering paradox raised by the data in (2) and (4) and predicts the correct interaction of Coalescence and *t*-Deletion in all cases. The second argument is that it predicts the otherwise problematic phonology/allomorphy interaction in (7) and is consistent with the restrictive and empirically well supported position that "allomorphy" is not replacement but selection (Lieber, 1987; Zwicky, 1986), and that "global" conditions on the selection of allomorphs are not allowed.

But recall that, as (2) shows, Coalescence applies in nonderived environments. It is thus an example of a cyclic lexical rule (significantly, an optional, although neutralizing, one) which applies across the board. The upshot is that the NDEB effect cannot be a property of all cyclic lexical rules.

2.2. NDEB in Word-Level and Postlexical Rules

A fair amount of evidence has already accumulated which shows the independence of NDEB and cyclic/lexical status in the other direction. NDEB effects have been found both in rules which apply noncyclically at the word level (Hargus, 1985, 1989; Hualde, 1989; Kaisse, 1986; Shaw, 1985: 199), and in postlexical rules (Clark, 1990: 117 ff.; Hargus, 1985; Iverson and Wheeler, 1988; Rice, 1988).

Many of the rules presented in the earlier literature as cases of "strict cyclicity" have turned out to be in reality noncyclic. For example, the Finnish assibilation rule (11) shows classic derived-environment behavior (Kiparsky, 1973). In a word like /tilat+i/ → *tilasi* 'ordered', Assibilation applies only to the second /t/, the one before a derived *i*. However, Assibilation must in fact apply at the word level. In derivations like (12) it is fed by a rule which raises *-e* to *-i* at the end of a word.

(11) *t* → *s* / — *i*

(12) a. /vete/ → *veti* → *vesi* 'water' (nom.sg.)
b. /vete+nä/ → *vetenä* (ess.sg.)

Since Assibilation is fed by a word-level rule, it must itself apply at least at the word level or later (though it may, as far as these data are concerned, also apply cyclically).

Another such rule in Finnish is Consonant Gradation, which degeminates double stops and weakens simple stops in the onset of a closed syllable. The examples in (13) illustrate the regular alternation between geminate and simple stops induced by Consonant Gradation in the word *hattu* 'hat'.

(13) a. *hattu* (nom.sg.), *hattu+a* (part.), *hattu+na* (ess.)
b. *hatu+n* (gen.), *hatu+ssa* (iness.), *hatu+sta* (elat.), *hatu+ksi* (transl.)

Both indigenous and borrowed vocabulary testify to the rule's failure to apply in nonderived environments.

(14) a. NATIVE AND NATIVIZED MORPHEMES: *sitten* "then", *kippis* "cheers!", *hellanlettas* (affectionate exclamation), *tattis* "thanks", Gen.Pl. *-tten* (e.g., *huone+i+tten* "rooms")
b. LOANS: *appelsiini* 'orange', *pikkelsi* 'pickles', *attentaatti* 'assassination (attempt)', *okkultaatio* 'occultation', *kettinki* 'chain', *rottinki* 'rattan', *appellatiivi* 'common noun', *opportunisti* 'opportunist', *hokkuspokkus* 'hocus pocus', *bakkantti* 'bacchante', *supportti* 'support (of a lathe)'

The following example illustrates all three cases in a single word, namely (taking the *tt*'s from left to right), (1) nonapplication in a nonderived environment, (2) application in a morphologically derived environment, and (3) application in a phonologically derived environment.

(15) /hottentotti+ttoma+ta/ → *hottentotti+ttom+ta* → *hottentoti+ton+ta* 'Hottentotless' (part.sg.)

I return to the derivation of such cases in Section 5.1.

I turn now to the evidence that Consonant Gradation is a word-level rule. That it must apply at word level is shown by the fact that it is fed by a rule which deletes word-final *-e* in polysyllables.[6] The closed syllable resulting from this word-level deletion process triggers degemination.[7]

(16) /vaatteCe/ → *vaatte*C → *vaate*C

That Consonant Gradation applies only at word level, not also in the cyclic phonology, is suggested by its interaction with the consonant deletion rule (8). Deletion by rule (8) bleeds Gradation in cases like (17).

(17) /hattu+n+si/ → *hattusi* (**hatusi*) 'your hat's' (hat+gen.sg.+2-sg.poss.)
/hattu+t+ni/ → *hattuni* (**hatuni*) 'my hats' (hat+nom.pl.+1-sg.poss.)

If Consonant Gradation were cyclic, it would wrongly apply at the stage *hattu+n, hattu+t,* before the possessive suffix is added on the last cycle, triggering the application of (8).[8]

Finally, I note that Consonant Gradation is lexical (this is actually inessential to my argument; the crucial point is that it is a word-level rule). It applies only within the morphological word, excluding clitics phonologically adjoined to it. This implies lexical status if we adopt Inkelas and Zec's suggestion that the "clitic group" is not a separate prosodic category but the postlexical incarnation of the phonological word (Inkelas, 1989; Zec, this volume), in which case application in (18) cannot be blocked by restricting the rule to a prosodic domain. A geminate arising across clitic boundary is not subject to Consonant Gradation.[9]

(18) /meneC#päs/ → *mene*[pp]*äs* (↛ **mene*[p]*äs*) 'go!'
/itseC#kin/ → *itse*[kk]*in* (↛ **itse*[k]*in*) 'self, too'

But if word-level rules are not constrained by the SCC, and Consonant Gradation applies at word level, what blocks it from applying in nonderived cases like (14)? The conclusion is that word-level rules can be restricted to derived environments exactly as cyclic rules can.

I turn now to the evidence that NDEB must also be countenanced for postlexical rules.

Evidence would be expected to be scarce for rules which apply ONLY postlexically, for such rules are normally nonneutralizing (in consequence of the strict domain hypothesis and structure preservation), and nonneutralizing rules are not subject to NDEB (for reasons to be explained later). Turkish final stop devoicing may be a case, however (Kaisse, 1986). But the point can be made equally well with rules which apply both lexically and postlexically. If NDEB were turned off postlexically, any blocking in their lexical applications would be overridden by their postlexical applications, and so they would effectively apply across the board. Yet many rules with this dual status do display NDEB.

The Sanskrit *ruki* rule has been cited as a showcase example of derived-environment behavior (Kiparsky, 1982). In Classical Sanskrit it applies strictly within the morphological/lexical word. In Vedic, however, it also applies optionally across clitic boundary (Macdonell, 1968:45–46; Selkirk, 1980; Wackernagel, 1895:237; Whitney, 1887:64) and (more rarely) between words within a phonological phrase.

(19) a. CLITIC BOUNDARY: *ṛcchánti ṣma* 'they went' (*RV.* 10.102.6)
b. WORD BOUNDARY: *nū́ ṣṭhirám* 'now the strong one' (*RV.* 1.64.15)

Application of the rule across word boundary in Vedic is certainly evidence that it applied postlexically in that dialect,[10] though not necessarily only postlexically. But the *ruki* rule was restricted to "derived environments" even in Vedic. Therefore, in order to block postlexical applications of the *ruki* rule in such morphologically simple words as *bisa* 'sprout', *busa* 'mist', it must be possible to restrict even postlexical rules to derived environments. Whatever principle is responsible for NDEB must stay in force postlexically here.

The proposal presented in the next section is designed to accommodate such cases without losing the respective theoretical and empirical virtues of previous accounts of the NDEB.

3. NDEB EFFECTS EXPLAINED AWAY

3.1. The Underspecification Account

I adopt the following assumptions.

(20) a. Underspecification (Kiparsky, 1982; Archangeli and Pulleyblank, 1989).
b. Default rules may be ordered to apply either cyclically, at the word level, or postlexically (Pulleyblank, 1986; Rice, 1988).
c. The optimal grammar is the simplest (Chomsky and Halle, 1968).
d. Structure-changing rules are to be decomposed into deletion (delinking) plus structure-building (Poser, 1982; Mascaró 1987; Cho, 1990).

For purposes of the argument, underspecification is understood in the strictest sense, that is, what Steriade (1987a) calls RADICAL UNDERSPECIFICATION, including the assumption of strict binarity of feature specifications in underlying lexical representations. In each environment, we can have at most [0F] and [αF], where [−αF] is the value assigned by the most specific rule (language-particular or universal) which is applicable in that environment. (That is, the relevant "environments" are defined by the rule system, including the markedness rules of universal grammar). The essence of my proposal could be maintained even under weaker versions of underspecification, however, as is shown below.

A corollary of (20c) and (20d) is that rules will be structure-building if possible (i.e., unless positive evidence requires positing a deletion rule). A corollary of (20c) and (20a) is that underlying representations are minimally specified.

My principal thesis is:

(21) NDEB is the result of structure-building rules applying to underspecified representations.

For example, the Finnish Assibilation rule (11) would be a structure-building rule that assigns the feature specification [+continuant] to a coronal obstruent before *i*. Elsewhere, coronal obstruents will be assigned the default specification [−continuant].

(22) a. $\begin{bmatrix} +\text{coronal} \\ +\text{obstruent} \end{bmatrix} \rightarrow [+\text{continuant}] \;/\; \_\_\, i$

b. $[+\text{obstruent}] \rightarrow [-\text{continuant}]$

Given these rules, the underlying representations for non-alternating /t/ and /s/ must be as follows.

(23)

	/t/	/s/
Before *i:*	[−cont]	[0cont]
Elsewhere:	[0cont]	[+cont]

In morpheme-internal /ti/ and /sa/ sequences, the consonants are specified as respectively [−continuant] and [+continuant]. The derivations in (24) show how this works (capitals denote segments unspecified for the feature [±continuant]).

(24) a. /tilaT+i/ → [tilas+i] [by (22a,b)]
b. /saTa/ → [sata] [by (22b)]

So the difference between the application of Assibilation in derived and non-derived environments follows directly from their different lexical representations and from the structure-building status of the rule. Both of these are in turn determined by the simplicity principle (20c). For lexical representations, simplicity enforces the minimal underlying feature specifications. Given that the feature [continuant] is distinctive and rules (22a,b) (the latter from universal grammar), the minimal system of representations must be as in (23). And the learner's assumption that Assibilation is structure-building is also a consequence of the simplicity principle, because (20d) guarantees that structure-building rules are the minimal (simplest) rules, which therefore will be chosen in the absence of contrary evidence. Contra Iverson and Wheeler, 1988, such underspecification does not involve the "ad hoc" "judicious manipulation" of the underlying representations. It is dictated independently of the NDEB effect by the requirement that the minimally specified underlying representations be selected, in accord with simplicity.

Under these assumptions, then, derived contexts are exactly those contexts in which the learner will assume that a rule applies. In sum, by divorcing NDEB from cyclicity/lexicality, and tying it instead to the structure-building versus structure-changing status of a rule (the latter being analyzed as the former with deletion), we get the NDEB effect essentially for free. In addition, the properties of NDEB immediately follow as well, as will now be shown.

I noted earlier that NDEB does not appear in optional rules or in nonneutralization rules. The former generalization can be derived in the following way. My assumption is that the simplest grammar results from maximally underspecified lexical representations and structure-building rules, and so more fully specified lexical representations and structure-changing rules will be set up only if positive evidence requires them. An across-the-board optional rule can be learned straightforwardly in conformity with these constraints, for its very optionality provides such positive evidence for more fully specified lexical representations, hence for the structure-changing character of the rule. For example, in the case of Finnish Coalescence [rule (1)], the positive evidence required for the learner to postulate lexical representations like /eä/ in a word like *pimee* is obviously the optional uncoalesced alternant *pimeä* [see (2a)]. On the other hand, a putative optional rule restricted to applying in derived environments can only be learned on the basis of NEGATIVE evidence, namely the nonexistence of one of the variants in nonderived cases. On general learnability grounds, such a system would be at least unstable.

As for why nonneutralization rules are not blocked in nonderived environments, the reason is that in the case of such rules the learner has distributional evidence for the "abstract" underlying form (with simplicity forcing the abstraction to be made). For example, in the simplest grammar of English, aspiration is unspecified in underlying representations and introduced on the basis of the phonetic context.

That rules should apply regularly in derived environments requires a further assumption, however, namely the strict binarity assumption. As a simple illustration of what is at stake in strict binarity, consider the interaction of the Assibilation rule (11) with the rule raising word-final *e* to *i*. Both are structure-building rules applying to underspecified archiphonemes. Their interaction is illustrated in (25), where /T/ represents a coronal obstruent unspecified for continuancy ($t \sim s$), and /E/ is a nonlow front vowel unspecified for height ($e \sim i$).

(25) a. /. . . Ti/: *lasi, lasi+na* 'glass'
b. /. . . ti/: *koti, koti+na* 'home'
c. /. . . TE/: *vesi, vete+nä* 'water'
d. /. . . sE/: *kuusi, kuuse+na* 'fir'

Binarity can be maintained if each environment shows at most a two-way opposition. This is clearly the case for continuancy, as shown in (26), where the columns represent, respectively, segments alternating between *t* and *s*, fixed *t*, and fixed *s*.

(26)

	/t~s/	/t/	/s/
Before /i/	—	[−cont]	[0cont]
Before /E/	[0cont]	—	[+cont]
Elsewhere	—	[0cont]	[+cont]

Suppose that, in addition to the four alternation patterns in (25), Finnish had a fifth pattern, exemplified by the made-up word in (27).

(27) /. . . tE/: **mati, *matena*

If this situation were to be represented in a purely phonological way, it would require a three-way contrast /TE/:/sE/:/tE/ for *vesi, kuusi, *mati* respectively. But such a three-way contrast would violate the strict binarity principle. So the absence of words like (27) would be predicted if we assumed strict binarity in addition to underspecification.

In the case of height, Finnish has a marginal three-way contrast.

(28)

	/e~i/	/e/	/i/
In env: ____]	[0high]	[−high]	[+high]
Elsewhere	—	[0high]	[−high]

The *e* to *i* rule fails to apply to a class of words comprising nursery words such as *nukke* 'doll', *nalle* 'teddy bear', hypocoristic names such as *Kalle* 'Charley', *Ville* 'Willie', and abbreviations such as *Yle* 'Public Radio' (from *Yleisradio*). Here the final vowels would be expected to raise as in (25c) and (25d).[11] The only way these words could be treated as phonologically regular on the present view is by lexically specifying their final vowel as nonhigh, and this would entail a three-way contrast as seen in the top line of (28). If they are specified as exceptions to the $e \rightarrow i$ rule, then all the right forms are derived in conformity with strict binarity. The marginal status of these stems makes this alternative quite reasonable. Similarly, the existence of hypothetical words like (27) would not force the abandonment of strict binarity, provided the correct way of accounting for them turned out to be as exceptions to rule (11).

Note that even if we were to compromise on strict binarity, our analysis of the NDEB effects in (25) could still be maintained. Allowing three-way distinctions would yield a formally coherent but weaker theory. We would, for example, lose the explanation for the nonexistence of the pattern in (27). Thus the viability of strict binarity and the proper explanation of NDEB are somewhat separate questions.

It is also clear why NDEB can persist in postlexical applications of rules which first apply in the lexical module, as in the previously cited cases. Postlexical applications are blocked in nonderived cases for exactly the same reasons that the lexical applications are blocked in them, that is, because the language does not have a structure-changing rule. This does not mean, however, that the blocking effect MUST always persist postlexically. It will not persist if the postlexical module contains, in addition to the structure-building rule which it shares with the lexical module, a structure-changing rule of its own which deletes or delinks the specifications of the same feature. This deletion rule will then create new inputs to which the other rule, still in structure-building mode, can apply. Examples for which this may be the appropriate analysis are discussed in Kiparsky (1985).

Finally, cases of nonfeeding order in cyclic rules, which have been cited as evidence for the SCC (Rubach, 1984: 13), will now be accounted for by the cyclic assignment of default rules (on which more in Kiparsky, 1992).

The way in which the proposed treatment accommodates the standard examples of strict cyclicity should now be clear.

3.2. Korean Palatalization

Another apparent lexical-cum-postlexical rule with "derived environment" behavior is Korean Palatalization. As presented in Iverson and Wheeler (1988), the Korean situation would match the Sanskrit *ruki* rule very closely. However, the additional facts brought to light by Hume (1990) and by Cho and Sells (1991) motivate a somewhat different analysis. For this reason I discuss it separately here.

The phonemic inventory of Korean includes the coronal consonants, /t, t^h, c, c^h, s, n, l/. The phonemes /t, t^h/ are normally realized as dental stops and /c, c^h/ are normally realized as postalveolar affricates. Before *i,* all coronals are palatalized; I will write the resulting prepalatal segments as [ţ, $ţ^h$, ç, $ç^h$, ş, ñ, λ]. Palatalization applies uniformly to all coronals before *i* regardless of whether the environment is derived or not.

(29) a. /si/ → [şi] 'poem'
/k'ini/ → [k'iñi] 'meal'
/p'alli/ → [p'aλλi] 'fast'
b. /os+i/ → [oşi] 'clothes-Nom.'
c. /pat^h ilaŋ/ → [paḑ iraŋ] 'ridge of a field'

In (29c), the stop is deaspirated in word-final position and voiced medially by a separate rule.

In addition to becoming palatalized, /t, t^h/ get affricated if the triggering *i* is within the same word, thereby coinciding with the allophones of underlying /c/ and /c^h/ in that environment.

(30) a. /pat^h+i/ → [$paç^hi$] 'field (nom.)'
/hæ tot+i/ → [hæ doji] 'sunrise (nom.)'
/mat+ita/ → [majida] 'eldest (copula)'
b. /tac^h+i/ → [$taç^hi$] 'anchor (nom.)'
/nac+i/ → [naji] 'day (nom.)'

Affrication only applies before a derived *i.* Before tautomorphemic *i,* /t, t^h/ are retained, as palatalized [ţ, $ţ^h$], contrasting with [ç, $ç^h$] from /c, c^h/ in that position. (It is these palatalized but unaffricated stops that the analysis proposed by Iverson and Wheeler neglects.)

(31) /mati/ [maḑi] 'knot', /canti/ [canḑi] 'grass'

/c/ and /c^h/ appear in lexical representations before all vowels and morpheme finally.

(32) *cuŋkuk* 'China', *-coc^ha* 'even', *nac* 'day', *kac-* 'to have', *tac^h* 'anchor'

The prepalatals are not phonemic and arise only from palatalization before /i/, which is automatic and obligatory.

(33) a. *[. . . şa . . .], *[. . . ñu . . .], *[. . . ţo . . .], *[. . . ça . . .]
b. *[. . . si . . .], *[. . . ni . . .], *[. . . ti . . .], *[. . . ci . . .]

Suppose that underlying /t, t^h/ are distinguished from /c, c^h/ by the feature [±anterior]. The minimally specified lexical representations of palatalized and nonpalatalized coronals are then:

(34)

	/t, t^h/	/c, c^h/	/s, n, l/
Before *i*	[+ant]	[0ant]	[0ant]
Elsewhere	[0ant]	[−ant]	[0ant]

Let us take the phonetic specifications of the palatalized and nonpalatalized coronals to be

(35)

	t	ţ	c	ç	s	ş
High	−	+	−	+	−	+
Anterior	+	−	−	−	+	−
Delayed release	−	−	+	+	−	−

and assume that Palatalization spreads the features [−anterior] and [+high] to coronal consonants from a following [+high] front vowel. (If we adopt the proposal of Clements, 1989, and Lahiri and Evers, 1989, that front vowels are [+coronal], we can simply take Palatalization to be spread of the Place node.) Palatalization applies freely to all coronals, both in the lexical phonology and the postlexical phonology. In the latter, it applies in feature-changing fashion. Although [−anterior, +high] coronals are not in the lexical inventory, structure preservation must not block Palatalization from applying lexically, perhaps because, in virtue of the linking condition (Hayes, 1986; Itô, 1986), the relevant lexical marking constraint is inapplicable to the multiply linked structures that result from spreading (Macfarland and Pierrehumbert, 1991). The different outcome of lexical and postlexical palatalization of /t, t^h/ is due to a word-level rule that specifies the [−anterior, +high] obstruent stops as [+delayed release].[12] Elsewhere, coronals are nonpalatal by the default rule (36).

(36) [+coronal] → [+anterior]

Moreover, some dialects (e.g., that of South Hamkyeng) have a lexical rule of vowel fronting (umlaut) triggered by a high front vowel or glide. According to Ramsey (1978) and Hume (1990), vowel fronting is blocked by any intervening coronal (hence palatalized) consonant. In terms of the present proposal, such dialects differ minimally from the nonumlauting dialects. In the latter, palatality spreads to the nearest C; in the umlauting dialects palatality spreads to the nearest eligible place node, whether C or V. That is, umlaut is simply a generalization of palatalization. This relationship between umlaut and palatalization could not be captured if the palatalization rule were split into a lexical and a postlexical part, as Iverson and Wheeler propose.

An apparent problem for the word-level status of Affrication arises in cases like (37), where the nominative case ending *-i* on the face of it appears to be syntactically attached to a phrase and phonologically cliticized to its last word.[13]

(37) *sup^h-kwa pa*[c^h]*-i* *p^{h}uli-ta*
forest-and field-nom. be green-decl.

However, Cho and Sells (1991) argue on independent grounds, including morphological evidence, that the endings in question really are lexical suffixes, even in cases like (37).

Most derived-environment rules discussed so far can be analyzed straightforwardly as structure-building rules applying to underspecified representations. In Section 5 I examine some trickier cases (including Finnish Consonant Gradation) and argue that, contrary to appearances, they are not structure-changing rule either.

Having shown how NDEB can be reduced to the application of structure-building rules to underspecified representations and how its main properties are thereby explained, I proceed to some more surprising consequences of this way of looking at the matter.

4. VACUOUSLY DERIVED ENVIRONMENTS COUNT AS UNDERIVED

A clear-cut empirical difference between the SCC and the underspecification account has to do with vacuously derived environments: environments not distinct from the underlying environment which arise in the course of the derivation.

On the classical SCC story, vacuously derived environments should trigger the application of lexical rules. In fact, the apparent confirmation of this prediction of the SCC was one of the most interesting results of Mascaró (1976).

The present proposal, though, makes just the opposite prediction. A feature specification which blocks a rule from applying in the lexical representation should block the rule equally when the same environment arises in derived forms.

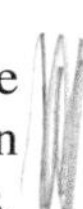

4.1. Finnish

The prediction that vacuously derived environments behave like underived environments is confirmed by the Finnish assibilation rule (11). It can be triggered by the past tense suffix *i* (38a). Certain final vowels, including *-i,* are truncated before it (38b).[14]

(38) a. *halut+i+vat* → *halusivat* 'they wanted'
b. *karsi+i+vat* → *karsivat* 'they pruned'

The /t/ in (38) is [−cont] because it precedes /i/ in the underlying representations. In the account proposed here, that makes it immune from assibilation before derived /i/ as well. On the SCC account, however, case 2 of the definition of "derived environment" should make it subject to assibilation. In fact, *t* is NEVER changed to *s* in such cases. Past tense forms of verbs in *-ti* thus furnish a case of a vacuously derived environment which supports my proposal over the SCC.

(39) a. *vaati+vat* → *vaativat* (**vaasivat*) 'they demand'
b. *vaati+i+vat* → *vaativat* (**vaasivat*) 'they demanded'

Since the /t/ in (39b) starts out preceding an /i/ in the same morpheme and ends up preceding an /i/ in a different morpheme, the structural condition for assibilation is met in a derived environment, and so, according to the older view of derived environment rules, assibilation should apply. On the present proposal, the /t/ must be lexically specified as [−continuant] for the reasons previously stated (otherwise it would be /s/), and this lexical specification will block the structure-building assibilation rule from applying in derived environments as well.[15]

What about the cases where it has been specifically argued that NDEB do disappear in vacuously derived environments? The two most impressive examples are Icelandic and Catalan.

4.2. Icelandic

The Icelandic rule of *u*-Umlaut, which turns *a* to *ö* if *u* follows in the next syllable (Anderson, 1969; Kiparsky, 1984; Orešnik, 1977) applies regularly in morphologically derived environments such as (40a) but is blocked morpheme internally in cases such as (40b).

(40) a. /harð+um/ → *hörðum* 'hard' (dat.pl.)
/saga+ur/ → *sögur* 'sagas' (nom.pl.)
/kalla+um/ → *köllum* 'call' (1-pl.)
b. /akur/ → *akur* 'field'

The vowel in the second syllable of words like *akur* is syncopated before syllabic endings, and when their *a* thereby comes to stand before *-u,* it does undergo *u*-Umlaut.

(41) a. dat.sg. /akur+i/ → *akr+i*
b. dat.pl. /akur+um/ → *ökr+um*

In Kiparsky (1984), the contrast between (40b) and (41b) was explained on the assumption that vacuously derived environments, unlike nonderived environments, are exempt from NDEB, which is contrary to the line we are developing here.

What is not explained on this analysis is why, in all words which show *u*-umlaut in vacuously derived environments, such as (41), the consonant after the non–umlaut-triggering *u* is *r.* Native stems ending in other final consonants have only *ö . . . u,* not *a . . . u* (e.g., *höfuð* 'head'), and the loans which have *a . . . u* do not seem to undergo syncope, such as *kaktus* 'cactus', *Bakkus* 'Bacchus'. It is suspicious, then, that precisely *-r* is subject to a rule inserting *u* before it in environments where it cannot be syllabified. And this epenthetic *u* also fails to trigger *u*-Umlaut, even though the environment is obviously derived.

(42) /dag+r/ → *dag*+V*r* → *dagur* 'day'

In previous analyses the failure of *u*-umlaut in (42) was handled by ordering Epenthesis after *u*-Umlaut. In the context of current phonological theory, epenthesis is more plausibly analyzed as insertion of an empty vowel slot, which fails to trigger umlaut because it has no feature content at the point where umlaut applies and is later assigned the features of *u.* Whichever of these options is taken, the non-Umlauting nature of epenthetic *u* immediately raises the possibility of representing *akur* as /akr/, with *u*-epenthesis, which would automatically yield the failure of *u*-umlaut. In the earlier analyses mentioned above, this possibility was rejected on the grounds that there is a class of stems which genuinely have this underlying shape, such as /lifr/ *lifur,* which differ systematically from stems like *akur* in their behavior, as Orešnik shows.

However, this conclusion may have been premature. Ottósson (1988) has now worked out a detailed analysis of Icelandic in the lexical phonology framework in which the case for vacuously derived environments disappears. In his proposal, the *u* of *akur* is analyzed as epenthetic, and the difference between the paradigms of the *akur* and *lifur* types is argued to be morphological rather than phonological. If this is accepted, then Icelandic *u*-umlaut, while showing standard NDEB effects, gives no support to the position that vacuously derived environments count as derived for purposes of the NDEB effect.

4.3. Catalan

Perhaps the most interesting case of vacuously derived environments apparently counting as derived is the Catalan Vowel Lowering rule, to which Mascaró devoted an extensive and insightful discussion in this theoretical context. He uncovered the generalization that Vowel Lowering (*o, e* → ɔ, ɛ) takes place before any suffix that assigns stress to the preceding syllable, and on that basis proposed the rule that it applies to stressed syllables. In order to block Vowel Lowering in unsuffixed stems, he assumed that stems bear underlying stress and invoked the SCC to block Vowel Lowering of syllables whose stresses are not derived. Stress vacuously assigned to the stem by the prestressed suffixes must thus count as derived for purposes of the SCC, on this analysis:

(43) *séntrə* 'center', *sɛ́ntr+ik*
direktó 'director', *direktɔ́r+i*

The assumption that stress in Catalan is marked in the lexicon is therefore crucial to Mascaró's analysis of Vowel Lowering. A recent study of Catalan stress, however, has considerably undermined this premise. Alsina (1987) argues that stress is not marked in the lexicon, but predictable.[16] The stress of all the words in (43) is thus "derived" in exactly the same way, namely simply by the application of the stress rule. Alsina observes that lowering can be formulated as a rule which assigns [+low] to vowels before any suffix at Level 1 (in fact, the environment might be simply before any syllable). This rule applies in structure-building fashion to vowels not already specified for the feature [low].

(44) a. /sEntrə/ → *sÉntrə* → *séntrə*
b. /sEntrə+ik/ → *sÉntr+ik* → *sɛ́ntr+ik*

Tha reason Presuffixal Vowel Lowering can simply apply before any suffix is that, unless the suffix is prestressed, the stem vowel will simply get reduced and the effects of Vowel Lowering will be undetectable.

Mascaró also argues for NDEB in a rule he motivates for Catalan which takes *o* to *u* and *e* to ə.[17] Let us refer to this rule as Mid Vowel Reduction. Certain words (unassimilated loans and learned words, it seems) do not observe Mid Vowel Reduction.

(45) [bóston] 'Boston'
[kátedrə] '(academic) chair'
[sopráno] 'soprano'

Mascaró suggests that these unstressed mid vowels fail to undergo Mid Vowel Reduction by the SCC (again on the assumption that they are underlyingly unstressed). Interestingly, stress-shifted derivatives of such exceptional words do undergo reduction.

(46) [bustun+yá] 'Bostonian'
[kətədrátik] 'holder of an (academic) chair'

Mascaró assumes that application of the stress rule on the derived word cycle causes the unstressed vowels to get vacuously respecified as unstressed, and that such vacuous respecification creates derived environments, so that the contrast between (45) and (46) is a case of the SCC at work. This case has a rather different character from the previously discussed Vowel Lowering case, however, for the words in (45) are, as Mascaró notes, exceptional. A reviewer suggests that what could be going on here is the elimination of exception features in derivatives (Kiparsky, 1973), as in French *Hitler* (with *h*-aspiré) versus *hitlérien* (regular).[18]

5. STRUCTURE-CHANGING RULES ARE NOT SUBJECT TO NDEB

Reducing NDEB to the operation of structure-building rules on underspecified representations predicts that structure-changing rules will never be subject to it, because they can delink a prespecified feature.

This prediction is independent of the claim of strict binarity of feature specifications in lexical representations. My analysis of NDEB is consistent with the existence of three-way lexical feature distinctions. What depends on strict binarity is the regularity of alternations in derived environments.

In the material examined so far, representing the standard types of cases cited in the SCC literature, it is fairly clear that we are indeed dealing with structure-building rules. For some rules this is not so obvious, though.

5.1. Finnish Consonant Gradation

The problem raised by Consonant Gradation is that, in a sequence such as /. . . VttVttVCCV . . ./, the result is /. . . VtVtVCCV . . ./ [see (15) for an example]. The middle /tt/ acts as a geminate since it triggers Gradation on its left, but itself undergoes degemination due to the closed syllable on its right. Such instances of multiple application make Consonant Gradation look like a structure-changing rule, because the /tt/ must be underlying to trigger the rule. But this is inconsistent with our claim that NDEB is a property only of structure-building rules.

A strictly structure-building account of degemination is possible by separating skeletal and melodic content. Suppose that the lexical representation of a morpheme consists of a melody (subject to OCP, and appropriately underspecified) and a skeleton (also perhaps underspecified). The association between the melodic elements and the skeletal slots is predictable by the standard association conventions and therefore not specified in the lexicon. (47) shows, using CV notation, how this would work for a word like *aatto* 'eve'.

(47)
```
V V C C V          V V C C V
              →     \|   \| |
  a    t o           a    t o
```

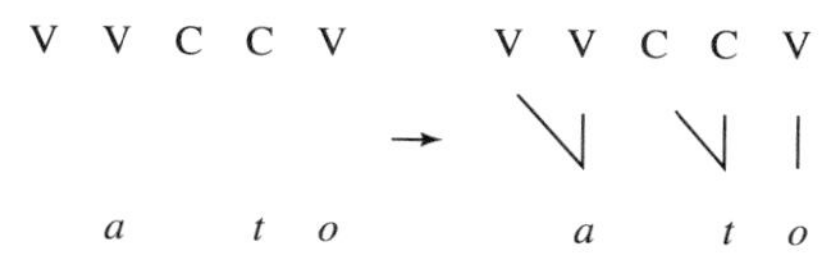

Consonant Gradation (degemination) is then simply the following Finnish-specific restriction on the universal association procedure.

(48) Before a VC rhyme, an obstruent stop is associated only to the onset.

If a -C or -CCV ending is added to the stem, (48) forces one of the adjacent C slots to remain vacant. Assuming that preference is given to onsets, this yields, for the genitive *aaton,*

(49) 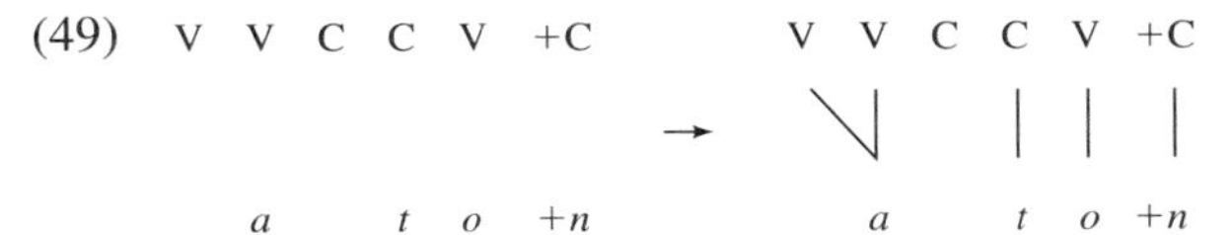

We know from other evidence that unassociated C-slots trigger Consonant Gradation and that they get deleted only postlexically, if at all. Both these assumptions are independently motivated by word-final "ghost consonants" (actually "ghost syllables," see Keyser and Kiparsky, 1984). For instance, in *aate* 'idea', the deletion of the word-final vowel in the nominative results in a syllable closed by an unassociated C-slot, causing Consonant Gradation.

(50) 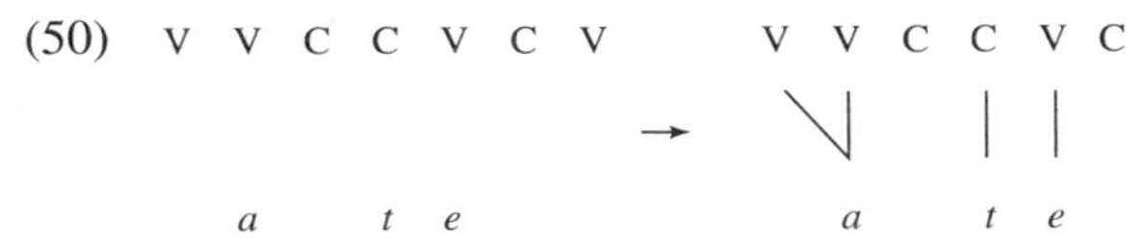

The final empty C-slot is not realized in isolation because it cannot be associated with any consonantal segment, but its persistence into the postlexical phonology is shown by the fact that a copy of the next consonant spreads onto it in sandhi, resulting in gemination, as in *aatev voitti* 'the idea won'. In genitive *aatteen,* the condition (48) is inapplicable, so association is maximal.

(51) 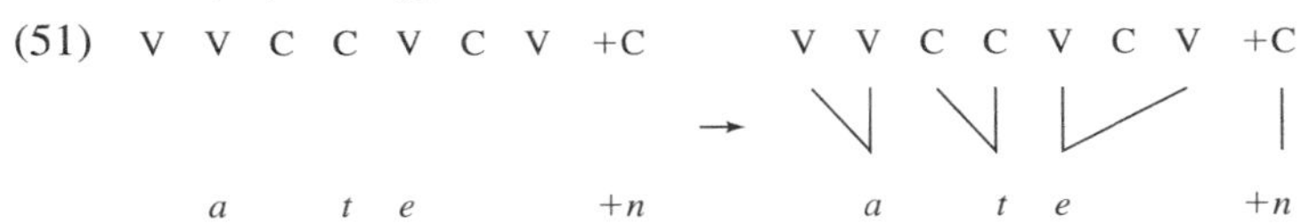

On this view of Consonant Gradation, cases with multiple degemination in consecutive syllables are not problematic any longer, as the derivations of *hatu+ttoma+na, hatu+ton* 'hatless' (ess. and nom. sg.) in (52) show. In the nominative, the V slot of the *-a* of the privative suffix /ttoma/ is deleted, again closing the syllable and causing degemination.[19]

(52) a. 

b. 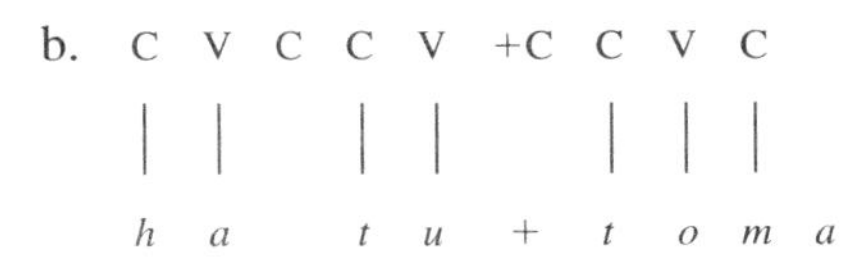

Geminates followed by tautomorphemic closed syllables [such as the first *tt* in *hottentotti;* see (15)] must then be lexically preassociated with the coda. Consequently they will not undergo gradation. As before, the possibility of such lexical preassociation of geminates elsewhere than before tautomorphemic closed syllables would be excluded by strict binarity (or more precisely, by its analog for nonfeatural information), which again raises the empirical issues discussed in Section 3.1.

5.2. Chumash Sibilant Harmony

An apparent derived-environment effect in a structure-changing rule of Chumash, a language formerly spoken along the central California coast, has been presented as a problem for the present proposal by Poser (1990). My reanalysis draws on his fuller earlier treatment (Poser, 1982), and on his source, Applegate (1972).

In Chumash, a process of Sibilant Harmony makes sibilants and affricates agree in laminality ([±anterior] in Poser, 1982, [±distributed] in Poser, 1990, and here) with the rightmost sibilant or affricate in the word. The rule is structure-changing and assimilates underlying apicals to laminals (53) as well as underlying laminals to apicals.[20]

(53)	/ha+s+xintila/	*hasxintila*	'his Indian name'
	/ha+s+xintila+waš/	*hašxintiliwaš*	'his former Indian name'
(54)	/p+iš+al+anan'/	*pišannan'*	'don't you two go'
	/s+iš+sili+uluaqpey+us/	*sis^{h}uleqpeyus*	'they two want to follow it'

Another rule of Chumash, Pre-Coronal Laminalization (PCL) (56), makes a sibilant laminal immediately before a nonstrident coronal (*t, l, n*):

(55)	/s+nan'/	*šnan'*	'he goes'
	/s+tepuʔ/	*štepuʔ*	'he gambles'
	/s+loxit'/	*šloxit'*	'he surpasses me'

(56) PCL: [+cor, +strid] → [+distr] / ___ [+cor, −strid]

Sibilants which become laminal by PCL trigger Sibilant Harmony, but they do not undergo it.

(57)	/s+is+lu+sisin/	*šišlusisin*	'they two are gone awry'
	/s+ti+yep+us/	*štiyepus*	'he tells him'

These data present an ordering paradox which Poser (1982) solves by decomposing sibilant harmony into a structure-changing delinking process and a structure-building spread process, and ordering PCL between them.

(58) a. Distributed Delinking: delink [±distr] from all strident coronals except the last in a word
b. PCL [rule (56)]
c. Distributed Spreading: spread [±distr] leftward

Given this ordering, laminals from PCL escape Distributed Delinking, and so the structure-building rule of Distributed Spreading cannot apply to them. Using S to symbolize coronals unspecified for laminality, we then derive cases like (57) as follows:

(59) /s+is+lu+sisin/ → (Distributed Delinking) *S+iS+lu+Sisin* → (PCL) *S+iš+lu+Sisin* → (Distributed Spreading) *šišlusisin*

Now the problem is that PCL exhibits NDEB effects. Morpheme internally, a contrast between *s* and *š* is preserved in the PCL environment:

(60) a. *stumukun* 'mistletoe'
slow' 'eagle'
wastuʔ 'pleat'
b. *wašti* 'of a flow, of liquid in motion'

While *š* from PCL does not undergo Sibilant Harmony, *š* before tautomorphemic *t* in words like (60b) (which on Poser's analysis would be underlying *š*) does undergo Sibilant Harmony:

(61) /s+wašti+lok'in+us/ → (Distributed Delinking) *S+waSti+lok'in+us* → (PCL) NA → *s+wasti+lok'in+us* 'the flow stops on him'

The contrast between (61) and (59) follows in Poser's analysis because PCL is assumed not to apply in nonderived environments, and because the [±distr] specifications in morphemes like those in (60) (which are fully marked in the lexicon) are detected by Distributed Delinking if a sibilant follows.

It might seem, then, that the apparent derived environment effect in the application of PCL cannot be reduced to blocking of a structure-building rule by specified representations. The reason is that, by the structure-changing operation of Distributed Delinking, all sibilants except for the last in a word get unspecified, including both derived cases like (57), to which PCL applies, and morpheme-internal cases like (60, 61), to which it does not apply. PCL therefore cannot distinguish between them on the basis of underspecification. But this contradicts our proposal that the difference between derived and morpheme-internal cases is encoded in the representation itself as a difference between the unspecified and the specified value of the relevant feature.

My idea can, however, be sustained by modifying Poser's analysis along the following lines. Suppose that a "shared feature convention" (Steriade, 1982) merges adjacent place nodes if they are identical.

(62)

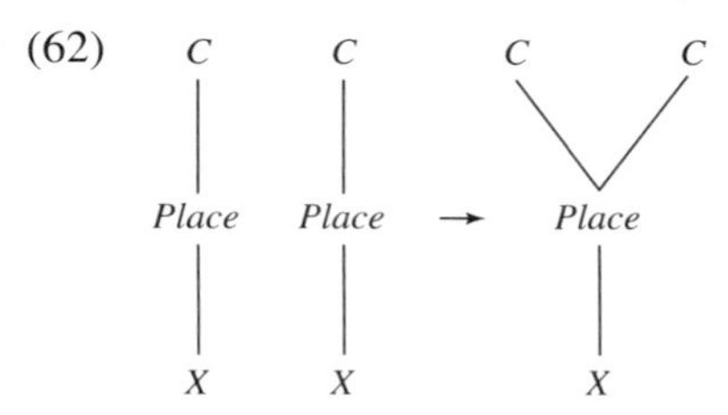

Suppose furthermore that this merger is restricted to tautomorphemic sequences, for reasons explored by McCarthy (1986).[21] Only remaining sequences of coronals with identical place nodes—in practice, heteromorphemic ones—are subject to PCL.[22]

(63)

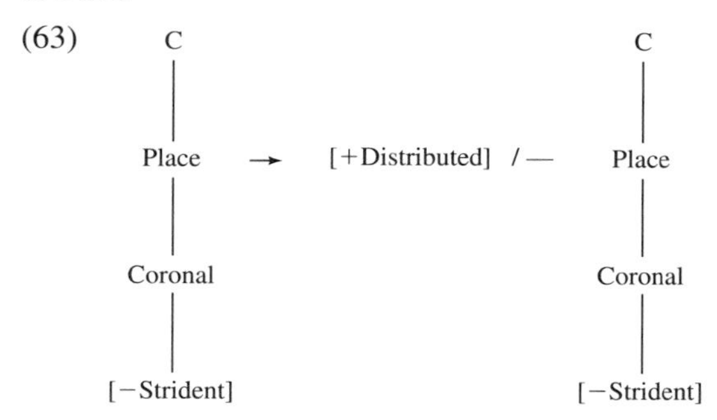

Distributed Spreading then applies iteratively leftward in structure-building mode.

(64)

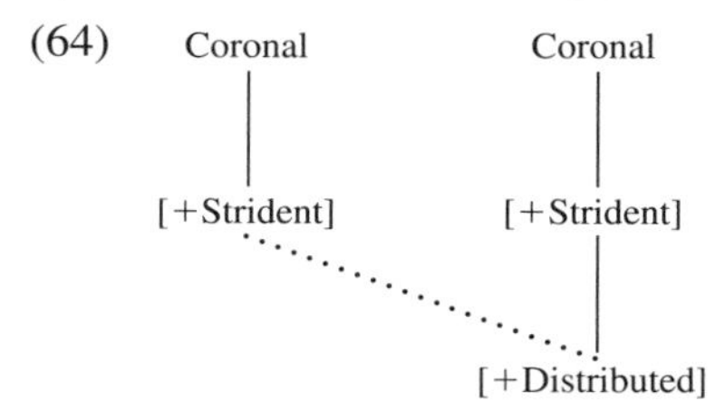

In the illustrative derivation below, I symbolize coronals unspecified for [±distributed] by S, T, and mark the result of applying the shared feature convention (62) to a coronal cluster by writing $\widehat{st}$.

(65)

underlying	*wašTi*	*S+wašTi+Lok'iN+uS*	*S+iS+Lu+SiSiN*
Distributed Delinking	—	*S+waSTi+Lok'iN+uS*	—
shared feature convention	—	*S+wa*$\widehat{ST}$*i+Lok'iN+uS*	—
PCL	—	(blocked)	*S+iš+Lu+SiSiN*
Distributed Spreading	—	—	*š+iš+Lu+SiSiN*
Default	*wašti*	*s+wa*$\widehat{st}$*i+lok'in+us*	*š+iš+lu+sisin*

On this analysis, Chumash is compatible with my claim that NDEB occurs only in non–structure-changing rules.[23]

5.3. Chamorro Vowel Lowering

Another "derived-environment" rule that apparently applies in structure-changing fashion is the rule that governs the distribution of high and mid vowels in Chamorro (Chung, 1983).

(66) Nonlow vowels are realized as
  a. *e, o* in stressed closed syllables.
  b. *i, u* elsewhere.

The following words illustrate the regular distribution of high and mid vowels.

(67) *mundóŋgu* 'stomach of a cow'
métgut 'strong'
písaw 'fishing line'

The shifting of stress by the cyclic application of stress assignment produces systematic alternations in derived forms between high and mid vowels, in accord with (66).[24]

(68)	*lápis*	*lapéssu*	'(my) pencil'
	hugándu	*hùgandóñña*	'(his) playing'

Although Vowel Lowering by (66a) "applies to the vast majority of noncomplex words, including virtually all native Chamorro words," Chung records "a handful of words" in which it unaccountably does not apply. Also, "a rather large class of loans" have low vowels in stressed open syllables, contrary to (66b). These two classes of cases where the normal distribution of vowel height is broken in nonderived environments are illustrated in (69).

(69) a. *húngan* 'yes', *asút* 'blue', *lístu* 'quick'
([+high] where [−high] is expected by (66a))
  b. *néni* 'baby', *ispéyus* 'mirror', *sitbésa* 'beer'
([−high] where [+high] is expected by (66b))

On my assumptions, the lexical representations of these morphemes would have [+high] and [−high] vowels respectively, while those of the morphemes in (67) would have [0high] vowels, which would be specified as [+high] and [−high] in the appropriate contexts by (66).

Is (66) structure-building or structure-changing? From what was said in the preceding paragraph, it seems that it must be structure-building, so it does not lower the specified high vowels in (69a) or raise the specified mid vowels in (69b). But it also seems that it must be structure-changing, for it does raise the specified open syllable mid vowels in (69b) when the stress shifts off them in suffixed forms.

(70) *néni* 'baby', *ninína* 'his baby'

We seem to have arrived at a contradiction.

The problem is only apparent. The height alternation is the result of two separate rules, a structure-building lowering rule (with [+high] default) conditioned by syllable structure, and a structure-changing raising rule conditioned by stress.

(71)) $[-\text{low}] \rightarrow \left\{ \begin{array}{l} [-\text{high}] \text{ in closed syllables} \\ [+\text{high}] \text{ (elsewhere)} \end{array} \right\}$ (non–structure-changing)

(72) [−low] → [+high] in unstressed syllables (structure-changing)

If these rules apply to the proposed lexical representations, both the height alternations and the distribution of unpredictable height are fully accounted for. If cyclic, these rules imply that [±high] is distinctive only in stressed syllables, and consequently, that NDEB effects with respect to Lowering occur only in stressed open syllables.

(73)

	/i/	/e/
Stressed closed syllable	[+high]	[0high]
Stressed open syllable	[0high]	[−high]
Unstressed syllable	[0high]	—

The prediction, which appears to be correct, is that there are no words with alternations like *hugándu* ~ **hògandónña,* as opposed to the type in (70).

The decomposition required by the underspecification account of the Chamorro vowel alternations is thus confirmed. Note also that strict binarity is again preserved.

6. NDEB EFFECTS IN PROSODIC RULES

6.1. Stress: Unifying FEC and NDEB

By attributing the blocking of rules in nonderived environments to their non–structure-changing status, we reopen the question of how to unify NDEB and "strict cycle" effects with the free element condition (FEC) (Prince, 1985).

(74) Rules of primary metrical analysis do not affect existing metrical structure.

Let us consider the distinction between rules of primary metrical analysis and rules of metrical reanalysis to be a special case of the more general dichotomy between structure-building and structure-changing rules. This would mean that FEC depends on the same property that I have just argued to be relevant for NDEB. Let us also assume as before that structure-building is the basic mode of rule application and that structure-changing rule application is the combined result of deletion and structure-building (where the deletion component of this combination could be either a deletion rule or a filtering/projection mechanism à la Halle and Vergnaud, 1987). The fact that rules of metrical reanalysis typically "reassert" the language's basic foot structure (Prince, 1985) independently confirms the principle that requires this decomposition, since it means that they must be viewed anyway as consisting of destressing plus reapplication of the rules of primary metrical analysis.

FEC effects come in two sharply different types, strong and weak. Strong FEC effects, documented for Greek (Steriade, 1988), Diyari and Warlpiri (Poser, 1986, 1989), Manam and Arabic (Halle and Kenstowicz, 1990), and Choctaw (Lombardi and McCarthy, 1990), involve absolute inviolability of all previously assigned metrical constituency. Weak FEC effects, seen in English (Kiparsky, 1982), Chamorro (Chung, 1983), Indonesian (Cohn, 1989), and Dakota (Shaw, 1985), involve the blocking of metrical structure reassignment in domains which are already footed in their entirety (as in *standardization*), while already footed syllables do get reassociated with as yet unfooted syllables (as in *solidify, original*). It was the weak FEC effects which were assimilated to the SCC in Kiparsky (1982), and more recently Kager (1989) has proposed reformulating the FEC itself so as to account for these cases.[25] But Kager's weakened version of the FEC has nothing to say about strong FEC effects, where foot boundaries constructed on previous cycles are entirely taboo for later foot construction.

The right move, then, would be to take the strong FEC as representing the basic NDEB syndrome in the domain of stress. The weak FEC is the result of composing stress assignment with partial deletion of metrical structure, specifically of bracketing (i.e., deforestation with retention of prominence marked by metrical grids). Proposals along these lines have in fact been made by Halle and Vergnaud (1987), Poser (1989), Steriade (1988), and Halle and Kenstowicz (1990) (though they differ substantially on how to do this, especially on the conditions under which metrical structure from previous cycles is retained and when it is changed). Accordingly, in the English/Chamorro/Dakota type of stress assignment there is deforestation in addition to the assignment of metrical structure. The strong FEC prohibits rules from changing existing metrical constituency or prominence relations (whether these originate in the lexicon or through the application of earlier stress rules). Stress assignment is thus structure-building in the strictest sense. If my proposal is right, this means that there is no "strict cyclicity" in stress rules other than what results from the FEC itself, and that the FEC is a special case of NDEB.[26]

If weak FEC effects are the result of deforestation, then they would in effect reduce to a ban on "prominence-changing." This requires a definition of what it means to change prominence. We must define a stress assignment as prominence-changing if and only if its input and output have incompatible prominence relations, where relative prominence is defined by grid height in the usual way.[27] The basic interpretation of grid height tells us, for example, that (75) asserts the prominence relations (76).

```
(75)  *    *
      *    *    *
     (a)((bc)(def))
```

(76) 1. $a, b, d, > c, e, f$
2. $c = e = f$
3. $a, b > d$

We must further assume that relative prominence among elements at the top grid level is undefined. Assigning superordinate metrical structure to the top grid level therefore does not assign incompatible prominence relations and is thereby structure-building, as desired.[28] For instance, (75) does not assert (77), but simply leaves the relative prominence of a and b unspecified.

(77) $a = b$

Also, metrically unassociated (unfooted) material must not have any prominence relations defined to it, so that adding metrical structure to such elements is not a structure-changing operation either.

Given these conventions, foot construction across a previously built foot is blocked, as in the third cycle of *standardization.*[29]

(78)
```
 *          *                         *      *       *
(stan dard) (iz) + a ⟨tion⟩ ↛ *(stan) (dar diz) (a) ⟨tion⟩
```

The English Stress Rule is correctly blocked here, since it would reverse the prominence relations in *-dardize-*. But it is free to apply in the second cycle of *solidity* and *original,* as desired.

(79)
```
 *                   *     *
(so)  lid + i ⟨ty⟩ → (so) (li di)  ⟨ty⟩
 *                   *     *
(ori) gin + ⟨al⟩ →  (o)  (ri gin) ⟨al⟩
```

In both these cases, the stress rule is free to apply on the third cycle because it does not change any of the prominence relations defined on the first, in the sense just defined.

Kager (1989: 127 ff.) has argued that two of the English destressing rules, Sonorant Destressing and the Arab Rule, actually belong in the subsystem of primary metrical analysis rules, in that they are ordered among them, and like them, are structure-building (hence subject to the FEC). From this he proposes to derive their restriction to nonbranching feet. We retain this result, for destressing of the disyllabic foot in (80a) is blocked because prominence relations are changed on *-nonga-*, but destressing of the monosyllabic foot in (80b) is permitted because no prominence relations are changed.

(80) a.
```
  *     *       *                    *          *
(Mo) (non ga) (he) ⟨la⟩ ↛ (Monon ga) (he) ⟨la⟩
```
b.
```
  *     *       *         *          *
(Ha) (cken) (sack) → (Hacken) (sack)
```

6.2. Quantity

Since NDEB effects with respect to quantity exist, a vowel or syllable must be capable of being lexically marked as distinctively short in environments where lengthening would apply to it, and conversely as distinctively long in environments where shortening would apply to it. Intrinsically privative representations are excluded for length just as for all other phonological properties. Itô (1990) reports that Japanese imposes a two-mora minimal foot requirement on derived words such as (81).

(81) a. Truncations: *choko* 'chocolate'
b. Reduplicated formations (two feet): *mi* 'look' → *miimii* 'while looking'

But it also has numerous monomoraic stems like (82), which, unless suffixed, surface as words consisting of degenerate feet.

(82) *su* 'vinegar', *ta* 'field'

As Itô points out, such stems must be lexically specified as short. Lexically specified subminimal feet will not be lengthened through the structure-building assignment of the canonical bimoraic foot. For instance, assuming a moraic representation of length, *su* would have the underlying representation (83),

(83)
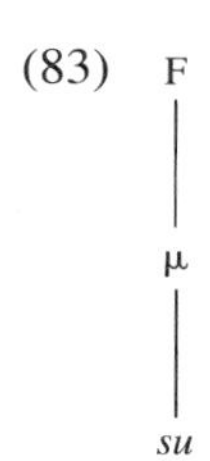

which escapes the minimal foot requirement in virtue of its lexically specified metrical structure. A stem conforming to the canonical pattern, such as *suu* 'number', has no metrical structure in the lexicon and gets assigned a full two-mora foot by the ordinary prosodic parsing processes operating on /su/. Finally, if truncation and reduplication superimpose their own foot patterns on the lexically specified prosodic structure of the stem (on the principle that affix properties supersede stem properties), they will effectively neutralize underlying lexical quantity.

6.3. Disharmony

The SCC has been used to account for idiosyncratically opaque segments in tone and harmony processes. The idea is to have the SCC block the morpheme-internal spread of a harmonic feature lexically associated to a segment[30] (Archangeli and Pulleyblank, 1989; Levergood, 1984; Pulleyblank, 1982; Steriade, 1987a). For instance, Archangeli and Pulleyblank propose for Yoruba a right-to-left spreading of [− ATR]. If present as a floating feature in the lexical representation, [− ATR] spreads maximally over all eligible vowels, e.g., *ẹkọ* 'pap'.

(84) *e k o* → *e k ọ* → *ẹ k ọ*

−A −A −A

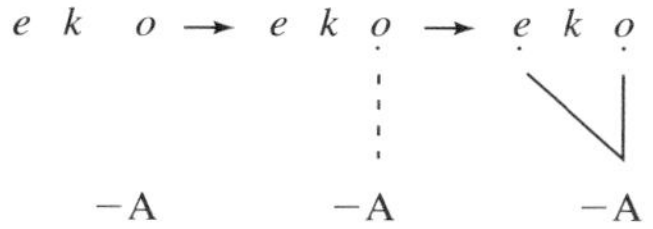

A disharmonic word such as *telọ* 'tailor' is treated as having its last vowel lexically preassociated with [− ATR].

(85) *t e l ọ* → *t e l ọ* tailor

−A +A−A

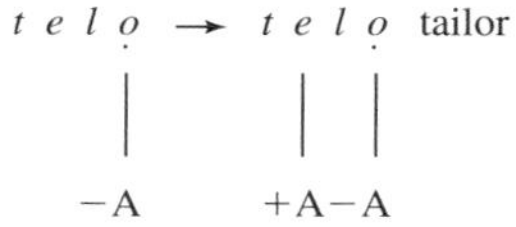

Leftward spreading of the prelinked autosegment in (85) is taken to be blocked by the SCC, and the unassociated vowel of the initial syllable is later assigned the default specification [+ATR], by the same rule which assigns it to regular harmonic [+ATR] words. We will want to retain the idea that disharmony results from there being more than one harmonic span and that vowels not reached by harmony get assigned their unmarked values of the harmonic feature by default. But clearly this implementation of it will not work without a specific principle such as the SCC, so it represents a potential problem for the proposal to explain away NDEB effects.

There is, however, an alternative approach to disharmony, which preserves the basic insight yet does not require stipulating blocking in nonderived environments. This is to mark off harmonic spans directly (see Hulst and Smith, 1986, for one treatment of this kind). In the normal case, the harmonic span is predictable; it is typically the phonological word. A regular word like *ẹkọ* constitutes one harmonic span, over which the harmonic autosegment spreads maximally. The exceptional nature of disharmonic words such as *telọ* is that they are marked as having two harmonic spans. Spreading then fails and [+ATR] is assigned by default.

(86) [*te*] [*lọ* −A] → [*te* +A] [*lọ* −A]

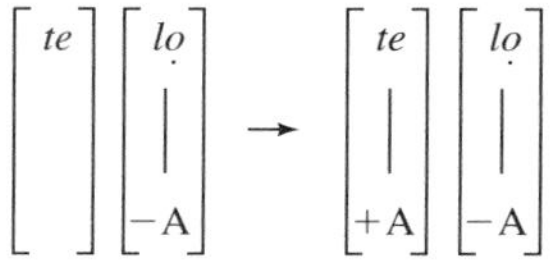

An argument in favor of this approach is that even words which are not disharmonic can fall into separate harmonic spans. For example, in Finnish, where *i, e*

are neutral, long words with back vowels followed by several neutral vowels, such as *karamelli,* nevertheless often take front suffixes.

(87) a. *väri+ä* 'color' (part.sg.)
b. *pari+a* 'pair' (part.sg.)
c. *karamelli+ä* ~ *karamelli+a* 'piece of candy' (part.sg.)

Since *i, e* are neutral, these stems are not intrinsically disharmonic, and so there is no lexically specified backness feature to preassociate. Adding [−back] to one of the neutral vowels for the sake of having something to preassociate would entail sacrificing a major generalization of Finnish phonology, that the neutral vowels are unspecified for backness. But the variation in these words is readily captured by allowing them to consist of two harmonic spans. It seems that such words normally consist of two stress feet, so that the generalization may simply be that the harmonic span in long stems is either the word or the foot.[31]

(88) a. [*karamelli* + *a*]
b. [*kara*] [*melli* + *ä*]

Additional justification for this treatment of disharmony can be found in a language like Turkish, which has both rounding harmony and backness harmony. The assumption of harmony spans makes sense out of the fact that rounding and backness disharmony never occur independently of each other in Turkish. The solidarity of rounding and backness would otherwise be puzzling since the two features spread by separate processes, as we can tell from the fact that nonhigh vowels block the spread of rounding but not the spread of backness. If rounding and backness disharmony are due to lexical linking of the respective features [round] and [back] to some vowel, then a hypothetical word of the nonexisting type where just one of these features fails to spread could be easily represented by lexically linking just that one feature. The result would be a range of disharmonic vowel sequences which in fact do not exist in the language. For example, since spreading in Turkish is left to right, in a word of the form . . . *u* . . . *ɨ* . . . , the feature [back] would be floating and the feature [round] lexically linked to the first vowel, and in a word of the form . . . *u* . . . *ü* . . . it would be the other way round. If disharmony is dealt with by delimiting harmonic spans as here advocated, then the systematic absence of such vowel combinations in Turkish is accounted for by the straightforward assumption that Turkish spreads rounding and backness in the same domain.[32] This works for all actually occurring disharmonic vowel combinations in the Turkish vocabulary listed by Clements and Sezer (1983). For example, a word like *muzip* 'mischievous' consists of two harmonic spans, the first associated with [+round] and [+back], the second unassociated and assigned [−round], [−back] by default.

There is yet another reason why prelinking with SCC–induced blocking of spread is not the right approach to disharmony. This is that it precludes the phonology from expressing the generalization, which holds for Turkish just as for any other language, that [+round] vowels are [+back] in the unmarked case. The vowel *u* in a monosyllabic word would be lexically marked as [+round] and assigned the feature specification [+back] by the universal default rule [+round] → [+back]. The same should be true for the *u* in a disharmonic word like *muzip*. But under the SCC treatment of disharmony, this cannot be done, because both [+round] and [+back] would have to be linked lexically in order to prevent them from spreading by harmony. In this way, the SCC forces us to abandon the underspecification analysis that other considerations demand. Under the span-delimitation solution, however, the underspecification analysis is available.

In addition, the latter solution affords a principled account of Clements and Sezer's generalization that only the five vowels *i, e, a, o, u* may be opaque in Turkish. This is of course just the subsystem of vowels which is unmarked for backness. For the other three vowels, *ɨ, ö, ü,* the value of the feature [back] is not predictable from the features [high] and [round]. In order to derive this distribution of vowels we need only assume, in addition, that the feature [back] is lexically distinctive only in initial spans. This restricts the vowels *ɨ, ö, ü* to the initial (possibly only) harmonic span of the word.

I conclude that opacity and disharmony do not provide evidence for the SCC or indeed for any principle which blocks the application of rules in nonderived environments.

7. CONCLUSIONS

Previous treatments of NDEB have not succeeded in reconciling empirical coverage with theoretical adequacy. The RAC provides a descriptively fairly accurate circumscription of the phenomenon, except that formulating the constraint as a categorical prohibition of absolute neutralization is probably too strong. The RAC is, however, clearly unsatisfactory as a principle of grammar, because of the formal indefinability of the class of "neutralization rules," the undesirability of having different principles for obligatory and optional rules, and the dubious status of the concept of "derived environment." The SCC, on the other hand, is preferable on general theoretical grounds but simply fails to match the facts in many specific instances. In this article I have presented a new interpretation which resolves this dilemma. It makes essential use of underspecification and of decomposition of structure-changing rules. Its main advantages are that it reduces the blocking effects to independent principles of grammar, predicts their restriction to structure-building rules and to nonvacuous rule applications, recaptures the empirical generalizations behind the original restriction of the alternation condition to obligatory neutralization rules, and correctly subsumes the FEC of prosodic phonology.

ACKNOWLEDGMENTS

I would like to thank Young-mee Cho for her helpful advice at several stages in the preparation of this article. It has also benefited from the pointed and constructive comments of Ellen Kaisse, John McCarthy, and an anonymous reviewer. I take responsibility for any remaining errors.

NOTES

[1] See also Giegerich (1988) for a different proposal to this effect.

[2] Recently, Hammond (1991) has also argued for an acquisition-based account of SCC effects, based on a "morphological WYSIWYG" principle. I hope to return to Hammond's proposal on another occasion.

[3] Consonant Gradation, as well as other cases which establish the same general point, is discussed at greater length below.

[4] Unless otherwise stated, I assume the analysis of Finnish word phonology presented in Keyser and Kiparsky (1984), complemented by the morphological analysis of Kanerva (1987). The reader is referred to those sources for the evidence supporting the rules and underlying forms which figure in the discussion below. I should add that I know of no reason to believe that these rules might belong to different levels of the lexical phonology, or indeed, that Finnish even has more than one level.

[5] The *-h-* is obligatory after a primary stress and after a long vowel, e.g., *maa+han* 'into the ground', *mi+hin* 'into what', *veesee+hen* 'into the toilet' (words of the latter type, with noncontracted unstressed long vowels, are loans, and they are often treated as contracted in nonstandard speech, e.g. *veesee+seen*). Otherwise, *-h-* is deleted, except in archaic, poetic, or dialectal usage.

[6] The deletion cannot be cyclic because it it is blocked by any following suffix, e.g., /vaatteCe+n/ → *vaatteen.*

[7] Detailed motivation for this analysis is presented in Keyser and Kiparsky (1984).

[8] The reader points out that these data could be reconciled with cyclic application of Consonant Gradation on the assumption that final consonants are cyclically extrametrical, and that rule (8) is ordered before it. Even on these assumptions, Consonant Gradation would have to apply at the word level as well (and extrametricality would have to assumed be turned off there), because of such cases as (16) and (49). Therefore, this alternative does not call into question the status of Consonant Gradation as a word-level rule subject to NDEB.

[9] The data in (18) represent the actual pronunciation. Postlexical gemination is normally

not shown in the spelling (*menepäs, itsekin*). For the evidence that clitics like *-kin* are syntactic elements and not attached lexically see Kanerva (1987).

[10]On the Zec/Inkelas assumptions mentioned above, so is application across clitic boundary. Moreover, on those assumptions both the fact that the *ruki* rule stopped applying across clitic boundary and the fact that it stopped applying across word boundary in classical Sanskrit can be seen as consequences of a single change, namely, that the rule became confined to the lexical phonology. This development represents a characteristic trajectory of phonological rules (Zec, this volume).

[11]As shown by the failure of sandhi gemination, and by forms like gen.sg. /nukke+n/ *nuke+n* (not /nukkeCe+n/ **nukkee+n*) and part.sg. /nukke+ta/ *nukke+a* (not /nukke-Ce+ta/ **nuket+ta*), there is no protective "ghost consonant" after them, as in (16) and in (50) below.

[12]The analysis is similar to that of English palatalization, which applies both lexically and postlexically, but with the lexical palatals undergoing (word-level?) spirantization, e.g., /edition/ [š] vs. /hit you/ [č] (Borowsky, 1986).

[13]Similar examples can be given for other endings beginning with *-i.*

[14]It is specifically the first vowel which is truncated, as shown by sequences of dissimilar vowels, e.g., /tunte+i+vat/ *tunsivat* 'they knew', /vaati+eCe/ *vaade* 'demand'.

[15]John McCarthy points out that even simple cases like /koti/ *koti* should constitute vacuously derived environments for $t \rightarrow s$, since raising would apply vacuously to the final vowel.

[16]It is immaterial for the point whether Stress Assignment is done along the lines proposed by Harris (1983, 1987) for Spanish, or following the somewhat different analysis developed by Alsina.

[17]Actually, this rule is formulated more generally as applying to the low vowels *ɔ, ɛ* as well, but in Mascaró's analysis these get raised to mid vowels in unstressed position anyway by the second Vowel Reduction rule, which brooks no exceptions whatever.

[18]A similar case of vacuously derived environments apparently counting as derived for the SCC was noted by Steriade (1987b note 23) for Yakan (data from Behrens, 1973: 25). Here unstressed *a* is raised to *i* in derived stems; on a Mascarovian account, the latter condition could be eliminated.

[19]Note also that if Consonant Gradation is not deletion but lack of association, it automatically follows that gradated consonants cannot undergo *t*-Deletion [rule (3)], in such words as *hatu+ton.* As John McCarthy has pointed out to me, ordering *t*-Deletion before Consonant Gradation would be problematic because the structural description of *t*-Deletion crucially refers to a combined prosodic and melodic context, which is not available until after Consonant Gradation, on the analysis suggested here.

[20]Geminate sibilants are realized as s^h, $\check{s}^h$.

[21]Some cases which at first blush seem to be exceptions to PCL could, if the proposed analysis is on the right track, be viewed as exceptionally undergoing the shared feature convention in the lexical phonology in spite of being heteromorphemic: *s+lu+skumu* 'it branches into four', *s+netus* 'he does it to him' (Applegate 1972: 120).

[22]Our formulation supposes that [distributed] is dependent on [strident].

[23]Applegate has many other examples of *š* ~ *s* alternations in *wašti*-type words (1972: 347, 351, 352, 367, 375), but none that clearly involve *wastuʔ*-type words. The derivation /ha p+xosloʔ+š/ → *apxošloš* 'you blow your nose' is given on p. 522, but no */xoslo/ is

actually cited (is /ha+s+noxš/ *ašnoxš* 'nose' somehow related?). The analysis I have proposed would actually predict that underlying /st/ does not undergo Sibilant Harmony, since the multiple link established by the shared feature convention would block spreading.

[24] Chung describes a pattern of optionality in the application of the high–mid alternation in vowels with secondary stress, which is of great theoretical interest but not directly relevant here.

[25] Kager's version of the FEC furthermore covers cases like *original(-ity)*, which were problematic for the SCC account.

[26] From this perspective, the distinction between strong and weak FEC effects is akin to that between stress-neutral and stress-dominant affixes. It is no accident, then, that clitic-triggered stress-assignment always displays strong FEC effects (Arabic, Manam, Greek), and that weak FEC effects are associated with stress subordination.

[27] A similar proposal was made by Bruce Hayes in a talk presented at a phonology workshop at the University of Massachusetts, Amherst, in 1983, of which I have seen only the handout.

[28] Contra Harris (1989:358).

[29] Adopting the notation of Kager (1989), I delimit feet by parentheses and extrametrical elements by angled brackets.

[30] With the no-crossing constraint blocking any spread across it.

[31] Finnish linguists sometimes characterize such long words as "quasi-compounds." There is no morphological support for this, in cases like (88) at least, but the intuition nevertheless has a real basis, to which my proposal also does justice, in that compounds similarly have at least two stress feet.

[32] This would be the unmarked situation, though different harmonic processes could potentially be restricted to different spans as well, a possibility which is apparently realized in some Turkic languages.

REFERENCES

Alsina, A. (1987). *Stress Assignment in Catalan.* Unpublished manuscript, Stanford University.

Anderson, S. (1969). An outline of the phonology of Modern Icelandic vowels. *Foundations of Language* **5,** 53–72.

Anderson, S. (1981). Why phonology isn't "natural." *Linguistic Inquiry* **12,** 493–539.

Applegate, J. (1972). *Ineseño Chumash Grammar.* Doctoral dissertation, University of California, Berkeley.

Archangeli, D., and Pulleyblank, D. (1989). Yoruba vowel harmony. *Linguistic Inquiry* **20,** 173–217.

Behrens, D. (1973). *Yakan Phonemics and Morphophonemics* (Papers in Philippine Linguistics 7). Australian National University, Canberra.

Borowsky, T. (1986). *Topics in English Phonology.* Doctoral dissertation, University of Massachusetts, Amherst.

Cho, Y. (1990). *Parameters of Consonantal Assimilation.* Doctoral dissertation, Stanford University, Stanford, Calif.

Cho, Y., and Sells, P. (1991). *A Lexical Account of Phrasal Suffixes in Korean.* Unpublished manuscript, Stanford University, Stanford, Calif.

Chomsky, N., and Halle, M. (1968). *The Sound Pattern of English.* Harper & Row, New York.

Chung, S. (1983). Transderivational relationships in Chamorro phonology. *Language* **59,** 35–66.

Clark, M. (1990). *The Tonal System of Igbo.* Foris, Dordrecht.

Clements, G. N. (1989). *A Unified Set of Features for Consonants and Vowels.* Unpublished manuscript, Cornell University, Ithaca, N.Y.

Clements, G. N., and Sezer, E. (1983). Vowel and consonant disharmony in Turkish. In *The structure of Phonological Representations* (H. van der Hulst and N. Smith, eds.) vol. 2, pp. 213–255. Foris, Dordrecht.

Cohn, A. (1989). Stress in Indonesian and bracketing paradoxes. *Natural Language and Linguistic Theory* **7,** 167–216.

Dresher, E. (1981). On the learnability of abstract phonology. In *The Logical Problem of Language Acquisition* (C. L. Baker and J. McCarthy, eds.). MIT Press, Cambridge, Mass.

Giegerich, H. J. (1988). Strict cyclicity and elsewhere. *Lingua* **75,** 125–134.

Halle, M. (1978). Formal vs. functional considerations in phonology. In *Festschrift for O. Szemerényi* (B. Brogyanyi, ed.). Benjamins, Amsterdam.

Halle, M., and Kenstowicz, M. (1990). *The Free-Element Condition and Cyclic vs. Noncyclic Stress.* Unpublished manuscript, Massachusetts Institute of Technology, Cambridge.

Halle, M., and Vergnaud, J.-R. (1987). *An Essay on Stress.* MIT Press, Cambridge, Mass.

Hammond, M. (1991). *Deriving the Strict Cycle Condition.* Unpublished manuscript, University of Arizona, Tucson.

Hargus, S. (1985). *The Lexical Phonology of Sekani.* Doctoral dissertation, University of California, Los Angeles.

Hargus, S. (1989). Underspecification and derived-only rules in Sekani phonology. In *Theoretical Perspectives on Native American Languages* (D. B. Gerdts and K. Michelson, eds.), pp. 70–103. State University of New York Press, Albany.

Harris, J. (1983). *Syllable Structure and Stress in Spanish: a Nonlinear Analysis.* MIT Press, Cambridge, Mass.

Harris, J. (1987). The accentual pattern of verb paradigms in Spanish. *Natural Language and Linguistic Theory* **5,** 61–90.

Harris, J. (1989). The stress erasure convention and cliticization in Spanish. *Linguistic Inquiry* **20,** 339–363.

Hayes, B. (1986). Inalterability in CV phonology. *Language* **62,** 321–352.

Hualde, J. I. (1989). The strict cycle condition and noncyclic rules. *Linguistic Inquiry* **20,** 675–680.

Hulst, H. van der, and Smith, N. (1986). On neutral vowels. In *The Phonological Representation of Suprasegmentals* (H. van der Hulst and M. Mous, eds.), pp. 233–279. Foris, Dordrecht.

Hume, E. (1990). Front vowels, palatal consonants, and the rule of Umlaut in Korean. Proceedings of the North Eastern Linguistic Society **21.**

Inkelas, S. (1989). *Prosodic Constituency in the Lexicon.* Doctoral dissertation, Stanford University, Stanford, Calif.

Itô, J. (1986). *Syllable Theory in Prosodic Phonology.* Doctoral dissertation, University of Massachusetts, Amherst.

Itô, J. (1990). Prosodic minimality in Japanese. Syntax Research Center, Cowell College, University of California, Santa Cruz, Technical Report, SRC-90-04.

Iverson, G. K., and Wheeler, D. W. (1988). Blocking and the elsewhere condition. In *Theoretical Morphology* (M. Hammond and M. Noonan, eds.), pp. 325–338. Academic Press, San Diego.

Kager, R. (1989). *A Metrical Theory of Stress and Destressing in English and Dutch.* Foris, Dordrecht.

Kaisse, E. (1986). Locating Turkish devoicing. *Proceedings of the West Coast Conference on Formal Linguistics* **5,** 119–128.

Kanerva, J. (1987). Morphological integrity and syntax: The evidence from Finnish possessive suffixes. *Language* **63,** 498–521.

Kean, M.-L. (1974). The strict cycle in phonology. *Linguistic Inquiry* **5,** 179–203.

Keyser, S. J., and Kiparsky, P. (1984). Syllable structure in Finnish phonology. In *Language Sound Structure* (M. Aronoff and R. T. Oehrle, eds.), pp. 7–31. MIT Press, Cambridge, Mass.

Kiparsky, P. (1973). Phonological representations. In *Three Dimensions of Linguistic Theory* (Osamu Fujimura, ed.). TEC, Tokyo.

Kiparsky, P. (1982). Lexical phonology and morphology. In *Linguistics in the Morning Calm* (Linguistic Society of Korea, ed.), pp. 3–91. Hanshin, Seoul.

Kiparsky, P. (1984). On the lexical phonology of Icelandic. In *Nordic Prosody III* (C. Elert, I. Johansson, and E. Strangert, eds.), pp. 135–164. Almqvist & Wiksell, Stockholm.

Kiparsky, P. (1985). Some consequences of lexical phonology. *Phonology Yearbook* **2,** 82–138.

Kiparsky, P. (1992). *Underspecification and Harmony Systems.* Unpublished manuscript, Stanford University, Stanford, Calif.

Lahiri, A., and Evers, V. (1989). Palatalization and coronality. In *The special status of Coronals: Internal and External Evidence* (C. Paradis and J.-F. Prunet, eds.), pp. 79–100. Academic Press, San Diego.

Levergood, B. (1984). Rule governed vowel harmony and the strict cycle. *Proceedings of the North Eastern Linguistic Society* **14,** 275–293.

Lombardi, L., and McCarthy, J. (1991). Prosodic circumscription in Choctaw morphology. *Phonology* **8,** 37–72.

Macdonell, A. (1968). *Vedic Grammar.* Indological Book House, Varanasi.

Macfarland, T., and Pierrehumbert, J. (1991). On ich-Laut, ach-Laut and structure preservation. *Phonology* **8**, 171–180.

Mascaró, J. (1976). *Catalan Phonology.* Doctoral dissertation, Massachusetts Institute of Technology, Cambridge.

Mascaró, J. (1987). *A Reduction and Spreading Theory of Voicing and Other Sound Effects.* Unpublished manuscript, Barcelona.

McCarthy, J. (1986). OCP effects: Gemination and antigemination. *Linguistic Inquiry* **17,** 207–263.

Orešnik, J. (1977). Modern Icelandic u-umlaut from the descriptive point of view. *Gripla* **2,** 151–182. Reprinted in *Studies in the Phonology and Morphology of Modern Icelandic* (J. Orešnik, ed., 1985). Buske, Hamburg.

Ottósson, K. (1988). *Fragments of the Lexical Morphology and Phonology of Icelandic.* Unpublished manuscript, University of Maryland, College Park.

Poser, W. (1982). Phonological representations and action-at-a-distance. In *The Structure of Phonological Representations,* part 2 (H. van der Hulst and N. Smith, eds.), pp. 121–158. Foris, Dordrecht.

Poser, W. (1986). Diyari stress, metrical structure assignment, and the nature of metrical representation. *Proceedings of the West Coast Conference on Formal Linguistics* **5,** 178–191.

Poser, W. (1989). The metrical foot in Diyari. *Phonology* **6,** 117–148.

Poser, W. (1990). *Are Strict Cycle Effects Derivable?* Unpublished manuscript, Stanford University, Stanford, Calif.

Prince, A. (1985). Improving tree theory. *Proceedings of the Berkeley Linguistic Society* **11,** 471–490.

Pulleyblank, D. (1986). *Tone in Lexical Phonology.* Reidel, Dordrecht.

Ramsey, S. R. (1978). *Accent and Morphology in Korean Dialects.* The Society of Korean Linguistics, Seoul.

Rice, K. (1988). Continuant voicing in Slave (Northern Athapaskan): The cyclic application of default rules. In *Theoretical Morphology* (M. Hammond and M. Noonan, eds.), pp. 371–388. Academic Press, San Diego.

Rubach, J. (1984). *Cyclic and Lexical Phonology.* Foris, Dordrecht.

Selkirk, E. (1980). Prosodic domains in phonology: Sanskrit revisited. In *Juncture* (M. Aronoff and M.-L. Kean, eds.), pp. 107–129. Anma Libri, Saratoga, Calif.

Shaw, P. (1985). Lexical phonology. *Phonology Yearbook* **2,** 171–200.

Steriade, D. (1982). *Greek Prosodies and the Nature of Syllabification.* Doctoral dissertation, Massachusetts Institute of Technology, Cambridge.

Steriade, D. (1987a). Redundant values. *Papers from the Regional Meeting of the Chicago Linguistic Society* **24,** 339–362.

Steriade, D. (1987b). *Vowel Tiers and Geminate Blockage.* Unpublished manuscript, Massachusetts Institute of Technology, Cambridge.

Steriade, D. (1988). Greek accent: a case for preserving structure. *Linguistic Inquiry* **19,** 271–314.

Wackernagel, J. (1895). *Altindische Grammatik,* vol. 1. Vandenhoeck & Ruprecht, Göttingen.

Whitney, W. D. (1887). *Sanskrit Grammar.* Harvard University Press, Cambridge, Mass.

Zwicky, A. (1986). The general case: Basic form versus default form. *Proceedings of the Berkeley Linguistics Society* **12,** 305–14.

ARE STRICT CYCLE EFFECTS DERIVABLE?

WILLIAM J. POSER

Department of Linguistics
Stanford University
Stanford, California 94305

1. DERIVED ENVIRONMENT EFFECTS

Derived environment effects, in which a rule fails to apply in nonderived environments that otherwise satisfy its structural description, are generally attributed to the strict cycle condition (Kean, 1974; Mascaró, 1976). Kiparsky (this volume) proposes to eliminate the strict cycle condition, arguing that derived environment effects result from the application of structure-building rules to underspecified representations. The purpose of this note is to present a case that appears to pose serious problems for Kiparsky's attempt to eliminate the strict cycle condition.

To illustrate Kiparsky's approach, consider his analysis of the well-known Finnish rule that takes /t/ to /s/ before /i/, which applies only in derived environments. Relevant forms, along with the proposed underlying representations, are given in (1).

(1)

	nominative	essive	underlying representation	gloss
a.	*lasi*	*lasina*	*laTi*	'glass'
b.	*koti*	*kotina*	*koti*	'home'
c.	*vesi*	*vetenä*	*veTE*	'water'
d.	*kuusi*	*kuusena*	*kuusE*	'fir'

The derived environment effect is illustrated by the contrast between (1b) and (1c). In (1b) /t/ precedes /i/ in the underlying representation and is unaffected. In

Phonetics and Phonology, Volume 4
Studies in Lexical Phonology

(1c) /t/ underlyingly precedes /e/, and it is only when /e/ raises to /i/ in word-final position that the preceding /t/ becomes /s/.

On Kiparsky's analysis there are two underlying non-low front vowels, /i/, which is [+high], and /E/, which is [0high]. There is no distinctively [−high] non-low front vowel as this is forbidden by principles of radical underspecification. The archisegment /E/ may receive a value for [high] either by the E-Raising rule (2) or by the default rule (3).

(2) FINAL E-RAISING:
[ ] → [+high]/ ____ #

(3) HIGH DEFAULT:
[ ] → [−high]

For [t] and [s] we have three underlying possibilities, /s/ ([+cnt]), /T/ ([0cnt]), and /t/ ([−cnt]). /s/ is permitted only before underlying /i/, while /t/ is permitted only when not preceding /i/, so that in no single environment is there an underlying distinction between [+cnt] and [−cnt]. Before /i/ we can have either /t/ or /T/; elsewhere we can have /s/ or /T/. The default rule supplies the value [−cnt], producing [t]. The rule that takes /t/ to /s/ before /i/ is a purely feature-filling rule and so applies to /T/, filling in the value [+cnt], but not to /t/, which is already specified [−cnt].

The derived environment effect results from the fact that derived [i] (that is, /E/) may be preceded either by /s/, which is always realized as [s], or by /T/, which is realized as [t] when /E/ is realized as [e], and as [s] when /E/ is realized as [i], while underived [i] (/i/) may be preceded either by /t/, which is always realized as [t], or by /T/, which before /i/ is always realized as [s].

The problematic example involves two rules of Chumash, a now extinct language of California. The data presented here are from the Ineseño dialect, described by Applegate (1972) on the basis of the field notes of John P. Harrington. The situation in the Ventureño dialect, described in the posthumously published Harrington (1974), is very similar. The analysis given here recapitulates that of Poser (1982), which may be consulted for additional examples and details omitted here.[1]

2. CHUMASH SIBILANT HARMONY

The first of the two relevant rules is Sibilant Harmony, which causes all sibilants (including affricates) to agree in laminality with the last sibilant in the word.[2] (4) illustrates the fact that the third person subject prefix surfaces as [s] when no other sibilant follows. But when the past tense suffix /waš/ is added as in (5), /s/ becomes /š/.

(4) *hasxintila* /ha + s + xintila/ 'his gentile'

(5) *hašxintilawaš* /ha + s + xintila + waš/ 'his former gentile'

Sibilant Harmony also causes underlying /š/ to surface as /s/. (6) shows that the dual subject prefix is underlyingly /iš/ since that is the form in which it appears when no other sibilant follows. In (7), where the last sibilant is /s/, the dual prefix harmonizes and surfaces as /s/.

(6) *pišanan?* /p + iš + al + nan?/ 'don't you two go'

(7) *sishuleqpeyus* /s + iš + sili + uluaqpey + us/ 'they two want to follow it'

These examples demonstrate that Sibilant Harmony is feature-changing, since it causes underlying /s/ to surface as /š/ and underlying /š/ to surface as /s/. For a harmony system to be purely feature-filling, it must be the case that harmonizing segments are unspecified for the harmony feature. Therefore, segments subject to harmony will all take on the same value, whatever value is supplied by the relevant default rule, when they lie outside the domain of a harmony trigger. In a case like the one at hand, in which the value of the harmony feature is unpredictable when not in the domain of a trigger, the value cannot be attributed to a default rule and therefore must be part of the representation of the segment, that is, must be specified. Since both /s/ and /š/ undergo harmony, the harmony rule must change underlyingly present feature values.

3. CHUMASH PRE-CORONAL LAMINALIZATION

In addition to Sibilant Harmony, Chumash has a second rule affecting the laminality of sibilants, which I call Pre-Coronal Laminalization (PCL). This rule, stated in (8), makes a sibilant laminal when it immediately precedes one of the non-strident coronals /t/, /l/, or /n/. The operation of the rule is illustrated by the examples in (9). In each case the third person subject prefix /s/ (apical) becomes [š] (laminal) before a nonstrident coronal.

(8) [+cor, +stri] → [+dist] / ____ [+cor, −stri]

(9) *šnan?* /s + nan?/ 'he goes'
štepu? /s + tepu?/ 'he gambles'
šloxit? /s + loxit?/ 'he surpasses me'

PCL creates a systematic class of exceptions to the generalization that all sibilants in a word agree in laminality with the last. Sibilants whose laminality is determined by PCL are opaque to Sibilant Harmony. In (10a) we see that the /š/

created by PCL fails to harmonize with the /s/ of /us/. In (10b) not only does the /š/ created by PCL fail to harmonize with the two /s/s of /sisin/, but it serves as a trigger with respect to the /s/ that precedes it.

(10) a. *štiyepus* /s + ti + yep + us/ 'he tells him'
b. *šišlusisin* /s + iš + lu + sisin/ 'they two are gone awry'

In Poser (1982) I argued that the opacity of /š/ created by PCL is incompatible with theories in which feature-changing rules directly change feature values. In such theories, if PCL applies before Sibilant Harmony, /š/ created by PCL should harmonize just like underlying /š/, since Sibilant Harmony has no way of distinguishing between underlying /š/ and those derived by PCL. If PCL applies after Sibilant Harmony, /š/s created by PCL will fail to harmonize but will not be opaque, for preceding sibilants will harmonize with the last sibilant in the word and will not harmonize with the /š/ created by PCL. In other words, if PCL applies after Sibilant Harmony, PCL will create islands, not opaque segments.

The same problem arises in the putatively non–feature-changing analysis of Avery & Rice (1989). In their discussion of Chumash (pp. 193f.) they do not directly address the evidence that Chumash is feature-changing, and they describe their analysis as not feature-changing. In one sense their analysis is not feature-changing, for it does not make use of explicit delinking or deletion rules or directly change one feature value into another. Their analysis is, however, feature-changing in another sense, namely, in that the harmony rule deletes underlyingly present information, and it is only for this reason that it can accomodate the evidence presented above that Chumash harmony is feature-changing. Their harmony rule fuses the Place node of the last sibilant with those of the sibilants before it. They explain the operation of fusion as follows (p. 181):

> Fusion is an operation which takes identical primary content nodes and fuses them provided that the nodes are non-distinct; i.e., both nodes do not dominate different secondary nodes. We assume that fusion is headed in that the secondary features of the triggering segment are maintained.

As the examples discussed on p. 182 make clear, not only are the secondary features of the trigger maintained, but the secondary features of the harmonizing segment are deleted. Thus, fusion of a [+dist] trigger with a [−dist] undergoer makes both [+dist], which is the equivalent of a feature-filling spreading operation, but fusion of a [−dist] trigger with a [+dist] undergoer causes deletion of the secondary features of the undergoer, making both segments [−dist], the equivalent of spreading accompanied by feature deletion. In the relevant sense, then, their analysis is feature-changing, and like more traditional feature-changing analyses, cannot account for the opacity of /š/ created by PCL, which they do not discuss.

The opacity of /š/ created by PCL can be accounted for in a theory like that of Poser (1982) in which feature-changing is the result of two distinct rules, one delinking or deleting feature specifications, the other inserting new feature specifications or spreading existing ones.[3] The proposed two-stage analysis of Chumash Sibilant Harmony orders PCL between Distributed Delinking, which delinks nonrightmost specifications of the feature [dist], and Distributed Spreading, which spreads the remaining rightmost specification of [dist] leftward.

(11) ORDER OF RULES:
Distributed Delinking
Pre-Coronal Laminalization
Distributed Spreading

/š/s created by PCL fail to undergo Sibilant Harmony because Distributed Delinking gets no opportunity to delink them, and Distributed Spreading is purely feature-filling.[4]

We now come to the crux of our argument, namely the fact that PCL is subject to a derived environment condition. As illustrated in (12), it fails to apply in tautomorphemic clusters.

(12)	*stumukun*	'mistletoe'
	slowʔ	'eagle'
	wastuʔ	'pleat'

Of course, it is possible for [š] to appear before nonstrident coronals morpheme internally, as in the morpheme /wašti/ 'of a flow, of liquid in motion'. Unlike instances of /š/ derived by PCL, which as we have seen are opaque to Sibilant Harmony, such underlying /š/s, which are not created by PCL, undergo Sibilant Harmony, as illustrated in (13) and (14). (13) illustrates the underlying /š/ that surfaces when no /s/ follows. (14) shows that this /š/ is not opaque to Sibilant Harmony.

(13)	*waštinanʔ*	/wašti + nanʔ/	'to spill'
(14)	*swastilokʔinus*	/s + wašti + lokʔin + us/	'the flow stops on him'

This is precisely what my analysis predicts: since underlying [+dist] specifications are wiped out by Distributed Delinking, unless PCL applies these sibilants remain unspecified for [dist] and therefore undergo Distributed Spreading.

The derived environment condition on PCL is predicted by the strict cycle condition, since it applies only when its environment is satisfied as the result of morphological composition. But it cannot be derived from constraints on underlying feature specification since, on my analysis of Sibilant Harmony, at the point at which PCL applies, both the sibilants that undergo PCL and those that fail to undergo PCL are unspecified for the feature [dist] as a result of the prior application of Distributed Delinking. It therefore appears to be impossible to derive strict cycle effects in all cases from underspecification.

This leaves open the question of whether the strict cycle condition must be maintained in its entirety, for it has two clauses. One clause classifies an environment as derived if the structural description of the rule comes to be satisfied as a result of morphological composition. The other classifies an environment as derived if the structural description comes to be satisfied as a result of prior application of a phonological rule. Kiparsky's proposal appears to derive successfully the known cases of derived environment effects due to prior application of a phonological rule. The force of the Chumash example may be that it is necessary to retain the first clause of the strict cycle condition, by which derived environments result from morphological composition, while dispensing with the second. This is a natural distinction, for this latter criterion requires information about the derivation of a sort not present in the representation, in contrast to information about morphological structure, which arguably is present in the representation.

NOTES

[1] Let me take this opportunity to correct an error in Poser (1982), where I glossed *haš-xintilawaš* as 'his former Indian name'. Actually, this form is the adjective meaning 'his former gentile' and has the given meaning only when combined with the noun *mastɨ "name". xintila* is a loan from Spanish *gentil* 'gentile, heathen'.

[2] In Poser (1982) I treated the distinction between Chumash /s/ and /š/ as a distinction between [+ant] and [−ant]. Here I adopt the proposal of Lieber (1987: 147) that it should be characterized as a distinction between [−dist] and [+dist], that is, as a distinction between apical and laminal.

[3] Lieber (1987) mistakenly credits herself with this proposal and attributes to Poser (1982) the metrical view of which it is a critique.

[4] A full formalization of this analysis requires a decision as to how to handle the transparency of the nonstrident coronals, which fortunately does not appear to be relevant to the points at issue here. For discussion of the transparency issue see Shaw (1991).

REFERENCES

Applegate, R. B. (1972). *Ineseño Chumash Grammar.* Doctoral dissertation, University of California, Berkeley.

Avery, P., and Rice, K. (1989). Segment structure and coronal underspecification. *Phonology* **6,** 179–200.

Harrington, J. P. (1974). Sibilants in Ventureño. *International Journal of American Linguistics* **40,** 1–9.

Kean, M.-L. (1974). The strict cycle in phonology. *Linguistic Inquiry* **5,** 179–203.

Lieber, R. (1987). *An Integrated Theory of Autosegmental Processes.* State University of New York Press, Albany.

Mascaró, J. (1976). *Catalan Phonology and the Phonological Cycle.* Doctoral dissertation, Massachusetts Institute of Technology, Cambridge.

Poser, W. J. (1982). Phonological representation and action-at-a-distance. In *The Structure of Phonological Representations,* part 2 (H. van der Hulst and N. Smith, eds.), pp. 121–158. Foris, Dordrecht.

Shaw, P. A. (1991). Consonant harmony systems: The special status of coronal harmony. In *Phonetics and Phonology,* Vol. 2 (C. Paradis and J.-F. Prunet, eds.), pp. 125–157. Academic Press, San Diego.

III

Applying the Theory to Historical Change

THE CHRONOLOGY AND STATUS OF ANGLIAN SMOOTHING

B. ELAN DRESHER

Department of Linguistics
University of Toronto
Toronto, Ontario, Canada M5S 1A1

1. INTRODUCTION

The Old English sound change known as Smoothing has been problematic in terms of both its chronology and status. Descriptively, Smoothing is a name given to the process whereby, in certain dialects, diphthongs were monophthongized before the velar consonants *k*, *g*, and *x*, when these followed either directly or with an intervening *r* or *l*. The observed changes are listed in (1).

(1) $$\begin{Bmatrix} \text{æa} \\ eo \\ io \end{Bmatrix} \rightarrow \begin{Bmatrix} \text{æ} \\ e \\ i \end{Bmatrix} \;/\; \underset{[+\text{stress}]}{\underline{\qquad}} \left(\begin{Bmatrix} r \\ l \end{Bmatrix} \right) \begin{Bmatrix} k \\ g \\ x \end{Bmatrix}$$

$$= / \; \underset{[+\text{stress}]}{\underline{\qquad}} \begin{bmatrix} +\text{cons} \\ +\text{son} \\ -\text{nasal} \end{bmatrix} \begin{bmatrix} +\text{obst} \\ +\text{back} \end{bmatrix}$$

The rule is somewhat unexpected, since some of these contexts were ones that had formerly caused diphthongization. Hence Smoothing appears to reverse the effects of earlier rules, which leads to the suspicion that one or the other is not a natural process. From the point of view of phonological theory, the rule, together with the processes it interacts with, provokes a number of interesting questions. My main concern here is with the results of the interaction of Smoothing with other processes and the extent to which these interactions bear on the theory of lexical phonology and vice versa.

Phonetics and Phonology, Volume 4
Studies in Lexical Phonology

In brief, I argue that there are a number of rules in Mercian Old English which apply quite regularly in weak verbs and nouns but not in strong verbs. Upon closer inspection, we find that the morphological contexts of the apparent exceptionality have a structural basis, in that certain rules systematically do not apply when their triggering context includes verb agreement suffixes. In terms of lexical phonology, this suggests that the phonology is partitioned into at least two levels. Moreover, the rules limited to the earlier level all have in common that they can be treated as persistent constraints. The facts suggest that certain types of rules are susceptible to be reinterpreted as constraints, thereby exhibiting complex interactions with other processes.

First, some preliminaries about the language under discussion. Smoothing applied in the Anglian dialects of Old English, that is, not in West Saxon, which is the dialect most familiar from the standard handbooks. The term "Anglian" groups together a number of dialects; the one we will be looking at is the Mercian dialect. Our knowledge of this dialect, and the various changes it underwent, comes from a series of texts from different periods. The largest and most consistent text is the *Vespasian Psalter* [Ps(A)], which dates from around 825. Earlier than Ps(A) are some glossaries that date from around 700–800; quite a bit later than it are a group of early Middle English texts from the early 1200s.[1]

A word about the vowels: Old English vowels as well as diphthongs could be either short or long. Diphthongs are all falling, with stress on the first part, which is always a front vowel. The second part of a diphthong is always back, written *o* when the first part is nonlow and *a* when the first part is low. We can take it to be some kind of schwa.[2]

I begin by reviewing some problems in determining the chronology of Smoothing. These problems are worth considering, even though the chronology of Smoothing relative to other rules is in fact easily determined by looking at the documents. Nevertheless, many traditional grammarians did not believe what the texts appear to be showing, because the interaction of Smoothing with some other rules was not what it should have been in terms of their theory of language change, which itself was connected to their theory of synchronic grammar. So a study of this case brings out clearly the interdependence between synchronic theory and the interpretation of diachronic developments, as well as turning up an interesting problem to which we can apply current theories. Let us turn, then, to the facts of this case.

2. THE CHRONOLOGY OF SMOOTHING

Smoothing applies fairly regularly to diphthongs in early texts, a fact which suggests that it predates them. A difficulty is posed by its interaction with the relatively late rule of Back Mutation, also known as "back umlaut" or "velar umlaut." Back Mutation diphthongizes short front vowels if a back vowel stands in the following syllable; the rule is given in (2). (In the first part of this article, all rules are written in informal linear format; these rules are meant to be descriptive only.)

(2) $$\begin{Bmatrix} \textit{æ} \\ \textit{e} \\ \textit{i} \end{Bmatrix} \rightarrow \begin{Bmatrix} \textit{æa} \\ \textit{eo} \\ \textit{io} \end{Bmatrix} \; / \; \underset{[+\text{stress}]}{\underline{\qquad\qquad}} \; \text{C} \; \underset{[+\text{back}]}{\text{V}}$$

Note that Back Mutation potentially conflicts with Smoothing when the intervening consonant is velar. A traditional assumption, going back to the Neogrammarians, is that a sound change, that is, what is in our terms a new rule such as Back Mutation, applies to surface forms.[3] This is equivalent to supposing that rules are added only to the end of the grammar. Therefore, if Smoothing is historically earlier than Back Mutation, as suggested by the manuscript evidence, we would expect to observe the diachronic sequence shown in (3).

(3)

a.	b.	
weorc	*dægas*	Earlier forms
werc	—	Smoothing
—	*dæagas*	Back Mutation

We expect Smoothing to apply to old diphthongs, as in (3a), but not to the new diphthongs created by Back Mutation (3b); that is, Back Mutation should apply freely before velars. In fact, though, it does not. What we actually find is variation between smoothed and unsmoothed forms, even at a time when Back Mutation applies regularly before other (i.e., nonvelar) consonants.

The interaction of Smoothing with Back Mutation thus does not accord with Neogrammarian assumptions about sound change, and traditional grammarians have had to propose a variety of extra mechanisms to account for it. For example, to account for the existence of smoothed forms, Luick (1964: §235.a.3) proposed that Back Mutation was prevented by back consonants in Anglian. Such an assumption, however, is hard to reconcile with the existence of forms where it did appply before back consonants. Moreover, the fact that both Smoothing and Back Mutation observe the identical restriction on diphthongs before back consonants would be unexplained. For these reasons, Campbell (1959: §247) argued for a relatively late date for Smoothing, following Back Mutation. He claims that the "complete absence in Anglian except in analogical forms of back umlaut before back consonants indicates that its effects were removed by smoothing, and that it in fact took place earlier than that change." Campbell therefore posits the diachronic sequence in (4).

(4)	a.	b.	
	dægas	*sprecan*	Earlier forms
	dæagas	*spreocan*	Back Mutation
	dægas	*sprecan*	Smoothing
		spreocan	Analogy

In this scenario, the earlier spellings with diphthongs predate Smoothing, while the later ones represent an analogical restoration after Smoothing.

One problem with this account is that there is no convincing basis for the analogical change in traditional terms. Also, Campbell's view does not accord with the evidence of the manuscripts, as has been shown by Ball and Stiles (1983), who find no texts which show Back Mutation but not Smoothing. They conclude that Smoothing preceded Back Mutation, and that Back Mutation of *æ* before velar consonants did take place "in some parts of the Mercian area." Thus they suggest that the variation is due to dialect mixture, where forms with diphthongs (*dæagas*) represent the contribution of the area which did allow Back Mutation before velars, while forms with monophthongs (*dægas*) are from the area which did not. This account, however, begs the question of why Back Mutation, the later rule, should ever have been impeded before velar consonants. Further, if the recorded forms reflect dialect variation, we would expect to find no systematic pattern to the variation; but the distribution of smoothed and unsmoothed forms in the same texts do not support this view, as we shall see.

Toon (1983) also demonstrates that Smoothing preceded Back Mutation in the texts he surveyed. He sums up his position as follows (p. 184): "Although velar umlaut and smoothing were synchronic forces in the same texts, smoothing began earlier and was complete before velar umlaut. . . . Smoothing had ceased to be a productive force in the language of the *Corpus Glossary:* [æə] could develop before the velar spirant. It was obviously not a productive rule in the phonology of the *Vespasian Psalter* scribe."

The situation in Ps(A) does not, however, support the view that Smoothing had become an unproductive rule. A look at the distribution of smoothed and unsmoothed forms reveals that the presence or absence of diphthongs has come to depend on morphological category: strong verbs and their derivatives do not in general show Smoothing in Back Mutation environments, but weak verbs, nouns, and adjectives do. This generalization holds with very few exceptions. The numbers of forms of each type are shown in (5).

(5) BACK MUTATION BEFORE VELARS IN Ps(A):

	Monophthongs	*Diphthongs*
Nouns	67	5
Weak verbs	15	0
Strong verbs and derivatives	3	69

Thus the synchronic rule order required to derive the strong verbs mirrors the diachronic order of Smoothing before Back Mutation (6a). However, a different synchronic order of application is required in the other major lexical classes (6b).

(6) REORDERING OF SMOOTHING AND BACK MUTATION:

a. Strong verbs

sprecan	Original Form
—	Smoothing
spreocan	Back Mutation

b. Weak verbs and nouns

cwæcade	*dægas*	Original Form
cwæacade	*dæagas*	Back Mutation
cwæcade	*dægas*	Smoothing

Classical generative phonology, in the style of Chomsky and Halle (1968), provides a richer apparatus in terms of which new rules can be integrated into the grammar. Thus rules may be added to the end of a grammar, or before the end; they may reorder, or become modified or lost. In this case, Smoothing preceded Back Mutation chronologically. Adding Back Mutation to the end of the grammar would give the sequence in (6a): Back Mutation should apply unimpeded by Smoothing. This may have been the initial situation; subsequently, the rules appear to have reordered in most lexical classes, creating the derivations shown in (6b).

Reordering by itself, however, does not adequately account for the facts of the case. First, the motivation for the reordering is unclear. In the putative original order, Back Mutation counterfeeds Smoothing; the reordering is into feeding order. To the extent that maximal application is a consideration, this order is an improvement. However, the order remains opaque, in the sense of Kiparsky (1973). In the original order, Back Mutation creates surface violations of Smoothing, so that it appears that Smoothing has underapplied. Reordering removes these surface exceptions to Smoothing but creates surface exceptions to Back Mutation, making it look like it has underapplied. Thus the synchronically later rule makes the earlier one opaque, in either order. Second, we cannot explain why the reordering was not carried through in the strong verbs. There are cases where an analogical change is impeded in a certain class of forms, and we could look for a reason why strong verbs resisted the change while weak verbs and nouns did not. Strong verbs had no particular disposition to diphthongal forms, however, nor did weak verbs particularly avoid them. In fact, it can be shown that analogy plays virtually no role in the distribution of diphthongs in Ps(A), which can in almost all cases be accounted for phonologically (Dresher 1978, Ch. 1). We can conclude that rule reordering does not suffice to account for the observed variability in these forms.

3. MORPHOLOGICAL CONDITIONS

Dresher (1978) assumed that Back Mutation and Smoothing had indeed reordered, that is, that the correct synchronic rule order for the Ps(A) dialect was that in (6b). The fact that Smoothing did not apply to the strong verbs was not accounted for by a different rule ordering, as in (6a), but rather was attributed to a failure of Smoothing to apply regularly in the strong verbs. This failure forms part of a wider generalization. There are a number of other rules in the Ps(A) dialect which distinguish between morphological categories in the same way: they apply regularly in weak verbs and nouns but not in strong verbs.

One such rule, like Smoothing, simplifies diphthongs, this time before the high vowel /i/. This rule accounts for the alternation we find in the stem vowel of the adjective ‘sharp’ (7a) as opposed to the weak verb ‘sharpen’ (7b).

(7)

a. Adjectives	b. Weak verbs	
/scærp+∅/	/scærp+i+d+un/	underlying
scæarp	*scæarp+i+d+un*	Breaking
—	*scærp+i+d+un*	*i*-Monophthongization
—	—	*e*-Raising
—	*scærp+d+un*	Vowel Deletion
—	—	*i*-Lowering
scæarp	*scerptun*	other rules

c. Strong verbs	d. Strong verbs	
/-werp+ið/	/swelg+ið/	underlying
-weorp+ið	—	Breaking
FAILS	—	*i*-Monophthongization
—	*swilg+ið*	*e*-Raising
—	—	Vowel Deletion
-weorp+eð	*swilg+eð*	*i*-Lowering
-weorpeð	*swilgeð*	other rules

The diphthong in the adjective is produced by the rule of Breaking, given in (8a), which diphthongizes a front vowel before the back continuants /w/ and /x/, as well as before the liquids /l/ and /r/ when these are followed by a consonant.

(8) a. BREAKING:

$$\begin{Bmatrix} \textit{æ} \\ e \\ i \end{Bmatrix} \rightarrow \begin{Bmatrix} \textit{æa} \\ eo \\ io \end{Bmatrix} \; / \; \underset{[+\text{stress}]}{\underline{\qquad}} \begin{Bmatrix} w \\ x \\ \{r,l\}\ \text{C} \end{Bmatrix}$$

$$= / \; \underset{[+\text{stress}]}{\underline{\qquad}} \begin{bmatrix} +\text{cont} \\ +\text{back} \end{bmatrix}$$

b. RETRACTION:

$$æ \rightarrow a \ / \ \underset{[+\text{stress}]}{\underline{\qquad}} \begin{bmatrix} +\text{son} \\ +\text{back} \end{bmatrix}$$

The adjective 'sharp' exhibits Breaking before a cluster of /r/+ consonant; the lack of a diphthong in the verb can be attributed to the effects of a rule of *i*-Monophthongization, given in (9); the presence of an /i/ in the morphology of weak verbs of this class can be independently motivated.

(9) $ə \rightarrow \varnothing \ / \ V \underline{\qquad} C_0 \ i$

But in the strong verbs, exemplified by *-weorpan* 'throw down' in (7c), *i*-Monophthongization fails to apply, although a potential triggering /i/ is present. We know that the vowel of the third person suffix *-eth* is underlyingly /i/ because it triggers other rules which apply before /i/, such as raising of the stem vowel /e/ of *forswelgan* 'devour' in (7d). A rule of *i*-Lowering lowers all underlying unstressed /i/s to *e*, giving the surface form of the suffix, *-eð*.

Another rule which often fails to apply in the strong verbs is *i*-Mutation, which fronts a stressed vowel when an /i/ follows in the next syllable.

(10) $V \rightarrow [-\text{back}] \ / \underline{\qquad} C_0 \ i$

Compare the derivations in (11) of the present indicative 3rd person singular of the strong verb *haldan* 'hold' and the weak verb *onhældan* 'lean down'. A rule of Retraction (8b) retracts *æ* to *a* before a back sonorant; then *i*-Mutation fronts the *a* in (11b) but fails in (11a).

(11) a. Strong verbs	b. Weak verbs	
/hæld+ið/	/-hæld+i+ið/	underlying
hald+ið	*-hald+i+ið*	Retraction
FAILS	*-hæld+i+ið*	*i*-Mutation
haldeð	*-hældeð*	other rules

We have thus seen a number of rules that fail in the strong verbs while applying in the weak verbs, nouns, and adjectives. If we assume noncyclic derivations of the sort illustrated above, it appears that this exceptional behavior is simply a property of the class of strong verbs: no phonological reason suggests itself. But there are interesting structural differences between strong and weak verbs which can be exploited by a lexical phonology. As is well known, strong verbs form their past tense by modification of the root (ablaut), while weak verbs add a dental past tense marker. More important to our analysis is another difference: weak verbs require a stem-forming extension in the form of a vowel. This extension is /i/ in weak Class I, and /a/ in weak Class II.

(12)

	Present	Past
Strong:	Root + AGR	Root (+Ablaut) + AGR
Weak:	Root + EXT + AGR	Root + EXT + TNS + AGR

EXT = /i/ in Class I, /a/ in Class II; TNS = /d/

Inspection of the various rules I have been discussing reveals a generalization: the rules in question fail when their environment crucially involves agreement (AGR); they do not fail when their context is the stem, that is, the root with extension if there is one. This is illustrated in (13a,b) for Smoothing.

(13)

a. Strong verbs	b. Weak verbs	c. Nouns	
sprec	*wæc-a*	*dæg*	stem domain
—	*wæac-a*	—	Back Mutation
—	*wæca*	—	Smoothing
sprec-an	*wæca-an*	*dæg-as*	word domain
spreoc-an	—	*dæag-as*	Back Mutation
FAILS	—	*dæg-as*	Smoothing
spreocan	*wæcian*	*dægas*	other rules

The same is true for the other rules, as shown in (14) and (15).

(14)

a. Strong verbs	b. Weak verbs	
werp	*scærp-i*	stem domain
weorp	*scæarp-i*	Breaking
—	*scærp-i*	*i*-Monophthongization
weorp-ið	*scærpi-d-un*	word domain
—	—	Breaking
FAILS	—	*i*-Monophthongization
weorpeð	*scerptun*	other rules

(15)

a. Strong verbs	b. Weak verbs	
hæld	*-hæld-i*	stem domain
hald	*-hald-i*	Retraction
—	*-hæld-i*	*i*-Mutation
hald-ið	*-hældi-ið*	word domain
—	—	Retraction
FAILS	—	*i*-Mutation
haldeð	*-hældeð*	other rules

We can account for the failure of the rules at word level by assuming that they do not operate at that level (cf. Kiparsky, 1985), as in (16).

(16) LEXICAL PHONOLOGY OF MERCIAN:[4]

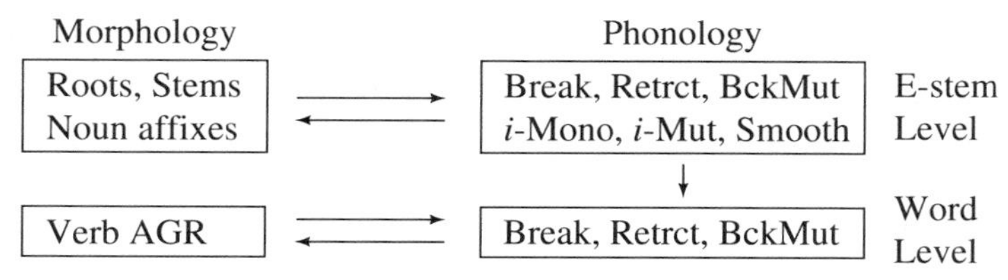

Something further must be said to account for the fact that nouns and adjectives undergo all the rules even when their context includes inflectional suffixes, as shown in (13c). Nouns and adjectives take suffixes indicating number, gender, and case. Noun inflectional suffixes act like verb stem extensions, in that Smoothing applies regularly. Evidently, the grammar does not treat noun inflection on a par with verb inflection. Thus for our purposes there is a domain which includes everything but agreement (AGR), that is, verb stems and nominals with number, gender, and person markings; I call this the E-STEM (for extended stem) level, as shown in (17).

(17) PHONOLOGICAL DOMAINS:

	Strong verbs	Weak verbs	Nouns
E-stem level:	*sprec*	*wæc-a*	*dæg-as*
Word level:	*sprec-an*	*wæca-an*	*dægas*

To sum up, a synchronic analysis of the Ps(A) dialect can account for much of the exceptionality of strong verbs by recognizing two lexical levels. The rules of Breaking, Retraction, and Back Mutation apply at both levels, while the rules of Smoothing, *i*-Monophthongization, and *i*-Mutation apply only at the E-stem Level.

4. RULES IN NONLINEAR PHONOLOGY

It is noteworthy that the three rules restricted to the E-stem level all share an interesting property: they all serve to undo the effects of other rules, a fact which becomes apparent when we consider their effects in parallel.

(18) RULE INTERACTION: E-STEM LEVEL:

	Input	Back Mutation	Smoothing
a.	*wæca*	*wæaca*	*wæca*

	Input	Breaking	*i*-Monophthongization
b.	*scærpi*	*scæarpi*	*scærpi*

c.	Input	Retraction	*i*-Mutation
	-hældi	*-haldi*	*-hældi*

The parallelism goes further, although it is obscured by the linear format in which the rules have been formulated. Consider the rule of Retraction (8b): this is a straightforward backness assimilation, in which the front low vowel *æ* is retracted to *a* before back sonorant consonants. Compare now Breaking (8a), which in a linear format looks quite different. However, diphthongization represents the addition of a back component to a front vowel when a back consonant follows. This, too, is a variant of backness assimilation. Breaking and Retraction occur under similar conditions: for example, where the Mercian dialect has Retraction before /l/ + consonant, as in (19a), West Saxon has breaking; hence Mercian *ald,* but West Saxon *æald,* both from **æld:*

(19) a. BREAKING AND RETRACTION:

Prim. OE:	**æld*	
Retraction:	*ald*	(Mercian)
Breaking:	*æald*	(West Saxon)

b. *a*-RESTORATION AND BACK MUTATION:

Prim. OE:	**hæfuc*	
a-Restoration:	*hafuc*	(West Saxon)
Back Mutation:	*hæafuc*	(Mercian)

Similar considerations hold for Back Mutation (2), which also creates diphthongs before back segments: in this case, the triggers are back vowels, and the rule can apply across an intervening consonant. Just as Breaking is paralleled by Retraction, there is a rule in West Saxon which operates in the same context as Back Mutation; but instead of turning a front vowel into a diphthong, it retracts it. This rule is called *a*-Restoration, and an example is given in (19b).

It is clear, then, that the diphthongization rules in question are a form of backness assimilation. In the case of Retraction (20), the assimilation is direct, in that the feature [BACK] spreads to the vowel. Breaking is similar (20b), the difference being that the spreading [BACK] is adjoined to the vowel, creating a diphthong. In these representations, *A* represents a low vowel apart from its specification for [BACK].[5]

(20) a. RETRACTION:

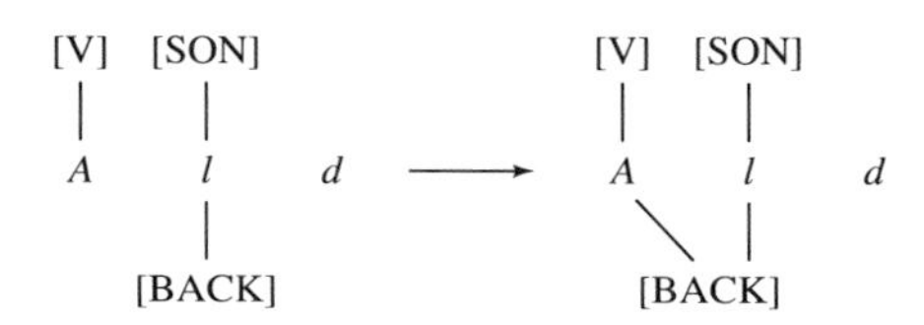

b. BREAKING:

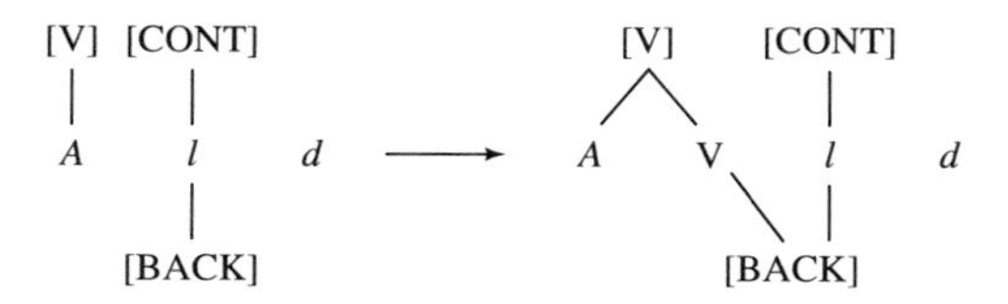

Similarly, *a*-Restoration and Back Mutation exemplify the two styles of propagation of [BACK] from a following vowel.

(21) a. *a*–RESTORATION:

```
   [V]  [V]                 [V]  [V]
    |    |                   |    |
f   A  t u      ------>   f  A  t u
         |                    \  /
      [BACK]                 [BACK]
```

b. BACK MUTATION:

```
   [V]  [V]                 [V]       [V]
    |    |                  / \        |
f   A  t u      ------>   f A  V   t   u
         |                      \     /
      [BACK]                     [BACK]
```

Let us turn now to the rules which apply only at the E-stem level of the lexical phonology. We observe immediately that *i*-Monophthongization and *i*-Mutation can now be subsumed under a single generalization, namely, delink a specification [BACK] to the left of /i/. This will have the effect of fronting a back vowel and voiding the second part of a diphthong. (Recall that the second element of a diphthong occupies no slot of its own [i.e., has no moraic value], so the loss of [BACK] causes it to meld into the front vowel.) We will call this unified rule *i*-Umlaut; its effects are illustrated in (22).

(22) *i*–UMLAUT:

a. *i*–Mutation:

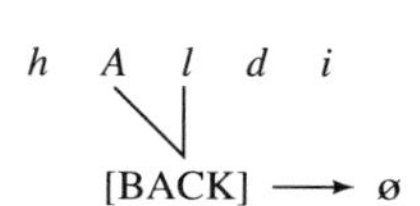

b. *i*–Monophthongization:

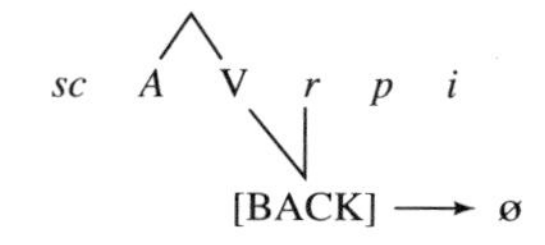

This leaves Smoothing. Up to now, all the rules we have been looking at have involved some kind of backness assimilation. By contrast, Smoothing removes a back diphthongal element before a back consonant and so appears to be a dissimilation rule, applying moreover, in some of the same contexts which cause backing.

Hogg (1992: §§ 93–102), in an interesting discussion of this issue, proposes that the consonants which caused Smoothing were by this time no longer velar but palatal, specified [– back]. Smoothing is thus brought into the fold of natural assimilation rules: monophthongization is treated as a type of fronting, triggered by a following [– back] feature.

There are a number of problems with this approach, however. First, Hogg's analysis needs a rather baroque mechanism of feature spreading to spread the feature [– back] from the first part of the diphthong onto the following velar consonant, vaulting over the intervening [+back] of the second part of the diphthong. Second, there is no clear evidence that the required palatalization ever occurred. Counting against it is the fact that in the same period when these consonants were causing Smoothing, they were also beginning to exercise a backing influence on low vowels, as shown by the forms in (23) from Ps(A).

(23) INCIPIENT GENERALIZED RETRACTION BEFORE VELARS [Ps(A)]

	Number of tokens with		
Form	*æ*	*e*	*a*
mæht	18		3
dæg	41	6	1
asagas	—		1
mægan	5		1
**plægian*	2		1
ah	—		44

We find the word *mæht* 18 times with the expected *æ,* but 3 times with *a; asagas* appears once, and it has *a* before *g* rather than the expected *æ,* and so on. The number of instances of *a* is not great, but there are more than we would expect as simply the result of scribal error. These occurrences gain in significance when we consider that in the Middle English dialect of *The Life and the Passion of Ste. Juliana,* considered a descendant of the Ps(A) dialect, we find that earlier *æ* generally became *a* before back consonants: *cwakien* 'quake' [Ps(A) *cwæcian*], *ahte* 'wealth' [Ps(A) *æhte*], *mahte* 'might' [Ps(A) *mæht*], and so on (d'Ardenne 1961: 182). Therefore we can consider the sporadic *a* spellings to indicate the beginning of the generalization of Retraction: originally triggered by back sonorants, Retraction is being generalized to occur before all back consonants. This account of Generalized Retraction requires that the same consonants which are responsible for Smoothing remained velar. Therefore assuming an intermediate stage of palatalized consonants to account for Smoothing will prevent us from giving a natural account of Generalized Retraction.

Let us return, then, to the idea that the consonants causing Smoothing did indeed remain velar, that is, [BACK], and reconsider rather the equation of monophthongization with fronting. While it is true that diphthongization is a species of backing, it does not thereby follow that monophthongization is always a species of fronting. It is important to note that, unlike *i*-Umlaut, the consonants which cause Smoothing do not ever cause fronting of a vowel. In terms of nonlinear representations, Smoothing never causes the feature [BACK] to be erased; rather, it simply delinks the feature from a diphthong, causing the loss of its second part, as shown in (24).

(24)

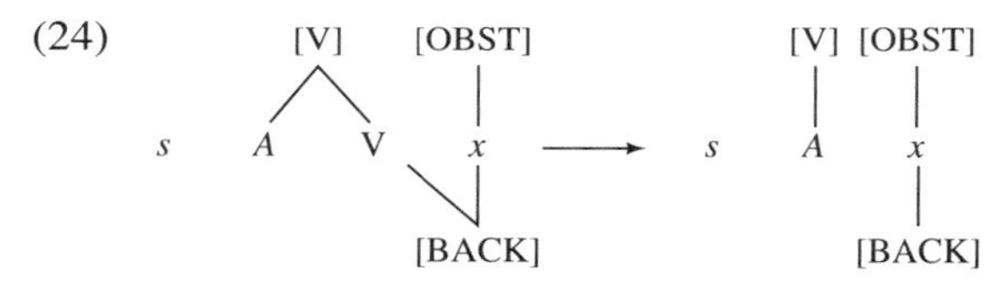

This delinking of a multiply-linked feature is a kind of OCP effect, in that it simplifies the transition from a front to a back element.[6] This is not an unnatural process, and so it is not necessary to suppose that Smoothing before a back consonant is paradoxical or problematic.[7]

5. RULES OR CONSTRAINTS

Having now recast the various rules into nonlinear terms, let us return to the E-stem level and the rules that are limited to that level. I began with three rules. I then united the two rules conditioned by /i/ into one rule of *i*-Umlaut. I can now generalize the parallelism in the derivations in (18): in each case a rule which spreads [BACK] to a stressed vowel is reversed, the [BACK] feature being delinked.

(25)	Input	Add BACK	Remove BACK
a.	*wæca*	*wæaca*	*wæca*
b.	*scærpi*	*scæarpi*	*scærpi*
c.	*-hældi*	*-haldi*	*-hældi*

The nature of these derivations suggests a reanalysis: instead of spreading [BACK] and then delinking it, why not block the spreading to begin with?[8] In classical generative phonology, there are a number of ways of doing this, but they all have drawbacks. One way is to simply exclude the restricted context from the rule directly, but this usually requires a more complicated rule. In this case, we can stipulate in the formulation of Back Mutation, for example, that spreading may not occur across a back consonant, thus incorporating Smoothing into the process. But this not only complicates the rule; it also misses the generalization that no diphthongs from any source are allowed in that context.

Another approach is to invoke metarules, persistent rules, filters, constraints, or, as they were once called, conspiracies. Work in lexical phonology has suggested a number of constraints on derivations, such as structure preservation, and has articulated a notion of levels or domains within which such constraints are in force or are turned off. From another direction, the representations and operations of nonlinear phonology lend themselves quite naturally to a theory in which configurational constraints and well-formedness conditions play a large role.[9]

Let us return, then, to the rules which are restricted to the E-stem level, namely Smoothing and *i*-Umlaut. We observe that we can reinterpret them as constraints, whereby the configurations in (26) are ruled out.

(26) a. Smoothing b. *i.*–Umlaut

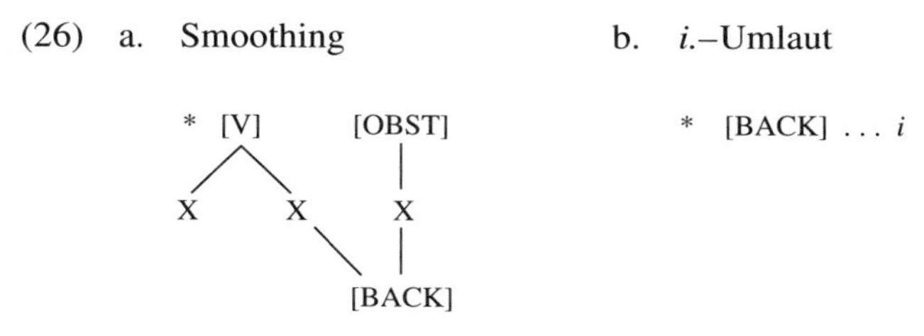

We assume that these constraints serve to block any rule that would create a violation of them. These constraints hold in the lexicon at the E-stem level but are turned off at the Word level, deriving the facts we observe in Ps(A).

6. LEXICAL PHONOLOGY AND DIACHRONY

We have thus arrived at an analysis which gives a better account of the synchronic facts as we find them, and the stage is now set for a better understanding of the diachronic developments as well. The following scenario suggests itself: Smoothing, whatever its original status, came to be interpreted as a constraint in the lexical phonology, that is, as a persistent rule, which like other such rules remains in force up to the Word level. Back Mutation was then added to the grammar; if it was not a lexical rule to begin with, it soon became one. As such, it was subject to the Smoothing constraint up to the Word level but was unimpeded by it thereafter.

7. CONCLUSION

This analysis makes sense of the synchronic and diachronic facts. Many questions remain, however, and I only raise three of them here.

First, it would be desirable to find independent evidence for the E-stem domain, in terms of either cross-linguistic or language-particular evidence from Old English.

A more general question concerns persistent rules, which have been appearing more and more in the literature. Basically, the difference between a rule and a persistent rule, or constraint, is that a rule has one chance to apply in a cycle, while a constraint can apply after, or during, every other rule. But in a theory with both kinds of rules, how do we distinguish one from the other? Why not make all the backing rules constraints also, say *[BACK] unlinked to stressed V in certain configurations? Of course, if everything is a constraint, we can no longer account for the apparent ordering, or the differences in level of application (E-stem and Word levels for backing rules, E-stem only for the others). We observe that, as formulated, the difference is between rules that spread a feature and rules that do not. Perhaps that plays a role in making the distinction.

Third, the constraints in (26) have been cast as filters, blocking devices which prevent certain configurations from arising. It is also possible to have persistent rules in the sense of Myers (1991): these have the format of rules but apply whenever their structural description is met. Rather than block the application of other rules, such rules act to repair any constraint violations as soon as they occur. It is difficult to determine whether the constraints in (26) have a blocking or repair function, as the two modes of application lead to the same results in the cases discussed here.

Despite these unresolved issues, it is nevertheless clear that current theories offer new and interesting perspectives on diachronic change.

ACKNOWLEDGMENTS

I would like to thank Peter Avery, Alana Johns, Keren Rice, Tom Wilson, and an anonymous referee for helpful comments.

NOTES

[1]For more on the language and texts, see Brunner (1965), Campbell (1959), Dresher (1978), Hogg (1992), Kuhn (1965), Luick (1964), and Toon (1983).

[2]Note that Old English texts typically spell the low diphthong [æa] as *ea*. There is little doubt that this was purely an orthographic convention, and for ease of exposition, I indicate it as *æa*.

[3]See Kiparsky (1988) for a review of Neogrammarian and contemporary issues in phonological change.

[4]The diagram allows for cyclic levels, but I have not shown this; the Word Level especially may not be cyclic.

[5]The representations in (20) and subsequently are schematic, and much structure is omitted. Gussenhoven and van de Weijer (1990) consider the spreading feature to be [+dorsal].

[6]Strictly speaking, this is what McCarthy (1989) calls anti-spreading, which often works together with the OCP to enforce cooccurrence restrictions.

[7]An anonymous referee suggests that Smoothing may have begun in fast speech, where the listener might be likely to interpret the second part of the diphthong as a mere formant transition to the consonant. Translating this perception backward to phonemic representations gives the effect of monophthongization. It is noteworthy in this connection that Brunner (1965) proposed that Smoothing is orthographic only, because the backness of the second part of the diphthong was already conveyed by the following consonant. I see no reason, however, to limit this effect to the orthography.

[8]We thus return in a way to Luick's suggestion that Back Mutation was prevented before velar consonants.

[9]See Singh (1987), Paradis (1988), Goldsmith (1990: Ch. 6), and Myers (1991) for recent proposals.

REFERENCES

d'Ardenne, S. R. T. O. (1961). *Þe liflade ant te passiun of seinte Iuliene* (Early English Text Society 248). Oxford University Press, London.

Ball, C. J. E., and Stiles, P. (1983). The derivation of Old English *geolu* 'yellow', and the relative chronology of smoothing and back-mutation. *Anglia* **101,** 5–28.

Brunner, K. (1965). *Altenglische Grammatik: Nach der Angelsächsischen Grammatik von Eduard Sievers,* 3rd ed. Niemeyer, Tübingen.

Campbell, A. (1959). *Old English Grammar.* Clarendon, Oxford.

Chomsky, N., and Halle, M. (1968). *The Sound Pattern of English.* Harper and Row, New York.

Dresher, B. E. (1978). *Old English and the Theory of Phonology.* Doctoral dissertation, University of Massachusetts, Amherst.

Goldsmith, J. A. (1990). *Autosegmental and Metrical Phonology.* Blackwell, Oxford.

Gussenhoven, C., and van de Weijer, J. (1990). On V-place spreading vs. feature spreading in English historical phonology. *The Linguistic Review* **7,** 311–332.

Hogg, R. M. (1992). *A Grammar of Old English. Vol. I: Phonology.* Blackwell, Oxford.

Kiparsky, P. (1973). Abstractness, opacity, and global rules. Part 2 of "Phonological Representations." In *Three Dimensions of Linguistic Theory* (O. Fujimura, ed.), pp. 57–86. TEC, Tokyo.

Kiparsky, P. (1985). Some consequences of lexical phonology. *Phonology Yearbook* **2,** 85–138.

Kiparsky, P. (1988). Phonological change. In *Linguistics: The Cambridge Survey. Vol. 1: Linguistic Theory: Foundations* (F. J. Newmeyer, ed.), pp. 363–415. Cambridge University Press, Cambridge.

Kuhn, S. M. (1965). *The Vespasian Psalter.* University of Michigan Press, Ann Arbor.

Luick, K. (1964). *Historische Grammatik der englischen Sprache.* Blackwell, Oxford.

McCarthy, J. J. (1989). *Guttural Phonology.* Unpublished manuscript, University of Massachusetts, Amherst.

Myers, S. (1991). Persistent rules. *Linguistic Inquiry* **22,** 315–344.

Paradis, C. (1988). On constraints and repair strategies. *The Linguistic Review* **6,** 71–97.

Singh, R. (1987). Well-formedness conditions and phonological theory. In *Phonologica 1984* (W. U. Dressler et al., eds.). Cambridge University Press, Cambridge.

Toon, T. E. (1983). *The Politics of Early Old English Sound Change.* Academic Press, New York.

RULE REORDERING AND RULE GENERALIZATION IN LEXICAL PHONOLOGY: A RECONSIDERATION

ELLEN M. KAISSE

Department of Linguistics
University of Washington
Seattle, Washington 98195

1. INTRODUCTION

How do grammars change from one generation to the next? The question engaged generative linguists deeply in the late 1960s and early 1970s. Interest in the theoretical characterization of sound change has since diminished, as the larger investigative paradigm has turned from rules, derivations, abstractness, and underlying forms to phonological representations and constraints. But many important and, in some cases, surprising results were achieved in the seventies and it is time to reconsider them in the light of a paradigm which has much new to tell us about rule ordering and rule types: the theory of lexical phonology, which forms the subject of this volume. The impetus for my reexamination of historical phenomena comes from Kiparsky's (1988) article surveying phonological change from the perspective of recent developments in phonological theory. In the latter part of this article, Kiparsky resolves the "Neogrammarian controversy" in a very satisfying way: he argues that changes in postlexical rules will result in sound changes which are regular, phonologically motivated, and in general obedient to the Neogrammarian hypothesis. But changes and additions to lexical rules will yield sound changes with exceptions, sensitivity to word structure, and so on, the hallmarks of lexical diffusion. If lexical phonology can strike to the heart of issues like this, which have caused consternation and strife among linguists for over a

Phonetics and Phonology, Volume 4
Studies in Lexical Phonology

century, it is obviously time to reconsider the other things we have learned about historical change in the terms of the theory. I make a small beginning here.

I consider two results of the diachronic investigations of the last twenty years and attempt to refine or explain them within the theory of lexical phonology. The first, which I refine, is the result that rules can be reordered with respect to one another and thus can be found out of their chronologically correct arrangement. We shall see that lexical phonology, with its ability to characterize a rule's position in the phonology by its characteristics, allows us a window into how and where rules move. Investigators of two decades ago could not ask some rather interesting questions about rule reordering, namely, which rule is moving, and where exactly is it ending up? But the divisions between strata and between lexical and postlexical rules now allow us to identify a rule's location not only by its order with respect to other rules but by a whole suite of other characteristics. We can now determine if a rule has moved from one stratum to another or even, in the case of a reordering in Cypriot Greek, from the lexical component to the postlexical component or the word level.

The second result that I reexamine is the somewhat astonishing conclusion, independently arrived at by two investigators (Bley-Vroman, 1975; Robinson, 1976), that when a rule generalizes, it does not do so in place, but rather at the end of the grammar, leaving its ungeneralized progenitor behind in its original position. Robinson terms a rule which has generalized in this way SCATTERED. I show that this apparently paradoxical rule ordering, with its odd displacement of the generalized form of a rule, in fact flows rather naturally from the conception of the grammar that is central to the lexical phonology model and is related to the increased access to feature specifications that rules may have as they apply at later levels. Once we have established that rules can move "down" in the grammar, and even out of the lexicon, we shall have an explanation for why rules do not appear to generalize in place. Ultimately, we can hope to explain a large class of rule generalizations as the result of reordering and the progressive specification of features. Moreover, we will have a clearer view of the progress of a rule through the grammar over time.

The direction of movement of a rule over time has been widely and correctly agreed to be "upward" (see Kiparsky, 1984, 1988, and references cited in the latter, and Zec, this volume): sound changes begin as variable rules of phonetic implementation, are gradually grammaticized as postlexical rules, and move into the lexicon as they are incorporated into the grammar, acquiring exceptions, reference to morphological information, a cyclic mode of application, and so forth. When we look in detail at the history of a rule of continuancy dissimilation in Cypriot Greek, we shall see an example of a rule that, having undergone the usual upward progression, has now moved DOWN again in the grammar, though reordering. Using the theory of underspecification, we shall see that a reordered rule should be expected to come to refer to feature values unavailable in the early strata of the lexicon (perhaps available only postlexically). Finally, we briefly reexamine one published case of rule "scattering" (Robinson, 1976) and one less familiar one (Kaisse, 1976) in terms of underspecification and lexical phonology and conclude that movement to a later stratum or component can explain the phenomenon of rule generalization that leaves behind the old version of the rule.[1]

It is possible that the two directions of movement for rules that I postulate can reconcile the opposite claims of Kiparsky (1984) and Halle and Mohanan (1985) with respect to the strong domain hypothesis. Halle and Mohanan (p. 58) state the following "Principles of Domain Assignment":

> a. In the absence of counterevidence, assign the smallest number of strata as the domain of a rule.
> b. In the absence of counterevidence, assign the highest possible stratum as the domain of a rule (where 'lowest' = stratum 1).

Given these assumptions, in the unmarked case all phonological rules apply at the postlexical stratum (b) and only at that stratum (a). We do not know at present whether there in fact exist languages where all phonological rules are restricted to the postlexical stratum. A footnote reads:

> Principles 1a,b are of course not the only ones conceivable. Alternatively, one might think of the following principles: (a) In the absence of counterevidence, assign the maximum number of strata as the domain of a rule. (b) In the absence of counterevidence, assign the lowest stratum as the domain of a rule.

The footnote implies that Halle and Mohanan have chosen their principles of domain assignment with some uncertainty. In any case, they give neither empirical not theoretical arguments for the choice they have made. In fact, Kiparsky (1984: 141ff.) makes almost precisely the opposite choice, assuming that the unmarked rule applies at Level 1 and that rules do not belong to particular domains unless explicitly restricted.

These issues, I would argue, cannot be understood nor resolved without taking historical factors into account. Halle and Mohanan are almost certainly correct if we are talking about rules near the beginning of their histories. Kiparsky indeed agrees that new rules are added as exceptionless postlexical ones. But as a rule ages, it extends its domain upward to earlier strata within the lexicon, perhaps curtailing its postlexical application as it moves. Thus the endpoint of a phonological rule is to be expected to be stratum 1, with the earlier strata the rule passed through possibly also subject to its action. Thus for older rules, Kiparsky is probably correct. Moreover I submit that parts (a) and (b) of Halle and Mohanan's principles are independent: we do not know the circumstances under which a rule will maintain its chronologically earlier, low-level domains of application while adding lexical ones. A rule might extend its domain upward while simultaneously shrinking its applicability in later strata. Similarly, rules might re-descend through the grammar, either extending their domains, so as to apply in early and late strata as well, or, instead, forsaking the older, earlier strata. The first type of descent should result in "sandwich" type rule application, where a newly extended rule can apply both before and after another rule. This is a characteristic part of the "scattered" rule phenomenon. The second type of descent will result in a rule which we describe as having "moved" or "reordered," for instance the Cypriot case of Section 3.

2. EXTENSION DOWNWARD OF MORPHOLOGICAL DOMAIN: KASKA *s*-DELETION

Before we turn to our central example from Cypriot Greek, let us consider a similar but simpler case (since it involves only one rule) from the Athabaskan language Kaska (Hargus, personal communication 1989, based on data from Moore, 1988). Like other Athabaskan languages, Kaska has an intricate set of prefixes which Athabaskanists divide into two sets: disjunct prefixes (those farthest from the stem, consisting largely of adverbial material) and conjunct prefixes, those closer to the stem, which include agreement and tense morphemes. The conjunct prefixes are further subdivided into sets, partially on the basis of their phonological behavior. (Most Athabaskanists recognize two divisions within the conjunct prefixes, but Hargus argues for three in Sekani.) Hargus (1988) argues that the outermost set of Sekani conjunct prefixes is added at level IV while the inner sets are added at levels II and III.

(1) $_{\text{V}}$[disjunct $_{\text{IV}}$[conjunct $_{\text{III}}$[conjunct $_{\text{II}}$[conjunct $_{\text{I}}$[stem

In all the languages of the family except Kaska, a rule of intervocalic deletion which deletes the /s/ of the conjunct prefix *ʔs(ə) (> s(ə) plus a distinctive tone in the daughter languages) applies only if the /s/ and the determinant vowels occur within stratum II; vowel-final prefixes added later, at stratum III, IV, or V do not supply the intervocalic environment for the rule to operate. Thus in the following examples from Sekani, /s/ is deleted in (2a,b) but not in (2c); in the former cases, the thematic prefix /zə/ and the inceptive prefix /də/ are shown by Hargus (1988) to fall within the level II morphology, while in the last case, the preceding prefix, /nə/ '2-sg. object', is in the level III conjunct prefixes.[2]

(2) a. /zə -ˋs-i-h-xį/ → [zěhxį] 'I kill (sg. obj.)'
thm-cnj-1sPf-clf-kill
b. /də-ˋs-i-ya/ → [děya] 'I started to walk'
incp-cnj-1sPf-go
c. /nə-ˋs-i-č'ǫ/ → [nə̀sič'ǫ] 'I shot you dead'
2sObj-cnj-1sPf-shoot'

Thus the extent of *s*-Deletion's domain in Sekani and the other Athabaskan languages is as illustrated in (3).

(3) I. stem } *S*-Deletion
II. conjunct prefixes }
III. conjunct prefixes
IV. conjunct prefixes
V. disjunct prefixes

In Kaska, however, the domain of *s*-deletion is extended to the environment between level III conjunct prefixes and the following material as well. Object pronouns in level III now trigger deletion of a following conjunct /s/. The critical comparison is between (2c) and the Kaska cognate in (4c). (4a,b) show that the Kaska rule continues to apply, as in Sekani, between a thematic level II prefix and the conjunct prefix, which Moore transcribes as /se/. (The [s] which appears in (4a,c) is the first person singular marker. I include a second person form in (4b) for comparison.)

(4) a. /de-\`se-s-h-hīn/ → *dêshīn*
thm-cnj-1sSub-clf-kill 'I kill sg. object'
b. de-\`se-n-tsīn/ → *dêntsīn*
thm-cnj-2sSub-make 'you made it for yourself'
c. /ne-\`se-'s-un'/ → *nes'un*
2sgObj-cnj-1sgSub-shoot 'I shot you'

So we see that it is possible for a phonological rule to reverse the normal historical progression upward to earlier strata and extend its domain. Indeed, in a survey of such changes in Athabaskan, Hargus (personal communication, 1989) finds no domain shrinking, several rules whose domain has been extended, several which are lost, and a few which have acquired morphological restrictions but not via domain shrinking. In fact, extension of a rule's morphological domain makes sense in terms of an increase in transparency: the rule applies increasingly where its phonological structural description is met. We shall see that transparency is also maximized in the Cypriot dialect by a reordering into feeding order.

Dumas's (1981) account of the development of vowel lengthening in Quebecois French appears to be another example of the downward movement of a phonological rule, in this case into the postlexical component.[3] While standard French lengthens the class of vowels which Dumas terms "tense" (higher mid vowels and nasalized vowels) in closed syllables only, Québecois lengthens these vowels in any syllable whatsoever, so long as the vowel is not absolutely sentence-final. Thus the rule has generalized, in losing the closed syllable requirement from its environment and, crucially, has become postlexical, since information about position in the utterance is not available within the lexicon. We see the logical connection between generalization and downward movement in later sections.

3. RULE REORDERING AND GENERALIZATION IN CYPRIOT GREEK

3.1. Continuant Dissimilation

A fairly simple generalization governs the distribution of obstruent clusters in all Modern Greek dialects: adjacent obstruents may not agree in continuancy. There is much to say about this rule (see Kaisse, 1989), but for our purposes, all we need to know is that it takes any sequence of stop plus stop or of fricative plus fricative and turns it into a sequence of fricative plus stop. Moreover, in the rare cases where a stop plus fricative sequence arises, both continuancy values are changed, yielding fricative plus stop; this fact suggests the existence of a template imposed as in (5) and indicates that the rule is not only dissimilatory, though this is certainly the effect it has in the vast majority of cases.

(5)

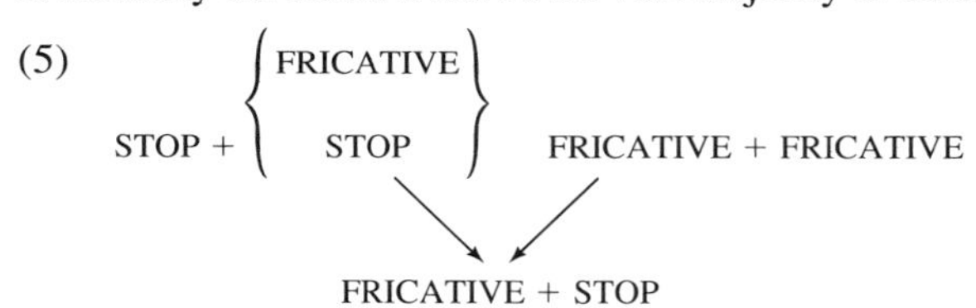

One's initial guess might be that Continuant Dissimilation is a syllable-based adjustment in sonority, but because it happens in onset clusters as well as between syllables, I reject this idea.

Since the subrules affecting stops and affecting fricatives cannot be collapsed using normal abbreviatory devices, and since, as I noted, sequences of stop plus fricative are also altered to fricative plus stop, I argue in Kaisse (1989) that the rule should be formalized as in (6).

(6) αcont βcont $\rightarrow$ +cont −cont

Here are examples of the application of the expansion of the rule where both α and β are set to minus, that is, where two stops come together.

(7) a. *ek-timo* → *extimo* 'esteem'
out-honor
b. *pep-to* → *pefto* 'fall'
fall-vbl
d. **okto* > *oxto* 'eight'

Fricativization of stops is clearly a lexical rule in standard Spoken Modern Greek, for it applies differently in different morphological environments and has exceptions in some of them. The rule is obligatory between stem and suffix and has applied invariably as a historical change within morphemes. (The fact that it is thus a morpheme structure condition on words of the spoken language thus argues for both values of continuancy being available in underlying representations.) However, between prefix and stem, fricativization applies to only some words. Consider the realizations of the prefix /ek/ exemplified in (7a). While the [x] there is the preferred colloquial pronunciation, phonologically similar words like *ektelo* 'carry out' cannot be spirantized for my informant. (I would expect just which words will and will not spirantize to differ among speakers to some extent.)

The operation of Despirantization, that is, the expansion of Continuant Dissimilation when α and β are set to plus, is illustrated in (8).

(8) a. *γraf-θike* → *γraftike* 'it was written'
b. *ef-xaristo* → *efkaristo* 'thank you'

Again, the rule operates differently at prefix–stem than at stem–suffix boundary. It is obligatory for all speakers (in colloquial speech) in the former environment, but only some speakers do it between prefix and stem. (Thumb, 1964, reports the form I give for 'thank you' and I have heard this myself, but my major informant shudders at it.) The despirantization portion of Continuant Dissimilation may be lexical by the test of failure to apply between words, but one is hard pressed to find examples which can argue this one way or the other. Unhappily, Greek words do not normally end in any obstruent except /s/, and /s/ is problematical.[4] However, if we are willing to consider despirantization after /s/ to be effected by the Continuant Dissimilation rule, we observe that interword application fails to occur: *tis θalassas* 'the seas' cannot become **tis talassas.*

Here are a few examples with reversal of stop plus fricative.

(9) a. /plek-θike/ → *plextike* 'it was knitted'
(cf. *plekete* 'it is knitted')
b. /para-lip-θika/ → *paraliftika* 'I was neglected'
(cf. *paralipome* 'I am neglected')

It is critical for the development of our argument that in every dialect of Modern Greek of which I am aware (Thumb, 1964, and Newton, 1972b, are remarkably complete and reliable sources), Continuant Dissimilation fails to apply in two cases where one might have expected it would: it does not apply to voiced fricatives and it does not apply to anything other than obstruents. The sole and telling exception to this generalization is Cypriot, to which I turn in the next section. The following examples from the standard dialect show sequences of voiced fricatives which regularly fail to show dissimilation and sequences of /r/ + fricative, where

/r/ is presumably [+continuant] on the surface (Halle and Clements, 1983) yet does not condition dissimilation.

(10) a. *avγo* ‘egg’
b. *vγ-o* ‘go out’
c. *erxete* ‘he comes’

In Kaisse (1989) I show that both these restrictions follow from the same thing: neither voiced fricatives nor sonorants are underlyingly specified for continuancy. This in turn follows from the theory of contrastive underspecification (Steriade, 1987). The lack of specification for sonorants is perhaps the more obvious of these two: Modern Greek, like most languages, does not use continuancy as the sole feature which distinguishes any pair of sonorants. There are, for instance, no fricative laterals or nasals in the language. Nasals, /l/, and /r/ are thus distinguishable by the features [nasal] and [lateral]. But what of my assertion that continuancy is not distinctive for voiced fricatives? This follows from the rather marked system of obstruents in Greek. There are underlying voiceless stops and there are both voiced and voiceless fricatives, but there are no voiced stops.[5] Thus voicing is distinctive for fricatives (but not for stops), while continuancy is distinctive for voiceless obstruents but not for voiced ones. Any voiced obstruent is redundantly [+continuant].

(11) CONTRASTIVELY UNDERSPECIFIED MATRICES FOR GREEK (lexicon) AND FULLY SPECIFIED (postlexicon):

	lexical						postlexical					
	t	θ	ð	n	l	r	t	θ	ð	n	l	r
vc		–	+				–	–	+	+	+	+
cnt	–	+					–	+	+	–	–	+
son	–	–	–	+	+	+	–	–	–	+	+	+
lat				–	+	–	–	–	–	–	+	–
nas				+	–	–	–	–	–	+	–	–

(12) REDUNDANCY RULES:

a. $+\text{son} \rightarrow +\text{vc}$

b. $-\text{son} \rightarrow \begin{bmatrix} -\text{lat} \\ -\text{nas} \end{bmatrix}$

c. $+\text{nas} \rightarrow -\text{cont}$

d. $+\text{lat} \rightarrow -\text{cont}$

e. $\begin{bmatrix} -\text{lat} \\ +\text{son} \end{bmatrix} \rightarrow +\text{cont}$

f. $\begin{bmatrix} -\text{son} \\ -\text{cont} \end{bmatrix} \rightarrow -\text{vc}$

g. $\begin{bmatrix} -\text{son} \\ +\text{vc} \end{bmatrix} \rightarrow +\text{cont}$

The redundant specifications for continuancy of the liquids (12d,e) will be important in the upcoming discussion and deserve some mention here. As I said, Halle and Clements (1983), by slightly modifying the Chomsky and Halle (1968) definition of continuancy, define /l/ as [−continuant] while /r/ is [+continuant]. Though they do not provide empirical evidence, I imagine that they have the following sorts of phenomena in mind. In many dialects of Spanish, voiced stops are realized as fricatives between vowels and also between an /r/ and a vowel. The process thus appears to be a spread of continuancy. Between nasals and a vowel or, crucially, between /l/ and a vowel, the stops emerge as stops.[6] Thus the lateral, like the nasals, behaves as a noncontinuant sonorant. Similarly, in Korean, underlying /l/ is realized as /r/ before a vowel. Here, /r/ appears as the result of continuancy spread. And Clements has himself worked on the distribution of intrusive stops in English, which, in some dialects, appear after a nasal or lateral but not after /r/. We shall see that the Cypriot liquids also give evidence for these opposing values of continuancy for /l/ and /r/.

3.2. The Obstruentization of /y/ in Cypriot

One of the striking facts about the Cypriot dialect is that it turns /y/ to the voiceless palatal stop [k^y] after a consonant. (After /r/, /y/ becomes [k]).[7] Informally,

(13) $y \rightarrow k^y$ / C ____

The following examples show alternations induced by the rule, involving, as they do, underlying /i/s which lose their syllabicity before another vowel and thus become subject to obstruentization.

(14) a. *aðelfi* 'brother'
b. /aðelfi+a/ (→ *aðelfya*) → *aðelfk^{y}a* 'brothers'
c. *teri* 'one of a pair'
d. /teri+azo/ (→ *teryazo*) → *terkazo* 'to match'

Just what needs to be specified in the formalization of the rule in uncertain—for instance, is the consonantality of the preceding C spreading with all the other changes following from redundancy rules? Is continuancy the critical change? Since /y/ is obstruentized after /r/ as well as after other obstruents, the purest form of the rule appears to involve spread of the feature [consonantal] only, with other features explained through redundancy or other means. The noncontinuancy of the output may even stem from the further operation of the continuancy template upon this new consonant, which is, of course, always in the second position of a consonant cluster. However, these issues are orthogonal to our main point, and I leave them unresolved here.[8]

(15) Obstruentization of *y:*

$$\begin{bmatrix} -\text{cons} \\ -\text{obst} \\ +\text{cont} \\ +\text{hi} \\ -\text{bk} \end{bmatrix} \rightarrow \begin{bmatrix} +\text{cons} \\ +\text{obst} \\ -\text{cont} \\ -\text{vc} \end{bmatrix} / \text{ C } \_\_\_$$

Now consider what happens when the consonant triggering Obstruentization is a stop: that stop itself becomes available as a focus for Continuant Dissimilation. In other words, there is a new, innovative feeding order between Obstruentization and Continuant Dissimilation.

(16)					
a.	*mati*	'eye'	$ma\theta k^y a$	'eyes'
b.	*spiti*	'house'	$spi\theta k^y a$	'houses'
c.	/pi/	'drink'	$nafk^y o$	'let me drink'

The following derivation illustrates this new order.

(17) /spiti + a/	
spitya	Glide Formation
$spitk^y a$	Obstruentization of *y*
$spi\theta k^y a$	Continuant Dissimilation

Continuant Dissimilation is an old pan-Greek rule, while Obstruentization of *y* is a relatively new innovation of Cyprus only. Because it is a well-recognized result of generative historical linguistics that rules are not added in the middles of grammars (King 1973),[9] and that new rules are added at the ends of grammars, we conclude that the synchronic order reflects a classic (Kiparsky, 1965, 1968) reordering into feeding order. But which rule moved where? Did Obstruentization move up or did Dissimilation move down? Or did they switch? If Continuant Dissimilation moved, how far "down" did it go? The answer I shall give is: Dissimilation moved down, most likely into the postlexical component, at least into a very late level of the lexicon where redundant feature values become available. (18) also incorporates the speculation that Obstruentization is lexical, since it applies before redundant values for voicing are assigned. This placement is upheld by the failure of any source on the dialect to cite application of Obstruentization between words.

(18)	I (Pan-Greek)	II (Proto-Cypriot)	III (Cypriot)
Lexicon:	Dissimilation	Dissimilation	
			Obstruentization
		Obstruentization	
Postlexicon:			Dissimilation

3.3. Motivation for Continuant Dissimilation in the Postlexical Component

Four seemingly unrelated changes in the Continuant Dissimilation rule in Cypriot argue that it has moved later in the grammar than in other dialects. The rule has generalized with voiced fricatives as either focus or determinant [illustrated in (19)] and with /r/ as determinant (20). Moreover, two previously apparently unrelated peculiarities about Cypriot come into focus: where other Greek dialects have *l* before a consonant (or where Cypriot has a borrowed word with the etymological sequence *l* + C), Cypriot has *r* (21). Furthermore, there are sporadic changes that go in the opposite direction, turning *r* to *l*. But those changes take place only when the original *r* is in the second (or final) position of a consonant cluster (22). I note the last phenomenon through a close reading of Kahane and Kahane's (1987) survey of the Cypriot vocabulary. *l*'s and *r*'s in other environments are stable in all 127 Cypriotisms cited in Kahane and Kahane, of which about 92 contain at least one instance of *l* or *r*. In other words, Cypriot does not show a random confusion of borrowed *l* and *r*. The only places where one is substituted for the other is in consonant clusters where the template [+continuant] [−continuant] will be instantiated [or, in the case of (21e, 22), approximated by giving the liquid the correct value for its position in the consonant cluster]. Incidentally, Kahane and Kahane speculate that the [l] in *spliverin* (22a) comes from dissimilation from the following [r]. But my reading of their vocabulary yields several words with two /r/s which do NOT dissimilate. The nondissimilating /r/s are in clusters where their continuancy value is already correct (*kourkourizi* 'rumble'). I conclude that dissimilation is neither a necessary nor a sufficient condition for the change of a liquid.

Where no source language is given below, the form on the left represents the reflexes found in non-Cypriot Greek dialects, which are conservative with respect to the consonantism. The final /n/s found in the Cypriot forms are a morphological conservatism, not relevant to our point here.

(19) a. *ravði* > *ravdin* 'stick'
b. *avγo* > *avgon* 'egg'
c. *evðomaða* > *evdomaða* 'week'

(20) a. *erxete* > *erkete* 'he comes'
b. *arxi* > *arki* ~ *arči* 'beginning'

(21) a. *belki* (Turk.) > *berki* 'perhaps'
b. *balkone* (Ital.) > *parkonin* 'balcony'
c. *poltos* (Anc.Gk.) > *portos* 'sweetmeat'
d. *coltello* (Ital.) > *kurtela* 'handle-less knife'
e. *aðelfi* > *aðerfi* 'sibling'

(22) a. *esprevier* (O.Fr.) > *spliverin* 'mosquito net'
b. *kriθari* > *kliθθarin* 'barley'

The "fricativization" of the liquids in (21) results in the fulfilment of the first part of the continuancy template: the first consonant becomes [+continuant]. Whether or not the full template is instantiated through this change apparently depends on whether the input sequence happened to already have a stop in second position. Ideally we would have expected [aðerpi]. Newton cites only this one word with an inherited *r* + fricative sequence, and I do not yet know what to make of the apparent failure of the /f/ to become [−continuant]. Similarly, while the failure of the /p/ of *esplevier* to spirantize may be explained by the preceding /s/, I do not know why the /k/ of *kliθθarin* does not spirantize. The import of the *l/r* alternation is nonetheless clear: it is almost certainly NOT an independent and unrelated peculiarity of Cypriot but yet another example of the availability of the redundant values for continuancy to the Continuant Dissimilation rule and hence an argument that Dissimilation is postlexical or word-level in this dialect.[10]

Note that in explaining rule generalization, I am not taking the formal tack of earlier generative phonologists, who saw generalization as the removal of features from a rule, so that it applied to a broader class of segments or in a broader class of environments. From that viewpoint, our Cypriot generalization would have consisted in the change illustrated in (23).

(23) a. UNGENERALIZED FORM:

$$\begin{bmatrix} +\text{obst} \\ -\text{voice} \\ \alpha\text{cont} \end{bmatrix} \begin{bmatrix} +\text{obst} \\ -\text{voice} \\ \beta\text{cont} \end{bmatrix} \rightarrow +\text{cont} \quad -\text{cont}$$

b. GENERALIZED FORM:

$$\alpha\text{cont}\ \beta\text{cont} \rightarrow +\text{cont} \quad -\text{cont}$$

Instead, we say that the rule has always had the "general" form of (23b). The class of segments affected by the rule becomes larger under generalization not because the rule has changed, but because of the characteristics of the stratum it has moved to. Our argument follows the path laid down in Kiparsky (1985). Kiparsky argues that Russian Voicing Assimilation applies more broadly in its postlexical applications than its lexical ones because values for voice become assignable to and spreadable from nondistinctively voiced sonorants. Similarly, we say that Cypriot Continuant Dissimilation affects and is triggered by the nondistinctively continuant segments when it moves to a later stratum. The innovation in my approach is to recognize this broadening as a primary mechanism of rule generalization. It may well be that not all rule generalizations can be reduced to this type—rule generalization by the actual removal of features from rules may yet be a valid mechanism of phonological change. But in the next two sections of this article, I sketch how two other rule generalizations, which had been treated as feature removal, can instead be seen as the result of the filling in of nondistinctive features.

My argument is, of course, only as strong as the theory of underspecification on which it rests, and if we are incorrect in thinking that noncontrastive and redundant feature values only become available late in derivations, most likely postlexically, this kind of argument cannot go through. However, the arguments for some version of underspecification seem to me very strong (Archangeli, 1988; Steriade, 1987). Thus we see that the availability of noncontrastive features in the generalized or reordered form of a rule argues powerfully for its relocation in late strata.

We have seen several strands of evidence indicating that Continuant Dissimilation has gained access to nondistinctive features. What we are lacking, and what is not available in the data reported in the literature, is corroborating evidence of other types which would pin down the position that Continuant Dissimilation has assumed in the grammar. I anticipate having access to further Cypriot materials and to informants shortly to gather the missing data.[11] If Continuant Dissimilation has become postlexical, I expect to find the following:

1. Unlike in other dialects, Cypriot Continuant Dissimilation should apply between words. Because the only word-final obstruent in Modern Greek is /s/, one would expect to observe this effect most clearly in the defricativization case, that is, in examples of the form *tis θalasses* (→ *tis talasses*), though the problematic nature of examples containing /s/ has been mentioned. Nasals can also be word final, but we have seen that nasals do not participate in the generalization of Continuant Dissimilation in Cypriot. A few words end in /r/, so we might also look for defricativization of word-initial consonants after *r*-final words. There may also be borrowed, clipped, or acronymic words which end in consonants other than /s/, /r/, and /n/ whose behavior in external sandhi I will investigate.
2. The exceptions to Continuant Dissimilation which I reported above for my Athenian informant should be absent in Cypriot.
3. The morphological conditioning on the rule, whereby application between stem and suffix is obligatory but application between prefix and stem is optional and lexically governed, should disappear.

We do not yet understand enough about the ordering of redundancy rules to be certain when features like continuancy in sonorants become available. Possibly they are filled in at the word level, possibly at the postlexical level. (See Borowsky, this volume, for evidence that structure preservation may shut off at the word level.) Corroborating evidence of the type I hope to collect will help to ascertain when redundancy rules operate.

4. A SCATTERED RULE IN SWISS GERMAN

It is appropriate that we take up here an example first made illustrious in Kiparsky's early (1965, 1968) work on rule reordering, namely, the relation between the rules of Umlaut and Lowering in several dialects of Swiss German. Kiparsky's original observations on this reordering were sharpened and expanded by Robinson (1976), who argues as follows. The generalized form of a rule lowering the mid back vowel, which applied in conservative Swiss dialects only before /r/ (+cor, −nasal, −lat), is generalized in the Schaffhausen dialect to apply before coronal stops and fricatives as well (but not before /l/). The surprising fact uncovered by Robinson is that the applications before /r/ continue to apply in their conservative position before Umlaut, while the innovative, generalized applications before coronal obstruents, apply after Umlaut. Thus Umlaut bleeds the innovative applications, by fronting the focus vowel before it can be lowered, but counterbleeds the older, ungeneralized form of lowering.

(24) Lowering before /r/
Umlaut
General Lowering

Robinson (1976: 148, 151) formulates the ungeneralized and generalized versions of Lowering as follows.

(25) a. UNGENERALIZED:

$$\overset{\text{V}}{\begin{bmatrix} -\text{high} \\ +\text{back} \\ -\text{long} \end{bmatrix}} \rightarrow [+\text{low}] \;/\; \underline{\quad\quad} \begin{bmatrix} +\text{son} \\ +\text{cor} \\ -\text{nasal} \\ -\text{lateral} \end{bmatrix}$$

b. GENERALIZED:

$$\overset{\text{V}}{\begin{bmatrix} -\text{high} \\ +\text{back} \\ -\text{long} \end{bmatrix}} \rightarrow [+\text{low}] \;/\; \underline{\quad\quad} \begin{bmatrix} +\text{cor} \\ -\text{nasal} \\ -\text{lateral} \end{bmatrix}$$

Our new viewpoint leads us to realize that in a simple consonant inventory like that of German, the features [-nasal] and [-lateral] are distinctive only for the sonorant, /r/, not for the obstruents. (I will not pause here to attempt to further underspecify the sonorants for these two features; the algorithm in Steriade, 1987, is indeterminate for narrowing the D-class for lateral and nasal further than to the sonorants. I discuss the issue more in the following section.)

(26)

	r	l	n	t	s
Nasal	−	−	+	0	0
Lateral	−	+	−	0	0

The features [lateral and [nasal] normally distinguish only sonorants except in languages with lateral affricates, nasal fricatives, prenasalized stops, and the like. They should become available for obstruents only in that portion of the grammar where redundant feature values may be referred to. As with the Cypriot case, the rule need not have changed but can always have had the generalized form in (25b). The "scattered" effect, where Lowering before /r/ is counterbled by Umlaut while Lowering before other coronals is bled by it, follows from the spread of Lowering's domain to the postlexical component.

We can now see how Robinson's result—that generalized forms of rules occur at the end of the grammar, separated from the ungeneralized rule from which they spring—follows from the lexical phonology model. It is not generalization that breeds scattering, as Robinson thought. Rather, the extension downward of the domain of a rule, as in the case of Lowering, automatically entrains generalization, for the rule has acquired a domain in which more information becomes available: in this case, nondistinctive features. Generalization is not the cause but the effect of reordering into a later stratum. The scattering effect results when instead of picking up and moving its domain downward, a rule merely expands its domains, applying in both lexical and postlexical strata.

5. LIQUID DELETION IN SAMOTHRAKI GREEK

The question remains whether domain extension and the concomitant availability of redundant features is the sole means of rule generalization, or whether the more traditional explanations must still be called on for some cases. Because it is difficult to determine the properly underspecified matrix for a given dialect without knowing its phonology thoroughly, I present the following example not as a definitive analysis but as a case where an underspecification solution, though pursuable, is not entirely convincing.

In the dialects of Modern Greek spoken in Samothrace (Newton, 1972b; Kaisse, 1976), a scattering similar to the Swiss German one has taken place. In the relatively conservative city dialect, intervocalic /r/ is deleted. In more innovative country dialects, both /l/ and /r/ are deleted. A vowel height dissimilation rule applies to the vowel sequences created by *r*-deletion but not by *l*-deletion.

(27) a. *or-a* (→ *oa*) → *ua* 'time'
b. *kol-a* → *koa* 'starch'

Just as in Swiss German, we can posit an apparent generalization at the end of the grammar.

(28) *r*-Loss
Vowel Height Dissimilation
General Liquid Loss

Let us attempt to write both *r*-Loss and its generalized counterpart, Liquid Deletion, as a single rule which applies more generally when it applies later.

(29) $$\begin{bmatrix} +\text{son} \\ +\text{cor} \\ -\text{nas} \end{bmatrix} \rightarrow \varnothing \,/\, \text{V} \_\_\_ \text{V}$$

Since Greek and German have the same inventory of sonorants, the simplest hypothesis is that they have the same feature matrix for those consonants.

(30)

	r	l	n
Nasal	−	−	+
Lateral	−	+	−

We did not think carefully about the specification of the sonorants in German, noting only that the features [nasal] and [lateral] were obviously necessary in some way to distinguish them from one another, while those features were not relevant for distinguishing obstruents. As I mentioned in the last section, Steriade's algorithm is indeterminate for deciding how fine a distinction one wants to make in determining D(istinctive) and R(edundant) classes. We could merely divide the consonants into obstruents and sonorants, as I did above, and state that the sonorants are the D-class for [lateral] and [nasal]. But it is possible to make finer distinctions, and this is the tack one would have to take in pursuing an underspecification solution along the lines we advocated for Cypriot and Swiss German.

We know that [lateral] is distinctive for the class of liquids, particularly since, like the other Greek dialects, Samothraki does not impose the continuancy template on sonorants. Thus continuancy cannot be the feature which distinguishes /r/ from /l/, and [lateral] is properly specified for both segments. But the rest is not so obvious; (30) still contains some redundant information. A more thoroughly underspecified matrix, if we follow Steriade's algorithm for determining D-classes, would be:

(31)

	r	l	n
Nasal	−		+
Lateral	−	+	

I derived (31) as follows. The feature that distinguishes /l/ from /r/ is [lateral]. Thus they are a D-class for lateral and receive plus and minus features respectively.

(32)

	l	r
Lateral	+	−

Steriade states that an R-class for a feature is that class of sounds for which one value of a distinctive feature is systematically excluded. For example, sonorants are usually an R-class for voicing because the value [−voice] is excluded for them. Following this reasoning, we see that while liquids are a D-class for [lateral], both features of lateral being assignable to them, nasals are an R-class for lateral, as the features [+nasal] [+lateral] are incompatible in normal feature inventories. Thus /n/ is [0lateral]. Continuing this reasoning for the feature [nasal], we see that [+nasal] is excluded for /l/ because, as we have said, [+lateral] is incompatible with [+nasal]. However, neither [+nasal] nor [−nasal] is excluded from segments like /r/ which are [−lateral], and indeed we need [−nasal] to distinguish /r/ from /n/.

The reader can now see where this argument is leading: rule (29) requires the feature [−nasal] in order to apply to a sonorant. In contrastive underspecification theory there is nothing special about a + value over a − value; a rule can require either equally well. In lexical applications, therefore, neither nasals ([+nasal]) nor laterals ([0nasal]) meet the structural description of the rule, and only /r/ undergoes deletion. The postlexical extension of Liquid Dissimilation will result in the nonnasality of /l/ becoming available, and /l/ thus will become subject to deletion.

Such an explanation may turn out to be tenable. However, I must point out several weaknesses in it. If the underspecification analysis is rejected due to these weaknesses, we will have to admit that there is more than one mechanism by which rules may generalize: our underspecification mechanism, and the more traditional method by which features are dropped from rules, allowing them to apply to a broader class of segments.

First, we must us ask whether /n/ and /l/ are distinct in (31). Pushing the contrastive underspecification algorithm led us to assign no − value to one for which a corresponding + was assigned to the other. So we must ask whether [+nasal] contrasts with [0nasal] and/or whether [+lateral] contrasts with [0lateral]. The only strong arguments for ternarily contrasting features come from situations typical to tone languages, where L- and H-toned morphemes contrast with alternating, 0-toned morphemes or, similarly, from harmony systems, where +F and −F vowels contrast with alternating, 0F vowels. Greek provides no evidence I know of for a ternary distinction within the feature [nasal] or [lateral]. Therefore, I tentatively conclude that an early redundancy rule must fill in at least the value [−lateral] on /n/ or [−nasal] on /l/. Which one is filled in appears to be arbitrary, or we might choose to fill in both. But of course our rule generalization will only work if we choose to fill in the value for [lateral] on /n/ early and leave /l/ unspecified for nasality until the postlexical component. Only in that way will /l/ escape deletion prior to Height Dissimilation and undergo deletion after Height Dissimilation. I find this indeterminacy worrisome. Without further evidence, we must wonder whether the availability of an underspecification solution for the Samothraki case is merely a result of the latitude provided by current theories of underspecification.

A second worrisome aspect of the solution sketched above concerns the status of the feature [nasal]. Steriade (personal communication, 1990) now suspects that [nasal] is a privative feature, not a binary one. Her evidence involves the absence of rules spreading [−nasal] and the frequency of rules spreading [+nasal]. If [−nasal] cannot be referred to by phonologies, Liquid Deletion (27) must be reformulated to apply to sonorants with no nasal node, that is, to the liquids. At no time does /l/ have a nasal node. Therefore, the nongeneralized form of the rule, which deletes only /r/, must specifically include the feature [−lateral], and we are back to the old analysis of rule generalization via the dropping of features from rules.

6. CONCLUSION

The theory of underspecification within lexical phonology allows us to understand the mechanism of rule generalization with greater clarity than was previously possible. It further allows us to link rule generalization to an underappreciated direction of rule reordering: movement downward in the grammar, including even re-entry into the postlexical component. We have seen cases of downward movement in Kaska, in Québecois French, in Cypriot Greek, in the Schaffhausen dialect of Swiss German, and possibly in Samothraki Greek as well. In the Kaska case, movement takes the form of extension of a rule's morphological domain one lexical stratum further, so that more sequences meeting the phonological description of the rule actually undergo it. The rule's transparency is thereby increased. The Kaska case would not typically be termed a rule generalization because it does not involve an extension of the natural class of segments undergoing or conditioning the rule. The case in Québecois French involves extension or movement into the postlexical component, since a Vowel Deletion rule gains access to information concerning the end of a sentence, that is, to the prosodic organization of constituents into intonational phrases and utterances. At the same time, the rule has acquired a generalized environment in no longer requiring its focus to appear in a closed syllable. The Cypriot, German, and Samothraki cases showed (in order of decreasing certainty on the part of this author) that a rule which is out of its chronologically correct order may gain access to redundant feature values. From this we concluded that such rules have moved downward with respect to the chronologically later rules they now follow. The analysis of Cypriot, for which we were able to bring the most evidence to bear, had the advantage of unifying several disparate facts about the dialect under the rubric of rule generalization. Moreover, it suggested that we might eliminate the subtraction of features from foci and determinants as a primary mechanism of phonological change. Instead, such generalization of rules can be subsumed under the independently needed mechanism of rule reordering. Within a theory which adopts level ordering, this reordering mechanism might further be expected to result in sandwich-type rule interactions, where an old rule both precedes and follows a new one. The Cypriot case does not appear to involve this sort of ordering paradox, the type that led Robinson to coin the term "scattered rule." But looking at "scattering" in Swiss German and in Samothraki Greek, I concluded that at least some cases of rule generalization which exhibit sandwiching fall out from the theory of rule reordering and underspecification I have developed here. Further investigation will tell us if all rule generalization can be reduced to a mere consequence of late rule application or if the elimination of features from structural descriptions must remain as an independent mechanism of phonological change.

NOTES

[1] The other case of rule scattering in the literature known to me is Bley-Vroman's (1975) treatment of Old Norse. In that language, umlaut of vowels in extra-heavy syllables applies before a vowel syncope rule. The generalized umlaut of vowels in any type of syllable applies after syncope. The treatment of this phenomenon in terms of rule movement is not obvious to me but might emerge from a close study of the form syllabification takes at different strata in Old Norse or of syllabification's ordering with respect to umlaut. The Québecois French case discussed at the end of this section also involves loss of a closed syllable requirement.

[2] In Sekani transcriptions, a vowel unmarked for tone is high. /i/ is an allomorph of the 1sg prefix used in the perfective of verbs having a zero or *-h-* classifier ('clf'). The grave accent preceding the conjunct prefix indicates a floating tone, realized as Low in Sekani and as High in Kaska.

[3] I am grateful to Doug Pulleyblank for directing me to this example. An anonymous referee suggests another interpretation of Dumas's facts, namely that the vowel lengthening rule has become optionally cyclic, so that it can optionally lengthen vowels that precede voiced fricatives that are word final prior to suffixation.

[4] The spirant partner of /t/ is /θ/, not /s/. And indeed /s/ acts asymmetrically with respect to other continuants. It cannot despirantize itself and causes despirantization of any fricative which precedes it, in violation of the continuancy template. Despirantization before /s/ is a very old rule, one found in Attic Greek. It is therefore unclear whether phenomena involving /s/ should be used as evidence in discussions of Continuant Dissimilation, and I will avoid such examples.

[5] Actually, the phonemic status of voiced stops is a more vexed question than my simple statement indicates, and Modern Greek scholars have argued over it at length. Voiced stops do appear as the result of voicing spread from a preceding nasal, and when that nasal is optionally lost, an apparently unconditioned voiced stop can appear on the surface. Voiced stops also appear in loanwords, though an etymologically incorrect nasal occasionally appears along with them. I cannot hope to resolve the issue here, but the reader may be

assured that the distribution of voiced stops is defective in Modern Greek and that credible analyses where these segments are lacking abound. Moreover, the evidence for the derived character of voiced stops is particularly weighty in Cypriot, where they are invariably preceded by nasals.

[6] An anonymous reviewer reminds me that /d/ does not spirantize after /l/, though /b/ and /g/ do. The complication may result from the fact that /l/ and /d/ are homorganic; the linking convention may prevent spirantization of stops sharing a place node with an adjacent consonant.

[7] Data in this and the following sections are taken from the excellent work of Newton (1972a,b), except where otherwise noted. My analysis of some rules differs. I discuss the spread of consonantality in Kaisse (1992).

[8] Pat Shaw points out to me that the emergence of *y* from this rule as a voiceless consonant indicates that the rule applies before the redundant values for voicing of glides and stops have been assigned. Obstruentization of *y* is therefore likely to be a lexical rule in Cypriot, and the value of voicing can be omitted from the actual structural change of the rule. The placement of Obstruentization in the lexicon is consistent with my claim that Continuant Dissimilation, which follows Obstruentization, is postlexical. It also suggests weakly that not only did Continuant Dissimilation move down, but that Obstruentization moved up. However, the movement of Obstruentization into the lexical component could of course have been independent of its reordering with Continuant Dissimilation. As we have said, the normal course of development for any new rule is for it to move into the lexicon.

[9] There are still a few controversial cases where rule insertion appears the best analysis, the most celebrated being Lachmann's Law.

[10] Nasals never seem to participate in the continuancy template; in fact, fricatives are disfavored after presumably [− continuant] nasals, since the normal historical development of aspirated and voiced stops to fricatives did not occur after nasals. I conclude that the value for continuancy for nasals is never specified within the phonology of Greek.

[11] The Gulf War prevented my planned visit to Cyprus in January 1991. I apologize to the reader for leaving you in suspense.

REFERENCES

Archangeli, D. (1988). Aspects of underspecification theory. *Phonology* **5,** 183–207.

Bley-Vroman, R. (1975). Opacity and interrupted rule schemata. *Papers from the Regional Meeting of the Chicago Linguistics Society* **11,** 73–80.

Chomsky, N., and Halle, M. (1968). *The Sound Pattern of English.* Harper and Row, New York.

Dumas, D. (1981). Structure de la diphthongaison québecoise. *Canadian Journal of Linguistics* **26,** 1–60.

Halle, M., and Clements, G. N. (1983). *Problem Book in Phonology.* MIT Press, Cambridge, Mass.

Halle, M., and Mohanan, K. P. (1985). Segmental phonology of Modern English. *Linguistic Inquiry* **16,** 57–116.

Hargus, S. (1988). *The Lexical Phonology of Sekani.* Garland, New York.

Kahane, H., and Kahane, R. (1987). A Cypriot etymologicum: comments to the glossary of Georgios Loukas. *Mediterranean Language Review* **3,** 71–104.

Kaisse, E. (1976). *Hiatus in Modern Greek.* Doctoral dissertation, Harvard University, Cambridge, Mass.

Kaisse, E. (1989). *Modern Greek Continuant Dissimilation and the OCP.* Unpublished manuscript, University of Washington, Seattle.

Kaisse, E. (1992). Can [consonantal] spread? *Language* **68,** 313–332.

King, R. (1973). Rule insertion. *Language* **49,** 551–578.

Kiparsky, P. (1965). *Phonological Change.* Doctoral dissertation, Massachusetts Institute of Technology, Cambridge.

Kiparsky, P. (1968). Linguistic universals and linguistic change. In *Universals in Linguistic Theory* (E. Bach and R. Harms, eds.), pp. 171–202. Holt, Rinehart and Winston, New York.

Kiparsky, P. (1984). On the lexical phonology of Icelandic. In *Nordic Prosody III* (C. C. Elert et al., eds.), pp. 135–164. University of Umeå, Umeå, Sweden.

Kiparsky, P. (1985). Some consequences of lexical phonology. *Phonology Yearbook* **2,** 82–136.

Kiparsky, P. (1988). Phonological change. In *The Cambridge Survey of Linguistics,* vol. 1, *Linguistic Theory: Foundations* (F. J. Newmeyer, ed.), pp. 363–415. Cambridge University Press, Cambridge.

Moore, P. (1988). *Kaska Verb Workshop.* Unpublished manuscript, Yukon Native Language Centre, Whitehorse.

Newton, B. (1972a). *Cypriot Greek: Its Phonology and Inflection.* Mouton, The Hague.

Newton, B. (1972b). *The Generative Interpretation of Dialect: A Study of Modern Greek Phonology.* Cambridge University Press, Cambridge.

Robinson, O. W. (1976). A "scattered" rule in Swiss German. *Language* **52,** 148–161.

Steriade, D. (1987). Redundant values. *Papers from the Parasession on Autosegmental and Metrical Phonology,* pp. 339–362. Chicago Linguistic Society, Chicago.

Thumb, A. (1964). *A Handbook of the Modern Greek Language.* Argonaut, Chicago.

RULE DOMAINS AND PHONOLOGICAL CHANGE

DRAGA ZEC

Department of Modern Languages and Linguistics
Cornell University
Ithaca, New York 14853

1. INTRODUCTION

This paper addresses a problem in historical linguistics, the problem of rule addition, from the perspective of lexical phonology and morphology (LPM). Rule addition played an important role in the debate of several decades ago on the characterization of language change in the generative framework (Halle, 1962; Kiparsky, 1965; King, 1969, 1973). Central in this debate was the ordering of a newly added rule with respect to other rules in the grammar. Within the LPM model, rule addition can be approached from a somewhat different viewpoint. This model proposes a set of possible rule domains, as well as a constrained mapping between rules and their respective domains. Thus, couched within the LPM model, the problem of rule addition can be formulated as follows: which of the domains available in the grammar may be selected by the newly added rule?

The case of rule addition to be studied here is accent retraction in the Štokavian dialects of Serbo-Croatian.[1] This historical process, dated around the 15th century (Belić, 1956: 161), significantly altered the accentual properties of the Štokavian dialects. However, not all Štokavian dialects have been affected by this process in the same fashion. In the Neo-Štokavian group of dialects this process has affected all accents and as a result entirely replaced the old accentual system with the new one. The Old Štokavian dialects fall into two subgroups. The conservative dialects preserve the accentual situation prior to accent retraction. The less conservative dialects have been affected by accent retraction only partially, so that they retain

Phonetics and Phonology, Volume 4
Studies in Lexical Phonology

certain properties of the old accentual system while also acquiring properties of the new one. My focus is on those dialects which have undergone accent retraction. The variation across this group of dialects provides an insight into various stages of this historical change. We will be able to observe how the addition of a rule interacts with phonological systems of essentially the same type yet differing in certain relevant details. In particular, dialects vary as to what rule domains are selected by accent retraction. Moreover, the cross-dialectal variation follows a clear pattern, which receives a straightforward account within the model of LPM. I now turn to those aspects of the model which are crucial to my analysis. The version of the LPM model I use here is that proposed in Kiparsky (1984, 1985).

In this model, the grammar is organized into distinct levels which provide successively larger rule domains; in Serbo-Croatian we need to posit at least those levels listed in (1).

(1)	Level 1		Cyclic
	Level 2		
	Level 3	Phonological word	Postcyclic
	Level 4	Phonological phrase	
		. . .	

The postcyclic levels posited for Serbo-Croatian are in fact universal; they are derived from, although not isomorphic with, syntactic domains (Hayes, 1989a; Nespor and Vogel, 1986; Selkirk, 1978, 1980). Postcyclic levels have thus been equated with the independently motivated hierarchy of prosodic constituents such as the phonological word, the phonological phrase, and so on. The levels preceding the postcyclic set can in principle be either cyclic or noncyclic. It so happens that in Serbo-Croatian all the earlier levels are cyclic (for arguments see Zec, 1988).[2]

A further property of this model crucial for us is the lexical/postlexical segregation. The lexical component includes levels smaller than the word, while the postlexical component includes levels larger than the word. The word is thus caught, as it were, at the intersection point between these two components. This is due to the ambiguity of the word domain, which belongs both to the syntax and to the morphology. This being the case, the phonological word could be created either lexically or postlexically. The facts presented here clearly show the dual character of the word.

Now, which of the levels in (1) belong to the lexical, and which to the postlexical component? The situation in the Štokavian dialects is not uniform in this respect; the phonological word may either be created lexically, as in (2), or postlexically, as in (3).

Let us start with the situation in (2), in which the phonological word is created lexically. It is no longer assumed, as it was in the early versions of LPM, that all postcyclic rules apply postlexically; at least one postcyclic domain, the level of the word, may have lexical properties, as argued in Kiparsky (1985) and Booij and Rubach (1987). A lexically created phonological word is also present postlexically and may combine with clitics. It is at this point that clitics enter the structure and are included into the phonological word, thus increasing its size.[3] In the lexicon, however, the phonological word can only appear in its smaller size, that is, without clitics.

(2)	Lexical	Level 1		Cyclic
		Level 2		
		Level 3	Phonological word (word-sized)	Postcyclic
	Postlexical	Level 3	Phonological word (clitic group)	
		Level 4	Phonological phrase	

If created postlexically, as in (3), the phonological word is manifested only in combination with clitics, never in its smaller size.

(3)	Lexical	Level 1		Cyclic
		Level 2		
	Postlexical	Level 3	Phonological word (clitic group)	Postcyclic
		Level 4	Phonological phrase	

We thus observe an asymmetry: if the phonological word is created lexically, it comes both in its smaller and in its larger size; if created postlexically, it comes only in its larger size. The domain often referred to in the literature as the clitic group corresponds to the phonological word in its postlexical guise. In fact, once the prosodic constituency is divided up into its lexical and postlexical subparts, it is possible to dispense with the clitic group as a prosodic level while retaining the rule domain of the clitic group size.[4]

Given this general design of the grammar, we will ask the following question: Which of the levels, or components, is chosen as the entrance gate for a phonological rule that is newly added to the grammar? Do rules enter a grammar with an arbitrarily specified domain, or does rule addition follow a more regular pattern? What I propose is comparable to the old claim, due to King (1973), that a new rule is added at the end of a grammar.[5]

(4) A new rule is added to the largest (i.e., highest) domain of a grammar.

Its further properties will then follow from the strong domain hypothesis (Kiparsky, 1984), which essentially makes the following claim.

(5) STRONG DOMAIN HYPOTHESIS: If a rule applies at level n, it also applies at level $n - 1$, but not necessarily vice versa.

Under optimal conditions, the newly added rule will then simply spread throughout the grammar. The case of phonological change to be studied here will show that the strong domain hypothesis governs both synchronic and diachronic aspects of the rule component, with one notable exception: rules of the domain limit type diverge from the strong domain hypothesis by choosing only the postcyclic domains.

The article is organized as follows. Sections 2–4 present the set of facts relevant for locating accent retraction within the Serbo-Croatian accentual system. In Section 2 accent retraction is analyzed as a tone spreading rule; Section 3 focuses on the postcyclic application of this rule in a representative group of dialects, while Section 4 provides arguments for its cyclic application. Section 5 develops a constrained view of postcyclic levels, which accounts for all cross-dialectal variation associated with accent retraction in terms of a single set of rule domains. Finally, Section 6 outlines a route of change that can be reconstructed for this case within the LPM model. The general view of Serbo-Croatian accent to be presented here is that developed in Inkelas and Zec (1988) and Zec (1988). While Inkelas and Zec (1988) focus on late lexical as well as postlexical processes, Zec (1988) looks into the relatively early lexical processes. The two accounts in many ways complement each other; moreover, both are based on Lehiste and Ivić's (1986) important study of the phonetic properties of Serbo-Croatian accent.

2. ACCENT RETRACTION AS A TONE-SPREADING RULE

According to traditional descriptions, the accentual difference between the Neo- and Old Štokavian dialects is manifested in the number of surface accent types: the Neo-Štokavian has four pitch accents, two rising and two falling, while the Old Štokavian has only the two falling pitch accents.[6] The difference between the two dialect groups has been attributed to the effect of accent retraction. In this section I outline the accentual properties of the two Štokavian dialect groups, and then show that the Neo-Štokavian dialects differ from the Old Štokavian ones in possessing the phonological rule which is the synchronic counterpart of accent retraction.

2.1. Neo-Štokavian Dialects

The Neo-Štokavian dialects are traditionally described as possessing four pitch accents: short rising, short falling, long rising, and long falling. Below are given examples for each of the accent types, marked by the traditionally used diacritics; in the righthand column are given the pitch properties associated with each of the accents:

(6) a. Short rising: *màrama* *mara|ma* 'scarf'
b. Short falling: *kȕćica* *ku|ćica* 'house (dim.)'
c. Long rising: *rázlika* *ra|azli|ka* 'difference'
d. Long falling: *râdnica* *ra|adnica* 'worker'

The relevant phonetic correlates of accent established by Lehiste and Ivić (1986) are pitch and duration. Taking duration to be a correlate of stress, and pitch a correlate of tone, Inkelas and Zec (1988) propose to decompose accent into tone and stress, as shown in the following autosegmental representation.[7]

(7) a. Short rising: *mårama* (H linked to *ma* and *ra*; L linked to *ma*)
b. Short falling: *kůćica* (H linked to *ku*; L linked to *ći* and *ca*)
c. Long rising: *råazlika* (L linked to *ra*; H linked to *a* and *zli*; L linked to *ka*)
d. Long falling: *råadnica* (H linked to *ra*; L linked to *ad*, *ni* and *ca*)

In (7), the pitch properties of each of the four accents are represented in terms of High and Low tones. As noted in Lehiste and Ivić (1986), pitch prominence is found on the only syllable bearing a falling accent and on the accented and the postaccentual syllables of the rising accent. This is captured in (7) in terms of the distribution of the High tones: a falling accent is associated with a High tone linked to a single syllable, and a rising accent with a High linked to two consecutive syllables. The leftmost syllable linked to a High tone bears stress, which is marked with an asterisk.

The representation in (7) is suggestive in several respects. If we factor out vowel length, the four accents can be reduced to just two—the falling H(L) and the rising (L)HH(L) type. Moreover, the two accent types can be kept distinct even if the Low tones are left out of the structure: the falling accents can simply be characterized as singly linked Highs, and the rising accents as doubly linked Highs.

(8) a. Short rising: *marama* (H linked to *ma* and *ra*)
b. Short falling: *kućica* (H linked to *ku*)
c. Long rising: *raazlika* (H linked to *a* and *zli*)
d. Long falling: *raadnica* (H linked to *ra*)

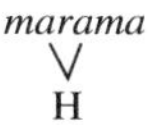

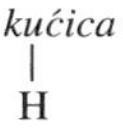

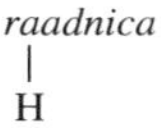

It is thus sufficient to represent only High tones in the lexical component; Low tones are introduced by a default rule, late in the postlexical component (for details see Inkelas and Zec, 1988).

The representation in (8) can be simplified even further: one of the two association lines linked to the High is redundant and can therefore be derived by rule. This brings us to the rule responsible for accent retraction, the phonological change focused on here. The synchronic counterpart of this process is a tone-spreading rule: a linked High tone spreads to the immediately preceding mora, deriving the forms in (8) from those in (10).[8]

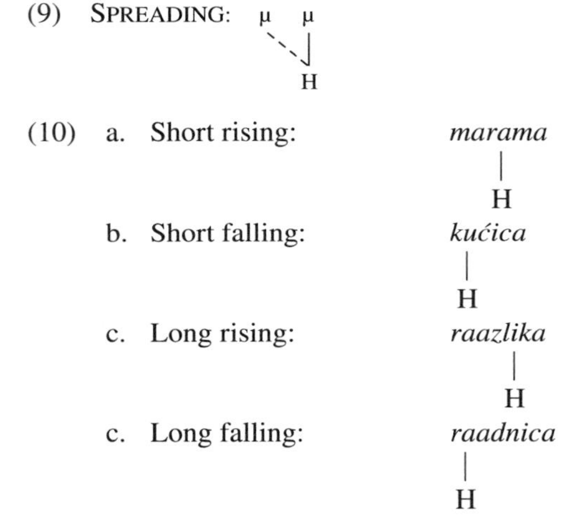

As formulated above, Spreading applies right to left. In support of this, we can bring up pairs of forms as in (11).

(11) a. *raadnik* 'worker'
H

b. *neraadnik* 'nonworker'
H

Crucial to our point is the fact that the singly linked High in (11a) spreads to the prefix in (11b).[9] Tone linked to a stem-final syllable would not spread in a similar fashion to the following suffix. The historical change of accent retraction also operated right to left, just like its synchronic counterpart.

Most importantly, Spreading alone accounts for the distribution of accents in the Neo-Štokavian. The distribution of the Neo-Štokavian accents is described in the literature as follows: (1) the falling accents appear only on word-initial syllables, (2) the rising accents appear on any syllable other than the final one, and (3) monosyllabic words can only bear a falling accent (see Browne and McCawley, 1965; Halle, 1971; Kenstowicz, 1974; Lehiste and Ivić, 1986, and the references therein). Given the formulation of Spreading, these distributional properties follow naturally. The falling accents occur on the word-initial syllable because this is the only position which can be occupied by an unspread High tone. The stressed syllable of a rising accent cannot occupy word-final position because the leftmost syllable containing a High tone will never be word-final in forms that have undergone Spreading. Finally, rising accents, which are a result of Spreading, cannot appear on monosyllabic words since they can only be associated with forms which possess at least two syllables.

Spreading thus creates a system with four pitch accents typical of the Neo-Štokavian dialects. In addition, Spreading identifies the tone-bearing unit in Serbo-Croatian. Since contour tones are found on long but not on short vowels, we are led to conclude that the tone-bearing unit is the mora and that tones are linked to tone-bearing units in a one-to-one fashion.

2.2. Old Štokavian Dialects

The Old Štokavian dialects have escaped the effect of accent retraction. The four Neo-Štokavian accents illustrated in (6) correspond to the following Old Štokavian accents.

(12) a. Short falling: *marȁma* *ma|ra|ma* 'scarf'
b. Short falling: *kȕćica* *ku|ćica* 'house (dim.)'
c. Short falling: *razlȉka* *raaz|li|ka* 'difference'
d. Long falling: *râdnica* *ra|adnica* 'worker'

The Old Štokavian thus possesses two accent types, the long falling and the short falling; and if we factor out vowel length, the range of accents is reduced to (L)H(L) as the only accent type. The phonetic properties of the pitch accents remain constant across dialects: the falling Old Štokavian accents can thus be represented in exactly the same fashion as the falling Neo-Štokavian accents.

(13) a. Short falling:

```
marạ*ma
 | |  |
 LH   L
```

b. Short falling:

```
ku*ćica
 | \/
 H  L
```

c. Short falling:

```
raazli*ka
 V   | |
 L   H L
```

d. Long falling:

```
ra*adnica
 | \/
 H  L
```

Once the representation is simplified by taking the Low tones out of the structure, we arrive at the lexical representations, which are identical for the two groups of dialects.[10]

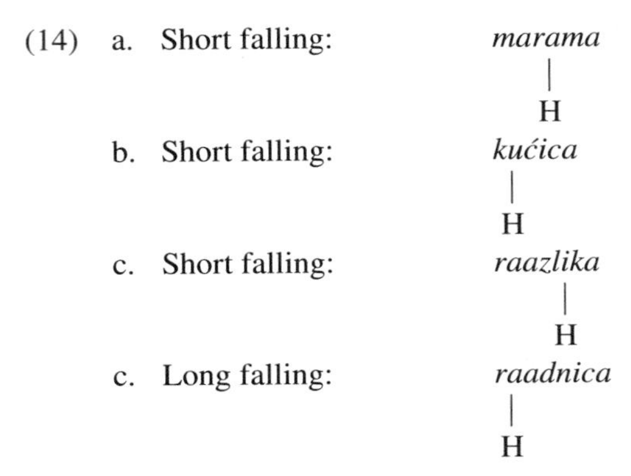

These are precisely the forms which in the Neo-Štokavian serve as input to Spreading. Spreading is thus solely responsible for the accentual differences between the two dialect groups. If we factor out the effect of Spreading, the two dialect groups become identical in their accentual properties.

2.3. Lexically Toneless Forms

In order to complete my account of the surface accentual properties in the two dialect groups, I need to introduce the distinction between lexically toneless stems and stems characterized by lexical tone. Note the difference in tonal properties between the sets of verbal forms in (15) and (16).

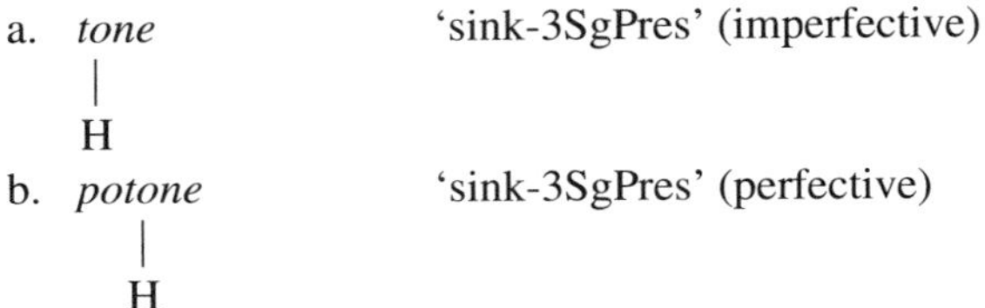

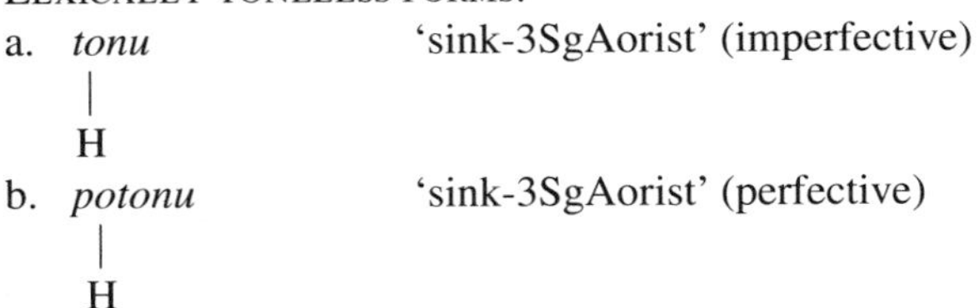

(16) LEXICALLY TONELESS FORMS:
a. *tonu* 'sink-3SgAorist' (imperfective)
H
b. *potonu* 'sink-3SgAorist' (perfective)
H

The situation in (15) is familiar: in the Neo-Štokavian dialects, the High on the stem in (15a) spreads to the prefix in (15b); in the Old Štokavian, the High remains on the stem and the prefix eventually receives a Low tone. This is in fact the pattern exhibited by those forms which are associated with lexical tone. The forms in (16a) and (16b), however, appear to undergo tonal rules separately. This pattern is to be found with toneless stems, that is, with those that lack lexical tone. The distinction between the forms in (15) and in (16) corresponds to the well-known bifurcation into accented and unaccented stems found in pitch-accent languages (see the analyses of Sanskrit and Lithuanian in Halle and Kiparsky, 1981; Kiparsky, 1973; and Kiparsky and Halle, 1977; as well as Poser's 1984 analysis of Japanese). The present tense verbal forms, those in (15), have lexical tone, while the aorist forms, those listed in (16), are toneless. Toneless forms receive tone by virtue of Initial High Insertion, a rule which assigns a High to their initial moras (for details, see Inkelas and Zec, 1988).[11]

(17) INITIAL HIGH INSERTION: $[\mu \rightarrow [\underset{\text{H}}{\overset{\mu}{|}}$

The effect of this rule is to ensure that, eventually, all forms obtain accent; in our terms, this means that lexically toneless forms will have to be supplied with a High tone at some point of the derivation. In sum, we distinguish two kinds of High tones—those that are associated with forms lexically, and those that are assigned by virtue of Initial High Insertion.

The rules proposed thus far account for the pitch properties that Lehiste and Ivić attribute to accent types in various Štokavian dialects. Location of the syllable whose vowel exhibits increase in duration is fully predictable from pitch: in all Štokavian dialects, this is the leftmost syllable that contains a High tone. Stress assignment is thus identical for the two groups of dialects; in those dialects that possess Spreading, this rule will have to precede the assignment of stress.

We now turn to the domains within which Spreading applies. It will be shown that this rule is associated both with the cyclic and with the postcyclic domains. Its postcyclic application is discussed in Section 3, and its cyclic application, in Section 4.

3. POSTCYCLIC APPLICATIONS OF SPREADING

In this section I focus on the postcyclic applications of Spreading in three Neo-Štokavian dialects, which differ in their choice of postcyclic domains for this rule. While all three dialects select the phonological word as a domain for Spreading, one of the dialects also selects the phonological phrase. Moreover, Spreading may apply either within the lexical or within the postlexical version of the phonological word. The phonological word in its postlexical size is referred to here, informally, as the clitic group; this term is taken to refer to a domain size rather than to an actual prosodic constituent.

Before turning to the postcyclic domains of Spreading, I will digress briefly to comment on the prosodic properties of Serbo-Croatian words. Following Inkelas (1989), I classify lexical items in Serbo-Croatian into those that are prosodically salient and those that lack prosodic salience. Prosodically salient forms will map into phonological words. Forms that lack prosodic salience are all clitics in Serbo-Croatian; they include certain personal pronouns, prepositions, conjunctions, and particles. Since Serbo-Croatian clitics subcategorize for the phonological word, they will be incorporated into this particular prosodic constituent, forming an enlarged domain.

I first examine the postcyclic domains of Spreading for the three Neo-Štokavian dialects to be discussed here and then compare them with those of Initial High Insertion. It will be shown that the domains of the two rules coincide in each of the dialects to be examined below. The domains of Initial High Insertion will in fact play an important role in determining the domains of Spreading for each of the dialects.

3.1. Domains of Spreading

The three Neo-Štokavian dialects described here are Neo-Štokavian 1 (NS1), in which Spreading operates within the clitic group, Neo-Štokavian 2 (NS2), in which this rule chooses the domain of the phonological word, and Neo-Štokavian 3 (NS3), in which Spreading applies both within the phonological word and within the clitic group.[12] Moreover, in NS1 Spreading also applies within the domain of the phonological phrase.

In NS1, a word-initial High spreads onto the preceding clitic, as in (18).

(18) NS1: *u kuću* 'into (the) house'
H

If the preceding clitic is disyllabic, Spreading will affect its second syllable.

(19) NS1: *ispred kuće* 'in front of (the) house'
H

As a consequence, words with an initial lexically assigned High exhibit the following alternation in NS1.

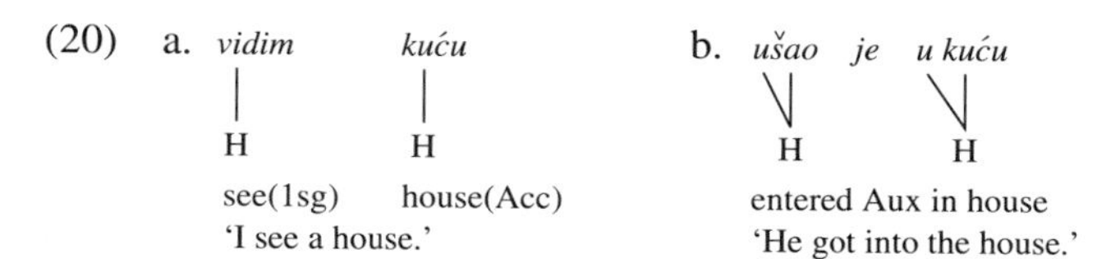

Tone spreading onto a proclitic is a highly general phenomenon in this dialect. In order to illustrate this, we give a few more examples (taken from Vuković, 1940). In (21a), tone spreads onto a preposition from a preceding adjective; and in (21b), a High linked to the initial syllable of a verb spreads to the complementizer.

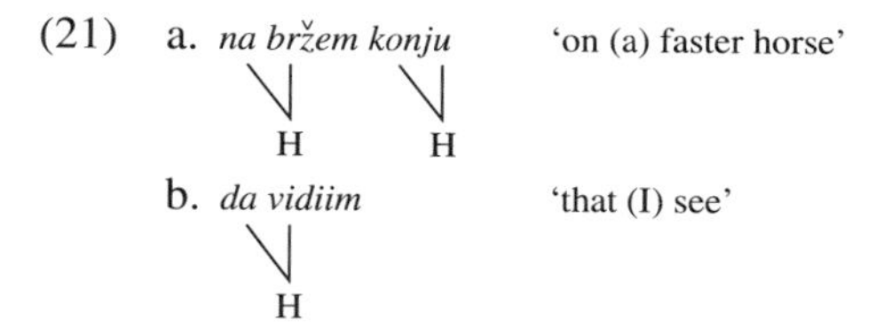

Moreover, in NS1 we also encounter applications of Spreading within the phonological phrase. Examples in (22) are taken from Vuković (1940), and those in (23) from Ružičić (1927).

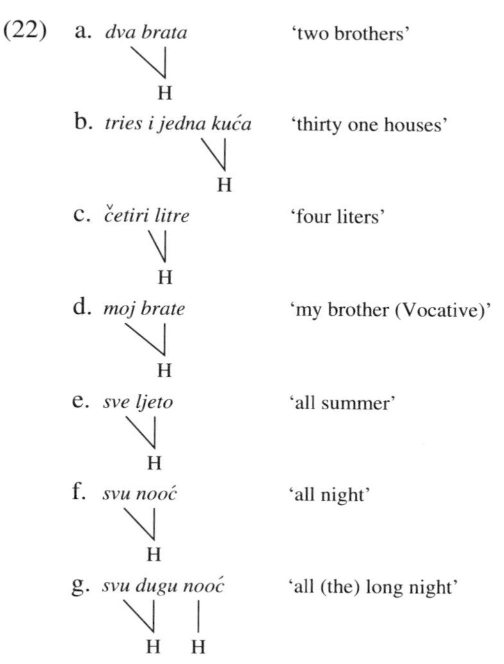

(22) a. dva brata 'two brothers'
H
b. tries i jedna kuća 'thirty one houses'
H
c. četiri litre 'four liters'
H
d. moj brate 'my brother (Vocative)'
H
e. sve ljeto 'all summer'
H
f. svu nooć 'all night'
H
g. svu dugu nooć 'all (the) long night'
H H

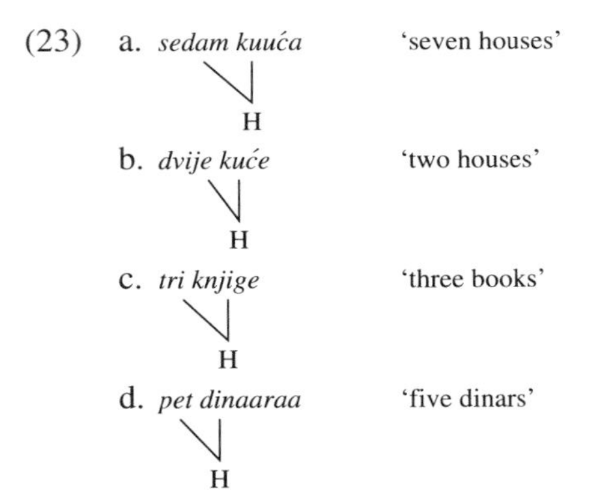

It should be pointed out that Spreading will not apply between just any two words in a phonological phrase. In all examples that have been reported, the target of Spreading is either a numeral or a nonclitic pronoun. These forms receive tone optionally in the dialect described by Vuković and Ružičić as well as in other dialects discussed in this article. Examples in (24), taken from Vuković, illustrate this point. In (24a) the pronoun *sav* 'all' is toneless, and in (24b) it is associated with an initial High tone; the numeral in (24c) is toneless, and that in (24d) is supplied with tone.

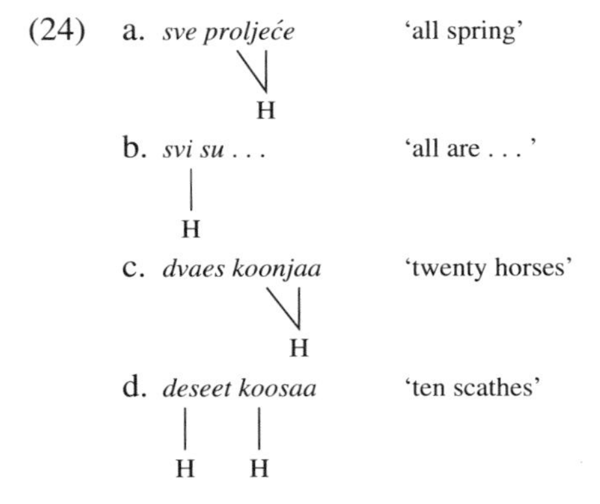

Only those forms that remain toneless will be targets of Spreading. The fact that forms linked to tone do not become targets of Spreading within the phonological phrase is consistent with the generalization that a word may be associated with at most one High tone (see note 11). Moreover, Spreading applies optionally within the phonological phrase; Ružičić lists alternants of (22f,g) in which the pronoun *sav* 'all' appears toneless.

In NS2, the next dialect we will describe here, Spreading is word-bounded. Word-initial Highs do not undergo this rule, as shown in (25); only those Highs that are linked to a noninitial syllable of a word are affected by Spreading in this dialect.

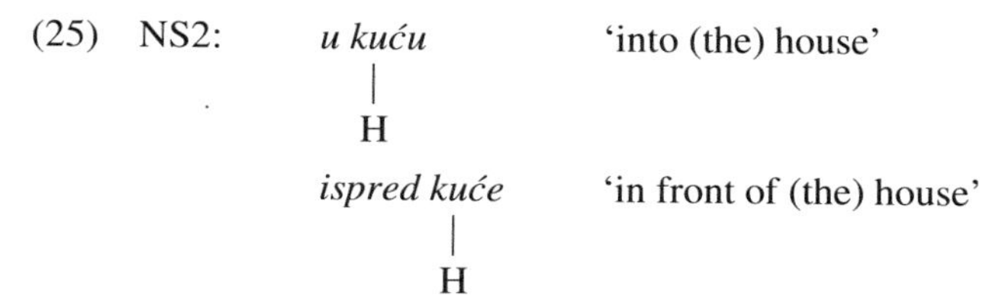

In this dialect, therefore, we encounter no alternation of the sort illustrated in (20), as shown by the following examples.

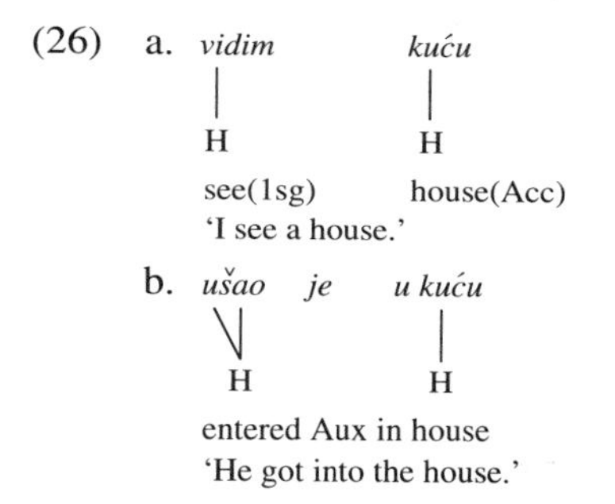

(26) a. vidim kuću
H H
see(1sg) house(Acc)
'I see a house.'
b. ušao je u kuću
H H
entered Aux in house
'He got into the house.'

Finally, NS3 possesses alternant forms like those listed in (27)–(28) (taken from Nikolić, 1970, and Moskovljević, 1927–28), which strongly suggests that Spreading applies both within the phonological word and within the clitic group.[13]

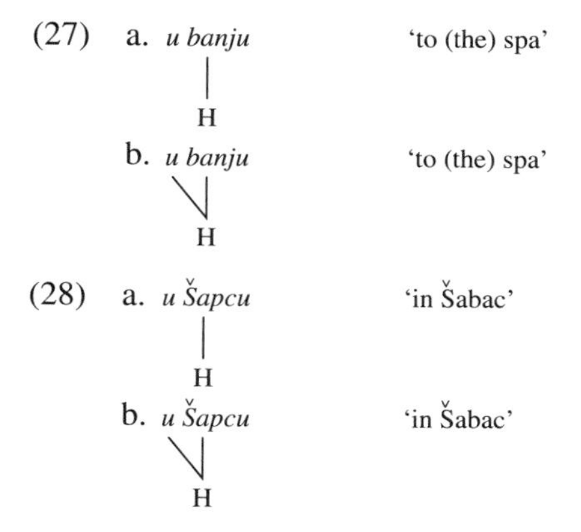

Variation that characterizes NS3 will be attributed to the optionality of rule application: in this dialect Spreading applies obligatorily within the phonological word, but optionally within the clitic group.[14]

The table in (29) summarizes the applications of Spreading in the three Neo-Štokavian dialects discussed here.

(29)

	NS1	NS2	NS3
Lexical phonological word (phonological word)	?	Yes	Yes
Postlexical phonological word (clitic group)	Yes	No	Yes(Opt)
Phonological phrase	Yes(Opt)	No	No

I have shown that in NS2 Spreading operates within the phonological word but not within the clitic group; and that in NS3 Spreading operates both within the phonological word and within the clitic group. Less clear at this point is what happens in NS1. While we have clear evidence for the application of Spreading within the clitic group and the phonological phrase, there is little evidence that this rule also applies within the phonological word. This problem is addressed in Section 5.

3.2. Comparison with Initial High Insertion

If we now examine the application of Initial High Insertion, a very interesting fact emerges. In each of the dialects, the domain of Initial High Insertion overlaps with that of Spreading: in NS1 the two rules meet in the domain of the clitic group, in NS2 they meet within the phonological word, and in NS3 they overlap both in the phonological word and in the clitic group. The facts presented below are in many ways a replication of those found with Spreading.

In NS1, Initial High Insertion assigns a High tone to the proclitic, if there is one in the structure.

(30) NS1: *u graad* 'in (the) town'
|
H

If the proclitic is disyllabic, tone is assigned to its first syllable. This follows from the way the rule is formulated in (17): tone is assigned to the leftmost mora of the relevant domain.

(31) NS1: *iza graada* 'behind (the) town'
|
H

In NS2, however, the rule ignores the clitic and operates on the word-initial mora.

(32) NS2:

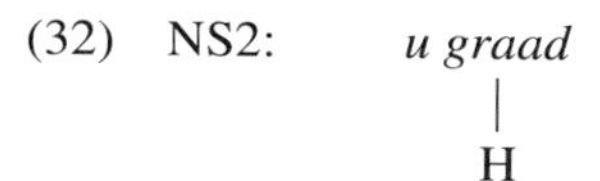

We thus find the following alternation in NS1 but not in NS2.

(33)

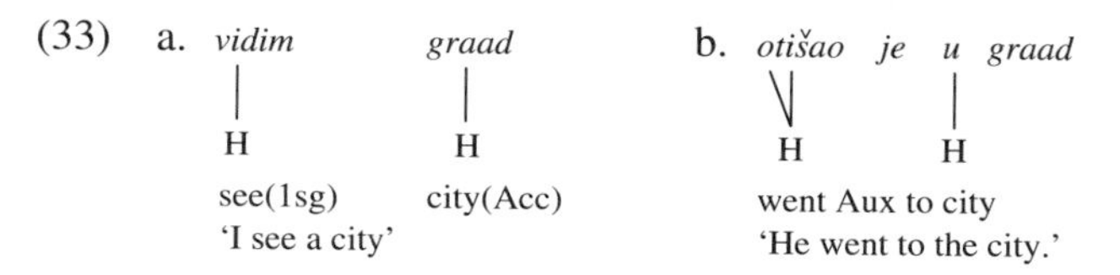

In NS3, we encounter alternant forms of the following kind, which I attribute to optional rule application in the lexical, although not in the postlexical, domain.[15]

(34) NS3: *u glaavu* (H on *u*) versus *u glaavu* (H on *glaavu*) 'into (the) head'

(35) NS3: *ispod leda* (H on *ispod*) versus *ispod leda* (H on *leda*) 'under (the) ice'

The applications of Initial High Insertion in the three Neo-štokavian dialects are summarized in (36).[16]

(36)

	NS1	NS2	NS3
Lexical phonological word (phonological word)	No	Yes	Yes(Opt)
Postlexical phonological word (clitic group)	Yes	No	Yes

3.3. Interaction of Spreading and Initial High Insertion

3.3.1. In NS3

In NS3, Spreading and Initial High Insertion apply both lexically and postlexically and could therefore potentially interact with each other. In particular, a High assigned to a phonological word by virtue of Initial High Insertion may spread to a proclitic within the domain of the clitic group. The following alternant forms, from Nikolić (1970), support this prediction.

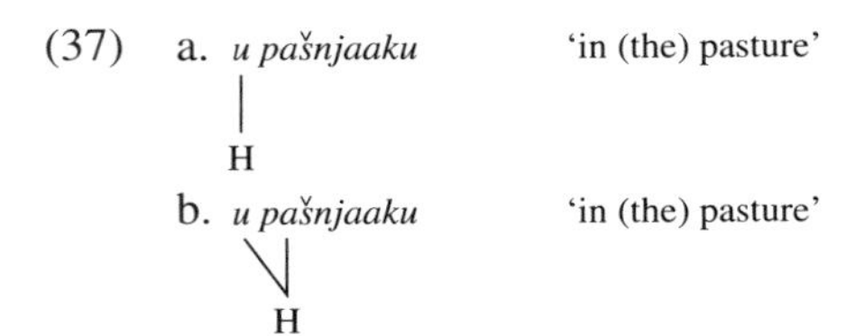

The alternation shown in (37) follows from the optionality of rule application: Initial High Insertion is optional within the lexical phonological word. Moreover, we also find three-way alternations as in (38) (again from Nikolić, 1970); (38c) is due to the optionality of Spreading within the postlexical phonological word (i.e., the clitic group).

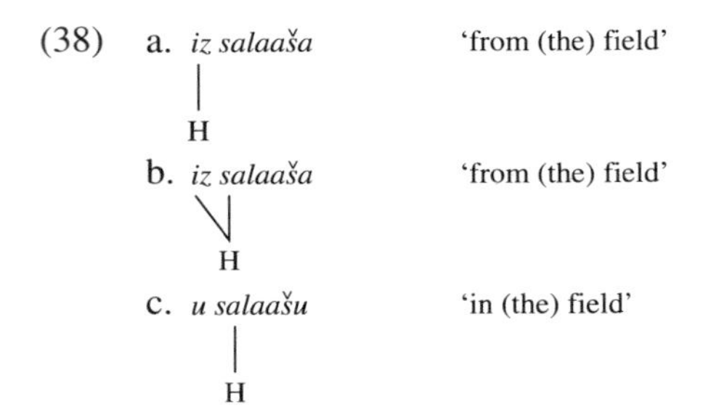

Below are given the derivations of forms in (38).

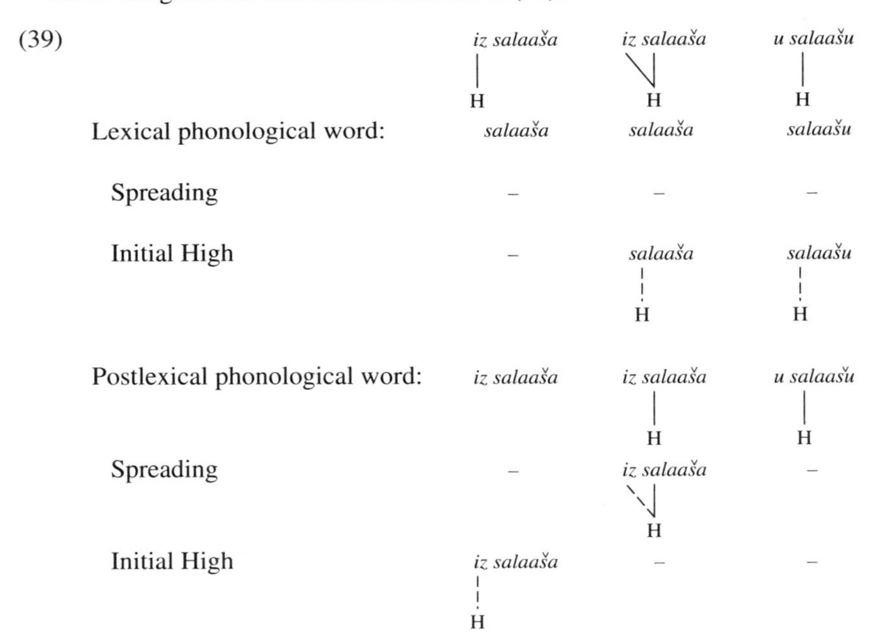

(39) iz salaaša iz salaaša u salaašu
Lexical phonological word: salaaša salaaša salaašu
Spreading – – –
Initial High – salaaša salaašu
Postlexical phonological word: iz salaaša iz salaaša u salaašu
Spreading – iz salaaša –
Initial High iz salaaša – –
H

Lexically toneless forms which spread their High onto the proclitic are treated in the literature as anomalous and accounted for in terms of analogy (Nikolić, 1970). Under the analysis developed here, however, there is no need to assume that such forms are in any way exceptional.

3.3.2. In NS1

In NS1, Spreading applies both within the phonological word and within the phonological phrase, while Initial High Insertion applies only within the phonological word. As a result, Highs assigned by Initial High Insertion at the level of the phonological word may undergo Spreading within the phonological phrase. Vuković (1940:271) lists several cases whose tonal patterns are accounted for straightforwardly if viewed as resulting from the interaction of Initial High Insertion and Spreading. Among the forms listed are pairs of forms as in (40), in which the word *noć* 'night', which is lexically toneless and therefore receives tone by virtue of Initial High Insertion, triggers different tonal patterns on the preceding word.

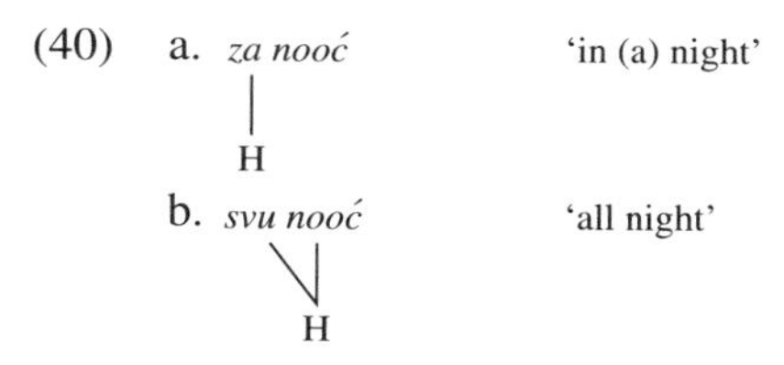

This difference is predicted under the analysis proposed here. In NS1, Initial High Insertion applies only within the postlexical phonological word, that is, within the clitic group. In (40a), this rule will apply to the entire prepositional phrase, which forms a postlexical phonological word, and will link the High to the proclitic *za;* and in (40b) it will apply only to the form *nooć,* which by itself constitutes a postlexical phonological word. The toneless form *svu,* which is an appropriate target for Spreading, undergoes this rule within the phonological phrase, that is, at the point at which it shares constituency with *nooć.* These steps are shown explicitly in the following derivation.

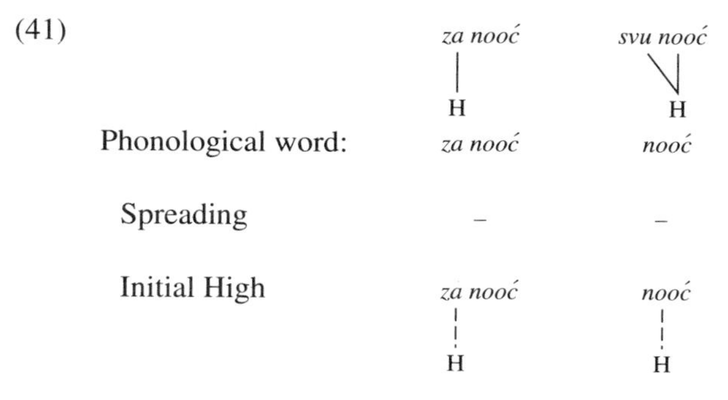

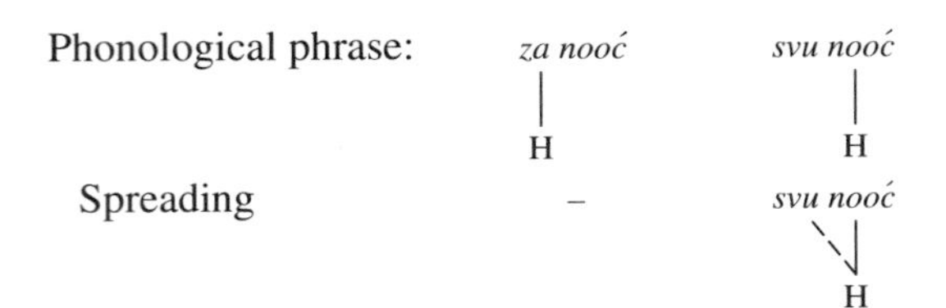

4. CYCLIC APPLICATION OF SPREADING

Thus far we have seen that the Neo-Štokavian dialects possess the rule of Spreading which is absent from the Old Štokavian group; and that the Neo-Štokavian dialects vary as to which of the postcyclic domains is selected by this rule. In this section I argue that, in the Neo-Štokavian group of dialects, Spreading applies not only postcyclically, as we saw in the previous section, but also cyclically. The argument itself will take us somewhat afield. We will again bring in the Old-Štokavian dialects, as a point of comparison for the Neo-Štokavian group. Evidence for the cyclic application of Spreading in the Neo-Štokavian is provided by accent shift in the genitive plural, which follows different patterns in the two major dialect groups. These diverging patterns will receive a simple characterization under the assumption that Spreading operates in the Neo-Štokavian dialects but not in the Old Štokavian ones. In order to demonstrate this, I need to digress into the territory of lexical tone. Sections 4.1 and 4.2 are devoted to the properties of lexical tone shared by the two dialect groups. In Section 4.3 I turn to accent shift in the genitive plural, which brings in accentual differences between the two groups of dialects.

4.1. Lexical Tone

It has generally been held that the distribution of Serbo-Croatian accents is fairly free, if not for the most part random (Browne and McCawley, 1965; Halle, 1971; Kenstowicz, 1974; Lehiste and Ivić, 1986). In keeping with this, Inkelas and Zec (1988) propose to reduce what appears to be random distribution of accent to random distribution of lexical tone; in their analysis, High tones are prelinked in the underlying form. Lexical tone, however, is not devoid of pattern. If tone is prelinked in the underlying form, then we will have to stipulate the absence of the following underlying configuration.[17]

(42)

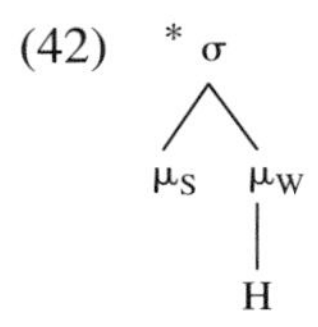

The prohibited configuration in (42) points to a gap in the distribution of lexical tone: a High tone may not be linked to the rightmost mora of a heavy syllable. In fact, Inkelas and Zec (1988) treat the prohibited configuration in (42) as a constraint on underlying form. This move, however, is redundant. Taking this gap as a point of departure, I will show that the distribution of tone is fully predictable.

The tonal configurations associated with lexical tone are those given in (43), and they are both characterizable by rule. I account for the configuration in (43a) in Section 4.1.1, by proposing a cyclic tone linking rule. The configuration in (43b) is attributed to a relinking rule to be discussed in Section 4.1.2.

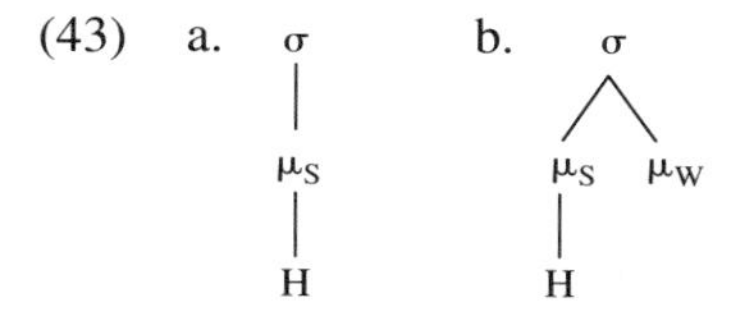

4.1.1. Tone Linking Rule

The accentual properties of various inflectional classes serve as principal motivation for the tonal rule which creates the configuration in (43a). Crucial for my argument is the contrast between forms with a light stem-final syllable, as in (44), and those with a heavy stem-final syllable, as in (45). The forms in (44) and (45) are all nominal stems, and this is the class of stems to which I limit myself here; the claims to be made extend naturally to the adjectival and verbal stems (for details see Zec, 1988).

Let us first examine the properties of stems that end in a light syllable. All the case forms in (44) (with the exception of the genitive plural, which is discussed in Section 4.3) have lexical tone linked to the final syllable of the stem.[18]

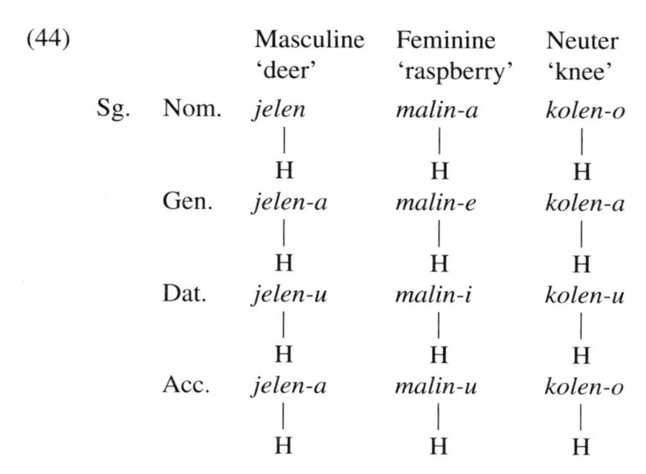

(44)
Masculine
'deer'
Feminine
'raspberry'
Neuter
'knee'
Sg.
Nom.
jelen
malin-a
kolen-o
Gen.
jelen-a
malin-e
kolen-a
Dat.
jelen-u
malin-i
kolen-u
Acc.
jelen-a
malin-u
kolen-o
H

```
         Instr.  jelen-om     malin-om     kolen-om
                   |            |            |
                   H            H            H
         Loc.    jelen-u      malin-i      kolen-u
                   |            |            |
                   H            H            H

Pl.      Nom.    jelen-i      malin-e      kolen-a
                   |            |            |
                   H            H            H
         Gen.    jelen-a      malin-a      kolen-a
                 |            |            |
                 H            H            H
         Dat.    jelen-ima    malin-ama    kolen-ima
                   |            |            |
                   H            H            H
         Acc.    jelen-e      malin-e      kolen-a
                   |            |            |
                   H            H            H
         Instr.  jelen-ima    malin-ama    kolen-ima
                   |            |            |
                   H            H            H
         Loc.    jelen-ima    malin-ama    kolen-ima
                   |            |            |
                   H            H            H
```

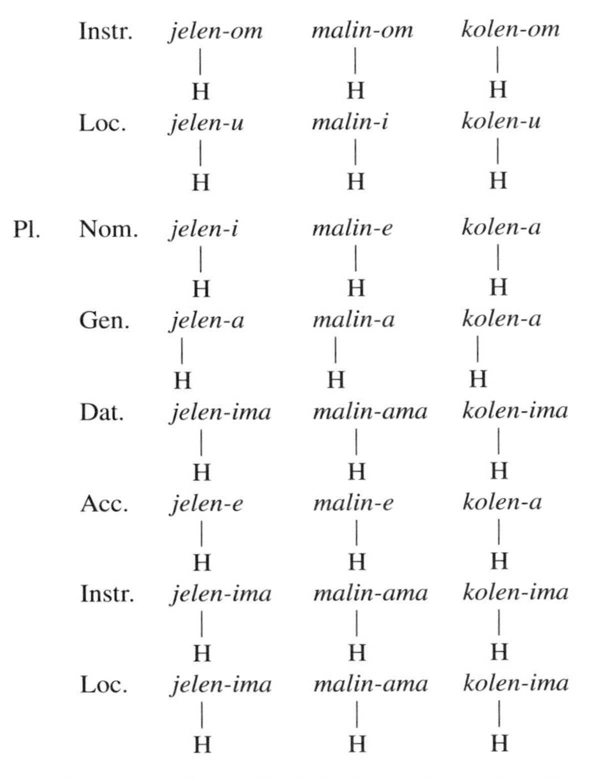

Forms whose stem-final syllable is heavy do not bear lexical tone on this syllable (with the exception of the nominative singular form, to be discussed in Section 4.2). Lexical tone appears, instead, on the suffix.

```
(45)             Masculine    Feminine     Neuter
                 'hero'       'guitar'     'principle'
Sg.      Nom.    junaak       gitaar-a     načeel-o
                    |               |             |
                    H               H             H
         Gen.    junaak-a     gitaar-e     načeel-a
                        |           |             |
                        H           H             H
         Dat.    junaak-u     gitaar-i     načeel-u
                        |           |             |
                        H           H             H
         Acc.    junaak-a     gitaar-u     načeel-o
                        |           |             |
                        H           H             H
```

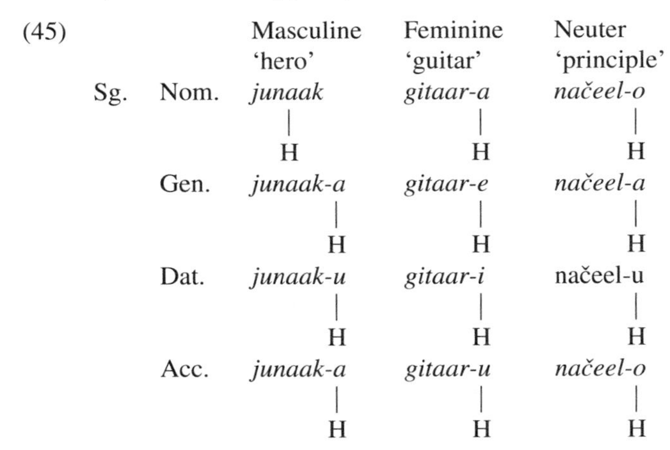

	Instr.	*junaak-om*	*gitaar-om*	*načeel-om*
		H	H	H
	Loc.	*junaak-u*	*gitaar-i*	*načeel-u*
		H	H	H
Pl.	Nom.	*junaac-i*	*gitaar-e*	*načeel-a*
		H	H	H
	Gen.	*junaak-a*	*gitaar-a*	*načeel-a*
		H	H	H
	Dat.	*junaac-ima*	*gitaar-ama*	*načeel-ima*
		H	H	H
	Acc.	*junaak-e*	*gitaar-e*	*načeel-a*
		H	H	H
	Instr.	*junaac-ima*	*gitaar-ama*	*načeel-ima*
		H	H	H
	Loc.	*junaac-ima*	*gitaar-ama*	*načeel-ima*
		H	H	H

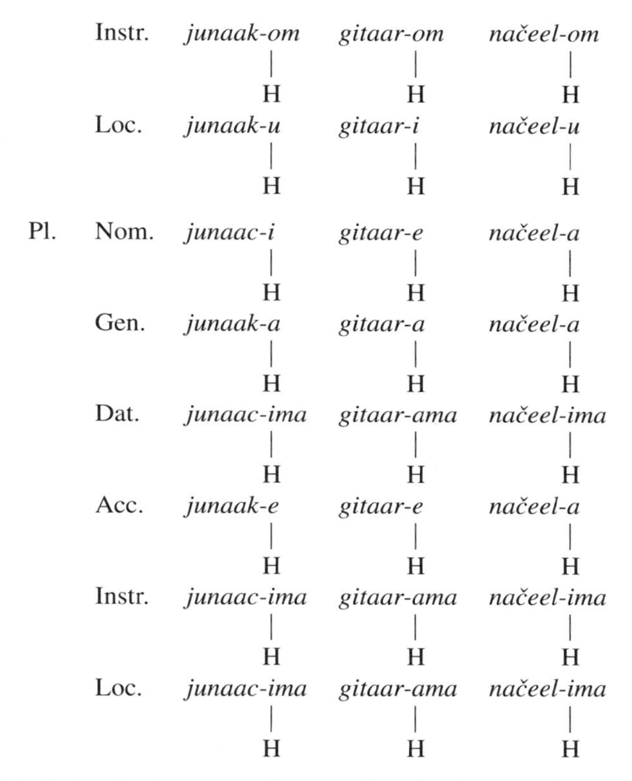

This distinction is captured by a cyclic rule of tone assignment. The bifurcation into accented and unaccented stems mentioned earlier becomes relevant at this point. This distinction is represented underlyingly as in (46).

(46) a. stem
H
b. stem

Accented stems are affiliated with a floating High in their underlying form, as in (46a), which keeps them apart from the unaccented ones. The rule responsible for the assignment of lexical tone will operate on accented stems, in the following fashion.[19]

(47) TONE LINKING RULE (informal): Link the floating tone to the stem-final syllable if and only if it does not branch.

This rule will link a High tone to the final syllable of the stem if this syllable is light, as in (44). If the stem-final syllable is heavy, the tonal rule will fail to apply on the stem cycle; but it will reapply on the next higher cycle, assigning tone to the suffix, as in (45). The relevant derivations are given in (48).

(48)

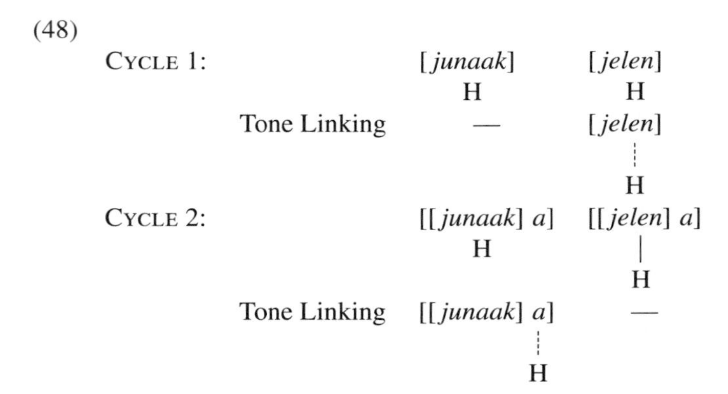

The tonal rule operates only on those forms which are associated with lexical tone. In contrast, toneless forms receive a High tone on their initial syllable, by virtue of Initial High Insertion (discussed in Section 2.3), as shown in the derivations of two toneless masculine forms, *oblaak* 'cloud' and *dever* 'brother-in-law'.

(49)

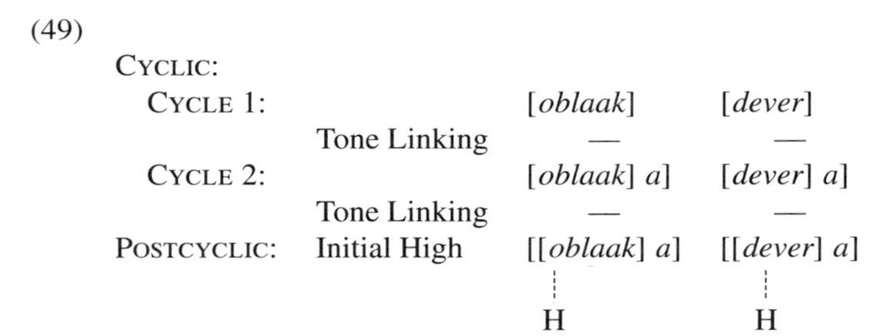

We thus observe clear tonal differences between toneless stems and stems which are lexically affiliated with tone.

The rule of Tone Linking is also responsible for the distribution of accent in derived forms. When the four stems in (48)–(49) are combined with the possessive suffix *-ov,* the pattern remains unaltered. Again, accented stems like *jelen* receive tone on the stem-final syllable, and those like *junaak,* on the first syllable of the suffix; unaccented stems receive tone by Initial High Insertion.[20]

```
(50)  [jelen] ov      versus   [dever] ov
          |                      |
          H                      H

(51)  [junaak] ov     versus   [oblaak] ov
                |                |
                H                H
```

The distinction between stems ending in a short vowel and those ending in a long one pervades a good portion of the accentual system; we find it in fact in all the forms which possess lexical tone. Furthermore, this generalization has interesting consequences for monosyllables: Tone Linking will assign tone to a monosyllabic stem whose stem syllable is light, as shown in (52a); otherwise the High is linked to the suffix, as in (52b).

(52) a. *jad-a* 'woe(gen.sg.)'
 |
 H

b. *dvoor-a* 'court(gen.sg.)'
 |
 H

Toneless stems obtain tone on the stem syllable by virtue of Initial High Insertion; as a consequence, only lexically toneless forms have tone linked to the heavy syllable of a monosyllabic stem.

(53) *graad-a* 'city(gen.sg.)'
 |
 H

Under the assumption that the place of accent is unpredictable, such regularities in the distribution of accent across inflectional paradigms would have to be treated as merely accidental.

4.1.2. Metatony

Tone Linking thus derives the well-formed configuration in (43a), in which tone is linked to the only mora of a light syllable, while excluding the illicit arrangement in (42) with tone linked to the nonhead mora of a heavy syllable. We now turn to the other well-formed configuration, that in (43b), in which tone is linked to the head mora of a heavy syllable. Evidence for this will come from the behavior of the nominative masculine singular form in (49) above. The relevant example is repeated in (54).

(54) *junaak* 'hero(nom.sg.)'
 |
 H

This is the only case form in the entire paradigm that lacks a phonologically realized desinence; furthermore, the High links here to the stem-final syllable although this syllable is heavy, which could be seen as a counterexample to the operation of Tone Linking. It is justified, however, to posit a vocalic desinence for the nominative singular, in the form of a *yer* vowel, an abstract segment generally associated with the vocalic systems of Slavic languages. In Serbo-Croatian this vowel appears on the surface only under a narrowly defined set of circumstances: a *yer* is vocalized as *a* if followed by another *yer,* otherwise it is lost. We will thus assume that the nominative singular ending is a *yer* vowel (Marked here as *ă*), as in (55).[21]

(55) [*junaak*] *ă*

Yer vowels play an important role in shaping the Serbo-Croatian accentual system (for details, see Zec, 1988). Moras headed by *yer* vowels can be linked to tone by virtue of Tone Linking; and if the *yer* vowel disappears from the structure, tone relinks in predictable ways. In particular, tone will relink to the left, to the nearest mora that possesses an *s* label. I refer to this relinking process as Metatony.[22]

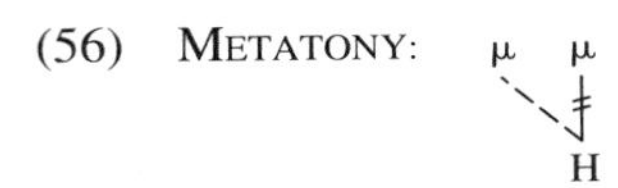

The accentual properties of *junaak* can now be accounted for in the following fashion: tone docks on the *yer* in the desinence, by virtue of Tone Linking; when the *yer* is lost from the structure (since it does not vocalize in this context), the mora it heads also delinks, and so does the tone linked to it. The High then relinks to the nearest mora that possesses an *s* label.

The derivation in (57) shows explicitly how tone is assigned to *junaak*. Moreover, in order to demonstrate that derivational suffixes containing *yer* vowels behave in exactly the same fashion as their inflectional counterparts, we also give the derivation of *junaački* 'heroic', formed with the suffix *-ăsk* which converts nominal stems into adjectives.

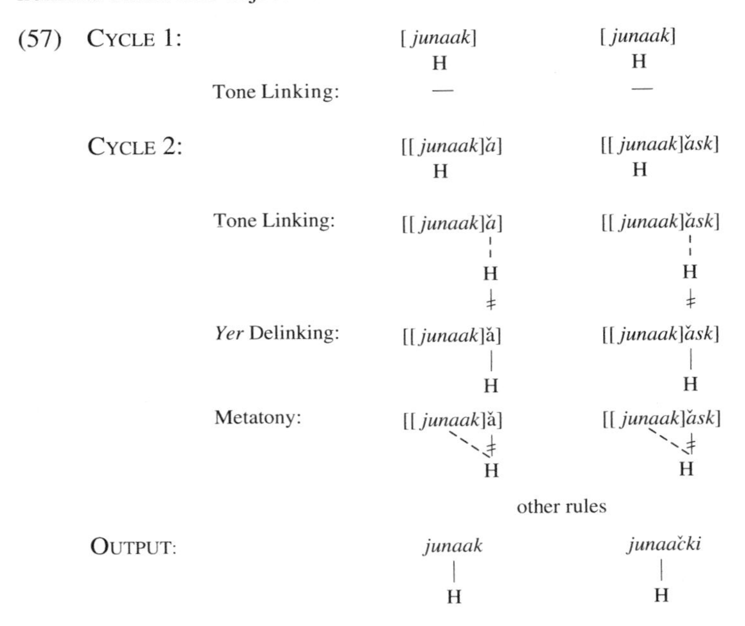

Crucially, tone relinks to the head mora of a heavy syllable, skipping over a nonhead mora.

4.2. Tone Linking and Syllable Structure

It is important to note at this point that Tone Linking and Metatony, on the one hand, differ in their mode of application from Spreading and Initial High Insertion, on the other. Both Initial High Insertion and Spreading can be stated solely in terms of moras and could hardly be stated in any other terms. Being oblivious to syllable structure, these two rules support the earlier observation that the tone-bearing unit in Serbo-Croatian is the mora. The Tone Linking rule, however, does make reference to syllable structure: tone is linked to a light but not to a heavy syllable. Metatony also needs to be characterized in terms of syllable structure: tone relinks to the only mora of a light syllable, or to the head mora of a heavy syllable. A way of sorting out these facts could be to say that Tone Linking and Metatony choose the syllable as the tone-bearing unit, while Spreading and Initial High Insertion make reference to the mora. This distinction can then be handled by level ordering, that is, by assigning Tone Linking and Metatony to the cyclic level, and Spreading and Initial High Insertion to the postcyclic level, as in (58).

(58) CYCLIC LEVELS: Tone Linking
Metatony
POSTCYCLIC LEVELS: Spreading
Initial High Insertion

The distribution across levels in (58) is compatible with the ordering of these rules, since Tone Linking and Metatony feed Spreading, and Initial High Insertion has to follow all the applications of Tone Linking in order to "know" which forms remain toneless.

An obvious solution, which ultimately proves unsatisfactory, is to stipulate that at the cyclic levels the tone-bearing unit is the syllable, while at the postcyclic levels it is the mora. This was in fact proposed in Inkelas and Zec (1988), in order to account for the fact that tone can only appear on the leftmost mora. The explanation offered was that, at the early levels, tone resides on syllables but percolates down to the head mora. This move, however, provides only a partial solution; while it could work for Metatony, it does not work for Tone Linking, since it does not explain why this rule operates only on light syllables. I therefore pursue a different path here, retaining the segregation into levels in (58), yet proposing that the mora is the tone-bearing unit at all phonological levels. The limited distribution of lexical tone is captured by the following positive constraint.

(59)

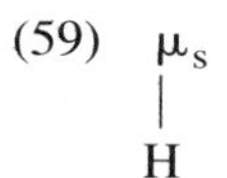

The constraint in (59) operates at the cyclic levels and is turned off postcyclically. As a result, lexical tone may link only to the *s*-labeled mora, that is, to the mora that acts as the syllable head. My claim, then, is that tone may be assigned only to moras, although not necessarily to all moras. The Tone Linking rule, stated informally in (47), can now be restated as in (60): the floating High is linked to the rightmost mora of the domain.

(60) μ]
⋮
H

This rule will be able to operate only if the domain-final mora is also the head mora, that is, if it possesses an *s* label. If the rightmost mora happens to be the nonhead mora, possessing a *w* label, the rule will fail to apply, since the mora targeted by the rule will not be able to receive tone. Thus, by assigning tone to only a subset of moras, we can derive the fact that the High that undergoes Tone Linking can be linked to a light but not to a heavy syllable.[23] Moreover, the constraint in (59) also explains the functioning of Metatony. Since only head moras may receive tone at the cyclic level, the delinked High can be relinked by Metatony only to the leftmost mora of the syllable. However, in the examples of Spreading that we saw earlier, either the head or the nonhead mora can be linked to tone. This is because Spreading applies in the postcyclic component, while constraint (59), which prohibits tone assignment to a nonhead mora, is operative only cyclically and is turned off at the postcyclic level. However, the fact that Spreading is a postcyclic rule does not exclude the possibility that it also applies cyclically. That this is indeed the case is shown in the following section.

4.3. Spreading as a Cyclic Rule

In the cyclic component, only the head mora, that is, the leftmost mora of the heavy syllable or the only mora of the light syllable, may be linked to tone. If Spreading applies at the cyclic level, it will have to operate within this level's constraints: it could apply as in (61a), but not as in (61b) or (61c).

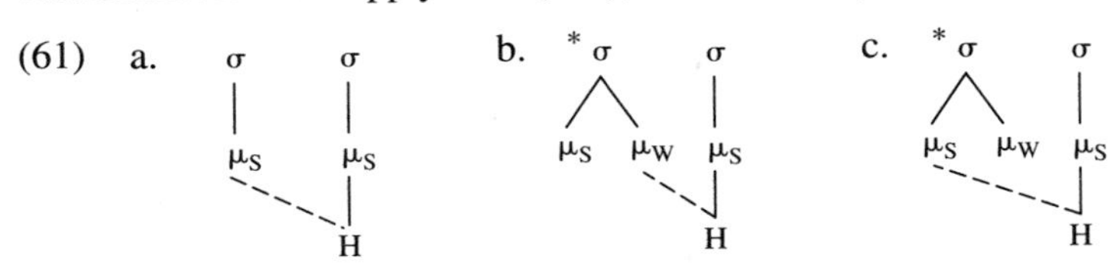

Application in (61b) is blocked by virtue of constraint (59), which prohibits tone assignment to a nonhead mora. Spreading cannot operate as shown in (61c) either, since skipping over a mora would lead to a violation of locality: a multiply linked tone may only be linked to adjacent tone-bearing units.

Thus, if Spreading applies at the cyclic level, the spread High will be able to link only to a light syllable; those applications in which the spread High links to the second mora of a heavy syllable will be incompatible with the cyclic component. Associating some of the applications of Spreading with the cyclic, and others with the postcyclic, component will have a theoretically desirable consequence: we adhere to the principle that a rule applies as early as possible. But a further advantage of placing Spreading among cyclic rules is that this provides a simple account of the accent shift induced by the genitive plural ending *-a*.[24] This accent shift operates differently in the Old and Neo-Štokavian dialects. In the former group accent will shift to any preceding syllable, while in the latter group it will shift only to a *light* preceding syllable.

I first present the situation in the Old Štokavian dialects: the High linked to the final syllable of the stem retracts one syllable to the left in the genitive plural form. The examples below are among those listed in Rešetar (1900) and Stevanović (1940).

(62)

```
a. jezik (nom.sg.), jezik-a (gen.sg.) versus jeziik-a (gen.pl.) 'tongue'
     |               |                     |
     H               H                     H
b. jelen (nom.sg.), jelen-a (gen.sg.) versus jeleen-a (gen.pl.) 'deer'
     |               |                     |
     H               H                     H
c. bubreg (nom.sg.), bubreg-a (gen.sg.) versus bubreeg-a (gen.pl.) 'kidney'
      |                |                        |
      H                H                        H
```

(63)

```
a. naarod (nom.sg.), naarod-a (gen.sg.) versus naarood-a (gen.pl.) 'people'
      |                |                        |
      H                H                        H
b. saabor (nom.sg.), saabor-a (gen.sg.) versus saaboor-a (gen.pl.) 'fair'
      |                |                        |
      H                H                        H
c. proorok (nom.sg.), proorok-a (gen.sg.) versus proorook-a (gen.pl.) 'prophet'
       |                 |                         |
       H                 H                         H
```

The pattern exhibited by the genitive shift can be captured by a morphologically conditioned delinking rule, in the spirit of Kenstowicz's (1974) proposal: a High linked to the stem-final syllable is delinked in the environment of the genitive plural ending *-a*.[25]

(64) GENPL DELINKING (OS): $\mu] - a_{\text{GenPl}}$ (delinked from H)

The delinked High tone will then assume its shifted position by virtue of Metatony, the relinking rule proposed in the previous section. In (65) are given the derivations of the genitive plural forms *jeleena* and *naarooda*.

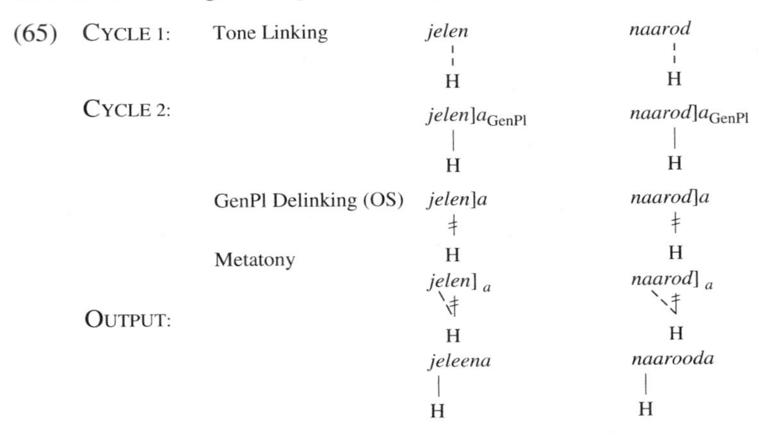

This analysis, however, does not extend to the Neo-Štokavian dialects, which exhibit a different pattern of the genitive shift: tone shifts to a preceding light syllable, but not to a preceding heavy syllable. Thus, forms in (66) retract their High in the genitive plural, while those in (67) fail to do so.[26]

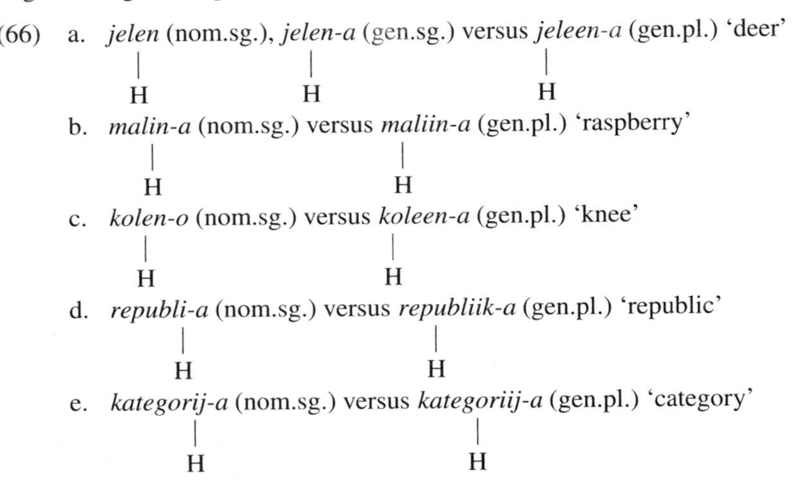

(66) a. jelen (nom.sg.), jelen-a (gen.sg.) versus jeleen-a (gen.pl.) 'deer'
H H H
b. malin-a (nom.sg.) versus maliin-a (gen.pl.) 'raspberry'
H H
c. kolen-o (nom.sg.) versus koleen-a (gen.pl.) 'knee'
H H
d. republi-a (nom.sg.) versus republiik-a (gen.pl.) 'republic'
H H
e. kategorij-a (nom.sg.) versus kategoriij-a (gen.pl.) 'category'
H H

(67)

a. *naarod* (nom.sg.), *naarod-a* (gen.sg.) versus *naarood-a* (gen.pl.) 'people'

H H H

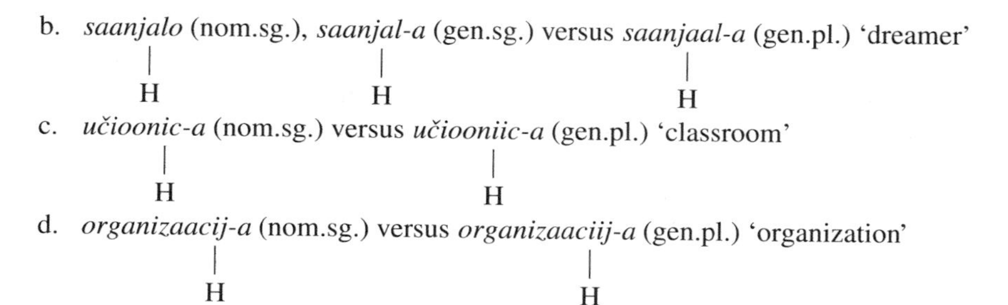

We could capture the difference between the stems in (66) and those in (67) by imposing an additional condition on the rule of Gen.Pl.Delinking: in the Neo-Štokavian this rule applies only in the environment of a light syllable. This condition, however, is highly suggestive. It distinguishes between forms that are subject to the cyclic version of Spreading and those that would fail to undergo this rule in the cyclic component. We can in fact account for the difference between the two sets of forms simply by including Spreading in the set of cyclic rules.

Consider the following possible scenario for deriving the Neo-Štokavian genitive plural forms. First, Tone Linking links the High tone to the stem-final syllable; next, the linked tone spreads to the preceding syllable; and finally, a doubly linked High tone loses its second link in the environment of the genitive plural suffix, by virtue of the following rule.

(68) GENPLDELINKING (NS): $\mu \quad \mu]\ \text{-}a_{\text{GenPl}}$ (H linked to both μ; link to the second μ delinked)

Under this scenario, the Neo-Štokavian version of the genitive delinking will not be able to apply to the forms in (63) and (67), since these forms do not undergo Spreading. This succession of moves is presented formally in (69).[27]

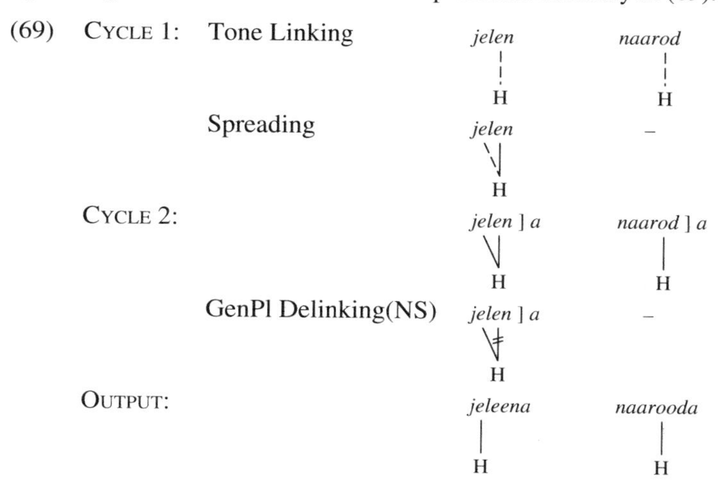

In sum, the Old Štokavian version of Gen.Pl.Delinking was reanalyzed in the Neo-Štokavian dialects due to the impact of Spreading. Once Spreading entered the cyclic component of the grammar, it was most likely reordered with respect to Gen.Pl. Delinking. And once this happened, two outcomes were possible, by virtue of an effect due to inalterability (Hayes, 1986): either Gen.Pl. Delinking could have applied only to forms that had not undergone Spreading, or the rule itself could have mutated so as to apply only to those forms that had undergone Spreading. It is this latter alternative that was realized in the Neo-Štokavian dialects.

5. SPREADING AND THE STRONG DOMAIN HYPOTHESIS

In the previous two sections I have traced the rule of Spreading through the various components of the grammar in the Neo-Štokavian dialects. In Section 4 it was argued that, in all Neo-Štokavian dialects, Spreading applies cyclically. Section 3 showed that, although all Neo-Štokavian dialects have Spreading in their postcyclic component, in NS1 this rule applies only postlexically, in NS2 it applies only lexically, and in NS3 it applies both lexically and postlexically. (70) summarizes the application of Spreading in the three Neo-Štokavian dialects we have examined.

(70)

	NS1	NS2	NS3
Cyclic	Yes	Yes	Yes
Lexical PW (phonological word)	?	Yes	Yes
Postlexical PW (clitic group)	Yes	No	Yes
Phonological phrase	Yes	No	No

NS1 requires a further comment. Recall that there are no compelling reasons to assume that in this dialect Spreading operates within the phonological word. Moreover, in this same dialect Initial High Insertion clearly fails to apply in this domain.

(71)

	NS1	NS2	NS3
Lexical PW (phonological word)	No	Yes	Yes
Postlexical PW (clitic group)	Yes	No	Yes

This strongly suggests that, in NS1, both Spreading and Initial High Insertion in some sense ignore the word-sized domain. One possibility might be that both Spreading and Initial High Insertion in fact skip over the word-sized domain, thus violating the strong domain hypothesis. But is it really likely that each of the rules independently chooses its domain, and that they just happen to go hand in hand?

This puzzle is resolved under the view of rule domains presented in the introductory part of the article. In particular, grammars may vary in whether the phonological word is created lexically or postlexically. This is precisely the difference between NS2 and NS3 on the one hand, and NS1 on the other. In the first case, the phonological word is created lexically, which yields (72) as the set of available rule domains.

(72)

Lexical	Level 1		Cyclic
	Level 2		
	Level 3	phonological word (word-sized)	Postcyclic
Postlexical	Level 3	phonological word (clitic group)	
	Level 4	phonological phrase	

In NS1, on the other hand, the phonological word is created postlexically, which results in the set of domains listed in (73).

(73)

Lexical	Level 1		Cyclic
	Level 2		
Postlexical	Level 3	phonological word (clitic group)	Postcyclic
	Level 4	phonological phrase	

The situations depicted in (72) and (73) are sufficient to account for the domains of Spreading in the three dialects. Thus, in NS1, in which the phonological word is created postlexically, Spreading applies as in (74).

(74)

Lexical	cyclic levels	yes
Postlexical	phonological word	yes
	phonological phrase	yes

In other words, NS1 simply lacks the word-sized domain, which explains why both Spreading and Initial High Insertion behave in the same fashion in this dialect, failing to apply in this domain.

The set of domains available in NS2 and NS3 is exactly the same. But while in NS3 Spreading applies in both the lexical and the postlexical components (just as in NS1), in NS2 it only applies lexically, as shown in (75).[28]

(75)

		NS2	NS3
Lexical	cyclic levels	yes	yes
	phonological word	yes	yes
Postlexical	phonological word	no	yes
	phonological phrase	no	yes

I am now in a position to explain why Spreading and Initial High Insertion go hand in hand in each of the dialects. The two rules overlap in the domain of the phonological word, and this domain varies from one dialect to the next. In NS1, Initial High Insertion cannot apply on the phonological word in its lexical size because this domain is formed only postlexically. In NS2 and NS3, however, where the phonological word is available in its smaller size, Initial High Insertion does apply lexically.

In some versions of the prosodic phonology (Hayes, 1989a; Nespor and Vogel, 1986), the set of prosodic domains includes the clitic group in addition to the phonological word and the phonological phrase. The clitic group thus corresponds to what we call here the phonological word in its postlexical guise; and the phonological word is treated as a strictly word-sized domain. Under this set of assumptions, however, the fact that the rules in NS 1 ignore the word-sized domain would raise the question of how universal are prosodic constituents such as the phonological word or the clitic group. In particular, NS1 would need to be characterized as lacking the phonological word domain, in which case the phonological word loses its universal status. The only way to salvage the universal status of the phonological word would be to assume its presence in NS1 and then treat as accidental the fact that both Spreading and Initial High Insertion skip over this domain, in violation of the strong domain hypothesis. This situation in which we have to abandon either the strong domain hypothesis or the universality of the phonological word will persist as long as we keep the clitic group in the inventory of prosodic constituents or of rule domains.

But once the prosodic constituency is divided into its lexical and postlexical subparts, it is possible to dispense with the clitic group as a prosodic level while retaining the rule domain of the clitic group size, as argued here (and in Zec, 1988). The clitic group is in fact the phonological word in its postlexical guise. This view of the clitic group is based on Inkelas's (1989) theory of prosodic constituency. By associating clitics with prosodic subcategorization frames, this framework provides theoretical foundation for the intuition that clitics are indeed "leaners." Serbo-Croatian clitics subcategorize for the phonological word, which explains why this domain automatically includes clitics in the postlexical component. Moreover, we have an account for the asymmetry in the possible sets of rule domains. The framework set up here predicts two types of cases: the phonological word is either manifested only in its larger size, or in both its smaller and its larger size. We thus exclude the case of the phonological word being manifested only in its smaller size (as long as a language possesses clitics that subcategorize for the phonological word).

Note that, in NS3, Spreading applies within the phonological word both lexically and postlexically. Kanerva (1989) points to a similar case of cyclicity in Chichewa, arguing that cyclicity of this sort follows from the specific properties of the phonological word; this is the only prosodic domain which is present in more than one component of the grammar.

6. THE ROUTE OF CHANGE

In the introductory part of the article I proposed that a new rule is added to the highest level, which corresponds to the largest domain of the grammar, and that it then enters all the accessible lower levels (which house successively smaller domains) by virtue of the strong domain hypothesis. However, Kiparsky (1984) also proposes that a rule may be turned off at a certain level of the grammar. I interpret this as a withdrawal of a rule from one or more of its higher, that is, larger, domains; this will again be viewed as a type of phonological change.

With these background assumptions, we are now able to follow up the phonological changes associated with accent retraction, or rather, with the addition of Spreading to the set of phonological rules. Each of the three Neo-Štokavian dialects examined here is viewed as a stage in this process of change. NS1 stands for the earliest stage, in which Spreading simply pervades all the components of the grammar.[29] In NS3 this rule has withdrawn from the higher levels of the grammar, choosing the phonological word as its highest level. And in NS2, the rule has withdrawn entirely from the postlexical component.

(76) STAGES OF THE PHONOLOGICAL CHANGE:

		NS1	NS3	NS2
Lexical	cyclic levels	√	√	√
	(phonological word)		√	√
Postlexical	phonological word	√	√	
	phonological phrase	√		

We thus see that the lexical/postlexical boundary is a relevant point at which rules may be turned off. In other words, if a rule is lexicalized (Kiparsky, 1984, 1988), its crucial reference point will become the lexical/postlexical boundary, even if this boundary happens to cut across one of the prosodic constituents, as is claimed here to be the case in Serbo-Croatian.

Another dimension along which the dialects differ is whether the phonological word is created lexically or postlexically. While this difference can be interpreted as another phonological change, I treat it as unrelated to Spreading. This view is supported by the fact that the domains of Initial High Insertion, a rule which is historically unrelated to Spreading, are also sensitive to the presence versus absence of the phonological word in the lexical component. Moreover, Initial High Insertion exhibits the same type of variation in the Old Štokavian dialects which entirely lack Spreading.

In order to complete the picture, I bring in at this point the application of Spreading in the Old Štokavian dialects. Several regional varieties possess a rule whose effect is close to the Neo-Štokavian version of Spreading, with one important difference: in this case, Spreading operates as a domain limit rule, affecting only the High tones linked to the rightmost mora of the domain. The Old Štokavian version of Spreading can be formulated as in (77).

(77) $\mu \quad \mu]_D$

H

I illustrate briefly how Spreading applies in the Old Štokavian dialect described in Ćupić (1977). The domain chosen by Spreading in this dialect is the phonological word. The operation of this rule is exemplified by the following paradigm.

(78) *naarod* (nom.sg.) *naarod-a*(gen.sg.) *naarod-ima* (dat.pl.) *'people'*

H H H

The rule applies only in the nominative singular form, whose High tone is linked to the final mora of the domain. It fails to apply in the genitive singular and dative plural forms, in which the High is linked to a nonfinal mora.

Furthermore, since this dialect possesses only the phonological word in its postlexical size, we also encounter alternations as in (79) and (80), in which the presence of an enclitic blocks the application of Spreading (from Ćupić, 1977: 205, 210).

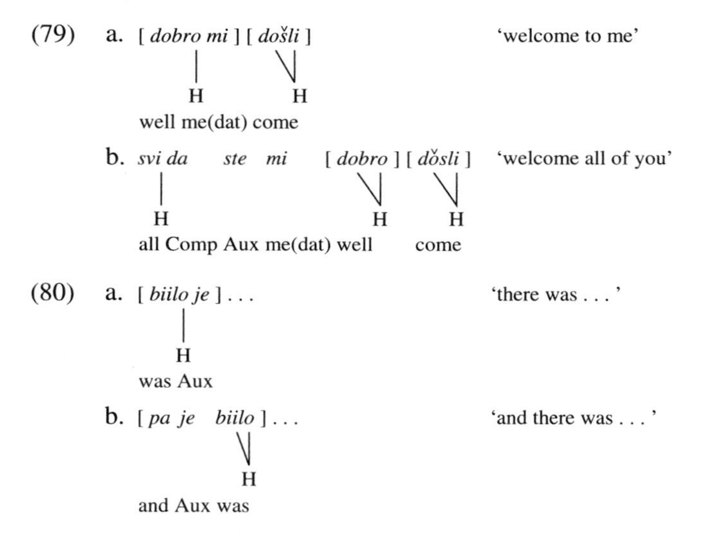

(79) a. [dobro mi] [došli] 'welcome to me'
H H
well me(dat) come
b. svi da ste mi [dobro] [dŏsli] 'welcome all of you'
H H H
all Comp Aux me(dat) well come
(80) a. [biilo je] . . . 'there was . . . '
H
was Aux
b. [pa je biilo] . . . 'and there was . . . '
H
and Aux was

Finally, tone will spread onto a proclitic only if its host is a monosyllabic word, which again follows from the formulation of Spreading in (77).

In this Old Štokavian dialect, then, Spreading selects the domain of the phonological word. We may assume that it applies at levels that house domains larger than the phonological word; this, however, cannot be demonstrated because the edge of any of the larger domains will coincide with the edge of the phonological word. However, rule (77) does not apply in any of the domains smaller than the phonological word; as we saw earlier, the Old Štokavian group of dialects lacks Spreading in the cyclic component. This is clearly a departure from the strong domain hypothesis. Moreover, Spreading is restricted to the postcyclic domains in just those dialects in which it operates as a domain limit rule. My hypothesis is that this departure from the strong domain hypothesis may well be related to the properties of domain limit rules in general; it could be that selecting one of the edges of a rule domain is permissible only in the postcyclic component. In support of this, I bring up two other Serbo-Croatian rules of the domain limit type which violate the strong domain hypothesis. First, Initial High Insertion, which makes reference to a domain edge, fails to apply at any levels with domains smaller than the phonological word; and second, a rule proposed in Inkelas and Zec (1988) that links a Low tone at the right edge of one of the larger domains, most likely the intonational phrase, clearly fails to apply within any of the lower levels.[30] While I have no explanation of why domain limit rules behave in this peculiar fashion, it will at least be possible to narrow down the class of rules which depart from the strong domain hypothesis to those of the domain limit type.[31]

But how are the Old and the Neo-Štokavian versions of Spreading related? That is, which of the two versions characterizes an older stage and which is an innovation? What seems to be a likely scenario is that Spreading entered the grammar in its Old Štokavian form, that is, as a domain limit rule. The crucial change that occurred in Neo-Štokavian is that Spreading lost its domain limit specification; and only then was it able to conform to the strong domain hypothesis, by becoming omnipresent in the grammar. Under the reversed scenario, Spreading would have to abandon the lexicon in its transition from the Neo-Štokavian to the Old Štokavian version. Had this happened, we would have expected to find traces of the cyclic version of Spreading in at least some of the Old Štokavian dialects; however, I am not aware of any evidence that would support the latter alternative.

The principles of the LPM model have thus enabled us to interpret the cross-dialectal variation associated with accent retraction as a succession of synchronic stages which characterize a phonological change. The Old Štokavian group of dialects records an earlier stage than the Neo-Štokavian group. Within the Old Štokavian, the innovative dialects are those that possess Spreading as a domain limit rule; and in the Neo-Štokavian dialects, Spreading lost its domain limit properties, which resulted in first its pervasion of and then withdrawal from the various subparts of the grammar. The set of stages posited here follow from the strong domain hypothesis and from the assumption that rules are added at the end of the postlexical component. Crucial for our claims, however, is a specific organization of the LPM model into levels which serve as rule domains.

ACKNOWLEDGMENTS

I am grateful to Sharon Inkelas, Ellen Kaisse, Paul Kiparsky, and an anonymous referee for most helpful comments on earlier versions of this article.

NOTES

[1] Serbo-Croatian is divided into three major dialects, the Štokavian, the Čakavian, and the Kajkavian. I cover the accentual situation in the Štokavian dialects, with the exception of those characterized by only one accent. The subdivisions within the Štokavian group of dialects adopted here are those proposed in Ivić (1958, 1985).

[2] I assume that rule domains are provided by morphological constituents at the cyclic levels, and by prosodic constituents at the postcyclic levels.

[3] Here I follow Inkelas (1989), where clitics are analyzed as prosodically dependent elements which subcategorize for prosodic domains. Serbo-Croatian clitics, both proclitics and enclitics, subcategorize for the domain of the phonological word.

[4] This proposal is made in Zec (1988), to account for the applications of several postcyclic rules in Bulgarian. Kanerva (1989) adopts this perspective in his analysis of clitics in Chichewa. Section 5 of the present article provides further arguments for this view of the phonological word. This position is originally due to Selkirk (1986), who assumes that clitics are included into the phonological word.

[5] According to King (1973), a new rule is necessarily added at the end of a grammar, that is, as the latest in the set of ordered rules (for other views in the debate on rule addition see Halle, 1962; King, 1969; Kiparsky, 1965; as well as Kaisse, this volume). However, while King focuses on the ordering of a newly added rule, my focus is on the new rule's domain.

[6] The situation in the Old Štokavian is somewhat more complex. While the more conservative Old Štokavian dialects are indeed characterized only by the falling accents (as in the regional variety described in Stevanović, 1940), the less conservative Old Štokavian dialects may also possess the rising accents. According to Ivić (1985), the crucial difference

between the Old Štokavian and the Neo-Štokavian dialects is in the distribution of the pitch accents, regardless of the number of accents they may possess. The less conservative Old Štokavian dialects are discussed in Section 6.

[7] Vowel length is marked throughout the article as gemination. This is the only departure from the standard orthography.

[8] Syllable weight in Serbo-Croatian is determined by vowel length: a syllable with a short vowel is light, and a syllable containing a long vowel is heavy. Consonants do not contribute to syllable weight. Furthermore, Serbo-Croatian does not have diphthongs; two unlike adjacent vowels belong to different syllables and are separated by a hiatus (Lehiste and Ivić, 1967).

[9] That the prefix *ne-* is not associated with a High tone if it escapes the effect of Spreading is shown by the pair of forms *pušaač* 'smoker' and *nepušaač* 'nonsmoker', both having lexical tone on their final syllables; the lexical High then spreads to the preceding syllable, which in *pušaač* is also the initial syllable. The prefix *ne-* in *nepušaač* remains toneless.

[10] In Inkelas and Zec (1988), lexical tones are prelinked in the underlying form. In Zec (1988), lexical tone is assigned by a cyclic tonal rule. This article adopts the latter analysis, which is presented in Section 4.

[11] In order to make sure that rule (17) applies only to toneless forms, we may invoke the OCP in its passive version (McCarthy, 1986), which will prevent the application of (17) to a form already linked to a High tone. Generally, Serbo-Croatian words may be associated with at most one High tone.

[12] NS1 is represented by what is known as the Vukovian norm, described in Daničić (1925); this norm is based on the east Herzegovian dialect (see Vuković, 1940, and Ružičić, 1927, for descriptions of two of its regional varieties). NS2 corresponds to the eastern standard, spoken predominantly in Belgrade (Miletić, 1952). NS3 is spoken in the regions of Srem and Mačva (see the descriptions of regional varieties in Moskovljević 1927–28 and Nikolić 1953–54, 1966, 1970).

[13] I have found no convincing evidence that Spreading applies within the phonological phrase in this dialect. Nikolić (1970:51) lists a single case of this type, *sto hektaara* '(one) hundred hectars' in which the High on the first syllable of *hektara* spreads onto *sto*.

[14] If Spreading applies lexically, it will not reapply in the postlexical component. The failure of Spreading to apply more than once can be attributed to inalterability (Hayes, 1986): given the statement of the rule in (9), only a singly linked High will undergo Spreading.

[15] Note that in NS3 Initial High Insertion is optional lexically, but obligatory postlexically. In other words, a phonological word has to be assigned tone within the phonological word domain. It was suggested by an anonymous referee that Initial High Insertion is a metrical rather than a tonal rule (see Halle, 1971) since the High assigned by this rule coincides with stress, and that it is metrical structure rather than tone that is obligatorily assigned within the phonological word. However, the High assigned by Initial High Insertion may undergo Spreading, as shown in Section 3.3, and in this case it will not coincide with stress. In fact, a metrical analysis would have to posit a stress shift in this case that would replicate Spreading. This demonstrates that a tonal analysis is to be preferred over a metrical one.

[16] I have found no cases of the application of Initial High Insertion within the domain of the phonological phrase. This is to be expected, I believe, since Initial High Insertion ap-

plies only within toneless domains (see note 11), and a phonological phrase can never be toneless by virtue of the fact that it has to contain at least one content word, which will have received tone by this point.

[17] Here I assume the moraic theory of syllable structure with a direct representation of moras, as in Hyman (1984), Hayes (1989b), Itô (1989), and Zec (1988), among others. I also adopt the labeling convention of marking the leftmost mora as s(trong), and the remaining moras as w(eak); the *s*-labeled mora is interpreted here as the head of the syllable it belongs to (for details see Zec, 1988).

[18] The forms in (44) and (45), as well as all other forms in this and the following subsections, are shared by the two dialect groups. In other words, we ignore the effect of Spreading.

[19] A formal version of the rule is provided in Section 4.2.

[20] The situation is actually somewhat more complex. Just like stems, affixes may either be toneless or have tone of their own. The suffix *-ov* is obviously toneless. If a toneless stem combines with an affix with its own tone, the derived form will be associated with tone. For example, the derived form *oblačić* 'cloud (dim.)' has a High on its final syllable; this High comes from the suffix *-ić,* which is affiliated with tone in its underlying form. When a toneless simplex stem is combined with a toneless suffix, the derived form remains toneless.

[21] It is worth noting that, at the earlier stages of the language, before the fall of *yers,* the nominative ending had exactly this form.

[22] Metatony is triggered by any process that delinks a High tone. A High may be delinked either by rule (see the case discussed in Section 4.3), or by virtue of vowel loss. This latter case could be motivated as follows: once the vowel is delinked from its mora, the mora in its turn delinks from the higher structure, which then leads to the delinking of tone. Tone delinking caused by *yer* deletion is only one such case; other cases are found in the verbal paradigm where a vowel other than *yer* is deleted when followed by another vowel (Zec, 1988).

[23] Zec (1988) posits two cyclic, that is, lexical levels, and associates Tone Linking with Level 2. The failure of this rule to apply at Level 1 is attributed to the prosodic setup of this level. Several phonological phenomena receive a unified account under the assumption that Level 1 includes only moras while Level 2 includes both moras and syllables. Since constraint (59) is operative throughout the cyclic component, it will preclude the linking of tone to a mora that does not bear the *s* marking, and such moras are not available before Level 2. Absence of relevant structure at some point in the grammar is the standard type of interference with the strict domain hypothesis (cf. Kiparsky, 1984).

[24] This type of accent shift is found only in the Štokavian dialects (Leskien, 1914: 221–222). The Čakavian dialects, which in many ways preserve an older accentual situation than that in the Štokavian, lack entirely the accent shift in the genitive plural form. Moreover, only the genitive plural forms taking the *-a* desinence are subject to this type of accent shift; no accent shift is exhibited by forms taking the *-i* desinence.

[25] This ending has another peculiar property: it lengthens the vowel of the immediately preceding syllable. The lengthening process, however, appears not to be responsible for the genitive accent, as the discussion below will make evident. This lengthening process is ignored in the derivations given below.

[26] I focus here only on those forms which do not contain *yer* vowels in the stem. Forms with *yers,* like *komaarac* (nom.sg.), *komaarca* (gen.sg.), *komaraaca* (gen.pl.) 'mosquito' exhibit a shift in the genitive plural which I believe is of a different sort. In this class of forms, tone is linked to the desinence in all case forms other than the genitive plural. Thus tone is delinked here from the genitive plural desinence rather than from the stem-final syllable. While I do not have an account for this set of forms, I will assume that the pattern they follow is distinct from that discussed here.

[27] We will have to assume that *yer* delinking operates before Spreading, in order to account for the fact that this process is not sensitive to syllable weight.

[28] Evidence for the postlexical version of the phonological word in NS2 comes from postlexical applications of Initial High Insertion. One class of forms, indefinite pronouns, is lexically marked as exceptional to Initial High Insertion and can thus undergo this rule only postlexically; as a result, the High is assigned to a proclitic. Thus the negated prepositional phrase *nȉ sa kim* 'not with anyone' has a High tone on the negative particle *ni,* which is a proclitic, rather than on the pronominal stem *kim.* Note that *ni* gets no tone in *ni sa Pȅtrom,* since *Pȅtrom* possesses a High tone on its initial syllable.

[29] I have no evidence for the application of this rule within any of the levels larger than the phonological phrase; however, it is reasonable to assume that the rule has bled itself, so to speak, beyond the phonological phrase level.

[30] This situation is not restricted to Serbo-Croatian. Hyman (1990) discusses several tonal rules of the domain limit type which apply postlexically. Two such rules in Kinande, for example, operate on the domains of the phonological and the intonational phrase, but not on any of the smaller domains.

[31] Kaisse (this volume) argues that a relatively new rule may be applying within larger (most likely, postlexical) domains while still failing to descend to the lexical domains; this most likely captures the progression of Spreading in the Neo-Štokavian dialects. However, while I agree with Kaisse that a relatively new rule may be applying in the larger but not in the smaller domains, I also believe that this kind of situation may become stable only in the case of domain limit rules. Initial High Insertion, for example, is a very old rule with deep Indo-European roots. As for the Old Štokavian version of Spreading, it is not clear whether it dates as far back as its Neo-Štokavian counterpart; if it does, then its failure to descend to smaller domains is due to its domain limit properties.

REFERENCES

Belić, A. (1956). *Osnovi istorije srpskohrvatskog jezika,* vol. 1, *Fonetika.* Naučna knjiga, Beograd.

Booij, G., and Rubach, J. (1987). Postcyclic versus postlexical rules in lexical phonology. *Linguistic Inquiry* **18,** 1–44.

Browne, W. E., and McCawley, J. (1965). Srpskohrvatski akcenat. *Zbornik za filologiju i lingvistiku* **8,** 147–151.

Ćupić, D. (1977). Govor Bjelopavlića. *Srpski dijalektološki zbornik* **23,** 1–226.

Daničić, Dj. (1925). *Srpski akcenti.* Srpska Kraljevska Akademija, Beograd-Zemun.
Halle, M. (1962). Phonology in generative grammar. *Word* **18,** 54–72. Reprinted in *The Structure of Language: Readings in the Philosophy of Language.* (J. A. Fodor and J. Katz, eds., 1964), pp. 334–352. Prentice-Hall, Englewood Cliffs, N.J.
Halle, M. (1971). Remarks on Slavic accentology. *Linguistic Inquiry* **2,** 1–19.
Halle, M., and Kiparsky, P. (1981). Review of *Histoire de l'accentuation slave* by Paul Garde. *Language* **57,** 150–181.
Hayes, B. (1986). Inalterability in CV phonology. *Language* **62,** 321–351.
Hayes, B. (1989a). The prosodic hierarchy in meter. In *Rhythm and Meter* (P. Kiparsky and G. Youmans, eds.), pp. 201–260. Academic Press, San Diego.
Hayes, B. (1989b). Compensatory lengthening in moraic phonology. *Linguistic Inquiry* **20,** 253–306.
Hyman, L. (1984). *A Theory of Phonological Weight.* Foris, Dordrecht.
Hyman, L. (1990). Boundary tonology and the prosodic hierarchy. In *The Phonology–Syntax Connection* (S. Inkelas and D. Zec, eds.), pp. 109–125. CSLI Publications and University of Chicago Press, Chicago.
Inkelas, S. (1989). *Prosodic Constituency in the Lexicon.* Doctoral dissertation, Stanford University, Stanford, Calif.
Inkelas, S., and Zec, D. (1988). Serbo-Croatian pitch accent: The interactions of tone, stress, and intonation. *Language* **64,** 227–248.
Itô, J. (1989). A prosodic theory of epenthesis. *Natural Language and Linguistic Theory* **7,** 217–259.
Ivić, P. (1958). *Die serbokroatischen Dialekte: Ihre Struktur und Entwicklung,* vol. 1, *Allgemeines und die stokavischen Dialektgruppe.* Mouton, The Hague.
Ivić, P. (1985). *Dijalektologija srpskohrvatskog jezika: Uvod i štokavsko narečje.* Matica srpska, Novi Sad.
Kanerva, J. (1989). *Focus and Phrasing in Chichewa Phonology.* Doctoral dissertation, Stanford University, Stanford, Calif.
Kenstowicz, M. (1974). Inflectional accent of the Serbo-Croatian noun. *Studies in the Linguistic Sciences* **4,** 80–106.
King, R. D. (1969). *Historical Linguistics and Generative Grammar.* Prentice-Hall, Englewood Cliffs, N.J.
King, R. D. (1973). Rule insertion. *Language* **49,** 551–578.
Kiparsky, P. (1965). *Phonological Change.* Doctoral dissertation, Massachusetts Institute of Technology, Cambridge.
Kiparsky, P. (1973). The inflectional accent of Indo-European. *Language* **49,** 794–849.
Kiparsky, P. (1984). On the lexical phonology of Icelandic. In *Nordic Prosody III* (C. Elert, I. Johansson, and E. Strangert, eds.), pp. 135–164. University of Umea, Umea, Sweden.
Kiparsky, P. (1985). Some consequences of lexical phonology. In *Phonology Yearbook* **2,** 85–138.
Kiparsky, P. (1988). Phonological change. In *Linguistics: The Cambridge Survey.* vol. 1, *Linguistic Theory: Foundations* (F. J. Newmeyer, ed.), pp. 363–415. Cambridge University Press, Cambridge.
Kiparsky, P., and Halle, M. (1977). Towards a reconstruction of the Indo-European accent.

In *Studies in Stress and Accent* (Southern California Occasional Papers in Linguistics 4) (L. Hyman, ed.), pp. 209–238. University of Southern California, Los Angeles.
Lehiste, I., and Ivić, P. (1967). Some problems concerning the syllable in Serbocroatian. *Glossa* **1/2,** 126–136.
Lehiste, I., and Ivić, P. (1986). *Word and Sentence Prosody in Serbocroatian.* MIT Press, Cambridge, Mass.
Leskien, A. (1914). *Grammatik der Serbo-Kroatischen Sprache.* Winter, Heidelberg.
McCarthy, J. (1986). OCP effects: Germination and antigemination. *Linguistic Inquiry* **17,** 207–263.
Miletić, B. (1952). *Osnovi fonetike srpskog jezika.* Znanje, Beograd.
Moskovljević, M. (1927–28). Akcenti pocerskog govora. *Južnoslovenski filolog* **7,** 5–68.
Nespor, M., and Vogel, I. (1986). *Prosodic Phonology.* Foris, Dordrecht.
Nikolić, B. (1953–54). O govoru Srema. *Južnoslovenski filolog* **20,** 273–287.
Nikolić, B. (1966). Mačvanski govori. *Srpski dijalektološki zbornik* **16,** 179–313.
Nikolić, B. (1970). *Osnovi mladje novoštokavske akcentuacije.* Institut za srpskohrvatski jezik, Beograd.
Poser, W. J. (1984). *The Phonetics and Phonology of Tone and Intonation in Japanese.* Doctoral dissertation, Massachusetts Institute of Technology, Cambridge.
Rešetar, M. (1900). *Die serbocroatische Betonung südwestlicher Mundarten.* Vienna.
Ružičić, G. (1927). Akcenatski sistem pljevaljskog govora. *Srpski dijalektološki zbornik* **3,** 115–176.
Selkirk, E. O. (1978). On prosodic structure and its relation to syntactic structure. In *Nordic Prosody II* (T. Fretheim, ed.), pp. 111–140. TAPIR, Trondheim, Norway.
Selkirk, E. O. (1980). Prosodic domains in phonology: Sanskrit revisited. In *Juncture* (M. Aronoff and M.-L. Kean, eds.), pp. 107–129. Anma Libri, Saratoga, Calif.
Selkirk, E. O. (1986). On derived domains in sentence phonology. *Phonology Yearbook* **3,** 371–405.
Stevanović, M. (1940). Sistem akcentuacije u piperskom govoru. *Srpski dijalektološki zbornik* **10,** 67–184.
Vuković, J. L. (1940). Akcenat govora Pive i Drobnjaka. *Srpski dijalektološki zbornik* **10,** 185–417.
Zec, D. (1988). *Sonority Constraints on Prosodic Structure.* Doctoral dissertation, Stanford University, Stanford, Calif.

LANGUAGE INDEX

E

F

G

H

I

J

K

L

M

SUBJECT INDEX

U

W

PHONETICS AND PHONOLOGY

Volume 1: Rhythm and Meter
edited by Paul Kiparsky and Gilbert Youmans

Volume 2: The Special Status of Coronals: Internal and External Evidence
edited by Carole Paradis and Jean-François Prunet

Volume 3: Current Issues in ASL Phonology
edited by Geoffrey R. Coulter

Volume 4: Studies in Lexical Phonology
edited by Sharon Hargus and Ellen M. Kaisse